MAGILL'S
LITERARY ANNUAL
2006

MAGILL'S LITERARY ANNUAL

2006

Essay-Reviews of 200 Outstanding Books
Published in the United States During 2005

With an Annotated List of Titles

Volume Two
L-Z

Edited by
JOHN D. WILSON
STEVEN G. KELLMAN

SALEM PRESS
Pasadena, California   Hackensack, New Jersey

LIBRARY OF CONGRESS CATALOG CARD NO. 77-99209
ISBN 1-58765-280-3 (set)
ISBN 1-58765-311-7 (vol. 2)
ISBN 978-1-58765-280-6 (set)
ISBN 978-1-58765-311-7 (vol. 2)

FIRST PRINTING

PRINTED IN CANADA

CONTENTS

CONTENTS

COMPLETE ANNOTATED LIST OF TITLES

VOLUME 1

COMPLETE ANNOTATED LIST OF TITLES

VOLUME 2

MAGILL'S
LITERARY ANNUAL
2006

LEGENDS OF MODERNITY
Essays and Letters from Occupied Poland, 1942-1943

Author: Czesław Miłosz (1911-2004)
First published: Legendy nowoczsenosci, 1996, in Poland
Translated from the Polish by Madeline G. Levine
Introduction by Jaroslaw Anders
Publisher: Farrar, Straus and Giroux (New York). 266
   pp. $25.00
Type of work: Essays
Time: 1942-1943
Locale: Warsaw, Poland

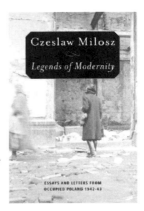

   In these essays, written during the Nazi occupation of Poland, Miłosz explores the roots of twentieth century literature and art and how certain aspects of modernism led to the horrors of fascism and Stalinism

Principal personages:
CZESŁAW MIŁOSZ, a Polish poet and essayist
JERZY ANDRZEJEWSKI, a Polish novelist

   In *Legends of Modernity*, a young Czesław Miłosz explores the sources of World War II in the literature and art of the modern era. Written between 1942 and 1943, the essays and letters in this book resulted from Miłosz's attempts to both explain and escape the nightmare of Nazi occupation through writing. In his note to the 1996 Polish edition, he describes using calm, intellectual prose as a way to distance himself from the war's anguish. In addition, he was also trying to understand why Europe had succumbed to the nightmare of World War II. The result is a highly articulate and penetrating study of the relationship of creativity to political extremism, a book that, while unpublished until 1996, formed the foundation for his classic essay collections such as *Zniewolony umysł* (1953; *The Captive Mind*, 1953), *Emperor of the Earth* (1977), and *Zaczynając od moich ulic* (1985; *Beginning with My Streets: Essays and Recollections*, 1991).
   When World War II began, Miłosz was twenty-eight, an accomplished poet, and a broadcaster for Polish State Radio in Warsaw. After Poland fell to the German Blitzkrieg, he escaped briefly to his home city of Wilno on Poland's eastern frontier, but when the Soviet Union captured Wilno, Miłosz returned to Warsaw. There he joined the resistance movement and for a while made a living transferring books from the bomb-damaged French Institute to the University of Warsaw library. As he saved the books, he read many of them, and this immersion in French literature became the centerpiece of *Legends of Modernity*.
   Nonetheless, the collection's first essay is "The Legend of the Island," a critique of a British novel, Daniel Defoe's *Robinson Crusoe* (1719). With this essay, Miłosz be-

Born in 1911, Czesław Miłosz spent World War II in Warsaw's anti-Nazi underground. Later, disillusioned by socialist Poland, he settled in the United States. A Nobel laureate, Miłosz is the author of more than thirty books, including The Captive Mind *(1953),* Rodzinna Europa *(1959;* Native Realm: A Search for Self-Definition, *1968), and* New and Collected Poems, 1931-2001 *(2001). He died in Kraków, Poland, in 2004.*

gins the overarching thesis of *Legends of Modernity*: that modern literary concerns resulted in the immoral excesses of fascism, Nazism, and Stalinism. In *Robinson Crusoe*, there is the metaphor of the island as a place isolated from society and all its problems. The salvation portrayed in the novel is individual rather than societal, revealing literature's growing obsession with unchecked individualism. Also present in *Robinson Crusoe*, from Miłosz's point of view, is the immorality of viewing people of a different race as separate and dispensable entities, the alien "other" or outsider, as found in Crusoe's lack of emotion at the murder of his faithful servant Friday toward the novel's end.

The next three essays, which form the book's core, focus on French literature and the evolution of modernism as represented in the works of Honoré de Balzac, Stendhal, and André Gide.

In "The Legend of the Monster City," Miłosz use Balzac's *La Comédie humaine* (1829-1848; *The Human Comedy*, 1895-1896, 1911) to explore the myth of the modern city as Leviathan. In this monstrous metropolis, the old religious basis for morality gives way to the modern belief that a human is simply an amoral animal seeking personal survival and gain. Thus, Balzac's nineteenth century Paris becomes a place of alienated individuals competing against one another in a capitalist frenzy.

"The Legend of the Will" drives Miłosz's thesis deeper with Stendhal's *Le Rouge et le noir* (1830; *The Red and the Black*, 1898). For Miłosz, the novel's protagonist, Julien Sorel, is the prime model for the "strong man," a character type who pursues his desires with a driving will that possesses no moral compass except victory and can only be stopped by violent death or execution. Miłosz sees in Sorel echoes of Napoleon, and by way of German philosopher Friedrich Nietzsche's admiration for Stendhal, ultimately one of the influences on Benito Mussolini and Adolf Hitler. Miłosz also discerns a literary line beginning with Stendhal that threads its way through the works of Fyodor Dostoevski and Gide, with dire consequences for European culture.

Gide serves as the central figure for the next essay, "Absolute Freedom." Miłosz argues that this French novelist, with his complete adoration of Nietzsche, is the epitome of modern literature's dangerous fixation on the irrational, the intuitive, and the realm of the unconscious—all of which lead directly to rise of fascism, and by a more circuitous route, revolutionary Marxism. Miłosz explains that Gide's urge for the extremes of human experience helps to inspire a program of action over thought, a central characteristic of fascist belief. Miłosz also warns against the common perception that literature is harmless, and he discusses how artistic theory influences politics through journalism, the university, and other sociocultural institutions.

With "Beyond Truth and Falsehood," Miłosz leaves French literature to explore American psychologist William James. Miłosz focuses primarily on James's *The Varieties of Religious Experience* (1902) as the prime example of modernism's urge to embrace the irrational and the conflict between faith and reason; whereas, Miłosz views these forces in the classical manner as complimentary forces. Miłosz detects in James's promotion of internal revelation the twentieth century's elevation of myth and its suspicion of absolute truth, which results in a chaotic relativism and the irruption of irrational political movements such as fascism.

Following this, "The Experience of War" and its Slavic subject matter establish *Legends of Modernity*'s final direction. In this essay, Miłosz proposes that Russian novelist Leo Tolstoy's *Voyna i mir* (1865-1869; *War and Peace*, 1886) is one of the best artistic representations of warfare, equaled only by the paintings of Spanish artist Francisco Goya. Miłosz believes that Tolstoy's classic novel about Napoleon's invasion of Russia portrays the way that warfare, with its bloodlust and mechanized brutality, erodes humanity's belief in civilization, creating a nihilistic vacuum all too easily filled by the extreme nationalism and racial fantasies of political movements such as National Socialism.

"Zdziechowski's Religiosity" centers on Polish author Marian Zdziechowski, one of Miłosz's professors at the University of Wilno. Zdziechowski, with his traditional Catholic unification of faith and reason, is for Miłosz the antidote to modernism's obsession with extreme individuality and irrationality. Unfortunately, coming from an older generation than Miłosz and his peers, Zdziechowski and writers like him found themselves largely ignored as Europe lurched toward the Holocaust of 1939-1945.

In *Legends of Modernity*'s longest and most elaborate essay, "The Boundaries of Art," Miłosz sums up the major themes of the book. He begins with the absurdist novels of Stanislaw Ignacy Witkiewicz, whose *Pożegnanie jesieni* (1927; farewell to autumn) and *Nienasycenie* (1930; *Insatiability: A Novel in Two Parts*, 1977) contain apocalyptic endings describing foreign invaders dismembering a decadent Poland swimming in depraved sex and strong opiates. For Miłosz, these novels foreshadow the fall of Poland's Pilsudski government to the Nazi onslaught. After describing this intersection of art and history, Miłosz argues that modern art has lost its sense of mystery and has replaced content rooted in philosophical truth with a fixation for exploring the deepest recesses of personal identity and individualistic expression. This degeneracy, Miłosz believes, begins with the impressionists and climaxes with cubism and the artistic and literary theories of Witkiewicz and Henri Bremond. These approaches lead artists to mythologize the past and embrace the concept of pure form—tendencies that Miłosz finds disturbing. He ends the essay with a reminder of poetry's power, a mystical power so strong that it influences civilizations more than the forces of science and politics. This is why, according to Miłosz, poetry must have boundaries that will keep form in balance with substance and thereby transform poetry into a force for order and cultural enrichment rather than disintegration and relativism.

Legends of Modernity closes with a set of nine essay length letters written by Miłosz and Polish novelist Jerzy Andrzejewski. These letters, composed in 1942 and 1943 and exchanged by hand at great risk in Warsaw's Aria Café, a center of anti-Nazi underground activity, chart the thoughts of these important Polish writers during the height of Poland's suffering under the Nazis. They serve as a coda to *Legends of Modernity*, repeating the collection's major themes in a more personal, argumentative format. These letters possess a certain irony, for when they were written, Andrzejewski was a conservative, Catholic nationalist responding to Miłosz's democratic socialist visions of art and politics. Later, Andrezejewski became a communist and supported the postwar Stalinist regime in Poland, writing his most famous novel, *Popió i diament* (1948; *Ashes and Diamonds*, 1962), as a favorable portrait of early Communist Party rule; while Miłosz, horrified by the abuses of power in Soviet-style postwar Poland, lived in exile in the United States and ultimately rejected socialism.

While the letters largely reiterate the themes Miłosz elucidated with greater eloquence in the essays, there are two new major contributions in them. In the third letter, Miłosz proposes that all people are innately ethical. However, Nazis and Stalinists twist such ethics through perverse definitions. Thus, if a Nazi defines a Jew as subhuman, he can be charitable and loving to his children or to a fellow German, while shooting a Jewish prisoner in the head after torturing him. This is what happens, Miłosz argues, when art and morality become indeterminate. In the final letter, the war comes to the forefront to a depth not seen elsewhere in the book. Miłosz laments the deaths of his friends who have been the war's victims and emphasizes again how terribly wrong Nietzsche was to embrace the irrational, stating that "audacity of thought is not always a guarantee of truth." He finishes with the genuine hope that intellectuals and artists will reform and embrace meaning, culture, and truth, thereby helping to bring about a more sane, compassionate, and meaningful European civilization.

Legends of Modernity is a powerful work, in part because it serves as a record of a major author's thoughts while living in the midst of probably one of the most oppressed cities in Nazi-occupied Europe. In the book, the war is mostly a subtext, rarely mentioned but always present as a dark undercurrent to Miłosz's literary and philosophical wanderings. More important, by collecting these essays and letters into a unified collection, Miłosz reveals the origins of the literary and intellectual concerns that blossom in his decades of writing essays and poems. Postmodern theorists state that literature and art are devoid of perennial truths, that the very concept of truth is a tainted fiction left over from the narrow confines of the Enlightenment and its triumph of absolute values. Miłosz stood in opposition to the relativism of deconstruction and championed the belief that for art to have power, both for the individual and for the society, it must embrace truth and culture as meaningful terms. For Miłosz, this central belief runs throughout his work, from an early book of essays such as *The Captive Mind* to a late collection of poetry such as *To* (2000). *Legends of Modernity* allows one to glimpse the sources of Miłosz's lifelong elevated vision in the depths of war-torn Europe, like a great flower blossoming from the ruins.

John Nizalowski

Review Sources

Kirkus Reviews 73, no. 16 (August 15, 2005): 900-901.
Library Journal 130, no. 17 (October 15, 2005): 56-58.
The Nation 282, no. 2 (January 9, 2006): 26-30.
Publishers Weekly 252, no. 33 (August 22, 2005): 53.

THE LETTERS OF ROBERT LOWELL

Author: Robert Lowell (1917-1977)
Edited, with endnotes, by Saskia Hamilton
Publisher: Farrar, Straus and Giroux (New York). 852
  pp. $40.00
Type of work: Letters
Time: 1936-1977
Locale: New England, New York City, England

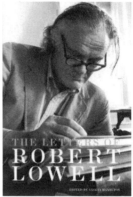

Saskia Hamilton presents 711 of Lowell's letters, arranged chronologically and annotated

Principal personages:
ROBERT LOWELL, a poet
RANDALL JARRELL, a poet, critic, and novelist
PETER TAYLOR, a novelist
EZRA POUND, a poet
ELIZABETH BISHOP, a poet
JEAN STAFFORD, a writer and Lowell's first wife
ELIZABETH HARDWICK, a novelist and Lowell's second wife
CAROLINE BLACKWOOD, a novelist and Lowell's third wife

In a letter to Beat poet Allen Ginsberg, Robert Lowell set out his theory of epistolary composition: "I think letters ought to be written the way you think poetry ought be. So let this be breezy, brief, incomplete, but spontaneous and not dishonestly holding back." The sampling of letters that editor Saskia Hamilton has assembled reveals the virtues and flaws of this approach. Lowell is not among the great letter writers, such as John Keats or Virginia Woolf. Prose was not his preferred medium. As he wrote to his good friend Elizabeth Bishop on April 15, 1976, he was having trouble composing an obituary on the philosopher Hannah Arendt because he felt "naked without my end-lines." Nonetheless, this volume of letters offers insights into Lowell's attitude toward poetry, his own life, and his attitudes toward other writers. Often, too, the writing is good fun.

This anthology begins with a letter dated May 2, 1936, which Lowell, an undergraduate at Harvard University, sent to Ezra Pound. Already one sees Lowell's dedication to the craft of poetry: He asks Pound to take him on as an apprentice. Pound refused, but this letter began a lifelong friendship grounded in mutual admiration. In the late 1950's Pound would tell Harry Meacham that Lowell was the best poet and the best human being in America. Lowell repeatedly visited Pound while the elder poet was being held in St. Elizabeth's Hospital in Washington, D.C. After World War II, Pound was a controversial figure because of the radio broadcasts he had made for Benito Mussolini's Fascist regime. When Random House thought about dropping Pound from its *Anthology of Famous English and American Poetry* (1946), Lowell informed the publisher that if Pound's work was removed, Lowell wanted his own deleted as well. Bennett Cerf, the president of Random House, relented.

The letters also show that Lowell was not, however, uncritical of the older writer. Pound was notoriously anti-Semitic, while Lowell had Jewish relatives. Pound had supported fascism; Lowell was a liberal (though he shunned being labeled anything). Even Pound's poetry was not immune to Lowell's criticism. Lowell found *The Pisan Cantos* (1948) excellent in places but over-long, an opinion which he expressed to Pound and others.

At the age of nineteen Lowell wrote to the poet Richard Eberhart that only "an etymological fanatic armed with a Websters dictionary" could get through Eberhart's "Alphabet Book" (1936). He was unflattering about Aldous Huxley's *Eyeless in Gaza* (1936), which he found unreadable. In the previously cited letter to Ginsberg, Lowell made clear that he did not care for that poet's approach to the craft, nor for Beat poetry in general.

> One of the inventors of confessional poetry, Robert Lowell was the leading American poet of the postwar period, winning two Pulitzer Prizes, the National Book Award, and the Bollingen Prize for poetry. He served as poetry consultant to the Library of Congress (forerunner of the poet laureateship) and taught at Harvard and Boston Universities and the University of Essex. Among his students were poets Sylvia Plath, Anne Sexton, and W. D. Snodgrass.

At least in the selection that Hamilton presents here, though, Lowell appears for the most part generous and gracious. He repeatedly expresses his admiration for the work of Bishop, Randall Jarrell, Peter Taylor, William Carlos Williams, Philip Larkin, William Empson, Adrienne Rich, Ted Hughes, John Berryman, Flannery O'Connor, and others. Even when his friend Allen Tate objected to Lowell and others about Lowell's turning to free verse, Lowell replied kindly to the older poet's strictures. However difficult Lowell may have been in person, these letters at least make him seem altogether kind and considerate.

One sees repeatedly in the letters how Lowell also tried to provide concrete assistance to other writers. In a 1956 letter to Bishop, Lowell recounts trying to secure the prestigious Bollingen Prize in poetry for either her or Jarrell. When he was poetry consultant to the Library of Congress (forerunner of the poet laureateship) he promoted the work of many fellow authors through recordings and readings. He encouraged Bishop to join him at the artists' colony of Yaddo. In a letter on January 18, 1949, Lowell recommended both Bishop and Jarrell to T. S. Eliot, editor at the British publishing house of Faber and Faber.

Lowell's poems tend to brevity; many are sonnets, and most do not exceed a page. This same concision characterizes the letters presented here, which display Lowell's epigrammatic skills. In a letter to Peter Taylor dated October 31, 1958, Lowell neatly encapsulates Allen Tate's biography as an "endlessly picaresque and phallic life." An earlier letter to Taylor shows the dissolute, decaying Dylan Thomas visiting the Iowa Writers' Workshop: "dumpy, absurd body, hair combed by a salad spoon, brown-button Welsh eyes always moving suspiciously . . . a great explosion of life, and hell to handle." In a letter to Bishop on November 29, 1953, Lowell relates Caitlin

Thomas's coming to New York in pursuit of her straying, dying husband. According to Lowell, Caitlin wanted both to murder and have sex with everyone she saw. His thumbnail sketch of Theodore Roethke captures the man in a sentence: "Poor thing, a mammoth, yet elfinlike, hairless, red-faced, beginning the day with a shot of bourbon, speechless except for shrewd quoted asides—behind him nervous breakdown, before him—what?"

Lowell could be equally good in writing about himself. Describing his life with Caroline Blackwood, his soon-to-be third wife, he writes to Peter Taylor on March 20, 1972, "The house is early eighteenth century Palladian, and very Old South messy, a just housebroken miniature dachshund, about a thousand children, numerous, very unreliable, even dangerous, Old South help, strangely dressed." He is always amusing when he describes the life and adventures of Harriet, the daughter he had with his second wife, Elizabeth Hardwick. One senses from these letters that the hardest part of his divorce from Hardwick was the rift that it created between Lowell and his daughter.

Lowell's poetry was confessional; this collection sheds even more light on his inner and outer life. An early letter to his parents anticipates Lowell's lifelong serial infatuation with a variety of women. On August 9, 1936, he sent his mother and father the sort of letter some parents have nightmares about receiving. Lowell states that Harvard is a waste of time; he sees no reason to get a job as the family has plenty of money; and he's going to marry his cousin (Anne Dick) even though his parents object.

Lowell did leave Harvard, but the next year he met the poet John Crowe Ransom, whom he followed to Kenyon College. In June, 1940, his parents received some welcome news: Lowell had graduated from Kenyon summa cum laude, Phi Beta Kappa, with highest honors in classics, and valedictorian. He even had a job at Louisiana State University. His relationship with Dick had ended in 1937; in April of 1940 Lowell married Jean Stafford.

This marriage ended in 1946, though the divorce proceedings dragged on for two years. The letters trace the difficult negotiations, as they do the later divorce from Hardwick, whom he married in 1949. Between Stafford and Hardwick, Lowell had affairs with Gertrude Buckman and Carly Dawson. Buckman was eager to marry him, but on February 19, 1948, Lowell wrote to her that he was not ready for another marriage. A month later he was writing to Dawson, asking to marry her. Throughout his more than twenty-year marriage to Hardwick he repeatedly would announce that the two were about to divorce and that he was planning to wed someone else. Often these infatuations were linked to his manic attacks, for which he was hospitalized many times. (An early hint of the onset of these illnesses was Lowell's writing large numbers of letters in a single day.) Even after affairs ended, Lowell often corresponded with and befriended his paramours.

Lowell's ability to remain on good terms with women after the end of a romance (or marriage) is nowhere more evident than in his relationship with Bishop as charted in these letters. In the summer of 1948, Lowell and Dawson visited Bishop in Maine. The Lowell-Dawson affair ended, and Lowell wrote to friends that he was planning to marry Bishop. While Bishop was to have a long-term lesbian relationship, she had also had affairs with men, though never with Lowell. At Yaddo that year, Lowell and Bishop quarreled, and in 1950 Bishop moved to Brazil with her partner. A decade later, Lowell and Bishop were together again in New England, though Bishop left after a few days when Lowell grew amorous, the effect of another manic attack. Yet for the next twenty years the two remained the best of friends and correspondents.

Disappointingly, Lowell wrote little about his own poetic theory or practice. He much admired the letters of the nineteenth century poet John Keats, but he did not imitate their insights into the life of writing. Still, he does make clear how important writing is to him. He tells Bishop on July 2, 1948, that nothing is as real to him as writing, and nearly thirty years later he notes that an entire day can vanish unnoticed when he is engaged in creating poetry. In an October 10, 1961, letter to Isabella Gardner, then married to Allen Tate, Lowell observes that writing is hell, but that there is always the surprise, the discovery of the unexpected. The next year he relates to Bishop that one surprise is his writing in strict meter, despite his theories about how poetry should be written. Later one sees him reflect on his turn to freer, and free, verse. Like any good writer, Lowell was an inveterate reviser; the letters show his wrestling with that hardest of all tasks, getting the words right.

This edition of letters is not without its flaws. While the 711 letters cover 670 pages, they also cover forty-one years, or fewer than 20 letters per year. This is a book of letters, not of a correspondence, and the notes often fail to include the letter or letters to which Lowell is responding. Indeed, the notes are deficient overall. One often turns to the back of the book for information only to find it unenlightening. Readers are sometimes referred to a manuscript at Harvard or Yale or told no more about a work than its date. A separate section of brief biographies of correspondents and others mentioned would be useful. People usually are identified in the notes when they first appear, but few readers are likely to read the letters from beginning to end or to remember where a name first occurred should they want to be reminded of a person's identity. Still, anyone interested in Lowell or in the literary scene of the mid-twentieth century United States will welcome this collection.

Joseph Rosenblum

Review Sources

Booklist 101, no. 14 (March 15, 2005): 1258.
Harper's Magazine 311 (July, 2005): 92-98.
The New Republic 232, no. 24 (June 27, 2005): 32-36.
The New York Review of Books 52, no. 11 (June 23, 2005): 4-10.
The New York Times Book Review 154 (June 26, 2005): 10-11.
Poetry 186, no. 3 (June, 2005): 248-254.
The Spectator 298 (July 9, 2005): 32-33.
The Times Literary Supplement, September 9, 2005, pp. 3-5.
The Virginia Quarterly Review 81, no. 4 (Fall, 2005): 269-284.

LIGHT FROM HEAVEN

Author: Jan Karon (1937-   )
Publisher: Viking Penguin (New York). 384 pp. $27.00
Type of work: Novel
Time: 2005
Locale: In and around Mitford, a fictional town in the
southeastern United States

*In this seventh volume of the Mitford series, Father Tim
starts to rebuild a small, rural church, unused for many
years, and becomes involved in the lives of his parishioners*

Principal characters:

FATHER TIM KAVANAGH, an elderly Episcopal priest whose quiet ministry touches
a great variety of small-town personalities

CYNTHIA KAVANAGH, wife and soulmate of Father Tim, a writer and
illustrator of children's books

AGNES MERTON, an elderly woman who has provided faithful mainte-
nance at Holy Trinity Church since its closure more than thirty years
ago

CLARENCE MERTON, son of Agnes, deaf from birth, a skilled craftsman
in wood

SAMMY BARLOWE, a teenage boy who runs away from his alcoholic
father and comes to live with the Kavanaghs; brother of Dooley from
the earlier Mitford books

DONNY and DOVEY, a brother and sister whose mother is in prison for
killing their abusive father

UNCLE BILLY WATSON, a parishioner in Mitford, known for his hilarious
jokes

Light from Heaven is the seventh in Jan Karon's series of books featuring Father
Tim. In the earlier books, Father Tim came to live and work in Mitford, a fictional
town that might be located in the author's home state of North Carolina. Karon's
strength as a writer has been to give a sympathetic portrait of life in a small town. People who have read any of the earlier books in this series will fondly recall Uncle Billy,
the joke teller, Emma, the overly efficient church secretary, the men who gather at the
Main Street Grill for food and conversation, and Father Tim's lengthy romance with
his neighbor Cynthia that eventually leads to his marriage at age sixty-three.

In the current book, Karon introduces her readers to a large cast of new characters
whose joys and tragedies are skillfully woven together. Each chapter may have a
dozen or more short anecdotes that move the individual life stories forward. Karon's
writing is like a large wall mural that contains many people drawn by the artist, each
one distinctively different. An elderly woman sitting in a rocking chair, a young cou-

ple walking together, a farmer busy with chores, a grandmother reading to a young child, an angry, drunken man pointing a gun at his frightened son, a construction worker building a chimney, a priest visiting a hospital room—these are a few of the vignettes to be found in *Light from Heaven.*

Father Tim has retired from his church work in Mitford. He and Cynthia are living on a nearby farm that is owned by some friends who will be away for a year. A hired man takes care of the sheep and chickens and other farm work. Cynthia is happily at work writing and drawing pictures for a new children's book. Father Tim finds himself at loose ends, with no defined duties. One day he receives a call from his bishop, who is also his close friend since seminary days, asking if he would be willing to take on a new responsibility. Not far from where he lives there is a church called Holy Trinity that has stood empty for more than thirty years. Would he consider trying to bring that church back into operation? Some money is available to help repair the building, but for everything else he would be on his own.

Jan Karon was an advertising executive before she started her career as a writer. The beginning volume in the Mitford series, At Home in Mitford, *was first published serially in a small-town newspaper. It became a book in 1994 and was a* New York Times *best seller.* Light from Heaven *is to be the last in the Mitford series. Karon has published sixteen books, including two for children.*

How does one start a new congregation? Where will the people come from? Father Tim, almost seventy years old, wonders if he has the energy to handle such an assignment. All of his previous work has been with established congregations. He has a strong need, however, to feel useful, to do something meaningful with his time. With the encouragement of his wife and the bishop, he finally agrees to accept the job, but with a time limit of one year. In his personal collection of quotations, he finds one by Will Rogers that seems appropriate to his current situation: "Go out on a limb—that's where the fruit is."

Father Tim makes his first trip out to the abandoned church to see what is left after many years of disuse. He drives along rural roads into the hill country, looking for the building. When he arrives, he is completely amazed. The grass has been mowed, the church pews have been dusted, the woodwork gleams with fresh polish, and the floor has been swept clean. Has someone been expecting him? Who has been doing all this maintenance work? No one is around. He notes that the pulpit is missing and that there is no cross above the altar. There are no hymnals or prayer books, so some work needs to be done.

On his second visit he meets Agnes Merton, a woman in her eighties who has been caring for the church since it was closed. Her story emerges slowly. Agnes and another young woman had been sent to Holy Trinity by the Missionary Society of the Episcopal Church. They came to teach school in this poverty-stricken region of Appalachia and to be the deaconesses for the church, which was too small to have a regular priest. Agnes says that her faith grew slowly, as a child's foot grows into a shoe that is too large.

Some years later, the church was closed, and both women left for other places. When Agnes's father died, she received a small inheritance. Agnes had a son, Clarence, who was born deaf. She decided to move back to Appalachia to raise her son. She felt a calling to maintain Holy Trinity Church as a penance until God sent someone to reopen it. The arrival of Father Tim was an answer to her patient prayers.

Agnes proposes to go with Father Tim for home visits to see who may want to make a fresh start at Holy Trinity. Through these visits, Karon introduces the reader to a diverse group of individuals, including a man who drives them away with a gun and two sisters who welcome them with tea and cookies. At one home, he meets Donny and Dovey, a brother and sister whose mother is in prison for killing their violent, abusive father. Dovey has been bedfast for a long time with a mysterious illness but refuses to go to a doctor. She has a talkative, five-year-old daughter who provides lighthearted, comic relief in these sad circumstances. After more home visits, Father Tim decides that the time has come to set a date for the first worship service. It is to be on Easter Sunday, the most significant day in the Christian calendar. When the day arrives, the congregation consists of seven people, including himself. Seeing them sitting in the pews, he expresses deep gratitude to God for their presence.

Through the following summer and fall, the congregation grows in size, and the congregants grow in mutual concern for one another. Clarence makes wonderful wooden toys which he freely gives away. With help from Agnes and a lively young boy, people start to learn sign language so that they can communicate with Clarence. Someone donates a piano to the church, and soon there is a choir of three people to lead the singing. The church has never had plumbing facilities, but during the offering one Sunday a construction worker announces that he will build an outhouse, and it will even have separate places for men and women.

Along with his new church duties, Father Tim still maintains a friendly camaraderie with some of his former parishioners and friends in Mitford. One of the colorful characters from Karon's previous books is Uncle Billy Watson, the man who had a joke for every occasion. Father Tim used to visit him and always came away refreshed by having had a good laugh. When Uncle Billy dies, Father Tim is called to conduct the funeral service. To celebrate the life of the deceased, he asks the congregation if any of them wish to share some memories. One person stands up and tells a funny story that he remembered hearing from Uncle Billy. Other people become encouraged to share their favorite Uncle Billy jokes, so gradually the funeral becomes an occasion for laughter. Father Tim has a favorite joke that he starts to tell, but halfway through it he is overcome by the emotion of losing this good friend and is unable to go on. Then Rose Watson, Billy's wife, stands up to finish the story and provide the punch line. It is a poignant moment.

In the earlier books, Father Tim had become the surrogate father for Dooley Barlowe, a boy from a dysfunctional family. Dooley has matured and is now in college. Sammy, a younger brother of Dooley, arrives one day at Father Tim's front door after running away from his domineering father. Sammy, sixteen years old, needs a place to live. Father Tim and Cynthia offer to take him in but insist on some house rules. It is their second time to deal with the stressful ups and downs of having a teenager in their home. Sammy says he wants to make it on his own, but Father Tim responds that no one can make it without help from others.

With the approach of Thanksgiving and Christmas, Father Tim's tenure as priest at Holy Trinity is coming to a close. Some loose ends remain to be tied up. The mysterious illness that had been afflicting Dovey is finally solved by a doctor who is willing to make a house call to gain her cooperation. Father Tim completes the legal requirements to formally adopt Dooley as his son. Sammy, Dooley's brother, very reluctantly agrees to be a shepherd in the Christmas pageant at church, a big step forward for him. A difficult parishioner who had been in prison for a crime he did not commit overcomes his anger and resentment as he accepts God's forgiveness. Finally, Kenny Barlowe, a brother of Dooley and Sammy who has been missing for many years, shows up unexpectedly at the Kavanagh house. It becomes a joy-filled Christmas.

Father Tim is portrayed as a warmly human and sensitive person. He has a special talent for listening to people's stories and making them aware of God's unlimited love. He prays frequently. His mission is to help each person move forward along their journey of faith. In difficult situations that seem to have no solution at all, he relies on a prayer that he says never fails, which is simply, "Thy will be done." He has the ability to relate to people of very diverse backgrounds and needs. In his book of favorite quotations that Father Tim keeps by his bedside is this powerful, inspiring thought from an unidentified sixteenth century poet: "Every saint has a past, and every sinner has a future."

Karon uses multiple story lines in each chapter. Someone who has not read any of the earlier Mitford books may find it difficult to keep track of the large cast of characters. However, their unique, diverse personalities provide memorable and entertaining portraits of the individual people. The Christian message of God's love and forgiveness is prominent in Father Tim's prayers. From the Mitford series, a reader can gain a greater appreciation for the role of a priest or pastor in the church and in the larger community.

Hans G. Graetzer

Review Sources

The New York Times Book Review 155 (November 27, 2005): 26.
Publishers Weekly 252, no. 42 (October 24, 2005): 30-31.

THE LIGHTHOUSE

Author: P. D. James (1920-   )
Publisher: Alfred A. Knopf (New York). 335 pp. $26.00
Type of work: Novel
Time: 2005
Locale: Combe Island, off England's Cornish coast

When Scotland Yard Inspector Adam Dalgliesh investigates a suspicious death on a private island off the English coast, he uncovers a complexity of intrigues among the island's residents as well as its closely screened visitors and is confronted with a double murder case

Principal characters:
ADAM DALGLIESH, a Scotland Yard detective
NATHAN OLIVER, a novelist
MIRANDA OLIVER, Nathan's daughter
DENNIS TREMLETT, Nathan's secretary-editor
ADRIAN BOYDE, an Anglican priest
RUPERT MAYCROFT, the Combe Island resident secretary
DANIEL PADGETT, the Combe Island handyman
DR. RAIMUND SPEIDEL, a former German diplomat
DR. GUY STAVELEY, the Combe Island physician
JAGO TAMLYN, the Combe Island boatman
DR. MARK YELLAND, a laboratory researcher

Authenticity of characters, setting, and motives is a hallmark of P. D. James's detective novels, in which realism invariably trumps gentility. Even in her first novel, *Cover Her Face* (1962), a traditional detective story in the Agatha Christie tradition, there is an atypical depth of characterization and development of milieu. James eschews the genteel deaths common in the works of her English forebears. In *A Mind to Murder* (1963), her second novel, a woman is killed with a chisel in her heart. In *Unnatural Causes* (1967), a victim is discovered with both hands severed. In *Original Sin* (1995) a victim is discovered with a stuffed snake crammed into his mouth. In *The Lighthouse*, one man is strangled and then hanged, and another has his face bashed to a pulp with his nose reduced to splintered bones.

Such departures from the old norms notwithstanding, much is familiar about *The Lighthouse*, which abounds with echoes not only of previous James mystery novels but also of her indebtedness to predecessors in the genre. Again as in the works of Christie and others appear such motifs as an isolated island setting, a gathering of apparent strangers, old grievances generating vengeance, people trying to escape or overcome past transgressions, and a narrative developed mainly by way of interviews interspersed with consultations among the sleuths. Neither this book nor James's previous ones, however, are mere exercises in armchair detection, for both Detective Inspector Kate Miskin and Sergeant Francis Benton-Smith, Adam Dalgliesh's young assistants, engage in dangerous physical feats as they pursue clues and ultimately corner their prey.

The many similarities that evoke tradition do not demean James's accomplishments in *The Lighthouse*, her seventh Adam Dalgliesh mystery, for throughout her career she has tested the parameters of the genre while adhering to its basic tenets. Consider, for instance, Dalgliesh, a career man who has risen through the ranks of the Metropolitan police force to the higher reaches of Scotland Yard. In his personal life he evolves from grieving widower through several liaisons to the threshold of marriage to Emma Lavenham, a university professor he met in *Death in Holy Orders* (2001). Poet and lover, this policeman is, above all, a sensitive human being. At a key point in *The Lighthouse*, he is laid low by the severe acute respiratory syndrome (SARS) virus—James's novels often reflect current events, an aspect of her realism—and cedes

P. D. James has been a Red Cross nurse, has managed psychiatric units for Great Britain's National Health Service, and was an administrator in Home Office forensics and criminal justice departments. She has held advisory positions with the Church of England and the British Broadcasting Corporation (BBC), has won many writers' awards, and was made Baroness James of Highland Park in 1991.

much of his responsibilities to his assistants, though he—while in sickbed—has the crime-solving epiphany. This illness (like the life-threatening one he is suffering when 1986's *A Taste for Death* begins) enriches the realism, focusing as it does on Dalgliesh's fallibility.

Similarly, James devotes a dozen pages to personal information about Miskin and Benton-Smith, matter with no direct bearing on the investigation except to suggest how their experiences inform their work. Though her sleuths (these three and Cordelia Gray elsewhere) may arrive on a crime scene like avenging deities sent by society's protective spirits, they are very different from the genre's more prevalent two-dimensional, eccentric sleuths. Far from being omniscient or intuitive, these detectives solve crimes almost entirely by legwork and a process of logical deduction from a plethora of clues, most of which are apparent to the careful reader.

Though London-based, Dalgliesh does most of his work in other places, for James often turns to the sea for her settings, either an isolated coastal venue or, in the present instance, privately owned Combe Island off southern England. Available to government officials and people of privilege in industry, the arts, and science as a secure retreat for rest and rejuvenation, the island has only a few permanent residents, most of whom are there to serve its visitors. Owned for centuries by the Holcombes, since

1930 a charitable trust has run it, though one remaining family member, Emily Holcombe, now eighty years old, lives there, tended for the past fifteen years by her manservant Roughthouse.

Others who more or less permanently reside on Combe are Rupert Maycroft, a former solicitor who runs the island on behalf of the trust; the resident physician, Dr. Guy Staveley, who abandoned his London practice after he made a wrong diagnosis that caused a child's death; his wife, who serves as his nurse; Adrian Boyde, an alcoholic Anglican cleric who lost his parish and works as Maycroft's assistant; Mrs. Burbridge, the housekeeper; handyman Dan Padgett, whose mother died soon after taking up a post on the island; and Jago Tamlyn, the island's boatman.

They are joined by a maximum of five visitors at a time, who may stay for just two weeks. Casual visitors are not permitted. The present guests are Dr. Raimund Speidel, a former diplomat; Dr. Mark Yelland, director of a research laboratory besieged by animal rights activists; and renowned novelist Nathan Oliver, his daughter Miranda, and his secretary-editor Dennis Tremlett. Oliver, a central figure in the narrative, was born on the island (his father was its boatman, and he lived on Combe until he was sixteen) and therefore has the right to visit anytime and to stay indefinitely. For years, Miranda has been his full-time companion cum housekeeper, a round-the-clock employee like Tremlett, traveling and living with him, catering to his every whim and manifestly subservient. An island intended as a haven for achievers seeking a respite from their cares has become a refuge for social misfits and failures.

When Nathan Oliver's body is found hanging from the lighthouse, Scotland Yard takes on the case of apparent murder because the prime minister plans to convene a top secret international meeting on Combe, so the matter has to be resolved with dispatch. Oliver, at the height of his career at age sixty-eight but fearful that his creative powers were waning, had become a frequent visitor and decided to make Combe his full-time home, hoping that "here his words would come back."

A crisis had occurred when the island's handyman, Daniel Padgett, apparently lost a blood sample from Oliver that was being sent to the mainland for analysis. Oliver's furious attack on Padgett, quite disproportionate to the event, terrorized the young man. The author then berated Maycroft for having hired the inept Padgett, announced his intent to remove the Combe Trust as a main beneficiary of his will, and made known his desire to live permanently on Combe, with Atlantic Cottage as his residence, indifferent to the fact that Emily Holcombe had lived in the house for years. When Maycroft told the old lady the news, she said, "Legally or illegally, he's got to be stopped. If no one else has the guts to do it, then I shall." Maycroft thought the Combe trustees would blame him for the Oliver residency debacle and that he would lose his job: "He wasn't ready to make yet another fresh start and dreaded the inconvenience and exertion."

Meanwhile, Miranda Oliver and Dennis Tremlett had become lovers, and when her father learned this, he threatened them. In addition, Dr. Yelland believed that an unfavorably portrayed character in Oliver's forthcoming novel was based on him and that the ensuing publicity would imperil his work; he intended to confront Oliver about it. Dr. Speidel had come to Combe to learn the truth about his father's death in

World War II and discovered that Oliver, albeit just a child, may have been culpable. In the same incident, Oliver's father may have killed Jago Tamlyn's father, then the island's boatman. Adrian Boyde, an alcoholic Anglican priest who found refuge on Combe as Maycroft's assistant, also had a grievance against Oliver, who one night gave him wine because "he was writing a book with a character who was a drunkard and he wanted to witness exactly what happened when you feed wine to an alcoholic"—an episode that almost undid Boyde's reformation.

James thus lays before the reader a series of grievances against Oliver, and the medical examiner determines Oliver's death to be a homicide. As many of the present occupants of this insular society have motive as well as opportunity, there are a number of suspects. The murder—by strangulation, with the body then brought to the top of the lighthouse and hanged from a window—requires physical strength and agility. Dalgliesh therefore eliminates most of the women as suspects.

While his aides try to ascertain the whereabouts of remaining suspects at key times, and Dalgliesh in his sickbed is reviewing what he has learned, another body is discovered, eliminating a suspect but complicating the case. The assumption is that Oliver's killer also committed the second murder, for typically in whodunits one crime begets another, often because an otherwise peripheral person is in the wrong place at the wrong time. That this second death, the brutal murder of Boyde at the altar of the island's chapel, is committed in a place of worship should not surprise; James previously has used chapels as murder venues, such as in *Death in Holy Orders* (2001). Her mysteries, not merely puzzles to be solved, are also studies of the nature and manifestation of evil, a power so strong that it even befouls consecrated places, with churchmen sometimes victims and sometimes perpetrators of this evil. In *The Lighthouse* James has two false sanctuaries, the island retreat itself and the chapel on it, just as in other books she shows how similar places—such as rest homes, psychiatric clinics, and the courts—fail to fulfill their traditional palliative purposes.

James enriches this Adam Dalgliesh novel in other ways. While the dysfunctional family is a staple of the genre, *The Lighthouse* has several such, whose problems are rooted in difficult relationships that span generations. In addition, because of its setting, the book inevitably recalls Christie's *Ten Little Indians*, and James may well intend *The Lighthouse* to be a parody of that 1939 classic, just as *Unnatural Causes* (1967) and *The Skull Beneath the Skin* (1982) may be parodies of the whodunit genre as a whole.

Further, rather than just the usual tidying up of loose ends in a concluding chapter, *The Lighthouse* has an epilogue whose mini-chapters, told from different narrative points of view, present the postcase musings of the detectives and erstwhile suspects. What is more, the prevailing tone is surprisingly bittersweet. When she sees Dalgliesh's reunion with Emma, Detective Inspector Miskin realizes the futility of her secret romantic longing for her boss. For Dalgliesh, too, there is not unalloyed satisfaction: "It hasn't been one of our successes, Kate. Adrian Boyde shouldn't have died. . . . If failure teaches us anything, it's humility." Not many fictional detectives react with such sober introspection at the end of a case.

In sum, after more than forty years, P. D. James continues to surprise with her varied approaches to the genre, leading readers to think about matters religious, familial, legal, and literary as well as challenging them to solve crimes in tandem with her sleuths.

Gerald H. Strauss

Review Sources

Booklist 102, no. 4 (October 15, 2005): 4-5.
Kirkus Reviews 73, no. 20 (October 15, 2005): 1110.
The New York Times 155 (December 1, 2005): E1-E9.
The New York Times Book Review 155 (December 25, 2005): 21.
People 64, no. 24 (December 12, 2005): 54.
Publishers Weekly 252, no. 41 (October 17, 2005): 43.
The Spectator 299 (October 1, 2005): 48.*The Times Literary Supplement*, October 7, 2005, p. 23.

LIGHTHOUSEKEEPING

Author: Jeanette Winterson (1959-   )
First published: 2004, in Great Britain
Publisher: Harcourt (Orlando, Fla.). 232 pp. $23.00
Type of work: Novel
Time: From the late eighteenth century to the late twenti-
eth century
Locale: Salts, on the northwest coast of Scotland; Bristol,
England; London; the Isle of Capri; Athens, Greece

*Two characters living a century apart both find that
only love gives meaning to existence*

Principal characters:
    SILVER, a ten-year-old orphan girl and the
      lighthouse keeper's apprentice
    PEW, the blind lighthouse keeper in charge of the Cape Wrath light, a
      storyteller
    THE REVEREND BABEL DARK, a minister in Salts
    MOLLY O'ROURKE, Babel's lover and the mother of his blind daughter
    JOSIAH DARK, Babel's father and the man who financed the lighthouse's
      construction
    DOGJIM, Silver's dog

Although Jeanette Winterson has been called England's best-known lesbian writer, her novels deal with far more profound issues than her own sexual orientation or her noted loathing of organized religion. *Lighthousekeeping* is about a universal problem, the difficulty of finding something or someone that can give life a meaning. The two major characters in this novel never do meet, for one of them lives in the nineteenth century and the other in the twentieth. However, they are both vitally involved in a search for enlightenment, and both come to the same conclusion: that a purposeful life depends on total commitment to another human being.

The novel begins as a first-person narrative, an informal account of the early years of the narrator, who is identified only as Silver. She does not know her father's name; he was a fisherman who happened by on a stormy night. She knows only that after giving birth to an illegitimate child, her mother was evicted by the people of Salts, and the two had to make their home in a lopsided house set into a cliff. When Silver was ten, her mother fell to her death, and no one would take in the orphaned girl except the Cape Wrath lighthouse keeper, a man called Pew, who made Silver his apprentice.

Although he permitted Silver to bring along her dog, at first Pew seemed unfeeling, and it did not help that because he was blind, he kept their living quarters in total darkness. As Silver puts it, there were two Atlantic Oceans, one inside and one outside. However, Pew was more aware of Silver's sense of loss than he had at first ap-

Jeanette Winterson won a Whitbread
Award for best first novel for
Oranges Are Not the Only Fruit
(1985), the John Llewellyn Rhys
Memorial Prize from the British
Book Trust for The Passion *(1987),*
and the E. M. Forster Award from
the American Academy of Arts and
Letters for Sexing the Cherry *(1989).*

peared to be, and he had a remedy for loneliness: storytelling. Soon Silver's request, "Pew, tell me a story," begins to appear regularly in intervals between chapters.

Because Silver is fascinated by the history of the lighthouse, she begins asking Pew about a man called Babel Dark, whose father, Josiah Dark, arranged for the construction of the lighthouse by a young engineer named Robert Louis Stevenson, who would someday be a famous author. Pew insists on introducing his story by comparing Babel Dark to Samson, a man doomed by his love of a woman but, more profoundly, destined to fall because he had placed himself too high.

In 1848, Pew continues, Babel Dark was a dashing young man from Bristol, who was pursuing the study of theology at Cambridge University. No one expected Babel to take holy orders; it was assumed that after he graduated, he would take over the business of his wealthy father, Josiah Dark. Josiah raised no objection when Babel began courting Molly O'Rourke, a pretty shopgirl, and when Molly became pregnant, Josiah urged his son to marry her. However, Babel became suspicious, denied having fathered her child, abandoned Molly, and hastened back to Cambridge. When he next appeared in Bristol, he had given up his former finery for gloomy garb and was announcing that he meant to go into the Church. Moreover, although through his father's influence he could have been assigned to a pleasant parish, he insisted on being assigned to Salts. In 1851, he married a gentle, well-connected local woman. However, Pew adds, it was rumored that Babel continued to see Molly and that he might finally have killed her. To Silver's question as to what happened to the child, Pew replies that no one knows.

From that point on, the novel moves between Silver's first-person narrative, which includes Pew's stories, and Babel Dark's account of his own life, related sometimes by an omniscient author, at other times as an interior monologue. Winterson's artistry is evident in the seamlessness of these transitions from one point of view to another and also in her deft handling of the thematic development of the novel.

One way to trace this development is to look at the headings of the nine sections into which *Lighthousekeeping* is divided. The first heading, "Two Atlantics," repeats the comment Silver made after she moved into the lighthouse and before she established her relationship with Pew. However, the phrase can also be applied to Babel Dark. When he coldly turns his back on Molly, he is beginning the process that will leave him as empty as the ocean itself.

Early in the second section, "Known Point in the Darkness," Silver defines the lighthouse in exactly those terms. Before it was constructed, Pew explains, wreckers would use lights to entice ships onto the rocks. Pew calls those lights lies, for, he says; only a true light can illumine one's path. Again, the narrative turns to Babel Dark, who has now realized that when he rejected Molly's love, he chose death over life, darkness over light. Ignoring what his professed faith could have revealed to him, the possibility of redemption, Babel begins to live as two people. One of them is the clergyman, whose behavior to his parishioners and to his wife is never more than perfunctory. The other is the man whose diary reveals the torment within, who recognizes the fact that his habitual mistreatment of his wife is an expression of the degree to which he despises himself.

"A Tenant of the Sun" quotes a conversation that Pew maintains he had with Babel Dark, during which the minister referred to the biblical tale in which human beings, aspiring to be gods, built a tower as high as the moon. Babel Dark comments that he feels an affinity for the moon; that barren landscape, he says, is where he belongs. This important conversation emphasizes two themes that are repeated throughout *Lighthousekeeping*. One is the danger of pride, the sin of Samson and of the tower-builders, and the other is the danger of isolation. For Winterson, the two are related. While she rejects conventional religious principles, which would define pride as attempting to make oneself equal to God, she does hold to the principle of the second great commandment, which commands Christians to love their neighbors as themselves.

In the section that follows, "Great Exhibition," it appears that Babel may find his lost happiness. On a trip to London with his wife, he sees Molly and her child, who is blind, presumably from the brutal beating Babel inflicted on Molly during her pregnancy. Now Babel embarks upon a double life. He marries Molly, buys her a house near Bristol, and as "Mr. Lux," he takes up his residence there for two months every year. However, against his orders, Molly comes to Salts, attends church, and learns that he has another wife there, as well as a son. The section ends with another crisis: Pew is informed that the lighthouse is to be automated, and his services will no longer be needed.

In "A Place Before the Flood," while rescuing his dog, Tristan, from a perilous ledge, Babel Dark finds a cave full of fossils. This discovery brings scientist Charles Darwin to Salts and leads Babel to reexamine his notions of God, whose very existence he has come to doubt. Meanwhile, Pew and DogJim vanish, leaving Silver with little more than nostalgic recollections of the time before "the Flood," in other words, before her world vanished. At this point, the book changes dramatically. The repeated phrase becomes "Tell me a story, Silver," for as Pew predicted, Silver has now learned how to transcend place and time through narrative. This skill enables her to make her way into the new world of adulthood.

In "New Planet," Silver is in Bristol, haunting the library and stealing a book because she needs to read the story. In "Talking Bird," she is on Capri, in Italy, stealing a talking bird. Thus Winterson emphasizes the importance of words. It is through words, through stories that Silver will connect with others and find happiness. Babel's prospects are less hopeful. Having heard of the fossil cave, Robert Louis Stevenson revisits Salts and talks with Babel Dark about the possibility of a person's having two diametrically opposed personalities.

"Some Wounds" begins with the story of Tristan and Isolde, who gave up their very lives for love. Then the narrative moves to Babel Dark, who is drinking tea with

Pew, who may well be Silver's Pew at an earlier age. Babel shows him the book he has just received from Stevenson, *The Strange Case of Dr. Jekyll and Mr. Hyde* (1886). Like the man with two selves in Stevenson's novel, Babel confesses that he has not just lived two different lives but that he is actually two different people. In Bristol, he not only went under the name of Lux, but he actually was Lux, or light. In Salts, he was a dark man named Dark. At this point the author explains why Molly came to Salts: She wanted Babel to leave Salts and go with her to France. In other words, she sought a real commitment. However, Babel Dark preferred to continue living as a hypocrite. Despite her pleas, he remained adamant, and Molly left.

Unlike Dark, Silver has the courage to commit herself to love. In Greece, she encounters a stranger, reaches out to her, and establishes a connection by telling her a story. "The Hut" is the account of their rendezvous in England, which Silver optimistically assumes is the beginning of a lifelong relationship. By contrast, Babel Dark now realizes that by being unwilling to give himself fully, he has forfeited love forever. He has learned too late that his initial suspicions of Molly were groundless, and even though she could forgive him for doubting her, he could not reciprocate by making the necessary commitment. Having denied love not once but twice, Dark seeks Molly in death.

The epilogue takes place twenty years after Silver left the lighthouse. Slipping away from the official tour group, Silver begins to explore her former home. Suddenly Pew appears. His purpose in coming back, it seems, is to make sure that Silver knows how to do two things, to tell stories and to tell her love. Once he is reassured on both points, Pew gets into his little boat and, with DogJim, he disappears into the mist.

Although *Lighthousekeeping* has a simple theme, it is not a simple book. It has a complex structure, a wide range of symbols, and a multitude of allusions. It draws on the traditions of Magical Realism, but it also resembles fable, fantasy, and folktale. With *Lighthousekeeping*, Winterson has again demonstrated why she is considered one of England's most innovative young writers.

Rosemary M. Canfield Reisman

Review Sources

Booklist 101, no. 11 (February 1, 2005): 943.
Kirkus Reviews 72, no. 24 (December 15, 2004): 1164.
Library Journal 130, no. 1 (January, 2005): 101.
New Statesman 133 (May 17, 2004): 55.
The New York Times Book Review 154 (May 1, 2005): 23.
Publishers Weekly 252, no. 4 (January 24, 2005): 218.
The Times Literary Supplement, May 7, 2004, p. 21.

LIKE A FIERY ELEPHANT
The Story of B. S. Johnson

Author: Jonathan Coe (1961-   )
First published: 2004, in Great Britain
Publisher: Continuum (New York). 486 pp. $30.00
Type of work: Literary biography
Time: 1934-1974
Locale: England

This first-person account of the experimental British novelist who took his own life at the age of forty is unconventional and engaging

Principal personages:
B. S. (BRYAN STANLEY) JOHNSON, a British
    novelist
SAMUEL BECKETT, one of his literary
    heroes
ZULFIKAR GHOSE, his confidant and fellow writer
STANLEY JOHNSON, his father
EMILY JOHNSON, his mother
VIRGINIA JOHNSON, his wife
JULIA TREVELYAN OMAN, a photographer and one of Johnson's collaborators on book projects
ANTHONY SMITH and TONY TILLINGHAST, Johnson's close friends
MURIEL STARKEY, Johnson's lover who rejected him
JOYCE YATES, one of Johnson's lovers and friends

Jonathan Coe is a novelist who has written an unconventional biography of an unconventional writer. B. S. Johnson believed in novels that did not lie. In his view, a novel was a form of writing, not a made-up story. In other words, the novelist's duty was to stick to the facts of his life as he understood them. Nothing was real unless the novelist had experienced it. When Johnson wrote about a sea voyage in his novel *Trawl* (1966) he actually went to sea in order to present an authentic account.

Furthermore, Johnson thought that, because life did not present itself as a neat plot, novels should not tidy up events and human characters in order to present pleasing fiction. The chaos of life—its randomness—had to be reflected in novels. In one instance, Johnson presented his readers with a novel unbound in a box, with the instruction that the novel should be read in any order whatsoever.

Samuel Beckett and the practitioners of the French new novel, who rejected conventional narrative and focused on the writer's interior life, heavily influenced Johnson. This is why Johnson, as Coe points out, so often favored the interior monologue. Only that form of writing could be true to the writer's personal experience.

With *Like a Fiery Elephant: The Story of B. S. Johnson*, Coe has attempted something like Johnson's approach to the novel by producing a biography that begins with

〜

*Jonathan Coe, born in Birmingham,
England, is an award-winning
novelist, biographer, and critic. His
novels include* What a Carve Up!
*(1994), which won the John
Llewellyn Rhys Prize and the French
Prix du Meilleur Livre Étranger;*
The House of Sleep *(1997), which
won the Writers' Guild Best Fiction
Award; and* The Rotters' Club
(2001). He lives in London.

〜

the biographer's first glimpse of his subject on television. This occurs long before Coe becomes one of Johnson's readers, and long before Coe even begins to think about writing Johnson's biography. Johnson did a good deal of work for television and the theater, and Coe, like many of Johnson's audience, confesses that his first encounter with the writer was mystifying.

Indeed, although mainstream publishers distributed Johnson's work, he had a small audience in Britain, and most of his work was not published in the United States because it was deemed too British (one of Johnson's favorite topics was the rigidity of the British class system) and esoteric. His kind of experimental prose hardly appealed to a mass audience. Johnson, a truculent author, blamed his publishers for not making his work better known.

Coe surmounts the difficulties of getting to know Johnson and his work by making the reader a kind of collaborator or interlocutor. The biography reads like a chatty conversation—or a story by Henry James, with the "industrious biographer" recounting how he foraged through his subject's papers. Coe jocularly refers to "our hero," who, "you will be pleased to learn," after a period of struggle achieved literary, if not popular, recognition.

At certain points Coe confesses he is "bored" with Johnson, especially with his subject's intense but narrowminded definition of the novel, which, the biographer notes, Johnson is not always able to fulfill in practice. In other words, Johnson does sometime fictionalize. *Trawl*, for example, while based on an actual sea voyage, was in all likelihood written mostly in Johnson's London flat, as Johnson was very seasick for most of his time aboard ship. Still Coe tempers his skepticism about Johnson's literary theories and provides fascinating detail on how they actually work out in the fiction. He also admires his subject's independence and tenacity.

A heavyset man—many figures in the book call him fat—Johnson was a rather awkward, if persistent, lover and a combative writer whose outspoken work got him into trouble with printers who objected to his use of profanity. During his early twenties, he supplemented his income by becoming a substitute teacher (a supply teacher in English terms). One of his students called him a "firy [sic] elephant," a phrase that captures both the majestic and the blundering aspect of Johnson's persona.

Like a good novelist, Coe provides vivid portraits of the important people in Johnson's life: his energetic mother, who coddled her only son; his shy, retiring father whose love of sports seems to have been the one bond with his son (who became quite a talented sportswriter); Johnson's wise and tolerant lover, Joyce Yates, almost twenty years his senior, who remained a mainstay of his life even after their affair ended; his beautiful wife, Virginia, an executive's daughter who was at first charmed by her working-class husband but then baffled by him; the novelist Zulfikar Ghose, who collaborated with Johnson on many projects and shared his ambition to shake up the world of British fiction; and friends such as Tony Tillinghast and Anthony Smith, who often tried to get Johnson to lighten up and not take himself quite so seriously.

Johnson was happy for a time with Virginia and their child, but his heart belonged to literature in a rather shocking way. Early on, he thought of himself as a captive of the "White Goddess," the term Robert Grave used in a book by the same title that described the poet as enthralled by his muse. Although Johnson sought realism in his fiction and his poetry, his view of the writer was romantic. He claimed to have had a vision of the White Goddess (although Coe is hard put to pin down exactly what this experience of the muse entailed) and a premonition that he would die at thirty. Johnson lived to forty, but there is plenty of evidence in his writing and from Coe's interviews with his friends that Johnson was often suicidal and that he believed the writer's lot was grim, even when his career was going well.

Unlike Johnson's unconventional novels, Coe's unusual biography is not that daunting. After his chatty introduction, he provides a chapter with brief but lucid descriptions of Johnson's novels and of how they related to his life. Only then does the biographer begin to provide a chronological account of his subject's life.

The conversational tone continues, with the biographer pointing out when evidence is scarce. He also lets Johnson tell part of the story by including extracts from Johnson's journals, fiction, and journalism. The result is a remarkable sense of intimacy—a bond that is formed not only between reader and subject but also between reader and biographer. Coe tosses in asides about his own career as a novelist, although in judicious fashion. He earns the reader's confidence by sharing with the reader the difficulties of researching and writing a biography, including those first confusing days as the biographer begins to sift through his subject's papers, seeking something that will make Johnson "come alive."

Although Coe certainly interprets his subject's life, he also knows that interpretation can obstruct events as much as it can illuminate them. Here, for example, is a passage on Johnson's tormented relationship with Muriel Starkey: "Anyway, Johnson and Muriel went out for a while, and then they split up: let's keep it as banal as that. She 'betrayed' him, in his parlance, and from then on he would usually refer to her in melodramatic phrases such as his 'dead love.'" Not only does Coe provide his view of the subject and the subject's view of himself, but by using the phrase "let's keep it as banal as that," he includes the reader as well—as if to say that Johnson can only come to life to the extent that the reader is willing to parley, so to speak, with the biographer. Biography, in Coe's hands, is a kind of negotiable document, with the biographer always searching for the right word, even when it turns out to be "banal."

A sense of doom hovers over Johnson, even though Coe does not belabor the point. One of Johnson's friends tells him, for example, that if he means to pursue an aesthetic that requires him to write about only what he has experienced, then his literary career will be a short one—perhaps five years. The remark is prophetic. After seven novels in not much more than a decade, Johnson could not go on. No person can live enough, experience enough, his friend told him, to make a sustained literary career by relying simply on his autobiography.

At various times friends tried to shake Johnson out of his solipsism. He should get over Starkey, for example, whose memory continued to plague him after his marriage. Johnson simply could not let go of any hurt, and therefore he could not get a perspective on his own experience.

This is what *Like a Fiery Elephant* is able to do: provide a context for Johnson's fraught life. The biography as conversation between reader and biographer is a kind of therapeutic exercise that illuminates Johnson—that most autobiographical of writers—in ways that he could not do for himself. This is an authorized biography. Coe thanks Johnson's wife and two children for their help, but he emphasizes that all interpretations of Johnson's life are his own. He has evidently had a free hand in creating an affectionate yet critical biography. That he dedicates his book to two of his sources, Joyce Yates and Julia Trevelyan Oman, suggests the kind of rapport he was able to establish with his interviewees. Yates and Oman become almost a kind of chorus in the book, commenting on the action and providing measured and memorable portraits of Johnson and his milieu.

With a writer such as Johnson, who is just coming back into print and who even in his heyday had a rather small following, it is also helpful to have Coe's notes and extensive bibliography of his novels, his collected shorter prose, his uncollected and unpublished prose, his collected and uncollected poetry, special editions of his work, anthologies, his writing for the stage, radio, television, and cinema, his journalism, theater and book reviews, his sports reporting, a B. S. Johnson Web site, and published interviews as well as a section on books and articles about Johnson, including several important memoirs. Both in terms of scholarship and style, this is an impeccable biography.

Carl Rollyson

Review Sources

Booklist 101, no. 18 (May 15, 2005): 1629.
Library Journal 130, no. 10 (June 1, 2005): 127-128.
London Review of Books 26, no. 15 (August 5, 2004): 11-13.
New Statesman 133 (June 21, 2004): 48-49.
Publishers Weekly 252, no. 17 (April 25, 2005): 51.
The Spectator 295 (June 12, 2004): 46.
The Washington Post Book World, June 5, 2005, p. 15.

LIKE A ROLLING STONE
Bob Dylan at the Crossroads

Author: Greil Marcus (1945-   )
Publisher: PublicAffairs (New York). 283 pp. $25.00
Type of work: Music
Time: The 1960's
Locale: The United States

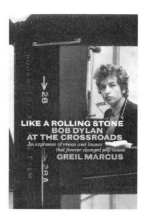

While at times disjointed and rambling, Marcus's book is a stunning portrait of Dylan's song "Like a Rolling Stone" and how its release changed the face of popular music

Principal personages:
BOB DYLAN, a songwriter and singer
TOM WILSON, a Columbia Records producer

Bob Dylan and his music have been part of the American fabric for more than forty years. In the early 1960's, Dylan established himself as one of America's most complex and insightful singer-songwriters. Since then, his lyrics have been scrutinized, fought over, and picked clean by scholars and fans alike. Over the years, much has been written about Dylan. There is a whole mythology about the man and his music that seems to have a life of its own. In 2004, Dylan published the first volume of his memoirs, *Chronicles: Volume One*. In this intriguing work, he makes it clear that he began his career with large ambitions. He wanted to become a songwriter who made a difference, who was a force of nature. He admired the likes of artist Pablo Picasso for being able to revolutionize the world that he inhabited.

Dylan's first record album, *Bob Dylan*, was released in 1962. At this point in time, the artist clearly was part of the folk tradition. He had been influenced by such American folk music legends as Woody Guthrie and Pete Seeger. Little did the music world know that by 1965, Dylan would become almost "larger than life." He shocked the folk music community at the Newport Folk Festival that year by playing an electric instead of an acoustic guitar. As evidenced by his performance, Dylan was not going to allow himself to be put into a restrictive box where innovation would be impossible. He was marching forward with a musical vision that would explode all preconceived notions of what a song could do.

During the late 1960's, his stature as a cultural icon grew in exponential fashion. For his 1965 album *Highway 61 Revisited*, Dylan wrote what has come to be considered one of the greatest rock songs ever to be recorded. "Like a Rolling Stone" opens the album with its cutting and cryptic lyrics "Once upon a time you dressed so fine/ Threw the bums a dime, in your prime/ *Didn't you?*" and "Never turned around to see the frowns/ On the jugglers and the clowns when they all did/ *Tricks for you*," Here

∽

*Greil Marcus has been writing
about popular music and culture
since the late 1960's. He spent
years as a staff writer at* Rolling
Stone *magazine. The many
notable books that he has
authored include* Mystery Train
(1975), Dead Elvis *(1991),*
Invisible Republic *(1997), and*
Double Trouble *(2000).*

∽

Dylan is in the listener's face, in the faces of all those who believe that they are better than others. The long, strange history of this song and how it finally saw the light of day is at the core of Greil Marcus's *Like a Rolling Stone.*

In the fall of 2004, *Rolling Stone* magazine published its list of the five hundred greatest rock songs of all time. "Like a Rolling Stone" was at the top. Marcus would concur with this ranking and, in his book, he gives the reader more than 250 pages of both persuasive and over-the-top arguments to make the case. Marcus began writing articles about Dylan in the late 1960's. As he must have realized, no one who was seriously interested in writing about popular culture in general, and rock music specifically, could ignore Dylan. Throughout the years, Marcus has been an enthusiastic proponent of rock music. He is first and foremost a fan of the musical form. His enthusiasm has always been a part of his writing style. No matter what critical points he may make in his writing, at its core is a healthy love for what rock music can do for the American psyche.

Marcus began his career as a music critic in the late 1960's at *Rolling Stone.* In 1975, his influential book *Mystery Train: Images of America in Rock 'n' Roll Music* was published. This landmark study of rock music was nominated for a National Book Critics Circle Award. Since the publication of this breakthrough study, Marcus has gained the reputation as being one of the most erudite writers of the music world. Over the years, he has continued to be interested in writing about American culture and how music fits into the cultural mosaic. Such cultural icons as Elvis Presley and Bob Dylan always have fascinated Marcus. These figures can be seen as musical beacons that shine brightly on the American landscape. While Dylan frequently has been the subject of Marcus's columns and essays, in 1997 he turned his complete attention to Dylan in the book *Invisible Republic: Bob Dylan's "Basement Tapes."* It seems fitting that the critic who chronicled the history of Dylan's *Basement Tapes* would write what certainly will become considered the definitive history of Dylan's "Like a Rolling Stone."

Marcus dedicates *Like a Rolling Stone* "to the radio." It is amazing to think that a song lasting six minutes and six seconds would not only be played on the radio but would also become a hit. Columbia Records released the song on July 20, 1965. It entered the *Billboard* singles chart on July 24, and on September 4 of that year "Like a Rolling Stone" reached number two. The song would not become number one, but the important thing to remember is that the song appeared at all and that it turned the music world upside down by the sheer force of what Dylan had done. After the Beatles had "conquered" America in 1964, Dylan realized that music was headed in a new direction and that he needed to push himself.

Marcus has divided *Like a Rolling Stone* into three parts and an epilogue. He opens part 1 with a chapter titled "The Day Kennedy Was Shot." After the assassination of

John F. Kennedy on November 22, 1963, the United States needed to find its bearings once again. The country could not remain oblivious to domestic social upheaval. Amid the headlines of racial strife and the Vietnam War, new musical voices spoke to the social turmoil that was brewing. The Beatles, the Rolling Stones, and Dylan pushed popular music in new directions. This section includes chapters about what Top 40 radio was like in the early 1960's and how Dylan was perceived by the press (or how he was misperceived, misread, and misunderstood). In part 2, Marcus moves toward the song itself, into the space that it inhabits. He emphatically states in chapter 6, "In the Air," that

> As songwriting, what's different about "Like a Rolling Stone" is all in its first four words. There may not be another pop song or a folk song that begins with "Once upon a time . . ."—that in a stroke takes the listener into a fairy tale, off the radio you're listening to in your car or on the record player in your house.

This is a grandiose claim, but Marcus is very persuasive, or at least his enthusiasm is hard to discount by anyone who is a serious student of the history of rock music.

While Marcus does take the necessary time to put "Like a Rolling Stone" on its rightful rock pedestal, his account of the recording session itself will amaze. Once again, fact truly is stranger than fiction. On several occasions, the reader is turning pages furiously, wondering whether this quirky song will ever get recorded, let alone released. Marcus is more than up to the task of setting the scene, and the dynamics of the production process make for a nail-biter. The reader gets to know the musicians who play on the session, including the guitarist Michael Bloomfield and the organ player Al Kooper, who would go on to form the band Blood, Sweat, and Tears. The song was produced by Tom Wilson. The reader learns that Wilson had produced the works of such jazz legends as John Coltrane and Cecil Taylor and that he was one of only a handful of African American producers working for a major record label. After the "Like a Rolling Stone" sessions, Columbia Records replaced him as Dylan's producer. He would die of a heart attack in 1978.

Marcus may lose his way on occasion, descending into hyperbole, but he maintains the story of the song at the heart of his narrative: Columbia Records had to be convinced that it should even be released, and Dylan stood firm, refusing to make the changes demanded by the record company executives. In his epilogue, Marcus reviews each of the twenty takes that were recorded on June 15 and 16. As he points out, the song still receives airplay forty years after it was recorded, and Dylan has continued to challenge himself, has continued to be relevant to the American popular culture that he played a crucial part in shaping.

Marcus is nothing if not an erudite interpreter of American culture, but at times he can be his own worst enemy. On occasion, his praise for the song can be discounted because it is so over the top. In the end, however, the patient reader will come away with a renewed appreciation for what Dylan did for music in the second half of the twentieth century. The book includes an instructive bibliography and index.

Jeffry Jensen

Review Sources

Booklist 101, no. 14 (March 15, 2005): 1255.
Choice 42 (July/August, 2005): 1996.
The Christian Science Monitor, April 12, 2005, p. 17.
Kirkus Reviews 73, no. 5 (March 1, 2005): 277.
Library Journal 130, no. 6 (April 1, 2005): 96.
Los Angeles Times Book Review, April 10, 2005, p. 6.
The Nation 280, no. 16 (April 25, 2005): 25-29.
New Statesman 134 (May 30, 2005): 49-51.
The New York Times Book Review 110 (July 3, 2005): 12.
Publishers Weekly 252, no. 8 (February 21, 2005): 169.
San Francisco Chronicle, April 21, 2005, p. E1.
Sunday Telegraph, May 15, 2005, p. 12.
The Washington Post, April 6, 2005, p. C10.

THE LIVES OF AGNES SMEDLEY

Author: Ruth Price (1951-   )
Publisher: Oxford University Press (New York). Illustrated. 498 pp. $35.00
Type of work: Literary biography
Time: 1892-1950
Locale: Colorado, New York, Berlin, Moscow, England, and various locales in China

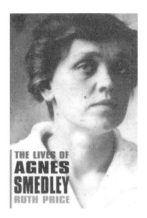

Price has written a detailed study of a writer who was near the center of several of the most important political and cultural movements of the twentieth century

Principal personages:
> AGNES SMEDLEY (1892-1950), a journalist and memoirist who covered revolutionary changes in Russia and China for twenty years
> MARGARET SANGER, an American pioneer of birth control and women's rights, a friend and supporter of Smedley
> VIRENDRANATH CHATTOPADHYAYA ("CHATTO"), the leader of the movement for India's independence from Britain, Smedley's lover
> RICHARD SORGE, a Soviet spy in China, Smedley's lover
> MADAME SUN YAT-SEN, a widow of the so-called father of the Chinese Republic who became an important Chinese leader after her husband's death in 1925
> CHIANG KAI-SHEK, the Chinese nationalist leader who fought both the Communists and the Japanese in the 1930's over control of China
> MAO ZEDONG, the Chinese Communist leader, Smedley's friend
> EDGAR SNOW, a journalist who gained fame in China, Smedley's friend and associate

In January, 1937, when the newly successful *Life* magazine published photographs introducing the Chinese Communists to Depression-era America, it included a shot of "Mao's American ally," Agnes Smedley. Two years later, the same magazine carried Smedley's photo essay on the new Chinese Fourth Army fighting the invading Japanese. Smedley was one of the first reporters to cover China from inside its border and, consequently, one of the world's most noted foreign journalists.

Author of the highly praised fictional memoir *Daughter of Earth* (1929), Smedley was also the journalist who over a decade of revolutionary change produced *Chinese Destinies: Sketches of Present-Day China* (1933), *China Fights Back, An American Woman with the Eighth Route Army* (1938), and *Battle Hymn of China* (1943). Ruth Price's exhaustive biography, *The Lives of Agnes Smedley*, details Smedley's full career. The book required at least fifteen years of research and interviewing; Price's

Ruth Price taught English for several years at the City University of New York, worked for New York city and state governments, and was press secretary for Congresswoman Bella Abzug. She has also published several works of fiction.

notes run to more than fifty pages, her index more than ten. What emerges is a complex portrait of a talented writer who gave her career to revolutionary causes, one of the most significant American women of the twentieth century, and someone who ultimately paid a price for her political commitments.

Smedley was born in Missouri in 1892 but was raised in Colorado. Her life there was partly determined by her exposure to the Colorado mining camps and labor wars she witnessed in the early 1900's, leading to the Ludlow Massacre of 1914. In the 1910's, she became involved in India's fight for independence from Great Britain and worked with several exiled Indian nationalists on the West Coast. When she moved to New York in 1917 she was almost at once caught up in several political and social movements based in Greenwich Village, especially the birth control campaign spearheaded by Margaret Sanger and various political movements spawned by Russia's Bolshevik Revolution of 1917.

In 1920 Smedley left for Europe for the first time (she would not return for thirteen years), and became a writer in Berlin, where she befriended other writers and artists. Her *Daughter of Earth* was an autobiographical novel based on her first thirty-odd years and proof of her acumen as a writer. In the 1930's, as the first Western journalist to cover the Chinese Communists, she traveled dangerously close to battle with Chinese soldiers and wrote three highly acclaimed books about the revolution in China.

In the 1940's Smedley returned to the United States. She spent time at the famed Yaddo writers' colony in upstate New York but increasingly was caught up in the anticommunist hysteria building after the end of World War II. After Smedley died in England, her ashes were interred in the People's Cemetery for Revolutionary Martyrs in Beijing—at the same time, she was being investigated by several military agencies and congressional committees in the United States.

Smedley's career can almost be charted by her relationships. She had an early and brief marriage to Ernest Brundin. Although the marriage did not last, Brundin's connections gave her access to Indian nationalists fighting in exile for their country's independence. She fell in love with Virendranath Chattopadhyaya ("Chatto") in Berlin; their relationship was not long-lived, but it propelled her into early work with European revolutionary leaders and, ultimately, into espionage.

Finally, her liaison with the Russian-born Richard Sorge in China confirmed her revolutionary sympathies. Sorge worked for Soviet military intelligence and the Comintern (as Chatto had as well), the militant international organization the Soviets had set up in the 1920's. Smedley's relationship with Sorge led her deeper into spy work in China as the Chinese Communists, with Soviet aid, tried to wrest power from the Nationalist forces under Chiang Kai-shek. "She would act as a mail drop and liaison," Price writes, "offer her home for meetings, and gather information and write reports on matters of interest to Sorge, which he said initially included 'the increasing importance of America's role in China and new American investment in Shanghai,' and which he forwarded to Moscow."

Smedley's greatest love affair, finally, was with China itself. She lived there for more than a decade, and during that period China was transformed into a revolutionary power. Smedley fell in love with its people—in fact, she tried to adopt a young Chinese boy who helped her in her work—and she had close relationships with a number of the revolutionary leaders who led China out of feudalism into the twentieth century. Smedley had, as the journalist James Bertram wrote of her in the late 1930's, "an unbounded admiration for the common Chinese people: the mill worker in Shanghai, the girl at the silk looms of Canton, the peasant who worked his fields (or another's) through drought and flood and famine, with a patient persistence that is sub or superhuman."

Smedley herself knew she could never really share the lives of the Chinese people and contented herself with writing about them. "I remain a teller of tales," she said, "a writer of things through which I have not lived. The real story of China can be told only by the Chinese workers and peasants themselves." In her writing, she tried to relay the human stories.

Almost all of her dozens of books and articles about China came out of contemporary and pressing political and military crises. Acclaimed as they were at the time, they have not stood the test of time. Her fictional memoir, *Daughter of Earth*, is an exception. The thinly veiled story tracing her hardscrabble childhood through her work in New York with Indian nationalists has an almost poetic power to it and has enjoyed a second life after being rediscovered and republished in 1973 by the Feminist Press. Its beauty points up one of the many contradictions in Smedley's career: While her best work was creative, she devoted most of her career to political and social journalism. At the end of her life, after she had returned to the United States and was spending extended periods at Yaddo, she began to turn again to that earlier creative strain in her work. Her health, however, and her almost constant persecution by government authorities, hampered her writing. When she died in 1950, in exile in England, she was remembered as a woman who wrote some of the first reports out of China, not as the novelist who had written the beautiful *Daughter of Earth* twenty years before.

All these themes and issues emerge in Price's biography but almost in spite of her focus. What stand out in Smedley's career for Price, and what Price has reveals in great detail for the first time, are the espionage roles that Smedley played during the 1920's and 1930's, in both Russia and China. Price has uncovered documentation of Smedley's activities in a number of new sources, including archives opened up in the last few decades in Moscow and Beijing. Price's discovery is that Smedley played a greater undercover role than her defenders allowed at her death. The documentation, however, almost overwhelms the life as Price presents it, and readers must wade through pages of complicated Soviet and Chinese history (including dozens of political acronyms—KPD, KMT, CCP, and so on) to get to Smedley's activities.

Smedley was committed to revolutionary work, especially in China. Like the China experts (for example, Owen Lattimore) who would be pursued, persecuted, and purged in the late 1940's because they enthusiastically predicted the victory of the Communist revolutionaries, Smedley was a believer. Her political work, in addition to taking her away from her creative writing, also bordered on espionage. Price is obsessed with that story, and at several places that fascination nearly sinks the narrative. As she focuses on her subject's political activities, she often ignores the journalism Smedley was publishing in *The Nation*, the *Manchester Guardian*, *Harper's*, and other prestigious magazines and newspapers around the world. That writing, incidental as it was, still deserves greater analysis in a work of nearly five hundred pages.

Smedley's complex character comes through Price's biography in spite of this obsession with her political work. Here was a woman who knew many of the most important political and cultural figures of the first half of the twentieth century, from revolutionaries such as Mother Jones and Emma Goldman through writers such as Upton Sinclair, Katherine Anne Porter, and Langston Hughes to international figures such as German artist Käthe Kollwitz and Chinese leader Madame Sun Yat-sen.

One of the first women to undergo psychoanalysis, which she undertook in Berlin in the mid-1920's, Smedley was anxious, neurotic, promiscuous, and hypochondriacal. Such traits can perhaps be forgiven in one who had J. Edgar Hoover reading her mail as early as 1921; her books would be removed from libraries three decades later. She never belonged to the American Communist Party, and yet she worked for Soviet intelligence and was truly dedicated to revolutionary political change. In one of the most moving depictions of her in Price's biography, she is staying with the revolutionary Chinese Communist military forces in caves in the mountains in the late 1930's—and teaching the officers to square dance and fox trot as well as advising Mao Zedong about romantic love. Probably no biography, not even one of five hundred pages, can do justice to a figure of this size.

David Peck

Review Sources

Booklist 101, no. 8 (December 15, 2004): 700.
Far Eastern Economic Review 168, no. 4 (April, 2005): 65-66.
Library Journal 130, no. 1 (January, 2005): 124.
National Review 57, no. 8 (May 9, 2005): 44-45.
Publishers Weekly 252, no. 5 (January 31, 2005): 64.
Weekly Standard 10, no. 19 (January 31, 2005): 34-36.

LIVING WITH POLIO
The Epidemic and Its Survivors

Author: Daniel J. Wilson (1949-   )
Publisher: University of Chicago Press (Chicago).
   300 pp. $29.00
Type of work: History of science, medicine, and science
Time: From the 1930's to the 1960's
Locale: The United States

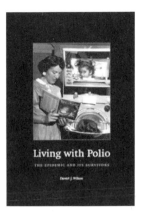

Prior to development of the polio vaccines in the 1950's, tens of thousands of children contracted polio each year; using interviews with survivors, the author, himself a survivor, relates their stories

Living with Polio
THE EPIDEMIC AND ITS SURVIVORS
Daniel J. Wilson

Principal personages:
DANIEL J. WILSON, the author, a history professor who relates his own story of polio
FRANKLIN DELANO ROOSEVELT, the president of the United States, 1933-1945; a polio survivor and role model
JONAS SALK, the developer of a killed poliovirus vaccine, the first effective measure to prevent the disease
ALBERT SABIN, the developer of a live, attenuated poliovirus vaccine

Though an ancient illness, poliomyelitis, or polio, became a significant epidemic disease only with the beginning of the twentieth century. The reasons are complex. Ironically, however, changes in the epidemiological pattern of polio had much to do with improvements in public health during the early years of that century. Polio was primarily a childhood disease; the relatively few who developed paralysis were generally young children, as reflected in a name often used for the illness: infantile paralysis. Though the likely viral etiology of the disease was demonstrated by the Austrian physician Karl Landsteiner in the first decade of the twentieth century, the mechanism for spread of the disease as well as the extent of inapparent infections remained obscure. Answers to such questions would come only in the 1930's, as better methods for study of the virus as well as improved methods of diagnosis became available.

As is true for many viral diseases, the age of infection played a critical role in the severity of the disease. Young children were initially provided a measure of protection by antibodies obtained from their mothers, either in utero or through colostrum if the child was nursed. Relative resistance to the infection often remained through early years of growth. The result was that exposure to the virus at a young age generally resulted in an inapparent infection, providing lifelong immunity to the child without development of any obvious symptoms. Probably 95 to 99 percent of natural infections fell into this category, and as long as the virus remained present in the human environment, a consequence of poor public health policies, this did not change.

~

Daniel J. Wilson is a professor of history at Muhlenberg College in Pennsylvania. He has also authored Arthur O. Lovejoy and the Quest for Intelligibility *(1980);* Arthur O. Lovejoy: An Annotated Bibliography *(1982);* The Cause of the South: Selections from "De Bow's Review," 1846-1867 *(1982), with Paul Paskoff; and* Science, Community, and the Transformation of American Philosophy *(1990).*

~

Changes in public health practices, including improvements in the quality of the water supply for most major cities, decreased the likelihood of early childhood exposure to the virus. Beginning with the second decade of the twentieth century, children were older when first exposed to the virus. Early resistance to infection had largely disappeared, and polio appeared with a vengeance. The first major epidemic in the United States appeared in 1916, initially in New York City, but the outbreak subsequently spread across the country. At least thirty thousand persons developed some level of paralysis, with a mortality rate approaching 25 percent. In subsequent years, the numbers of cases abated somewhat and were accompanied by changes in the age distribution as well. Whereas most cases of polio in 1916 were in children under the age of four, epidemics in later years affected older children.

While sporadic epidemics continued to appear on a yearly basis, major outbreaks began in the early 1940's and continued until development of the Salk and Sabin vaccines in the 1950's. As noted by the author, between 1944 and 1955, the last year for a major epidemic, nearly 416,000 cases of polio were reported. While other epidemic diseases such as tuberculosis, whooping cough, and scarlet fever actually affected larger numbers of children, the nature of polio, particularly the onset of (often permanent) paralysis, lent itself to a fear among the population which went far beyond specific numbers. Polio season, the summer months, was a time of dread, and numbers published in the newspapers reinforced widespread fears among the populace.

This is not to say research into preventing the disease or dealing with its aftermath was neglected. In 1938, the National Foundation for Infantile Paralysis, under the direction of President Franklin Roosevelt and headed by his lawyer and friend Basil O'Conner, was established, both to fund research into the disease and to provide funds for hospitals and private citizens. Purchases of equipment such as the "iron lung" to keep patients alive and braces or tractions to enable victims to return to society were largely funded by the organization. A yearly "March of Dimes" was established, both to provide a means to obtain funding and to allow private citizens to feel they personally were involved in fighting the disease. Roosevelt, of course, was a polio survivor, and though the public rarely saw the extent of his paralysis, he remained a role model in demonstrating that even polio could not deter a person determined to live an active life.

In *Living with Polio*, author Daniel J. Wilson, himself a polio survivor, taps into the fear that existed throughout the American population. The primary premise of the book involves interviews with some 150 people who, like the author, survived polio and its aftermath and continued on with their lives. Roosevelt is not among those sin-gled out in the book, primarily because his wealth and support groups were atypical of experiences encountered by the average person. Roosevelt's support for the foundation as well as the symbolism of the rehabilitation facility he developed in Warm Springs, Georgia, must not be understated, but the general public had little understanding of the extent of Roosevelt's challenges.

The author clearly conveys the dread exhibited by family members that accompanied symptoms of illness in a child which could too easily result in a diagnosis of polio. Illnesses in general were, and continue to be, common in childhood. The early symptoms of polio, headache, fever, nausea, were no different from those of colds, influenza, or any of a number of common illnesses. The difference was that rather than responding to medications such as aspirin available to the population at the time, polio symptoms only continued to become worse. Compounding the problem was that, during these early stages of disease, children were just as likely to be attending school or playing with friends as resting in isolation at home. The reality was that siblings or other family members could still be infected and become carriers of the polio virus even in the absence of any discernible illness. Either way, the virus could be spread through the community.

Physicians faced large challenges. Diagnosis of the early stages of polio was often difficult given the generality of the symptoms. If a doctor failed to diagnose polio, a child might remain in the local community, passing the virus to others. Diagnosis might also involve the use of a spinal tap, a painful procedure which most physicians preferred to avoid if possible. In contrast, an incorrect diagnosis of polio would subject the family to unnecessary fear and dread for the future health of the child. A final diagnosis was sometimes delayed for several reasons, some of which Wilson discusses. By delaying a firm diagnosis, the physician would allow a measure of hope to exist among family members, while at the same time preparing them for the worst. In addition, by waiting until hospital tests could be completed, the physician could allow someone else to provide the news to the family.

The bulk of the book provides firsthand accounts of diagnosis of the disease, treatment, and the level of recovery among the subjects. Once a child was conclusively diagnosed as having polio, he or she usually was admitted to a hospital where, in the absence of parents for long periods, the child was in the care of hospital staff. As one reads these accounts, one is reminded that sufferers were mostly children. Hospital staff, nurses and others, did what they could to provide both physical and psychological comfort to their patients. Some treated their duties as simply a job, but the subjects of the author's interviews also relate the kindness and caring nature of many of their heath care workers, despite being overworked and often overwhelmed by the stress of their jobs. It was not unusual, even after a shift was completed, for a nurse to stay and talk with children.

It is easy to overlook the fact that in these pre-television days, often the only "entertainment" for these children was either a radio, if one was available, or socialization with other children. Interviewees related how they would invent songs which mocked the staff or even their own conditions. The "polio jitterbug," movement of eyes or nose in conjunction with music on a radio was one type of entertainment among hospital-bound children to relieve the boredom and tedium. Former patients also related a variety of pranks. For example, some discovered that after stabbing the paper coverings of straws into butter, they could blow the paper toward the ceiling and it would stick. Spitball fights were also common among young patients.

In some cases, survival was dependent on a relatively new invention, the so-called iron lung. In the days before respirators, paralysis of the muscles associated with breathing often resulted in the child being placed in what could only be described as an iron barrel. Increase and decrease of pressure within the contraption allowed the child to inhale or exhale air.

Rehabilitation followed recovery from the illness itself. In some cases paralysis eased, and children could eventually resume normal activities. Many of the subjects, however, left their hospital beds and learned to become mobile on wheelchairs or on crutches. During these years, a large number of rehabilitation facilities were established to allow such children to become adept in moving themselves and to work their ways back into society. The cost of much of this rehabilitation was supported by the National Foundation, although it could do little to combat the fear which caused society too often to continue to fear, or at least prefer to avoid, the former patients.

The polio survivors describe other milestones on the road to recovery. To be able to discard leg braces provided a strong psychological boost, and many did so as soon as possible. In some cases, removal of braces was in contradiction to the orders of the physician. Medical concerns, however, were overridden by the desire to again "feel normal."

Polio survivors had every expectation of their lives returning to a semblance of normality as they approached middle age and beyond. By the 1970's, however, an increasing number of survivors began to experience mild symptoms of the disease: fatigue, pain, and difficulty in carrying out tasks. While the historical medical literature did contain occasional reference to what became known as post-polio syndrome, it was only after polio as an epidemic disease had largely disappeared that the widespread nature of the problem became apparent. The precise cause or nature of the syndrome remains elusive, but the large numbers of such survivors who relate their conditions supports the idea that nature has played a cruel joke. The author relates the physical and psychological difficulties encountered by many of these victims as they relate their frustrations in accepting the reality of the illness and their challenges in dealing with it.

In the end, this book's accounts add up to more than a recounting of the events associated with a terrible and frustrating childhood disease. The stories reflect the ability of children to accept their condition and to overcome its associated difficulties. The development of vaccines, first by Jonas Salk and then by Albert Sabin, resulted in the elevation of these scientists into icon status; in these stories, one understands why.

Richard Adler

Review Sources

The Economist 375 (June 18, 2005): 79-80.
JAMA: Journal of the American Medical Association 294, no. 10 (September 14, 2005): 1277.
Library Journal 130, no. 7 (April 15, 2005): 111.
Publishers Weekly 252, no. 11 (March 14, 2005): 59.
The Times Literary Supplement, May 27, 2005, p. 24.

A LONG WAY DOWN

Author: Nick Hornby (1958-   )
Publisher: Riverhead Books (New York). 333 pp. $25.00
Type of work: Novel
Time: 2005
Locale: London

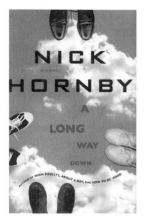

This comic novel brings together four would-be sui-cides

Principal characters:
    MARTIN SHARP, a disgraced television
      celebrity
    MAUREEN, the worn-down mother of a
      severely brain-damaged twenty-year-old
      son
    JESS, the nineteen-year-old daughter of a
      Labour Party minister
    JJ, an American musician

It was inevitable, after so many books wrapped in yellow covers as bright as their happy endings, that the writer often credited with inventing "lad lit," or at least lad lit lite, would eventually receive not just a bad review but a scathing one. Scathing, in fact, hardly describes Michiko Kakutani's review of Nick Hornby's fourth novel and eighth book overall, *A Long Way Down*. "A maudlin bit of tripe," Kakutani calls it, nowhere more so than in the "sappy and predictable ending to [this] sappy and predictable novel." Her vehemence, however, suggests a willful blindness that, in so single-mindedly attacking the novel's weakness, perversely points the way to its greatest strength, one that the marketing hype of the dust jacket and author's Web site entirely misrepresent.

The clue to Kakutani's blind spot and Hornby's achievement is in Kakutani's review of Zadie Smith's 2005 novel *On Beauty*. Clearly, Smith's and Hornby's novels are quite different, and not just in that Kakutani loves one and loathes the other. Where *On Beauty* is ambitious to a fault, albeit a fault that has endeared it to many reviewers, *A Long Way Down* is, marketing hype aside, a decidedly small book in almost every way that counts: language, scope, cast. For all the praise of Smith's characterizations, it is Hornby's novel that sticks to human scale.

Hornby's usual subjects are here: the obsessiveness, the emotional clumsiness, the sense of not belonging and of being a loser. Where this novel differs from the earlier ones is in its extending Hornby's tinkering with point of view among his four main characters. Martin Sharp is a former television celebrity whose sexual encounter with Danielle ("5'9", 36DD, fifteen years and 250 days old") results in the breakup of his marriage, a three-month prison sentence, and his being relegated to hosting *Sharp Words* on FeetUp!TV, "Britain's worst-rated cable TV station." He is narcissistic, sarcastic, fast-thinking, and self-loathing but (this being a Hornby novel) not altogether unlikable, even if he has trouble distinguishing between his two daughters. Maureen, early fifties, is dull, dutiful, and, as a practicing Catholic, guilt-ridden. Her twenty-year-old, severely brain-damaged son, Matty, is less an obligation than a penance for Maureen's only sexual act, with the fiancé who promptly abandoned her. Jess is the impulsive, foul-mouthed daughter of a junior minister in Prime Minister Tony Blair's government. She is annoying as only an alternately in-

~
Nick Hornby's first two books, the critically acclaimed novel High Fidelity *(1995) and the memoir* Fever Pitch *(1997), as well as their film versions, have come to define the educated, anxious middle-class man in the late twentieth or early twenty-first century in a state of prolonged adolescence.*
~

dulged and neglected upper-middle class nineteen-year-old can be. In search of the boyfriend who abandoned her, Jess is no less in search of family. JJ is a young, American musician and autodidact whose accent grates on English ears. After losing his band, then his girlfriend, JJ works illegally for a pizzeria—the least educated among a delivery staff of immigrant doctors, lawyers, and the like.

What brings together this foursome is nothing more or less than each being depressed and showing up—two by design, two by chance—on New Year's Eve at a building known as Toppers House because so many people have flung themselves from its roof. As Hornby has pointed out, *A Long Way Down* is not really about suicide. It is about people whose sense of self-worth has hit rock bottom (another "long way down"). These four are not even real would-be suicides. Martin has come prepared, knowing he would need a ladder and wire cutters to breach the fence constructed to prevent suicides, but once over the top he sits on the ledge and starts drinking. Maureen has made sure Matty will be taken care of that night and subsequent ones, but the extent of her preparations ends there. Jess never intended to attempt suicide, only to search for her ex-boyfriend at a party in a building she did not know was a known suicide spot. JJ just happens to be delivering pizzas at the building.

Until page thirty-six, the four characters' stories are more or less separate. After that, each is interwoven with the others, advancing here, backtracking there, complementing this, correcting that. The suicide plans of each having been scotched by the presence of the others at Toppers House, the four form a tentative band of sorts on an episodic odyssey that takes them to a party in Shoreditch, to Martin's flat in Islington (where the usually abstemious Maureen vomits the wine she drank at the party and where Martin's sometime lover Penelope has been awaiting his return), and from there to a café for breakfast. Having nothing better to do, they agree to meet again on Valentine's Day. The following day, however, when a tabloid newspaper runs a story linking a former celebrity and a minister's daughter in a suicide pact, they all find themselves thrown together much more quickly than they had hoped or planned. The four never quite form a cohesive group but, thanks in large part to Jess's efforts, they do stay together like a genially dysfunctional family. Taking an approach borrowed from Alcoholics Anonymous, of living one day at a time, they make it first to Valentine's Day, then to a 90th Day party, after which the future is unclear.

Martin is still alive but still very much Martin, splendidly cynical about the underclass youth named Pacino whom he mentors. Jess has taken up with an old geezer she names Nodog, who is, in fact, a step up from her father, the consummate technocrat and politician. JJ is happy—sort of—with his new life as a busker. Maureen has a job at a newsagent and a place, as an alternate, on a pub-quiz team. These are minor triumphs, to be sure, ensuring nothing, or at least very little, making the book's ending at once more tentative and more believable than the endings of Hornby's three earlier novels. There is more than a note of whimsy and willed optimism, weighted by the slight but persistent echo of Samuel Beckett's grim and grimly funny existential credo, "You must go on I can't go on I'll go on." At novel's end, JJ asks, "I'm sorry. I was just wondering, you know. Why we're still here"—the "here" meaning both still alive and at Toppers House for their 90th Day party.

> "Thanks," said Martin. "Thanks for that."
> In the distance we could see the lights on that big Ferris wheel down by the river, the London Eye.
> "We don't have to decide right now anyway, do we?" said JJ.
> "Course we don't," said Martin.
> "So how about we give it another six months? See how we're doing?'
> "Is that thing actually going around?" said Martin. "I can't tell."
> We stared at it for a long time, trying to work it out. Martin was right. It didn't look as though it was moving, but it must have been, I suppose.

The ending is a little sweet but forgivably so, for two reasons. First, it is entirely in keeping with Hornby's overall vision of the contingency of human life. Second, whatever symbolism Hornby may have intended, the monstrous size of the tourist attraction known as the London Eye, a high-tech Ferris wheel referred to as an observation wheel, serves to underscore the human scale of Hornby's work. The sudden leap from Topper's House has been replaced by a slow, step-by-step descent to solid ground. Martin, Maureen, Jess, and JJ will probably make it, not quite together, but not quite alone either.

Robert A. Morace

Review Sources

The Atlantic Monthly 296, no. 1 (July/August, 2005): 148.
Booklist 101, no. 14 (March 15, 2005): 1246.
The Boston Globe, April 22, 2005, p. D6.
The Christian Science Monitor, June 28, 2005, p. 17.
Kirkus Reviews 73, no. 5 (March 1, 2005): 249-250.
Library Journal 130, no. 7 (April 15, 2005): 73.

Los Angeles Times, June 15, 2005, p. E3.
The New York Times Book Review 154 (June 12, 2005): 26.
People 63, no. 22 (June 6, 2005): 49.
Publishers Weekly 252, no. 14 (April 4, 2005): 41.
USA Today, June 23, 2005, p. D7.
The Washington Post, June 26, 2005, p. T06.

LOST IN THE FOREST

Author: Sue Miller (1943-   )
Publisher: Alfred A. Knopf (New York). 247 pp. $25.00
Type of work: Novel
Time: The late 1980's
Locale: Napa Valley, California

The sudden death of a beloved husband, father, and stepfather dramatically alters the dynamics of a Napa Valley family

Principal characters:
 EVA ALBERMARLE, a bookstore owner,
  wife, and mother of three
 JOHN ALBERMARLE, her second husband, a
  book publisher
 MARK, her first husband, a wine-grower
 DAISY, Eva and Mark's troubled fourteen-year-old daughter
 EMILY, Eva and Mark's popular seventeen-year-old daughter
 THEO ALBERMARLE, Eva and John's three-year-old son
 DUNCAN, a fifty-three-year-old furniture designer
 GRACIE, Eva's best friend and Duncan's wife

Lost in the Forest is an intimate story of one family's loss, which resonates with the universal concepts of grief, romance and sex, family dynamics, and painful adolescence. When John Albermarle steps off the curb a split second too soon one afternoon, his family's universe suddenly shifts, and relationships are irrevocably altered and broken. While minutely examining the ramifications of this particular death, Miller offers insights into the human condition that will resonate with readers of all ages and backgrounds.

The novel opens with the violent death of John Albermarle, second husband of Eva, father to three-year-old Theo, and stepfather to Emily and Daisy. As he steps off the curb while walking with his wife and son in the small Napa Valley town of Saint Helena, John is hit by a car and sent flying into a nearby lamppost. His untimely demise provides the catalyst for subsequent events, plunging all those affected into their own personal crises, revealing the fault lines lying dormant beneath the surface of their relationships and shifting the connections between them. The reader gradually learns, through flashbacks, that John was the most mature, well-balanced person in his family, upon whom all the others depended for a sense of stability and comfort. When the foundation upon which this happiness rests suddenly disappears, the aftershocks are cataclysmic.

Told from three different points of view—Eva's, her former husband Mark's, and her younger daughter Daisy's—the family's history unfolds via flashback. Eva and Mark's marriage ends when, in a misguided confessional mood, he reveals to her that he recently ended a nearly year-long affair with a local barmaid. Hoping his confession would somehow deepen their relationship, Mark is instead kicked out of the house and out of the marriage. Eva, still in love with Mark and devastated by his betrayal, begins life anew with their two daughters, who see Mark only on occasional weekends, as he becomes immersed in work and an active sexual life.

Eva eventually falls deeply in love with and marries the soft-spoken book publisher John, the antithesis of the sexy, charming bad boy Mark. Emily, and particularly the shy, awkward Daisy, adore John, who is interested in their opinions and makes them feel as if they matter to him. Thus, John gracefully steps into the role that their own father has essentially abdicated, and a new family, with baby Theo, is created.

Sue Miller was born on the South Side of Chicago and attended Harvard University. She began writing seriously after separating from her husband in 1971 and published her first story in 1981. Miller received a Bunting Fellowship from Radcliffe from 1983 to 1994, during which time she wrote The Good Mother *(1986). This work was followed by several novels, a collection of short stories, and a memoir,* The Story of My Father *(2003).*

This family, established after the wreckage of Eva's first marriage, is blown apart by John's death, as each member processes the loss differently and alone. Eva retreats into her immense grief, leaving Emily and old family friend Gracie in charge of keeping their daily lives on track. Emily, a bright, popular, well-adjusted teenager, handles grief quickly and gets on with enjoying her senior year in high school. Theo continues to believe his father will return until, finally, standing with his mother at the intersection where his father died, he remembers how his father flew into the air, "like an angel," and realizes he is not coming back.

It is fourteen-year-old Daisy, however, left completely adrift by her beloved stepfather's death, who suffers the deepest scars from John's loss. Tall, gawky, and uncomfortable, Daisy lives in the shadow of her petite, pretty, self-possessed older sister. Entering her first year of high school right before John's death, she feels cautiously optimistic about her future. She hopefully auditions for chorus, basketball, and the literary magazine, and, knowing that her high school career would be very different from that of her cheerleader sister, she is nonetheless determined to find like-minded friends and succeed on her own terms. John's death, however, destroys these plans. "Daisy . . . felt herself stop inside after John died. For months it was simply as if she were frozen." She quits basketball, neglects her classes, and gives up her sanguine hopes for school.

Eva, distracted by her own grief, and Mark, preoccupied with his reemerging romantic and sexual feelings toward his former wife, convince themselves that Daisy's difficulties are simply those of a typical adolescent, and leave her to her own devices.

As she becomes more estranged from school, friends, and family, Daisy begins lying about her whereabouts and regularly pilfering small amounts of money from Eva's bookstore, where she has a part-time job.

Caught in the act by Duncan, Gracie's caustic husband, she is gradually drawn into a bizarre sexual relationship with him, and the fifteen- and fifty-three-year-old begin to meet regularly in his secluded studio. Daisy enjoys for once being someone's center of attention and also takes pleasure in the sense of power the relationship confers upon her. "She felt he offered her a new version of herself, one she more and more carried with her into her real life. She felt uplifted, in a sense; she felt an elevation over the daily ugliness of high school. She was less afraid, less shy." For the first time Daisy experiences the power of sex, which she had heretofore only observed secondhand in the breakup of her parents' marriage after Mark's affair, and in Eva's overwhelming grief at John's death. "Duncan exposed the underpinnings of adult life, sexual life, to Daisy, though there wasn't a way for her to have articulated that at the time."

Mark, who had nearly abdicated his role as father to John, also finds his life changed because of John's absence. He is once again thrust reluctantly into the role of father, this time to young women rather than girls, and as a substitute father to Theo as well. He feels that, "now that they were young women, he felt confused about how to do it, not ready yet to be a parent to them." He soon realizes that "He'd left it to John. . . . Because he didn't *want* to understand this. Because he wouldn't have known—because he *didn't* know—how to be a father to them through all this."

As he begins to sense that something is going on between Daisy and Duncan, however, Mark finally accepts his role as father and "rescues" his daughter, willing finally to be the father she has been missing since John died. Miller's grasp of family dynamics is formidable—her portrayal of husband/wife, mother/daughter, father/daughter, and sibling relationships is razor-sharp. Daisy's simultaneous feelings of hero worship and envy toward her older, more self-possessed sister and Emily's conflicting emotions of disgust and protectiveness toward Daisy are particularly astute, and the reader understands that these daughters of divorce are close in a way that can never be destroyed, because they were thrown upon each other for comfort and security. Also insightful is Miller's portrait of Eva's troubled relationship with Daisy. She brilliantly captures the strained exchanges, slammed doors, and anger so often found between mothers and their adolescent daughters.

Miller's vivid depiction of grief is particularly moving and will be recognized by readers who have experienced a great loss. Eva's grief is described as almost "like being in love. . . . It was like the way you were stunned with love when you were young. . . . There was that same sense of having lost yourself, of being taken over by some feeling you weren't in control of." She pours orange juice on her cereal instead of milk, forgets where she is going when she gets into the car, cries through her parent-teacher conference, and "Sometimes in the first months after John's death, she woke in the night and staggered into the bathroom and threw up, threw up even when there was nothing more there." Finally, as her grief begins to subside, bit by bit, she fears its loss, and "began to grieve for her very grief, her letting go of John." Her grief has become her last connection to her late husband, and she mourns its passing.

Miller's frequent use of fairy tale as a motif underscores Daisy's perilous journey through adolescence, as she negotiates the tricky world of adult sexuality amid her grief for her stepfather and the loss of her family as she has known it. She is indeed Little Red Riding Hood, lost in the woods at the mercy of the big bad wolf, in desperate need of rescuing. This use of Jungian motif is underscored by the family's habit of telling stories at dinner to keep Theo happy, each person adding a bit to the tale as it passes around the table, as they spin yarns of white horses rescuing lost little boys from the forest.

Lost in the Forest, with its penetrating and sensitive examination of family dynamics, rates among Miller's best works as it demonstrates how easily the delicate balance of family life can be destroyed and how difficult it is to rebuild. Miller's ability to portray the endless ripples set off by one tragic event and probe the complex web of relationships in one small family unit makes her an exceptional chronicler of domestic life.

Mary Virginia Davis

Review Sources

Booklist 101, no. 11 (February 1, 2005): 917.
Kirkus Reviews 73, no. 3 (February 1, 2005): 142.
Library Journal 130, no. 3 (February 15, 2005): 119.
The New York Times Book Review 154 (May 1, 2005): 9.
People 63, no. 15 (April 18, 2005): 49.
Publishers Weekly 252, no. 7 (February 14, 2005): 50.
Vogue 195, no. 4 (April, 2005): 253.

LUNAR PARK

Author: Bret Easton Ellis (1964-   )
Publisher: Alfred A. Knopf (New York). 308 pp. $25.00
Type of work: Novel
Time: The early 2000's
Locale: An anonymous suburb in the northeastern United
States

Ellis includes himself as the central character in a metafictional horror novel

Principal characters:
> BRET EASTON ELLIS, a successful author in
> his forties
> JAYNE DENNIS, his fictional film star wife
> ROBERT MARTIN ELLIS, his father, who
> died in 1992 and haunts Ellis throughout
> the novel
> AIMEE LIGHT, a graduate student with whom Ellis has an affair
> JAY MCINERNEY, the real-life author of *Bright Lights, Big City* (1984)
> often associated with Ellis in his youth
> ROBBIE, Ellis's eleven-year-old estranged son
> SARAH, Jayne Dennis's five-year-old daughter from a previous relation-
> ship
> PATRICK BATEMAN, the serial killer and central character of Ellis's
> *American Psycho* (1991)
> CLAY, the central character of Ellis's *Less than Zero* (1985)
> DONALD KIMBALL, a detective with the Midland County Sheriff's
> Department
> ROBERT MILLER, a paranormal investigator
> MITCHELL ALLEN, a supporting character in Ellis's second novel, *The
> Rules of Attraction* (1987), who now lives next door to him in the
> suburbs

In 1985, at the age of twenty-one, Bret Easton Ellis created a sensation when he published *Less than Zero*. A California novel influenced by the deadpan style of Joan Didion, *Less than Zero* depicted in a nonjudgmental way the youthful nihilism, drug use, and music video culture of its time period. After its success, Ellis found himself rapidly becoming part of the so-called Brat Pack of young authors, including Jay McInerney and Tama Janowitz, who were often seen clubbing together in New York City. Since that heady early period, Ellis has had to work to approximate the level of his youthful success.

After his second college novel, *The Rules of Attraction*, earned less notice but still sold well, Ellis's third work, *American Psycho*, with its portrait of a rich New York serial killer, scandalized Simon & Schuster's editors so much that they refused to

publish it. Sonny Mehta of Knopf bought the rights
to the work, and it quickly became one of the most
reviled, criticized, and best-selling novels of its day.
As Ellis received death threats, Norman Mailer came
to the book's defense in *Vanity Fair*, and the novel
was boycotted by the National Organization for
Women (NOW) for its graphic sexual crimes. Since
then, *American Psycho* has been the subject of numerous critical studies, in part because of its extreme
portrait of Reagan-era consumerism. After the controversy died down, Ellis published a collection of
short fiction, *The Informers* (1994), and another ambitious conspiracy novel, *Glamorama* (1998), which
juxtaposed the fashion industry with terrorism.

*Once labeled the voice of the
MTV generation, Bret Easton
Ellis is the author of several
best-selling novels, including
Less than Zero (1985), The
Rules of Attraction (1987),
American Psycho (1991), and
Glamorama (1998).*

Now entering his forties, Ellis can no longer hold
the title of the voice of transgressive youth, and he
must make the awkward transition to adulthood.
For *Lunar Park*, he has chosen to fictionalize himself as a protagonist so that he can satirize the
media-constructed image of himself as a rebellious
and wildly successful author. He also turned to one
of his favorite writers of his youth—Stephen King—
to supply him with a horror genre. The result is a kind of hybrid metafictional novel of
dread that borrows liberally from Ellis's life and his estranged relationship with his
father to form a kind of postmodern William Shakespeare's *Hamlet* (pr. c. 1600-
1601) of the New England suburbs.

Given such juicy material to satirize—his own celebrity—Ellis begins the novel in
a highly self-conscious form. He begins by calling attention to the relative concision
of the opening sentence, "You do an awfully good impression of yourself," then compares it to the opening sentences of his previous novels, which he then lists in order.
Next, he gives a succinct overview of his scandal-mongering career, exaggerating the
excesses of his fame to humorous effect. He notes how *Less than Zero* "was mistaken
for autobiography" but was largely comprised of scenes taken from "lurid rumors that
whispered through the group, [he] hung with in L.A." In the same way, he creates fictions about his own fame that gently lampoon the press's interest in him and its distor-
tions. Thus, the Brat Pack's "antics included food fights, hurling lobsters and hosing
one another down with bottles of Dom Perignon" in New York's fanciest restaurants.

The big difference, however, between this mock-Ellis and the real one is that in the
course of the fictional Ellis's career he has fathered a child, Robbie, with a film star
named Jayne Dennis. He disputes his parenthood, claiming in court that the child's father is actually Keanu Reeves, who was starring in a motion picture with Dennis at the
time, but DNA tests have proven him the father. Later, after his rock-star excesses of
drugs and depravity have brought him to a new low after the grinding international
reading tour promoting *Glamorama*, Ellis abruptly marries Jayne, takes responsibil-

ity for his estranged son, now eleven, and Jayne's daughter from another union, five-year-old Sarah. They all move to the New England suburbs to try to lead a normal life. Ellis begins to write a new novel titled *Teenage Pussy*, takes on a small creative writing teaching post at the local college, and settles down to upper-class suburbia, which he calls "a refuge for the less competitive: it was the minor leagues." Given that Ellis's protagonists have usually defined themselves as distinctly urban and hiply single socialites, usually along the axis between Los Angeles and New York, it is funny to see Ellis try to adjust himself to family life—trick or treating with his children and attending couples therapy sessions. He finds that he does not mind the suburbs as much as he thought he would: "Passing by someone pruning a shrub did not spark the powder keg of regret I expected."

Following these interludes, the horror story starts off with an ostentatious but also sinister Halloween party, and as a consequence the novel becomes both more focused and less plausible. The story line covers a twelve-day period between late October and November, during which Ellis's characterization of himself commits various indiscretions, including hints of a sexual relationship with a graduate student named Aimee Light, cocaine use, and binge drinking. Suddenly, he finds that a toy bird his daughter owns has developed a sinister ability to fly, a mock gravestone outside mysteriously carries his deceased father's name, and the furniture in his household keeps shifting around to resemble his childhood home. Ellis describes his father as "careless, abusive, alcoholic, vain, angry," and "paranoid," but ironically "the pain he inflicted on" Ellis—"verbal and physical—was the reason [he] became a writer." Ellis's father showed him how the "world lacked coherence," and now it seems as if he has returned in spirit, or demonic form, to communicate something either to Bret or to his son, Robbie. That this visitation may allude to *Hamlet* can be guessed from the fact that Ellis begins the novel with an epigraph from the play. Also, his fictive house is on Elsinore Lane not too far from the Fortinbras mall.

Whether or not the increasing menace inside the Ellis household is effective will depend on how much the reader accepts the conventions of Stephen King-style horror novels. The fictional Ellis keeps seeing the same cream-colored 450 SL Mercedes car around the neighborhood that his father bequeathed to him upon his death. A young man strongly resembling Clay from *Less than Zero* appears in Ellis's office to drop off a manuscript, and he may have appeared dressed as Patrick Bateman, the serial killer from *American Psycho*, at the Halloween party. A detective named Donald Kimball arrives to investigate a rash of murders in the area which strongly resemble the murders in *American Psycho*. Then the fictional Ellis goes next door to a dinner party, where he observes how suburbia has "zapped" the "youthful edge" of his male friends, who are "early-middle-aged and bored." Ellis notes how his hedonistic days of youth are sadly over, and while the women talk inside, the men get stoned, but then Ellis spies an intruder inside of his house across the way. When he goes to try to save his children and the baby-sitter from the stranger, he ends up scaring his family, and Jayne accuses him of allowing his drug use to help him imagine things.

As the novel continues, several problems come to light. First, middle-aged drunken high jinks are less amusing than youthful ones. Whereas the drugs taken were important for the atmosphere of his earlier novels, now they seem gratuitous and less integrated into the plot line. As a user, Ellis enjoys making himself the butt of his own jokes, and he thus turns his celebrity excess into a cartoon, but this kind of humor is hard to sustain. Second, compared to the evil of *American Psycho*, narrated from the point of view of a serial killer, Ellis's father is remote and not fully realized. Even at the end of the novel, it is not clear what his father wants to say to his son or his grandson, perhaps something about the sins of the father being repeated in Ellis's mistreatment of Robbie. Whereas the return of his father may carry resonance for Ellis, it has not been sufficiently dramatized for the reader. Finally, the novel lacks credibility. It tries to turn an individual dislike for his father into a universal evil, and the increasingly otherworldly phenomena are not plausible. Ellis draws on his unpublished juvenalia to create one creature who attacks his fictional double and his son and daughter in the night. A short monster, covered with hair, with no eyes, and teeth at the top of its head, rushes headlong at the family as the lights go out. Then the disbelieving police arrive, and the trio retires to a hotel.

In the midst of the schematic horror effects, however, one can still find interesting details about Ellis's take on middle-aged life and writing. He notes the contradiction between trying to succeed as a responsible father and the darker side of his imagination. He summarizes his creative efforts as "the world of teenage flameout and the curving murals of scorched corpses," but now adult responsibilities oblige him to make moral choices and serve as an example to his children. As he tries to protect them from both common and metaphysical evils, he points out how "the half world of the writer's life encourages drama and pain, and defeat is good for art." As a character who is also the author, Ellis embodies both the pleasure in destruction and the desire to survive. The detective asks him, "You're not a fictional character, are you Mr. Ellis?" In this way, Ellis calls attention to the fictionality both of his media presence and the way in which he has always catered to this "dangerous" persona. As this is his novel, however, the threat never seems all that real. As his family gets menaced and falls apart, Robbie runs away and seems to join a group of other runaway boys in the same community. Ellis's character cries and indulges in hysterics for much of the latter half of the narrative, but it is hard to believe that the evil will amount to much within his metafictional hall of mirrors.

By the end of the novel, Ellis manages to forestall the visitation of his father's ghost by agreeing to scatter his ashes, which have been locked up in a safe deposit box in a Bank of America back in Los Angeles. As he puts his father to rest, Ellis the author ends the novel with a lyrical passage reminiscent of the coda of James Joyce's short story "The Dead," where the ashes cover all the memories of his youth, and father and son are happily resurrected one last time:

> The ashes were collapsing into everything and following echoes. They sifted over the graves of his parents and finally entered the cold, lit world of the dead where they wept across the children standing in the cemetery. . . . From those of us who are left behind: you will be remembered, you were the one I needed, I loved you in my dreams.

Whether or not Ellis has earned this kind of elegiac conclusion in an otherwise ironic horror novel depends upon the reader's ability to immerse himself or herself seriously in Ellis's mock drama. The novel as a whole is awkwardly poised between a nostalgia for youthful revolt and a bid for something more mature, literary, and lasting.

Roy C. Flannagan

Review Sources

Booklist 101, nos. 19/20 (June 1, 2005): 1712.
Kirkus Reviews 73, no. 11 (June 1, 2005): 602.
Library Journal 130, no. 12 (July 1, 2005): 66.
The New York Times 154 (August 11, 2005): E8.
People 64, no. 9 (August 29, 2005): 52.
Publishers Weekly 252, no. 26 (June 27, 2005): 38.
Time 166, no. 8 (August 22, 2005): 66.
The Times Literary Supplement, October 7, 2005, p. 21.
The Washington Post Book World 35 (August 21, 2005): 6.

A MANNERED GRACE
The Life of Laura (Riding) Jackson

Author: Elizabeth Friedmann (1941-   )
Publisher: Persea Books (New York). Illustrated. 571 pp.
  $37.50
Type of work: Literary biography
Time: 1901-1991
Locale: New York City; London, England; Deya,
  Mallorca, Spain; New Hope, Pennsylvania; Wabasso,
  Florida; Watrous, New Mexico

*Friedmann compiles a detailed record of the American
writer who was one of the earliest modernists and who
lived nearly half a century after she renounced poetry*

Principal personages:
> LAURA RIDING (later JACKSON), one of the first modern poets, whose
> work and reputation were overshadowed by her relationship with poet
> Robert Graves
> LOUIS GOTTSCHALK, her first husband
> ROBERT GRAVES, the English poet and critic with whom Riding lived for
> almost thirteen years
> GERTRUDE STEIN, one of the many writers whom Riding knew and with
> whom she corresponded in the modernist heyday of the 1920's and
> 1930's
> SCHUYLER JACKSON, a writer whom Riding married in 1941 and with
> whom she collaborated in her later dictionary projects

Laura Riding Jackson rode one of the most mercurial careers in twentieth century
literary history. The formative Fugitive poets called her the "discovery of the year" in
1924, when she was only twenty-three. In the following twenty years, she published
more than two dozen books of poetry and criticism, often in collaboration with the
English writer Robert Graves, with whom she lived in the 1930's in Deya, Mallorca.
In the 1940's, she moved back to the United States, married and settled in Florida, and
renounced poetry but continued her work on language. As the reputation of Graves
grew, Riding's fame shrank, until she was omitted from the literary histories. In the
last twenty years of her life—Graves died in 1985, Riding in 1991—the tide was reversed. Readers began to rediscover her earlier poetry, and critics began to reassess
her role in twentieth century Anglo-American literature and criticism.

Elizabeth Friedmann's biography *A Mannered Grace* is clearly part of this latter
effort. Researched and written over a period of ten years, the book draws on a number of literary archives and Riding's voluminous correspondence. ("According to
her record-keeping, from early 1974 through mid-July 1986," Friedmann notes at
one point, "Laura wrote more than eight thousand letters.") Friedmann herself be-

〜

*Elizabeth Friedmann has published
articles on Laura Riding Jackson
and coedited* First Awakenings: The
Early Poems of Laura Riding *(1992),
a new edition of Jackson's* Four
Unposted Letters to Catherine
(1993), and The Word "Woman,"
and Other Related Writings *(1994).
In 2000, Friedmann was also guest
editor of a special issue of* Chelsea
devoted to Jackson's later work.

〜

gan corresponding with Riding in 1980, began visiting her in 1985, and during Riding's final years worked with her and kept notes on their activities and conversations. By the time Riding died, Friedmann was a member of the board Riding had appointed in her will to oversee her literary estate. Such intimate knowledge of her subject means that Friedmann's biography gets as close to this creative life as is possible. Unfortunately, the result is more a detailed compilation of biographical facts and figures than the literary history and analysis readers might expect in the study of such a pivotal creative figure.

Laura Reichenthal was born in New York on January 16, 1901, and was a student at Cornell University by the time she was seventeen. She flourished in the academic environment and produced a great deal of poetry. She married a graduate student in history, Louis Gottschalk, and at the same time started using the name Riding, considering it softer sounding than Reichenthal, as her middle name. By 1924, she had dropped out of Cornell, followed her husband to several teaching posts, and started to publish her work in magazines such as *Poetry*, the important journal edited in Chicago by Harriet Monroe. Riding's real success came with the Fugitives, the seminal group of southern writers centered in Nashville around Donald Davidson, John Crowe Ransom, and their magazine, *The Fugitive*.

As her marriage foundered, Riding became a contributor to *The Fugitive*. At the time . . . only three women had been published in the seven previous numbers of the poetry journal. She also began an affair with one of *The Fugitive*'s young stars, the poet and critic Allen Tate. From the beginning, Riding's poetry was preoccupied with the metaphysical questions raised by the nature of human existence. "Though technically unpolished at times, her poems startled with their originality, their unconventionality, their verbal audacity." She also began to publish criticism with the essay "A Prophecy or a Plea" in *The Reviewer* in 1925.

One of the first people to notice her was the English writer Robert Graves, who wrote the editors of *The Fugitive* from London after they published her poem "The Quids." When her marriage and her affair both had ended, Riding found herself in the heady world of Greenwich Village in the mid-1920's, where she met many of the writers responsible for the recent renaissance of American literature, most notably the poet Hart Crane, whose poetry had much of the same intellectual intensity as Riding's. She tired of Village life rather quickly, however, and when Graves wrote and invited Laura to accompany his wife, four children, and himself to Cairo, where he had taken a temporary teaching position, she readily agreed. Graves's job did not last long, but by the time they all returned to England, Laura was part of a ménage à trois. Nancy Graves was apparently happy with the arrangement (even supplying the couple with contraceptives), but this "marriage of three" did not last long. In a few years, Laura and Robert would leave England and settle in the village of Deya on the island of Mallorca.

For the more than thirteen years of Graves and Riding's relationship, they would produce a number of important literary works, including chapbooks produced through their own Seizin Press, the first volume of which was a collection of Riding's poetry, *Love as Love, Death as Death* (1928). A year earlier, they had completed *A Survey of Modernist Poetry* for Heinemann, the analysis and criticism of which would "influence the way poetry was written, read, and reviewed" and, with their "passionate attention to the poem's verbal and syntactical makeup," help forge the critical revolution called the New Criticism for the remainder of the twentieth century. While she was publishing poetry such as her *Collected Poems* (1936) and criticism (often in collaboration with Graves) such as *Anarchism Is Not Enough* (1928) and *Four Unposted Letters to Catherine* (1930), Graves was writing his popular autobiography *Goodbye to All That* (1929) and the best-selling historical novel *I, Claudius* (1934). They were also at the center of a web of literary connections emanating from Mallorca that included Gertrude Stein, Jacob Bronowski, Tom Matthews, and many other English and American writers and intellectuals.

In the fall of 1936, their idyll ended when the Spanish Civil War broke out, and they were rushed from Mallorca by the authorities with one suitcase apiece. (Graves would return in the 1940's to the home they had built in Mallorca.) Their sexual relationship had ended some years earlier (in 1933 Riding wrote that she thought "physical relations between men and women immoral"), and soon their collaboration ended as well. After a few years in Europe, they sailed to New York. After they arrived, Riding met Schuyler Jackson, the poetry editor for *Time* magazine, and for the second time in her young life, she entered a relationship with a man who abandoned his wife and children for her. The two married, and for several years, Laura Riding Jackson and her husband lived in New Hope, Pennsylvania, working the Jackson farm. They then moved to Wabasso, Florida, where for a few years they maintained a mail-order fruit business, with frequent trips to a second home in the isolated village of Watrous, New Mexico.

The basis of their relationship, as had been the case with Riding and Graves, was writing. Laura, however, in "her final apprehension of the flawed nature of poetic utterance," renounced poetry in the 1940's, and concentrated instead on language, including working on several dictionaries with Schuyler. Her poetry had become increasingly cut off from her emotional and sensory life, intellectual and difficult, and her work on thought and language was a natural continuation of her search for linguistic purity and truth. The dictionary work did not go well, however: Deadlines were missed, contracts cancelled, and in the end the only published result of their collaborative work was *Rational Meaning: A New Foundation for the Definition of Words*, which did not appear in its entirety until 1997, when both creators had been dead for some years.

Schuyler was ill for much of their marriage and died in 1968, but Laura would outlive him by several decades, and this period is perhaps the most interesting part of Friedmann's narrative. As Laura Riding Jackson retired from poetry, Graves became a larger and larger presence in postwar Anglo-American literature, and studies of him airbrushed her from the record, exaggerating her worst personal traits and citing books that the two had written together without her name. The English critic William Empson, to cite one example, omitted any reference to her in his discussion of *A Survey of Modernist Poetry* in the second edition of his influential *Seven Types of Ambiguity*. In 1970, he wrote to apologize to her for his mistake.

It was in 1965, in fact, that the tide first began to turn, when the American poet John Ashbery asked Laura Riding Jackson for permission to reprint one of her earlier stories for the journal he was editing in Paris, *Art and Literature*. Other poets, including Sylvia Plath and Ted Hughes, acknowledged her importance. At the same time, critics and historians began to reassess her role in the thought and writing of Robert Graves, and her poetry was finally reprinted by Faber in 1970 in *Selected Poems: In Five Sets*. This revival was capped in 1991, the year of her death, when Riding was awarded the prestigious Bollingen Prize from Yale University.

Friedmann's biography is clearly in favor of this revival. She establishes that during "their close association Robert Graves had become increasingly dependent upon Laura Riding for both intellectual guidance and creative inspiration." Any future evaluation of either writer will have to consult this study. At the same time, Friedmann is fairly facile with her literary history and analysis. There is little here on the ideas and poetic forms that influenced Laura Riding Jackson, or the literary elements that made up the modernism of which she was a vital part, and almost nothing on what was behind the massive dictionary work which she and her last husband spent decades working on. Friedmann has eighty pages of notes, many of them citing the various archives of her voluminous correspondence but only a two-page list of "Major Works of Laura (Riding) Jackson," and no other bibliography. The complex fabric that was modernism, including the ideas and literary models which were so formative in the 1920's and 1930's, and so influential in the later decades of the twentieth century, find little room here. The linguistic studies upon which the Jacksons were apparently drawing are missing. The biography, ultimately, is an interesting life of an important, if minor, writer; as literary history and linguistic analysis, it is rather thin.

David Peck

Review Sources

American Book Review 26 (July/August, 2005): 5.
Booklist 101, no. 12 (February 15, 2005): 1051.
Library Journal 130, no. 5 (March 15, 2005): 85.

MAO
The Unknown Story

Authors: Jung Chang (1952-   ) and Jon Halliday
(1939-   )
Publisher: Alfred A. Knopf (New York). Illustrated.
832 pp. $35.00
Type of work: Biography and history
Time: 1893-1976
Locale: China

Through meticulous research, the authors demonstrate the evil, quintessentially selfish, brutal, and power-hungry nature of Mao Zedong, the man who united China under communism and whose climb to power and twenty-seven years of rule caused the deaths of more than seventy million Chinese

Principal personages:

MAO ZEDONG (MAO TSE-TUNG), the chairman of the Chinese Communist Party, 1931-1976

CHIANG KAI-SHEK, Mao's Nationalist adversary, director general of the Guomindang (Kuomintang), 1938-1975

JOSEPH STALIN, the general secretary of the Soviet Communist Party, 1922-1953

ZHOU ENLAI (CHOU EN-LAI), the prime minister of the People's Republic of China, 1949-1976

JIANG QING (CHIANG CH'ING), Mao's fourth wife, known as Madame Mao

Mao: The Unknown Story focuses on the vast dark side of Mao Zedong (Mao Tse-tung in Wade-Giles transliteration), the Chinese Communist leader who rose to power to rule a unified mainland China for twenty-seven years until his death in 1976. The authors passionately demonstrate that Mao was driven by selfish goals, quickly developed a penchant for brutality, and ruthlessly sought to achieve supreme power, often relying on bloody purges. With considerable historical justification, the authors hold Mao responsible for the deaths of seventy million Chinese in peacetime.

At the end of 2005, Mao was still officially venerated in the People's Republic of China, his portrait looming over Tiananmen Square and printed on China's currency. Jung Chang and Jon Halliday's book is a welcome antidote to the idea that history is written by the victors. In the West, for too long, lack of free access to mainland Chinese sources and archives and, until 1989, those of the former Soviet Union, led too many to rely on Mao's propaganda machine in order to form a somewhat benign picture of the man. While his responsibility for the murderous Great Famine of 1958-1961, which killed approximately thirty-five million people, and his reveling in the

~

Jung Chang moved to England from China in 1978. She reaped international fame with her award-winning book Wild Swans _(1991), a memoir chronicling the lives of three generations of women in twentieth century China. Her first book,_ Mme Sun Yat-sen _(1986), is a biography written with Jon Halliday. Halliday is an accomplished Irish author and academic fluent in Russian. He is a retired Senior Visiting Research Fellow at King's College, London, and has contributed to eight previous books as editor, coauthor, or author, many with an Asian topic._

~

carnage of the Cultural Revolution has generally been acknowledged, the true nature of his rule and personality has still been often glossed over. After reading _Mao_, one hopes that any lingering affection for Mao and Maoism can be duly extinguished.

Mao begins by debunking the myth that its subject came from poor peasants and had a lifelong sympathy for their harsh lot. Mao's father, Mao Yichang (Mao Yi-chang), through hard work became one of the richest men of his village, one of the kind his son would later exhort his followers to murder. His privileged start in life enabled young Mao to study during the heady days when China became a republic in 1912. Still, Mao showed no liking of the peasants. In a surviving essay of 1917-1918, the year of the Russian Revolution when he turned twenty-four, Mao wrote that "there are people and objects in the world, but they are all there only for me." Envisioning himself as a kind of Nietzschean superhuman, he claimed for himself the right to stand above all morality and ethics. Chillingly enough, _Mao_ proves, he would live up to his student-day vision of himself, at the cost of millions of Chinese lives.

With postrevolutionary China still in turmoil, in June, 1920, Mao met a professor in Shanghai who would become a founder of the Chinese Communist Party (CCP) after Mao had left the town. Typical for Mao's later forgery of the historical record, the founding of the CCP was officially dated forward to 1921, when Mao was part of its first congress. What further lured Mao to the party, _Mao_ argues, was a generous Soviet stipend for its leaders. In turn, Mao proved exceedingly loyal to Moscow's line, got to live with his new wife in a house with servants, and ousted all those who opposed his local rule, relying on friends to do the operative party work. As Chang and Halliday prove, this set the pattern for his early party career.

Rather free from ideological concerns, _Mao_ shows its subject frequently shifting course to gain maximal power among the Communists. A rural tour of rebellious Hunan countryside in March, 1927, awakened in Mao a lifelong lust for blood. In his unpublished report of the tour, deposited in the CCP Archive Study Office and CCP Hunan Committee, he wrote feeling a "kind of ecstasy" at the sight of extrajudicial killings and torture of the peasant victims, calling this "wonderful" and authorizing further murders. Executions would remain a lifelong passion of Mao.

Mao's opportunity to engage in more atrocities began after April, 1927, when the leader of the Nationalists, Chiang Kai-shek, attacked the Communists. In October, 1927, Mao joined mountain bandits with his Communists, took a new wife, and terrorized the area under his control for fifteen months. In the following years, the authors paint a devastating picture of a man, now in his thirties, placing his own power

above everything else, scheming to amass more troops and not even stopping at sacrificing his former wife, who was executed by the Nationalists.

In his quickly expanding area of control Mao instigated the first of his famous
bloody purges in November, 1930. He used Communist terminology to justify torture
and mass killings of those he saw as blocking his path to power. Saved from destruction by Chiang Kai-shek when Japan invaded Manchuria in 1931 and Chiang reluctantly sought an armistice with the Communists which they, contrary to their later legend, refused to enter, Mao formed his own Communist state and made himself
chairman on November 7, 1931.

Chang and Halliday point out strongly how Mao's ineffective inaction in the face
of Nationalist pressure nearly cost him his position in the early 1930's. All of this con-
tradicts the propaganda myth of Mao as the great military leader. Instead, it was
others such as Zhou Enlai (Chou En-lai) who saved the Communists, and only Mao's
superb relations with Moscow's leader Joseph Stalin saved him.

Taking on one of the greatest myths of Maoism, the Long March of the Communists to safety in the far Northwest, *Mao* presents a devastating historical picture of
Mao's true behavior. Pressed by the Nationalists in their southern stronghold, the
Communists decided to move out in October, 1934, after executing thousands of "unreliable" comrades. Mao had himself and his friends carried in bamboo chairs the
whole way—a very different picture from that painted by Communist mythology. Those who have read Chang's previous memoir, the widely acclaimed *Wild
Swans* (1991), and remember how, on a different Communist march, her own father, a devoted Communist, prohibited her pregnant mother from being carried, insisting on equality with the masses, will realize the depth of the authors' contempt
for Mao.

The authors further challenge Communist propaganda by asserting that Mao's
Communists were let go, rather than breaking out. This, they reason, was because Stalin held hostage Chiang's son in Russia and because Chiang felt that pursuing the
fleeing Communists would let his army enter the fiefs still held by independent war-
lords. This issue needs further historical scrutiny, as well as the authors' review of
Mao's crossing of Dadu Bridge. Communists claim the bridge was stormed under
fire; *Mao* argues, based on an eyewitness account, that the Nationalists did not block
the crossing, as Chiang also wanted a small Communist force surviving as backup
against Japanese invaders.

Chang and Halliday continue to challenge Chinese Communist propaganda at every turn of their biography of Mao. They provide sources that show that he deliberately led rival Communist forces to their death in hostile terrain and had the surviving
comrades buried alive, and offer compelling evidence that he had a rival leader shot
from behind. *Mao* shows that, far from Mao's later claim that the Communists hated
Japanese more than their Chinese Nationalist enemies, Mao insisted on attacking
Chiang Kai-shek's forces even after China's declaration of war on invading Japan in
1937. Forced by Stalin to stop these attacks, in 1937 Mao married a former Shanghai
actress, Jiang Qing (Chiang Ch'ing), who would enter history as the infamous Madame Mao, a driving force behind the devastating Cultural Revolution.

Backed by substantial evidence such as the absence of documented military battles between them, *Mao* shows that Mao held back Communist forces in China's war against Japan from 1937 to 1945. Chang and Halliday insist that while Mao was more bent on expanding the area of his control than fighting the aggressors, the West swallowed his propaganda lies to the contrary. Even more historical research will be needed to clarify this issue.

Mao boldly claims that Chiang Kai-shek lost the Chinese Civil War (1945-1949) due to American dislike of Chiang Kai-shek and, most important, the deliberate military sabotage of key Communist moles in Chiang's service. Openly acknowledging the widespread corruption that severely tainted and undermined Chiang Kai-shek's regime, Chang and Halliday nevertheless affix final blame for the Nationalists' disaster to betrayal. While it will be difficult to establish the truth regarding the alleged moles, historical forces played straight into the hands of Mao. He had created a monumental image of himself as leader of an ideological movement that promised a much better future. Some of the bitterness with which Chang and Halliday, a self-professed atheist Socialist, judge their subject may result from this sense of so many positive ideas such as social justice, national self-determination, and women's rights being hijacked by a ruthless, evil man using them to obtain personal power.

Mao's persuasive, well-documented chapters on the chairman's disastrous plans for the People's Republic of China that saw tens of millions of Chinese die during the artificially created Great Famine, and the unspeakable barbarities and atrocities of the Cultural Revolution chill the reader. Once in power after founding the People's Republic of China on October 1, 1949, Mao became a monster nearly unchecked. Only the depth of disaster in the midst of the Great Famine led to him being reined in by his comrades after the "Conference of the Seven Thousand" ended on February 7, 1962. Yet he and his wife Jiang Qing stormed back to center stage, unleashing the Cultural Revolution in June, 1966. Great purges consumed all of Chinese society, and for a decade normal life ceased to exist. Misery descended on people on a hitherto unbelievable scale. Hundreds of millions of Chinese were affected by denunciations, forceful deportations, stints in prisons, labor and reeducation camps, public executions, and endless humiliation.

Mao shows how the aging and ailing Mao, after having turned China into a barren state devoid of all real culture and enjoyment, moved to the international stage to raise his flagging status. American President Richard Nixon's visit to China in 1972 boosted Mao's ego and turned him into an international statesman, but at a steep price for China. Any country whose leader showed up in Beijing and asked for it would be rewarded with aid; tiny Mediterranean Malta got a present of twenty-five million dollars in 1972 when its prime minister returned home wearing a Mao badge.

Unrelenting in setting the historical record straight, the authors show how Mao was jealous to his death. He forbade Zhou Enlai cancer treatment so that Zhou would die a few months before him. For his wife Jiang Qing or any other hardliners who would survive him, he showed little concern, promising restless reformers they could move ahead once he was dead. His death came on September 9, 1976.

Mao: The Unknown Story is the result of over ten years' research by its two authors. The acknowledged goal of their biography is to debunk the myths about Mao that the Chinese Communist dictator dedicated a lifetime to establishing. The authors focus on the evil side of Mao and find more than sufficient proof for their strongly advocated thesis. Theirs is a truly important book about one of the most influential men of the twentieth century whose misrule caused suffering among more than half a billion people.

R. C. Lutz

Review Sources

Booklist 102, no. 1 (September 1, 2005): 47.
The Economist 375 (May 28, 2005): 83.
Foreign Affairs 84, no. 6 (November/December, 2005): 153-154.
Maclean's 188 (October 31, 2005): 52-53.
The New Leader 88, no. 5 (September/October, 2005): 24-26.
The New York Review of Books 52, no. 17 (November 3, 2005): 23-24.
The New York Times Book Review 155 (October 23, 2005): 1-11.
Publishers Weekly 252, no. 35 (September 5, 2005): 51.
Time 166, no. 18 (October 31, 2005): 82.
The Times Literary Supplement, July 22, 2005, pp. 22-23.

THE MARCH

Author: E. L. Doctorow (1931-   )
Publisher: Random House (New York). 363 pp. $26.00
Type of work: Novel
Time: November, 1864, to April, 1865
Locale: Milledgeville and Savannah, Georgia; Columbia,
   South Carolina; Fayetteville, Bentonville, and
   Goldsboro, North Carolina; and Washington, D.C.

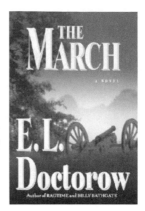

*Doctorow fictionalizes General Sherman's famous
march to the sea and its effects upon the Confederacy and
the South's newly freed slaves*

Principal characters:
   MAJOR GENERAL WILLIAM TECUMSEH
      SHERMAN, the commander of the Union
      Army of the West
   PEARL JAMESON, a newly freed "white" African American from a Geor-
      gia plantation
   STEPHEN WALSH, a Union soldier and Pearl's love interest
   COLONEL WREDE SARTORIUS, a German-born Union Army surgeon
   ARLY WILCOX, a Confederate soldier and would-be assassin
   WILL B. KIRKLAND, a Confederate soldier and Arly's companion

It is easy to understand why the American Civil War would appeal to a gifted fiction writer such as E. L. Doctorow. This immense conflict began in 1861 and ended in
1865, a period that saw the destruction of much of the American South and the manumission of its slaves. What is more difficult to grasp in a time of such tumult is its impact upon individuals. It is true that participants in the American Civil War were perhaps the most literate group of soldiers in history up to that time. They generally wrote
well, and they wrote often; however, the historical record is largely silent regarding
those who were simultaneously the most marginalized and the most deeply affected
by the conflict, African Americans. Unlike modern wars, a relatively small number of
civilians died as a direct result of the conflict, but few were untouched by the economic and cultural maelstrom it created.

Without question, the most chaotic period of the war—and the portion most devastating to the South—was the long march of Union General William Tecumseh Sherman and his sixty thousand-man army to the sea in the closing months of 1864. The
general's goal was twofold: to subdue the forces of Confederate General Joseph
Johnston and to destroy the South's ability to wage war by pillaging large sections of
it. In addition to the turmoil one would normally expect from war, there was also the
matter of thousands of newly freed but homeless slaves. All of this is fertile ground
for fiction. Doctorow has covered similar ground before. In *Ragtime* (1975), he dealt
with the turmoil of early twentieth century America, with its waves of immigrants and

explosive race relations. It is appropriate that Doctorow has selected the Civil War South as the setting for *The March*, for in it one can find the seeds of the racial oppression so painfully elucidated in *Ragtime*.

Up until November of 1864, when *The March* begins, the Confederacy had resisted the overwhelmingly superior forces of the Union Army, despite the fact that its cause was all but hopeless. Sherman's solution was to bring the horrors of war to the farms and large plantations whose products enabled the Confederacy to survive. While Sherman's forces had standing orders to seize whatever goods were deemed necessary without causing collateral damage, in practice the Army of the West had carte blanche to lay waste to anything in its path. To Sherman, this was a necessary act of war; to the slaves, the Union Army was a force of liberation.

The novel opens at the center of this whirlwind, with a young slave girl named Pearl viewed at the moment of manumission. Doctorow's description of the approach of Union forces is masterly and is worth quoting: "And, as they watched, the brown cloud took on a reddish cast. It moved

E. L. Doctorow's books include Ragtime *(1975),* Loon Lake *(1980),* World's Fair *(1985), and* Billy Bathgate *(1989). Among his awards are the National Humanities Medal, the National Book award, the PEN/ Faulkner Award, the National Book Critics Circle award, the William Dean Howells Medal of the American Academy of Arts and Letters, and the Edith Wharton citation for fiction.*

forward, thin as a hatchet blade in front and then widening like the furrow from the plow. . . . When the sound of this cloud reached them, it was like nothing they had ever heard in their lives."

Pearl Jameson is that most unusual product of slavery, a "white" Negro; that is, she has the physiognomy of her African American mother but with the pale flesh tones of her slaveholding father. Doctorow has chosen his character well, for she embodies the two-fold dilemma concomitant with the arrival of Sherman's troops. Manumission leaves the former slaves free but homeless in a society that is rapidly collapsing. Pearl, as the illegitimate child of her slave-owning father, would seem to be in the worst of all possible worlds. Given her light completion, she might have been able to assimilate into the white population of the South had she been acknowledged by John Jameson as a rightful heir; however, Jameson never regarded her as anything more than an embarrassing byproduct of his relations with Pearl's mother. He and his family flee Sherman's forces without the slightest consideration for this young woman, who is left to face an invading army with neither food nor shelter.

Appropriately, the only aid comes from Roscoe, a fellow slave who tosses his life savings to Pearl as he flees with his master. It is to Doctorow's credit that he allows this poignant moment to develop fully while preventing it from descending into melodrama or even mawkishness. The elements of the scene are convincing, especially young

Pearl's manner of speech, which captures the paucity of her education without denying her humanity. One of the pleasures of reading *The March* is how well it demonstrates that speech is a marker not of race but of class, something that is fluid and subject to change. Indeed, the Southern plantation dialect with which Pearl begins the novel is a kind of linguistic shackle that she is as intent upon breaking as the bonds of slavery. One can measure the maturity of her character by the determined manner with which she models her speech after that of her Union Army liberators throughout the novel.

Pearl's position, of course, is even more precarious than that of her fellow African Americans. While her race has excluded her from white Southern society, her light completion condemns her as an outcast among other freed slaves. Unlike others newly manumitted, Pearl accompanies Sherman's forces not in the transient mode of a refugee seeking shelter but as a means of entering white society. She initially poses as a Union drummer boy, thus forcing her to deny both her true race and gender. It is an irony as pervasive as it is trenchant. Pearl's pliant racial and sexual identity forms the core of the novel, a quality that captures the uncertainty of life in a time of war. It also functions as a potent metaphor for the other major characters who are also compelled to cross hitherto sacrosanct boundaries. In effect, Doctorow suggests that if the boundary of racial identity can be crossed—a seemingly impermeable wall—then all the other barriers that affect the characters can be traversed.

At the most obvious level, it is evident that the Civil War as a whole represented the division between North and South, a conflict between freedom and enslavement. That neat division held through much of the conflict. While the Union Army had fought major battles in the South in prior years, the clear separation between these two distinct cultures remained. With Sherman's foray into the South, the separation between the two societies was suddenly called into question. This was not a straightforward matter of capturing enemy territory. On the contrary, the Army of the West brought the North into the very heart of the Deep South. For the slaves, this meant liberation from a life of involuntary servitude, but it was a liberation that was solely dependent upon the presence of Union forces, the guarantors of their freedom. Understandably, former slaves who had successfully traversed the division between enslavement and freedom had no wish to return. One of the more interesting aspects of the novel is the skill with which Doctorow deals with the irascible Sherman and the seemingly endless train of African Americans following his army.

The permeable barrier of Pearl's racial identity also has echoes in other characters, both great and small. In Union Army Colonel Wrede Sartorius, Doctorow effectively creates a character who crosses the barrier of time and points the way to the future. While he astonishes his medical colleagues with the superiority of his surgical techniques, Sartorius decries the primitive nature of medicine and predicts the invention of antibiotics to combat infection. For Confederate soldiers Arly Wilcox and Will B. Kirkland, the invasion from the north offers possibilities both comic and deadly. When these condemned men are offered a pardon in return for continued wartime service, they pose as Union soldiers while their ill-equipped brothers-in-arms are annihilated.

Although these minor characters may at first appear to be a kind of afterthought by Doctorow, they are essential to the thematic structure of the novel. The wartime utility of these picaresque characters is nugatory. When Arly and Will attempt to save themselves by donning Union Army uniforms, it results in their recapture by Confederates, which is followed by their pretense of being Confederate prisoners-of-war when the Union Army returns. Their efforts at survival are so laughably incompetent that they provide comic relief to Pearl's more serious journey. They constitute a kind of foil to Pearl and underscore her development as an independent woman. In addition, they also highlight the fluid boundaries of the opposing sides during Sherman's March. Southern towns such as Milledgeville, Georgia, became Union territory while in the possession of the Union Army, only to revert back to the Confederacy once Sherman had moved on.

Arly and Will are distinguished from Pearl on two levels, one relating to the differing nature of their respective dilemmas and the other having to do with their ultimate goals. As Confederate soldiers, Arly and Will would most likely have volunteered for wartime service, a fact which clearly distinguishes them from Pearl, who was born into involuntary servitude. Despite the mishaps that plague them, Arly and Will possess the option of deserting the war and returning home, an option that is unavailable to Pearl. She, too, dons a uniform, first as a Union drummer boy and later as a kind of unofficial nurse. Unlike Arly and Will, she remains consistent with her choice of sides and her goal of an unfettered existence. As the novel unfolds, it becomes clear that Arly's aim is not to extricate himself from the conflict but instead to assassinate Sherman, a mission that undermines his sanity and eventually destroys the two men.

Doctorow's long experience in novel writing is much in evidence here, for he carefully matches the deterioration of the two men with the steady elevation of Pearl's character. The novel's conclusion finds Pearl planning a life in the North with Union soldier Stephen Walsh, possibly as a white doctor. While she regrets the prospect of concealing her true racial identity, it would enable Pearl to fulfill her role of transcending the most formidable barrier imposed by society, that of class. With its deft characterization and plotting, *The March* memorably captures the chaos and the triumph of the Civil War.

Cliff Prewencki

Review Sources

Booklist 101, no. 22 (August 1, 2005): 1952.
The Economist 377 (October 22, 2005): 88.
Kirkus Reviews 73, no. 14 (July 15, 2005): 752.
Library Journal 130, no. 1 (August 15, 2005): 67.
The Nation 281, no. 14 (October 31, 2005): 32-36.
New York 38, no. 31 (September 12, 2005): 77.
The New York Review of Books 52, no. 16 (October 20, 2005): 21-23.
The New York Times 155 (September 20, 2005): E1.
The New York Times Book Review 155 (September 25, 2005): 1.
The New Yorker 81 (September 12, 2005): 98.
Publishers Weekly 252, no. 28 (July 18, 2005): 177.

MARK TWAIN
A Life

Author: Ron Powers (1941-   )
Publisher: Free Press (New York). 722 pp. $35.00
Type of work: Literary biography
Time: 1835-1910
Locale: Hannibal, Missouri; the American West; Hartford, Connecticut

Powers's massively documented historical biography is based on new archival material, which should place it among the standard lives of Twain

Principal personages:
SAMUEL LANGHORNE CLEMENS (pen name
    MARK TWAIN), the most famous nineteenth century American writer
OLIVIA LANGDON (LIVY) CLEMENS, his wife
OLIVIA SUSAN (SUZY) CLEMENS, his oldest daughter
CLARA CLEMENS, his middle daughter
JEAN CLEMENS, his youngest daughter
JANE LAMPTON CLEMENS, his mother
ORION CLEMENS, his older brother
HENRY CLEMENS, his younger brother

It is difficult to overestimate Mark Twain's place in American literature. With *Adventures of Huckleberry Finn* (1884), he established the vernacular voice in American literature. He is quoted more often than any other writer except William Shakespeare. His friend William Dean Howells called him "the Lincoln of our literature." Twain's life spanned the American nineteenth century, from the antebellum period through the Gilded Age into the beginning of the twentieth century. Twain said of himself, "I am not an American, I am *the* American." With the assistance of the Mark Twain Project at the University of California at Berkeley, biographer Ron Powers has been able to incorporate many recently discovered letters and notebooks in his massive new historical work, *Mark Twain: A Life.*

In his prologue, Powers emphasizes the importance of the November, 1869, meeting in the Boston offices of the publisher Tichnor & Fields, between Twain and Howells, the young editor of *The Atlantic Monthly.* This encounter would blossom into a close literary friendship which would connect the Brahmin tastes of American high literary culture with Twain's vigorous, new American vernacular style. Twain was a deeply subversive figure, ridiculing and mocking American genteel attitudes and tastes in his first book, *The Innocents Abroad* (1869). It is to Howells's credit that he recognized the enormous talent behind Twain's unprepossessing veneer of a shambling, drawling, ill-dressed bohemian. The Howells-Twain friendship enabled Twain to contribute regularly to *The Atlantic Monthly*, a bastion of Brahmin literary tastes, and to extend his literary reputation. Through his friendship with Howells, Twain was able to break into "the ranks of New England literary culture" and in the process reinvigorate American literature.

The Powers biography departs from the standard theoretical/interpretative perspective of many Twain biographies, most notably Justin Kaplan's award-winning *Mr. Clemens and Mark Twain* (1966), and offers instead a historical/interpretive perspective which places Twain within his time period and milieu. The forty-five chapters of his massive, exhaustively documented new biography march the reader through Twain's life in short increments, offering much new factual material based on the enormous archives of the Mark Twain Project at Berkeley, with its eleven thousand Clemens letters, fifty-odd notebooks, six hundred unpublished or unfinished manuscripts, and many other memorabilia. Powers

Critic Ron Powers has won a Pulitzer Prize and an Emmy. He is the author of numerous books, among them The New York Times *best seller* Flags of Our Fathers *(2000) and* Dangerous Water: A Biography of the Boy Who Became Mark Twain *(1999).*

also corrects many of the factual errors and misconceptions in Albert Bigelow Paine's authorized three-volume *Mark Twain: A Biography* (1912) and the heavily edited, posthumous *Mark Twain's Autobiography* (1924) that Twain largely dictated to Paine.

What Powers offers is a rich social and political biography that places Twain within the center of the cultural changes in post-Civil War America. In *The Gilded Age* (1873), his collaboration with Charles Dudley Warner, Twain exposed the sordid political climate in Washington, D.C., and in Congress. With his popular stage appearances, Twain became the first American literary celebrity, achieving the equivalent of almost rock-star status. His hunger for public approbation enabled him to play upon his audiences' sensibilities to a remarkable degree, with his distinctive Missouri drawl, dramatic pauses, shuffling gait, hoaxes, burlesques, and other humorous devices. Though humorists were generally held in low repute, he developed his stage and literary humor into a distinctively American genre. Through his Western vernacular frontier sketches and his persona of the "American vandal" in *The Innocents Abroad*, Twain became the voice of a newly emergent and outwardly self-confident America, though his mockery of European culture and tradition reveals an underlying sense of cultural inferiority. His friend Howells also noted the anger beneath Twain's humor, his indignation at injustice, and his incisive social criticism.

The private Sam Clemens was also complex and contradictory, as Powers demonstrates. An auburn-haired man with bushy eyebrows and mustache, an aquiline nose, and a curious shuffling gait, Twain presented a striking image. Ten years older than his wife, Livy (Olivia Langdon Clemens), and in many ways totally different from her in temperament and class, Clemens remained devotedly in love with her, and they were an exemplary literary couple. His 189 courtship letters to her are models of eloquence and devotion, which she returned, calling him "Youth." He was not an easy husband to live with, however, with his explosive temper and violent, unpredictable mood swings which left his family afraid of him. He was unaware of his impact on his family until his favorite daughter, Suzy, informed him of it in her childhood biography of him.

Clemens was gregarious and extroverted and loved having friends and family around him but always made himself the center of attention, often performing impromptu humorous dances, skits, or songs at dinner. He disliked the dishonesty of sham sentimentality, though he could be quite sentimental himself. He had a great genius for friendship, with many enduring friendships with Howells, Joe Twitchell, Will Bowen, and many others, but he could be unforgiving and vindictive if crossed. He was hungry for money and commercial success, though he saw through the tawdry materialism of American life as well as anyone of his time. Though he seemed unconscious of these personal contradictions, which may perhaps have been accentuated by his mood swings and bipolar tendencies, he could use them for creative purposes. Throughout his life, Twain was obsessed with the theme of twins and reversed identities—the Dandy and the Squatter; Bixby and Brown; Tom and Huck; the Prince and the Pauper; Chambers and Tom; and the "Twins of Genius."

Twain was a Southerner who spoke out passionately against slavery, though he never fought in the Civil War. He became the friend and confidant of president and former Union general Ulysses S. Grant, whose war memoirs Twain helped to publish, saving the Grant family from financial ruin. Twain was also the first American writer publicly to endorse a presidential candidate, Rutherford B. Hayes in 1872. A compassionate social reformer who championed the rights of African Americans, women, and Chinese immigrants, he never got over his early prejudice against American Indians. In 1884, Twain toured the United States with fellow Southern writer George Washington Cable as "the Twins of Genius," speaking out against Jim Crow racism and lynching.

Twain's style and values also straddled the contradictions of his age. He was a frontier writer who courted acceptance by the Boston Brahmins; he was a southerner who lived in the North, in an extravagant mansion in Hartford, Connecticut. He was at the same time a romantic and a realist, a spokesman for the American frontier and a writer nostalgic for English customs and traditions, a public adherent of the "genteel code" and a private author of bawdy tales, a champion of international copyright laws who borrowed many of his ideas from others, an imagined playwright who adapted several works for the stage but who depended on his characters to carry the drama. He was a prodigious letter writer who wrote more than eleven thousand letters in a graceful and fluent hand, yet he was fascinated with the new typewriter and was one of the first authors to type a manuscript. He imagined himself a shrewd businessman but bankrupted his family with his unwise investments in the hopelessly intricate Paige typesetter. He outlived all of his beloved family except his daughter Clara, who grew estranged from him, and he died a lonely old man in his Redding, Connecticut, mansion, itself a manifestation of his desperate attempts to recapture the happiness of his Hartford years.

In April, 1882, Twain headed west for a month-long nostalgic trip on the Mississippi River that would renew his creative vigor and allow him to complete *Adventures of Huckleberry Finn*. He briefly relived his days as a steamboat pilot before the Civil War and felt sufficiently liberated by his time on the river that his writing flourished. In his greatest works, "Old Times on the Mississippi" (1875), *The Adventures of Tom Sawyer* (1876), *Life on the Mississippi* (1883), and *Adventures of Huckleberry Finn*, Twain recaptured the post-Civil War American nostalgia for an idyllic childhood past that never really existed, but he also invented a new vernacular style that came to define American writing.

It is interesting to consider that Twain was working on *Adventures of Huckleberry Finn* and *The Prince and the Pauper* (1881) alternately at about the same time and could sustain such utterly different styles and sensibilities. At the time, based in part on his wife's genteel tastes, Twain came to prefer the artificiality of his genteel historical romances to the social realism of *Adventures of Huckleberry Finn*. Perhaps it was only in *A Connecticut Yankee in King Arthur's Court* (1889) that Twain was able to combine, to a degree, his interest in social satire with his taste for European historical romance. Hank Morgan became Twain's "American Vandal" who returns to Europe to turn medieval England upside down with his nineteenth century American inventions, factories, bureaucratic efficiency, and modern weapons of destruction. Twain found a new god in the Machine and Industrial Progress. Unfortunately, he could not sustain this critical vision, and with its return to historical naïveté and sentimentality, *The Personal Recollections of Joan of Arc* (1896) marks the beginning of the decline of Twain's literary gifts.

After the bankruptcy of his publishing company in 1894, Twain relied on his new friend Henry H. Rodgers for financial guidance and undertook an exhausting round-the-world lecture tour to pay off his debts. With the sudden death of his favorite daughter, Suzy, in 1896, followed by the loss of Livy in 1904 and his daughter Jean in 1909, his vision grew darker and more pessimistic. He was lionized everywhere and saluted as a great man, but fame could not console him for his personal losses. In late 1896, he had gathered together the remainder of his family in England. Before returning to the United States in 1900, he and his family restlessly moved around Europe, living in apartments and hotels in such places as Berlin, Vienna, Florence, and London. After Livy died, Twain and his daughter Clara moved to an apartment on Fifth Avenue in New York, where he could be seen on Sunday mornings strolling with his daughter in his trademark white suit.

Meanwhile, Twain continued to speak out against racism, imperialism, and jingoism and to explore the dark side of his consciousness in "The Man That Corrupted Hadleyburg," "The Mysterious Stranger," *Letters from the Earth* (1962), "What Is Man?" and "To the Person Sitting in Darkness." He spoke out against American imperialism in the Philippines and Belgian colonialism in the Congo, becoming a pacifist by 1905 with his famous "War Prayer." He became the American Voltaire, writing his barbed social criticism "with a pen warmed in hell," as he skewered sham and hypocrisy. His view of village life darkened considerably, from the nostalgic charm of St. Petersburg to the provincialism of Hadleyburg.

Unfortunately, Twain also increasingly drifted toward a personal nihilism that viewed humankind and its world as meaningless specks in a larger, unknowable universe. His last years were marked by honorary degrees from Oxford, Yale, and the University of Missouri. On April 21, 1910, Twain went out with the same Halley's comet that had greeted him in 1835. Though not breaking any critical new ground, Powers has written an expansive new life of Twain, rich in detail.

Andrew J. Angyal

Review Sources

Booklist 101, no. 22 (August 1, 2005): 1982.
The Christian Science Monitor, September 27, 2005, p. 11.
Library Journal 130, no. 13 (August 15, 2005): 86.
National Review 58, no. 1 (January 30, 2006): 54-55.
The New York Times 155 (September 21, 2005): E1-E6.
The New York Times Book Review 155 (October 2, 2005): 13-14.
Publishers Weekly 252, no. 30 (August 1, 2005): 60.
The Washington Post, October 9, 2005, p. T4.
Weekly Standard 11, no. 1 (September 19, 2005): 53-56.

MARRIAGE, A HISTORY
From Obedience to Intimacy: Or, How Love Conquered Marriage

Author: Stephanie Coontz (1944-   )
Publisher: Viking Penguin (New York). 432 pp. $30.00
Type of work: Anthropology, history, psychology, and
    sociology
Time: From prehistory to 2005
Locale: Worldwide

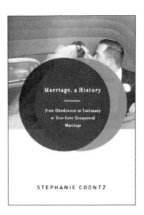

*An extensive and detailed look at marriage since the
Stone Age and how the concept of marriage has changed
dramatically in the past two hundred years, making matrimony both more satisfying and more fragile*

In her thorough and lucidly written book, Stephanie
Coontz examines the institution of marriage across the
globe and throughout history. *Marriage, a History* is not only a major piece of scholarship but also a work that provides a crucial understanding of the central institution
in modern culture.

Coontz begins by demonstrating that the idea of marrying for love is a construct
peculiar to the last two centuries. She argues that for most of human history, the idea
that anyone should choose a marital partner based on something as irrational as love
was inconceivable. For example, in ancient China, as elsewhere, strong love between
husband and wife was considered a threat to the established social order. Some Greek
and Roman philosophers believed that a man who loved his wife with excessive ardor
was an adulterer. Even today, in places such as Kenya marriage is considered too important to be entered into because of love.

Moreover, sexual fidelity was not always held in high regard. Coontz cites an an-
thropological study of 109 past societies in which only 48 forbade extramarital sex to
both husbands and wives. Love was a rare element in the history of marriage, and
even today the definition and function of marriage are not entirely fixed. One legally
accepted, though challenged, definition describes marriage as an arrangement in
which a man and a woman live together, engage in sexual activity, and cooperate economically. Coontz lists other arrangements, such as those in Africa and Indonesia
where husbands and wives live in separate houses, and in other societies where married couples do not even eat together.

Some anthropologists have reasoned that marriage has historically involved a set
of legal rules governing goods, social status, and titles, especially the issue of legitimate heirs. There are, however, important exceptions to this concept. The Japanese
language, for example, until 1868 contained no equivalent to the English word
"bastard." Polygamy, considered deviant in the Western world, is not uncommon
worldwide. In some areas of India a woman might be married to several men at once.
In China women are sometimes married to ghosts or dead people.

Stephanie Coontz teaches history
and family studies at Evergreen
State College. The author of four
previous books, she is the
recipient of numerous awards.
She has also appeared on several
national television talk and
interview programs.

For Coontz, apparently the single most important function of marriage throughout history has been the establishment of a tie between families and larger groups, what she calls the necessity of acquiring the right set of in-laws. In other words, marriages were arranged by the parents or guardians of the young couple so that one or more families could gain advantage by uniting their land holdings or wealth: A kingdom might be enlarged, a business funded, or a set of specialized skills acquired.

The author demonstrates this practice by examining stories of such famous relationships as that of Marc Antony and Cleopatra VII, presenting evidence that the marriage of those two rulers had more to do with controlling the Roman Empire than with passion. Even the suicides of this husband and wife came about because Antony had lost Rome to Octavian's army. Like the marriage of Antony and Cleopatra, most unions in the classical world could be made or broken depending on the need to strengthen or loosen ties with in-laws. It was not only the nobility who arranged marriages. All classes of parents tried to find gain for themselves by arranging marriages that consolidated the right set of in-laws.

The emergence of Christianity in Rome had little initial impact on marriage, for early Christians did not hold the marital union in very high esteem compared to the spiritual union in celibacy with Christ. As the Catholic Church became the single most important institution in medieval Europe, it turned its attention to matrimony. In an effort to reduce bloodshed when marriages were broken or misused by various rulers seeking new lands to control, the Church supported monogamy and sharply limited divorce and remarriage. It would be some time, however, before these new restrictions saw widespread adherence.

Among well-known attempts to circumvent Church law were those of King Lothar II of Lorraine. Lothar had a son by his consort Waldreda, but he put her aside to marry Theutberga, whose brother controlled important lands immediately south of Lorraine. When Theutberga had no children and her brother proved less than friendly, Lothar divorced her and married Waldreda, justifying the split by claiming that Theutberga had engaged in incestuous relations with her brother. There was much argument in various Church courts, but ultimately the pope ordered Lothar to return to his first wife, establishing clearly the Church's support of monogamous marriage.

As Coontz stresses, monogamous marriage did not limit the husband's practice of extramarital sex, and illegitimate sons often became a man's chief supporters. Lothar aside, powerful men had found a way to legitimate divorces: incest. If incest could be proven—up to the seventh degree of separation—then the marriage could be annulled. Many bishops were willing to cooperate with such claims, especially for financial gain. A simpler cause for annulment was to argue that the marriage had never been consummated. This was a widespread practice until the Church was reminded in the twelfth century that Mary and Joseph, the biblical parents of Jesus, would not have had a legal marriage under this provision.

The Church also cooperated with parents by frowning on clandestine marriages. Ultimately, however, by the sixteenth century, the Church recognized the importance of young people's consent to marriage, while continuing to maintain that a wife was subordinate to her husband. Even women in loving marriages were expected to address their husbands as "sir." Throughout medieval culture, husbands were expected to discipline their wives, by force if necessary. The Protestant Reformation saw some changes in marriage laws, especially those granting to Protestant priests and ministers the right to marry. King Henry VIII of England broke with the Roman Catholic Church and established the Anglican Church so that he could obtain a divorce in order to marry Ann Boleyn, the mother of Queen Elizabeth I. Coontz records increasingly frequent mention of the words "love" and "marriage" in combination as the seventeenth century draws to a close.

By the eighteenth century, a change in Western marriage ideals from union of the workforce to a union of two souls is clearly visible, according to Coontz. There remained inequalities in early "love marriages," for the husband was still considered the master and economic engine of the household. The wife, however, had now emerged as the spiritual and sentimental core of the home. As the ideal of a love marriage gained strength, so also did the ideal of relative equality between the sexes. The French and American Revolutions favored such a the trend; for example, French divorce laws were greatly altered in favor of women, introducing a woman's right to retain her children after a divorce. Such social phenomena frightened those who feared that the movement toward women's rights would lead to such social disorders as children's rights and even rights of unborn babies. Fortunately for the conservatives, economic opportunities had not evolved along similar lines and thereby favored the male-as-breadwinner marriage. Employment opportunities for women existed only within such low-paying positions that families could save more money by having the woman stay home to care for the children while the husband worked.

Another way to control the implications of the love-match marriage was to repress women by making them into sexless puritans. This spin represents a radical change from that employed several centuries earlier, in which women were said to have uncontrollable sexual urges. The entirely virtuous wife and mother became a cultural invention of the nineteenth century, most widely held up for example in the Victorian period. In the late decades of the nineteenth century, Coontz tells the reader, women sheltered their new purity in the protective barrier of clothing, the average weight of a fashionable outfit totaling thirty-seven pounds. Basing marriage on love and centering it around the image of woman given over to affection more than sex and ready always to do the bidding of her husband was to produce, in Coontz's metaphor, a society of hidden volcanos. Ultimately, women would begin to erupt from the prison of marriage as Nora did in Henrik Ibsen's famous play *Et dukkehjem* (pr., pb. 1879; *A Doll's House*, 1880), a story of a wife who walks away from a marriage in which she was treated by her domineering husband as if she were only a little wiser than a child.

Contrast to the Victorian vision of the pure woman was to be found in the second decade of the twentieth century, called the Roaring Twenties. Young women known as flappers made open statements of their sexuality while dancing the Charleston, and intellectuals across the Western world were discussing the sex theories of Sigmund Freud. Young men and women of every social class began going on dates, and the widespread ownership of automobiles meant that unmarried couples might find convenient places to park and kiss or engage in more daring sexual activity. Marriage for love remained the ideal, however, and with the economic health of the early twentieth century, income in all social classes increased sufficiently so that husbands could be sole breadwinners, while wives remained at home to care for the house and children.

This domestic situation became increasingly prevalent, while women continued to be discriminated against in the workforce so that it still made the best fiscal sense for them to remain at home. The economic depression of the 1930's served to intensify the concept of the superiority of the male as a breadwinner. In the United States males were given job preference in federally funded programs such as the Works Progress Administration. World War II would soon challenge the forces that relegated women to being homemakers.

As men went off to war, women took up their jobs in shipyards and other defense occupations. Men became soldiers; wives became career women, and some even became soldiers. At the end of the war, many women were reluctant to give up their newfound freedom and return to their secondary status as homemaker. Many marriages were threatened, and the divorce rate climbed steeply, with one out of three unions ending in divorce. Just when the very concept of marriage seemed endangered, trends reversed themselves. The prosperous 1950's saw marriage enter what Coontz calls a golden age. Almost all who married wed for love, and growing numbers of younger people were marrying. By the end of the 1950's, almost half of American women married by age nineteen, and men of about the same percentage were married by age twenty-four. The divorce rate was also dropping precipitously. By 1960, 95 percent of all adults in Western Europe and North America were married, and a major baby boom was under way.

The golden age was to end in the second half of the twentieth century. By 1980, the divorce rate climbed to 50 percent, and by the end of the century 43 percent of first marriages ended in divorce within fifteen years. Moreover, one child in three was born to an unwed mother. As women gained new independence and equality, marriage was not always desirable. Many people today live together before marriage, or live together with no intention of marrying. Indeed, cohabitation has in many ways become indistinguishable, legally and socially, from marriage. The issue of same-sex marriages was thrust into headlines in the early years of the twenty-first century, and controversy over it is sure to continue.

Today, as Coontz concludes, society faces a major revolution in the institution of marriage. While love is still clearly at the base of most Western marriages, there are less clear concepts of husbands' and wives' roles within marriage. Indeed, as Coontz observes, there exists a much clearer idea of what those roles should not be.

What the future will hold for this long-lasting and significant human institution is not apparent, but Coontz's history should be required reading for anyone contemplating marriage.

August W. Staub

Review Sources

Booklist 101, no. 16 (April 15, 2005): 1417.
Harper's Magazine 310 (June, 2005): 83-88.
Kirkus Reviews 73, no. 5 (March 1, 2005): 271.
National Review 57, no. 13 (July 18, 2005): 45-47.
The New York Times Book Review 154 (June 12, 2005): 20.
The New Yorker 81, no. 16 (June 6, 2005): 101.
Newsweek 145, no. 23 (June 6, 2005): 51.
Publishers Weekly 252, no. 11 (March 14, 2005): 56.

MATISSE THE MASTER
A Life of Henri Matisse: The Conquest of Colour, 1909-1954

Author: Hilary Spurling (1940-   )
Publisher: Alfred A. Knopf (New York). Illustrated. 544
    pp. $40.00
Type of work: Biography
Time: 1909-1954
Locale: Paris, Nice, Venice, and the United States

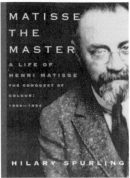

The second volume of this massive biography of Matisse analyzes his artistic contributions and provides fascinating details about his personal relationships and his unique contributions to modern art

Principal personages:
    HENRI MATISSE, an artist
    AMÉLIE MATISSE, his wife
    OLGA MEERSON, one of his favorite models
    LYDIA DELECTORSKAYA, another of his favorite models, his close friend
        and secretary
    PABLO PICASSO, an artist and Henri's close friend
    CLARIBEL and ETTA CONE, sisters and art collectors

Since his death in 1954, Henri Matisse has been largely ignored by potential biographers. Hilary Spurling's is the first major account of the life of this artist. Matisse, often neglected by a public and by other artists who failed to understand his work, was considered by many too dull and his work too shallow to be an appropriate subject for full biographical treatment.

Spurling, whose account of Matisse's life is challenging and fascinating, has shown that those who belittled her subject were quite wrong. Matisse once said that if the true story of his life were ever recorded fully and truthfully, it would amaze everyone. To a considerable extent, readers of this biography will experience some of the amazement of which Matisse spoke.

In *Matisse the Master*, the second and final volume of her biography, Hilary Spurling continues to describe neglect and occasional antagonism shown toward Matisse in Paris's art circles. One early champion of his work was Pablo Picasso, who became Matisse's lifelong friend. Not only was Picasso able to glimpse into the turmoil from which many of Matisse's creations erupted, but he also came to look upon Matisse as one might an elder brother. Theirs was a symbiotic relationship from which Picasso derived significant artistic benefits. Spurling suggests that Picasso veered into cubism largely as a result of his exposure to some of Matisse's early paintings. Ironically, the influential Parisian art world looked upon Picasso as a revolutionary painter but dismissed much of Matisse's work as decorative art, lacking depth and essentially dull.

Spurling's research in the Matisse correspondence, to which his survivors gave her unrestricted access, led her to the conclusion that Matisse was one of the most fluent and effective letter writers of the twentieth century. He wrote to his wife nearly every day whenever the two were apart, and he also carried on a colossal correspondence with other family members and friends. He reserved at least an hour each day for his correspondence, resulting in a vast archive of letters that, according to Spurling, could fill ten volumes.

The Matisse that Spurling depicts was at times a seething volcano within. He sometimes dressed badly, in a worn black sheepskin coat. However, Spurling observes, "As his paintings grew bolder and more disturbing, his dress and manner became quieter and more restrained." If a Jekyll-and-Hyde personality lurked within him, art became his means of releasing his more destructive forces. Spurling also notes, "The figures on his canvas grew beneath his brush into a great elemental surge of release and liberation. At times he seemed to be unleashing forces" that "frightened even him."

Hilary Spurling's first volume of her two-part biography of Henri Matisse, titled The Unknown Matisse *(1998), covers the years from 1869 to 1908. It was named an Editors' Choice book of* The New York Times. *Educated at Oxford, Spurling has published biographies of writers Ivy Compton-Burnett and Paul Scott. In 2005, she organized an exhibition on the importance of textiles to Matisse at London's Royal Academy that later moved to New York's Metropolitan Museum of Art.*

Clearly, painting was Matisse's means of controlling something within him that was at heart explosive and even terrifying. His surface demeanor changed as he found artistic relief and, in a very real way, transferred his inner strife to paintings that many viewers found profoundly disturbing. When Spurling chose to use the term "the conquest of colour" as a part of her subtitle, she might with equal validity have chosen, "the conquest of demons," because through his art and particularly through the intensity of his colors, Matisse was controlling, even killing, his inner, personal demons.

As he aged, Matisse dealt with these demons much better than he had in his earlier life; they seemed to trouble him less as he became increasingly obsessed with color, enthralled with the power inherent in it. Through his experiments with color, he was able to think more clearly. He learned a valuable and necessary lesson: "to manipulate without danger the *explosives* that are colours" (Matisse's italics).

The young Matisse was torn between music and art. He played the violin and loved music. When he was twenty, however, his mother gave him his first box of paints. Spurling describes this as the turning point in Matisse's life. She refers to this moment as "the great animal uprush of feeling" that this first introduction to color evoked.

Among the many intriguing details of Spurling's biography is her account of Matisse's relationship with the Cone sisters, Claribel and Etta. The heiresses to a textile fortune, they lived together in Baltimore but visited Paris most summers. They were friends of Gertrude Stein and Alice B. Toklas and, through them, acquaintances of Picasso, who looked upon them as silly old hens. Picasso regaled people with stories of how he sold his pencil sketches and other disposables to the Cone sisters when he would otherwise have thrown them away.

Picasso had a chauvinist attitude toward women, convinced that they were inferior beings. He dominated the women in his life, of whom he created either glorified goddesses or hapless doormats. Matisse, on the other hand, admired spunky women and valued his give-and-take relationship with Etta Cone. Spurling says that when Etta told Matisse that she had made him what he was, he replied that she was wrong: He had made her what she was. There was a modicum of truth in both statements. At a time when few people were interested in buying Matisse's art, Etta became a regular customer and avid collector. Matisse saved his best canvases for her inspection on her annual trips to Paris, and she usually bought two or three of them.

Matisse not only depended upon her for the income these sales produced but also for a more important reason: Etta intended to bequeath her collection to the Baltimore Museum of Art, and at the rate she was buying, she would likely have the largest and most significant Matisse collection in the world upon her death. The display of this collection in a major museum would assure Matisse of the kind of immortality of which most artists only fantasize.

In this volume, Spurling dispels two common misconceptions about the artist, both of which have affected the appreciation of his work through the years. One is that Matisse collaborated with the Axis invaders of France during World War II. It is true that he remained in Nice after most of the French residents and tourists had departed for fear of an onslaught from Italian forces. With property values in Nice dropping precipitously, at a time when everyone else was fleeing, Matisse went so far as to buy two adjacent apartments in the about-to-be renovated Excelsior-Regina Palace, a hostelry in which England's Queen Victoria had sometimes stayed. There exists no evidence, however, that, as the war continued and as the Axis powers moved in to occupy France, Matisse consorted with the enemy. Rather, he kept a low profile and continued his artwork.

A second misconception Spurling dispels is the assumption that an oversexed Matisse exploited his two most frequent models, Olga Meerson and Lydia Delectorskaya, sexually. Although a closeness existed between the artist and these two Russian models, Spurling's exhaustive detective work in the various Matisse archives, which she was given almost total freedom to explore, produced no evidence of a sexual relationship between Matisse and his models. Although Henri and Amélie's married life was far from serene, Spurling denies that Matisse was sexually involved with his models.

His wife, however, did issue an ultimatum to which her husband paid scant attention: Choose between Lydia and me. As a result, Lydia moved out of the Matisses' apartment but not out of Henri's life. She continued to serve as his secretary and lived in lodgings close to the Matisse residence.

As the clouds of war gathered over Europe, Matisse was approaching his seventieth birthday. He suffered from ill health and had barely survived a severe case of bronchial pneumonia in the winter of 1938. By this time, his wife, Amélie, had been something of an invalid for nearly two decades, more psychosomatically ill than actually infirm.

In February, 1939, Amélie's lawyer drew up a bill of separation. It provided for the equal distribution between husband and wife of all Matisse's artwork. In May, 1939, eight lawyers and their agents arrived in Matisse's Paris studio, where they conducted a thorough search and made an inventory of everything there. Eventually Matisse was persuaded to meet with Amélie, and in July they met in a Paris café. Matisse sat in silence, staring at his wife for half an hour, while she refused to meet his eye. No words were exchanged, but this meeting marked the final dissolution of a marriage that had once been close and cohesive. Immediately after the artist's death, Amélie appeared in Nice as his widow to oversee the distribution of his property.

Some critics contend that Spurling's book provides too much detail about Matisse's domestic life and its complications. The detail she presents, however, helps to create in her Matisse a round character, a flesh-and-blood Matisse with whom readers can readily identify.

Matisse spent his final years in Nice at Cimiez. He worked regularly at his various art projects, completing a stained glass window for Nelson Rockefeller in memory of his mother, Abby Aldrich Rockefeller, one of the founders of the Museum of Modern Art. The Rockefellers had been among Matisse's greatest admirers and supporters.

Matisse continued to work on the color cut-outs with which his later art is often associated, and that evoked from some art critics the accusation that Matisse was doing decorative art rather than serious art. Delectorskaya remained with Matisse throughout his illness and seldom left his bedside after he suffered a small stroke.

On November 2, 1954, Matisse asked Delectorskaya for something on which to draw. She gave him a ballpoint pen and some writing paper, on which he drew his final sketch of her. He died the following afternoon. Lydia and his daughter, Marguerite Matisse Duthuit, were at his side.

This book is enhanced by twenty-two pages of exquisite color reproductions of Matisse's work gathered in two sections. Throughout the text, there are 159 additional black and white illustrations, many of them depicting Matisse, his family, and his friends. Many more illustrate what the text on a particular page is discussing.

R. Baird Shuman

Review Sources

The Christian Science Monitor 97 (September 13, 2005): 14, 16.
The Economist 374 (March 12, 2005): 79.
Kirkus Reviews 73, no. 11 (June 1, 2005): 628.
Library Journal 130, no. 13 (August 1, 2005): 82-83.
New Statesman 134 (March 28, 2005): 50-51.
The New York Times Book Review 154 (September 4, 2005): 7.
The New Yorker 81, no. 25 (August 29, 2005): 78-83.
Smithsonian 36 (October, 2005): 72-80.
The Times Literary Supplement, April 1, 2005, pp. 3-4.
Vogue 194, no. 9 (September, 2005): 579-580.

A MATTER OF OPINION

Author: Victor S. Navasky (1932-   )
Publisher: Crown Pantheon Books (New York). 397 pp.
   $27.00
Type of work: Memoir
Time: 1932-2005
Locale: The United States

This account of the author's educational background and professional life as an editor and publisher of The Nation *is accompanied by his thoughts on the importance to a functioning democracy of journals of opinion*

Principal personages:
   VICTOR S. NAVASKY, the editor (1978-
      1995), editorial director (1995-2005),
      and current publisher emeritus of *The Nation*
   FREDA KIRCHWAY, the editor of *The Nation*, 1937-1955
   CAREY MCWILLIAMS, the editor of *The Nation*, 1955-1975
   HAMILTON FISH, the current publisher of *The Nation*

"Art always was, and is, a force of protest of the humane against the pressure of domineering institutions." —Theodor Adorno

Substitute "journal of opinion" for the word "art" in Adorno's quote (selected by the author to conclude his manuscript) and one has, in a nutshell, the rationale for Victor Navasky's life's work. Part autobiography, part business history, with plentiful doses of politics, philosophy, humor, and practical advice thrown into the mix, he jokingly calls the memoir a "How-Not-To" book. Nevertheless, Navasky takes pride in *The Nation*'s relative health under his stewardship. While the book contains no subtitle, the original working title was "Reflections on the Role of the Journal of Opinion in the Age of Electronic, Conglomerated, Transnational Communications." It could have been subtitled "The Making of a Successful Liberal Entrepreneur."

Surprisingly, *A Matter of Opinion* contains little mention of modern politics, but one can always find that in *The Nation* itself. While liberalism has supposedly lost its luster, Navasky makes no apologies for his viewpoints. The grandson of Russian Jews, he attended progressive schools that put on assemblies featuring folksingers of the caliber of Pete Seeger and Woody Guthrie. The antifascist, Spanish Civil War songs he listened to stirred his soul. At Swarthmore, Navasky wrote an article ridiculing his college's Victorian dormitory visitation policy. Satire became an outlet for channeling his anger or disgust at the inequalities and absurdities of modern life.

Drafted in 1954, Navasky moonlighted for the *53rd Infantry News* in Alaska. The Anchorage *Daily News* editor got him credentials for the 1956 Democratic convention, and there he witnessed corporations co-opting the press corps with free food, drinks, and other sundries. Navasky was attending Yale Law School when liberal anticommunist Joseph L. Rauh spoke at Yale about ten things wrong with the House Committee on Un-American Activities (HUAC). Rauh was upset to learn that the sponsoring group, the Emergency Civil Liberties Committee (ECLC) allowed so-called Reds on its board and disparaged the organization from the podium. Navasky's favorite law school professor, Thomas Emerson, rose to defend the ECLC.

∾

A professor of journalism at Columbia University, Victor S. Navasky is publisher and editorial director for The Nation, *as well as the author of* Kennedy Justice *(1971) and* Naming Names *(1980), winner of the National Book Award.*

∾

Not counting law review articles, Navasky's first publication (in *Frontier* magazine, which *The Nation* later absorbed) took a California court to task for ruling against comedian Jack Benny's spoof of the film *Gaslight* (1944), titled *Autolight*. Navasky's point was that parody should not be confused with plagiarism. He then helped launch *Monocle*, whose motto was: "In the land of the blind, the one-eyed man is king." One of its parodies took the form of the board game Monopoly, the object being to advance from a log cabin to the White House. Navasky opted to channel his creative energies into keeping the satirical "rag" afloat rather than practice law, putting out occasional "Emergency Bulletins" on issues of the day. "Ink for Jack" chided President John F. Kennedy for reneging on promises to end public housing segregation "with the stroke of a pen."

During a New York newspaper strike, *Monocle* produced parodies of the *Post*, called the *Pest*, and the *Daily News*, called the *Dally Noose*. The staff turned down as too trenchant a Ralph Nader piece in which a fictitious automaker rationalized the policy of planned obsolescence to stockholders. Although Kennedy's assassination set back political humor, *Monocle* supported a mock-1964 Republican candidacy against Arizona senator Barry Goldwater, who had opposed the Civil Rights Bill banning segregation in public places, based on the Republican Party's platform of a hundred years before. While researching *Kennedy Justice* (about Attorney General Robert F. Kennedy), published in 1971, Navasky free-lanced on related subjects for *The New York Times Magazine* and in 1970 became an in-house editor.

Clearly uncomfortable maintaining a pretense of neutrality, the self-described "left-liberal" chafed when editors forbade the characterization of Judge Julius Hoffman ordering Black Panther leader Bobby Seale manacled during the Chicago Eight conspiracy trial as "brutal," even though they had approved the word when applied to an Afghanistan warlord. He quipped: "One's ability to tell the truth was inversely proportional to one's distance from West Forty-third Street [*Times* headquarters]." After managing to shepherd into print Merle Miller's "On Being Different: What It Means To Be a Homosexual," he left to research *Naming Names* (1980), a book about informers. Even though it dealt with the post-World War II "Red Scare," the idea stemmed from his outrage at Attorney General Kennedy releasing a nefarious thug for the express purpose of gathering evidence against Teamster boss Jimmy Hoffa. For him, the end did not justify the means.

Hamilton Fish, liberal grandson and namesake of the anti-New Deal congressman from Franklin Delano Roosevelt's New York home district, lured Navasky into becoming *The Nation*'s editor. At the time, Navasky's mentors were modern-day muck-raker I. F. Stone (whom he talked into becoming a contributor) and predecessor Carey McWilliams, who bequeathed bound volumes dating back to 1965.

Perusing the premier issue, Navasky discovered a startling statement by founding editor E. L. Godkin: "The week has been singularly barren of exciting events." The nerve of the man, he thought. A chapter titled "Looking Backward" traces the maga-zine's proud history under four prolific and ruthlessly honest editors. Godkin's suc-cessor, Oswald Garrison Villard, grandson of abolitionist William Lloyd Garrison and son of railroad magnate Henry Villard, made it a New York *Post* Sunday insert. The government seized the September 14, 1918, issue on grounds of sedition on ac-count of its criticism of President Woodrow Wilson, an action that boosted subse-quent circulation.

The magazine changed hands during the mid-1930's. Villard remained a contribu-tor until the publication abandoned isolationism under Freda Kirchway. An antifas-cist and advocate for a Mideast Jewish state, the editor took issue with President Harry S. Truman's Cold War policies, believing that the threats of communist expan-sion and internal subversion were greatly exaggerated. McWilliams, who began a twenty-year tenure in 1955, seamlessly continued the gadfly tradition. What had first attracted Navasky to *The Nation*, incidentally, was a Dalton Trumbo piece about the Hollywood blacklist (being on it, screenwriter Trumbo worked under assumed names). As editor, he struggled to implement policies consistent with the journal's heritage yet relevant to changing business conditions.

Contributor Calvin Trillin quipped that *The Nation* was a "pinko" publication "printed on very cheap paper." (Photocopies often looked better than the butcher block original.) The overriding priority, Navasky believed, was to interpret the mean-ing of news events in a coherent, engaging manner. Mainstream detractors labeled the publication ideological, but he believed the charge baseless unless narrowly defined as a shared body of beliefs, which could equally apply to his detractors. Indeed, the stable of *Nation* regulars was rarely of one mind.

In a chapter titled "The Legal Landscape," Navasky recalled that the magazine ob-tained an advance copy of former president Gerald R. Ford's memoirs. He approved an article that summarized the newsworthy parts and used a few quotes. Harper & Row successfully sued for $12,500, the amount lost when *Time* backed out of printing excerpts. Another controversy involved Allen Weinstein's *Perjury* (1978), which purportedly proved that former State Department official Alger Hiss had been a Soviet agent. *The Nation* writers (with one exception) had previously defended Hiss, despite his having been convicted of lying under oath about his past. Navasky claimed to have had open mind on the subject but was shocked at the sloppy logic and documentation, not to mention Weinstein's questionable claim that he originally be-lieved Hiss. His negative review resulted in anticommunist conservatives accusing him of being in denial, but he believed they were too hasty to proclaim *Perjury* as de-finitive.

Starting in 1985, self-made maverick multimillionaire Arthur Carter helped keep *The Nation* solvent during a ten-year period of ominous corporate mergers. Ironically, subscriptions increased with Republicans in the White House. The one time Carter raised a ruckus was over a "penis poster" ad. Women staffers protested a David Levine cartoon of former National Security Council adviser Henry Kissinger atop a naked women (representing the Caribbean basin), believing it to be sexist and demeaning in that it stereotyped women as passive. It ran anyway, but Navasky arranged a productive meeting between the cartoonist and the feminists.

After a *Nation* article linked Kissinger to Argentina's oppressive right-wing regime, Navasky ran into the former secretary of state at a party hosted by Arthur Carter. "How is it," Kissinger asked, "that a short article in an obscure journal such as yours . . . resulted in sixty people holding placards denouncing me . . . when I got off a plane in Copenhagen?" Navasky, straight-faced, replied, "I guess we have readers in Denmark."

When the magazine endorsed "territorial compromise" between Israelis and Palestinians and opening negotiations with Yasser Arafat, Kenneth Bialken of the Anti-Defamation League complained to Carter, who replied: "What do you think we are? It's *The Nation*, not the Jewish Federation newsletter." In the 120th anniversary issue, writer Gore Vidal criticized editor Norman Podhoretz of *Commentary*, an organ of the American Jewish Committee. Podhoretz responded by labeling Navasky "a self-hating Jew who edited an anti-Semitic magazine."

The Nation declined to break an exclusive story of Congressman Henry Hyde's past adulterous affair at the time when the accused chairman of the House Judiciary Committee was drawing up articles of impeachment against Bill Clinton stemming from the president's dalliances with Monica Lewinsky. Too sensationalistic was the editorial verdict, even though some staffers believed the Republican deserved to be outed as a hypocrite. Instead, an on-line magazine broke it.

The final chapters document multitudinous fund-raising efforts to keep Navasky's "baby" afloat, including a fruitful lunch with actor Paul Newman and his wife, Joanne Woodward. While on sabbatical Navasky took a Harvard Business School course in which *The Nation* was one of the case studies. He wrote: "I got a big laugh and a lot of little snickers when I mentioned that unions can increase productivity." Matthew Rothschild, editor of *The Progressive*, marveled that Navasky had increased subscriptions sixfold (to about 184,000) and, after many years in the red, in 2002 finally made a quarter-million-dollar profit.

Predictably, liberals praised *A Matter of Opinion*, while conservatives panned it. Labeling him "a happy ringmaster for revolutionists, apologists for terrorism and/or left-wing dictatorships, professionally angry blacks, women, homosexuals, environmentalists, [and] pacifists," *Commentary* reviewer Nell Rosenthal concluded his review with this: "Nothing in Navasky's universe, it seems, has ever been sufficiently cataclysmic to shake his steady faith in the goodness of socialism and the evil of American capitalism." *National Review*'s Neal B. Freeman, after proclaiming the author wrong on most issues save the decriminalization of marijuana (which both supported), was more charitable, terming the memoir an "absorbing account of his long stewardship" that "kept the democratic conversation going." Indeed, articulate Americans owe Navasky a debt of gratitude. He did not just preach to the converted, as some critics asserted, but won untold numbers of modern-day idealists to progressive causes ranging from ecology to respect for First Amendment guarantees.

> I need to ask you a favor. I'm stuck in Abbeville, Louisiana, and I want to move, but I want to move somewhere where I can see a Democrat before I die. It occurs to me that you might be able to rummage up a place where people are actually subscribers to *The Nation*, where I would have somebody to talk to. I don't want their names or anything. I just want a town where there are a few kindred souls. —A letter to Navasky from a sixty-eight-year-old widow

Among the many charms of *A Matter of Opinion* are its telling anecdotes. Navasky proudly mentions a couple about to be married who met on an Internet dating service. What attracted the woman to her future husband was his handle "nationreader."

James B. Lane

Review Sources

Booklist 101, no. 17 (May 1, 2005): 1550.
Commentary 120, no. 2 (September, 2005): 81-84.
Kirkus Reviews 73, no. 4 (February 15, 2005): 217.
The Nation 280, no. 20 (May 23, 2005): 48.
National Review 57, no. 10 (June 6, 2005): 51-52.
The New Leader 88, no. 3 (May/June, 2005): 19-21.
The New Yorker 81, no. 15 (May 30, 2005): 91.
Progressive 69, no. 8 (August, 2005): 46-52.
Time 165, no. 20 (May 16, 2005): 77.

MELVILLE
His World and Work

Author: Andrew Delbanco (1952-   )
Publisher: Alfred A. Knopf (New York). 415 pp. $30.00
Type of work: Literary biography
Time: 1819-1891
Locale: New York City, Massachusetts, and Pacific
Ocean islands

This modestly proportioned but authoritative biography of one of the greatest American writers interprets his life and work in the context of the significant events of his time

Principal personages:
HERMAN MELVILLE, a nineteenth century
novelist, story writer, and poet
ELIZABETH SHAW MELVILLE, his wife
EVERT DUYCKINCK, a magazine editor and promoter of Melville's work
NATHANIEL HAWTHORNE, a novelist, Melville's most distinguished literary friend
LEMUEL SHAW, a Boston judge who became Melville's father-in-law

Briefly lionized as a young writer of South Sea romances, neglected by critics throughout most of his writing career, and unacknowledged as a literary genius until thirty years after his death, Herman Melville has since become the subject of an enormous amount of critical attention and several substantial biographies, including Hershel Parker's comprehensive two-volume life, published in 1996 and 2002. Andrew Delbanco has wisely chosen not to compete with Parker, whose life of Melville approaches two thousand pages. Rather, Delbanco has concentrated the results of what has clearly been a long and thorough study of his subject into 322 pages of text. The relative brevity of Delbanco's book is one of its virtues, though not the most important one. How much, not just of Melville's "work," but of his "world," as the subtitle promises, can be told in such a compass? The answer is: a great deal.

Delbanco immediately reveals himself as a connoisseur of Melville appreciators (and depreciators) in a preliminary seven-page selection of "Extracts, supplied by a Sub-Sub-Sub-Librarian"—a witty parody of Melville's send-off of *Moby Dick* (1851), of course. They range from Allan Melville's observation that his seven-year-old son Herman seemed "backward in speech" and "somewhat slow in comprehension" to a *New York Times* editorial from May, 2005, comparing New York mayor Michael Bloomberg to Captain Ahab. Some of these Melvillian allusions come from sources seemingly far afield, for instance the television series *The Sopranos*, where Billy Budd becomes the subject of dialogue, or Richard Clarke's confession to Condoleezza Rice that he was becoming Ahab-like in his obsession with Osama bin Laden. Collectively, these allusions seem to indicate that despite the modern paucity

~

*Andrew Delbanco is Julian Clarence
Levi Professor in the Humanities
and the director of American studies
at Columbia University. The author
of many books and essays, he was
named a Fellow of the American
Academy of Arts and Sciences in
2001.*

~

of common literary points of reference, allusions to Ahab and Bartleby and Billy Budd still give readers welcome shocks of recognition.

Delbanco focuses his twelve chapters on the way his subject confronts the personal challenges and cultural currents of each stage of his life and—in those chapters dealing with his literary career—the way those challenges and currents pervaded or modified his writing at the time. More often than not, each chapter has a major theme that governs and limits the details therein.

In his second chapter, for instance, dealing with the period of Melville's Pacific adventures, Delbanco concentrates on Melville's and his contemporaries' notions of civilization in the 1840's. For most Americans, and for Melville before his seafaring, the Indians that the federal government was then busy relocating epitomized primitive or uncivilized humankind. A scattering of Romantics theorized that noble savages might perhaps not be so savage after all, and a few ethnologists (to use a term just coming into use) were commencing investigations that challenged Western Europeans' and Americans' supposed monopoly of civilization. Delbanco quotes an 1838 writer, Abner Kneeland, who reported that Hottentots excise one of the testicles of every male child, while Parisians (for instance) do not. Each, Kneeland pointed out, is appalled at the other, not because their practice is unreasonable but simply because it is different. Kneeland, Delbanco notes in one of the captivating asides sprinkled through his book, was the last man to be prosecuted for blasphemy in New England, and Melville's future father-in-law, Lemuel Shaw, presided at the trial. Delbanco's point is not that the young Melville's weeks among the Polynesians turned him into a full-fledged cultural relativist but that what he experienced there began the process of rousing him from mental lethargy.

The next chapter, "Becoming a Writer," traces Melville's progress from casual teller of anecdotes of Tahitian and Hawaiian life to author of enormously popular early novels, *Typee: A Peep at Polynesian Life* (1846) and *Omoo: A Narrative of Adventure in the South Seas* (1847). N. P. Willis, in his 1849 review of Melville's novel *Redburn: His First Voyage* (1849), reported that Melville's initial audience, once he returned from his years at sea, was his family. Applying more specifically an idea broached by Elizabeth Hardwick in her modern biography of Melville, Delbanco calls this storytelling Melville's "rehearsal" for the writing career on which he was shortly to embark. Delbanco then recapitulates *Typee*, still a siren song, even for readers who have learned to recognize the tale as inferior Melville, but notes that the book is important as a manifestation of an author learning his trade.

Chapter 4, "Escape to New York," offers considerable detail about the city to which Melville and his new bride, Elizabeth Shaw, the daughter of a prominent Boston judge, repaired in 1847. Conceding that Melville is not often regarded as a New York or urban writer, Delbanco argues that he was "deeply affected, indeed *in*fected, by the tone and rhythm of the city," although the fiction that he was writing at the time continued to be primarily nautical in nature. Delbanco believes that Melville also began *Moby Dick* in New York; most of it, however, was composed in the Berkshires, to which he moved his family in the summer of 1850. Delbanco even sees a New York influence on his new novel in the person of a minor Knickerbocker writer named William Cox, who, in writing on the value of getting away from home, forming "odd acquaintances," and developing "universal toleration," may have contributed something to the chapter in which Ishmael learns to share a bed with the outlandish Queequeg in the New Bedford inn.

Delbanco has many shrewd observations about *Moby Dick* in the following two chapters, but one of his themes is an unusual one. In chapter 5 he follows those critics who have stressed the importance of Melville's reading in mid-century while *Moby Dick* was in progress. More surprisingly, in the following chapter, he emphasizes the part Melville's political awareness played in his thinking. The towering political event, of course, was the Compromise of 1850, with its forceful reaffirmation of the Fugitive Slave Law, which Melville's father-in-law, Judge Shaw, was obliged to enforce. Delbanco goes as far as calling South Carolina's John C. Calhoun, the foremost spokesman for slavery in the United States Senate, one of the models for Captain Ahab and *Moby Dick* "a book about politics."

After a chapter titled "Herman Melville Crazy"—a way of explaining *Pierre, or the Ambiguities* (1852) in the minds of some contemporaries, and also a way of classifying the protagonist of his brilliant "Bartleby the Scrivener," Melville's most thoroughgoing New York story, which appeared the following year in *Putnam's Monthly Magazine*—Delbanco discusses the remarkable *Benito Cereno* in a chapter called "The Magazinist." *Putnam's*, where it also first saw print in 1855, had developed a reputation as a strong antislavery publication given to editorializing fiercely against the recent Kansas-Nebraska Act, which, by annulling the Missouri Compromise of 1820, permitted slavery to flow into Kansas Territory.

Melville based *Benito Cereno* on Amasa Delano's published recollection of his encounter with a Spanish slave ship in 1805. Delano, the captain of an American merchant vessel, boarded the Spanish ship to find its crew and captives perishing of thirst and hunger. The Spanish captain's unwillingness to part with his slave attendant, even when he asked for a private interview, puzzled Delano. After he left the ship, the Spanish captain, Don Benito, jumped from his ship and, after being rescued, told Delano that the slaves had taken over his vessel. The slave "attendant" had actually become his master. In 1839, in an incident that many of Melville's readers could have been expected to remember, another Spanish ship, the *Amistad,* was also seized by its human cargo. Later an American naval ship captured the *Amistad*, but John Quincy Adams subsequently defended the slaves successfully in the United States Supreme Court.

Melville's Delano is even denser and less comprehending than his historical counterpart. He suspects nothing, even when the leader of the insurrection holds a razor to Don Benito's throat in the guise of shaving his "master," a chilling scene brought to the stage in Robert Lowell's 1964 dramatization of the story. (Delbanco includes a photograph of this stage version as one of dozens of incidental but telling supplements to his text.) Delbanco characterizes Delano's failing as "the kind of moral opacity that seems still to afflict America as it lumbers through the world creating enemies whose enmity it does not begin to understand" and judges Melville the first "classic" American writer to plumb the depths of slavery in America and delineate what it did to both oppressed and oppressors.

Benito Cereno also exemplifies Melville's ability to summon and put to telling use the more or less chance observations he had made over time. On a European trip in 1849, Melville had visited the Hôtel de Cluny, a Paris museum, where he saw—and recorded in his diary—medieval ivory carvings that included one of Judas whispering in Jesus' ear and several Resurrection scenes. Six years later, Melville drew upon these ivories (one of which Delbanco pictures) to create an image of Delano as a "savior" who ironically cannot, in his ignorance, save. Instead of taking Melville into that museum at its chronologically correct time in his narrative and merely providing a pedestrian account of what he saw there, the biographer saves the Hôtel de Cluny carvings for the time when they matter. Delbanco, it might be added, exhibits the same skill.

Melville's novel *The Confidence Man* (1857) was the last published in his lifetime. At thirty-seven years of age, this is a very early swan song for a novelist; his friend Nathaniel Hawthorne published his first novel at forty-six. The world of this 1857 book—Delbanco calls it Melville's "most time-bound"—is the world of P. T. Barnum, of swindlers and confidence men, and of a public willing and even eager to be conned. The work baffled readers and critics, not least because it was so difficult to distinguish the swindlers from the swindled. It is a duplicitous book about duplicity. At this point there remained for Melville a trip abroad, a return to residency in New York City, a decision to concentrate his literary efforts on poetry, and, in 1866, a job as inspector at the New York Custom House, which he would hold for nearly twenty years. Finally, near the end of his life, he plunged one last time into fiction.

Billy Budd, the young man whose stammer keeps him from defending himself verbally against an unjust accusation and thus impels a subsequent, and unfortunately fatal, physical assault on his accuser, was destined, years after Melville's death, to become, along with Ahab and Bartleby, one of the author's, and literature's, most intriguing characters. For Delbanco the contemporary ingredients of *Billy Budd, Foretopman* (1924) include a background of industrial violence, of strikes that turned violent and savage retaliations. The New York of Melville's old age was a city of millionaire capitalists and oppressed immigrant laborers. The theme of Melville's final story, Delbanco alleges, is "the loss of the democratic ideal." On a more personal level for the aging Melville, the city, constantly rebuilding itself, was thereby effacing many of the old, familiar features. Dedicated to Jack Chase, Melville's friend of the 1840's, *Billy Budd, Foretopman* is for the biographer "a work of remembrance." If these factors seem less relevant to the work at hand than some of those Delbanco proposed as background for Melville's earlier works, he is probably on safe ground in relating the death of a beautiful young man of twenty-one years to Melville's loss of his own two sons, Stanwyx, who had died recently at thirty-six, and Malcolm, who, years earlier, had shot himself at age eighteen.

Even where Delbanco seems to be reaching a bit far in linking Melville's world to his work, one cannot help admiring his resourcefulness. Both text and documentation reveal knowledge both wide and deep. He has fashioned a most valuable book for serious students of Melville and one that can be read with pleasure and profit by those barely acquainted with this great writer.

Robert P. Ellis

Review Sources

Booklist 102, no. 1 (September 1, 2005): 41.
The Boston Globe, September 18, 2005, p. E6.
Kirkus Reviews 73, no. 13 (July 1, 2005): 716-717.
Library Journal 130, no. 13 (August 15, 2005): 84.
The Nation 281, no. 19 (December 5, 2005): 43-46.
The New Republic 233, nos. 26-28 (December 26, 2005): 25-29.
The New York Review of Books 52, no. 19 (December 1, 2005): 6-12.
The New York Times Book Review 155 (September 25, 2005): 24.

MEMORIES OF MY MELANCHOLY WHORES

Author: Gabriel García Márquez (1927-   )
First published: Memoria de mis putas tristes, 2004, in
   Spain and Mexico
Translated from the Spanish by Edith Grossman
Publisher: Alfred A. Knopf (New York). 115 pp. $20.00
Type of work: Novel
Time: 1960
Locale: Unnamed town in Colombia, South America

   On his ninetieth birthday, a Colombian newspaper col-
umnist arranges to go to bed with a young virgin; for a
year he visits her chastely and falls in love with her

> *Principal characters:*
> THE NARRATOR, an unnamed ninety-year-
>   old journalist
> AN UNNAMED FOURTEEN-YEAR-OLD GIRL, whom the protagonist calls
>   Delgadina (little slender one)
> ROSA CARBACAS, the madam of the local house of prostitution
> DAMIANA, the protagonist's longtime servant

   When Gabriel García Márquez contracted lymphatic cancer in 1999 and published
the first volume of his projected three-part autobiography, *Living to Tell the Tale*
(2002), many of his admirers thought this was his swan song, that he would never
write fiction again. Now, in *Memories of My Melancholy Whores*, his first book of fiction in ten years, a novella of a little over one hundred pages, he returns to a fairy-tale
form that he has used in short fictions in the past. Some may see this novel as a sort of
new breath of life for García Márquez, who seems to have successfully triumphed
over his cancer. Others may see it as the perverse dream of an old man who has nothing to look forward to other than death; at the time of the book's publication, García
Márquez was seventy-eight years old. Even before the official publication of *Memoria
de mis putas tristes* in Spain and Latin America, the little book was eagerly anticipated, with street vendors hawking pirated copies. To protect their investment of a
million-copy release, the Spanish-language publishers were quick to report that
García Márquez had made significant changes at the last minute to the final chapter.
   The plot of *Memories of My Melancholy Whores* is quite simple, summed up in the
initial sentence, in which the unnamed, first-person narrator says simply that on his
ninetieth birthday he wants to give himself the gift of a riotous night of lovemaking
with an adolescent virgin. The remainder of the book recounts the results of this decision by the narrator, a journalist in a Colombian town. The most important result is
that the elderly hero does not engage in a night of sexuality with a young girl, but instead sits by her bed, watching her as she sleeps. For the remainder of his ninetieth
year he returns to the brothel night after night, continuing to watch the girl sleep,

hardly ever touching her and hearing her voice only once. However, he falls helplessly in love with her and, as improbable as it may seem, she ultimately falls in love with him. They finally come together as a most unlikely couple on the last page.

Some critics have chastised the author and the novel's hero as dirty old men who have no social conscience about the exploitation of young women in developing nations, but it is a misunderstanding of the tradition of *Memories of My Melancholy Whores*, as well as García Márquez's obvious intention, to label this a perverted book about an old man's wicked lust for a teenage girl. As García Márquez has suggested in previous works, visiting a brothel does not have the same unsavory aspect in Colombia as it does in the United States. Indeed, the author of the classic *Cien años de soledad* (1967; *One Hundred Years of Solitude*, 1970) has praised the brothels of Bogota, where he studied law, even

Gabriel García Márquez, the master of the Latin American movement called Magical Realism, was born in Colombia. He won the Nobel Prize in Literature in 1982, largely for his celebrated novel One Hundred Years of Solitude *(1967).*

though he was once beaten up there for failing to pay a prostitute. There is no sordid reality of young women made chattel to men with money in the book. Rather, the story is about enrapt attention, fantasy, the romantic dream of pure ideal love.

Although the protagonist realizes that sex is merely a consolation for not having love, he has never been able to experience love; indeed has never had sex with a woman unless he paid for it. That the final object of his desire is a fourteen-year-old girl has nothing to do with the social issue of preying on the helpless and innocent. Neither love nor sex in this novel has anything to do with social reality; the story is rather a complete romantic idealization of the art-like object of desire. The romantic nature of the old man's silent observation of the girl as he watches her each night can be compared to the famous metaphor that opens the quintessential Romantic adoration of an untouched object—John Keats's "Ode on a Grecian Urn." For the young girl in García Márquez's novel is a frozen work of art, not to be approached if the true nature of ideal romantic love is to be sustained. She is indeed Keats's "still unravished bride of quietness," a "foster-child of silence and slow time." The protagonist knows that he does not want her to awaken, does not want to hear her voice, does not want to see her in daylight but rather wishes only to watch her in silence.

Memories of My Melancholy Whores inevitably will be compared to Vladimir Nabokov's paean to passion for a child, *Lolita* (1955), but it is Dante's celebration of a similar love for his Beatrice that invented this kind of romantic love story. Gabriel Aschenbach's tragic love for the young Tadzio in Thomas Mann's *Death in Venice* (1912) is perhaps the most famous twentieth century model. The most immediate comparison is suggested by García Márquez's opening epigraph from Yasunari

Kawabata's "The House of the Sleeping Beauties" (1926), another classic story of idealistic love of an older man for a young girl. "The House of the Sleeping Beauties" centers on a brothel visited by old men who can no longer perform sexually. Forbidden to have sex with the young women, and thus free of sexual expectations, they lie down with beautiful young virgins who, under the influence of a sleeping potion, are unaware of their visits. The central character is a man who does not tell the madam that he is still able to function as a man, and his visits are tormented by the fact that he desires more than the girls are allowed to give. As he lies by different girls each night, he remembers his youthful adventures and contemplates his own future impotence as he grows older.

The difference between Kawabata's story and García Márquez's new novel is that, whereas Kawabata is concerned with the inevitability of growing old and the longing for death, García Márquez holds out for the romantic ideal of never being too old to fall in love. *Memories of My Melancholy Whores* is not a fairy tale for the aged but rather a fable for the romantic.

The unlikely hero of the novel says he is ugly and shy and seems proud to admit that he has never gone to bed with a woman he did not pay. He was even voted client of the year two different times in the red-light district he frequents. He says by the time he was fifty, he had slept with 514 women. Then he simply stopped counting. He lives in an old ancestral mansion, has no wife, no children, no kin, no pets. He is cultured, surrounding himself with great literature, listening to classical music. Each week he writes in longhand a weekly column for the local Sunday newspaper, and he is fairly well known in the town. At one time in his youth he was engaged to be married, but at the last minute he hid from his bride and never again made a commitment to a woman.

The virgin the madam arranges for him to visit is a poor girl who works by day sewing buttons in a clothing factory. She lives with her crippled mother and provides for her brothers and sisters. She is afraid of sex because a friend once bled to death when she lost her virginity. The madam gives her some bromide and valerian that makes her sleep during the protagonist's visit. Each night he lies beside her, listening to her breath, imagining the blood flowing through her veins. Neither he nor the reader ever sees her awake. He sometimes speaks to her in her sleep, but she does not respond. Her only sentence is the sleep-laden cryptic remark, "It was Isabel who made the snails cry." On one other occasion, she writes an enigmatic sleepwalking message on the mirror when she goes to the bathroom about the tiger not eating far away. He reads to her and eventually begins to write love letters to her that he publishes as his columns. It is appropriate that the protagonist reads fairy tales by Charles Perrault to the young girl, for she is the classic Sleeping Beauty, untouched and untouchable; to waken her would be to make her merely human, and that is not what the protagonist falls in love with. Realists may say that it is immature to fall in love with a child, with someone you can never have, with someone you have hardly spoken to; however, most great love stories in Western culture, from Tristan and Isolde to William Shakespeare's *Romeo and Juliet* (pr. c. 1595-1596), share such characteristics.

The old man's idyll is interrupted by an intrusion from the real world when an important banker is stabbed to death in the brothel, and the investigation and bad publicity shuts it down for months. The protagonist watches for the girl on the street, even though he knows he would not recognize her dressed and in daylight. He imagines her in what he terms her "unreal" life, caring for her brothers and sisters, sewing buttons at her work. He feels he is dying for love, but he also knows that he would not trade his suffering for anything in the world. During this separation from his beloved, the protagonist happens to see his long-ago bride-to-be, aged and infirm. He meets with an old sexual companion who advises him not to die without knowing the wonder of having sex with someone he loves. He is anguished by jealousy, thinking that the madam Rosa Carbacas has sold his loved one to someone else, and he flies into a rage when it seems that his romantic fantasy love has been contaminated by sordid reality. However, he cannot stay away from his "Delgadina."

On the morning of his ninety-first birthday, he and Rosa make what they call an old people's bet—that whoever survives keeps everything that belongs to the other one. The madam says instead that when she dies everything will belong to the young girl, which will amount to the same thing, for, she tells him in the final improbability of this most romantic novel, that the poor girl is head over heels in love with him. Radiant, he feels that finally he is experiencing real life, with his heart condemned to die of happy love. García Márquez thus ends his romantic fable in the classic fairy tale manner, leaving the reader hopeful that the couple will live happily ever after.

Charles E. May

Review Sources

Booklist 101, no. 22 (August 1, 2005): 1953.
Boston Herald, October 24, 2005, p.40.
Esquire 144, no. 5 (November, 2005): 56.
Kirkus Reviews 73, no. 14 (July 15, 2005): 754.
Library Journal 130, no. 14 (September 1, 2005): 130.
Los Angeles Times, November 6, 2005, p. R7.
The Nation 281, no. 19 (December 5, 2005): 51-53.
The New York Times 155 (November 22, 2005): E1-E8.
The New York Times Book Review 155 (November 6, 2005): 14.
The New Yorker, November 7, 2005, pp. 140-145.
Publishers Weekly 252, no. 33 (August 22, 2005): 34.
The Washington Post Book World, November 6, 2005, p. T07.

THE MEN WHO STARE AT GOATS

Author: Jon Ronson (1967-   )
Publisher: Simon & Schuster (New York). 259 pp.
    $24.00
Type of work: History and psychology
Time: From the 1970's to 2005
Locale: The United States and Iraq

As part of a strange and apparently ongoing history of the United States military's fascination and experimentation with psychic and supernatural ideas, this work describes the attempts of certain military figures to train psychic soldiers, as revealed through interviews with current and past participants

> *Principal personages:*
> JON RONSON, the author, who has the amazing ability to extract information from people
> MAJOR GENERAL ALBERT STUBBLEBINE, the U.S. Army's chief of intelligence in 1983, who oversaw the attempt to train psychic soldiers
> URI GELLER, a famous psychic known for his alleged ability to bend metal spoons with his psychic powers
> GLEN WHEATON, a retired sergeant first class and onetime Special Forces psychic spy
> JIM CHANNON, a retired lieutenant colonel and the author of *The First Earth Battalion Operations Manual*

Jon Ronson is a British documentary filmmaker and journalist who lives in London. His first book, *Them: Adventures with Extremists* (2002), was an international best seller that examined fringe hate groups around the world. *The Men Who Stare at Goats* is his second book. Ronson engages in on-the-site reporting, but he is not particularly objective about his politics or his reactions to what he learns. Neither does he attempt to persuade the reader to adopt his point of view.

The Men Who Stare at Goats opens in the year 1983. Major General Albert Stubblebine is frustrated at his inability to walk through his office wall. He believes that this should be possible, that one day it will be "a common tool in the intelligence-gathering arsenal." Stubblebine, the United States Army's chief of intelligence, is a soldier of the Cold War, with the memory of the U.S. military's failure in Vietnam still painfully fresh. Stubblebine is rebuffed when he tries to share his ideas with Special Forces, but he does not know that the Special Forces are already deep into their own experiments with psychic warfare.

The most amazing part of Ronson's book may be that any of these people talked to him at all. Stubblebine shares part of the story of the military's attempt to harness psychic powers in its soldiers but not all of it. He does provide Ronson with intriguing an-

ecdotes that are, surprisingly enough, verified by
other people Ronson manages to track down. In
the first chapter, one learns that these antics involving psychic warfare have been revived in
President George W. Bush's so-called war on
terror.

    In his second chapter, Ronson meets with Uri
Geller, who has long claimed to have been a psychic spy for the Central Intelligence Agency

*Jon Ronson is a British
documentary filmmaker and the
best-selling author of* Them:
Adventures with Extremists *(2002).*
The Men Who Stare at Goats *is his
second book.*

(CIA). At first Geller denies ever having made such claims, but Ronson's file from
the 1970's and 1980's proves that Geller did make such statements in interviews.
Then Geller surprises Ronson by informing him that he has been reactivated but refuses to reveal anything more, including what organization extended the offer. He
mentions only a mysterious "Ron," whom the author attempts to find.

    This quest for "Ron" puts Ronson on the trail of Glen Wheaton, who lives on a
large estate in Hawaii and appears to be a hearty, healthy fellow. Wheaton immediately confronts Ronson with the idea of the "supersoldier." He speaks about a Project
Jedi, an attempt by Special Forces to train soldiers to become supersoldiers with su-
perpowers. The goals of this training are expressed as "levels." Wheaton explains that
the first-level soldier would have the ability to be instantly aware of every detail of his
or her surroundings. The second level involves developing one's intuition to guide
unfailingly the soldier's decisions. The third-level soldier could become invisible.
The soldier of the next level would be able to stop the heart of a goat just by thinking
it, by applying his or her powers of concentration. Wheaton claims that one of his soldiers actually could do this.

    Inside Goat Lab, perhaps as many as a hundred goats were subject to Special
Forces experiments. At first, the goats were purposely wounded and served as patients in battlefield surgical training for Special Forces soldiers. Later, Special Forces
supersoldier trainees targeted these same goats in their attempts to cause death through
the power of their minds. Wheaton reveals the name of the soldier whom he claims
was successful, and the author sets out to find this man who can stare a goat to death.

    Ronson's research into the background of this man, Michael Echanis, reveals that
he was briefly a soldier in Vietnam, with twenty-nine confirmed kills. Upon being
wounded, Echanis was sent back to the United States. After his recovery, he became
a practitioner of a Korean martial arts system and trained Special Forces soldiers at
Fort Bragg. A former colleague of Echanis describes him as psychotic. He became a
soldier of fortune known to be operating in Nicaragua. Ronson is unable to interview Echanis, as he has been killed, although there are several versions of how his
death occurred. Yet in all the author's attempts to link Echanis with goat staring, he
was unsuccessful because none of Echanis's associates would discuss anything to do
with psychic powers. Ronson begins to doubt that Echanis is the man for whom he is
looking.

    The military's fascination with psychic abilities and the possibility of training psy-
chic soldiers, however, can be traced to a work written by Jim Channon, a retired

lieutentant colonel. Channon's experiences in Vietnam had convinced him that soldiers needed to be more "cunning," an ability he found sadly lacking in those he commanded. He proposed a fact-finding mission, and the Pentagon approved, paying his salary for the duration of the project. Channon traveled extensively, visiting many New-Age practitioners, including another man interviewed by the author, Steven Halpern, a composer specializing in meditation and subliminal recordings. Later Ronson uncovers a link between Halpern's subliminal message tapes and practices used on detainees at Guantanamo Bay and in Iraq.

Another group Channon visited was the Gentle Wind World Healing Organization, which filed a lawsuit in 2004 against former members who claimed that the secret ingredient in their special healing bar consisted of group sex.

When Channon finished his journey, he returned and wrote a report for his superiors that he titled *The First Earth Battalion Operations Manual.* Channon envisioned a future world in which many of the New Age values of harmony and conservation of natural resources were commonplace, normal behaviors. His "Warrior Monk" army would conquer an enemy with kindness and love. Music would be used to try to pacify the crowd, but if unsuccessful, discordant sounds would replace the pleasant ones. He envisioned instruments that could project positive energy into crowds, although he acknowledged that lethal force might still need to be used if these methods failed. Channon's new vision was seen as a promising new direction for a military chastened by Vietnam and immobilized by the Cold War.

The military's initial attempts to train their supersoldiers by inviting "peak-performance guru[s]" from California failed. Ronson located Dr. Jim Hardt, who was hired by the Special Forces to tune the minds of the soldiers with his alleged mind-reading devices. Hardt describes working with the soldiers but does not know what happened to them after his treatment.

In his journey to discover the truth about staring at goats, Ronson uncovers some interesting, though failed, weapons that the military attempted to develop for nonlethal confrontations. One of these is Sticky Foam, designed to be sprayed upon someone or something. The foam expands and then hardens, immobilizing whatever it covers. Unfortunately, Sticky Foam has not proved to be useful in deployment. Rioting inmates can be immobilized with it, but then they cannot be moved from their cells once the foam hardens. Canisters of Sticky Foam were taken to Iraq, supposedly to coat the weapons of mass destruction when they were found, but no opportunity for such use was found, or for any other use, to Ronson's knowledge. The evidence of the foam and other nonlethal weapons comes from a leaked 2002 Air Force report. The trail leads Ronson to the coauthor of this report, Colonel John Alexander, who lives in the suburbs of Las Vegas. Alexander proves to be the source for which Ronson has been looking. Echanis was not the soldier who stared the goat to death, Alexander claims. The one Ronson wants is Guy Savelli.

Ronson tracks Savelli down and finds yet another martial arts enthusiast and instructor. Savelli claims he was recruited by Special Forces in 1983, after a hiatus in the special training following the death of Echanis in Nicaragua. Savelli tells the author that he did, indeed, cause a goat to drop dead. Then he plays a tape that is supposed to show him doing the same thing to a hamster. Ronson watches the hamster fall over, and then recover fifteen minutes later. When he points out that the hamster did not die, Savelli claims his wife warned him not to show Ronson the tape of the hamster actually dying from Savelli's power. At the end of their meeting, Savelli reveals that he has been contacted by the military and asked to participate in a sting operation involving teaching Muslims to stare goats to death. He reports his visits to Ronson but does not tell his handlers that Ronson is aware of what Savelli is doing. Just after he says he is going to tell them, Ronson loses contact with him altogether.

The most troubling part of the book describes an incident reported in the media, in which Iraqi prisoners were supposedly being tortured. They were held in shipping containers and subjected to loud playing of Barney the Dinosaur's famous "I Love You" song. Instead of expressing outrage at this treatment, the media made the incident out to be some sort of joke, while at the same time not denying that it had actually happened.

Ronson reports a harrowing tale about a man who was involved in the CIA's experiments with LSD and ended up jumping out of a hotel window to his death in 1953. The name Sidney Gottlieb kept turning up in this story, and Ronson finally remembers that Gottlieb was the other administrator of the "secret psychic spies." Gottlieb has been linked with more well-known, but less effective plots to disable or kill enemies of the United States, including the failed attempt to poison Fidel Castro's cigars.

Graduates of the psychic program did not always keep their secrets. Major Ed Dames actually founded a school to train people to use the psychic ability called remote viewing. Someone with this ability can supposedly view any place at any time on earth, even from the other side of the globe. It is not hard to see the advantages this would give to military operations. Dames appeared often on a popular radio show that discussed unidentified flying objects and other strange topics. Some of Dames's students credulously supported the false rumor that a mysterious companion accompanied the Hale-Bopp comet, which may have indirectly contributed to the mass suicide of the Heaven's Gate cult near San Diego.

Copies of *The First Earth Battalion Operations Manual* may have found their way into Iraq and Afghanistan. Jim Channon was pleased that "[Donald] Rumsfeld has now openly asked for creative input on the war on terrorism." For a peaceful system, the ideas seem to have harsh implementation. Ronson points out the juxtaposition of nearly comical, clownish attempts at assassinations and mind control with the real evidence of torture going on in Iraq and Guantanamo Bay. This book alleges plenty of quirky goings-on behind the walls of the Pentagon. One can only speculate about what Ronson was not able to uncover.

Patricia Masserman

Review Sources

Entertainment Weekly, April 15, 2005, pp. 87-88.
Kirkus Reviews 73, no. 4 (February 15, 2005): 219.
The New York Times 154 (April 7, 2005): E9.
Newsweek 145, no. 2 (January 10, 2005): 49.
The Village Voice 50 (April 13, 2005): 86.

METHODISM
Empire of the Spirit

Author: David Hempton (1952-   )
Publisher: Yale University Press (New Haven, Conn.).
  278 pp. $30.00
Type of work: History and religion
Time: The eighteenth, nineteenth, and twentieth centuries
Locale: The British Isles and America

*In this brief, formidable volume, Hempton analyzes the
rise and decline of Methodism in the British Isles, America,
and throughout the world, within social contexts that both
influenced and were influenced by the movement*

David Hempton

Principal personages:
    JOHN WESLEY (1703-1791), the English
        Anglican clergyman who founded Meth-
        odism
    CHARLES WESLEY (1707-1788), his brother, who helped found Meth-
        odism
    JABEZ BUNTING (1779-1858), the most influential leader of Methodism
        in England after the death of John Wesley
    FRANCIS ASBURY (1745-1816), the most influential leader of Methodism
        in America after Wesley's death
    RICHARD ALLEN (1760-1831), the organizer and first bishop of the Afri-
        can Methodist Episcopal Church in America

In earlier works David Hempton has discussed Methodism, first as an English movement and later as a British Isles movement. In *Methodism: Empire of the Spirit*, he explores Methodism's spectacular expansion across national borders, explaining why the movement flourished when and where it did throughout the world. He examines Methodism's appeal across national, ethnic, racial, class, social, and gender boundaries and the social, economic, and political factors that fostered its growth, as well as its failure to thrive in unsuitable conditions and its decline when environments changed.

Methodism began after John Wesley, an Anglican clergyman, experienced a spiritual awakening, when his heart was "strangely moved" at an Aldersgate Street society meeting in London in 1738, and he felt the full assurance that his sins were forgiven. Wesley was a member of a religious society at Oxford University that met methodically to study and worship in the 1730's. With the help of his brother Charles, he and other followers spread the message of Methodism. It became a significant international religious force, a virtual empire of the spirit, and accomplished the most remarkable missionary movement of the 1800's. By 1909, Methodist worshipers numbered about thirty-five million worldwide and had become the largest Protestant

∼

David Hempton directs the "History of Christianity" program at Boston University. His other works include Methodism and Politics in British Society, 1750-1850 *(1984), winner of the Royal Historical Society Whitfield Prize, and* The Religion of the People: Methodism and Popular Religion, c. 1750-1900 *(1996).*

∼

denomination in the United States. American Methodists accounted for more than 75 percent of the total membership, including more African American Methodists than the entire Methodist population in Europe.

Hempton compares the expansion of Methodism to the rise of a political empire. He seeks to penetrate the essence of the movement, using various themes. Competition and symbiosis, a biological metaphor, is one theme used to explain the growth and adaptation of Methodism to certain environments. Competing with other ideologies, Methodism provided something other religions did not provide; it took what it needed from the environment to survive and thrive; and it changed and was changed by its environment. Established religion in preindustrial England, suffering from internal decay and threats posed by the Counter-Reformation, rationalism, and deism, had become out of touch and irrelevant. Methodism was a new religious "species" that won popular appeal through a distinct theology—free will, grace for all, the assurance of forgiveness of sins, and the possibility of complete sanctification. Wesley's aim was to reform the Anglican Church and spread the love of God and neighbor. Responding to the needs of the poor, sick, imprisoned, and spiritually hungry, Methodists established schools, orphan houses, clinics, and opportunities for worship. "It was a cultural revolution from below."

Treated with relative tolerance within the Anglican Church, Methodists took what they needed from the Anglican tradition. Methodism's success in Ireland was mainly among the English settlers. In the new American frontier, says Hempton, "Methodism offered a more enthusiastic religion for Anglicans in an environment unsuitable to liturgical and moralistic refinement." In Canada, it received a boost when Loyalists, British immigrants, and disbanded British military settled there in the wake of the American Revolution. Methodism's global outreach in the nineteenth century benefited from British and American military, commercial, and cultural expansion, adapting to cultural variations in each area. It had little appeal in settled, longstanding Anglican strongholds, but it thrived among mobile populations, soldiers, sailors, immigrants, pioneers, and slaves, expanding with trading routes and migration patterns. "Eighteenth-century Methodism, throughout the English-speaking world, was essentially a sub-species of Anglicanism, but with a greater capacity to adapt to the changing conditions of a new world order." Democratic revolutions and expanding markets strengthened its appeal. Economic uncertainty and political change—major environmental changes—accounted for its success as much as its message, enthusiasm, and the mobility of its messengers. Following informal outreach by lay people, missionary societies were officially formed in Britain and America and sent missionaries throughout the world. Through hard work, education, and self-discipline, Methodists, who began as outsiders everywhere, became part of the establishment, especially in America.

Hempton addresses the dialectical friction or tension between enlightenment and enthusiasm, or rationalism and the direct inspiration of the Holy Spirit, that generated the energy of Methodism. A voluntary movement of free people caught up in ecstasy and enthusiasm, Methodism seemed to be emotional and irrational, but it was a movement characterized by sobriety, rules, and discipline, rooted in reason and responsibility for individual self-improvement and the improvement of society. John Wesley was an enthusiast who looked for signs of divine inspiration and intervention. He preferred religious excitement and vigorous faith to dull orthodoxy. He was also a rational logician, educated at Oxford, who was opposed to slavery, defended religious tolerance, and believed in human progress. He believed in the Anglican High Church authoritarian ecclesiastical hierarchy and organized Methodism within that church. Conferences, annual minutes, and many small groups to provide Christian nurture, as well as lay preaching and itinerant leadership, were the "bricks" of the movement he built. Wesley's administrative genius kept Methodism from becoming just another irrational and extremist populist religion.

Another theme of Hempton's is the Methodist message and the way it was delivered—how it spoke to men, and especially, to women, in the eighteenth and nineteenth centuries through its hymns, sermons, love feasts, camp meetings, and classes. Wesley objected to the religious skepticism of the Enlightenment and the Deists. He found Calvinism, with its angry God who predestined human beings to everlasting punishment, morally repugnant. He took Christ's command to "be perfect" literally and expected believers to "work out" their own salvation. His theology was "a moving vortex, fueled by scripture and divine love, shaped by experience, reason, and tradition, and moving dynamically toward holiness or Christian perfection." Sermons emphasized the blessings of faith. Hymns, an integral part of all gatherings, were a powerful means of communicating the message to hearts and minds. Charles Wesley, a poet and also a clergyman, wrote many hymns, and the Wesley brothers issued some thirty hymnals in fifty years. Their first hymnal, published in 1737, was the first Methodist hymnal, the first Anglican hymnal, and probably the first hymnal published in America. Methodism was a noisy, life-affirming movement that used revivalism to change hearts and political reform to create a better life. It changed subtly from place to place, as it adapted to local culture and traditions, but it was always based on a personal religious experience, spiritual egalitarianism, and a message of grace.

Hempton points out that studying occasions of vigorous opposition to Methodism and conflicts within the movement reveals its inner relationships, relationships with the community, and the importance of the movement. Although Wesley hoped to keep Methodism within the Anglican Church, eventually Methodists were not welcome there. They were hated for their refusal to participate in the reveling associated with village sports and festivals and accused of promoting ignorance, orgies, promiscuity, and divisions in families and villages. In eighteenth century Ireland and Britain, they were often attacked by violent mobs, especially during times of social instability or warfare. The law offered little protection. The abuse was often the work of drunken ruffians who intended to humiliate, rather than seriously injure, but serious riots broke out in northern England in 1748 (where John Wesley himself was a victim) and Cork City in Ireland in 1749. Wesley's legal connections and appeal to the law slowed the intensity and number of attacks thereafter. In America, Methodists were harassed or imprisoned for failing to support the Revolution, but their numbers increased as they took advantage of opportunities to preach to soldiers and prisoners. Anti-Methodist opposition in America also focused on their undemocratic church structure and emotionalism.

After Wesley's death in 1791, conflicts within Methodism revealed broader social stresses and tensions. Secessions in both England and the United States after the Revolution resulted over the issue of whether the church would have a democratic or authoritarian government. In America, attacks on the episcopacy and its appointment of preachers to circuits without their agreement challenged the authority of the English-born, first American Methodist bishop, Francis Asbury. Asbury, a farmer's son and former metalworker's apprentice, had a remarkable rapport with preachers and asked no more of them than he would of himself. He maintained that the episcopacy was the best government for furthering the mission of the church. Dissident congregations, numbering about thirty thousand members, withdrew in 1835. The church in England fared worse, when Jabez Bunting, an ecclesiastical bureaucrat ridiculed as "the Methodist pope," gained the upper hand. Bunting feared popular radicalism and revivalism, and his autocratic control in the late 1840's provoked counterattacks and schisms from which Methodism in Britain has not recovered.

Clashes between "traditionalists" and "modernists" in the 1800's, related to style and strategy, were common; but issues related to class predominated in England, and issues of race and slavery were by far the major issues in the United States. Wesley was opposed to slavery, and Methodism, offering a sense of community, deliverance, spiritual power, ecstatic rituals and lively worship, made sweeping gains among African Americans. Discrimination and segregation frustrated many African American Methodists, however. Denied access to power, Richard Allen, an African American preacher, left the church to form an independent black church in Philadelphia in 1794. In 1816, he founded the African Methodist Episcopal Church and became its first bishop. Other African American denominations were later formed, and the schism in 1844 over the issue of slavery split the northern and southern church in the United States.

Financial issues—how money was raised, for what purposes, decisions about owning property and financing missions—provide another perspective revealing the distribution of power within Methodism and its shift over time from its roots in revivalism to a mainline denomination. "The church's nineteenth-century investments in property, education, publishing, and ecclesiastical organization along with its inculcation of personal qualities of work discipline, sobriety, self-improvement, and civic responsibility among its members allowed Methodists to achieve a more central position in the cultures of most of the countries in the North Atlantic region." As Methodism became more mainstream and less of a countercultural movement challenging the norms of established religion and society, it lost its otherworldly zeal and energy, according to Hempton. Society became more accepting of Methodism, and it became more accepting of society. This accounts for Methodism's declining growth rate in the twentieth century even more than the secularization of society. The Methodist holiness tradition continues, however, in the global expansion of Pentecostalism.

Hempton's research on the global expansion of Methodism is impressive, and his thoughtful and scholarly interpretations of events provide fresh insights into an intriguing topic. His book assumes a basic knowledge of key personalities, major events, and theoretical debates, but its style is totally engaging. *Methodism: Empire of the Spirit* bears reading and rereading by those interested in deepening their knowledge of the history of Methodism.

Edna B. Quinn

Review Sources

The Christian Century 122, no. 22 (November 1, 2005): 26-31.
International Bulletin of Missionary Research 29, no. 4 (October, 2005): 210-211.
Journal of Church and State 47, no. 3 (Summer, 2005): 631-632.
The Times Literary Supplement, May 27, 2005, p. 10.

MIGRATION
New and Selected Poems

Author: W. S. Merwin (1927-   )
Publisher: Copper Canyon Press (Port Townsend,
   Wash.). 545 pp. $40.00
Type of work: Poetry

   This generous selection of poetry spans more than fifty
years in the career of one of America's most respected
poets

   W. S. Merwin published his first volume of poetry, *A Mask for Janus*, in 1952. Since then, he has released more than twenty highly regarded poetry collections. Also the author of several books of prose, he is considered a brilliant translator of poetry as well. Over the years, Merwin has been awarded numerous honors, including the 2005 National Book Award for Poetry for *Migration: New and Selected Poems*. Always one to experiment with language, Merwin shows himself in this collection at every turn of his career as a poet. Poems from fifteen volumes are included in *Migration* as well as eight new poems.

   Merwin's first collection, *A Mask for Janus*, is represented with merely one poem. The poem is "Dictum: For a Masque of Deluge," and the opening lines, "There will be the cough before the silence, then/ Expectation; and the hush of portent/ Must be welcomed by a diffident music/ Lisping and dividing its renewals," are an appropriate introduction to *Migration*. The words "expectation," "renewal," and "migration" are all strong expressions of Merwin's poetic style. Over the years, he has refused to stand in place, to become complacent with his craft. Diversity of approach always has been at the forefront of Merwin's poetic style.

   Although he was born in New York City, he grew up in Union City, New Jersey, and Scranton, Pennsylvania. His father was a Presbyterian minister. Merwin has stated that his parents believed in discipline and had little regard for humor. He was a child when he wrote his first poems; these earliest attempts at verse were written to impress his very sober father. During his years at Princeton University, Merwin became intrigued by the poetry of Ezra Pound. Through his introduction to Pound's work, he became interested in translation. He left the United States in 1949 in order to immerse himself in what European cultures had to offer. Merwin became an expert translator of Spanish, Latin, French, and Portuguese. During the early 1950's, he worked for the British Broadcasting Corporation (BBC) as a translator. His ability to mold foreign-language poetry into English helped immensely with his own growth as a poet.

   In 1952, Merwin was selected by judge W. H. Auden as the winner of the Yale Series of Younger Poets Award for *A Mask for Janus*. Although Merwin undeniably showed early promise as a poet, his 1950's collections were criticized by such noted poets as Robert Bly, James Dickey, and Thom Gunn for various failings, including wordiness, flat language, and an absence of intensity. Merwin bore the brunt of criticism for the formality of the verse he wrote during the early years of his career. By 1960, he was showing a willingness to experiment, to take chances, to migrate in a new poetic direction. After such changes began creeping into his work, he wrote the majority of the poems found in the current collection.

While he has evolved as a poet stylistically, he has remained steadfast in his examination of the human condition. In one of Merwin's more important poems of the 1950's, "Leviathan," he takes his inspiration from Old English poetry. While the poem takes a look at the contemporary human condition, Merwin employs techniques that were widely used hundreds of years earlier. The poem was included in the 1956 collection *Green with Beasts*, Merwin's third published volume, and it includes a number of gripping dramatic monologues. The leviathan of the poem is a whale. Because of its size, the whale is "Frightening to foolhardiest/ Mariners." Merwin

W. S. Merwin is one of the most respected and influential American poets of his generation. Over more than fifty years, he has published numerous volumes of poetry. Merwin also is a talented translator of poems and a noted prose writer. He has won several major awards, including the Pulitzer Prize in poetry and the National Book Award for poetry.

describes the impact of such a creature on the world around it. For the poet, humanity takes over the role of the leviathan. At one time it was a whale that wrecked havoc on the world, but now it is humans who have taken the place of the giant beast. As the whales were feared, so now are humans. This fear isolates humankind, sets it apart from all the other creatures. The poet makes the point that humans are boxed in by their dominance, forced into empty existence in the vast darkness that surrounds them. In addition to "Leviathan," fourteen other poems from *Green with Beasts* are included in *Migration. Green with Beasts* can be looked at as being a transitional volume of poetry. The poems found in this 1956 collection do not have the detachment of Merwin's first two collections; their riches can be traced to the poet's conscious decision to live in the poems and not merely rely on description.

For Merwin, success as a poet starts with freshness—not repeating himself, not settling for imitation of even himself. He has stated that he is not interested in what he has already written but in what he has not written. If he is to write another poem, then that "next poem" is what is of prime importance to him. Merwin does not take it for granted that he will write another poem; he believes that a poem only can come out of the not knowing. At times, Merwin has known that he will not write for some undetermined period of time. He understands that if he forced himself to write, then he would merely repeat himself. He decides to wait for one period of writing to end before he can make a fresh start in a new direction. After finishing *The Drunk in the Furnace*

(1960), Merwin patiently waited for inspiration. Eventually, he began writing again, and the 1963 collection *The Moving Target* took shape.

During the 1960's, Merwin's poetry became more loose, more casual. The poetic forms that had served him well during the 1950's were shed like old skin. In 1967, Merwin published *The Lice*. It is evident in this collection how he has become more comfortable in the skin of his new, more relaxed style of poetry. One of the most extraordinary examples of his growth as a poet found in this collection is the lyric "In the Winter of My Thirty-eighth Year." In this work, Merwin employs twenty-two lines of free verse. He has abandoned all punctuation. The poem ends with the piercing lines "Of course there is nothing the matter with the stars/ It is my emptiness among them/ While they drift farther away in the invisible morning." Poetry cannot be planned, cannot be intellectualized before it is even written. The poet must be intelligent enough not to impose a shape on the natural world from which poetry emerges. Merwin wishes to be drawn toward what he does not completely understand, wishes to have his mind "in open contact with that which escapes understanding—that which always requires further understanding, with one horizon reached only to divulge another, and another."

His 1970 collection, *The Carrier of Ladders*, won the Pulitzer Prize for poetry. The strength of this collection stems from Merwin's recognition that each individual needs renewal and rebirth. No matter how deep and pervasive his despair over the human condition may be, he must find a way out of the darkness in order to continue to be a creative person. For his very survival, he must process life as more of a participant and less as a judge who can remain aloof. In the poem "The Piper," Merwin reveals that "It has taken me till now/ to be able to say/ even this/ it has taken me this long/ to know what I cannot say/ where it begins/ like the names of the hungry." He is aware of all of his shortcomings. He also is aware of all that there is to learn and absorb. In the last stanza of the poem, Merwin states that "I am here/ please/ be ready to teach me/ I am almost ready to learn." With every small revelation comes the realization of how much more there is to know. In the poem "Words from a Totem Animal," Merwin seeks a new way of seeing. His own eyes "are waiting" for him as he feels his "way toward them." During the 1970's, the poet continued his journey toward self-knowledge. He also was obsessed with the prospect of living in harmony with the natural world around him. In the late 1970's, Merwin and his wife, Paula, settled in Hawaii. His new home would become a sanctuary, which he only would leave when it was absolutely necessary.

In 1979, Merwin was awarded the prestigious Bollingen Prize. Never one to rest on his laurels, Merwin continued to stretch himself as a poet during the 1980's. Included in his 1983 collection, *Opening the Hand*, is a touching poem about his relationship with his parents. In the poem "Yesterday," Merwin is criticized by a friend for not being "a good son," for not always being attentive to his father's needs. He understands the criticism. He realizes that he really did not have to leave in order to do "important work." The poet leaves his father anyway, leaves "though there was nowhere I had to go/ and nothing I had to do." Merwin of the 1990's continues to forge ahead, to travel in new directions.

The collections from the 1990's forward are well represented in *Migration*. More than twenty poems are included from each of the following volumes: *Travels* (1993), *The Vixen* (1996), *The River Sound* (1999), and *The Pupil* (2001). It is clear that Merwin feels much more of an affinity toward what he has recently written. He writes poignantly about mortality in the poem "The Hours of Darkness" from *The Pupil*. The poem opens: "When there are words/ waiting in line once more/ I find myself looking/ into the eyes of an old/ man I have seen before/ who is holding a long white cane/ as he stares past my head/ talking of poems and youth." He ends the poem with "how small the day is/ the time of colors/ the rush of brightness." One of the most memorable of the eight new poems found in *Migration* is the poem "To Impatience." Merwin remembers the good advice given to him by his mother and how extremely hard it was to follow. She told him not to "wish your life away." A man of many talents, Merwin is a brilliant American poet, and *Migration* should be savored by all serious students of American poetry.

Jeffry Jensen

Review Sources

Booklist 101, no. 16 (April 15, 2005): 1425.
The Hudson Review 58 (Autumn, 2005): 498.
Library Journal 130, no. 4 (March 1, 2005): 89-90.
Los Angeles Times Book Review, February 27, 2005, p. 10.
The New York Times Book Review 154 (August 14, 2005): 26.
Poetry 187, no. 2 (November, 2005): 137.
Publishers Weekly 252, no. 14 (April 4, 2005): 57.
The Yale Review 93 (October, 2005): 172.

MONOLOGUE OF A DOG

Author: Wisława Szymborska (1923-   )
First published: Monolog psa zaplątanego w dzieje,
   2002, in Poland
Translated from the Polish by Clare Cavanagh and
   Stanisław Barańczak
Foreword by Billy Collins
Publisher: Harcourt (New York). 96 pp. $22.00
Type of work: Poetry

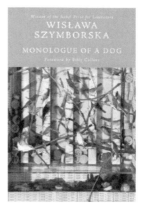

This collection of new poems by Szymborska further re-
fines the spare, lean style of the poetry she has written
since winning the Nobel Prize

In spite of the proliferation of prizes in the literary community, a phenomenon studied by James F. English, who
has determined that there are about one hundred prizes for every one thousand books
published in the United States, the Nobel Prize in Literature stands far above and beyond the others, coveted by writers regardless of their nationality and conveying both
prestige and, at least temporarily, the imprimatur of the world's literati. Some of the
recent selections by the Swedish committee have been not only unknown to most
American readers but inaccessible and even baffling to many. The Italian playwright
Dario Fo's award in 1997 drew anger and confusion, while the award to the Austrian
novelist and playwright Elfriede Jelinek in 2004 led to a response of "Who?" from
even readers with a solid cultural context. Wisława Szymborska's award in 1996, on
the other hand, while initially startling many serious readers, has been generally acknowledged as a superb choice as more people in the Anglo/American literary community have become familiar with her work.

While a European writer such as Günter Grass, the Nobel laureate of 2002, has
been received with appreciation and understanding in the United States since the publication of *Die Blechtrommel* (1959; *The Tin Drum,* 1961), the subject matter and sensibility of writers such as Fo and Jelinek—even when their work has found a comfortable equivalent in English translations—has not reached readers beyond a small core
of specialists. For Szymborska, however, the benefit of several excellent translators
(most notably Clare Cavanagh and Stanisław Barańczak, working together, and
Joanna Trzeciak), plus a unique ability to convey a sense of the contemporary world
previously inarticulate for Americans yet resonating significantly with them, has
made her work both admired and enjoyed by a considerably wider range of readers
than customarily exists for a writer with a background such as Szymborska's.

Perhaps most crucially, Szymborska's poetry is clear and readable, communicat-
ing on a primary level of understanding without the need for analysis or exegesis.
American poets laureate Robert Haas and Billy Collins, in his lucid introduction to
Monologue of a Dog, have testified to the inviting availability of her work. As pleas-

ing as these qualities are, though, they would not be sufficient to interest the Nobel Committee— or Haas and Collins either—were it not for several additional distinguishing characteristics. Born in 1923, Szyborska endured the agony of World War II and then the oppression of her country during the Cold War. The full title of the poem which gives the book its name is "Monologue of a Dog Ensnared in History," a modern working of a medieval allegory, deriving from her experiences under the Nazi and communist conquests. Szymborska's first book was suppressed by the puppet government in Poland in 1948 on the grounds that it was "too obscure for the masses." The effect of these trials has resulted in a way of seeing that carries a moral gravity built on a confrontation with the worst in human behavior, joined to a persistent faith in the worth of human existence, a very difficult combination to convey in suitable language. Her poem "Photograph from September 11" is heartbreaking in its description of a much-too-familiar scene:

Wisława Szymborska has been publishing poetry and translations since 1952. Well known in Poland since that time, she became internationally famous when she won the Nobel Prize in Literature in 1996, and her stature as a poet has continued to advance with subsequent publications.

> They jumped from the burning floors—
> one, two, a few more,
> higher, lower.
>
> The photograph halted them in life,
> and now keeps them
> above the earth toward the earth.

This indelible image remains shattering no matter how much it has been reproduced. Szyborska's description touches on human mortality in its implications of a destiny that reaches all human beings. The poem continues with devastating details and concludes with what seems like an exceptionally appropriate response, the instinct to assist terribly thwarted, the idea of assistance offering the only consolation available. Szymborska's paradox is especially poignant in its urge to accomplish the impossible: "I can do only two things for them—/ describe this flight/ and not add a last line."

The subject here requires a somber tone, one which is not uncommon in many of Szymborska's poems, but much of her work has a kind of comic slant that is startling and disconcerting, as well as heartening in way, partially thanks to its occurrence in poems where no trace of humor is expected. It enables Szymborska to inject a kind of highly qualified optimism that recalls Samuel Beckett, whose well-known injunction "Ever tried. Ever failed. No matter. Try again. Fail again. Fail better," is a reflection of hard-won courage in the face of facts that discount any reason to be encouraged, and operates in accordance with her idea that "Generally speaking, life is so rich and full of variety; you have to remember all the time that there is a comical side to everything." In "A Contribution to Statistics," Szymborska begins with a complete sample, somewhat akin to a government report, "Out of a hundred people," and then, in a matter-of-fact tone, divides the sample statistically, into "those who always know better/ —fifty-two;" continuing each short stanza—a consistent feature of her work— with the results of the study, as "those who" are

> doubting every step
> —nearly all the rest,
>
> glad to lend a hand
> if it doesn't take too long
> —as high as forty-nine,
>
> always good
> because they can't be otherwise
> —four, well, maybe five,

The accumulative effect of this catalog is to present a knowing, realistic but not quite resigned portrait of humanity, from the dark vision of "those who" are "living in constant fear/ of someone or something/ —seventy-seven" to the far fewer who are "capable of happiness/ —twenty-something tops," onto the final stanza, which summarizes "mortal/ —a hundred out of a hundred./ Thus far this figure still remains unchanged."

The "thus far" carries the glimmer of a better world which inhabits Szymborska's poetry in all but the worst circumstances and resides even in those by implication in the context of the entire volume. It becomes apparent quickly that the numbers in the separate stanzas exceed "a hundred," so the categories are not absolutely confining, suggesting the multiple possibilities of human existence, and a resistance to the compartmentalization of totalitarian regimes. The seemingly casual asides, delivered in a vernacular as "better not to know," or "just a couple more," or "I wish I were wrong" contrast sharply with the impression of meticulous calculation and lead to a comic mood through the sharp juxtaposition of disparate observations. It is this subtle manipulation of tone that is the hallmark of Szymborska's poetry, and just how delicately and deftly it has been managed can be perceived in a comparison of the translation by Cavanagh and Barańczak of "First Love" with Trzeciak's rendition.

The first three lines are identical: "They say/ the first love's most important./ That's very romantic." Cavanagh and Barańczak conclude the stanza with "but not my experience," while Trzeciak has it "but it's not the case with me." The my/me variant determines a degree of distance from the subject, while Trzeciak's line has an iambic swing that the much blunter version in the book cuts short. From there, the two English poems are fairly similar, so that each alternate choice strikes a distinctly different chord. Cavanagh and Barańczak begin the third stanza "My hands never tremble," while Trzeciak proclaims "My hands don't tremble," again underscoring the distance of the poet from the subject by contrasting an immediate present with an ongoing, recollective one. Defining "First Love" as the "something " that "transpired and expired" (Trzeciak) or "went on and went away" (Cavanagh and Barańczak) sets the finality of end rhyme against a softer, less conclusive alliterative repetition. Although most English-understanding readers will not have sufficient Polish to make the original on the facing page useful, in this case it is interesting to consider the lines that led to "expired" or "went away": *Coś między nami było i nie było,/ działo się i podziało.* Because its end-rhyme is apparent, while its internal rhyme is also evident, the translator must make a choice dependent on the full flavor of the poem.

This becomes clear in terms of the ways in which the last line, *oswaja mnie ze śmiercią,* has been translated. Trzeciak's rendering of this line, "it accustoms me to death," is a summary of everything about "First Love" that the poem contains. Cavanagh and Barańczak's "it introduces me to death" is also a summary, and here the word choice demarks the difference between the abrupt jolt of an introduction and the deepening distribution of an emotion that gradually pervades consciousness. These "minute particulars" (as Allen Ginsberg described them in a commentary on Emily Dickinson) are the telling touches that give Szymborska's poetry its signature and account for the voice in her later poems which is discernibly distinct, identifying Szymborska alone even among the company of the other great international writers—Czesław Miłosz, Zbigniew Herbert, Pablo Neruda—whom Collins cites as her peers.

The concentration on history and linguistic nuance, on a wry, ironic kind of wit in other meditative poems such as "Plato, or Why," "A Few Words on the Soul," or "Clouds" might suggest that Szymborska's poetry lacks the lyric impulse which is at the root of song/poetry itself. When appropriate, Szymborska reveals a singing strength which carries her poems into emotional realms that can connect a reader (or listener, as in the sublimely evocative "The Courtesy of the Blind"), through the power of a vivid image, toward the beauty that John Keats so forcefully argued is "its own excuse for being." In "Among the Multitudes," the first stanza is a characteristic statement of being, a philosophical proposition calling for metaphysical contemplation in the spirit of centuries of thought: "I am who I am./ A coincidence no less unthinkable/ than any other." The poem proceeds from this bold assertion with a smooth shift toward the realm of nature, the "I" or essential, unadorned Self taking its form from "Nature's wardrobe" which "holds a fair supply of costumes," a joining of René Descartes and W. B. Yeats, one might say. The linking of the individual's consciousness with elements of the landscape leads to a series of metaphors that extends the philosphical concept in terms of:

> A tree rooted to the ground
> as the fire draws near.
>
> A grass blade trampled by a stampede
> of incomprehensible events.
>
> A shady type whose darkness
> dazzled some.

Presenting herself as "something swimming under a square of glass" focuses attention on the correspondence between the human and other forms of life, as well as maintaining the conceit of sentience as an aspect of a nonhuman organism. The succession of images in this poem takes the philosphical proposition into the tangible world, one of the most important and traditional of artistic tasks. It is a way for Szymborska to carry an existential outlook out of or beyond the language of its discipline (as Albert Camus did) and into the active world of immediate human experience, something she does prominently in "List" ("I've made a list of questions/ to which I no longer expect answers") and "The Ball" ("As long as nothing can be known for sure") and which reaches a kind of ultimate clarity and compression in "The Three Oddest Words":

> When I pronounce the word Future,
> the first syllable already belongs to the past.
>
> When I pronounce the world Silence,
> I destroy it.
>
> When I pronounce the word Nothing,
> I make something no nonbeing can hold.

As in many of the poems in this collection, the most abstract and theoretical of philosophical concepts—intellectually removed from the fundamentally human—is emphatically redefined through the use of language in terms of the most personal of pronouncements, the "I" of the poet as maker of meaning.

Leon Lewis

Review Sources

Booklist 102, no. 5 (November 1, 2005): 14.
Library Journal 130, no. 16 (October 1, 2005): 81-82.

MY NAME IS LEGION

Author: A. N. Wilson (1950-   )
First published: 2004, in Great Britain
Publisher: Farrar, Straus and Giroux (New York). 506
    pp. $26.00
Type of work: Novel
Time: Early in the twenty-first century
Locale: London, a provincial estate

A *corrupt newspaper propels a dazzling array of characters toward their individual fates in a horrifying, postmodern London*

Principal characters:
    LENNOX MARKS, publisher of *The Daily Le-
        gion*, a newspaper; eventually Lord
        Marks of the Lower Pool
    MARTINA FAX MARKS, his wife
    FATHER VIVYAN CHELL, an activist monk
    LILY D'ABO, a Bahamian-born nurse
    MERCY TOPLING, her sexy daughter
    PETER D'ABO, also known as TULI and PIET, Mercy's illegitimate son, a
        schizophrenic
    GENERAL JOSHUA BINDIGA, the dictator of the African state of Zinariga
    MARY MUCH, a columnist for *The Daily Legion*
    L. P. WATSON, a columnist for *The Daily Legion*
    DEREK WORLEDGE, an editor of *The Daily Legion*
    SINCLO MANNERS, in his thirties, an employee of *The Daily Legion*
    RACHEL PEARL, the twenty-eight-year-old arts editor of *The Daily
        Legion*

A. N. Wilson may be England's most prolific writer. He has written biographies of
Jesus, the Saint Paul the Apostle, Leo Tolstoy, Hilaire Belloc, and the members of the
British Royal Family. Recently he penned an unflattering portrait of the distinguished
novelist Iris Murdoch. He is a novelist of distinction himself, beginning with scandalous comedies such as *The Sweets of Pimlico* (1977) and moving on to the five-novel
Lampitt Chronicles and to the story of a pedophile, *Dream Children* (1998). The
comic achievement of *Incline Our Hearts* (1988), first of the Lampitt novels, would
by itself make him a major author and make any new novel of his an event.

My Name Is Legion is such an event. It is a long novel, telling an involved story
that takes place in England, mainly in London, over a fairly short period of time.
Flashbacks take the reader to Zinariga, an African country rich in copper, where the
grandfather of Lennox ("Lennie") Marks established copper mines. Lennie was born
in Zinariga and as a boy fell under the spell of an Anglican monk, Father Vivyan
Chell. Chell, an aristocrat, came to Zinariga as a military officer, was overwhelmed

~

A. N. Wilson is the author of several novels and biographies of such subjects as John Milton, C. S. Lewis, Leo Tolstoy, Jesus, and the Apostle Paul. He has been a columnist on the Evening Standard, a London tabloid newspaper.

~

by a transient feeling of God's presence, became a monk, and returned to Zinariga to do good. Under Father Vivyan, Lennie briefly became devoted to the good, but when he went to the United States for his education, he lost most of his ethical principles. He retains, however, a belief in God and a taste for theological disputes.

In the present, perhaps forty years later, one finds Lennie the owner and publisher of *The Daily Legion*, a powerful London tabloid newspaper. He enjoys his power and lusts after a peerage. Lennie's wife is Martina, a former East German whore who keeps his conscience numbed. Martina's best friend and occasional lover is Mary Much, and both women are columnists for *The Daily Legion*. Lennie's publishing empire is supported by money from the Zinariga's copper mines, now controlled by a boyhood friend who has become the country's dictator, General Bindiga. In return for this support, *The Daily Legion* ignores Bindiga's flagrant human rights abuses and backs him editorially.

Physically, both Lennie and his wife are nauseatingly unattractive. Lennie is short and very fat. He wolfs down huge quantities of caviar and lobster. His speech is larded with obscenities. Martina may appear sexy at a distance, but her face has been lifted so many times that she can scarcely smile.

Early in his life as a monk, Father Vivyan wrote a book that made him famous as a Christ-like figure. By the time the central action of *My Name Is Legion* begins, he has returned to England to take over a parish in the nastiest part of South London— Crickledon. He has opened the vicarage to a mixed bag of unfortunates—asylum seekers from Eastern Europe, young criminals and terrorists, homeless men and women. He himself lives an austere life, counseling these people and saying Mass. He preaches against the rich and powerful practitioners of global industrial capitalism, Lennox Marks and General Bindiga in particular. His secret vice is lust for women.

Enter Peter d'Abo, a sixteen-year-old young man whose life will affect all the others in the novel. When Peter was born, his mother, Mercy, could not be sure who his father was—and her list of four possibilities included both Lennie and Father Vivyan. Peter assumes many names, and he has an even more complicated inner life. His brain contains many shifting voices: P. G. Wodehouse's Bertie Wooster, a Coldstream Guards major, The Murderous Moron, and the wise Tuli (a gang leader). Not only do these characters talk to one another, but Peter often assumes their voices when he talks to other people. He is capable of nasty tricks and obscene and heartless violence. Mercy finally tells him that Lennie is his father.

The novel begins with a short, solemn preface describing the death of Father Vivyan; the reader thereby knows that the story will not end with his triumph. Lennie Marks arrives smelling of sausages but too late to see Father Vivyan alive. He punctuates the scene with jarring obscenities.

Then the story proper begins, perhaps a year before Father Vivyan's death. Martina Mark is at her house in a fashionable part of London. The house is filthy because all of her servants left a week before; they could not stand her abusive behavior. She has sent out for food, but the delivery boy she admits is not the real delivery boy (who has had an ear cut off) but Peter d'Abo, speaking in several of his voices. Peter threatens her with a knife, but she finds a gun and forces him to clean her house. He continues to work there, even though his mother, Mercy, and grandmother Lily worry about what he is doing. At *The Daily Legion*, the columnists continue to bend the facts to support General Bindiga and to defame Lennie's opponent, Father Vivyan. A new and nastier editor, Worledge, brings in a reign of terror.

In the opinion of some reviewers, most of them fellow journalists, the novel is a bitter and telling satiric exposé of London tabloids. Wilson's characters are easily identifiable versions of real people, and the real newspaper world is as corrupt as the one Wilson describes. Whatever the truth of these assertions, in the novel that world is horrible. By means of a doctored audiotape, *The Legion* tells its readers that Father Vivyan has molested Peter; subsequently the monk is removed from his job.

However, two comparatively nice people get ahead. Rachel Pearl is arts editor, though she finds that her boss understands "the arts" as mainly cases of Hollywood scandals. (Her lover, L. P. Watson, a once-promising writer who has sold out, is thought to be Wilson's self-portrait.) The innocent abroad, Sinclo Manners, who once wrote an honest article about Zinariga, is promoted to be a gossip columnist. As the novel proceeds, it focuses more and more on these characters. Rachel breaks with her lover and quits her job. Although she is an atheist, she becomes a resident of Father Vivyan's vicarage and converts to some of his ascetic views. Sinclo, hopelessly in love, pursues her.

As the novel draws to a close, General Bindiga arrives in London for a state visit. Father Vivyan sees him riding in a carriage with the queen and is struck by what is the novel's climactic vision of how corrupt England has become—a vision so vivid it is hard to think that Wilson himself does not share it: "The Queen, no longer a radiant young woman, now looked like an old frump made out of pastry, grumpy and about to crack into floury powder. . . . That decent, brave, good place of his childhood . . . now seemed a mean, ugly, filthy little fraud of a place."

Back in Crickledon, the story races to an end. The young terrorists, including Peter, take refuge in some almost-abandoned vegetable gardens. They murder a man and store their weapons and ammunition there. These gardens merge into a crumbling cemetery. Peter hides in a mausoleum, and when Rachel arrives, he take her prisoner and comes close to mutilating her. The police converge. Father Vivyan arrives. Peter shoots Father Vivyan. Father Vivyan shoots Peter dead. Father Vivyan lingers long enough to participate in the scene that forms the preface to the novel. After his funeral, as Mercy is being driven home, she realizes that she still loves her evil son. Looking into the back seat of the car, she sees the hopeful sight of Rachel and Sinclo embracing.

Despite this happy ending, and despite its many comic touches, *My Name Is Legion* can hardly be called a conventional comedy. It is rather a long, angry, energetic, phantasmagoric, postmodern vision of what A. N. Wilson thinks has happened, not only to newspapers but also to England. Although the author's opinions are not always obvious because the novel changes points of view at every turn, his control is maintained by many agile shifts in tone and by very frequent and disruptive chapter breaks. (The novel has seventy-nine chapters.)

The novel's title is taken from the biblical Gospel of Mark, where Jesus meets a man possessed by demons. The man says "My name is Legion: for we are many." That describes the novel well. The most obvious person possessed by evil demons is Peter, though almost all the other characters are possessed by evil in one way or another. The only characters with some human goodness are Mercy, Lily, Rachel, and Sinclo. The others participate in a pageant of joyless sex, child abuse, defecation, fraud, duplicity, greed, depravity, and violence.

Wilson's London includes vivid actual or contemplated acts of desecration of the human body, including chopping off ears, tongues, and breasts and violating both male and female genitals. The high point of this vision is when a conceptual artist is blown up as he sits on a see-through toilet on a pedestal in the courtyard of the Royal Academy of Arts. To make the atmosphere complete, much of the action takes place in the seedy district of Crickledon, two main characters die in a grotesque cemetery, and it rains without letup for the year or so it takes to complete the action of the novel. Significantly, the sun comes up only in the last chapter when Mercy, Rachel, and Sinclo are in the automobile.

The novel is kept from being disgusting by its lack of true realism. Except for Rachel, Lily, and Mercy, the characters have no more complexity than those found in comic books. At first, Lennie seems to have a mixture of traits. Greed and gluttony are contrasted with his interest in theology, but many readers will not find that mixture convincing. Characters such as Martina and Mary Much are little more than stick figures. Peter, on the other hand, is too complex to convince. Although some readers may yearn for the humane vision of the early Lampitt novels, that does not mean that in the world of this novel the characters are not effective. Peter is genuinely frightening, and Father Vivyan's vision of the metamorphosis of the queen is powerful.

The most interesting side of this novel may be its theological one. Wilson was once a seminarian, and he has various characters say many cogent things about humanity and its relation to God. Oddly enough, Lennie is one of the only believers in the novel, and even he wonders why God chose to create anything at all. Father Vivyan has based his life on an overwhelming but never-to-be-repeated sense of God's presence. Later he realizes that now "What he meant by faith . . . was the preparedness to live as if God really were there." Readers will not find a coherent system here, but they will get a sense of what it is like to live in a world that is godless but in which some still yearn for God.

George Soule

Review Sources

Booklist 101, no. 17 (May 1, 2005): 1573.
Commonweal 132, no. 9 (May 6, 2005): 28.
The Guardian, April 3, 2004, p. 27.
The Independent, March 26, 2004, p. 25.
Kirkus Reviews 73, no. 5 (March 1, 2005): 259.
Library Journal 130 (January, 2005): 76.
The Nation 190, no. 13 (March 26, 1960): 280-281.
Publishers Weekly 252, no. 11 (March 14, 2005): 44-45.
Sunday Times, April 24, 2005, p. 46.
The Times Literary Supplement, April 2, 2004, p. 22.

MY NOISELESS ENTOURAGE

Author: Charles Simic (1938-   )
Publisher: Harcourt (New York). 65 pp. $22.00
Type of work: Poetry

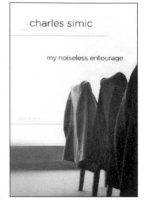

In this collection, Simic revisits some familiar (albeit surreal) landscapes familiar to readers of his earlier work, and he enters some new territories using American settings and a less detached voice

The images evoked by the title of Charles Simic's newest collection of poems, *My Noiseless Entourage*, serve as an effective introduction to this book, suggesting the silent, perhaps even invisible followers that haunt many of these poems. Such presences will seem familiar to readers of Simic's earlier work; they could appear in many of his settings, silent except for their breathing witness to things which can scarcely be named. Simic's readers have often noted a sort of central European sensibility in his work; part of that sensibility rises from the vague sense of threat such noiseless watchers create.

Often Simic's poems hint at violent events which are about to take place just outside the viewer's sight. "Shading Exercise" from the first section of this volume sets a typical scene. It begins with a sun-baked street on which a child plays, alone except for his shadow. Indoors, his parents sit in a darkened room in a house where the cellar stairs are rarely used anymore, the speaker says, as if they have earlier been put to some unspeakable purpose and now must be avoided. When evening's shadows arrive, they are "like a troop of traveling actors dressed to play *Hamlet* [pr. c. 1600-1601]," a play by William Shakespeare marked by unspoken suspicions, madness, and death. In the poem's last quatrain, the speaker introduces an aesthetic issue: "What to do with the stones in the graveyard?" The graveyard has not been mentioned before, perhaps because, as Simic notes, it seems incompatible with the sun's glare that opened the poem. "The sun doesn't care for ambiguities," Simic says, "But I do. I open my door and let them in." Those ambiguities, shapeless terrors, nameless threats, insistent graveyards create the world of Simic's poems and perhaps hint at central Europe's history of dark events.

These settings are both familiar and always new. In "To Dreams," the speaker says that he is "still living at all the old addresses,/ Wearing dark glasses even indoors." They are addresses where neighborhood shops are open into the night for solitary shoppers, where shabby theaters show "grainy films" of the speaker's life. In "The Alarm," this is an urban world where windows are filled with faces of those who seem to see an invisible disaster. Although some cover their children's eyes, their voices are calm when they call out, as if they live somewhere in a past time "less violent than ours," as if the bloodshed of the times has inured them to crisis.

"Fabulous Species and Landscapes," as its title suggests, is a series of glimpses into nightmarish settings and events. An arm rises from an undertaker's basement to steal a watch. A birdcage holds only a disembodied tongue which asks how long the restless night will last. In a dream, the sea is like a trinket peddler and the moon, a pork butcher. In the poem's last section, "you sit/ Like a rain puddle in hell / Knitting the socks/ Of your life" while the world itself dreams that you are turned on a spit like a roasted pig. Ingmar Bergman, the Swedish film director,

Born in Yugoslavia, Charles Simic came to the United States at the age of sixteen. He received the Pulitzer Prize in poetry in 1990 for The World Doesn't End. *His volume* The Voice at 3:00 A.M.: Selected Late and New Poems *was a finalist for the National Book Award in 2003. He lives in New Hampshire.*

and the fifteenth century painter Hieronymus Bosch seem to have joined forces to make the images for these poems, whose appeal rises from the ambiguities which Simic has invited in (what sort of life can be knitted out in mere socks?) and from the sense of impending threat they carry with them, perhaps the very threat one senses in today's headlines.

Simic's poems carry more than a sense of growing doom, however, and this volume offers the reader a generous sample of his humor, which sometimes surprises the reader with outright joking. In "Used Book Store," for example, the speaker examines first a novel, then a memoir about growing up on a farm and a balloon ride over Lake Erie, even a tome of theology. At last his imagination is fired by a guide to Egypt. He examines it for sand and then finds a dead flea, thinking that it might be the very flea "that once bit the ass of the mysterious Abigail," the woman who used an eyebrow pencil to write her name in the cover. She seems even more intriguing than Egypt itself. Simic's humor is sometimes as surreal as his settings, as in "Kazoo Wedding," which pictures an entire wedding party, including guests and minister playing kazoos, to the mystification of the hard-of-hearing grandfather. "Midnight Feast" offers a mad list of dishes ("cuckoo-clock soup," "peep-show soufflé") found on a late-night take-out menu.

More often the laughter is slyly satiric. In "The Absentee Landlord," Simic pictures God as the title character about whom one asks fruitless questions. Where is he? What does he want? Instead he has left one wondering about the meaning of lives here on earth "Where nothing works/ And everything needs fixing." God could at least have left a sign on his door, "AWAY ON BUSINESS," Simic suggests; perhaps he could have hung it on "the graveyard where he collects the rent." Simic uses the same tone of voice in "To Fate," where he wryly pictures Fate as a personage who is busy setting the stage for the meaningless tragedies—birth defects, motorcycle accidents—that inform human lives. Such events seem as random as the fortunes which come from gumball machines, and one remains vulnerable to whatever Fate offers; one is a piano hung by rope and dangling out of a window. In "My Turn to Confess," Simic offers his ironic smile and a metaphor to explain his role as poet: "A dog trying to write a poem on why he barks. . . . " It is an impossible task, of course, especially for a dog, nor is it regarded highly by the librarians, he says; nevertheless he is driven to the task by his powerful master, that muse which asks him to interpret the world he sees, even when it contains things he cannot bear to name and leaves him growling on the floor.

Some poems in this volume seem to represent a sort of departure for Simic, particularly those that seem to claim a distinctly American setting. "Hitchhikers," for example, as its epigraph indicates, is based on a Depression-era Walker Evans photograph of a couple walking down an empty road, carrying their possessions—a bedroll, a frying pan, a suitcase, all they can manage to take into their bleak futures. The scene is familiar to anyone who has seen an American history book. Simic moves from physical description of the couple to their psychology, the combination of shame and hope that leads them to hitch rides from strangers. The poem's last stanza sketches a future for them, describing them first as laborers, then as a sort of Bonnie-and-Clyde team, robbing banks, fleeing in fast cars, and even stopping to give a ride to the reader, "If you are down on your luck yourself."

"Talk Radio" records a talk-show caller who claims to have been protected by his Bible when aliens abducted him. The poem's listener is incensed; "America, I shouted at the radio,/ Even at 2 A.M. you are a loony bin!" This is quintessentially American radio, and Simic's reaction is one many Americans have shared. He then goes on to replace the madhouse image with another, more ambiguous metaphor that pictures America as a stone cemetery angel, blind and deaf even while it stands in the snow, apparently listening to the geese that fly far overhead. Still another poem, "Battling Grays," describes a series of gray tones which mingle images of a beaten landscape with a picture of a Civil War soldier. The country road Simic pictures is marked by abandoned houses whose weedy yards are parking lots for rusty cars. The very hills look like piles of cigar ash from the general on the war monument whose wound makes the only red in a gray world. "Meeting the Captain" places the speaker in a seaside town in "soot-stained December." As he hurries home in the growing dark, he catches a glimpse of a figure in a stovepipe hat on the stairs to the speaker's room. In this poem, the reds of the sunset sky hint at bloodshed, so it is not surprising that the speaker might search under his bed for any number of troubled (or troublesome) characters, only to find a copy of Herman Melville's *Moby Dick* (1851).

At the same time Simic seems to have located a growing number of poems in present-day America, he seems also occasionally to have added a more personal voice, although it is a well-known fallacy for readers to assume that a poem's speaker is in any great sense the author himself. Although many of Simic's speakers call themselves "I" and may even make references to elements of personal life (the room one lives in, a wife, a father), most maintain a cool distance from both the poem's subject and the reader. This distance is part of the ambiguity which the poet claims as his territory. It is also true that any poet is personally present in his selection of subjects and point of view. With these cautions in mind however, it still seems possible to find a newly intimate tone in some poems in this collection. The protest against the absentee god, the ironic "poet as dog" in "My Turn to Confess," the joined images of Dresden and Atlanta and the panhandling Vietnam veteran in "The Tragic Sense of Life" all seem to suggest a narrower distance between poet and reader than the "I" who is haunted in "My Noiseless Entourage." In any case, the perfect evoker of a world where potential disaster still haunts, as it always has, every town and landscape and "The more innocent you believe you are,/ The harder it'll be for you"—that speaker is still teaching readers to share his love for ambiguity. It is a valuable lesson.

Ann D. Garbett

Review Sources

Antioch Review 62 (Winter, 2004): 44.
Booklist 101, no. 13 (March 1, 2005): 1133.
The Economist 376 (July 23, 2005): 78.
Iowa Review 34 (Fall, 2004): 170.
Library Journal 130, no. 7 (April 15, 2005): 93-95.
Paris Review 47 (Spring, 2005): 266.
Publishers Weekly 252, no. 4 (January 24, 2005): 236.

MYSTERIES OF MY FATHER
An Irish-American Memoir

Author: Thomas Fleming (1927-   )
Publisher: John Wiley & Sons (Hoboken, N.J.). 341 pp.
    $25.00
Type of work: History and memoir
Time: From the 1880's to 1998
Locale: Jersey City, New Jersey

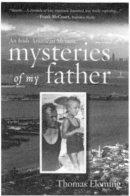

A son looks into his family's history, illuminating the experiences of Irish Americans in the early twentieth century and the political machines that helped shape their lives

Principal personages:
THOMAS FLEMING, the author
TEDDY FLEMING, his father
DAVEY FLEMING, his paternal grandfather
MARY GREEN FLEMING, his paternal grandmother
KITTY DOLAN FLEMING, his mother
TOM DOLAN, his maternal grandfather
MARY FITZMAURICE DOLAN (NANA), his maternal grandmother
FRANK HAGUE, the longtime mayor of Jersey City and boss of the Sixth
    Ward

In the multilayered memoir *Mysteries of My Father*, Thomas Fleming presents the tale of his parents' troubled marriage, his own growth as a man and a Roman Catholic, and the struggles of both lower-class and middle-class Irish Americans to gain acceptance in a Protestant-dominated society, against the background of ward politics in New Jersey.

Fleming, a prolific author and noted historian, began his quest to understand more about his family, especially his father, after an intriguing e-mail message was forwarded to him in 1998. The message had originated in France, where photographer Gil Malmasson had found a ring inscribed "From Mayor Frank Hague to Sheriff Teddy Fleming 1945." Hoping to return the ring to Fleming's family, Malmasson had tried for years to learn who Hague and Fleming were. An article he found on the Internet about Hague's long service as mayor of Jersey City led him to contact the city hall. Coincidentally, the city's director of communications had attended high school with author Thomas Fleming and knew he was Teddy Fleming's son.

The ring had been lost by Thomas Fleming three decades earlier, when he was in France to write an article for the fiftieth anniversary of the bloody World War I battle of Argonne. Fleming returned to France to reclaim the ring. Upon his return home, he delved into his family's personal history and did extensive research into the ward politics in which his father had been involved. With both his mother and his father dead, he relied on his own recollections, conversations with relatives, and diary entries by his mother. He expected that confronting his past would be painful, but he found that doing so enabled him to realize the depth of his father's love.

Fleming begins his story by re-creating the lives of his parents' parents, both from Irish American families but of vastly different classes. His paternal grandfather, Davey Fleming, was strong, illiterate, hot-tempered, and unbending in his hatred for the English. From County Mayo on the impoverished West Coast of Ireland, he raged about the Great Famine and the heartless English landowners. His wife, Mary Green Fleming, a petite, cheerful woman, wanted her three children to grow up American rather than focus on the tragedies of the old country.

~

Thomas Fleming is a noted historian and the author of more than forty novels and nonfiction books. He is a fellow of the Society of American Historians and has been chairman of the American Revolution Round Table and president of the American Center of PEN.

~

A poorly paid day laborer in the United States, Davey saw his fortunes sink further in 1893 when the country suffered an economic collapse. To avoid moving his family to the unsanitary, overcrowded almshouse, he began working for the Democratic political machine, voting several times under fake names and intimidating voters who favored the other side. His two sons worked also; Teddy, the author's father, sold newspapers before school from the age of ten and was known as one of the toughest fighters in the neighborhood. One reason for the family's continuing poverty was widespread discrimination against the Irish. Many Protestants refused to hire Irish Catholics; when they were hired, it was often at lower wages than other workers received.

Teddy's rise through the ranks of Sixth Ward politics was interrupted by World War I. The courage and nerve he had exhibited in the ward translated into fearless but compassionate leadership in the Army. His service at the battle of Argonne, one of the decisive battles in France, won him promotion to lieutenant and made him feel validated as an American, but the carnage and random death he saw there weakened his faith in the loving God in whom he had been raised to believe. The horror of the battle of Argonne, as seen through Teddy's eyes, is brought vividly to life in Fleming's hands.

Fleming's mother, Kitty, grew up in a pleasant, middle-class neighborhood of mostly Protestants. Her father, Tom Dolan, was born in the United States to Irish immigrants; her mother, Mary Dolan, had emigrated from County Wicklow and worked in a mansion before marrying her father. Unlike the Flemings, the Dolans were educated, spoke standard English without a brogue, and had little interest in U.S. politics or the situation in Ireland. Their life seemed charmed, until their first three daughters died in a typhoid epidemic in 1889. Tom began drinking heavily, refusing to quit even after the births of two more children, Kitty and George. Only help from Tom's relatives enabled the family to maintain their comfortable existence.

Tom and Mary's marriage was greatly strained by their constant arguments over his drinking, and Kitty was torn between her devotion to her father and her mother's constant criticism of him. Pretty, lively, and smart, Kitty's dreams of marrying into high society were dashed when her sweetheart was stricken by a debilitating disease.

She still longed to marry a prosperous, cultured man, but as a schoolteacher in her late twenties, Kitty was in danger of becoming an old maid.

Kitty met the Flemings when her cousin Al married Teddy's younger sister, Mae. Mae, who had been pushing Teddy to give up his bachelor ways and settle down, quickly decided that Kitty was the perfect woman for him. Mae arranged for them to meet "accidentally" as soon as Teddy returned from overseas. Despite their huge differences in background, education, and values, each saw in the other something they wanted. Teddy realized that a cultured and educated wife by his side would be the final proof that he had arrived in American society. Kitty thought the strong, confident war hero could provide her with security and stability. She also believed that, with her guidance in grammar and manners, Teddy's political ambitions could go beyond ward politics to state or even national office, which would give her the social status she craved.

Their early years together were warm and loving, even passionate, but when their first child, a girl, died at birth, Kitty realized that her husband could not ensure the charmed life she expected. In 1927, Thomas was born, and life returned to normal for a time. Pregnant again in 1930, Kitty was absolutely convinced that she would finally have a daughter and became hysterical when she learned she had another son. Her grief and rage were exacerbated by an anonymous letter claiming that Teddy was having an affair with an attractive young neighbor. Although Teddy denied the accusation, and there was no evidence that it was true, the gulf between husband and wife widened.

Kitty continually berated her husband, angry that she did not have more spending money and resentful that his ties to the Sixth Ward prevented them from moving to a neighborhood that she considered finer. As Kitty's loyalties to her parents had been divided by her mother's determination to make her an ally against her father, Kitty now tried to make her older son her confidant and companion. She could not see that her tirades against her husband were damaging to the self-esteem of a son who needed a masculine role model and craved the admiration of his father.

Thomas Fleming was a bookish child who excelled in school; nevertheless, he went into the Navy right after high school. His motivation for enlisting was less to serve his country or prove himself than to escape from a Jesuit teacher in his high school who, encouraged by Kitty, was pressuring him to enter the seminary to study for the priesthood.

In contrast to his father's experiences in World War I, Thomas Fleming's naval service during World War II was uneventful. The Japanese had surrendered shortly before he went to sea, and he was in no battles. Still, the experience forced changes in his outlook. The devastation and poverty he saw in Japan and China were beyond what he could have imagined.

On a deeper level, Thomas's friendship with the ship's chaplain opened his eyes to philosophies and viewpoints he had never encountered in his strict Catholic upbringing. Chaplain Benson, a Baptist, also edited the ship's newsletter, on which Fleming worked. Learning of Fleming's Jesuit education, Benson leant Fleming books by German philosophers, espousing ideas far different from those he had studied in high school. Just as the battles Teddy Fleming had experienced changed his view of the

Roman Catholic faith, his son Thomas's complete acceptance of Catholicism was reshaped by his wartime encounters, although much more gently.

In addition to telling his family's story, Fleming does a wonderful job of illuminating both the rampant corruption and the fierce loyalties inherent in the political machines that controlled many big American cities from the late nineteenth to the mid-twentieth century. The tightly knit Catholic community in the wards created an insular but effective political force. "Floaters" such as Teddy voted several times in their own ward before being bused off to vote in other cities. Their discipline in getting out the vote for their party gave them access to officeholders at higher levels, even enabling them to influence the selection of their party's presidential candidates. Even church officials took part in, and were influenced by, the local political machine.

Ward "bosses" such as Frank Hague ensured that service to the ward was rewarded with jobs for the loyal "soldiers" and their family members. Bosses provided not only jobs, food, and parties for the community but also important social services. In the Sixth Ward, Hague built a modern medical complex with funds from the Works Progress Administration (WPA), staffed it with excellent doctors, and included a maternity ward available to all women in the ward, regardless of ability to pay. As a result, the Sixth Ward had an unusually low infant mortality rate.

The ward played a central part in Teddy's life from his childhood. He identified with the Sixth Ward more than with his church or, ultimately, with his wife. She resented his nights at the ward's social club and his loyalty and devotion to Frank Hague, whose grammar and manners were typical of the lower-class Irish Americans from whom she wished to distance herself. She refused to accept that her family's status, as well as its income, came from her husband's loyalty to the ward and its leader and made every effort to avoid the social obligations that came with her husband's position. She also ignored her husband's argument that the Republican Party machines used the same tactics and extracted the same price of their people. Her childhood family had been torn apart by her father's drinking and lack of employment; her adult family was consumed by conflict over her husband's politics and chosen field of work.

Mysteries of My Father provides a loving but honest portrait of three generations of Irish American assimilation into the fabric of American life, laced with heartache and humor, as well as an unflinching look at the political machinations that helped to bring them into the mainstream.

Irene Struthers Rush

Review Sources

American Heritage 56, no. 3 (June/July, 2005): 16.
Commonweal 132, no. 14 (August 12, 2005): 32-34.
Library Journal 130, no. 8 (May 1, 2005): 83-84.
Publishers Weekly 252, no. 9 (February 28, 2005): 49.
The Wall Street Journal 246, no. 13 (July 20, 2005): D10.

THE MYSTERIOUS FLAME OF QUEEN LOANA

Author: Umberto Eco (1932-   )
First published: Misteriosa fiamma della Regina Loana,
  2004, in Italy
Translated from the Italian by Geoffrey Brock
Publisher: Harcourt (New York). 469 pp. Illustrated.
  $27.00
Type of work: Novel
Time: 1931-1991
Locale: Northern Italy

Eco's fifth novel tells the story of a bookish man who re-
discovers his identity by reading the books he loved as a
child

Principal characters:

GIAMBATTISTA BODONI, nicknamed YAMBO, an antiquarian bookseller,
  aged sixty
PAOLA BODONI, his wife of thirty years, a psychologist
CARLA and NICOLETTA, their daughters
DR. GRATAROLO, Yambo's physician, a neurologist
GIANNI LIAVELLI, his friend of nearly fifty years
SIBILLA, a young Polish woman, his assistant
AMALIA, the caretaker of his country house

By any standard, Umberto Eco is a bookish man. His townhouse in Milan resembles a private research library that specializes in early printed books; his country house near Rimini serves as a warehouse for books. His weekly column in the Italian newspaper *L'Espresso* is as often concerned with books at it is with more recent communications media such as radio, television, and the Internet. His scholarly books on language, literature, and culture are invariably concerned with other books. His first five novels all have bookish heroes.

In *Il nome della rosa* (1980; *The Name of the Rose,* 1983), a literary sleuth must work out the classification system of a medieval monastic library. In *Il pendolo di Foucault* (1988; *Foucault's Pendulum,* 1989), editors get caught up in a conspiracy that they have largely created with their choices of titles for a New Age series. In *L'isola del giorno prima,* (1994; *The Island of the Day Before,* 1995), an early explorer trying to measure longitude is comically hobbled by the book learning of his time. In *Baudolino* (2000; English translation, 2002), late medieval explorers seek the eastern kingdom described in a famous literary hoax. It should be no surprise that Eco's protagonist in *The Mysterious Flame of Queen Loana* is a man made of books.

Giambattista Bodoni (whose name is that of an eighteenth century Italian type designer) awakens in a fog. Yambo, as he is known to his friends, is recovering from a medical "incident" and has developed an unusual form of amnesia. He does not know his name and recalls nothing from his previous life, but he remembers everything he has ever read. His mental fog is also linguistic, a pastiche of lines about fog in several European languages. In the first chapter alone, the English of Charles Dickens, the French of Charles Baudelaire, the German of Hermann Hesse, the Italian of Eugenio Montale, and the Spanish of Federico García Lorca all intertwine with words of famous authors and facts from encyclopedia articles. Yambo's attending physician, Dr. Gratarolo (whose name is that of a sixteenth century physician and alchemist), suspects disturbance in the area known as Broca's brain, which governs the use of language.

Yambo's partial amnesia makes for an unusual first-person narrative. "Apparently I am well-off," he notes on returning home in chapter 2. When he learns that he has had extramarital affairs, he agonizes over his relationship with Sibilla, the beautiful young assistant at his antiquarian bookshop. When he is attracted to a stranger in the street, he can only guess what their relationship has been. Meanwhile his wife, Paola, has taken charge of his recovery. A clinical psychologist, she sets small tasks for him to perform. One day they visit a street market where they find a reproduction of one of the first Mickey Mouse comics published in Italy. Without opening the book, Yambo summarizes the story, convincing Paola that his memory is not entirely verbal. She decides that he should spend time alone at their summer house in the Italian Piedmont, where he still has the books from his childhood.

Umberto Eco is the most influential thinker in Italy today and one of the world's leading intellectuals. He has taught at the universities of Florence, Milan, and Turin and, since 1971, has been professor of semiotics at the University of Bologna. English translations of his studies in popular culture include The Role of the Reader *(1984),* Travels in Hyperreality *(1991), and* Apocalypse Postponed *(1994). The* Mysterious Flame of Queen Loana *is his fifth novel.*

Like a sonata, this novel is divided into three parts. The first part, just summarized, is titled "The Incident." The last is *oi nostoi*, Greek for "The Return" or "The Return Pain," the sort of "nostalgia" that Odysseus experienced on returning to Ithaca in Homer's *Odyssey* (c. 725 B.C.E.). The middle portion, which contains ten of the novel's eighteen chapters, is "Paper Memory," Paola's name for her husband's strange condition. Yambo's summer house once belonged to his grandfather, a dealer in used books, and Yambo lived there as a child during World War II. The grandparents' living space has been sealed off, like a shrine, but a loyal cook and housekeeper named Amalia has kept it clean and orderly.

As he explores the old family quarters, Yambo works through one group of material after another: pulp fiction he consumed as a child, old records and their covers, newspaper clippings and magazines from World War II and the years leading up to it, postcards, and elementary school readers, all with their idealized images of Italian youth. He is taken by the popular art as well as the writing and discovers that his paper memory is visual as well as verbal. This is "An Illustrated Novel," as the subtitle promises, and the pages abound with colorful images of magazine, record, and book covers as well as commercial art from the packages of products his family consumed.

Probing further, Yambo discovers the secret entrance to the family chapel, sealed off during the war to create a hiding place for antifascists. In the chapel he finds the comic books he collected as a child. Some are as American as Flash Gordon; others are Italian and profascist. There are film magazines and romance magazines. There are Fascist newspapers, including one containing Ezra Pound's byline. There is even a first edition of the Italian Mickey Mouse comic, the book that started him on the quest. Moreover, there are his first poems, aching with love for a girl he never won, as his friend Gianni informs him during a telephone conversation. As he reads the once-forbidden comics, Yambo realizes how much they helped to shape his ethical and even his aesthetic values. If Dick Tracy was "degenerate" art by Fascist standards, then he was destined to love Picasso. In addition to the personal discoveries, there is a book that will secure his fame as an antiquarian. The shock of discovery causes Yambo's already elevated blood pressure to shoot up, and it seems to cause another medical "incident." The last part of the novel finds Yambo in an altered state of consciousness which is, at the least, a near-death experience.

All of his reading has made Yambo something more than the walking encyclopedia of trash culture that Paola feared he would become. In the final chapters, the images from Yambo's reading converge in a series of visions, and the visions lead to memories of who he really is. They also converge on the page in a series of full-page collages (*elaborazioni*) prepared by Eco himself, presumably with a scanner and image editing software. It all comes back: the heroic gestures that his grandfather made to fight fascism and the little ones that he struggled to make as a schoolboy. Here the story dovetails with that of Belbo in *Foucault's Pendulum*, who first encountered conspiracy in the resistance efforts of wartime Italy.

The Mysterious Flame of Queen Loana takes its title from a comic book in Yambo's summer house based on H. Rider Haggard's African novels *She* (1887) and *Ayesha* (1905). The words "mysterious flame" have stuck with Yambo, who uses them to tell Dr. Gratarolo about the warm glow he feels when something strikes close to his heart. The childhood reading has influenced Yambo more than he suspects. He discovers that he has chosen the names for his children and pets, as well as his own nickname, from works he thought he left behind when he went on to college and professional life.

The new novel is worlds away from earlier Eco novels, based on books from earlier periods or present-day occult books, but it actually represents a kind of homecoming for Eco. As a scholar, he was among the first to write seriously about popular culture and perhaps the first to write a learned essay on Superman or Steve Canyon or the comics of Maoist China. Eco has written about television series and James Bond films as well as the aesthetics of Thomas Aquinas and James Joyce, all in an effort to understand the cultural artefacts that define society. Given his scholarly approach to media of all sorts, one should not be surprised to find a nineteen-page list of sources or to see that most of the illustrations are from copies in the "author's collection."

Response to the English version of the novel has been remarkably favorable on both sides of the Atlantic Ocean, considering that the book has only one fully developed character and that it refers to writers unknown outside of Italy or even outside of Eco's generation. Although *The Evening Standard* calls it "magnificently boring," in a review titled "Eco Too Clever for His Own Good," *Booklist* finds that it approaches "the pacing of a thriller." *The Village Voice* calls it Eco's "most hypertextual novel to date," noting that the endless references could only have been traced on the Internet, a medium which Eco says he uses with caution. *Harper's* suggests it may be "the closest he will ever get to an autobiographical novel." Indeed, Eco's essay "How I Write," included in his collection *On Literature* (2004; *Sulla letteratura*, 2003), reveals that his fiction grew directly from early efforts in the genres that Yambo loves.

The American poet Geoffrey Brock, who is translating Eco's work for the first time, has provided a very accessible text. He has restored the original English of passages from British and American authors whose words Eco translated into Italian, and has made good English versions of the many Italian songs that Yambo recalls or hears on an old record player. Brock has created a suitable peasant dialect for Amalia and even translates a political broadside. There is one small irony in the translation, however. The title, here translated from the Italian, was first translated from English in the 1930's, along with a "Tim Tyler" story by the Chicago-born cartoonist Lyman Young, whose brother Chic created the iconic comic stip Blondie.

Meanwhile, Harcourt has produced a book with the same look as the original, even the same typefaces. The only possible objection is that the larger page format of hardcover edition makes for somewhat faded, pixilated results with the full-page images.

Thomas Willard

Review Sources

America 193, no. 5 (August 29, 2005): 25-26.
Booklist 101, no. 13 (March 1, 2005): 1102.
Entertainment Weekly, June 3, 2005, p. 91.
Kirkus Reviews 73, no. 4 (February 15, 2005): 190.
Library Journal 130, no. 6 (April 1, 2005): 85.
The New Leader 88, no. 3 (May/June, 2005): 36-38.
New Statesman 134 (June 20, 2005): 53-54.
The New York Review of Books 52, no. 10 (June 9, 2005): 25-26.
The New York Times Book Review 154 (June 12, 2005): 38-38.
Publishers Weekly 252, no. 12 (March 21, 2005): 34.
The Times Literary Supplement, June 10, 2005, pp. 26-27.

THE NARNIAN
The Life and Imagination of C. S. Lewis

Author: Alan Jacobs (1958-   )

Publisher: HarperSanFrancisco (San Francisco). 342 pp. $26.00

Type of work: Literary biography

Time: The first half of the twentieth century

Locale: Belfast, Ireland; Oxford and Cambridge, England

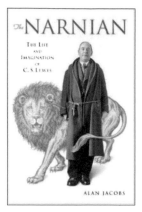

This work analyzes the intellectual, particularly the imaginative, development of writer Lewis

> *Principal personages:*
> C. S. LEWIS, a medieval and renaissance scholar, Christian apologist, and fantasy writer
> WARREN "WARNIE" LEWIS, his brother
> MRS. JANIE MOORE, his lover for thirty-three years
> MRS. JOY DAVIDMAN GRESHAM, a correspondent and eventual wife of Lewis
> J. R. R. TOLKIEN, a friend and fellow Oxford professor who helped Lewis reconcile Christianity and mythological storytelling

In his public career, C. S. Lewis was known as a gifted professor, scholar, Christian apologist, radio voice, and celebrity who was featured on the front page of *Time* magazine in 1947. However, his own preference was for solitude and a private imaginative world. He was, according to Alan Jacobs, a Narnian before Narnia was created.

With *The Narnian: The Life and Imagination of C. S. Lewis*, Jacobs has written what he terms "almost a biography." A chronicle of the development of Lewis's mind, the book dispenses with conventional details of a life story in favor of insights that might shed light on the imaginative writer. Essentially, Jacobs finds that the young Lewis's mind was divided between analytical and imaginative sides. Trained in the skepticism and atheism of late nineteenth and early twentieth century thought, Lewis found it difficult to reconcile faith with modernity. With the help of Christian friends such as J. R. R. Tolkien, he eventually found a means to include Christian faith as an essential part of a new synthesis. Consequently, Lewis's thought became unleashed, and he produced the outstanding writings for which he is known.

Born in 1898, Clive Staples Lewis grew up a Protestant in Belfast, Ireland. At age four, he determined that he wanted to be called Jack or Jacksie, and was. His brother Warren (Warnie), with whom he would live most of his life, was three years older than he. His mother died when he was nine, and his father became remote. Having lost the security that his mother represented, Lewis describes himself as withdrawing into solitude. In his autobiography *Surprised by Joy* (1955), he explains that his ideal was the solitude such as one experiences when recovering from an illness, for it allowed

him precious time for reading, imagining, and reflection.

He was certainly not happy without his solitude.
In the various preparatory and public schools he attended he erected a defense against social snobbery
by becoming an intellectual snob. Fortunately, his
father found a tutor, named William T. Kirkpatrick,
with whom Lewis could board. According to Lewis,
Kirkpatrick was a purely logical entity from whom
he learned argumentative skills and skepticism, but
eventually he would discover the inadequacy of
pure logic for a life of faith.

*Alan Jacobs is a professor of
English and director of the Faith
and Learning Program at
Wheaton College in Illinois. He
is the author of* Shaming the
Devil: Essays in Truthtelling
(2004) and A Theology of
Reading: The Hermeneutics of
Love *(2001).*

Nicknamed the Great Knock, Kirkpatrick taught Lewis many of the influential
texts of the late nineteenth century, and those works tended toward atheism rather
than Christianity. Arthur Schopenhauer, for example, recounted the suffering of life
to prove that there could be no loving and benevolent God. And *The Golden Bough*
(1890) by Sir James Frazer made the case that Christianity shared so many of the attributes of other myths about dying gods that it could not be regarded as anything
more than a variation of that theme. At this early point in his life, Lewis had few alternatives to counteract his educational training. Certainly any Christian beliefs he had
were ineffectual.

World War I did nothing to make Lewis a believer. He was wounded by three
pieces of shrapnel at the northern French town of Arras in the spring of 1918, after
only three and a half months at the front. In his free time at the front and later during
convalescence, he worked on writing a sequence of lyric poems which would eventually be published as *Spirits in Bondage* (1919). Although the poems are professedly
atheistic, Jacobs notes that Lewis spends a great deal of time cursing the God in whom
he claims not to believe.

As Lewis settled into his postwar life, several different factors combined to launch
a very productive career as a Christian writer. Paradoxically, central to his life during
this period was his mysterious relationship with Mrs. Janie Moore, a staunch atheist.
At Oxford before the war, Lewis had roomed with Paddy Moore, a fellow cadet and
Irishman. They made a pact that if either failed to return from the war while the other
did, the survivor would take care of the other's parent. When Paddy was killed, Lewis
fulfilled his part of the bargain, spending the following thirty-three years with Mrs.
Moore, or Minto, as she was nicknamed. The nature of the relationship was kept secret by Lewis, although Jacobs provides sufficient evidence to prove that it was a romantic one. At any rate, Minto, Lewis, and Warnie would share a home at the Kilns,
near Oxford, until her death. Although several of Lewis's friends appreciated Minto,
to Warnie she was tyrannical in her demands on his brother. Jacobs believes that some
of the passages in Lewis's writing about the resentment Christians face in their homes
from nonbelievers were a direct consequence of his relationship with her.

Lewis's life focused, besides on Minto, on Oxford University, to which he had received a scholarship before the war. Returning afterward, he received the equivalent

of a degree in philosophy and then sought a second degree in English. To Jacobs, to pursue this course of study was a critical decision because it would eventually nurture Lewis's imaginative side, which he had been neglecting. Additionally, his choice of medieval and Renaissance studies exposed him to the charms of narrative poetry. In 1924, he became a don, or tutor, and teaching would become his lifelong career.

Jacobs argues that Lewis had the gift of faith, although his conversion did not come easily or quickly. With his return to Oxford, Lewis was still faced with his inability to reconcile the imaginative and analytical sides of his mind. As he writes in *Surprised by Joy*, "Nearly all that I loved I believed to be imaginary; nearly all that I believed to be real I thought grim and meaningless." A difficulty for Lewis was reconciling the dying god myth with the story of Jesus Christ's sacrifice. In his early years as a tutor at Oxford, his friendship with Tolkien helped him to conclude that myth did provide a truthful connection to God's universe. Nevertheless, Lewis describes himself after his 1929 conversion as "the most dejected and reluctant convert in all England." Still, after the conversion, Jacobs notes a new style of writing, an exuberance, and a fluency not present in the younger Lewis. He developed the remarkable ability to articulate his maturing Christian thinking in a variety of genres: literary scholarship, Christian polemic, science fiction, and the fantasy of the Narnia books.

One immediate change in his output was that he shifted from poetry to prose. His first work of prose was *The Pilgrims Regress* (1933), an updated version of John Bunyan's *The Pilgrim's Progress from This World to That Which Is to Come* (1678, 1684), critical of modern trends. Lewis's first great scholarly book, *The Allegory of Love* (1936), appeared during this period as well as his first science-fiction work, *Out of the Silent Planet* (1938). His first apologia was *The Problem of Pain* (1940) followed by the popular *The Screwtape Letters* (1941).

In both his teaching and his writing, he relentlessly challenged his audiences to dispense with what he called chronological snobbery: assuming that the ideas of one's own time are superior to an entirely discredited past. In fact, he argued, although some ideas of the past might justifiably have been discredited, others were not—although they might have gone out of style—and might be a superior alternative to modern notions. In *The Problem of Pain*, he noted that people in every culture have unbalanced ethical developments. They might be acutely aware of some virtues but insensitive to others. Modernity, for example, had discredited heroism and even the notion of truth and encouraged a faithless skepticism. Progress had become more important than humanity, so much so that Lewis feared that humankind might become irrelevant. His book *The Abolition of Man* (1943) takes issue with a modern textbook that urged teachers to teach children skepticism, or what Jacobs terms disenchantment. Under the guise of objectivity the textbook's authors, in fact, simply presented their own values without skepticism as a replacement for traditional ones.

During World War II, Lewis became a well-known radio personality through broadcasts he did for the British Broadcasting Corporation (BBC). In them, he advocated a transdenominational orthodoxy, something he would phrase "mere Christianity" and use as the title of the book in which he collected those broadcast lectures in 1943. The gist of these lectures was that most orthodox Christians have common core beliefs, whatever their particular sect. He found that those who objected to his ideas were too liberal to be included in any denomination. He received abundant letters in response to these lectures, and he conscientiously tried to answer every one of them. (Jacobs notes that he wrote 138 letters to one correspondent alone.)

However, it was never sufficient for Lewis to be a scholar or a Christian defender of the faith. Paradoxically, he began to believe that nothing could be more dangerous to his beliefs than argumentation. A belief in Christianity depended on faith, not argument. That is why, just at the peak of his reputation as a Christian apologist, he would decide to resort to story and myth. Jacobs believes that, although argument had opened the way for his becoming a Christian by disposing of philosophical objections, Lewis soon realized that logic alone could not make him a believer. Thus, having fulfilled his responsibility to the British people during the war, and facing overwhelming pressures in his life—Minto's illness, Warnie's alcoholism, the burdens of teaching and his correspondence—as well as confronting new doubts raised by his intellect, he turned to writing the fantasies of Narnia for children. To Jacobs, Lewis always needed a story to capture his imagination.

When he began writing *The Lion, the Witch, and the Wardrobe* (1950), Lewis felt freed from what he called the expository demon. He promised himself that he would not analyze or argue. He trusted that the images he would create would reflect a believing soul. In fact, the Narnia books were a truer depiction of his spiritual state than his apologetics were. As Jacobs points out to further his contention that Lewis's diverse activities were remarkably unified, Lewis's fantasies simply followed the storytelling conventions of two of his favorite Renaissance authors—Sir Philip Sidney and Edmund Spenser—but instead of writing to illuminate their ideas, as he did in literary criticism, he wrote to discover what lay at the center of his own soul.

Many changes occurred in the midst of the composition of the Narnia books. Minto died in 1951, *Surprised by Joy* was written, and Lewis's history of sixteenth century literature was finally completed. Unable to secure an endowed chair from Oxford, which would have increased his pay and reduced his workload, he eventually accepted a chair from Cambridge University, at the urging of Tolkien.

The greatest influence in Lewis's later years was the American Joy Davidman Gresham. She and Lewis began corresponding in 1950 when she wrote to thank him for influencing her conversion to Christianity. She came to England in 1952, he married her in a civil ceremony so that she could remain in England, then he married her before a priest at her sickbed in 1957. She died of cancer in 1960. Lewis took responsibility for her two children's educations. The last Narnia book was published in 1956, he had a heart attack in 1962, and he died in 1963.

Before his death, Lewis wrote a final polemic responding to what he believed was a wrongheaded approach to literary criticism by his colleague at Cambridge, F. R. Leavis. Leavis's great tradition of novelists was too exclusive for Lewis. In addition, he was opposed to Leavis's belief that literature was able to do what the church had failed to do (build character and spirituality). In *An Experiment in Criticism* (1961), Lewis fiercely defends reading independence, particularly for children. He pictures a boy secretly poring over Robert Louis Stevenson's *Treasure Island* (1883)—a book decidedly outside Leavis's great tradition—for the love of reading, and argues that imaginative literature, fantasy, myth, and adventure are as much a means to character formation as books recognized by an intellectual elite. To Jacobs, Lewis's position in this final book is indicative of the unity of his thought over the years. The independent imagination was a critical component of his faith and creative inspiration.

The Narnian is a thought-provoking study and also offers an excellent background to C. S. Lewis's life. Throughout the biography, Jacobs does an excellent job of explaining concepts ranging from Schopenhauer's pessimism to the causes and effects of World War I, from the structure of English schools and Oxford's colleges to the public debates of G. K. Chesterton and George Bernard Shaw. One would have to do a great deal of research to derive such comprehensive and usefully concise accounts. Most important, the thesis advanced in this book about the nexus of belief and the imaginative power of literature is ably defended and interestingly presented.

William L. Howard

Review Sources

Christianity Today 49, no. 12 (December, 2005): 34.
Kirkus Reviews 73, no. 15 (August 1, 2005): 829.
The New Republic 233, nos. 26-28 (December, 26, 2005): 29-34.
Publishers Weekly 252, no. 32 (August 15, 2005): 48-49.
The Spectator 299 (November 5, 2005): 77.
The Wall Street Journal 246, no. 79 (October 15, 2005): P13.

THE NEUTRAL
Lecture Course at the Collège de France, 1977-1978

Author: Roland Barthes (1915-1980)
First published: Le Neutre, 2002, in France
Translated from the French by Rosalind E. Krauss and
 Denis Hollier
Text established, annotated, and presented by Thomas
 Clerc
Publisher: Columbia University Press (New York). 280
 pp. $29.50
Type of work: Literary theory

Barthes explores a previously neglected area of literary theory in arguing that Western civilization's reliance on binary oppositions (good/evil, true/false) as structures of thought is usefully amended and enhanced by consideration of the role of "the Neutral" in producing cultural meaning

Any new book by Roland Barthes is an event, and the lectures in *The Neutral,* given at the Collège de France in Paris during the 1977-1978 academic year, reaffirm his position as a consistently insightful, as well as remarkably accessible, practitioner of literary theory. Whereas contemporaries such as Jacques Derrida, Michel Foucault, and Jacques Lacan often seemed to be vying for the title of most obscure high priest of literary speculation, Barthes's willingness to address a nonspecialist audience in works such as *Mythologies* (1957; English translation, 1972)—which includes essays on "The World of Wrestling," "Soap-Powders and Detergents," and "Steak and Chips"—attracted a much wider readership.

At the same time that Barthes became an influential analyst of the meaning of everyday cultural phenomena, however, he earned the respect of his fellow scholars with groundbreaking conceptual formulations that helped to reorient the course of academic literary studies. His idea that writers do not possess a privileged understanding of the meaning of their work, summed up in the somewhat misleading phrase "the death of the author"—it is the author's authority over her interpretation, not her existence, that Barthes believes to be "dead"—has been instrumental in encouraging subjective approaches to literary criticism that emphasize the importance of the reader's response to what is being read. Conversely, Barthes's essay "The Structural Analysis of Narrative" (1966) and *S/Z*'s (1970; English translation, 1974) development of the concept of narrative coding gave critics a rigorously objective toolkit for the systematic dissection of written texts.

The idea of the neutral has been touched upon previously in Barthes's work, notably in the concept of the "zero degree" developed in *Writing Degree Zero* (1953), which cleared a small space for nonpolarized phenomena amid the clash of dueling

~

*Roland Barthes was a French
literary critic and philosopher whose
lucid examinations of value systems,
narrative, and the sociocultural
implications of everyday phenomena
appealed to scholars and general
readers alike. His more than twenty
published titles include* Writing
Degree Zero *(1953)*, Mythologies
(1957), A Lover's Discourse *(1977)*,
and Camera Lucida *(1980)*.

~

binaries. The subsequent influence of deconstructionist forms of literary analysis and their emphasis on the binary oppositions that structure people's communication with one another—in which Barthes was for a time an active and eager participant with such works as *Elements of Semiology* (1968) and *The Pleasure of the Text* (1973)—have tended, however, to crowd out any serious or extended consideration of the role of the neutral. The idea that the literary critic proceeds by the identification of the dominant and subordinate terms in binary relationships, and then illuminates the ideological implications of these relationships by reversing their polarities and making the subordinate term dominant, has become a formula for the generation of deconstructive interpretations of texts, and often a rather mechanical and contrived one. In the volume under consideration here, Barthes engages with what had in effect become a kind of tyranny of the binary opposition, as he returned to his earlier interest in searching for signs that there are in-between, unappropriated, and essentially neutral places that have escaped the domination of discourse by dichotomous thinking.

The organization of *The Neutral* reflects its origin as the contents of a college course, but any fear that this might result in some dry-as-dust academic tome is subverted by some of its author's engagingly idiosyncratic touches. After a brief outline of how the course will proceed, Barthes makes a typically frank admission of what it is about: It is "The Desire for Neutral," he reflects, that might better describe what he is seeking here, thus acknowledging the personal interest that underlies the book's normative academic sequence of readings and lectures. This quintessentially Barthesian move, which both confesses and foregrounds the role of autobiography in his work, is the first in what will be a series of intimate disclosures that engagingly humanize an intellectually demanding text. Thus an apparently mundane anecdote about knocking over a bottle of the pigment "Neutral" ties Barthes's domestic and scholarly activities together in a way that is both amusing and intellectually suggestive. More seriously, his thoughts on the consequences of the death of his mother depict a writer who is well aware that postmodern playfulness is not unbounded by the basic conditions of human existence. For someone so closely associated with the idea that authors are in some sense "dead," *The Neutral*'s autobiographical episodes serve as a salutary reminder that "the death of the author" is a figurative concept rather than a literal one.

Barthes continues by examining twenty-three "figures," various conceptual and behavioral terms that he suggests might also be thought of as "traits" or "twinklings," which to some degree seem to embody aspects of the neutral. He explains that these were chosen in no particular order but rather set down as they came to him, with the idea that this would keep him from imposing some preexisting meaning on the material of the course. Although a suspicious reader might suspect that there is in fact some secret significance hidden within the organization of these figures-traits-twinklings, it is more likely that Barthes's audience will be charmed as well as disarmed by a sequence that begins with such rather homely notions as "Benevolence," "Weariness," and "Silence," follows "Tact" with the somewhat surprising "Sleep" and "Retreat" with the even more surprising "Arrogance," and concludes by setting up the bisexual figure of "The Androgyne" as an ambiguous combination of male and female binaries that results in something neutral. There is a sense in which *The Neutral* consists of Barthes taking an extended meander through a wide range of miscellaneous topics and in the process demonstrating the ubiquity of the neutral through its manifestation in such a remarkable variety of forms.

During this deliberately discursive journey, Barthes, in addition to indulging in passages of autobiographical reflection, exchanged notes and letters with the students in the class and provided some more formal "supplements" concerning matters that arose during class discussions. Despite this apparently haphazard methodology, however, *The Neutral* does not seem disorganized or disjointed; its eclecticism in fact operates as a kind of inductive validation of its author's hypothesis that the neutral appears in many different forms and guises, much as a random number table ensures the widest possible representation of the material within a delimited domain. Barthes's ability to make convincing connections between the most apparently disparate "figures" also contributes much to the book's coherence, as does its uniformly engaging tone of congenial conversation about a varied but related series of significant ideas and actions that seem to partake of the neutral.

Turning to the figures themselves, "Tact" serves as an appropriate characterization of his discourse as well as the occasion for some eloquent as well as persuasive analysis. Defining tact as "elegant and discreet flight in the face of dogmatism," Barthes demonstrates that this seemingly innocuous form of social politeness is capable of both suspending and postponing the dogmatic speech of an interlocutor, which in turn creates a sensation of pleasure in those who employ it and thus further reason for the continuation of a state of neutrality. A strict deconstructionist view of this situation would identify dogmatism and tact as the, respectively, dominant and subordinate poles of a binary opposition and would interpret his defensive use of tact as a reversal of this polarity that highlights the social dynamics operating in such conflicts. Barthes, however, building on his observation that suspension and postponement increase in prominence as tact continues to parry dogmatism, convinces one that there are in fact places in which such figures of the neutral come to occupy positions that are outside the control of binaries.

His examples range from the everyday to the metaphysical: The Japanese tea ceremony, and its salient characteristics of the prolonging of the tea-making experience and the assigning of different meanings to each successive cup of tea, clears a domestic space for the elaboration of the neutral. In contrast, the Daoist doctrine of the immortality of the body—in which, through proper thought, the body's material organs are over time replaced by immortal substitutes—results in the cultural practice of substituting a sword or cane in the deceased's coffin in order to signify the immortal body's passage elsewhere. Thus it creates a spiritual realm that likewise harbors a form of the neutral in its refusal to choose either the life or death poles of one of the most basic binary oppositions.

The figure of "The Adjective" is another instance in which a seemingly unpromising concept is developed in a way that reveals to the reader a remarkably complex and suggestive world of possibilities. Here Barthes's characteristic concern with the functions of language, and particularly with its structuration of the situations that people encounter as individuals, is readily apparent in the grammatical analysis that he performs upon adjectives and their place in the syntax of sentences. Unlike the postponement of conflict between binaries that occurs when one exercises "Tact," refinements of description employing adjectives create new, complex terms that operate as "conflictual Neutrals" which complicate rather than suspend the discourse of binary oppositions. Adding "good" or "bad" to the property of having "heat" or "cold," for example, creates new binaries ("good heat" versus "bad heat," "good cold" versus "bad cold") that can be made even more complex through the addition of other adjectives. One might evade such ensnarement by the operations of language, Barthes playfully suggests, if one purged one's discourse of adjectives. This would, however, "pasteurize to the point of destruction" the content of what people have to say to one another, and so the acceptance of this conflictual form of the neutral seems to be a condition of preserving one's ability to describe and discriminate.

The editorial team responsible for the translation and presentation of *The Neutral* has done an excellent job of organizing Barthes's lectures into a coherent volume, and the supporting notes and bibliography are particularly extensive and helpful. In terms of its significance for its author's work, *The Neutral* is perhaps best thought of as a useful corrective to the common misconception that Barthes was some sort of fellow-traveling deconstructionist who applied the more rigorous ideas of Jacques Derrida and others to less respectable topics drawn from popular or mass culture. There is certainly no lack of intellectual rigor exemplified in these pages, but they are also continuously invigorated and supplemented by a style of presentation that blends wit, verbal dexterity, and an impressive range of references into a powerfully effective text. There is nothing "neutral," in other words, about this sophisticated exploration and elaboration of what is meant by "the Neutral," and anyone interested in experiencing a fresh approach to language and literature should appreciate its mature and considered wisdom.

Paul Stuewe

Review Sources

Library Journal 130, no. 12 (July 1, 2005): 83-84.
London Review of Books 27, no. 18 (September 22, 2005): 13.

NEVER LET ME GO

Author: Kazuo Ishiguro (1954-   )
Publisher: Alfred A. Knopf (New York). 288 pp. $24.00
Type of work: Novel
Time: From the 1970's to the 1990's
Locale: England

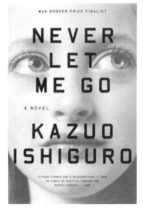

As a young woman reviews her school days, she explores the realization that she and her fellow students were cloned for purposes of organ donation and will not live out their normal life spans

Principal characters:
> MISS EMILY, the headmistress of Hailsham,
> a school for cloned children
> KATHY H., a former student at Hailsham
> School, now a caregiver to clones in the
> process of donating their organs
> RUTH, a manipulative best friend of Kathy H. at Hailsham
> TOMMY D., a short-tempered Hailsham student
> MISS LUCY, a rebellious teacher at Hailsham School
> MADAME MARIE-CLAUDE, a mysterious figure who collects Hailsham
> students' artwork

Although *Never Let Me Go* is structured as a mystery in which much is concealed from the reader, its most important plot point is disclosed about a third of the way through the novel—namely, that the narrator has been cloned by a society which intends eventually to harvest her vital organs. The postponement of this crucial piece of information in the novel's first one hundred pages allows the reader to bond with the narrator, the sensitive and intelligent Kathy H., who might otherwise be greeted by the reader in the same way her society sees her—as other than human. Additionally, the initial withholding of such information indicates Kathy's reluctance to confront the reality of what is going to happen to her and to her friends, fellow clones who have been educated at the seemingly exclusive Hailsham School.

The school, in an isolated rural setting that segregates the clones from the rest of the society, also serves as a buffer for the children, protecting them to some extent from their true situation while they receive an education, develop creatively, and form close friendships. Despite Hailsham's good works, however, Kathy's retrospective monologue exposes a ruthless and conspiratorial aspect to the school, as if the institution were a sham predicated on repression and denial and calculated to lull the students into a false sense of security.

Miss Emily, the headmistress, is most concerned with protecting the children from a clear knowledge of their fates; it is she who represents the consensus among the guardians at the school that the children should not told about what is going to happen

Kazuo Ishiguro is the author of five previous novels, including The Remains of the Day *(1989), which won the Booker Prize and became an international best seller. His work has been translated into twenty-eight languages. In 1995, he received an Order of the British Empire for service to literature, and in 1998 he was named a Chevalier of the Order of Arts and Letters by the French government. He lives in London with his wife and daughter.*

to them. Only one renegade teacher, Miss Lucy, especially galled by the children's unsuspecting innocence, explicitly tells them how little they can expect from life. Miss Lucy's outspokenness notwithstanding, Kathy comes to feel that, on a deep level, all the students had seen some glimmerings of the truth of their situation.

When she is assigned to look after the psychological well-being of those who are in the process of donating their organs, Kathy confronts the reality of death for the first time. She finds that the constant nearness to the suffering and death of her fellow clones compels her to look back on her life at Hailsham, a reevaluation in which she recognizes not only the strangeness of her years there but the degree to which the peculiarity of the students' situation is masked by a veneer of normality.

Evaluating her childhood in the light of her knowledge of what will be her fate, she develops a double perspective, so that the more innocent way she once saw her childhood competes with the way she has revised her impressions now that she is an adult. For instance, Kathy begins to recognize the level of deception practiced at Hailsham, and, even more, begins to comprehend the puzzling behavior of her two closest friends, whose characters, like her own, have been formed by the psychological pressure implicit in their circumstances.

Kathy and her friends, Ruth and Tommy, know they will never marry, never have children, never have real jobs, and that, soon after leaving Hailsham, they will be placed in a hospital for the purpose of organ harvesting. This knowledge has damaged each of their personalities in different ways. Kathy responds by becoming muted and passive. Her best friend, Ruth, rebels against the message that her existence is of little value and compensates with self-serving fantasies, self-aggrandizing power plays, and attempts at entitlements of one kind of another. Determined to make herself special in any way she can, she blocks the naturally developing romance between Kathy and Tommy until it is almost too late, keeping Tommy as her own lover and scheming against the trusting Kathy behind her back.

While Ruth becomes manipulative and selfish, Tommy responds to his situation at Hailsham with anger, which, in an environment that socializes its students to compliance, establishes him as an undesirable outsider. Tommy also refuses to cooperate with Hailsham's emphasis on creativity, refusing to produce the works of art expected of the students. It is the artwork of the students that preoccupies the third major adult figure at Hailsham, Madame Marie-Claude, whose job it is to collect the best of the students' works for a mysterious gallery intended to demonstrate that the Hailsham clones, contrary to popular opinion, have human souls. Madame Marie-Claude's reaction is one in which sympathy barely disguises her actual revulsion, suggesting the limits—even the hypocrisy—of her seemingly humane effort to prove students' soulfulness though the excellence of their artwork.

When free from the coercive environment of Hailsham, in which the pursuit of art is part of a larger socializing process, Tommy does create little works of art—drawings of animals that are impossible to decipher close to the eye but, when held at a distance, are easily comprehensible. Tommy's little animals suggest the narrative strategy of the novel itself, which is an accretion of seemingly unimportant and unrelated everyday details and episodes that, when seen from Kathy's retrospective position, reveal larger, shocking patterns.

In addition to the way in which Kathy's story reveals the complex relationships among schoolchildren, as well as her tragic destiny and that of her schoolmates, her tale also inferentially develops a revealing picture of the outside world that has bred the clones for its own purposes. Author Kazuo Ishiguro places this society not in the future but in the near past, positing an alternative history in which modern society has made great strides in biological engineering. Such technologies are not part of some futuristic dystopia, but, it is suggested, already exist—or have the potential to exist—in real time. The reader comes to understand that the system of cloning is so well-established that it is not subject to interrogation, so that few realize that such technology represents not only the triumph of science over ethics but, even more, establishes the absolute power of a scientifically advanced society to subject the individual to its will.

Ironically, the clones are sacrificed so that the larger population can evade illness and prolong their years—but despite the realization that health is indeed the goal of this society, it becomes clear that, in an insidious way, the society's use of science has become deeply evil.

Never Let Me Go does not rest, however, as an interrogation of scientific advances that require the sacrifice or devaluation of designated segments of the population. The slightly surreal, parabolic quality of the narrative allows the story of Kathy also to point to other themes which move beyond that of a dubious technological progress which permits cloning for the purposes of organ harvesting. For instance, the passivity of the clones—their eagerness to be a good students, good caregivers, and eventually good donors—points to a theme Ishiguro has explored in his other novels, namely, the way in which individuals can be conditioned to accept the terms of a given society, even as these terms work against their own interests. Kathy and her friends never question their situation—they have been born to serve their society in this way, and they see their sacrifice as perfectly sensible, taking some pride in performing their duties as well as possible.

Another important theme in the novel is that of the nature of childhood—its innocence, its character as a protected zone in which one is shielded from certain harsh realities, foremost of which is mortality itself. This is a reality that is not specific to the situation of the clones—the brevity of the lives of the seemingly "different" clones does not alter the fact that the rest of the human race shares exactly their awareness of mortality, especially its inescapability.

At the same time the novel faces both the power of society to limit the individual and the existential reality of death, however, it also explores what makes life worth living. At the end of the novel, when Hailsham has been suddenly shut down and when Kathy has lost Tommy and Ruth, she thinks about her own future, reflecting on what it was that she was supposed to be doing. On one level, the dramatic closing out of Kathy's childhood points to the way in which as an adult it will be her society and her socialization into a society that dictate the behavior and the destinies of all its citizens. On the other hand, Kathy's awareness of her oncoming mortality leads her to reflect on what it was in her life that mattered to her as an individual and not simply to her society.

From this perspective, the reader experiences Kathy's sense of regret for missed chances and wrong turns, especially with regard to Tommy and the love affair that comes too late. The reader understands that Kathy's sadness at the passing of herself and her friends is grounded in all the things about life that were valuable, such as love, friendship, childhood innocence, and creativity. Alone at the end of the novel and facing a grim future, Kathy nevertheless feels that she was given a happy childhood. Despite the irony with which Kathy has deployed the words "lucky" and "privileged" with regard to her time at Hailsham, Ishiguro demonstrates that, even if her society is uncomprehending, Kathy has transcended her role as a dutiful clone, revealing the emotional and perceptive woman she really is and affirming her value as an individual. That Kathy has become someone who is able to reveal her deep humanity suggests that she can indeed count herself lucky.

Kathy becomes attached to a recording of an old song called "Never Let Me Go," also the novel's title. The song lyrics are subjected to a number of different interpretations, including that of motherlessness, childlessness, and the loss of the sheltering world of Hailsham. In defiance of the assumption that the clones are soulless monsters with expendable lives, the phrase also refers to the deep human connection among Tommy, Ruth, and Kathy. In fact, Kathy's recognition of her humanity and that of her fellow clones may shape the way she countenances the awful future her society has prepared for her.

While the understated, ordinary surface of this story suggests traditional realism, *Never Let Me Go* reveals itself eventually as a surreal, unsettling parable that is as much symbolic as it is literal. It has been favorably compared to Ishiguro's earlier success, *The Remains of the Day* (1989), and indeed there are similarities between the life of service and sacrifice scripted for Kathy and that of the devoted English butler in the earlier novel. What is strikingly original in *Never Let Me Go*, however, is its deployment of the conventions of both alternate history and dystopian science fiction. Combined with the insights into the human heart Ishiguro brings to all of his novels, *Never Let Me Go* succeeds as both an important modern fable and as a powerful psychological study.

Margaret Boe Birns

Review Sources

Booklist 101, nos. 9/10 (January 1-15, 2005): 783-784.
The Chronicle of Higher Education, May 13, 2005, p. B6.
The Economist 374 (March 19, 2005): 87-88.
Kirkus Reviews 73, no. 1 (January 1, 2005): 11.
London Review of Books 27, no. 8 (April 21, 2005): 21-22.
The Nation 280, no. 19 (May 16, 2005): 28-31.
National Review 57, no. 11 (June 20, 2005): 53-54.
The New Republic 232, no. 18 (May 16, 2005): 36-39.
The New York Times 154 (April 4, 2005): E1-E8.
The New York Times Book Review 154 (April 17, 2005): 16.
The New Yorker 81, no. 6 (March 28, 2005): 78-79.

NEW YORK BURNING
Liberty, Slavery, and Conspiracy in Eighteenth-Century Manhattan

Author: Jill Lepore (1966-   )
Publisher: Alfred A. Knopf (New York). 323 pp. $27.00
Type of work: History
Time: 1700-1741
Locale: Colonial Manhattan

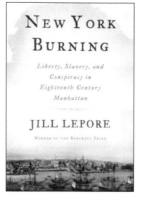

This study of a series of fires in colonial Manhattan is based on primary records of the trials, convictions, and, in many cases, executions of the alleged conspirators, mainly members of the city's free and slave African American population

Principal personages:

> DANIEL HORSMANDEN, the author of *A Journal of the Proceedings in the Detection of the Conspiracy* (1744) and presiding judge during the conspiracy trials
> JOHN HUGHSON, a white cobbler and tavern keeper accused of and executed for assisting the black conspirators
> MARY BURTON, Hughson's sixteen-year-old white servant, principal accuser of the conspiracy participants who were arrested and tried
> CAESAR, accused as a conspiracy leader, convicted and executed by burning at the stake
> PRINCE, accused as a conspiracy leader, convicted and executed by hanging

In 1741 the population of Manhattan was ten thousand, two thousand of whom were free or enslaved African Americans. In the appendix to *New York Burning*, Jill Lepore reports the basis for this fact and all the material about the colonial city that painstaking research in sources from the period has yielded. Lepore is careful to distinguish what is objective and what is subjective in her narrative. The result is a measured yet remarkable analysis of the political and cultural life of one city. The work gives clues to the forces at work in an emerging nation where the enslaved and the free coexisted.

The demographic and physical information about New York City that Lepore researches and reports gives a rich context to the historical events she chronicles. Maps and period portraits accent the text. Lepore's prose style, while scholarly, has a lively vocabulary and a common-sense tone that engages the reader of this complex historical narrative.

At the heart of the difficulty Lepore faced in writing about the 1741 fires that plagued New York City is the authority of the single available record of event. Daniel Horsmanden's *Journal of the Proceedings in Detection of the Conspiracy Formed by Some White People, in Conjunction with Negro and other Slaves, for Burning the*

City of New York in America, and Murdering the Inhabitants (1744) is his subjective record of confessions and testimony related to the arrests, confessions, trial, and convictions. Horsmanden writes it to defend himself against growing criticism of the judicial process he supervised.

~

Jill Lepore is a Harvard University professor of history. She won the Bancroft Prize and Phi Beta Kappa's Ralph Waldo Emerson Award for her book In the Name of War: King Philip's War and the Origins of American Identity *(1998).*

~

In her attempt to sift fact from fiction in this record, Lepore relies on other political, cultural, social, and historical findings about the period. She concludes that the conspiracy event and the flawed trial of the accused are worthy of restoration to history. Moreover, a close look at the event aids an understanding of the continuation, indeed growth, of slavery and racism in the American colonies, even as the cry for freedom grew within the white population: "Perhaps the paradox, the mystery, of liberty and slavery can never be solved. But in [this new analysis] a lantern can be held up to it," says Lepore.

What happened? According to Horsmanden's record, in early 1741, shortly after one of the fiercest winters the colonial city had known, ten fires broke out in Manhattan over a short period of time. In explanation of this event, a rumor grew that the fires had been set by a conspiracy of black slaves working under white men's leadership. In her prologue, titled "The Plot," Lepore puts together from Horsmanden's *Journal* the story of the conspiracy's origin as confessed to by the accused.

Thus, on a Sunday evening in January, 1741, free and slave black men and a group of Hispanic sailors came together at cobbler John Hughson's tavern, meeting with Hughson, a white man, and three white women: Sarah, his wife; their daughter; and Peggy Kerry, a lodger. Hughson put out a tablecloth and gave them drinks of potent rum and a good meal. By the gathering's conclusion all had sworn freely or under duress to set fire to Manhattan, murder all white men and carry off the white women as wives. In Horsmanden's *Journal* accused slaves confessed to this meeting and many more, some including card games and cockfighting, fiddle music and dancing. Hughson explained the apt timing of their plan. England's wars with Spain and France had thinned the militia present in New York; the Spanish and French would come to the aid of the black rebels. As one slave testified, *"After they had conquered . . . they would know what it was to be free men."* Hughson would be king; Cuffee or Caesar, alleged plot leaders, would be governor.

In consequence of the alleged conspiracy, a total of 152 slave and free black persons were arrested, eighty-one accused. Eighty confessed. Over several months of the trial of the accused, "thirteen black men were burned at the stake. Seventeen more were hanged, two of their dead bodies chained to posts . . . left to bloat and rot. . . . Two white men and two white women, the alleged ringleaders, were hanged." Pardons were granted to seven white men on condition of banishment. Eighty-four men and women were sold to slave owners in the Caribbean region.

Horsmanden is the sole portrayer of the conspiracy and was judge at the conspirators' trial. He also interrogated the prisoners and set the sentences of the guilty. What were his motives, asks Lepore. First, Horsmanden was a politician, and his politics are one key to his pursuit of the conspiracy theory and the conspirators. Four of the first five fires occurred in buildings owned by members of his political party, the Court Party. Did he worry that his political rivals, the Country Party members, were behind the fires? Lepore theorizes that he did and that he wanted to dispel the latent power of an opposition party. The anti-British Country Party had grown in influence during the year 1735 when, in a much better known New York City event, Peter Zenger had been arrested, tried, and found not guilty. Lepore suggests that Horsmanden saw in the 1741 fires a means to unite the anti-British Country party with his pro-British Court party by bringing everyone together against the slaves and their rebellious and property-damaging conspiracy of fires.

He could do this in part, Lepore theorizes, because a culture of slavery raised both guilt and fear in the hearts of the masters. She argues that whenever one group of persons is enslaved by another group, the latter suffer from an unease about depriving someone of his or her liberty, treating another human being as property, and also from a fear of rebellion. Charging the slaves with conspiracy played on the ever-present fear of a slave revolt. New Yorkers had heard or read about numerous earlier slave rebellions: in Barbados in 1676, in New England from 1675 to 1676, and in 1736 in Antigua. Writes Lepore, "The paranoid style of American colonial life might just as easily be termed a realistic assessment of the perils of empire." Moreover, says Lepore, Horsmanden wrote with "fiery racial hatred" that gives rise to suspicion about the objectivity of his account. This further supports Lapore's view that Horsmanden was stoking his constituents' racism to achieve his own ends. Lepore theorizes that Horsmanden's account stretches the truth, especially when he describes a gathering at Hughson's tavern where, supposedly, the conspiracy was formed.

Lepore uses other lenses besides politics and racism to view the 1741 New York slave conspiracy. One such lens is the idea of "conspiracy" in America's intellectual history. She questions why immediate suspicion was cast on a conspiracy among the city's slave population. Lepore posits that in addition to politics and racism the answer is found in the eighteenth century view that behind everything that happened lurked a plan, indeed a conspiracy. She contrasts this rational or enlightened view of cause and effect with earlier views of the hand of God, or providence, behind all events, typical of Puritans of the seventeenth century. Did the slaves actually conspire? Yes, says Lepore, but the conspiracy was slow-growing. She finds evidence of 1737 gatherings that parodied Masonic rites of initiation. At these black men in imitation of white men engaged in swearing of oaths, crowning of kings, and plotting. Such meetings were celebrations in which "black men feasted on veal and goose, as if they were gentlemen, a world where whites served blacks, the vulgar affected refinement, and slaves would be free." Lepore conclude that the so-called conspiracy began as a joke in 1737 but, given the reality of the oppression of the African American population in New York, what began as a "mockery of Masonry" became a real plot.

Slaves did not like being slaves, and such beginnings could have yielded a plot conspired in by a few that eventually took the form of the 1741 fires. Such a plot was not difficult to spread in colonial New York. Urban slaves lodged in the attics and basements of houses owned by their masters, often separated from their spouses and children. Urban slaves labored long hours in tandem with white workers. Urban slaves were errand runners, walking long ways through the city. Urban slaves rose early to go out to the water pumps and bring a supply back to their owner's family. Proximity to nonslaves and ease of meeting with fellow slaves across the city was clear fodder for hatching a conspiracy to rise up against the powerful.

So although Horsmanden's account of the conspiracy stretches the truth, there was a conspiracy of sorts among Hughson and some of the city's slave population. There were ten fires. There were arrests, confessions, convictions, and executions. Horsmanden records the details, but Lepore, who attempts to unravel the daily happenings over this period, finds grave weaknesses in the prosecution and conviction of those arrested and tried. One obvious weakness is that the accusers were rewarded for accusing, and the accused were rewarded for accusing still more of conspiracy.

A second weakness was the testimony of Mary Burton, Hughson's sixteen-year-old white servant whose story of the conspiracy feast at her employer's tavern, although ever-changing, formed Horsmanden's evidence for the initial and ongoing arrests. Lepore notes Burton began reluctantly, and over the weeks and months of the trial her memory kept improving; that is, adding more and more details to the gathering and names to the list of conspirators.

A third weakness was that Horsmanden was the initial questioner of all the accused, put all of their confessions in writing himself, and was also the principal Supreme Court judge. Many who were questioned denied their guilt when questioned, but after more questioning and time in the filthy basement that was their prison, confessed and gave additional names. Many died, including Prince and Caesar, still denying their alleged crimes.

No clear truth about guilt or innocence of those who suffered under New York's judicial process for the fires that struck the city in 1741 is possible now. In Appendix B, however, Lepore lists by name all the accused, from Adam, owned by Captain Joseph Phoenix, to York, owned by Peter Van Ranst's widow. Using Lepore's lens, the reader wonders at the power of enslavement, racism, fear, and Horsmanden to be at play in a colonial America just beginning to raise the cry of liberty and justice for all.

Francine Dempsey

Review Sources

America 194, no. 1 (January 2, 2006): 24-25.
Booklist 101, nos. 19/20 (June 1, 2005): 1745.
Library Journal 130, no. 13 (August 15, 2005): 100-102.
The Nation 281, no. 17 (November 21, 2005): 37-39.
The New York Times Book Review 155 (October 2, 2005): 28.
Publishers Weekly 252, no. 18 (May 2, 2005): 183.

THE NIAGARA RIVER

Author: Kay Ryan (1945-   )
Publisher: Grove Press (New York). 72 pp. $13.00
Type of work: Poetry

The short, pithy poems in this collection reveal Ryan's attitudes about life's "givens," the limits people place upon themselves, the blighting of nature, and the hope that enables people to come to terms with their problems

Kay Ryan's *The Niagara River* is comprised of about sixty short—usually one page, two or three sentences long—poems that concern the schism between people and nature. The title poem provides an apt introduction to the work. The poem begins with a simile that ultimately proves to be untrue: "As though/ the river were/ a floor." Operating on that assumption, the speaker and her colleagues, presumably seated in a boat, act if they were in charge, rearranging furniture and "calmly" gazing at the passing scenery as if "dining room paintings/ were being replaced." The emphasis is on the actions of the people, not on the flow, the force, the current, or even on the falls in the river. They are so removed from the physical reality of what a river is that the speaker has to state, "We do/ know this is the/ Niagara River." Knowing, however, is not enough because "it is hard to remember/ what that means." Time has created a breach between the speaker and nature, much like the gap between the instinctive response to nature in childhood and the more mature understanding that, in William Wordsworth's words, "little we have in nature that is ours." Ryan is a nature poet, though she does not overwhelm her readers with concrete details about nature; rather, she uses nature as a means of self-exploration.

In "Green Hills," a similar poem, the speaker denies the link between the hills and humankind at the same time that she personifies the hills with their "flanks," "breast," and "shoulder," which are, "we tell ourselves," not our "flesh." Yet despite the speaker's denials, the hills share with people a common life, one that is vernal and reproductive: The green fields are the fields of spring and regeneration. The breasts, flanks, and shoulders have a "languor" when they roll over which is akin to the movements of the human sexual act.

Some of the "high places" in nature are inaccessible to people, despite their somewhat arrogant assumptions about conquering nature, bending it to their will, in this case naming them, defining them in human terms. In "No Names" the speaker states that these places do not "invite us," that our attempted relationship with them "refuses to take." She states that "Some/ high lakes are not for us," that they resist attempts to name and, by extension, own them. Yet the speaker persists, "giddy with thinking/ where thinking can't stick." There are limits to thought, just as there are limits to people's expectations. In "Expectations" "we expect rain/ to animate this/ creek," to shape it and order it in line with notions about how creeks should move and look, notions gained from pictures or past experiences; but "The bed is ready/ but no rain yet." The rain will come when it comes, and the picture of that "animated" creek may or may not square with one's "expectations."

Part of people's problems stem from a willingness to overdramatize their limitations and weaknesses and to be bound by them. In "Shipwreck," the speaker elaborates on a quotation from Fernando Pessoa: "I was shipwrecked beneath a stormless sky in a sea shallow enough to stand up in." For the speaker, being shipwrecked or "lost" is a self-inflicted state, an illusion, a kind of stage performance, "just one's fancy." The "articulation" of despair is comic because the shipwrecked state is so exaggerated: The water in the "tub" is filed with "our own tears"; the mast is of breadstick, capable of being destroyed by a muse; and "shackles" are made of flimsy paper. The speaker suggests that people wallow in this "shipwrecked" state rather than take action to "step/ off the island."

Kay Ryan has published five other collections of poems, two of them, like The Niagara River, *in Grove Press's Poetry Series. She has won the Ruth Lilly Poetry Prize and has also received awards from the National Endowment for the Arts, the Ingram Merrill Foundation, and the Guggenheim Foundation.*

According to the speaker, one does not know why one fails to act. Using a clothes metaphor, the speaker suggests that one decks oneselves in tragic trappings that can easily be cast off, just as actors can step out of their roles and accept the applause of an appreciative audience.

That clothes are not so easily shed is the theme of "Caps." In this poem the speaker states that people ought to be "open on top" so that they can be "sopped" up or read by other people. Instead, one is "capped," shut off from the outside, so that one spends all one's time "trying/ to get our caps off." Citing the storybook lad who wants to doff his hat to the king as a sign of respect, only to find that another hat has replaced it, the speaker suggests that this happens "over and over." Like the boy, people cannot act clearly because of the different hats they wear, out of choice or by force. One's hats are one's different identities and roles, all of which make it difficult for people to express their true selves and for others to interpret their actions accurately. Many of the hats that people don indicate their status, are "brightly feathered," but the accumulation of these different identities or poses "pile up so high they bury us." As a result, people cannot be "open on top."

Ryan seems to take a perverse delight in turning things inside out, in having it both ways, in reexamining what seems established. In "Weak Forces" she validates the "weak forces," those things that people have traditionally viewed as being negative. A weak faith can easily be shaken, but it can also be easily regained. Drifting, with its lack of purpose or direction, is positive, not negative; the "untrainings of the mind" cause people to lose not only the good but also the bad; and the "sift" that remains after resolution, whether good or bad, weakens is not necessarily negative. The most telling reversal is in her reworking of Robert Frost's "A Road Less Traveled By," in which one does not know "if this is the road taken/ or untaken." Certitude and resolution may lead to arrogance, unlike the questioning, vacillating, and adjusting that are more positive attributes. The "soft affinities" of weak forces are like "moonlit/ hints" or "pink/ glowy spots that are not/ the defeat of something,/ I don't think." After extolling the value of weak forces throughout the poem, Ryan's last line qualifies and undercuts her entire argument.

A similar kind of reversal occurs in "Rubbing Lamps," a reference to Aladdin's lamp with its attendant genie granting wishes. The speaker asserts that other "things" grant wishes, wishes of a more significant kind. A turned knob or a dish washed with a cloth produce "something/ so odd and/ full of promise," something at once vague but full of possibilities that "you spend/ your only wish / wishing someone else/ could see it." The focus is not on self-gratification but on the desire to share a special moment or apprehension with another person. The idea that beauty sometimes occurs, rather than is created, also appears in "The Light of Interiors." In this poem the light that enters a house is "muffled," "buffeted," and "baffled" as it progresses throughout a house that is marked by "loose fits, leaks,/ and other breaches/ of surface." The house, not of the *House Beautiful* variety, has experienced both the "scatter and order/ of love and failure," but the light, mingled with the silence, creates an "island" of the table with flowers. Beauty can emerge from the most unlikely sources.

In "Felix Crow" the speaker puns on quid pro quo, a phrase about substitutes, with her "felix [happy] crow," an attendee at "crow school." Crows are negatively described as leading "unenlightened" lives, driving away "the sweeter species" of birds, and "swaggering" down the street; but, despite the behavior, "I like him/ when we meet."

Apparently, something there is about a crow, perhaps the swagger, that appeals. Considering the references to school, the "naming" of the crow, the personification, and Ryan's own career as a teacher, the crow is perhaps a substitute for the "swaggering" student who is nevertheless somehow appealing.

A woman's plight or fate is the subject of "Things Shouldn't Be So Hard." At the end of one's life there ought to be a mark or a track to indicate one's passage through life. The places where those marks should appear are those associated with traditional women's work, most notably where she stood before the sink. The speaker asserts that the "passage/ of a life should show," that something "however small" and "scarred" (the references to abrasions and wearing down attest to the woman's hard life) should remain after one makes the "grand and/ damaging parade." Once again, the speaker couples antithetical adjectives and ways of seeing things, suggesting the complexity of evaluating a person's life.

One's awareness of the passage of time and the progress of life stages is the subject of "Chart," which begins by depicting how the male figure (she also includes women) crawls as a child, walks as an adult, and bends over as an elderly person. While the chart or the stages of life are familiar, the speaker suggests, they are, when people are young, "remote," much as the evolutionary chart depicting progress from ape to humankind can seem to be an abstract theory without application to life. However, as one nears or engages in the bending stage, that chart becomes "the realer part" because one experiences what one only saw.

In *The Niagara River*, Ryan has playfully yet seriously explored a variety of topics and suggested different ways of looking at things, ideas, and "givens," often fusing contradictions, reversing herself, and demonstrating technical precision and a keen intellect. Ryan rarely uses the first-person voice in her poems, using instead a more omniscient tone, but she makes her readers know where she as an individual stands. Many of the poems begin with an outrageous title ("Weak Forces," "Desert Reservoirs," "Repulsive Theory") that turns out to perhaps have some validity. Others are clichés ("Home to Roost," "The Other Shoe," "Hide and Seek") that Ryan takes in unusual directions. Whatever conclusions she seems to draw from, her material is open to question with the reader being forced to evaluate and then reevaluate the poem.

Thomas L. Erskine

Review Sources

The New York Times Book Review 155 (December 25, 2005): 20.
Publishers Weekly 253, no. 36 (September 12, 2005): 43.

NO COUNTRY FOR OLD MEN

Author: Cormac McCarthy (1933-   )
Publisher: Alfred A. Knopf (New York). 309 pp. $25.00
Type of work: Novel
Time: 1980
Locale: The borderlands of Texas and Mexico

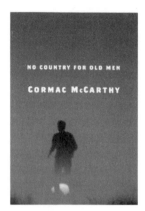

A young man out hunting antelope finds the gory tableau of an ill-fated drug deal; on impulse he takes a satchel with millions in cash and goes on the run from both drug kingpins and law enforcement

Principal characters:
 LLEWELYN MOSS, a Vietnam War veteran
  who works as a welder
 ED TOM BELL, an aging Texas sheriff who
  served in World War II
 ANTON CHIGURH, a psychopathic hired killer

Before the publication of *No Country for Old Men*, the four decades of Cormac McCarthy's writing career could be divided somewhat neatly into two phases, each of them comprising twenty years and four novels. The "southern" books, commencing with *The Orchard Keeper* in 1965, are set in Appalachia and weave indescribably dark, gothic themes of murder and sexual deviance. For the "Western" series, begun with the huge and ambitious 1985 novel *Blood Meridian; Or, The Evening Redness in the West*, McCarthy moves his landscape to America's historical Western frontier during the most bloodthirsty years of North American settlement.

The first five books earned him an intense cult following as "a writer's writer," working in the traditions of William Faulkner and Herman Melville, while simultaneously breaking new ground for American literature. Sales figures were modest, befitting the highly literary efforts. It was his sixth novel, the slender and elegiac 1992 volume *All the Pretty Horses*, that launched the author into best-sellerdom, feature film, and the popular imagination. He followed it with two more books that would make up his Border Trilogy: *The Crossing* in 1994 and *Cities of the Plain* in 1998.

Over the decades, it was McCarthy's use of language that remained ascendant—an odd and unmistakable blend of sparse, white-hot dialogue and long, soaring descriptions of the natural world whose style at times echoes both William Shakespeare and the King James Bible. Novelist Rick Moody has written of *Blood Meridian*: "Few books are more bloodthirsty, few more hieratic, and rarely has the dark side of Western expansion been depicted with as much ruthless courage. *Blood Meridian* is one of those rare books by which one measures the literature entire of the generation that follows." Literary critic Harold Bloom has declared McCarthy one of the four major contemporary American novelists, alongside Don DeLillo, Thomas Pynchon, and Philip Roth.

In advance of McCarthy's ninth book, the rumor in publishing circles (the author himself is famously private, shunning publicity and most interviews) was that it would mark a return to his southern roots, with a story set in present-day New Orleans. Instead, McCarthy has surprised readers and critics with a taut, compact literary thriller that unreels against the background of urban sprawl in south Texas at the dawn of America's "War on Drugs." *No Country for Old Men* is at once controversial, a change in direction, and yet redolent of themes, threads, and preoccupations from his earlier work.

Cormac McCarthy lives in Santa Fe, New Mexico, with his wife and son. He is active in its academic community, especially at the Santa Fe Institute, which was founded by his friend Murray Gell-Mann. No Country for Old Men *is McCarthy's ninth novel.*

Llewelyn Moss, a former sniper in the Vietnam War, is stalking antelope in the Texas wilderness near his home when the view in his binoculars suddenly reveals vehicles and corpses riddled by machine-guns, the apparent aftermath of a drug deal gone wrong. Moss inspects the carnage firsthand and finds one of the shooting victims barely clinging to life. The man asks him for water, but Moss has none. Nearby, he finds a leather satchel containing almost two-and-a-half million dollars in unmarked bills and takes it home.

He is well aware that taking the money will propel him into a dangerous new life on the run—"You have to take this seriously," Moss tells himself, "You can't treat it like luck"—but his conscience pains him, and he cannot resist going back to the scene after dark with a jar of water for the dying man.

It is during that hasty errand of mercy that Moss's main pursuer first spots him and opens fire with a rifle. Emblematic of the novel's bleak tone, it is not the theft itself that sets the violent chase in motion but rather Moss's gesture of empathy. In any case, the thirsty victim is already dead.

In the headlong action that follows, the fleeing Moss does not fully comprehend how dark his personal situation is. He has no way of knowing that the man trailing him is a professional killer of mythical proportions named Anton Chigurh (it rhymes roughly with "Sugar"), of whom one character later observes, "Even if you gave him the money, he'd still kill you. There's no one alive on this planet that's ever had even a cross word with him. They're all dead. These are not good odds."

Leagues beyond amoral, Chigurh is such a ruthlessly efficient killing machine that some of the people in his growing death toll bore him no threat whatever but were only momentary obstacles on his path to Moss and the satchel. Paradoxically, he is a psychopath with a strong metaphysical bent who apparently sees himself in the service of some cosmic reckoning of order that is beyond his power to question or control. In a narrative that has no shortage of grotesque violence and graphic gore, some of the most disturbing scenes are bloodless ones—Chigurh's rare conversations with his potential victims about their fates. In this passage, he forces a young woman to call an ominous coin toss:

> Heads, she said.
> He lifted his hand away. The coin was tails.
> I'm sorry.
> She didn't answer.
> Maybe it's for the best.
> She looked away. You make it like it was the coin. But you're the one.
> It could have gone either way . . .
> You wouldn't of let me off noway.
>
> I had no say in the matter. Every moment of your life is a turning and every one a choosing. Somewhere you made a choice. All followed to this. The accounting is scrupulous. The shape is drawn. No line can be erased. I had no belief in your ability to move a coin to your bidding. How could you? A person's path through the world seldom changes and even more seldom will it change abruptly. And the shape of your path was visible from the beginning.
>
> She sat sobbing. She shook her head.

Anton Chigurh's philosophical musings echo an earlier McCarthy character, a man in *Blood Meridian* known only as the Judge. A genteel, thoughtful, and scholarly figure who contrasts vividly with the rough ways of the surrounding cowboys, he is nonetheless the epicenter of a rampage of unspeakable violence and terror that exponentially outgrows the group's initial purpose, which is to collect a massive quantity of Indian scalps for bounty purposes. Like Chigurh, the Judge considers himself accountable only to some higher order that is beyond human understanding and oblivious to basic human needs and emotions. As the Judge phrases it in *Blood Meridian*:

> I tell you this. As war becomes dishonored and its nobility called into question those honorable men who recognize the sanctity of blood will become excluded from the dance, which is the warrior's right, and thereby will the dance become a false dance and the dancers false dancers. And yet there will be one there always who is a true dancer and can you guess who that might be? . . . I will tell you. Only that man who has offered up himself to the blood of war, who has been to the floor of the pit and seen horror in the round and learned at last that it speaks to his inmost heart, only that man can dance.

In recent years a growing number of academic books and essays have attempted to show parallels between the philosophies of McCarthy's characters and an ancient system of thought known as Gnosticism, a word derived from the Greek term for knowledge, *gnosis*. Such movements—some of them allied with orthodox Christianity or Buddhism, others in opposition to them—were most active during the first centuries of the common era and were often expressed as occult religious sects who claimed special access to arcane knowledge of a divine nature. Though the potential Gnostic framework is probably not as prevalent in *No Country for Old Men* as it is in some of McCarthy's other writings, it is still enough of a factor that scholars will no doubt use it to continue the intriguing conversation that speculates on the author's worldview— or at any rate, the world as viewed from inside his works of fiction.

As for the language and tone of *No Country for Old Men*, one reviewer convincingly describes it as McCarthy's "first indoor book." James Browning writes in *The Village Voice:*

> "Brown walls. Same chenille bedspread." may not be the most moving description you've ever read of a motel room. . . . But taking *No Country* as the fourth book in a Border Tetralogy, brown walls are a tragic substitute for the bloodred sun and open air breathed by McCarthy's other exiles . . . . Indeed, its most chilling image is of a drug lord's office furniture in a Houston skyscraper (exotic in McCarthydom as a horse would be in a novel by Nicholson Baker), a breaking of prose to death: "The desk was of polished stainless steel and walnut and there wasn't anything on it. Not a picture or a piece of paper. Nothing."

There are still passages of luminous nature writing here, albeit more constrained than in *All the Pretty Horses* and other descriptions of unspoiled landscape in the 1950's West. Though much of the chase takes place in the open air, it is clear that the landscape and the society have changed dramatically from decades past, and not for the better.

The job of embodying the contrast between those different eras falls to the novel's third main character and its most problematic one: an aging Texas sheriff named Ed Tom Bell, who is in desperate pursuit of both Llewelyn Moss and Anton Chigurh as the trail of the killer's victims grows ever bloodier.

Bell is a man haunted—by his combat experiences during World War II and by what he sees as a categorically new breed of conscienceless criminal (represented by Chigurh) who threatens justice and civil order to a degree that old-fashioned law officers such as himself cannot match.

No Country for Old Men is by far the most cinematically constructed of McCarthy's novels, and *Variety* reports that directors Joel and Ethan Coen—best known for such darkly humorous epics as *Fargo* (1996) and *O Brother, Where Art Thou?* (2000)—have signed to create the film version for a 2007 release. The story's blistering pace is interrupted only by italicized excerpts of Sheriff Bell's interior monologues on such topics as his wartime service, his beloved wife, his profession, and what he considers a dispiritingly changed America.

This pairing works better in some sections of the book than others. Though Bell is highly believable and an appealing human being, many of his observations seem too mundane to serve as an appropriately weighted dramatic counterpoint to the careening nihilism of Chigurh's world. Of the initial popular reviewers who expressed mixed feelings about the novel's success, nearly all mentioned the voice of Sheriff Bell as a likely weak link.

With a talent as distinctive and multifaceted as Cormac McCarthy's, even novels that may at times seem technically flawed are nonetheless gifts to American literature and reading experiences that are not to be missed.

Carroll Dale Short

Review Sources

America 193, no. 13 (October 31, 2005): 26-27.
Booklist 101, no. 18 (May 15, 2005): 1614.
Kirkus Reviews 73, no. 9 (May 1, 2005): 500.
Library Journal 130, no. 11 (June 15, 2005): 59.
The Nation 281, no. 7 (September 12, 2005): 38-41.
The New Leader 88, no. 4 (July/August, 2005): 31-32.
New Statesman 134 (November 14, 2005): 54-55.
The New York Review of Books 52, no. 16 (October 20, 2005): 41-44.
The New York Times 154 (July 18, 2005): E1-E4.
The New York Times Book Review 154 (July 24, 2005): 9.
The New Yorker 81, no. 21 (July 25, 2005): 88-93.
Time 166, no. 3 (July 18, 2005): 73.

THE NOODLE MAKER

Author: Ma Jian (1953-   )
First published: Lamianzhe, 1991, in Hong Kong, People's Republic of China
Translated from the Chinese by Flora Drew
Publisher: Farrar, Straus and Giroux (New York). 181 pp. $21.00
Type of work: Novel
Time: 1990
Locale: An unnamed city on the coast of China, modeled after Qingdao

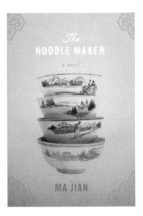

Through his protagonist's observations of city life, Ma offers a view of everyday absurdities in China during the year following the bloody suppression of demonstrators at Tiananmen Square

Principal characters:
>SHENG, a professional writer charged to write a communist propaganda novel
>VLAZERIM, a professional blood donor, friend of Sheng
>THE ENTREPRENEUR, a businessman who runs a private crematorium
>SU YUN, an actress who stages her own suicide
>OLD HEP, an editor of a literary magazine, punished by his wife for acquiring mistresses
>THE STREET WRITER, a writer who pens love letters for other men
>THE WOMAN WITH BEAUTIFUL BREASTS, an employee driven to despair by jealous coworkers
>THE PAINTER, Su Yun's boyfriend
>THE SURVIVOR, the painter's talking three-legged dog

The Noodle Maker, the second of Ma Jian's novels translated into English, offers an unflinching, sometimes humorous look at the trials and tribulations of the denizens of an unnamed coastal city in China in 1990. The novel, chapters of which have appeared in *The New Yorker,* opens as a professional writer, Comrade Sheng, is charged to write a short communist propaganda novel. He is told his piece should introduce a hero resembling Lei Feng, an idealized communist martyr of the 1960's. Sheng's hero should be drawn from the people around him and should sacrifice himself for a comrade at the end of the novel.

To his friend, a professional blood donor who visits him once a week to share the good food and drink that his profession allows him to buy, writer Sheng complains that he only knows people whose lives would never be allowed to serve as propaganda models. In the following chapters, such lives that are narrated, a literary sleight of hand that allows Ma to portray the suffering, disillusionment, and coping measures

~

*Ma Jian, who writes in Chinese,
published his first novel in Hong
Kong in 1986 and has continued to
write in London since 1987. His
partner Flora Drew translated his
novel* Red Dust *(2001) while Ma
wrote it; it won the prestigious
Thomas Cook Travel Book Award in
2002. Ma Jian's translated short
stories,* Stick Out Your Tongue, *was
published in 2006.*

~

of urban Chinese people living in the immediate aftermath of the post-Tiananmen Square government crackdown of 1989. At the end, in a moment of postmodern self-reflection, Sheng feels that the human models for his characters are strings of dough, pulled into white threads by an invisible noodle maker in his head.

The first of Sheng's acquaintances and neighbors whose life is presented is the entrepreneur. By buying a used kiln from an art school and setting up his own crematorium in the suburbs, he is taking advantage of the Open Door Policy often alluded to by the characters of *The Noodle Maker*. After the death of Mao Zedong in 1976, his successor Deng Xiaoping ended the dramatic excesses of the Cultural Revolution and began to promote a policy of limited economic reform. However, political power remains in the ironclad hands of the Communist Party, which still seeks to control people's private lives. In turn, Ma's characters, warped by their government's policies, use the party as a tool to enact revenge born of jealousy and pettiness, as they inform on their enemies. This creates a situation, the novel insists, in which eyes that look "gentle and kind" have all but disappeared in China, together with "all similar expressions of pity, compassion and respect." Thus, the entrepreneur can only experience the love of his old mother when he is about to cremate her. Still alive, she prefers to be reduced to a heap of shiny white bones rather than continue to suffer the squalid pettiness that permeates her life, even as her son achieves limited economic success.

Like all characters in *The Noodle Maker*, actress Su Yun leads a life inevitably tied to politics. At sixteen, she was a star in the operas of the Cultural Revolution, the only mass entertainment allowed by Mao's wife Jiang Qing in those years. When politics changed and people no longer desired asexual revolutionary figures, Su Yun engaged in love affairs but only got hurt in the process. After having brief affairs with Sheng and the blood donor, she truly fell in love with a painter. He then started to neglect her when he acquired a three-legged dog. Symbolic of the difficulties of sharing love after the very idea of romance had been outlawed for more than a decade, Su Yun demonstrates the fate of a person unprepared to experience sexuality.

In despair over her boyfriend's neglect, Su Yun writes a play about their relationship, which Ma embeds in *The Noodle Maker*'s text, successfully mixing genres and bringing alive the literary activities of his own characters in best postmodernist fashion. Su Yun decides to commit suicide by allowing a tiger to maul her to death in the avant-garde Open Door Club at 3 A.M. on June 4, 1990. Not coincidentally, this is the exact date of the first anniversary of the Tiananmen Square massacre, when government tanks literally crushed the students demonstrating for democracy in that Beijing square. Not alluding directly to that event, *The Noodle Maker* does not point out the significance of this date; readers must determine it for themselves.

As in the novels of Ma's fellow exiled Chinese writer Ha Jin, such as *War Trash* (2004), the following chapters of *The Noodle Maker* show the harshness of life under communism that drives characters to use the party's policies for personal gain and to try to destroy their enemies or competitors. Critics have likened Ma's writing to that of Chinese Nobel Prize laureate Gao Xingjian. Ma's novel *Red Dust* (2001), has been often compared to Gao's *Ling Shan* (1990; *Soul Mountain*, 2000). Yet many of the characters of *The Noodle Maker* have a personal edge that is closer to the bitter, brutalized characters of Ha Jin's literary universe than that of the somewhat gentler Gao Xingjian.

Old Hep, for instance, misuses his position as editor of the city's literary magazine to extract sexual favors from women poets vying for a place to publish their work. Old Hep's story reveals a world of unceasing combat and rivalry that naturally extends to the family. His wife adored and married him for his literary fame, won with propagandistic pieces. When she gains her own success, she surpasses him sexually as well as literarily. Taking advantage of the post-Mao relaxation of sexual prudery, she applies red polish to her fingernails. Her husband recoils from her "blood-stained hands!", and she calls him an idiot. At home, Old Hep is reduced to the position of domestic servant, until he begins to exploit his official position. After brutally rejecting and kicking a female admirer, the young woman contacts Old Hep's wife. In turn, she viciously kicks Old Hep and uses the party authorities to have her husband denounced and punished. She also uses love letters written to him in her own fiction. Sheng reveals that she slept with him once to gain material for her writing.

Even though most of the chapters of *The Noodle Maker* could stand alone as short stories, toward the end of his novel Ma brings together the characters in an interesting fashion. The cremated mother of the entrepreneur reappears as a ghost in the story of a street writer who now inhabits her old lean-to shack, introducing an air of the supernatural that is used for satirical intent. As the street writer pines for one of the young women to whom he has written love letters, as well as a final note of rejection in the pay of an illiterate suitor (ironically continuing a profession with roots in imperial and prerevolutionary China), the ghost appears looking for a piece of cloth she overlooked when alive. She scolds the man for writing "obscene" love letters. Finally the mother of Su Yun appears and sleeps with him, bemoaning the suicide of her daughter. Earlier, the mother had asked that he write Su Yun a letter to warn her of love. In their intercourse, *The Noodle Maker* depicts much of the despair felt by most of its characters, who live in a world devoid of redemption.

The social ostracism that haunts a young woman who suffers from the jealousy of her female colleagues is indicative of the bitter competitiveness in a brutalized society. Because her coworkers are unwilling to believe that the woman's beautiful breasts are natural, caused neither by medicine or male fondling, they taunt her to the brink of insanity. People's viciousness toward each other is revealed with unflinching clarity in this episode. The story of a man who plans to abandon his mentally handicapped daughter so that he and his wife can be allowed another pregnancy permit under China's one-child policy, but refuses in the end because he loves her too much, is a rare example of human kindness in *The Noodle Maker*.

The last chapter of the novel ties together many strands of the narrative in an often surprising fashion. It is here that Ma introduces the surreal with the character of the survivor, a speaking three-legged dog. Surrealism has always been frowned upon in Communist China, and only very few writers have dared writing in this vein, such as novelist Can Xue, whose *Canglao de fuyun* (1986; *Old Floating Cloud*, 1991) is a surreal tour de force. In *The Noodle Maker*, the dog is given a home by the painter, Su Yun's neglectful boyfriend. Hidden on the terrace of his apartment block, where pets are illegal, the dog reveals to the painter that he bears the reincarnated soul of one of the corpses burnt in the entrepreneur's crematorium.

Ma uses the speaking dog as a device through which *The Noodle Maker* voices much veiled criticism of post-1989 China. Reflecting on the scope of the political changes that factional fighting within the Communist Party can force on the people, the dog says that if dogs were to run the town, assimilation for humans would be easy: "You will simply have to change your motto from 'Serve the People' to 'Serve the Dogs.'"

After the painter and the dog witness a brutal gang rape in the streets below the terrace, the authorities enforce an eerie calm upon the city, a clear allusion to the brutal tranquility following the deaths at Tiananmen Square. Like the students who were crushed by the tanks of the People's Liberation Army, the dog suggests that the rape was started by the girl's boyfriend. Once authorities intervene, life appears normal, but violent "accidents" continue. As a consequence of the crackdown, the illegally housed dog is destroyed while the painter is at a conference. When its stuffed pelt is admired in Beijing it is given a posthumous medal, in another subversive allusion to the absurdities and brutalities of life under communism. When the narrative returns a final time to the professional writer and the blood donor, they exchange roles, with the donor getting ready to write the novel the writer could not bring himself to start.

In *The Noodle Maker*, Ma has produced an intricate and haunting work that depicts life in a period of Chinese history when the great horrors of the Cultural Revolution were replaced by a more mundane everyday despair. Many of the characters consider themselves lost victims of the previous upheavals that have left them without direction, hope, or sense of belonging. As they struggle in Deng Xiaoping's China of the Open Door Policy, where the limits of freedom were drastically curtailed again in 1989, Ma's characters are close to succumbing to either despair or a feral competitiveness and bitter jealousy.

Drew has done a superb job making accessible in English this earlier novel of Ma Jian that chronologically follows his autobiography *Red Dust*. *Stick Out Your Tongue*, translations by Drew of Ma's short stories, was published in 2006. It will be rewarding to follow the author as he continues to tackle the intricacies of life in a China emerging from decades of Communist Party control over even the most private aspects of life.

R. C. Lutz

Review Sources

Booklist 101, nos. 9/10 (January 1-15, 2005): 819.
Kirkus Reviews 72, no. 19 (October 1, 2004): 932-933.
London Review of Books 26, no. 13 (July 8, 2004): 12-13.
The New Leader 88, no. 1 (January/February, 2005): 31-32.
The New York Times Book Review 154 (March 27, 2005): 23.
Publishers Weekly 251, no. 47 (November 22, 2004): 37.
The Times Literary Supplement, May 7, 2004, p. 22.

OGDEN NASH
The Life and Work of America's Laureate of Light Verse

Author: Douglas M. Parker (1935-   )
Foreward by Dana Gioia
Publisher: Ivan R. Dee (Chicago). Illustrated. 316 pp.
    $27.50
Type of work: Literary biography
Time: 1902-1971
Locale: Rye, New York; New York City; Baltimore; and
    Hollywood

Drawing on Nash's papers as well as interviews with his family and friends, Parker has written a fast-paced, readable biography of the man he calls "America's laureate of light verse"

Principal personages:
OGDEN NASH, a poet
EDMUND NASH, his father, a successful businessman
FRANCES LEONARD NASH, his wife
LINELL NASH, his elder daughter, writer and illustrator
ISABEL NASH, his younger daughter, writer
SID J. PERELMAN, a humorist
HAROLD ROSS, the founding editor of *The New Yorker*
ROGER ANGELL, Nash's editor at *The New Yorker*
KURT WEILL, a composer

Frederick Ogden Nash was born in Rye, New York, on August 19, 1902. His father, Edmund, was such a successful businessman in the first years of the twentieth century that the New York, New Haven, and Hartford commuter train made a special stop for him at the edge of his fifty-acre estate, Ramaqua, in Rye, where Ogden grew up. Though the family would experience some financial difficulties in the 1910's, Nash throughout his life remained part of the genteel tradition in both his life and his writing. Indeed, Parker's book suggests that Nash's high living would impel some of his not-so-high writing throughout his life.

Nash's fondness for light verse appeared early and was encouraged by his family. When he was ten, he was allowed to read a poem at his sister Gwen's wedding. The piece began, "Beautiful spring at last is here!/ And has taken my sister, I sadly fear," and ends, "the mother of the playful cat/ Is always anxious on her behalf." Nash also proved a good student; when he graduated from St. George's School in Newport, Rhode Island, he received the Binney Prize, the institution's highest academic award, and matriculated at Harvard University. After a year of college and another of teaching at his old high school, he moved to New York, like Nick Carraway in F. Scott Fitzgerald's *The Great Gatsby* (1925), to sell bonds.

The world of finance was not his ideal milieu. In eighteen months he sold one bond (to his godmother). He then turned to writing streetcar advertisements for the Barron G. Collier firm, which a few years earlier had employed another Ivy League drop-out, Fitzgerald. Nash was rooming with Joe Alger; together they wrote a children's book, *The Cricket of Carador*, which Doubleday, Page & Company published in 1925.

An alumnus of Cornell University and Cornell Law School, Douglas M. Parker practiced law in New York and Washington, D.C. He also served in the Office of Counsel to the President and in the Department of Housing and Urban Development. Now retired, he lives on Cape Cod.

The most important consequence of this success was that it landed Nash a job with Doubleday, first in advertising, then in detective fiction, and finally as a literary editor. In this capacity he saw a lot of bad poetry but also recognized that there was a market for humorous verse. Parker observes that one book Nash saw at Doubleday was Roland Young's *Not for Children* (1930), which contained short poems about animals, and Parker links Young's verses to Nash's similar work, such as "The Turtle," which appeared in Nash's first volume of poetry, *Hard Lines* (1931):

> The turtle lives twixt plated decks
> That practically conceal its sex.
> I think it clever of the turtle
> In such a fix to be so fertile.

One of the delights of Parker's book is its reprinting of many of Nash's pleasure-giving lines.

While Nash was working at Doubleday, his boss, Dan Longwell, introduced him to the prolific Christopher Morley, a leading man of letters in the early twentieth century. Morley owned two theaters in Hoboken, New Jersey, and encouraged Nash to write for the stage. Nash's efforts in this field failed, as did his attempt to write for radio. However, on December 31, 1929, Nash received a check for twenty-two dollars from *The New Yorker* for "Invocation," which appeared in the January 11, 1931 issue. Nash would continue to publish with *The New Yorker* for the following forty years; his last poem for the magazine, the 353d of his that appeared in its pages, was printed posthumously on May 29, 1971.

"Invocation" made fun of Senator Reed Smoot of Utah (best known for his ill-conceived tariff legislation) for a bill objecting to the importation of salacious literature. Nash's poems also satirize the Daughters of the American Revolution, prudish religious figures, gossip columnist Walter Winchell, and politicians of all stripes. Most of Nash's work, however, deals with the slings and arrows of daily life, and his commentary is genial rather than strident.

Harold Ross, legendary editor of *The New Yorker*, admired Nash's verse, as did the magazine's literary editor Katherine White; both repeatedly asked Nash for more poems. When Ross's managing editor Ralph Ingersoll left for *Fortune*, Ross offered the post to Nash. Initially reluctant, Nash accepted the job on December 3, 1930. Parker demonstrates that Nash was right to be hesitant: He lasted at the job three months, though he and Ross had an amicable separation that did not diminish the latter's admiration for Nash's work.

Nash returned to book editing with Farrar and Rinehart, but as the Depression worsened, so did Nash's salary. By the spring of 1933 he was earning only twenty-five dollars a week from his job. Meanwhile, his poetry was gaining a large audience. In 1933 *Redbook*, the *New American*, and the *Saturday Evening Post* all gave him contracts guaranteeing a substantial income, and *The New Yorker* raised his fee to two dollars a line. Nash now was able to quit his editorial post and devote himself full time to his writing.

He moved from New York to Baltimore, the hometown of Frances Leonard, whom he had married on June 6, 1931. Like the Nashes, the Leonards were well-off and gave a house to the couple, soon to be a foursome with the births of two daughters, Linell and Isabel. Though Parker denies that the names were chosen with rhyming in mind, one cannot but wonder. The girls provided matter for verse, such as Nash's comment, "Isabel's chiffle/ In spite of her sniffle." Demonstrating both his humor and his understanding of how his daughters might react negatively to appearing in his poetry, Nash wrote in "My Daddy,"

> I have a funny daddy
> who goes in and out with me,
> And everything that baby does,
> My daddy's sure to see
> And everything that baby says,
>
> My daddy's sure to tell.
> You must have read my daddy's verse,
> I hope he fries in hell.

In fact, his daughters responded good-naturedly to his use of their words and deeds.

In 1935 Nash published 125 poems in magazines and was doing well financially, but the following year he listened to the siren song of Hollywood when Metro-Goldwyn-Mayer's Irving Thalberg beckoned. Despite the Depression, Hollywood had money: In the 1930's Louis B. Mayer was earning more than any other man in America. A screenwriter could earn five thousand dollars a week. No wonder, then, that William Faulkner, Fitzgerald, Thornton Wilder, John O'Hara, Aldous Huxley, J. B. Priestley, and P. G. Wodehouse all migrated to Southern California. While the money was good, the work was frustrating.

Nash's Hollywood experience matched that of almost all other authors who went there. His work for the studios was rewritten by others or was not produced. In his spare time he wrote little. In 1937-1938, Parker writes, Nash wrote two new poems. Nash returned east at the end of 1938. In the following two years he published fifty poems in magazines, and in 1941 he published forty-two. Two collections of his verse also appeared in these years, *The Face Is Familiar* (1940) and *Good Intentions* (1942).

During World War II Nash took up selling bonds. He fared better than he had in the 1920's: Parker quotes Julian Street's crediting Nash with $170 million in sales. Nash also enjoyed his one great theatrical triumph at this time. In Hollywood, Nash had become friendly with fellow humorist and *New Yorker* contributor Sid J. Perelman. Together they wrote *One Touch of Venus* (1943), with music by Kurt Weill. Starring Mary Martin, the show enjoyed 567 performances on Broadway. Nash's subsequent theatrical efforts failed for various reasons. *Two's Company* (1952) came closest to succeeding but had to close after eighty-nine performances on Broadway when its star, Bette Davis, became too ill to continue with the show.

Even though Nash's royalties from 1938 to 1961 totaled some $200,000, and by the late 1950's *The New Yorker* was paying him $400 for a twenty-line poem, Parker points out that Nash was always looking for new ways to make money. In the 1950's he appeared regularly on the television show *Masquerade Party*, which earned him a respectable $350 and then $450 a week. He endured grueling lecture tours, and for a decade starting in 1957 Nash wrote for Hallmark Cards. In that year he also published his first book for children since 1925, *The Christmas That Almost Wasn't*, illustrated by his daughter Linell, who also provided the pictures for Nash's *Custard the Dragon* (1959) and *Custard the Dragon and the Wicked Knight* (1961). Both Linell and Isabel went on to write children's books of their own, and Nash created an additional dozen books for young readers. In 1965 he sold his papers to the Harry Ransom Humanities Research Center at the University of Texas for ten thousand dollars.

Parker quotes Clifton Fadiman's 1955 comment that Nash was "the laureate of the age of friction." Nash's poems certainly addressed the frictions of daily life, such as consumerism, aging, and parenthood. In the late 1950's and the 1960's, however, he seemed out of touch with the changing literary and social worlds. His appearances in *The New Yorker* declined, while rejections from the magazine increased. Parker counts seventeen poems sold to that publication in 1956, ten in 1957, and another ten in 1959. Some associated with the magazine blamed the poetry editor Howard Moss, who had joined *The New Yorker* in 1950, for the large number of rejection notices Nash was receiving from 43d Street, though Moss was not Nash's editor. Nash usually was able to place his work somewhere, including *Playboy*, an anomalous choice for someone generally unsympathetic to the sexual revolution of the 1960's.

In his foreword, poet Dana Gioia likens Nash to Vachel Lindsay, Carl Sandburg, and Archibald MacLeish, all of whom attracted a wide readership but lacked the critical prestige of their contemporaries T. S. Eliot and Wallace Stevens. This analogy might be extended to suggest that Nash, Lindsay, Sandburg, and MacLeish are, *pace* Fadiman, not poets of an age of friction but rather reflect the attitudes of a more innocent and cheerful time. To steal one of Nash's rhymes, he is nearly always chiffle, and life's problems rarely elicit from him more than a sniffle. He is charming but lacks profundity. The same might be said of Parker's biography.

Joseph Rosenblum

Review Sources

Booklist 101, no. 15 (April 1, 2005): 1336-1337.
The Christian Science Monitor, April 26, 2005, p. 15.
Kirkus Reviews 73, no. 2 (January 15, 2005): 108.
The New York Times Book Review 154 (June 5, 2005): 26.
Publishers Weekly 252, no. 7 (February 14, 2005): 65.
The Times Literary Supplement, November 4, 2005, p. 7.
The Washington Post Book World, May 8, 2005, p. 2.

THE OLD BALL GAME
How John McGraw, Christy Mathewson, and the New York Giants Created Modern Baseball

Author: Frank Deford (1938-   )
Publisher: Atlantic Monthly Press (New York). Illus-
trated. 241 pp. $24.00
Type of work: Biography and history
Time: 1891-1934
Locale: Various major league baseball cities, especially
New York

Two baseball luminaries from sharply contrasting back-
grounds forge a close personal relationship while making
the New York Giants an early twentieth century success

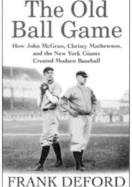

Principal personages:
JOHN MCGRAW, the manager of the New
York Giants, 1902-1932
CHRISTOPHER MATHEWSON, the star pitcher
for the New York Giants, 1900-1916
BLANCHE SINDALL MCGRAW, the manager's second wife
JANE STOUGHTON MATHEWSON, the pitcher's wife

Both of Frank Deford's fabled subjects in *The Old Ball Game* have attracted previous biographers, but what particularly interests Deford is the interplay between two
men totally different in background, temperament, and appearance. John McGraw,
born in the upstate New York village of Truxton, was the eldest child of an Irish immigrant father and a mother who died when John was eleven. Not long afterward, the
boy, beaten by a father unable to cope with the demands of five young children, ran
away from home and lodged in a local hotel where he earned his keep by doing
chores. Small of stature but rough, aggressive, and brimming with athletic talent, he
was playing major league baseball at the age of nineteen.

Christy Mathewson emerged from a small Pennsylvania town which Deford describes as bucolic. He grew up in a happy family, earned excellent grades in school,
behaved admirably, and gave his mother some reason to hope that he would enter the
Baptist ministry. By the time he entered Bucknell College in 1898 he was tall, handsome, and accomplished. He excelled in analytic chemistry, starred in baseball, football, and basketball, and was elected president of his class. As a church elder he could
not tell a lie. A story circulated that he once slid into home plate in a cloud of dust so
thick that the umpire could not make a call. "He got me," Mathewson volunteered,
whereupon the umpire called him out. He resembled McGraw in one important way:
He exuded talent for playing baseball.

Fate brought the two men together in 1902 when McGraw, after a decade of starring as third baseman for the Baltimore Orioles, was named manager of a team that

*Frank Deford is a senior
contributing writer at* Sports
Illustrated *who has been chosen
Sportswriter of the Year six times
by his fellow sportswriters. He
has also been similarly honored
by the* American Journalism
Review. *In addition, he reports
on sports for both National
Public Radio (NPR) and HBO.*

had been something of a major league joke up to that time: the New York Giants. Mathewson, then in his second full season with the Giants, won fourteen games and lost seventeen for his new manager but proved his mettle by pitching eight shutouts. For the next dozen years, in perhaps the most remarkable sustained stretch of pitching success in major league history, he would average twenty-seven wins a season. The Giants, still a doormat in McGraw's initial season at the helm, thereupon proceeded to win five pennants and finish second five times in the following twelve years. Only World Series championships tended to elude the team of Matty and Muggsy—the year 1905, when Mathewson pitched three shutouts over Connie Mack's Philadelphia Athletics, being the lone exception.

Mutual success on the diamond was not the only factor uniting the rowdy manager and the upright Christian pitcher. In a time of a social gulf between the few college-educated baseball players and the majority who did not complete high school, McGraw and Mathewson were friends. In 1903 the two men and their wives amicably shared a New York apartment. Blanche McGraw noted that she and Jane Mathewson performed wifely duties together while the two men spent their spare time talking baseball. McGraw, an old third baseman, was fascinated by the art of pitching—an art that Mathewson had mastered at a young age. Also, unlike many of the uneducated players, who tended to resent "college boys," McGraw respected academic attainments. In the 1890's, while playing for Baltimore, he had spent four winters coaching the baseball team at Allegany (the future St. Bonaventure) College, and in return was allowed to enroll in English, history, and mathematics courses. Although he never attained a degree—for that matter, neither did Mathewson—McGraw was proud of his own limited college experience. The age difference between the two men, only seven years, cast McGraw into a role somewhat like that of a big brother. Surviving their husbands by many years, their wives continued their friendship.

Deford deplores the fact that great athletes are so often forgotten or remembered imperfectly for single, often uncharacteristic, incidents. Two of McGraw's players, both named Fred and both ill-fated participants in games that Mathewson pitched, constitute two of baseball's most famous examples. Fred Merkle's name has become indelibly associated with the word "boner," for in a late-season game between the Giants and the Chicago Cubs as the two teams battled for the National League pennant in 1908, this fine all-around player neglected to do a simple thing. As a runner on first base with two outs, and the apparent winning run having scored ahead of him, he neglected to touch second base. With the Giant fans already celebrating the expected victory, an alert Cub called for the ball and stepped on second. The umpire called Merkle out, negating the run. By this time most of the players had left the field, jubilant Giant fans swarmed over it, and the game was declared a tie. Needless to say, when this pennant-deciding game was replayed, the Giants lost—all allegedly because of Merkle's boner.

Another single word sums up Fred Snodgrass: muff. Four years later Fred Snodgrass dropped an easy fly ball in the center field in the seventh and deciding game of the World Series, leading to a Boston Red Sox rally that carried them to victory over the Giants. The fact that the same Snodgrass made a spectacular catch of a ball hit by the very next batter was easily forgotten. Mathewson, the losing pitcher, pointed out that without Snodgrass's contributions, the team probably would not have been in the World Series at all. McGraw, displaying an aspect of his personality greatly overshadowed by his notorious truculence, generously rewarded each of these mortified players with raises after their unhappy experiences.

Far from whitewashing McGraw, however, Deford presents him as a complex man who unfortunately has been remembered mainly for his less attractive character traits. Mathewson offers the writer a different sort of problem. In his time a charismatic figure idolized by fans and eagerly sought after by commercial interests, Mathewson projected a squeaky-clean image and a relatively colorless personality that has made him seem, to use Deford's term, passé. Baseball fans in general know that he was a Hall of Fame righthander, that he spent his career almost entirely with the Giants— but not much else. To enlarge and thus nourish the memory of this odd couple of a century ago, the author re-creates their era both on and off the playing field. From reading *The Old Ball Game* it is possible to acquire such tidbits as the reason for the Giants' home field being called the Polo Grounds although polo was never played there. The author's local color branches out: Readers are informed that the Waldorf Astoria hotel had 765 baths, that the first New Year's ball descended in Times Square in 1908, and that New York of that day had twenty-five thousand prostitutes.

Deford's style is eclectic, his diction ranging from rarefied to demotic. In virtually the same breath he can refer to German Americans' *gemütlichkeit* and their inclination to "guzzle suds." He employs occasional archaisms such as "plighting their troth" and that once heavy-duty adjective of enthusiasm, *swell* (Mathewson's parents had "a swell house"); on the other hand, he can press adjectives into service as nouns ("a sweet, almost cherubic handsome") in the casual manner. He is exceedingly fond of the redundant adverb "thusly." Overall, the informal Deford predominates in *The Old Ball Game.*

The author injects some interesting comments on nicknames. McGraw acquired two, both well known and both appropriate. "Muggsy" and "the Little Napoleon" disclose how others saw him; his dislike of the former and approval of the latter suggest how he saw himself. The origin of Mathewson's nickname "Big Six" is more mysterious. Deford admits his inability to decide among several explanations. On the topic of nicknames, Deford overstates his point about their decline in baseball. He is probably correct in attributing the change to television's "utter visualization of sport at the expense of imagination," but to write that "Willie Mays and Pete Rose were essentially the last baseball superstars with original sobriquets" is to ignore or forget more recent names such as Roger Clemens, "the Rocket," and Randy Johnson, "the Big Unit," a nickname thoroughly in the tradition of "Big Six" for Mathewson and "the Big Train" for Walter Johnson.

The claim made in Deford's subtitle—that McGraw and Mathewson "created modern baseball"—is another overstatement. McGraw's boast that he and Wee Willie Keeler "revolutionized" baseball by such tactics as the hit-and-run play to move base runners along perhaps has some validity, but it was a revolution cut short by the feats and influence of Babe Ruth beginning in 1920. In fact, Deford admits in the twenty-second of his twenty-four chapters what is axiomatic among baseball buffs: that Ruth, by popularizing the home run, deserves the most credit for establishing the modern game. The sacrifice, the hit-and-run, and "hitting them where they ain't" are still part of the game, but offense today is more a matter of hitting them where the fans are—those sitting between the two foul lines.

The author is on safer ground in maintaining that Mathewson changed the game by inspiring more educated men to seek careers in professional baseball. In making it more difficult for parents to convince their athletic sons that baseball was a haven of disreputable characters, Mathewson contributed to an obvious social change in the game by proving that "college boys" could fit in. It helped, of course, that he was a superlative pitcher, for what teammate could deny the contributions of a man, no matter how educated, who could win two thirds of the games he pitched?

If McGraw and Mathewson did not "create" modern baseball, their exploits are a forceful reminder that the New York team that dominated baseball in the first quarter of the twentieth century, with ten pennants in the twenty-one-year span between 1904 and 1924, was not the Yankees but the Giants. This is a fact easily lost sight of by those who remember chiefly later editions of the Giants that could manage only two pennants in their last twenty years in the Polo Grounds before the franchise was whisked across the continent to San Francisco.

Deford's lively book also reminds one of how precarious and fleeting even great athletic careers can be. Mathewson turned thirty-four in the summer of his last great season. Two years later he was finished. Nine years after that he died. With reconstructive surgery, pitching careers can last much longer today. Given present-day medical advances, people's lives can last much longer. Although Mathewson succumbed to tuberculosis, his condition was probably exacerbated by poison gas that he ingested in World War I—not in combat but as a concomitant of his duty as a training officer. McGraw lived until the age of sixty, but his playing career, except for a few years of part-time duty, ended while he was still in his twenties. Injuries and an immoderate lifestyle rendered him an "old thirty," Deford observes. His tenure as a manager, thirty-two years, all but the first two-and-a-half with the Giants, was a long one by any standard, but there were no pennants after 1924. By that time the Yankees under Miller Huggins, not McGraw's Giants, were the toast of Gotham.

Robert P. Ellis

Review Sources

Booklist 101, no. 12 (February 15, 2005): 1050.
Kirkus Reviews 73, no. 2 (January 15, 2005): 97-98.
Library Journal 130, no. 2 (February 1, 2005): 88-90.
The New York Times Book Review 154 (May 1, 2005): 13.

ON BEAUTY

Author: Zadie Smith (1975-   )
Publisher: Penguin Press (New York). 446 pp. $26.00
Type of work: Novel
Time: The first decade of the twenty-first century
Locale: London and a suburb of Boston

In this Booker Prize finalist, a middle-aged liberal white professor and his mixed-race family interact with a conservative black public intellectual and his family in London and on the campus of an American liberal arts college

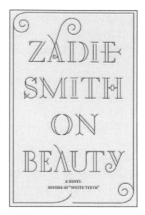

Principal characters:

> HOWARD BELSEY, a white, fifty-six-year-old professor of art history at Wellington College in Massachusetts
> KIKI SIMMONDS BELSEY, his African American wife
> JEROME BELSEY, their eldest son, a sophomore at Brown University
> ZORA BELSEY, their daughter, starting college at Wellington
> LEVI BELSEY, their youngest son, attending high school
> SIR MONTY KIPPS, a black visiting professor at Wellington College
> CARLENE KIPPS, his wife, originally from the Caribbean region
> MICHAEL KIPPS, their son, a yuppie businessman
> VICTORIA ("VEE") KIPPS, their eighteen-year-old daughter
> CLAIRE MALCOLM, poet and creative writing professor at Wellington
> CARL, a young African American from the ghetto, attractive to Zora Belsey
> CHOUCHOU, a poor Haitian immigrant to whom Levi Belsey is drawn

The British novelist Zadie Smith's debut novel, *White Teeth* (2000), appeared when its author was twenty-five years old; she was favorably compared to the likes of Salman Rushdie and Charles Dickens. The book became a best seller, a prizewinner, and a television adaptation aired on the Public Broadcasting Service (PBS). *White Teeth*, which was written during Smith's final student year at Cambridge University, was a boisterous, multigenerational novel set in a north London multiracial neighborhood of blacks, Asians, and whites much like the Willesden, where Smith grew up as the daughter of a black Jamaican mother and a white English father. Smith's second novel, *The Autograph Man* (2002), did not equal the expectations set by its predecessor; it concentrated on a smaller cast of characters, focused on a young autograph dealer, and explored the effects of fame as its action shuttled between suburban England and New York City.

On Beauty, Smith's third novel, was short-listed for Britain's coveted Man Booker Prize and may be poised to surpass the success of *White Teeth*—the British company

FilmFour purchased the motion-picture rights. As in *The Autograph Man*, the action of *On Beauty* also spans the Atlantic Ocean, this time between London and suburban Boston, with the preponderant share of its events occurring in the United States. Its American setting is the fictitious college town of Wellington, an academic environment that owes much to Smith's year as a fellow at Radcliffe/ Harvard (2002-2003). The title of the novel also acknowledges the influence of the distinguished Harvard professor Elaine Scarry, whose book *On Beauty and Being Just* (1999) argues that over the preceding two decades, aesthetics (beauty) has lost too much ground to political correctness (being just)— which is not to say that Scarry is an ivy-cloistered aesthete, for her publications have included speculations on electromagnetic interference (EMI) as a cause of air crashes and on the currently vexed topic of torture in her work *The Body in Pain* (1985).

Zadie Smith was born in London and has made her home there. Her best-selling debut novel, White Teeth *(2000), won the* Whitbread First Novel Award *and was a finalist for the* National Book Critics Circle Award. *Her second novel,* Autograph Man, *was published in 2002. She is a graduate of Cambridge University and has been a fellow at Radcliffe/ Harvard.*

Another influence on Smith can be seen in the book's opening narrative, its ensemble of characters, its concatenation of events, and its spirit of liberal humanism—the influence of E. M. Forster. In fact, Smith has, in the most honorific postmodern sense and in a wittily inventive fashion, appropriated Forster's *Howards End* (1910), thereby providing an intriguing dialogic reading experience for those familiar with Forster. The matter of *On Beauty*, however, is substantively Smith's. Primarily, her novel raises very American issues about the culture war between liberals and conservatives, about class and race, and about what women purpose with their lives.

Just as *Howards End* begins with letters followed by anger, so does *On Beauty* commence with a flurry of e-mails followed by pique. The e-mails reveal that two young people have experienced infatuation to the point of an engagement, whereupon an alarmed family elder is dispatched to end the undesirable match. The e-mails do demonstrate the advances that humanity has made in the technology of communication, but the pique demonstrates the persistence of humanity's penchant for misunderstanding, miscommunication, and taking offence.

The two young people are from families of opposed sociopolitical beliefs. The Belseys are a suburban, mixed-race American family of liberal persuasion (like Forster's Schlegels). The Kippses are a knighted, distinguished black family of Caribbean origins settled in London and of decidedly conservative views (like Forster's Wilcoxes). Howard Belsey, his clan's fifty-six-year-old paterfamilias, is a professor of art history who is struggling to complete a book deconstructing Rembrandt. Sir Monty Kipps is a distinguished intellectual who has completed a best-selling book praising Rembrandt's genius. The two men have so far been cordial enemies.

Complications arise when Jerome, the virginal collegiate Belsey son, becomes a Christian (against his atheist father's objections), takes a summer job in London as Kipps's intern, and becomes briefly engaged to Victoria, the Kipps's teenage daughter. Howard flies to London to break up the match which, unknown to him, has already spontaneously broken up, and the seriocomic scenes of misunderstanding and miscommunication further deepen the ill will between the patresfamilias.

After Howard has had a few months to recover from his embarrassment, the battle between him and Kipps is again joined when Kipps arrives at Wellington College, Howard's university, and proposes a course of lectures titled "Taking the Liberal out of the Liberal Arts." Howard wants to ban or at least vet these lectures because Kipps's published record of homophobic pronouncements, anti-equal-opportunity stances, and antifeminist positions are tantamount, in Howard's view, to hate speech. Kipps, however, stands his ground on the principle of free speech. The two battle it out at a mock-heroic faculty meeting held, ironically, in an auditorium named after the speechless Helen Keller.

A deeper irony is that while these two men argue about principles, the events transpiring in the novel show them to be rank hypocrites: Howard's lofty idealism is undercut by his uncontrollable sexual indiscretions (which bear resemblance to those of several prominent liberals in American government), and Kipps's principled tone is undermined by his bad faith regarding his wife's dying wishes, his cupidity, and his sexual harassment. On balance, both the liberal and the conservative are shown to be deeply flawed, though Belsey is perhaps more sympathetic (or pitiful) because he is merely weak, whereas Kipps is cold and calculating.

Another of the novel's major themes is race. Smith does not rehearse the usual black-white take on race; both of the feuding families are black. Rather, the novel examines race through the lens of class. Where this becomes clearest is in the characters of the younger Belsey siblings. Levi Belsey, the high-school-age younger son, enjoys all the comforts and advantages of a middle-class suburban African American upbringing. Levi is also in youthful revolt. He has set his mind to being cool, hip, and street smart. His inspiration is the rap and hip-hop that is constantly piped into his head by his omnipresent iPod.

To add authenticity to his image, Levi falls in with a group of down-and-out Haitians, street venders who hawk illegal knockoffs of designer accessories on Boston sidewalks. Levi is teamed up with Chouchou, a spectacularly scarred and abuse-hardened Haitian refugee who maintains his distance even as Levi attempts to get close to him. Eventually Levi does visit Chouchou's pad in the squalid, verminous depths of the ghetto. Overwhelmed, Levi realizes that he has glamorized and romanticized black poverty and that he (privileged as he has been) cannot genuinely negotiate the chasm of class difference between himself and Chouchou.

Zora Belsey (whose name is one of *On Beauty*'s several allusions to Zora Neale Hurston) is the college-age daughter who becomes sexually attracted to Carl, a toothsome black ghetto youth who does spoken-word gigs on the street and at open-mike nights. Pygmalion-like Zora takes him in hand and makes him her project. First, she wangles a rare seat for him as a nondegree auditor in her creative writing course. Then she maneuvers him into a music librarian's position in the Black Studies department. Unfortunately, Zora's feelings are not reciprocated by Carl. He is attracted to Victoria Kipps instead. When Zora reproaches him for his ingratitude, he bitterly accuses her of being excessively proprietary and controlling, and he quits the campus entirely: "People like me are just toys to people like you. . . . I'm just some experiment for you to play with. You people aren't even black any more . . . don't know *what* you are. . . . I can't do this no more."

The third major theme of this novel is a womanist teleology, an exploration of the purposiveness of women's lives. To elaborate this theme, Smith provides a spectrum of individual female characters ranging from Monique (the Belseys' Haitian maid) to Kiki Belsey (her employer). Of middling significance are a younger generation of women represented by the Belsey and Kipps daughters. Zora Belsey is the type of woman who exploits the politics of every situation, who finagles and contrives and cajoles, who takes control and assumes power,. Her coeval, Victoria Kipps, possesses all the physical allure of a Cleopatra and all the moral sensibility of a slut of Babylon—after she has slept with a young man, she seduces his father on the night of her own mother's funeral.

The major women characters are the matresfamilias Kiki Belsey and Carlene Kipps. Kiki was a blooming, spirited black woman from Florida (Zora Neale Hurston's state) who separated herself from her native African American community when she married her white English husband and settled in the suburbs. As if to emphasize this loss of spirit, Smith has this character weighing in at 250 pounds. After thirty years of marriage, raising three children, and working as a hospital administrator, Kiki discovers that her husband has cheated on her with their longtime friend, his colleague Claire Malcolm. In addition, he has had sex with an eighteen-year-old, currently his student.

As her life begins to crumble about her, there enters into it Carlene Kipps. They become friends in short order. Almost mystically they connect. ("Only connect" had been Forster's motto in *Howards End*.) Carlene, even more exclusively than Kiki, has devoted her life to her marriage and her family, whose members are a disappointment in terms of their values and their integrity, despite all of their outward trappings of success and recognition. Like Kiki's obesity, the symptom of Carlene's life disappointment manifests itself bodily—but invisibly—in the form of a cancer which she keeps hidden even from her own family. In contrast to their warring husbands, these two women connect in friendship during an afternoon of tea and pie. When Carlene dies, she wills a precious Haitian painting to her new friend, an act that will expose the greed and bad faith of the conservative Kipps family as well as the ineffectual and wrongheaded idealism latent in the liberal Belsey family.

Thus in the midst of a world fraught with misunderstanding and anger, chaos and meaninglessness, promiscuity and hypocrisy (conditions all too reminiscent of Forster's panic and emptiness), Smith shows her readers that there is one simply amazing saving grace—friendship. For Smith, friendship is a grace as beautiful and true and strong as it had been for Forster—who had proclaimed on the eve of World War II that if he had to choose between his country and his friend, he hoped that he would have the guts to choose his friend. In the end, it is of this core liberal, humanistic truth that Smith's novel beautifully and importantly reminds its readers.

C. L. Chua

Review Sources

Booklist 101, no. 22 (August 1, 2005): 1953.

The Economist 376 (September 10, 2005): 81-82.

Harper's Magazine 311 (October, 2005): 83-88.

Kirkus Reviews 73, no. 15 (August 1, 2005): 812.

Library Journal 130, no. 13 (August 15, 2005): 73.

The Nation 281, no. 10 (October 3, 2005): 25-28.

The New York Times 154 (September 13, 2005): E1-E8.

The New York Times Book Review 155 (September 18, 2005): 1-11.

The New Yorker, October 3, 2005, pp. 99-101.

Newsweek 146, no. 12 (September 19, 2005): 62.

Publishers Weekly 252, no. 30 (August 1, 2005): 44.

The Times Literary Supplement, September 2, 2005, pp. 10-11.

ORDINARY HEROES

Author: Scott Turow (1949-   )
Publisher: Farrar, Straus and Giroux (New York).
  371 pp. $25.00
Type of work: Novel
Time: 2005 and 1944-1945
Locale: Kindle County, in the United States, and Western
  Europe

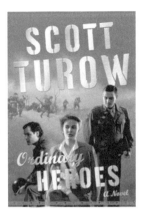

A man discovers the nature of his father's involvement in political and military intrigue during the last days of World War II and tries to unravel what happened

> *Principal characters:*
> STEWART DUBINSKY, the narrator, who
>   explores his father's participation in the
>   events of the closing months of World
>   War II
> DAVID DUBIN, his father, a military lawyer accused of crimes during
>   World War II
> GIDEON BIDWELL, an enlisted soldier in World War II who served with
>   David Dubin
> BARRINGTON LEACH, a military lawyer who defends David Dubin
> GITA LODZ, a woman whom Dubin encounters during his service in
>   Western Europe
> ROBERT MARTIN, an officer in the Office of Strategic Services during
>   World War II, whom Dubin is sent to find
> ROLAND TEEDLE, a general who was Dubin's superior and the author of
>   the mission to find Robert Martin

Scott Turow has achieved an admirable reputation as the author of novels based on lawyers and cases in fictional Kindle County, a place resembling modern Chicago. A lawyer himself, Turow has crafted intricate plots that reveal the workings of the legal system while also posing important moral and ethical questions. His latest book, *Ordinary Heroes*, has no trial scenes, nor does it deal with crimes committed in peacetime in the United States.

Instead, the action of the book occurs during the last year of World War II, in the Battle of the Bulge and afterward, as American troops fight their way into Nazi Germany. The book's major figure, David Dubin, a military lawyer, has been sent into the war zone to locate and arrest an officer, Robert Martin, in the Office of Strategic Services (OSS), a forerunner of the modern Central Intelligence Agency. From that assignment flows the main action of the novel, as Dubin finds his bravery tested in bitter combat against the counterattacking Germans. He also learns the complexity of Robert Martin's official and personal missions in wartime Germany.

Scott Turow, a Chicago attorney, is the author of such novels as Presumed Innocent *(1987),* Pleading Guilty *(1993), and* Reversible Errors *(2003), as well as the nonfiction study* Ultimate Punishment *(2003).*

This book is far from being merely a wartime thriller with an overlay of romance. It is framed after David Dubin's death in February, 2003, when his son, Stewart Dubinsky, learns that his father's military career culminated in a court-martial in which he faced the death penalty. This information, unknown to the son until after his father's passing, send Stewart Dubinsky on a quest to find out what happened to his father during World War II. Unlike his father, Dubinsky is not a lawyer. He is a retired journalist who turns his investigative skills to unraveling the mysteries of his father's life.

Until his discovery of the court-martial, Dubinsky had held a reassuring grasp on the past of his parents. His father had fought bravely in World War II, met Stewart's mother during the liberation of a concentration camp, and raised his family as a prominent attorney in Kindle County. The family did not talk about what David Dubin had experienced. It was, Stewart remembered, "an unpleasantness too great for discussion throughout our lives." Yet, as Stewart learns, family history can sometimes arise in ways that children do not anticipate.

As in Turow's other novels, the past carries secrets that affect the present, and Dubinsky finds out more than he expected to in his desire to understand his father's background. Stewart encounters his parents as young people through the documents they preserved and the recollections of his father's lawyer, Barrington "Bear" Leach. A key piece of evidence is the long written explanation that Dubin provided to Leach during the course of his military trial. That tale is a harrowing account of what befell the young military lawyer in the crucible of the war in Western Europe.

David Dubin's adventures also brought him a friendship and an even deeper relationship with Gita Lodz, a woman who was fighting with Robert Martin's band of OSS guerillas. Convinced at first that Godz and Martin are lovers, Dubin learns of the woman's past in the struggles against the Nazis. Dubin's personal involvement with her fate adds another dimension to his wartime story.

One of the great strengths of *Ordinary Heroes* is Turow's use of historical details of the fighting in France and Germany in 1944-1945. Into his narrative are woven extensively researched accounts of soldiers fighting and responding as the Germans retreat in late 1944 and then counterattack at the Bulge. Six decades after the end of World War II, the result now seems foreordained. To the soldiers who faced the Germans in 1944-1945, the battles were bloody engagements that persisted almost until the final collapse of the Wehrmacht in the spring of 1945. Turow's ability to convey the dangers of combat and the fears of the GIs imparts a strong sense of immediacy and tension to his narrative.

War is not glorious or heroic in this narrative, though there are ample acts of heroism by Dubin and his comrades. For example, Dubin and Gideon Bidwell parachute into the besieged town of Bastogne during the height of the Battle of the Bulge. Amid the tragedy of the moment, there are some comic aspects to the heroism of the two men, who have never jumped from a plane before. Yet Turow makes one understand that men looked for humor in their predicament as a way to deal with the carnage all around them.

The confusion of war, the capricious dealing of life to some and death to others, and the effort to find meaning amid the destruction—all these themes raise *Ordinary Heroes* above the literary level of a mere thriller. Like the best historical novels, Turow's story puts the reader back in time, into a specific place and amid real events.

With great skill, Turow also integrates into his story several political themes. The issue of race relations in World War II is presented in a matter-of-fact manner that makes its later appearance in the book quite striking and moving. Dubin learns how racial questions he had not previously thought about affect the Americans who live with prejudice every day. The tensions that shape race relations at home spill over into the interaction among officers and enlisted men in Europe. Without preaching the point in an obtrusive fashion, Turow illustrates the dysfunctional and self-defeating nature of discrimination, both at home and at the front.

As a Jew, Dubin confronts the possibility of capture and worse at the hands of the Germans. The Holocaust and its awful secrets provide another thread among the events that reshape Dubin's life. The revelation of German atrocities in World War II and the growing realization among the Americans about what was at stake in the conflict adds further richness and insight to the narrative.

Still other layers make Dubin's odyssey even more fascinating and complex. As the end of World War II neared, many Americans in the government and the military anticipated a conflict with the Soviet Union over the future of Europe. In that context, allegations of one's being a communist or having sympathies for Moscow could destroy a career. Turow folds that element into his account, as one of the reasons for attempting to arrest Robert Martin is his alleged communist allegiance. Martin is an enigmatic figure in the story, and his motivations are not always sketched as well as they could have been. His bravery in combat and the idealism that drives him to his course of action are asserted but not really fleshed out in detail.

An even deeper theme emerges as Dubin learns what Martin's real intentions are in German-occupied territory as the war grinds to its conclusion. Martin is seeking to ascertain the secret Nazi goals with regard to terror weapons and the capacity to deal even more devastation upon the world. So *Ordinary Heroes* engages the great themes of World War II, when civilization was in the balance.

This novel may not please fans of Turow who are looking for another one of his legal cases along the lines of *Presumed Innocent* (1987). Though his new book is likewise grounded in the legal setting of Kindle County, Turow broadens his range to deal with American and European history during the twentieth century. The narrative is securely based in the experiences of his individual characters but always conveys the sense that these men and women are caught up in the larger drama of their time.

Turow's ability to carry his themes forward over the course of sixty years attests to his development as a popular author of continuing depth and insight.

There are some rough edges in the book, and when the surprise revelation for Stewart Dubinsky comes, it does not seem as much of a shock as the author may have intended. The main figure of Roger Martin remains somewhat ambiguous and shadowy as even David Dubin examines him during their shared experiences. Martin's fate is more of a hook on which to hang Dubin's story than the compelling tale that Turow meant it to be.

For the most part, however, this is an exciting story on many levels, well told, with a good sense of historical context and the significance of Dubin's story in the panorama of World War II. Turow has done a significant amount of research into the nature of combat in Europe, and his details ring true. Especially in writing about the Battle of the Bulge, he conveys an excellent sense of the confusion and panic that affected some American troops when the Germans burst out of the Ardennes Forest in mid-December, 1944. In this way Turow makes the eventual American victory, led by men such as Dubin, even more impressive to read about after the passage of sixty years.

Turow's title echoes in the mind of the reader. The generation of Americans that Dubin represents were heroes in the challenge of World War II. The author makes clear that Dubin did not think of himself as a special warrior; he was a soldier doing the job he had been trained to do as a lawyer. He then found himself immersed in one of the great, climactic battles of World War II. As Dubin meets the demands of finding Robert Martin, defending Bastogne, and examining his own character and that of Gita Lodz, Turow transforms his main character's story into an epic drama of World War II. Future work by this author of unusual gifts will be awaited with high anticipation. *Ordinary Heroes* is Turow's best book so far, and it augurs even more rewarding reading from this distinguished author in the years to come.

Lewis L. Gould

Review Sources

Booklist 102, no. 1 (September 1, 2005): 8.
Chicago Sun-Times, October 30, 2005, p. B12.
Entertainment Weekly, November 4, 2005, pp. 78-79.
Kirkus Reviews 73, no. 17 (September 1, 2005): 942.
Library Journal 130, no. 16 (October 1, 2005): 70.
The New York Times 155 (October 27, 2005): E1-E9.
The New York Times Book Review 155 (November 6, 2005): 30.
People 64, no. 22 (November 28, 2005): 68.
Publishers Weekly 252, no. 37 (September 19, 2005): 42.
The Washington Post Book World, October 30, 2005, p. 7.

THE PEABODY SISTERS
Three Women Who Ignited American Romanticism

Author: Megan Marshall (1954-   )
Publisher: Houghton Mifflin (Boston). 602 pp. $28.00
Type of work: Biography
Time: 1804-1843
Locale: Salem and Boston, Massachusetts

Marshall breaks new ground in her biography of three dynamic sisters who each made important contributions to the nineteenth century American Renaissance

Principal personages:
ELIZABETH PALMER PEABODY, an educator, author, and publisher
MARY PEABODY MANN, an educator, abolitionist, and reformer
SOPHIA PEABODY HAWTHORNE, an artist and sculptor
ELIZABETH (ELIZA) PALMER PEABODY, an educator and writer, mother to Elizabeth, Mary, and Sophia
HORACE MANN, an educator and reformer, husband of Mary
NATHANIEL HAWTHORNE, an author, husband of Sophia

"When I decided to write the Peabody sisters' story," Megan Marshall comments in the introduction to *The Peabody Sisters: Three Women Who Ignited American Romanticism*, "I set out to read everything they ever wrote in letters and diaries and in print, along with most of the books they read and cared about. I wanted to know who they were in the inside, who they wanted to be, and who they became." Marshall's magisterial biography of Elizabeth (1804-1894), Mary (1806-1887), and Sophia (1809-1871) succeeds in illuminating the private world and the public personas of the remarkable siblings. At the heart of Marshall's account are entries from the sisters' diaries, plus hundreds of handwritten letters they exchanged with one another and with illustrious contemporaries such as Ralph Waldo Emerson, William Ellery Channing, Horace Mann, Nathaniel Hawthorne, and Margaret Fuller. The result of twenty years of research, Marshall's biography offers an intricate profile of the often complicated relationship the women shared as well as a fresh look at the era known as the American Renaissance.

Marshall's interest in the Peabody sisters began as a result of her reading of Louise Hall Tharp's *The Peabody Sisters of Salem*, written in 1950. Tharp also drew on the women's private papers for her well-received biography but did not have access to the newly discovered sources Marshall enjoyed. The result of Tharp's efforts was an interesting but limited portrait of the women. Marshall was determined to go beyond Tharp's stereotyping of Elizabeth, Mary, and Sophia as "the brain," "the beauty," and "the invalid" to create an intimate portrait of the sisters who were so influential in the

~

Megan Marshall has worked as an editor and an educator. She has published numerous articles on women's history and New England history.

~

religious, social, political, philosophical, and literary debates of their day. Her discovery of previously unknown letters and journal entries ten years into her research, in her words, "dramatically altered the way I viewed these women," and provided information that not only revealed the identity of Elizabeth's relationship to a mysterious suitor (a man whom Tharp tried, and failed, to identify) but also shed new light on the triangular love relationship of Elizabeth, Sophia, and writer Nathaniel Hawthorne.

The book begins and ends with an account of the wedding of Sophia Peabody and Nathaniel Hawthorne in 1842. Sandwiched in between is a detailed chronological narrative of the sisters' struggle to live outside the social constraints that bound women of their time and, in Elizabeth's words, to "be myself and *act.*" Although liberal-thinking men and women viewed each other as intellectual and social equals, it was difficult for women to live independently because few professions were open to them. The girls, however, had a magnificent role model in their mother, the indomitable Eliza Palmer Peabody.

Born into an old, and at one time prosperous New England family, Eliza discovered early on the allure of learning, as she devoured the volumes in her grandfather's extensive library. Under the pseudonym Belinda, she wrote and published feminist poetry which was admired by a wide audience, including President John Adams. Her disappointing marriage to Dr. Nathaniel Peabody, who was variously a physician, dentist, farmer, and businessman, thwarted her literary ambitions and taught her the importance of self-reliance. The family, which included three ne'er-do-well sons in addition to the brilliant sisters, relocated often in search of fresh opportunities to escape their genteel poverty. In each place they lived, which included Salem, Lancaster, and Boston, Massachusetts, Mrs. Peabody kept the family afloat financially by opening a school for children of the local elite. Prefiguring twentieth century feminist ideals, she encouraged her daughters to establish their own identities and develop their talents so that they would never have to depend on the dubious support of men. She believed it was more important for her to girls reach "a decent independence" rather than "learn to sew a shirt or bake a pudding."

Although the three sisters were heavily influenced by their mother's progressive views, as well as by the rigorous classical education she provided them, Elizabeth was perhaps the one most to embody Eliza's feminist philosophy. Brilliant, bossy, and controlling, Elizabeth was a precocious young woman who sparred with and learned from the Boston intelligentsia. At thirteen, she debated theology with eminent Unitarian minister William Ellery Channing. Her friendship with Ralph Waldo Emerson blossomed when, as a young theology student at Harvard, he tutored her in Greek. Her voracious intellect led her to attain the equivalent of a college education in spite of the fact that she was barred from the university because of her gender.

Following in Mrs. Peabody's footsteps, she became an accomplished and innovative educator and later pioneered the kindergarten movement in the United States.

She also assisted Bronson Alcott, the father of writer Louisa May Alcott, in running his revolutionary Temple School in Boston. As the Transcendentalist movement evolved, Elizabeth became a key proponent of its ideas. In the summer of 1840, she made her "debut in the mercantile world" when she became the first female book-seller in Boston, having opened a foreign-language bookstore and lending library. Her enterprise was much more than a bookstore, however. It became the primary gathering place for free-thinking Transcendentalist writers, clergy, and reformers. Elizabeth also published the Transcendentalist magazine *The Dial* and promoted the early works of up-and-coming writers such as Hawthorne and Margaret Fuller.

Although she possessed an intellect equal to her older sister's, Mary could not have been more different in personality and interests. Considered the beauty of the family, Mary often felt that she was judged on her striking good looks instead of her considerable talents. Mary's appearance also provoked resentment within the family. Elizabeth once remarked in a journal entry, "My sister Mary was very small & very beautiful. . . . I constantly heard of her beauty." Although Elizabeth claimed she was not jealous of Mary, it was plain that she felt inferior. She later noted, "I did not like my own looks," and became careless of her appearance, perhaps reacting against the attention Mary garnered because of her looks.

While Elizabeth believed she could not compete with Mary's beauty, Mary felt cowed by Elizabeth's overbearing personality and impressive intellect. She retreated into a world of popular romantic fiction, which fueled her fantasy of meeting a man who would reflect her conception of "ideal perfection." Her romantic notions were no impediment to her intellectual growth, however. When her father tutored Elizabeth in Latin, Mary was informed that she was not up to the task of studying the language. She secretly "borrowed" Elizabeth's textbook and clandestinely learned on her own. Eventually her quest for knowledge bore fruit. She became an accomplished writer, contributing essays, poetry, and reviews in her self-published literary magazine, the *Salem Recorder.* Later she authored several books on education and even wrote a ro-mance novel.

Nevertheless, as a young woman Mary often lived in Elizabeth's shadow, defer-ring to her older sister's wishes. To supplement the family income, Elizabeth turned to teaching, and she pressured Mary to join her in the classroom. Although Mary ini-tially disliked teaching, she could not say no to Elizabeth and partnered with her in opening schools in Maine and Massachusetts. Elizabeth also arranged for her to travel to Cuba with Sophia, where Mary toiled as a governess for two years while her youn-ger sister sought a rest cure for her maladies.

Sophia was plagued by ill health from childhood. It is possible that her frequent and severe migraine headaches were caused by repeated use of mercury, initially prescribed by her father for teething difficulties when she was a toddler. To quell her headache pain, she took opium, which was then not widely known to be addic-tive. Like her sisters, she was independent and willful, and Marshall suggests that her relentless migraines may have given her the opportunity to wield as much power within the family as Elizabeth, without appearing outwardly domineering. On the fre-quent occasions Sophia was indisposed, her parents and siblings would shower her with attention and sometimes tiptoe through the house in order to avoid disturbing her.

Unlike her sisters, who were primarily educators, Sophia was a painter and a sculptor, although she occasionally tutored art students. Her work drew praise from Emerson, Channing, and fellow artist and mentor Washington Allston. Despite Sophia's debilitating headaches, Elizabeth expected her to use her artistic talent to contribute to the family coffers. She frequently conceived of money-making schemes that involved Sophia, sometimes without consulting her first. Like Mary, Sophia gave into Elizabeth's demands. Also like Mary, Sophia was something of a romantic and fantasized about sharing her life with a hypothetical fellow artist who remained "unknown yet known."

The sisters were not so intellectually preoccupied that men and marriage never entered their minds, although both subjects proved to be problematic. Their mother and father's union was hardly an endorsement of the institution of marriage. The siblings looked down on women whose "principle desire . . . is to get married" and who, in Sophia's words, would "shine by borrowed light" if they were fortunate enough to wed prominent men. Those women became the trophy wives of their day, and the Peabody sisters would have none of it. They all turned down proposals from men who could have provided them a secure future, both emotionally and financially. The sisters wanted more. The Peabody women gravitated toward men who valued them for their intellectual gifts as well as for their femininity. Each woman found love. In Elizabeth's case, however, she did not experience long-lived happiness in her relationship.

Mary discovered her soul mate in widower Horace Mann, "the father of American education" and later the first president of Antioch College, but not before Elizabeth established a quasi-romantic liaison with him first. When Mann was in mourning for his first wife, Elizabeth offered him comfort and support. Out of respect for his grief and perhaps because the relationship between Mann and Elizabeth was not clear, Mary carefully hid her love for him. Eventually Elizabeth and Mann mutually concluded that they shared an intense friendship, nothing more. Finally Mann overcame his depression and turned his attention to Mary. Ten years after they met, he and Mary married and lived happily together until his death in 1859.

Although Elizabeth could have been in love with Horace Mann, Marshall argues that she definitely formed a romantic attachment to Nathaniel Hawthorne. After Hawthorne and Elizabeth became acquainted in November, 1837, she found herself enamored of the handsome writer. Elizabeth had promoted his works after reading *Twice-Told Tales* (1837), but their business relationship quickly evolved into something far more personal, until finally as Marshall states, they reached an "understanding: they would marry."

Marshall supports her contention in an extensive end note, citing evidence of a probable engagement revealed in Mary Van Wyck Church's unpublished biography of Elizabeth, as well as Elizabeth's own comments about her relationship with Hawthorne. Brenda Wineapple in her 2004 biography, *Hawthorne: A Life*, also addresses this subject. While she, too, leans toward the theory that Hawthorne and Elizabeth were engaged and that he later jilted her for Sophia, Wineapple leaves some room for doubt. In any event, it does seem that Elizabeth harbored deep feelings for Hawthorne. She witnessed the first meeting between Sophia and Hawthorne and later confessed that when Hawthorne looked at Sophia with such "intense" interest, Elizabeth was "struck with it, and painfully." She recognized that this was one battle with her younger sister that she could not win and removed herself from the situation by relocating to Newton Corner.

Covering the first half of the sisters' lives, Marshall's biography leaves the reader in medias res. Still, this engrossing work offers much fodder for students of American history, literature, and women's studies, as well as general readers, to contemplate and explore on their own. Individual biographies such as *Elizabeth Palmer Peabody: A Reformer on Her Own Terms* (1999) by Bruce Ronda and Patricia Dunlavy Valenti's *Sophia Peabody Hawthorne: A Life, Vol. 1, 1809-1847* (2004) may satisfy the curiosity of readers who want to know more, but Marshall's meticulously researched study is sure to set the standard by which future works on the sisters are judged.

Pegge Bochynski

Review Sources

Booklist 101, no. 14 (March 15, 2005): 1260.
Kirkus Reviews 73, no. 4 (February 15, 2005): 214.
Library Journal 130, no. 6 (April 1, 2005): 103-104.
The New Republic 233, no. 15 (October 10, 2005): 27-31.
The New York Times 154 (April 20, 2005): E10.
The New York Times Book Review 154 (April 17, 2005): 18.
People 63, no. 20 (May 23, 2005): 56.
Ploughshares 31, no. 1 (Spring, 2005): 210.
Publishers Weekly 252, no. 9 (February 28, 2005): 55.

PEARL

Author: Mary Gordon (1949-   )
Publisher: Pantheon (New York). 354 pp. $24.95
Type of work: Novel
Time: Christmas, 1998
Locale: New York, Dublin, and Rome

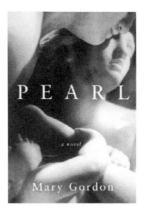

On Christmas, 1998, Maria Meyers receives a telephone call informing her that her daughter has chained herself to a flagpole outside the American Embassy in Dublin and is starving herself over the death of a young Irish boy

Principal characters:
PEARL MEYERS, a twenty-year-old American studying in Dublin
MARIA MEYERS, a fifty-year-old single mother devoted to liberal causes
JOSEPH KASPERMAN, a lifelong friend of Maria and foster father to Pearl
STEVIE DONEGAN, a dim-witted boy whose accidental death haunts Pearl
BREEDA DONEGAN, Stevie's mother and Pearl's friend

Pearl opens abruptly with the State Department phoning Maria Meyers on Christmas night with the news that her daughter Pearl, a student in Dublin, has chained herself to an embassy flagpole and is dying of a hunger strike. Maria phones her friend Joseph Kasperman in Rome, and the two resolve to meet in Dublin.

Pearl has carefully planned her demonstration, leaving letters for her mother, Joseph, and the press, and declaring that she is bearing witness to the death of Stevie Donegan, an obscure person, and to the virtue of the Good Friday Peace Accords that ended violence in Northern Ireland. Pearl resists all efforts to save her until she can no longer resist the police and is sent to the hospital. There she once more resists efforts on her behalf but is slowly nursed back to health.

Divided into three concentric narratives, the book also concentrates on her mother's attempts to come to terms with her own life and her daughter's incomprehensible decision to sacrifice her life. She battles with Pearl's attending physician for the right to visit her child. She visits Pearl's friends, who can shed little light on the girl's motivations. Meanwhile Joseph ponders what he can do to save the girl he has always regarded as a surrogate daughter and decides that by marrying her he can protect her from her mother and the threats of world with which he has never fully engaged himself.

The novel engages a number of complex themes, the first and most prominent of which is the notion of family bonds and inheritances. Neither Maria nor Joseph was particularly close to their respective parents. Maria, for instance, rebelled against her father and his confining version of parenting. "Maria hated the surveillance of her own childhood, the privileged enclosure, being kept from the world as if she were a fragile and precocious object." Although she convinces herself that she has created a life of freedom and openness for Pearl, the girl's Wellesley College education, study abroad, and personal affluence breed a sense of guilt and exclusivity. Where her mother is a devotee of every noble social cause or movement, Pearl is diffident and uninvolved, a shy, retiring antithesis to her mother's confidence and assertive righteousness.

As well as in her other novels, author Mary Gordon traces the links between generations in families; for all of their apparent differences, these generations inevitably replicate one another. Maria worships Roman Catholic saints; Pearl becomes enamored of a secular saint, Bobby Sands, a modern Irish icon of resistance and self-sacrifice. In her own dramatic gesture, Pearl reveals herself truly to be her mother's daughter, living a life of abnegation and service to others. When an adolescent Maria tells a Jewish neighbor that "you must lose your life in order to gain it," she augurs her child's self-destructive gesture. Just as sorrow and defeat is bred in the MacNamaras of Gordon's *The Other Side* (1989), devotion to others and to a grand cause are Maria and Pearl's congenital dispositions.

Mary Gordon published her first novel, Final Payments, *in 1979; it was followed quickly by* The Company of Women *(1980). After the birth of two children, she published a third novel,* Men and Angels *(1985), a best seller. The Other Side (1989) is a magnum opus about Irish emigration and assimilation. Gordon has published numerous other books and is a member of the faculty at her alma mater, Barnard College.*

As she has done in so many of her novels and essays, Gordon examines cultural differences, especially those between Ireland and America, and she implicitly questions what culture represents for Americans, a people who the are the product of a heterogeneous mix of cultures and attitudes. The Irish in *Pearl*, at least those given the most exposure, are pathetic people who want a sense of political urgency in their lives. They are convinced the 1998 peace accords are little more than political co-option, yet aside from drinking and railing they have no agenda or concrete political alternatives. Nevertheless, they possess a sense of urgency, a notion of history, however fractured, and a conviction which defines their lives.

By contrast, the Americans, and especially Pearl, have no ideology, no sense of history, no compelling sense of a world outside their private concerns. The narrator suggests as much when posing the rhetorical question, "Do we look in coils of our heritage?" Although Pearl's actions suggest devotion to a political cause, her motives are inspired by deeply personal feelings of betrayal and the human capacity for unkindness.

One of the novel's most arresting features is the unnamed narrator, whose voice Gordon foregrounds as a subjective consciousness that has almost complete omniscience of events and characters. The narrator constitutes a nearly palpable presence in the story and, while never identified, is a focus of attention. It could be argued that Gordon has simply appropriated an old convention of many chatty Victorian novels.

Pearl's narrator assumes a number of curious postures—ultimate authority, purveyor of crucial information, and conversational accomplice with the reader. The narrative is often punctuated by informal asides, "[Pearl's letters] sound rather different in some ways, don't you think, one from the other," invocations seeking the audience's tolerance, "You have to trust me," or announcements of changes in narrative focus, "We will leave Pearl for a little while, because this is not her story only but the story of three people, and we have not attended to Joseph and Maria for quite some time."

In matters of opinion about the characters or their actions, the narrator often avoids resolution in favor of inclusive consideration: "What do you think? And which side, you may wonder, am I on? I am on both sides." The narrator's profound engagement extends beyond the characters to the audience as well, and the result is an atmosphere of rare narrative intimacy. Readers may question, however, why such an intrusive, distracting device is used.

In part, Gordon is relying on ancient Irish traditions of storytelling, preserved to this day in the practices of the *shanachie*, who continue to rely on the techniques of an oral tradition paramount among which is the intimacy of the storyteller's physical presence. In such a tradition the voice of the narrator, with all its inflections, asides, and prevarications, is as much a part of the narrative experience as the story itself. The narrator of *Pearl* admits as much when commenting, "It has occurred to me that sometimes a story is more a tine than a tale," and indeed atmosphere—emotional and spiritual—is crucial to this story.

A similar aesthetic informs the yearnings of an abused Irish woman, Breeda, when she wishes to be "able to speak just as she liked, to tell stories the way she wanted to, not strung together by events but by the look of a thing, a smell, snatches of a song." Thus Gordon provides not only the tale—who did what, when, how, and why—but the highly nuanced texture of what it means to be in the world and struggle with the challenges and conflicts that ultimately define lives.

As readers of Gordon's other fictions realize, her Roman Catholic faith informs—often uneasily and antithetically—all of her works, and thus it should not be surprising that *Pearl* has a strong religious subtext, the most obvious aspect of which is the creation of a decidedly secular analogue to the Holy Family. Thus one finds a mother named Maria, a Jewish foster father named Joseph, and a single child, in this case a daughter, whose name may be an oblique reference to Christ's parable about the man who sacrificed all to purchase the "pearl of great price."

More significant than biblical parallels, in which the novel abounds, are the spiritual issues the book interrogates. For instance, the idea of martyrdom, a central concept in Catholic dogma which emphasizes the Passion of Christ and lives of the saints finds repeated expression in a more secular context. Bobby Sands, a martyr to a political ideal, inspires Pearl to martyr herself for a personal ideal of simple human kindness and compassion. Maria has martyred herself at the altar of social justice and made it a passion as strong as her love for her child. Joseph sacrificed his ambitions for a Ph.D. in art history to assume the reins of the Meyer family business to protect Maria and Pearl.

The theme of purity, an almost obsessive concern of the Catholic Church, is also given center stage in the novel. Here it becomes an ideal in a variety of shapes: For Pearl's Cambodian father it represents the order and orthodoxy of Pol Pot's murderous regime; for Maria it amounts to revolutionary revisionism; for Joseph it is his seemingly unselfish commitment to serving the Meyers; and for Pearl it defines a quality of action designed to remediate against selfishness and callous disregard of others. While many of these definitions may be self-serving or delusional, they are nonetheless essential. As Gordon says in an interview, "It we don't have that image of purity, we don't become our best selves."

A third crucial religious theme is that of penance and atonement. Pearl seeks to atone for her impatience with and criticism of Stevie Donegan, which she is convinced has occasioned his death. Maria, in watching her child nearly die, remembers her father's passing and finally forgives him and herself for all of their resentments. Perhaps the most unselfish forgiveness comes from Stevie's mother, Breeda, who absolves Pearl of responsibility in her son's death. As the narrator asks, "If Breeda has forgiven her is she no longer unforgivable?"

Once again Gordon has constructed a complex, deeply moving, and at times profoundly philosophical book which probes the great verities without preachiness or dogmatism. In such a deeply spiritual novel, perhaps the overarching question is that posed by the narrator when it asks, "Can you lose your faith and hold on to what that faith insists on? Isn't that, in fact, the purest of faith, faith without faith? Faith without hope? Faith without the possibility of faith's consolation?" The novel's resolution of that dilemma is at once so simple and so profound.

David W. Madden

Review Sources

Booklist 101, no. 3 (October 1, 2004): 282.
The Boston Globe January 16, 2005, p. C7.
The Christian Century 122, no. 8 (April 19, 2005): 24-25.
Kirkus Reviews 72, no. 20 (October 15, 2004): 977.
Library Journal 129, no. 17 (October 15, 2004): 53-54.
Ms. 14, no. 4 (Winter, 2004/2005): 89-90.
The New Leader 87, no. 6 (November/December, 2004): 33-35.
The New York Times Book Review 154 (February 20, 2005): 28-29.
The New Yorker 80, no. 43 (January 17, 2005): 91.
Publishers Weekly 251, no. 42 (October 18, 2004): 45.
The Washington Post, January 30, 2005, p. T6.

THE PEOPLE'S TYCOON
Henry Ford and the American Century

Author: Steven Watts (1952-   )
Publisher: Alfred A. Knopf (New York). 616 pp. $30.00
Type of work: Biography
Time: 1863-1947
Locale: Michigan, near Detroit

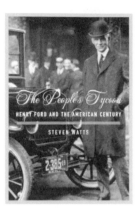

Watts's biography of the man who pioneered mass production and put America on wheels will stand as one of the best books written about Henry Ford

Principal personages:
HENRY FORD, an automobile manufacturer
EDSEL FORD, his son
HENRY FORD II, his grandson
CLARA BRYANT FORD, his wife
HARRY BENNETT, Ford's head of security

Perhaps no invention has influenced American culture as profoundly and changed the landscape so much as the automobile. Henry Ford, in a few short decades, transformed this turn of the twentieth century mechanical curiosity into a necessity of modern living.

From an early age, Ford exhibited a remarkable mechanical ability. He was fascinated by machines, especially watches, and soon became an expert at repairing them. His interest in gasoline engines began with his experience working with farm machinery at his Michigan home. Ford became aware that the tremendous labor-saving potential of machinery could free the farmer of much drudgery and long hours of work in the fields.

It was Ford's encounter with a crude, steam-powered wagon on a road between Dearborn and Detroit, Michigan, that fired his interest in automobiles. Leaving his father's farm at age sixteen, he moved to Detroit to find work in a machine shop. Working as a machinist by day and repairing watches at night, Ford had already begun dreaming about mass production—of watches at first. His skills with machine tools would be of the greatest importance to his future, and he soon began to envision a revolution in transportation. His goal was to produce a gasoline engine that could be a true source of mobile power. For such a "horseless carriage" to become a reality, Ford would have to build, from scratch, an engine that was lightweight, safe, and reliable.

As his first vehicle, the "quadricycle," became a familiar sight on the streets of Detroit, Ford attracted business investors. With a sizable cache of capital and the newly found fame which came from his building of race cars, Ford began assembling cars in 1903. His intent was to build a "car for the masses"—affordable, reliable, light, and sturdy. Eventually the ideal car was designed: the Model T, which put even

ordinary Americans on wheels in the early twentieth century and changed American culture forever.

The secret to Ford's success was the use of
the assembly line to build his cars. Although this
manufacturing technique was already in use in
many industries, it was Ford who perfected it.
Carefully studying the motions of workers, Ford
refined the assembly line, cutting costs, speeding
up production, and increasing profits. As thousands of autos began to roll off the assembly
lines, the Model T truly became the "universal

*Steven Watts is professor of history
at the University of Missouri. He is
the award-winning author of four
books, including* The Magic
Kingdom *(1997), a biography of
Walt Disney. His many articles have
appeared in the* Journal of
American History, *the* American
Quarterly, *and* American Studies.

car" that Ford had envisioned, making him a hero of the farming and working class, as
well as one of the richest men in America. His folk hero status rose to a level of almost
religious reverence, and Ford found himself a living symbol of American industrial
power and prosperity. As a result, he began to see himself as not only an industrialist
but a social reformer as well.

He saw work as a stabilizing force in civilization. To Ford, a steady job and a
decent salary were the foundation of a stable family life and a moral society. To demonstrate this concept, he stunned the United States and the world by giving his assembly-line workers a salary of five dollars a day—nearly twice the normal rate in such
industries. It was Ford's belief that money should be spent and not saved; it was the
flow of money, not the mere accumulation of it—that would produce economic
growth and happiness.

Observers noted that Ford, in his personal life, practiced what he preached. Slim,
athletic, indulging in neither alcohol nor tobacco, and with a seemingly perfect family
life, he was the epitome of the successful businessman. He extolled the virtues of hard
work, distrusted college-educated engineers, dismissed academic subjects such as
history as "bunk"—merely the stories of the triumph of the rich and powerful at the
expense of the common folk. Ford's five-dollar day and his homespun populist attitude made him a hero among the working class and one of the most revered men in the
United States. Soon there was talk of his running for the U.S. Senate or even the presidency. As his stature grew, however, his weaknesses began to show.

Ford's autocratic management style, in which no decisions, even small ones, were
to be made without his approval, led to dissent among his managers as the Ford Motor
Company grew. His ignorance of politics quickly became apparent when he chartered
a "peace ship" in 1915 to sail to Europe and negotiate an end to World War I. Confident that he could lead a successful peace conference in a neutral country, he instead
quickly showed that he was in over his head in the political arena.

Even worse for Ford's fortunes was his insistence that the Model T would remain
the sole product of the Ford Motor Company. By the mid-1920's, other auto manufacturers, such as General Motors and Chrysler, began marketing cars at slightly higher
prices but offering more choices, luxury, comfort, and power. As his market share began to dwindle, Ford drove his assembly-line workers relentlessly, destroying their

morale. By the time the new Model A was announced, it would take a massive retooling effort and thousands of layoffs to accomplish its manufacture. Ford Motors would never again dominate the automobile market.

Cracks also began to appear in his personal life. He took a mistress half his age and likely fathered a child with her. In the meantime, he emotionally neglected his only son, Edsel. Even when the younger Ford rose to the presidency of the company, Henry Ford would criticize his son's lifestyle, which he considered lavish compared to his own, and constantly undermine his son's authority. The withering abuse from his father eventually led Edsel to relinquish the presidency of Ford, but not before he fell gravely ill from stress and overwork. He would die of stomach cancer in 1943 at age forty-nine.

It was during his most powerful years that a terrible stain on Henry Ford's character emerged: a rabid anti-Semitism. Blaming the Jews for most of the economic and social ills of civilization, Ford's outright bigotry and ignorance shocked those who had placed him upon such a high pedestal. In his company-owned newspaper and later in a book, he preached anti-Semitism to the world, even earning the admiration and praise of Adolf Hitler. It is not clear where Ford's intense hatred of Jews originated. In *The People's Tycoon*, author Steven Watts speculates that it was probably the result of one of Ford's famous "hunches"—widely incorrect opinions formed by his own ignorance, vague perceptions, and an impulsive personality that frequently led him to jump to wild conclusions. Although Ford later attempted to blame the anti-Semitic tirades on the Ford-employed publisher of his newspaper, it was clear to most people that the ideas had come directly from him.

The low point of Henry Ford's career came when his workers attempted to unionize during the Great Depression. He dispatched a squad of armed men led by Harry Bennett, Ford's head of security, and a bloody confrontation ensued at the huge Ford plant, dubbed the "Dearborn Massacre" by the newspapers. Led by the ruthless Bennett, union organizers were spied upon, beaten, and fired. Ford steadfastly refused to negotiate with his workers until his wife, Clara, sickened by the continuing violence and loss of life, sternly ordered her husband to capitulate and recognize the union. The use of unscrupulous men such as Bennett clearly showed that Ford was losing control of his company.

As he grew older, Ford seemed to mellow a bit but lost interest in the day-to-day operations of his company. His enormous wealth left him free to pursue his personal projects. He was intensely interested in improving American education, especially in the skilled trades. He also began to idolize and glorify the past. How ironic, notes Watts, that the one man who was perhaps most responsible for the rapid industrialization and modernization of American life, and the end of a slower, less complicated, simpler society, was now extolling the virtues of a way of life that he, more than any other, had helped bring to an end.

Ford's real estate development, named Greenfield Village for the old township where his wife had grown up, would be an idealized American town as well as a living history museum. Ford spent so much time in its construction that the Ford Motor Company now seemed more of a distraction than anything else. As Ford dabbled with his pet project, powerful executives within the company attempted to gain control. As his grasp of reality began to wane, the Ford family, especially his wife, moved to take over the motor company. They convinced Henry to resign and placed his grandson, Henry II, in command. Although Henry II was only twenty-eight years old in 1945 and had just been recalled from active duty in the U.S. Navy, his grandfather's namesake would quickly assert himself, purging the company of its unscrupulous executives and restoring order. He would serve as president until 1960.

In the last few months of his life, Henry Ford had lost most of his mental faculties. Although he lived a healthy and robust life well into his late seventies, he then deteriorated rapidly, passing away in 1947 at the age of eighty-four. He had lived through the horse-and-buggy days of nineteenth century America and, almost more than any person, revolutionized transportation, manufacturing, and daily life in the twentieth century. His life stands as an example of the impact that one person's ideas can have on the stream of history and progress.

The task of the biographer is a difficult one. To capture the essence of a person's life between the covers of a book is an attempt to bring that person back to life for a new generation. In this case, Watts has overwhelmingly succeeded. This work will stand as the best of the Ford biographies yet written. In addition, Watts has revealed the importance of the executives and confidants on whom Ford depended but frequently overruled. In the end, as Watts observes, it was Ford's dogged determination that made him succeed, but the resulting unbending, autocratic leadership style would become his undoing. As with most people, Henry Ford had his strengths as well as his weaknesses, both physical and mental. His was blind to the limits of his intellect. His anti-Semitism was irrational, his harsh treatment of his son was unwarranted, yet his creative genius in the world of motors and gears transformed the world. Watts's candid, exhaustively researched, and balanced account of how these forces of talent, persistence, hard work, as well as moral failings shaped this giant of the twentieth century is the best yet of the man who put America on wheels.

Raymond Frey

Review Sources

Booklist 101, nos. 19/20 (June 1, 2005): 1729.
The Boston Globe, August 21, 2005, p. D2.
Fortune 152, no. 2 (July 25, 2005): 201.
Library Journal 130, no. 10 (June 1, 2005): 144.
Los Angeles Times, August 26, 2005, p. E18.
The New York Times Book Review 154 (September 4, 2005): 9.
Publishers Weekly 252, no. 26 (June 27, 2005): 53.
St. Louis Post-Dispatch, August 7, 2005, p. C10.
Washington Monthly 37, nos. 7/8 (July, 2005): 55-58.

A PERFECT RED
Empire, Espionage, and the Quest for the Color of Desire

Author: Amy Butler Greenfield (1969-   )
Publisher: HarperCollins (New York). 338 pp. $27.00
Type of work: History
Time: From earliest human history to 2005
Locale: Spain, Mexico, Italy, France, Germany, the Netherlands, England, the United States, Haiti, Guatemala, and Peru

The history of the red dye cochineal is traced from its discovery in Mexico to the spread of its use in Europe

Principal personages:
> HERNÁN CORTÉS, a Spanish conquistador
> CHARLES V, the king of Spain
> ROBERT DEVEREUX, the earl of Essex, an English courtier
> ROBERT TOMSON, an English merchant
> ANTONI VAN LEEUWENHOEK, a Dutch scientist and developer of the microscope
> JAN SWAMMERDAM, a Dutch scientist
> MELCHIOR DE RUUSSCHER, a Dutch natural historian
> NICOLAS-JOSEPH THIERY DE MENONVILLE, a French botanist
> JOSEPH BANKS, an English botanist
> JOSÉ ANTONIO ALZATE Y RAMÍREZ, a Mexican priest and scientist
> WILLIAM HENRY PERKIN, an English chemist
> AUGUST HOFMANN, a professor at the Royal College of Chemistry

Since the Middle Ages, Western societies have been fascinated by brightly colored, especially red, clothing. In *A Perfect Red*, historian Amy Butler Greenfield, the granddaughter and great-granddaughter of dyers, traces the lengthy European quest for the source of a perfect red, with success finally being found in sixteenth century Mexico.

"An affinity for red seems almost hard-wired into us," writes Greenfield. As proof, she explains that most languages had a word for red before any other colors except black and white. Various cultures from the time of the Neanderthals have had strong psychological, religious, and political associations with the color. Primitive societies equated red with magical powers, from curing illnesses to exorcising demons, and most cultures have associated it with courage, danger, violence, war, divinity, martyrdom, sin, or passion. Greenfield is most interested in red as a symbol of wealth, power, and status.

Since the Cro-Magnons used ochre in their cave paintings, a perfect red has been sought for use in art and commerce. Cinnabar was used in ancient Chinese scrolls and on the frescoed walls of Pompeii, but this source of a brilliant red was expensive and poisonous. It often turned black when exposed to light. By the thirteenth century, the center of the red world was Lucca, near Florence, where elaborately designed taffeta, damask, and brocade fabrics were created. The heavily controlled Lucchese silk trade prescribed death for anyone trading outside the city during the Renaissance, when textiles became a major European industry as merchants and lawyers emulated the fashions of the aristocrats and people of lower status bought more and more cloth. In Renaissance Europe, gray and beige were the colors of poverty, and bright clothing became a symbol of power.

Amy Butler Greenfield graduated from Williams College and was a Marshall Scholar at Oxford University. While writing her graduate thesis on the introduction of chocolate into Europe, she discovered the history of cochineal. As Amy Butler, she has written Virginia Bound *(2003), a historical novel for children, which was named one of the best children's books of the year by the Bank Street College of Education.*

A major drawback to the increasing popularity of bright colors was the instability of dyes made from plants. Few textiles could hold up to extensive wear and washing. Chemical binding agents known as mordants helped dyes adhere to cloth, but each produced different colors from the same dyestuff. The dyeing process itself was expensive. In fourteenth century Italy, most dyers' equipment cost four hundred gold florins at a time when a small farm could be bought for twenty florins. In the fifteenth century, the scarlet cloth worn by England's Henry VI cost more per yard than a month's wages for a master mason. The expense was part of the attraction, and Renaissance artists and merchants wore scarlet turbans as proof of their success. During a 1525 revolt in Germany, peasants demanded the right to wear red.

Europe's most common source of red, madder, had been used in ancient China and Egypt but was unstable, often resulting in coral and russet colors rather than the desired crimson and scarlet. Some dyers tried to improve it by combining madder with rancid olive oil, cow dung, and even blood, but the quality suffered. Other sources of red included archil, made from lichens found on coastal rocks; lac, made from an insect found in Asia; and oak-kermes, derived from a similar insect. The reds they produced varied in quality and were expensive. For Florence dyers, kermes red could cost ten times that of sky blue.

The major breakthrough finally occurred in 1519 when Spanish conquistadors in Mexico found Aztecs selling cochineal. A member of the scale family, cochineal insects are a third of the size of ladybugs and range from silver-gray to red-black. The insect feeds exclusively on the branches of cacti known as nopals or prickly pears. The female cochineal insect spends its whole life eating and produces carminic acid to ward off ants and other predators. This acid also produces a blood-red dye that adheres to cloth better than any other natural source of red.

Some evidence indicates use of cochineal as a dye in Mexico two thousand years ago. In addition to growing beans, maize, and squash, Mexican farmers discovered how to breed cochineal insects for size and color. Greenfield describes the harvesting and drying process in which seventy thousand dried insects produced one pound of cochineal. Aztecs were especially fond of red and used cochineal, called "blood of the nopal," to dye the feathers used in their colorful costumes. Aztecs also added cochineal to foods and medicine, practices that soon extended to Europe.

Hernán Cortés, leader of the Spanish expedition to Mexico, was amazed by the colors on display in marketplaces and notified his sovereign, Charles V. The first shipment of cochineal to Spain arrived in 1523, but the Spanish did not know how to market it and were reluctant to ask the Indians how to cultivate it.

By the 1540's, Italian dyers were experimenting with cochineal, finding it much more potent than kermes, and were the first to use it on silk. Cochineal gradually became New Spain's biggest export after silver, and by 1580, it dominated the European textile market, then the biggest industry on the continent. The Spanish Crown enacted laws to protect its monopoly. Because other countries could not produce cochineal themselves, they set about stealing it from the Spanish fleet. One of the more successful raids was led in 1597 by Queen Elizabeth's favorite, Robert Devereux, the earl of Essex, who stole fifty-five thousand pounds of the dyestuff. His sailors included a young John Donne, who later wrote of cochineal pirates in his poetry. Cochineal, writes Greenfield, was not only a highly valued commercial asset but a symbol of power: "To possess cochineal was to possess the color of military prowess and imperial glory."

The prominence of cochineal helped Mexico as well as Spain. Oaxaca, the chief cochineal-producing region, became Mexico's most culturally diverse state. For Mexicans, cochineal was less a product than "a living legacy from their ancestors."

One of the most compelling aspects of Greenfield's story is her account of the controversy over the source of cochineal. Robert Tomson, an English merchant who had been to Mexico, presented himself as a cochineal authority, explaining that the dye came from a berry. The Dutch scientist Antoni van Leeuwenhoek, developer of an early microscope, concluded that his instrument proved cochineal came from a seed. His countryman Jan Swammerdam used his microscope to determine that the source was indeed an insect, comparing cochineal to the larvae of bees. By 1704, Leeuwenhoek had improved his microscope sufficiently to see the truth and produce the first detailed drawings of the insect, though some disputed their accuracy. Another Dutchman, Melchior de Ruusscher, published a natural history of cochineal in 1729, finally providing conclusive proof that the color was derived from an insect.

One of Greenfield's most fascinating stories is that of Nicolas-Joseph Thiery de Menonville, a French botanist who convinced his government to fund his efforts to establish the country's first cochineal plantation in Haiti. A romantic adventurer, Thiery was willing to sacrifice his life in the effort. After a clandestine trip to Mexico, he returned to Haiti to begin cultivating the insects he proudly stole from Spain, only to ruin his physical and mental health. After he died of a fever, the project failed.

English botanist Joseph Banks, a favorite of George III, attempted to cultivate cochineal in Australia in 1787, with unexpected results. The nopals on which the insects thrived overran a hundred thousand square miles of eastern Australia, making the land useless for farming or grazing. Not until a South American moth whose larvae feed on the cactus was introduced in the 1920's did the problem come under control. Banks also attempted to grow cochineal in India, but the results were inferior.

In 1777, José Antonio Alzate y Ramírez, a Mexican priest and scientist, wrote the most comprehensive account of cochineal biology and cultivation. The patriotic Alzate claimed cochineal for Mexico and became the champion of Mexican science, lauding the botanical knowledge of ancient Mexicans in the face of Spanish indifference and ridicule. He enjoyed calling attention to the errors made by European scientists describing American phenomena.

Following the French Revolution, scarlet gowns and crimson velvet coats fell out of favor in France and elsewhere in Europe, and Mexican production of cochineal declined considerably. The revolutionary struggle in Mexico brought production to a standstill in 1812. During this period, cochineal was successfully introduced in Guatemala, which became Britain's main supplier, and by 1851, Guatemala produced twice as much cochineal as Mexico.

The public turned increasingly against red during the nineteenth century, as women began to associate scarlet with sin. A character in Charlotte Brontë's *Villette* (1853) considers red clothing unsuitable for respectable gentlewomen. An Emily Dickinson poem describes the products of cochineal as being "a tint too Red" for the tastes of her New England neighbors. English fashion manuals prescribed red as suitable only for married women.

The biggest impact upon cochineal during the nineteenth century came not from the mandates of fashion but the inevitable introduction of a synthetic source of red. In 1856, eighteen-year-old William Henry Perkin, a student at London's Royal College of Chemistry, was trying to synthesize quinine, only to create a purple dye that came to be called "Perkin's mauve." Realizing his discovery could transform the textile industry, Perkin labored for months to find a cheaper means of producing the dye, new technologies for improving its consistency, and a method for binding it to cotton, innovations considered even more important than discovering mauve itself. Luckily, mauve was favored by such trendsetters as the French Empress Eugenie, and by 1859, Perkin's mauve could be seen all over England. Perkin's mentor, August Hofmann, inspired by his student's success, created a synthetic crimson.

Such advances began the slow decline of the cochineal market. Cochineal, however, remained in some demand, especially because many of the synthetic dyes caused rashes and other ailments. Matters gradually improved for the new products, and by 1900, most textile manufacturers had stopped using cochineal. By the 1960's and 1970's, concern about the carcinogenic qualities of dyes and the increasing vogue for natural products resulted in a new demand for cochineal. Today, Peru is the main exporter of cochineal, which is also cultivated in the Canary Islands, Bolivia, Chile, and South Africa. The cochineal industry in Mexico has dwindled to a minor factor in the economy of Oaxaca.

Greenfield touches on the significance of red in folklore, its use by artists, references in literature, and its psychology but does not go into any of these subjects in detail. Rembrandt used cochineal to create depth for the bride's dress in *The Jewish Bride*. In *Candide* (1759), Voltaire uses cochineal as proof that humans were living in the best of all possible worlds. Greenfield notes that there are biological and cognitive differences in how cultures and individuals respond to red.

Greenfield has used her extensive sources quite well. She includes thirty pages of notes and a twenty-six-page bibliography. Her publisher, however, stints on the illustrations, offering only eight pages of color plates, depicting twelve images. Because the book is about color, many more illustrations would be an asset. Greenfield describes in detail a portrait of Essex that hangs in the National Portrait Gallery, but HarperCollins does not include it. This omission does not diminish Greenfield's achievement of weaving together the details of commerce and history to create a vivid image of red as a political and social symbol.

Michael Adams

Review Sources

Booklist 101, no. 15 (April 1, 2005): 1332.
Kirkus Reviews 73, no. 4 (February 15, 2005): 211.
Library Journal 130, no. 6 (April 1, 2005): 108.
Los Angeles Times Book Review, May 8, 2005, p. 7.
Natural History 114, no. 7 (September, 2005): 48-50.
The New York Times Book Review 154 (June 5, 2005): 26.
Publishers Weekly 252, no. 11 (March 14, 2005): 55.
The Times Literary Supplement, July 22, 2005, p. 28.
The Washington Post Book World, July 24, 2005, p. 8.

THE PERFECTIONIST
Life and Death in Haute Cuisine

Author: Rudolph Chelminski (1934-   )
Publisher: Gotham Books (New York). 354 pp. $27.50
Type of work: Biography
Time: From the 1930's to 2005
Locale: Saulieu, France

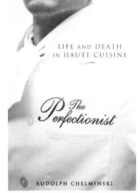

Chef Bernard Loiseau's hotel-restaurant in the French countryside reached the pinnacle of three Michelin stars before Loiseau committed suicide

Principal personages:
> BERNARD LOISEAU, the owner and chef of La Côte d'Or
> PATRICK BERTRON, Loiseau's *second,* or most important chef
> PAUL BOCUSE, the owner and chef at Restaurant Paul Bocuse, Loiseau's professional and personal role model
> HUBERT COUILLOUD, the *second maître d'hôtel* at La Côte d'Or, Loiseau's closest friend
> ALAIN DUCASSE, a celebrity chef who, at twenty-seven, was the youngest to ever win two Michelin stars
> BERNARD FABRE, Loiseau's accountant
> MICHEL GUÉRARD, the inventive owner and chef of Pot au Feu
> CHANTAL LOISEAU, Loiseau's first wife
> DOMINIQUE LOISEAU, Loiseau's second wife
> JEAN-BAPTISTE and PIERRE TROISGROS, brothers in whose Roanne restaurant Loiseau served his apprenticeship
> CLAUDE VERGER, an entrepreneur who hired Loiseau to run La Côte d'Or and eventually sold it to him

When Bernard Loiseau killed himself on February 24, 2003, his death was reported on every French newscast and in every French newspaper. Three thousand mourners attended his funeral. According to a survey, nine out of ten French people knew Loiseau's name. In the United States, however, the passing of the chef and owner of La Côte d'Or in Saulieu, a man who had appeared on the cover of *Time* magazine, went largely unremarked. Only in France, as Rudolph Chelminski explains in *The Perfectionist: Life and Death in Haute Cuisine*, does a masterful chef command the same celebrity as an athlete or a rock star does in the States—even among the many people who could never pay up to a thousand dollars for dinner for two.

How Loiseau rose from relatively humble beginnings to being the operator of a three-star restaurant and inn, and how his story illuminates the wider world of French cuisine, is the subject of *The Perfectionist.* Chelminski has been over some of this ground before, in decades of magazine articles and in *The French at Table: Why the*

Rudolph Chelminski is a journalist who has written for national magazines including Time *and* The Atlantic Monthly. Life *magazine sent him to Paris more than thirty years ago, and he continues to live and work there. He is the author of* The French at Table *(1985).*

French Know How to Eat Better than Any People on Earth and How They Have Gone About It, from the Gauls to Paul Bocuse* (1985). In this earlier book, Chelminski visited famous and little-known restaurants throughout France, demonstrating an educated palate and a pleasant demeanor that has made him a welcome patron. He appreciates good food and the hard work that goes into producing it.

In Loiseau's case, the hard work began with an apprenticeship arranged by his father in 1968, when the boy was seventeen years old. In the kitchen of the Troisgros brothers, Jean-Baptiste and Pierre, he spent twelve-hour days doing what every beginning kitchen apprentice does: hauling coal from the cellar, washing counter tops and ovens, and scrubbing the firebox with a wire bush, in addition to chopping vegetables and, after months of training, killing frogs by swinging their heads against the edge of a work table. Only fifteen days after Loiseau went to work at Les Frères Troisgros, the restaurant was awarded a third Michelin star, the highest award for cuisine in France. It was the beginning of Loiseau's dream of one day running a three-star restaurant himself.

To help his readers understand the significance of this dream—and the boldness of it—Chelminski pauses for a history of *Le Guide Michelin*, the guidebook that rates French restaurants according to a strict and mysterious system of secret inspectors and hidden criteria. Long recognized as the indisputable scorekeeper of French haute cuisine, the Michelin Guide began in 1900 as a simple listing of names and addresses of places motorists might like to visit. Issued by the Michelin tire company, the goal of the guide was to encourage people to drive their newfangled automobiles more frequently, so they would need more tires. Restaurants a few hours away from Paris received special attention, because people out for a day of recreational driving needed good, reliable food to break up their trips. In 1933, the guide began rating restaurants according to their quality, awarding two stars to places with "excellent cooking, worth a detour," and three stars to those with "exceptional cuisine, worth a special journey." Only a few restaurants were deemed worthy of three stars (though Michelin has always denied having a set limit); after Loiseau's death there were only twenty-four three-star chefs in all of France.

To be worthy of three stars, a restaurant must be nearly perfect in every detail: setting, service, atmosphere, china, silverware, presentation, and especially the food. Chelminski clearly understands and delights in food. He devotes paragraph after paragraph to describing complex and expensive dishes, and his prose is nowhere more elevated and yet whimsical than when he is praising haute cuisine. One sentence, from his tale of Loiseau's spiritual grandfather, Fernand Point, will suffice to demonstrate this aspect of Chelminski's style:

> Point was perfectly capable of strutting his stuff with showpieces like *turbot à l'amiral*, which required two sauces, one based on white wine and the other on red, or the even more complex *filets de sole Brillat-Savarin*, a creamy lobster mousse jacketed in sliced truffles, surrounded by poached filets of sole on puff-pastry *croustades*, each filet topped with a lobster tail scallop and a ruinously thick slice of *T. melanosporum*, the black truffle that does for French cuisine what a Wonderbra does for an ambitious ingénue.

It was at the top of the world of such cooking that Loiseau sought to find his place. Completing his apprenticeship, he soon found himself cooking at a bistro owned by Claude Verger outside of Paris. Verger knew talent when he saw it, and he saw in Loiseau the kind of personality he could coach to stardom. Although Loiseau had trained only a few years under the Troisgros brothers—not for many years under many chefs, as was the norm in the old days—Verger gave him more and more responsibility until, a few career bumps later, Loiseau was running La Côte d'Or, the past-its-prime hotel-restaurant Verger had purchased in the town of Saulieu. Once a three-star restaurant, La Côte d'Or was now a humble no-star place, but Verger saw potential. At first, the place was run entirely in Verger's image. He instructed Loiseau in his own style of food preparation, and he reserved for himself and his wife the apartment above the dining room, which they used on their infrequent long weekends in Saulieu, while Loiseau lived in a small room at the back. It was clear to the staff, and to the critics, who was in charge. Gradually, though, Loiseau did become a star, serving plain regional cooking prepared of the highest quality ingredients, and he was able to buy Verger out.

The core of the book is dedicated to the evolution of *le style Loiseau*. Moving away from Verger's and the Troisgros brothers' specialties, Loiseau's ideal was simplicity: the freshest ingredients, perfectly prepared, "always just three ingredients and three savors on the plate, complementing one another, tied togther by a sauce that hid nothing." For a while he deglazed pans only with water, rather than with the wine or stock that others used, because he found the resulting sauces purer. Others found them curiously yet attractively bland. To present only the authentic taste of each ingredient, he developed complicated multistep techniques for preparing caramelized cauliflower, a puree made of boiled celery, and the perfect veal chop. Somehow it worked, and for years people made the drive to Saulieu just to dine under Loiseau's watchful and dynamic gaze. While Loiseau's food was simple, his dining room and his hotel suites were not, at least not after he had borrowed millions of dollars to make renovations.

La Côte d'Or won its first Michelin star in 1977; its second came in 1981. Many chefs lead happy and contented lives with only one star to their credit; they know who they are and what kind of work they want to do. Loiseau was driven by forces even he may not have understood, and though he was respected and loved he does not seem to have been happy. Finally, in 1991, when Loiseau was awarded his third star, he declared, "This is the greatest day of my life." The tragedy of Bernard Loiseau is that this happiness did not last long. Having reached the top of his profession, he felt no less pressure to perform and to please than he ever had, and now the fear of losing his stars haunted him as much as his desire to win them had before. He drove himself to exhaustion, doing radio and television interviews, traveling to Japan, even forming a corporation to keep the money flowing and the borrowed money in check.

By the middle of the 1990's, the world that had so embraced Loiseau was starting to bypass him. Driving, for most, was now a chore, not an adventure, and restaurants in the countryside could no longer count on customers who would make a day of having lunch or dinner. A weakened economy meant fewer diners could afford lavish meals. Terrorist attacks, especially those in the United States on September 11, 2001, led to a decrease in international tourists. New tastes and new health concerns called for new styles of cooking—styles that Loiseau would not, and could not, imitate. As his accountant, Bernard Fabre, explained, "His cuisine was what it was, and he couldn't make it into anything else. He couldn't change, he couldn't add foreign flavorings, and he couldn't invent gimmicks." Meanwhile, the critics kept up a constant demand for new foods, new seasonings, new combinations, new presentations. Loiseau had always been a brilliant promoter, a generous and gracious host, a careful and demanding stylist—a perfectionist—but the fact remained that he was not adept at basic cooking skills, and he would not have known how to invent truly new dishes even had he so desired.

Compounding Loiseau's troubles was something that he managed to keep hidden from all but his closest associates: He suffered from bipolar disorder, experiencing manic highs and debilitating depressions. Chelminski, who knew Loiseau socially and dined as his guest several times, recounts that as early as the mid-1980's he noticed the chef's exceptionally manic energy one day and asked whether he ever felt down. "You've got no idea," Loiseau replied, "how far down I go when I fall." Chelminski was among many of Loiseau's acquaintances who did not understand the significance of the chef's moods until after his death. Sadly, Loiseau was spiraling downward at the same time that he heard a rumor that La Côte d'Or was about to be demoted to only two stars. His increasing phobias and paranoia, and the threat of losing the most important marker of his worth, led him to take his own life.

Chelminski is first and foremost a reporter, and the thoroughness of his research for this book is impressive. He seems to have interviewed everyone who ever worked closely with Loiseau, and his own affection for the chef clearly inspired affectionate reminiscences from those he interviewed. In addition, he has studied the history of the Michelin guide and its competitors; the lives and careers of Loiseau's culinary ancestors; and the mutually dependent, mutually destructive relationship between critics and artists. Bringing enormous empathy to his tragedy of one great chef, Chelminski has written the story of many great, obsessed perfectionists, and their ultimate inability to find satisfaction and peace.

Cynthia A. Bily

Review Sources

Booklist 101, no. 16 (April 15, 2005): 1421.
Kirkus Reviews 73, no. 6 (March 15, 2005): 327.
Library Journal 130, no. 7 (April 15, 2005): 112-114.
The New York Times 154 (June 1, 2005): E1.
The New Yorker 81, no. 7 (April 4, 2005): 88-92.
Publishers Weekly 252, no. 13 (March 28, 2005): 65.
Smithsonian 36, no. 5 (August, 2005): 103.
The Times Literary Supplement, March 4, 2005, p. 25.
The Washington Post Book World 35 (May 29, 2005): 2.

THE PLANETS

Author: Dava Sobel (1947-   )
Publisher: Viking Press (New York). 270 pp. $25.00
Type of work: History of science and science
Time: The first through the twenty-first centuries
Locale: The solar system

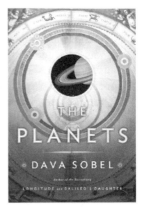

*Sobel surveys traditional views and modern theories of
the planets and the solar system as a whole*

Principal personages:
> PTOLEMY (c. 85-165), the Greek geographer
> and astronomer who devised a geocentric
> theory of planetary motion and mapped
> the earth using astronomical observations
> NICOLAS COPERNICUS (1473-1543), the Pol-
> ish astronomer who formulated a helio-
> centric theory of planetary motion
> GALILEO GALILEI (1564-1642), the Italian astronomer who confirmed
> Copernicus's theory
> JOHANNES KEPLER (1571-1630), the German mathematician and astron-
> omer who formulated the laws of planetary motion
> GERARD KUIPER (1905-1973), the Dutch American astronomer who pre-
> dicted the existence of numerous planetoids at the edge of the solar
> system

Dava Sobel's talent for portraying scientific advances within their cultural contexts made her earlier books international best sellers. In *Longitude: The True Story of
a Lone Genius Who Solved the Greatest Scientific Problem of His Time* (1995), she
dramatized not only John Harrison's invention of the chronometer and but also his agonizing struggle for recognition. In *Galileo's Daughter: A Historical Memoir of Science, Faith, and Love* (1999), she illuminated Galileo Galilei's unfailing devotion to
his religion and family as well as to science. In her recent work *The Planets*, she once
again explores the human dimension of her subject, combining her personal attraction
to the study of planets with a survey of their factual and not infrequently fabulous cultural dimensions.

Modern astronomers have employed technology to refine scientific descriptions of
the planets, the sun, and the solar system as a whole, providing new data that reverber-
ate with cosmic energy. In *The Planets*, Sobel reveals how traditional notions of the
heavens relate to these new discoveries. Her chapter titles suggest her method, as she
discusses the Sun in "Genesis," Mars in "Sci-Fi," Uranus and Neptune in "Night Air,"
and so on.

Sobel opens by recalling the origins of her fascination with the planets in the chapter "Model Worlds." During elementary school in the 1950's, she became enamored

of the planets, seeing them as reliable yet exotic beings where unlimited strangeness was circumscribed
by the unusual qualities of the number nine. Nine
planets could not be reckoned in pairs or dozens
or manipulated with zeroes or fives but could be
counted on the fingers. Her initial attraction to the
planets was intensified by activities that included
constructing a shoebox diorama for a science fair,
appearing in a class play as "Lonely Star," and visiting the Hayden Planetarium. Viewing the enormous
Willamette meteorite awakened her to the possible
threat to Earth from the skies above.

The author of Longitude *(1995)*
and Galileo's Daughter *(1999),*
Dava Sobel has excelled as a
science journalist in her thirty-
year career, contributing articles
to such periodicals as
Astronomy, Audubon, Discover,
Harvard Magazine, The New
Yorker, *and* Omni. *She won the*
National Science Board's
prestigious Individual Public
Service Award in 2001.

Sobel's memoir lays the groundwork for appre-
ciating the enormous progress of more recent space
exploration. Within the past few decades, unmanned
space probes have revealed previously unknown
details about the planets, including the existence of
"new" moons and multiple rings around Jupiter,
Saturn, Uranus, and Neptune. "Model Worlds" concludes with a reference to exoplanets—planets that
astronomers have calculated to exist in other solar
systems. In effect, current knowledge of Earth's
planetary system has become the basis for detecting
many other systems.

In "Genesis," Sobel relates the biblical story of creation to the big bang theory of
creation. Scientists attribute the beginning of the universe to the emergence of a hot
light bursting from a dark and timeless void. As the light rapidly cooled, it created an
entire universe of matter and energy. Sobel describes the stages of development of the
solar system, in which the Sun draws itself into being, amassing 99.9 percent of the
available matter swirling in a remote corner of a remote galaxy and leaving a mere
1 percent for all the planets. Her portrait of the Sun continues with a discussion of sunlight, solar winds, and eclipses.

The structure of Sobel's book extends from the Sun to the outer planets, with individual chapters devoted to the "terrestrial planets" of Mercury, Venus, Earth, and
Mars. In "Mythology," Sobel notes that Mercury (the Roman name for the Greek
messenger-god Hermes) is probably so-named because of the planet's swift and brief
appearances at or near the horizon. Ancient astronomer Ptolemy plotted the orbit of
Mercury as traversing the earth just beyond the orbiting moon, but Sobel discusses its
true profile in regard to orbit, rotation, and heat—the fevered light of the Sun always
bearing down directly on Mercury's equator.

Mercury's proximity to the Sun has historically caused astronomers difficulty.
Even Copernicus, developing his theory that the planets revolved around the sun, was
unable to see Mercury well enough to predict its orbit as accurately as he would have
liked. Johannes Kepler determined the laws of planetary motion by using data col-

lected earlier by his colleague Tycho Brahe. Later astronomers and mathematicians continued to struggle with Mercury's unusual orbiting behavior and speed, even proposing that another planet (dubbed Vulcan) caused these anomalies. The concept of Vulcan was dropped when Albert Einstein resolved the problem mathematically in 1915 by proving that the sun's extreme gravitational pull was the cause. Satellite Mariner 10 collected photos of Mercury's battered surface in the 1970's, and the planet's unique properties will be closely scrutinized once more by the space probe *MESSENGER*, scheduled to approach Mercury in 2008. (*MESSENGER* is an acronym for *ME*rcury *S*urface, *S*pace *E*nvironment, *GE*ochemistry, and *R*anging.)

Sobel's chapter on Venus, titled "Beauty," offers a roundup of ancient legends and examines a number of reverent poems written by earthbound admirers. There is no doubt that the planet's prominence in mythology and planetary lore is the result of its frequent, shimmering dominance of the night sky. Its appearance as the "evening star" or "morning star" (a designation it shares on occasion with several other planets) has resulted in generations of endearments. Thanks to his improvements to the telescope, Galileo was able to chart the phases of Venus. Future poets may be more constrained in their portraits of the planet, as it is now known that its surface is washed with sulfuric acid rain.

"Geography," as Sobel calls the section on Earth, delivers a sweeping summary of the exploration of the planet after presenting an overview of Ptolemy's use of astronomy in mapping it. In "Lunacy," a segment on the moon, she replaces the beloved and legendary champion of romance with a portrait of a dry, dark, and dusty satellite whose reflected light is never quite bright enough to engender color within the range of human vision. Also, thanks to intense studies of the red planet, the "sci-fi" vision of Mars has given way to a harsher, if no less exotic, view: It is now known that its iron-oxide surface poses a deadly threat to life and that its solidified iron core is incapable of generating a magnetic field.

The gas planets of Jupiter, Saturn, Uranus, and Neptune stretch outward in space from the terrestrial planets. In the chapter "Astrology," on Jupiter, the facts, as opposed to planetary lore, prove astonishing. Jupiter's volume is one thousand times that of the earth, and it retains a cloudy cover made up of countervailing winds and jet streams, visible as dark belts and bright swaths, features that are constantly metamorphosing in centuries-long storms. Its colorful clouds obscure the dense inner sea of liquid hydrogen, so compacted in the depths of the planet that its liquid turns into an electrically charged metallic substance that actually composes the bulk of the planet.

Turning to "Music of the Spheres," Sobel frames her discussion of Saturn musically, beginning with the English composer Gustav Holst's 1916 orchestral suite *The Planets*. In this work, Saturn is characterized as the "Bringer of Old Age," a role that Holst claimed entailed not only the decline of physical well-being but also a sense of fulfillment. In fact, as Sobel explains, the rings of Saturn incorporate distinct harmonic resonances.

Sobel cites the beauty of the Saturnian ring system as capable of attracting viewers to a lifetime interest in astronomy. Saturn's resplendent rings (composed of dust and ice crystals) vary in visibility with the planet's changing position in orbit, being fully displayed to viewers on Earth only every fifteen years. Following Galileo's unfulfilled study of the rings, Dutch mathematician and astronomer Christiaan Huygens was able to prepare a diagram in 1659 revealing how the planet's 29.5-year elliptical orbit actually progressed. The rings of Saturn resonate in relationships that accord with the rules of pitch developed by ancient Greek mathematician and astronomer Pythagoras. The resonance effect of the rings separates them, leaving empty spaces between, as proven when the *Cassini* spacecraft flew between the two rings known as F and G upon reaching Saturn in 2004.

Pluto, which Sobel dubs "UFO," is now considered by some to be too small to fit planetary criteria, but it remains dominant in its region. Gerard Kuiper first predicted the existence of Pluto's companions, icy exiles rejected from the inner solar system during its formative period and orbiting in what is known as the Kuiper Belt in honor of its discoverer. Scientists hope to learn more about the early formation of the universe from these planetoids.

Sobel explicates exciting new discoveries about the planets handily in her more straightforward scientific passages, and the celestial residents shine in splendor in her more poetic descriptions. However, her creativity sometimes results in overly cute and potentially misleading features. A Martian meteorite, fallen to Earth near the South Pole during the last ice age, narrates "Sci-Fi." "Night Air" consists chiefly of a fictional letter from astronomer Maria Mitchell to fellow astronomer Caroline Herschel. Sobel's previous work as translator of the 2001 volume *Letters to Father: Suor Maria Celeste to Galileo, 1623-1633* may lead readers to assume that Mitchell's letter is likewise authentic; only the "Details" section of seemingly random notes at the end of the book informs them otherwise. In "Astrology," Sobel's discussion of Galileo's horoscope, as well as the inclusion of a natal chart for the space probe Galileo, may lead the unwary to infer that astrology is on a par with astronomy. More sophisticated readers may weary of Sobel's tendency to anthropomorphize planets, meteorites, and even space probes.

Other readers, perhaps newly enchanted with the solar system thanks to Sobel's succinct summary of astronomical data, may find such distinctions inconsequential. For many, Sobel's brief tour of the solar system will provide a wealth of unexpected information concerning the planets' motion, composition, and moons. Her descriptions of astronomical discoveries and breakthroughs will entertain readers unfamiliar with astronomical history. For better and occasionally for worse, Sobel's mixture of science, myth, folklore, history, biography, science fiction, music, and astrology exercises its appeal at many levels.

Margaret A. Dodson

Review Sources

Atlanta Journal and Constitution, October 2, 2005, p. L5.
Booklist 101, no. 22 (August 1, 2005): 1950-1951.
Kirkus Reviews 73, no. 14 (July 15, 2005): 783.
Library Journal 130, no. 13 (August 15, 2005): 118.
Los Angeles Times, October 30, 2005, p. R6.
Nature 437 (September 29, 2005): 623.
The New York Times 155 (October 19, 2005): E9.
Publishers Weekly 252, no. 40 (October 10, 2005): 22-23.
Sky & Telescope 110, no. 4 (October, 2005): 104-105.
The Wall Street Journal 246, no. 90 (October 28, 2005): W6.

POL POT
Anatomy of a Nightmare

Author: Philip Short (1945-   )
Publisher: Henry Holt (New York). Illustrated. 539 pp.
$30.00
Type of work: Biography
Locale: Cambodia

Short analyzes how Pol Pot rose from obscurity to lead the Khmer Rouge regime that committed many of the twentieth century's worst crimes against humanity

Principal personage:
POL POT (1925-1998), born SALOTH SAR, the dictator of Democratic Kampuchea

The empire established in the fifth century by the Khmers, the aboriginal people of Cambodia, peaked with the construction of Angkor Thom and ruled the entire Mekong Valley as well as its neighboring Shan states. Annamese and Siamese conquests after the twelfth century left the Khmers vulnerable to outside domination; Khmer yearnings for independence and restoration of their previous glory remained. In the 1970's, the Khmer Rouge (Communist or "Red" Khmers) turned those hopes into one of history's most destructive revolutionary movements.

Philip Short's biography of Pol Pot shows that the Khmer Rouge leader does not rank very far below Adolf Hitler, Joseph Stalin, and Mao Zedong when one considers the twentieth century's perpetrators of mass murder and crimes against humanity. *Pol Pot: Anatomy of a Nightmare* contains important warnings. It documents how easily violence and barbarism can arise when dogmatic political theory is ruthlessly put into practice.

Short begins by observing that "history is to a great extent detective work." For at least two reasons, that judgment understates the challenge he confronted in researching his subject. First, Pol Pot's origins scarcely pointed to his becoming a murderous dictator. Second, no single person working alone could have implemented the policies that resulted in the massive slaughter of the Cambodian population that took place between April, 1975, and January, 1979, in ironically christened Democratic Kampuchea.

When the Khmer Rouge took power on April 17, 1975, Cambodia's population was about seven million. Although exact statistics for the number of Cambodians who perished under Pol Pot do not exist, one-and-a-half million deaths—those of one-fifth of Pol Pot's own people—are estimated by Short. It has been said that every civilian family in the nation suffered deaths and losses. Most of the victims died from the starvation and disease that resulted from Pol Pot's revolutionary policies, which were as unrealistic as they were radical, but some two hundred thousand Cambodians

Philip Short has been a foreign
correspondent for the British
Broadcasting Corporation (BBC).
He lived in Cambodia and China in
the 1970's and early 1980's. In
addition to writing for The Times
(London) *and* The Economist, *he is*
the author of Mao: A Life *(2000).*

were executed outright by the Khmer Rouge as well.

Apparently Pol Pot was not a "hands-on" killer. He could appear mild-mannered, polite, and smiling, but he ruled by terror and fear nonetheless. His reign, Short argues, made ideology primary. Thus, the Khmer Rouge regime required that its leaders and followers to do everything that was necessary to ensure that "principle won out, regardless of the material cost." The guiding principle was that Democratic Kampuchea was to be, in Pol Pot's words, "a precious model for humanity" whose egalitarian ways would erase human inclinations for exploitation, including the need for money and profit-making markets.

This dream was disastrous. To determine how and why the catastrophe was allowed, however, Short could not concentrate on Pol Pot alone. His biographical work became much more than that of a detective who has to track the actions of one complicated and elusive individual. Short's daunting problem was also to assess the historical, geographical, cultural, political, and international contexts that could produce not only Pol Pot but also the cadres of leaders and followers who were willing to destroy so much of their own Cambodian culture.

Short's narrative is as complex as it is detailed and compelling. For example, the radical nature of the Khmer Rouge movement meant that it operated in secrecy and with levels of mistrust that reached paranoia. Keeping track of names alone takes Short and his readers into a labyrinth that can be mapped only in part by the book's helpful pages that list and identify the key players. The name Pol Pot was an alias, the best known of several used by the Khmer Rouge leader, who was born Saloth Sar. In his youth, Cambodia was a French protectorate. Coming from a relatively prosperous family that enjoyed favor with the Cambodian royalty who were allowed some autonomy under French colonialism, Sar went to French-language schools. Popular but inconspicuous, he did not achieve academic distinction, although his record and connections were sufficient to win him the coveted scholarship that took him to Paris in 1949.

Radio technology was Sar's official field of study in Paris, but it was eclipsed by revolutionary politics as he found his way into the Cercle Marxiste, a group of young communist-inspired Cambodian intellectual-revolutionaries, and then into the French Communist Party. By 1952, his scholarship revoked, Sar was back in Cambodia, which achieved independence from France two years later. Officially, Cambodian political authority belonged to King Norodom Sihanouk, a wily practitioner of political expediency. The first to use the term "Khmer Rouge" to refer to the Cambodian Communists, Sihanouk sometimes opposed them and sometimes aligned with the Khmer Rouge. Meanwhile, Sar's influence grew. He became head of the Communist Party of Kampuchea (CPK) in 1963, although he tended to remain in the background, taking on the alias Pol Pot several years later.

Short convincingly depicts Pol Pot as a communist utopian of a peculiar kind. He wanted to restore Cambodia's national identity and pride. His exposure to French history and culture helped to form his extreme version of the French Revolution's emphasis on liberty, equality, and fraternity. In his Cambodia, capitalist-inspired individualism and exploitation would disappear. New freedom would be found as the Khmers worked together, dismantling old ways, sharing and sharing alike. Short identifies other influences as well. While in Paris, for instance, Pol Pot read the works of Russian anarchist Peter Kropotkin, who focused three of Pol Pot's lifelong convictions: Revolution depends on an alliance between intellectuals and peasants; revolution must go forward to the end without compromise; communism's core is egalitarianism.

In Short's view, neither Mao nor Stalin were Pol Pot's "ideological soul mates," but he took instruction from them both. Mao's Cultural Revolution in China suggested that social transformation could take place swiftly. Pol Pot acknowledged that Cambodia lacked the industrialization and proletariat that classical Marxist political theory regarded as necessary for revolutionary success, but he believed that an alliance between intellectuals and Cambodian peasants could rapidly bring about a new society, even in a region that was ravaged by the Vietnam War. The war in Vietnam spilled into Cambodia to such an extent that American planes dropped more than half a million tons of bombs there—an amount, according to Short, that was "three times the total tonnage dropped on Japan, atom bombs included," during World War II.

Stalin's "purges" in the Soviet Union convinced Pol Pot that a successful revolution required unrelenting vigilance against deviation and betrayal from within. If it took deceit and terror to get a pan-Cambodian consensus, or to eliminate those who would not agree, he was willing to pay that price. As Short points out, Cambodian tradition did not provide a strong base for resisting those who had gained power. That tradition emphasized obedience to authority and acceptance of the hand that history dealt—inclinations, Short believes, that were encouraged by the Theravada Buddhism that informed Cambodian spiritual life. Given the circumstances in which Pol Pot emerged from obscurity, this mixture was the recipe for a catastrophe that was utterly opposite to the utopia that Pol Pot so misguidedly envisioned.

As late as the spring of 1970, Short argues, there was little to suggest the horror that would be unleashed five years later. The times, however, were changing. In 1970, an American-backed coup displaced Sihanouk and elevated Lon Nol to power in the Cambodian capital, Phnom Penh. Eventually, the Khmer Rouge ousted Lon Nol, and at last, on April 17, 1975, Pol Pot and the Khmer Rouge got to implement their radical vision. At first, most Cambodians welcomed Pol Pot's black-clad men as liberators from the miseries of war and Lon Nol's corrupt government. In the newly named Democratic Kampuchea, their optimism, especially that of Phnom Penh's two million people, was short-lived. City dwellers were forced into the countryside to join agricultural communes. Free choice and wages virtually disappeared. Anything smacking of individualism was subordinated, if not crushed completely, so that Pol Pot's social transformation could advance.

Short contends that Pol Pot and the Khmer Rouge created "a slave state, the first in modern times." A grievous lack of planning and common sense made conditions go from bad to worse, as hunger and illness took escalating tolls. Pol Pot and his followers never gave up the conviction that their plan was right. Any shortcomings were due not to Khmer Rouge miscalculation or brutality but to the failure of the Cambodians to work hard enough, to sacrifice long enough. Those failures had to be corrected by punishment, which often meant starvation, or by death through execution, which, Pol Pot believed, would deter slacking. All the while, Pol Pot guarded Khmer Rouge loyalty jealously and vindictively. The slightest sense that his leadership was questioned or threatened led to murderous purges within his own ranks. Unsustainable though it was, Pol Pot's regime lasted long enough to inflict untold agony.

The end of the regime of terror came at the hands of Pol Pot's hated Vietnamese. When it seemed in their interests to do so, the Vietnamese Communists had supported the Khmer Rouge, but historically, and more often than not, the Vietnamese and the Cambodians have been at odds. Fighting between Cambodia and Vietnam flared in late 1977; by the next year full-scale war was under way. Victory would come, Pol Pot insisted, when every Cambodian soldier killed thirty Vietnamese. Instead, the Vietnamese invasion swept the Khmer Rouge from power as Pol Pot fled to Thailand.

Pol Pot eluded justice. Under the protection of Thai forces and the remains of his Khmer Rouge army, he lived in the forests of Thailand and northern Cambodia, periodically traveling to Bangkok or Beijing for cancer treatments. The exact circumstances of his death remain unclear, but his life ended on April 15, 1998. Before his death, Pol Pot acknowledged that he had made mistakes, but only in trying to implement his vision too fast. It is unlikely that he ever questioned his basic aspirations, for he expressed no apology or remorse for anything he had done.

Short ends his book on notes that are more arguable and controversial than the thoroughly researched historical analysis that precedes them. Contrary to what is often said about Pol Pot and his followers, Short does not believe that they should be indicted for genocide. His assessment is as follows: The actions of the Khmer Rouge do not meet the key conditions that define genocide in international law, for they did not attempt to annihilate, in whole or in part, a national, ethnic, racial, or religious group. Instead, says Short, "they conspired to enslave a people. That they did so believing that their ends were noble is irrelevant. Such an undertaking, carried out on so grand a scale and with such unrelenting savagery, is by definition, if words have any meaning, a 'crime against humanity.'"

Short thinks that the international community, especially the United States, has a vested interest is mislabeling Pol Pot's regime as genocidal. He points out that there would have been no Khmer Rouge reign of terror if there had been no Vietnam War. In that war, he suggests, far too many crimes against humanity were committed on multiple sides. By singling out Pol Pot and the Khmer Rouge as perpetrators of genocide, other nations can "regain the moral high ground" and divert attention from their own crimes against humanity in those woeful times and places.

This argument, problematic though it may be, is not intended to remove the spotlight from Pol Pot and his death-dealing regime. Short laments the fact that so little justice has been done, and he attributes much of that shortcoming to Cambodian governance that he disgustedly describes as rotten. Short's study does not leave him hopeful about the human condition. He does not expect events to repeat themselves in Cambodia, but he doubts that history has seen the last of political power abuses akin to those of Pol Pot. "The fire next time," he concludes, "will be somewhere else."

John K. Roth

Review Sources

Booklist 101, no. 8 (December 15, 2004): 703.
Kirkus Reviews 72, no. 22 (November 15, 2004): 1084.
Library Journal 129, no. 20 (December 1, 2004): 138.
Los Angeles Times, July 31, 2005, p. R8.
The New York Review of Books 52, no. 10 (June 9, 2005): 28-31.
The New York Times 154 (February 18, 2005): E33-E41.
The New York Times Book Review 154 (February 27, 2005): 8-9.
The Washington Post, February 27, 2005, p. T10.

PRINCE OF FIRE

Author: Daniel Silva (1960-   )
Publisher: G. P. Putnam's Sons (New York). 369 pp.
    $26.00
Type of work: Novel
Time: Around 2000
Locale: Cairo, Egypt; Tel Aviv, Jerusalem, Tiberias, and
    Tel Megiddo, Israel; Rome and Fiumicino, Italy; Paris,
    Marseilles, Aix-en-Provence, and Troyes, France; Sur-
    rey, England

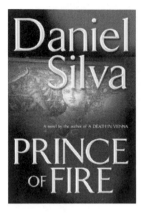

*Gabriel Allon, art restorer and terrorist hunter, tracks
down the organizer of a Palestinian attack on the Israeli
embassy in Rome*

Principal characters:
> GABRIEL ALLON, an art restorer and Israeli intelligence operator
> ARI SHAMRON, a special adviser to the Israeli prime minister on security
> and intelligence
> LEV AHRONI, Shamron's successor as director of the Israeli intelligence
> service
> SABRI AL-KHALIFA, the Palestinian Black Septembrist terrorist master-
> mind of the 1972 Olympic Village massacre
> PAUL MARTINEAU, the pseudonym of Sabri al-Khalifa's son, the terrorist
> Khaled al-Khalifa
> YASIR ARAFAT, the Palestinian president and sponsor of terrorism
> MAHMOUD AWISH, also known as COLONEL KEMEL, a double agent
> murdered by Arafat

When terrorists blow up the Israeli embassy in Rome in Daniel Silva's *Prince of Fire*, the Israeli prime minister tells Ari Shamron, his seventy-five-year-old, chain-smoking special adviser, that he wants the instigator's head "on a stick." Shamron immediately reaches Gabriel Allon in London, where Allon is en route from Venice to visit his wife, Leah, in a private psychiatric hospital in Surrey. Leah was wounded in a terrorist blast in Vienna, but Allon will not divorce her to marry his Italian lover, Chiara Zolli, daughter of the chief rabbi of Venice. Allon is a brilliant art restorer, currently working on Bellini's San Giovanni Crisostomo altarpiece, an undertaking he abandons when Shamron arrives in Venice and orders him back to Jerusalem.

Shamron promptly assembles a team for Allon, led by an intelligence analyst known only as Yossi and a woman named Dina with a complete file of terrorist activities in her head. It is Dina's acute instincts that lead Allon to Khaled al-Khalifa, and at this point the narrative switches back to Turkish-ruled Palestine in 1910. Khaled's grandfather, Asad al-Khalifa, was a young man in the Jewish settlement of Petah

Tikvah and a brutal criminal who robbed Jews and
Palestinians alike. When the Arab Revolt broke out
in 1936, Asad quickly became a nationalist and began a series of assassinations with his long, curved
knife. By 1938, however, the revolt had destroyed
itself by clan conflicts, and Asad was lying low in
Damascus. In 1947 he was summoned by Haj Amin
al-Husseini, the grand mufti of the Arab Higher
Council, to lead a campaign of massacres until in
1948 he was tracked down in a cottage near Lydda
and killed by the young intelligence officer Ari
Shamron.

~

*Prince of Fire is Daniel Silva's
fifth novel featuring Gabriel
Allon, the talented art restorer
who takes on some of Israeli
intelligence's most difficult
assignments. Silva lives in
Washington, D.C., with his wife,
NBC* Today *correspondent
Jamie Gangel.*

~

The story then picks up again with a flashback to Amman, Jordan, in June, 1967.
There a young man approaches a Fatah recruiting officer and announces his name as
Sabri al-Khalifa. He is Asad's son, who proved a talented Fatah intelligence officer
and a special favorite of Yasir Arafat. Sabri married a young Palestinian woman
named Rima and they had a son born in September, 1970, an "ominous" date. When
Arafat wanted revenge on the Jordanians, the Black September unit was created, with
Sabri al-Khalifa as the de facto mastermind. After several bloody attacks on Jorda-
nian officials in Cairo, London, and Bonn, as well as the murder in May, 1972, of
twenty-seven people in Israel's Lod Airport by Japanese Red Army terrorists acting
for Black September, Sabri sent six Palestinian terrorists over the fence at the Olympic Village in Munich the following September. This daring act led to the deaths of
eleven Israel athletes. Under Prime Minister Golda Meir's orders, Ari Shamron was
again assigned to kill a man named al-Khalifa. Shamron's team, code-named Wrath
of God, ferreted out and eliminated twelve of Sabri's Black Septembrists, but Sabri
himself remained alive. At this point, Gabriel Allon assumed the chase, tracing Sabri
through his girlfriend to her flat in Paris, where Gabriel lay in wait and fired eleven
shots into Sabri, one for each Olympic victim.

These events lie in the background of the Rome bombing, as it becomes clear to
Gabriel's team that it is Sabri's son, Khaled al-Khalifa, virtually Arafat's adopted
son, who is now running the Palestinian terrorists. The astute Dina pulls all the strands
together when she tells the story of the small Arab village of Beit Sayeed being dyna-
mited by Israelis on April 18, 1948, at seven in the evening, the same date and hour of
a truck bombing in Buenos Aires in 1994 that killed eighty-seven people at a Shabbat
meal, and of another car bombing at Istanbul's main synagogue in 2003 that claimed
twenty-eight lives. Moreover, Gabriel assassinated Sabri on March 4, the same date
that Rome was hit. From this reconstruction, Dina deduces that Khaled al-Khalifa
plans another attack in twenty-eight days, or on April 18.

Meanwhile, Khaled al-Khalifa, respected in his professional world as Paul Martineau, adjunct professor of archaeology at the University of Aix-Marseille III, is
winding up his dig in Provence with his graduate student girlfriend, Yvette Debré, before driving the A51 Autoroute to Marseilles. Parking his Mercedes on the Boulevard
d'Anthènes, Khaled walks to a coffee house in a dim neighborhood, where on the

second-floor landing a man in a galabia gown throws open the door. The man greets him with *Maa-salaamah*, and Khaled answers, *As-salaam alaykum*.

Gabriel begins his mission with a trip to the Mukata, Yasir Arafat's West Bank outpost in Ramallah. He is chauffeured by Shamron's son, Yonatan, a colonel in the Israeli army, and they are greeted and led to Arafat by a one-eyed Palestinian security officer named Colonel Kemel. The meeting produces little, but Gabriel is awakened early the next morning by a summons to Jerusalem, where he is told that Mahmoud Arwish, a spy inside the Mukata, wishes to talk to him in a small village on the West Bank. The informant turns out be Colonel Kemel, who is whisked away from his house in a spray of harmless gunfire and who explains his betrayal of Arafat as the price he paid for getting medical treatment for his cancer-afflicted wife. Arwish, or Colonel Kemel, gives Gabriel a photograph of Khaled al-Khalifa, confessing that Khaled orchestrated the Rome attack and is in frequent touch with Arafat. When Khaled communicates by telephone, however, it is always a woman who does the talking, Kemel confides.

A young Caltech-educated technology hotshot named Natan Hofi has listened to this woman's conversations and briefs Gabriel on her. She calls herself Madeleine when posing as French, Alexandra when British, and Lunetta when Italian. She speaks excellent Arabic but is probably from southern France, and in one of her conversations with Arafat she refers to an organizer called Tony and an upcoming rally in Paris of the Center for a Just and Lasting Peace in Palestine. Armed with this information, Gabriel acquires a German passport identifying him as Johannes Klemp and flies to Cairo, where he books himself into the Intercontinental Hotel.

Gabriel's contact in Cairo is Peter Quinnell, a former correspondent for a London daily, now washed up by "too much drink and too many women" and posing as an Arab sympathizer much favored by television station Al-Jazeera. He is familiar with the Cairo nightlife and suggests that Gabriel begin his search for Khaled al-Khalifa at a nightspot called Mimi's Wine and Jazz Bar, after its proprietor, Mimi Ferrere: "Everyone knows Mimi, and Mimi knows everyone." When Mimi approaches him at one of her tables and introduces herself, Gabriel identifies the voice immediately as that of the Madeleine on Natan's tapes. Enlisting Quinnell's help, Gabriel breaks into Mimi's apartment, bugs her telephones, and downloads data from her computer. A week later Gabriel flies to Frankfurt and telephones one of his recordings from Mimi's phones to an agent in Brussels, who confirms Mimi's identity and gives the name and address of the person she had called, Monsieur Paul Véran in Marseilles.

While Gabriel is following his clues to the man Mimi has called Tony, really Khaled al-Khalifa and also known as Paul Martineau and Paul Véran, the object of his search is holed up in Marseilles with the man in the galabi, Abu Saddiq, scheming to avenge the long-ago deaths in Beit Sayeed of his father and grandfather. Saddiq is in charge of the Paris operation. At this same time, a woman named Mira Assa is penetrating security at the Stratford Clinic, killing the bodyguard, and with the help of an accomplice, kidnapping Gabriel's helpless wife, Leah.

Gabriel has been ordered to a safe house in Rome where he finds coded instructions that order him to Sardinia to meet Shamron, who is waiting on a yacht, *Fidelity*, fully equipped as a command post. The *Fidelity* is to proceed to Marseilles and position Gabriel to carry out a plot to execute the man at 56 boulevard St-Rémy, Monsieur Paul Véran. Hours of monitoring the entrance to Khaled's apartment building pay off when he appears with his girlfriend. Gabriel quickly prepares for the hit, not knowing that at this time both Quinnell and Colonel Kemel are being executed by order of Arafat and that the whole scenario has been cleverly scripted by Arafat to trap Gabriel. So when Gabriel and his driver make their move on a Marseilles street they are unexpectedly thwarted by a Mercedes that obstructs their path, leaving Gabriel to pursue the now-vanished Khaled on foot.

Gabriel learns that he is the victim of Arafat's scheming when a young woman appears and tells him that the terrorists have Leah but that if he accompanies her Leah will come to no harm. Gabriel is driven to a house in the Arab quarter of the French town of Martigues, stripped naked, and brutally beaten before being ordered by the woman, Palestina, to drive the Mercedes on a long, circuitous route that concludes in Paris. By this time Khaled is in Montmartre, booking passage on an evening train to Aix-en-Provence. As they drive, Gabriel questions Palestina about her background and learns that she was born in the village of Sumayriyya, a tiny settlement in Western Galilee razed by Israeli forces on May 13, 1948. History repeated itself in June, 1982, when Palestina's home in the Lebanese town of Ein el-Hilweh was destroyed and her two brothers and her mother killed as Israeli paratroopers annihilated the village in a crackdown on the Palestine Liberation Organization.

Arafat's scheme plays out as Palestina leads Gabriel to the Gare de Lyon and he learns that three terrorists are ready to blow up the station in three minutes, at precisely 7:00 P.M. When instructed to dial a number from a phone booth, Gabriel reaches a gloating Mimi and sees Khaled walking toward the track for Marseilles. With ten seconds to go, Gabriel wrenches Palestina's pistol from her bag and shoots two of the suicide bombers before racing to Track D, where Leah has been abandoned to die in her wheelchair. The third bomber explodes his deadly suitcase, but Gabriel makes it safely to the Mercedes with the dazed Leah.

An Israeli agent spirits Leah off to Israel via Warsaw, and Gabriel reunites with Shamron in Jerusalem. Gabriel has intuited that the now-dead Palestina had been in love with Khaled, and he reasons that he can find clues to Khaled's whereabouts if he can track down anyone with ties to Sumayriyya and Ein al-Hilweh. With luck and the help of a Lebanese con man greedy for money, Gabriel learns that Palestina's real name was Fellah al-Tamari and that she had become an archaeologist. The denouement then works itself out rapidly. Gabriel enlists the expertise of an archaeologist named Eli Lavon, who discovers the cover that Khaled operates under, and the rest is simple. Gabriel wraps up his mission at a dig in southern France, where Paul Martineau dies an assassin's death like his father and grandfather.

Although *Prince of Fire* is fiction, it clearly reaches out in spots to the deadly history of Jews and Arabs. Silva notes that Asad and Sabri al-Khalifa, for instance, have rough historical antecedents in Ali Hassan Salameh and "his famous father," Yasir Arafat; and there was a village of Sumayriyya destroyed, just as recounted to Gabriel by Palestina. Clearly, Silva identifies Arafat as the architect of the misery in the Middle East, and he is frequently generous in his presentation of the suffering endured by many Palestinians, such as the inhabitants of the obliterated Sumayriyya.

Frank Day

Review Sources

Booklist 101, no. 11 (February 1, 2005): 917.
Library Journal 130, no. 3 (February 15, 2005): 121.
The New Yorker 81, no. 4 (March 14, 2005): 137.
Publishers Weekly 252, no. 4 (January 24, 2005): 221.

THE PRINCE OF THE CITY
Giuliani, New York, and the Genius of American Life

Author: Fred Siegel (1945-   ), with Harry Siegel
Publisher: Encounter Books (San Francisco). 386 pp.
  $27.00
Type of work: Biography and history
Time: 1951-2001
Locale: New York City

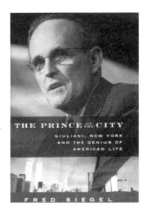

  This political history of Mayor Rudolph Giuliani focuses on New York City's twentieth century decline and subsequent rise

Principal personages:
RUDOLPH GIULIANI, the Republican mayor
  of New York City and a catalyst of its
  renascence
DAVID DINKINS, the first African American mayor of New York City
EDWARD KOCH, Dinkins's predecessor as mayor
MICHAEL BLOOMBERG, Giuliani's Republican successor as mayor
MARK GREEN, the first holder of the office of Public Advocate; a failed
  Democratic candidate for mayor in 2001
MARIO CUOMO, the Democratic governor of New York State
GEORGE PATAKI, the Republican governor of New York State
AL SHARPTON, a clergyman and political activist
CHARLES RANGEL, a congressman, leader of the Harlem political
  machine

John V. Lindsay, who in 1965 became the first Republican to hold the New York City mayoralty since Fiorello La Guardia left office twenty years earlier, was best known among New Yorkers for his statement that the city was ungovernable. He made this remark after riots in Harlem, Brooklyn, and Queens, after the deficit spending of his administration had driven New York to the point of bankruptcy, and after street crime had made much of the city unsafe.

Lindsay, a former congressman from the Bluestocking District of the Upper East Side, had ridden to his mayoral victory as the Republicans' answer to Robert Kennedy and to the political corruption of Tammany Hall. Periodic scandals within the administration of Robert F. Wagner, coupled with the electorate's desire for charisma rather than substance, had made Lindsay mayor. A crippling two-week transit strike beginning the first day of his administration, a two-week sanitation strike, and two weeks without snow removal in the outer boroughs following a twenty-inch snowfall were only the beginnings of Lindsay's undoing. He won a second term on the Liberal Party ticket only because he had so many opponents that default prevailed.

Lindsay attempted to salvage his political career by switching parties in 1971 and running for the Democratic nomination to the presidency. Even the Peter Principle

Fred Siegel is a professor of history at Cooper Union for Science and Art in New York City as well as a senior fellow at the Progressive Policy Institute in Washington, D.C.

(the theory that employees or public servants will advance to their highest level of competence and then ascend to and remain at a level at which they are incompetent) has some limits, however, and after his conspicuous and comprehensive failures, Lindsay retired from public life.

Lindsay's tragedy is New York's tragedy, and the city had seen the scenario replayed in variation ever since the Great Depression. What should be, and often is, New York's major asset, its diverse population, frequently becomes gangs of special interests courted by nearly all candidates for the mayoralty. Fred Siegel makes an excellent point in *The Prince of the City*, his political biography of Rudolph Giuliani, when he notes that until the 1980's, New York's municipal government behaved as though the Depression was an ongoing event. For example, through the 1970's, rent control applied to all apartments within city limits. Until this law was modified during the administration of Edward Koch, landlords could not increase the rent of continuing tenants. Tenants who had signed apartment leases in 1940 were still paying 1940's rates thirty years later. What is more, such tenants could transfer their leases to immediate family members, who would continue the boondoggle.

One can argue, and Siegel comes close to doing so, that New York runs with something approaching passable efficiency only when a benevolent tyrant, a philosopher-king, or a feisty billionaire administers it. Indeed, the very title of his book evokes the most famous political catechism of all, *Il principe*, (wr. 1513, pb. 1532; *The Prince*, 1640) of Nicolò Machiavelli. Before Giuliani and Bloomberg, the prevailing mythology was willing to settle for an honest machine bureaucrat such as Abraham Beame, who was mayor from 1974 to 1977, or a colorful but honest character such as Koch, who held the office from 1978 to 1989. The endearing image of La Guardia reading the Sunday comics to a radio audience during a newspaper strike softened the fact that such disruptions occurred with dismaying regularity.

Circumstances have always favored Giuliani in his public life, just as they continually opposed him in his personal affairs. As United States attorney in the Southern District of New York, Giuliani had untiringly prosecuted organized crime. As a congressman, he had acquired a reputation for hands-on involvement with his district's concerns. His encyclopedic knowledge of relevant statistics and ongoing events continually impressed those who heard him speak. His love of opera and of baseball endeared him to the arts community, the Metropolitan Opera, Yankee fans, and George Steinbrenner, billionaire owner of the Yankees.

What people tend to forget in the aftermath of his outstanding leadership following the terrorist attacks on Washington, D.C., and New York on September 11, 2001, is that Giuliani was not a popular mayor among many constituencies of New Yorkers. Advocates for the homeless cried foul when Giuliani routed the homeless from conspicuous public places. His nemesis, Brooklyn minister Al Sharpton, repeatedly censured Giuliani for an authoritarian management style that disregarded the poor and allowed the police free rein. The torture of Abner Louima by arresting officers in 1997 and the death by police gunfire of Amadou Diallo in 1999 gave Giuliani's critics further ammunition.

Giuliani did not become a wealthy man during his eight years as mayor, but he had wealthy friends and political allies. The symbiosis of Giuliani's administrative gifts coupled with the technology boom that fueled Wall Street in the 1990's created a New York its longtime residents barely recognized. Seemingly overnight, graffiti disappeared from public buildings; trash collection actually occurred on its scheduled days; though not reduced, taxes stabilized, and Giuliani even had the temerity to declare that the city's sales and nonresident income taxes were regressive and should be abolished.

This was heady stuff for New Yorkers used to municipal corruption, crushing welfare and debt-service obligations, and destructive special interests. Then came September 11, and all bets were off. Uncertainty ruled the day, but Giuliani was there. In fact, it appeared he was everywhere: in the Twin Towers even as they were falling, at Ground Zero during recovery efforts, and at the funerals of literally hundreds of firefighters and police officers. In the months before, he had battled through an ugly public divorce with his second wife, Donna Hanover, had suffered the tabloid revelations of his affair with his aide Judith Nathan, and had withdrawn from his race for the Senate following discovery of prostate cancer. What the New Yorkers remember, though, is Giuliani's decisiveness and indefatigable optimism.

The September 11 attacks occurred on the very day of the New York mayoral primary. Giuliani was not eligible to run for a third term because of City Charter revisions, which prohibited city officials from holding more than two consecutive terms. The primary was postponed for two weeks because of the attacks. Then, what had been predicted to be a close race between communications executive Michael Bloomberg and Public Advocate Mark Green became a landslide for Bloomberg, Giuliani's favored candidate. Green, a perennial candidate for almost every office in the state, in effect ended his political career under the Bloomberg steamroller. True to form, Giuliani had suggested that both candidates agree to his remaining as mayor for six months into the term of his successor so that he could stabilize the city. Bloomberg immediately agreed; Green, much to his own detriment, did not. Green immediately became the anti-Giuliani candidate in many voters' minds.

In imperial Rome, those elected to the office of aedile were wealthy men, because their position required them to finance the public athletic games. Bloomberg may well be the only political candidate in New York history entirely to finance his own campaigns, his second and last to the tune of twenty-six million dollars. Bloomberg is personally incorruptible, and this is a good start for anyone who aspires to the office of mayor of the City of New York. He is nominally a Republican, but he changed his party affiliation from Democrat only two months before his first campaign for mayor.

The beleaguered Republicans of New York City did not mind in the least that Bloomberg has proved more Democrat businessman than bluestocking east-sider.

Bloomberg had to deal with a crushing shortfall in city revenue in his first term immediately following the September 11 attacks. He did this in the tried-and-true New York way of increasing real estate and nonresident income taxes. The extraordinary paradox of the real estate tax increase has been the annual rebates of four hundred dollars paid to homeowners since the increase became effective. The outer boroughs that originally supported Giuliani's heir, then cried out for his blood when their taxes rose, annually sing his praises when the rebate checks arrive just one month before elections.

Siegel and his son Harry Siegel develop these ideas and more in their political history of the Giuliani years and their aftermath. The exponential theme that they trace is one of selfishness and self-interest versus the occasional flash of independent brilliance mixed with a touch of good luck. They demonstrate how, frequently, what favors an individual's fortunes places collective well-being at risk. Somehow, one feels that New York has always survived at one degree below chaos. New Yorkers hope it continues to do so, even if it is forever at Code Orange.

Robert J. Forman

Review Sources

Booklist 101, nos. 19/20 (June 1, 2005): 1746.
Commentary 120, no. 1 (July/August, 2005): 77-79.
The Economist 376 (July 30, 2005): 76.
National Review 57, no. 12 (July 4, 2005): 40-42.
The New York Post, June 7, 2005, p. 36.
The New York Times 154 (August 4, 2005): E7.
The New York Times Book Review 154 (July 10, 2005): 1-11.
U.S. News & World Report 138, no. 23 (June 20, 2005): 58.

THE PROPHET OF ZONGO STREET

Author: Mohammed Naseehu Ali (1972-   )
Publisher: Amistad/HarperCollins (New York). 212 pp.
   $23.00
Type of work: Short fiction
Time: From the 1970's to the early 2000's
Locale: Kumasi, Ghana; Long Island, New York; New
   York City

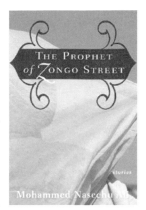

*In ten narratives that sometimes feature the fantastic or
the supernatural, sometimes focus on extraordinary events
in ordinary life, Ali tells the stories of his Ghanian characters*

Principal characters:
   UWARGIDA, a ninety-one-year-old widow of
      a Hausa king, the storyteller in "The
      Story of Day and Night"
   KUMI, a mail clerk, the title character in "The Prophet of Zongo Street"
   SHATU, a woman from Ghana, now a live-in maid on Long Island, the
      protagonist of "Live-In"
   MR. RAFIQUE, a newly married man who must face "The Manhood Test"
   ZULAIKHA, Mr. Rafique's wife
   YARO, the narrator of "Ward G-4"
   FELIX, a Ghanian painter living in New York, the protagonist of
      "Rachmaninoff"
   MALLAM SILE, a short, naive forty-six-year-old tea seller, the title char-
      acter in "Mallam Sile"
   ABEEBA, Sile's huge, strong-minded, and powerful new wife, a woman
      in her late thirties
   SAMADU, a sixteen-year-old boy, the bully of Zongo Street and Sile's
      tormentor
   SUF-YAN, the central character in "Faith," a man conscious of his many
      sins
   SURAJU, a drunkard, a bully, and a scam artist who pays for his sins in
      "Man Pass Man"

The Prophet of Zongo Street is framed by four stories that describe the intrusion of
the supernatural into the everyday world. Although the other six stories in the collection are realistic in form, they, too, demonstrate how anyone's life can suddenly take a
totally unexpected turn. The author does not commit himself as to whether such rever-
sals are merely chance occurrences or whether in these cases, too, there are extraordinary powers at work.

   In "The Story of Day and Night," with which the book begins, the author asserts
the authority of storytellers, at least on Zongo Street. As the first and oldest of the
wives of the late Hausa king, Uwargida is the respected matriarch of her household.

Mohammed Naseehu Ali, a native of Ghana, moved to New York in 1988. After graduating from Bennington College, he soon established himself both as a musician and as a writer. Although his essays and his short fiction have appeared in a number of publications, The Prophet of Zongo Street *is his first book.*

The other widows are her devoted attendants, and though she ordinarily tells stories each night to the children who collect in the courtyard to hear them, Uwargida may choose not to appear. Her status as the "mother" of the house and, in a sense, of the Hausa people, underlines the importance of what the unnamed narrator identifies as the "mother of all stories." The ongoing battle between Mewuya and the fetish priest Kantamanto does not merely explain the alternation between light and dark; it accounts for the constant struggle between good and evil. According to Uwargida, when one of the two combatants wins over the other, the world will end. Uwargida functions as a bard or a priestess, repeating stories to the young generation that represent the accumulated wisdom of the past.

In the title story, the narrator describes what happens when a man turns his back on tradition, abandons his community, and invents his own belief system. Kumi, the gentle, flower-loving mail clerk, is transformed into someone to be avoided. After his solitary death, only the fourteen-year-old narrator believes that Kumi was, indeed, something of a prophet.

The last two stories in the book deal with the definition of sin and its consequences. In "Faith," the Day of Judgment comes to Manhattan, and though Suf-yan is convinced that for his many sins he will be sent to Hell, he is less concerned about his own fate than that of his beloved Pas-cal. To Suf-yan's amazement, however, it is those who most criticized others who are damned, while those who broke the religious laws but did no harm to others, such as Suf-yan, are sent to Heaven. By contrast, Suraju, the bully and scam artist in "Man Pass Man," is caught in his own trap and sentenced to an existence filled with terror.

The principle of poetic justice operates just as efficiently in "Mallam Sile." The title character is a man who is too naïve and too gentle to succeed as a shopkeeper on Zongo Street. Mallam Sile is short of stature and long on patience. He does not have either the physical strength or the aggressive personality that would enable him to deal with the thieves and the bullies who haunt his tea shop, ridiculing him and stealing whatever they see. He does not even attempt to collect money from all those who take advantage of his good nature by leaving the shop without paying for what they have consumed. Even when he closes the tea shop in order to remodel it, no one expects his venture to become more profitable. Then, to everyone's amazement, after a short absence Sile reappears with an amazing wife. Abeeba is a woman in her late thirties, as large as her husband is small, as stern as he is gentle. In the shop, the atmosphere is now different. Abeeba will not put up with insolence or thievery. Samadu, the adolescent boy who is one of Sile's chief tormentors, has not yet paid his arrears. Abeeba sets out to find Samudu, does battle with him, and leaves him defeated and humiliated. Sile never does figure out why from that time on he is treated with respect or why his creditors now pay him on time. He simply gives the credit to Allah, and perhaps he is right.

For better or for worse, no one on Zongo Street can afford to ignore public opinion. This fact is illustrated by one of the funniest stories in Ali's collection, "The Manhood Test." At thirty-eight, Mr. Rafique has been unwise enough to marry a spoiled, nineteen-year-old girl, Zulaikha, or Zulai. He was one of the few suitors who did not desert her after her sexual exploits became common knowledge. Perhaps because he had already proven his manhood by fathering a son, perhaps because as a twelfth-grade graduate he felt himself to be generally superior to those around him, Mr. Rafique was undeterred by Zulai's reputation. However, after the wedding he discovers that when he is in bed with the sexually aggressive Zulai, he cannot perform.

The two of them try to be patient. Mr. Rafique thinks that his problem may be a punishment sent from Allah and that in time he will be blessed. Zulai tries to be patient because she fears that if the situation becomes known, her reputation will suffer even more then it has already. Eventually, however, the husband and wife come to blows, and the community becomes involved. A public test of Mr. Rafique's manhood is scheduled; if he fails, Zulai will be given a divorce. At the last minute, Mr. Rafique refuses to take part in the test. The love he feels for Zulai cannot erase his memories of the weeks since their marriage, nor can he envision a future in which he will always feel that he is a prisoner. Mr. Rafique decides that only by renouncing Zulai, sex, and the community's directives can he ever feel truly free.

Though it is difficult to feel free in the midst of a gossipy, judgmental community, it is almost inevitable that those who leave will feel that something is missing from their lives. In the poignant story "Live-In," Shatu has left her family behind in Ghana because she knows that there she cannot make enough money to support them. As a live-in maid on Long Island, she has an easier life, more comfortable surroundings, and, most important of all, a good salary to send back to Zongo Street. Unfortunately, Shatu's elderly employer is demanding and suspicious, and her employer's nephew, though seemingly kind, appears to have ulterior motives. Shatu can endure her situation only by vowing that eventually she will go back home.

Initially, the first-person narrator of "The True Aryan" does not appear to realize that he, too, yearns for the community he left behind. As a jazz musician, he has opportunities in New York that would not be available in Ghana. At the end of a gig, he is too tired to crave conversation, much less a cab driver's encomiums on his native Armenia. At the end of the story, however, the cab driver reaches out to the Ghanaian in a gesture of fellowship, and for a moment, the two exiles recognize their need for community.

"Rachmininoff" is another story that focuses on the plight of the exile. Though in a community such as Zongo Street there is little privacy and less freedom of action, there are always people available to provide guidance as to what should be done in a particular situation. In New York, the Ghanaian painter Felix does not know where to turn for help in an emergency. After a night of alcohol, drugs, and sex, the rich, blond American woman he brought home tells Felix that she is dying and begs him to call an ambulance. However, the friend Felix reaches advises him to avoid the authorities. In desperation, Felix tries out the remedies his friend suggests and, despite them, the woman lives. Felix is lucky; alone and unwise, he could well have killed her and ruined his own life.

By contrast, though they are at least as vulnerable to the perils of this world, the people of Zongo Street find security in the presence of the past, in their ties to their community, and in their strong family bonds. Nowhere is that truth so evident as in the three first-person narratives that recall childhood experiences. In "The Story of Day and Night," the children can contemplate the end of the world because they hear it in a family setting. After the storytelling session is over, Ali points out, they all go to the rooms of their mothers. In "The Prophet of Zongo Street," the father of the fourteen-year-old narrator takes him to Kumi's funeral, thus in effect freeing the boy to consider the ideas in the book the "prophet" gave him. "Ward G-4" is narrated by Yaro, a boy who, at eight, became convinced that he could see approaching death in the eyes of others. At twelve, Yaro himself becomes ill, and after treatment by a local quack and the family remedies fail to improve his condition, he is taken to the hospital. Because of his family's standing in the community, he is seen and admitted immediately. In the days that follow, Yaro is reassured by his mother's presence, though the death of his elderly roommate proves that the Angel of Death is indeed present. His father's arrival with the transistor radio Yaro wanted is another good omen; that day Yaro is discharged. At least for now, he can stop worrying.

Even in the stories that are set in Ghana, Ali does not provide much in the way of an exterior landscape. His interest is in the relationships of his characters to their spouses, their families, their community, and the communal past. Beyond that, Ali looks at their inner beings, the sense of self, and their most profound beliefs. Although almost all the characters in *The Prophet of Zongo Street* are Ghanaian Muslims, the book owes its appeal to the fact that the issues Mohammed Naseehu Ali raises in his stories apply to all of humanity.

Rosemary M. Canfield Reisman

Review Sources

The Baltimore Sun, August 7, 2005, p. F10.
Booklist 101, no. 22 (August 1, 2005): 1989.
Kirkus Reviews 73, no. 9 (May 1, 2005): 489.
Los Angeles Times, August 1, 2005, p. E8.
The New York Times Book Review 154 (August 14, 2005): 13.
People 64, no. 8 (August 22, 2005): 52.
Publishers Weekly 252, no. 24 (June 13, 2005): 31.
San Francisco Chronicle, August 21, 2005, p. F3.

REDEMPTION
The Life of Henry Roth

Author: Steven G. Kellman (1947-   )
Publisher: W. W. Norton (New York). Illustrated. 372
    pp. $26.00
Type of work: Literary biography
Time: 1882-1998
Locale: Eastern Europe; the Lower East Side, Harlem;
    Maine; New Mexico

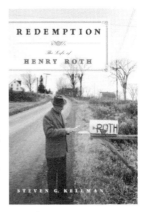

   The first full-length biography of the author of Call It
Sleep *(1934) uncovers the mystery of Roth's sixty-year silence, as well as the guilt and suffering that lay behind his
fragmented career*

Principal personages:
> HENRY ROTH, the author of *Call It Sleep*, whose second novel would
>   appear sixty years later
> HERMAN and LEAH ROTH, his parents, Galician Jewish immigrants
>   to the United States
> MURIEL PARKER ROTH, his devoted wife for more than half a
>   century
> JEREMY and HUGH, their sons
> LARRY FOX, the lawyer and bibliophile who became Roth's literary
>   executor and a member of his surrogate family at the end of the
>   writer's life

Like Edgar Allan Poe and Emily Dickinson, Henry Roth has become one of the
great legends of American literature, Steven G. Kellman writes in the introduction to
his engrossing new biography, *Redemption*. A Galician Jew growing up on the lower
East Side of Manhattan in the first years of the twentieth century, Roth created one of
the most memorable accounts of that immigrant childhood before he was thirty—and
then fell into sixty years of almost complete literary silence. *Call It Sleep* was rediscovered in 1964, when Avon brought out the first paperback of the novel which would
sell more than one million copies in thirty subsequent printings. Like a phoenix, Roth
at the age of fifty-eight began to rise out of the ashes of his tortured life and burnt-out
career. By the 1990's he was completing a tetralogy to continue the fictional retelling
of his early life. He died at the age of eighty-nine, just as the final two volumes were
being published.

   What Kellman has done, in this first book-length study of the writer, is strip the
legend of its fabrications, to sort out fact from fiction. In the process, he has uncovered a tormented literary life steeped in guilt and suffering but saved in the end, as his
title describes it, by the author's final redemption, a redemption which pulls together
the broken fragments of Roth's life into something almost whole.

Steven G. Kellman is a professor of comparative literature at the University of Texas at San Antonio and the author of The Translingual Imagination *(2000) and* Loving Reading: Erotics of the Text *(1985), among other works. His essays and reviews have appeared in numerous periodicals, including the* Texas Observer, The Atlantic Monthly, *and* The New York Times Book Review.

Roth was born in Tysmenitz, Galicia, in 1906—an area of what had historically been Poland, and today lies in western Ukraine—and emigrated with his mother, Leah, to the United States the following year, to join his father. His early life was not happy, for his parents were horribly unsuited for each other. Roth's father, Herman, was an insecure, violent man who failed at a number of careers, his mother a woman who teetered on the edge of mental instability for years before falling over in the late 1950's. The family was Roth's whole life, for four years on the lower East Side and then for more years in Harlem, and its anxieties and tensions became his own even after he escaped its hold in his twenties.

Roth, never a very good student, was expelled from Peter Stuyvesant High School. He was at best a mediocre student later at City College New York. His life changed in 1924, however, when he met Eda Lou Walton, a poet, editor, and English instructor at New York University, and for the following thirteen years she would be his mother, his teacher, and his sometime lover. Most important for Roth's career, Walton introduced him into her circle of writer friends—which included Hart Crane, Thomas Wolfe, Horace Gregory, Margaret Mead, and Ruth Benedict—supervised his reading, and led him to literary influences such as T. S. Eliot and James Joyce. Writing *Call It Sleep*, which was dedicated to Walton, actually liberated Roth from his dependency on her, for in reconnecting to his childhood roots through the novel, Roth finally found his own adult identity.

The novel met mostly favorable reviews but, published at the bottom of the Depression, it went the way of a number of serious works of the 1930's. *Call It Sleep* tells the story of the young David Schearl, from his arrival at Ellis Island in 1907 at the age of two until when, as an eight-year-old in August, 1913, just before the outbreak of World War I, he pushes a metal milk ladle into the electrical streetcar line and is knocked unconscious. Roth, Kellman shows, pioneered Joycean literary techniques such as stream of consciousness and Freudian themes such as the Oedipal conflict. In retrospect, critics and literary historians now recognize the role the novel also played in laying the foundation for the Jewish American novel which would become so important in the second half of the twentieth century in the work of Saul Bellow, Bernard Malamud, Philip Roth, and many other writers.

Call It Sleep immortalized the lower East Side and recorded the traumas the Old World underwent coming to the New, in an English that was "a subtle instrument for rendering the collision of languages." It was, as the literary historian Walter B. Rideout wrote in 1956, "the most distinguished single proletarian novel" of the Depression, and as the critic Irving Howe echoed when the novel was reissued in paper a decade later, "one of the few genuinely distinguished novels written by a 20th-century American." Roth became "the chronicler of a dying culture," Kellman concludes, and "his elegaic novels trace an American Jewish life shaped by profound loss."

What happened to Roth after this first novel is where the legend begins. Surely a victim of the Depression, when writers were pulled between fiercely political literary poles—one of the few negative reviews of his first novel had, ironically, come from the Marxist *New Masses*—Roth joined the Communist Party in 1934, and tried to make his next fiction fit the leftist mold. (Even Mike Gold, the Communist editor of the *New Masses*, faced hostile critics on the left when his own *Jews Without Money* was published four years earlier.) Roth was also the victim of his own insecure upbringing and a tendency to depression which followed him all of his life. Finally, in his youth he was sexually involved with his sister Rose and his cousin Sylvia, and the guilt of those years tormented Roth throughout his career. Roth slid further into depression after *Call It Sleep* was published. He burned the manuscript of his second novel.

His life picked up again when he met his future wife, Muriel Parker, at Yaddo, the artists' colony in Saratoga Springs, in upstate New York. They were married in 1939. Roth held several manual jobs, digging ditches for the Works Progress Administration and later working as a precision grinder in a series of machine shops, but he finally fled New York with his young family in 1946. For the following twenty years he barely scraped by in rural Maine, as a mental hospital attendant, and, most famously, as the operator of a plant for killing and plucking ducks and geese. His exile in Maine was clearly meant to end his identity as a writer, and for a second time, he burned his manuscripts. His wife, likewise, had given up a promising musical career to struggle with him.

As Kellman shows, however, Roth's silence was hardly total. Although he did suffer severe cases of writer's block for long periods of time, he continued to publish stories in *The New Yorker*. (The closest parallel, Kellman notes, is Ralph Ellison, whose *Invisible Man* appeared in 1952 and whose second novel, *Juneteenth*, was published posthumously in 1999.) In 1939, Roth's "Broker" appeared, and he placed later stories in the magazine in 1940, 1956, and 1966. When Avon republished *Call It Sleep* in 1964 (with an afterword by the British critic Walter Allen calling it "one of the best novels of our time"), Roth's rebirth really began. Awards and tributes followed the paperback reprint, trips to Spain and Israel inspired him, and "Roth had begun the final act of reconnecting with his people. From now on, his fiction would reaffirm his continuity with the immigrant boy on the lower East Side."

Roth projected a six-volume work to be titled *Mercy of a Rude Stream*, of which he would finish four—*A Star Shines Over Mt. Morris Park* (1994), *A Diving Rock on the Hudson* (1995), *From Bondage* (1996), and *Requiem for Harlem* (1998)—several published to considerable praise; the third volume of the tetralogy was a finalist for the National Book Critics Circle prize. "No one ever wrote so vividly about the ordeals of greenhorns on the lower East Side," Kellman suggests, "yet he was also the chronicler of uptown immigrant life less familiar to succeeding generations." In these last novels he finally revealed the incest of his youth and began to work out his personal and literary redemption. "Roth's tetralogy," Kellman concludes, "is a pared twilight encounter with elemental truths about Eros and Thanatos."

Roth's life story is not an easy one. Abused by his father, he abused others, including his own sons, Jeremy and Hugh, who were later understandably estranged from their father. His wife, Muriel, gave up her own career to devote her life to him, in New York, in Maine, and in their final, happier years in New Mexico. Fortunately, when Roth began his own regeneration, Muriel returned to composing music and performing and had several successes before her death in 1990. Roth was supported until his own death in 1995 by a loyal group of friends and fans, such as Larry Fox, who became a substitute family member and helped him to complete his final works.

In the end, Roth's books survived his terrible life, "the weight of their pages a victory over frailty and mortality," Kellman concludes his study. "Roth opened eyes to terrible shared truths about being human. If readers nod, it is not because they call it sleep. One might as well call it redemption." Kellman tells this terrible story with subtlety and compassion. He describes the pain of Roth's life fully, but he also has a wider cultural perspective that allows him to put the writer into context. His opening chapter on the immigrant experience is a brilliant historical summary. His descriptions of Roth's incest are tempered with his understanding that it was also "a dramatic manifestation of immigrant insecurity, the newcomers' inability to invest their emotions in anything beyond the reassuring confines of the clan." Throughout this literary biography, Kellman counters legend and sensation with a keen understanding of the forces at work in American life, as in the broken life and career of Henry Roth, and the ways that they shaped the American novel, in particular its Jewish American version, in the twentieth century. His biography is a model of clarity and comprehension, aided by pages of photographs and uncluttered indices of notes, chronology, and works.

David Peck

Review Sources

Booklist 101, no. 21 (July 1, 2005): 1890.
The Boston Globe, September 11, 2005, p. E9.
Kirkus Reviews 73, no. 14 (July 15, 2005): 777-778.
Library Journal 130, no. 13 (August 15, 2005): 86.
Los Angeles Times, August 15, 2005, p. 8.
The New York Times Book Review 154 (August 21, 2005): 9-10.
Publishers Weekly 252, no. 29 (July 25, 2005): 66-67.
The Washington Post Book World, August 21, 2005, p. T10.

RETURN TO WILD AMERICA
A Yearlong Search for the Continent's Natural Soul

Author: Scott Weidensaul
Publisher: North Point Press (New York). Illustrated.
  394 pp. $26.00
Type of work: Environment
Time: 1953-2003
Locale: The United States, Newfoundland, and Northern
  Mexico

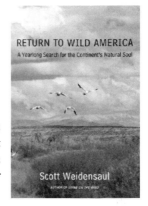

Weidensaul follows the pioneering route across North America that Roger Tory Peterson and James Fisher took in 1953 and records the environmental gains and losses in the half century since the publication of their best seller Wild America *(1955)*

In the spring of 1953, Roger Tory Peterson and James Fisher set out on what would become a legendary three-month journey across North America. Peterson was the noted naturalist who had published his groundbreaking *Field Guide to the Birds* in 1934, and in the intervening twenty years, this and his subsequent field guides had sold more than ten million copies, as interest in the environment steadily grew. His friend James Fisher was well known in Britain, through his writings and British Broadcasting Corporation (BBC) broadcasts on nature study. *Wild America* (1955), which was the result of their thirty-thousand-mile journey, became part of a growing environmental movement marked by works such as Aldo Leopold's *A Sand County Almanac* (1949) and Rachel Carson's *Silent Spring* (1962), books which reminded Americans of the beauty of the wilderness they so easily took for granted, warned of its fragility, and helped lay the groundwork for the conservation efforts and legislation that in the following half century—as the word "ecology" became part of the national lexicon—worked to protect this irreplaceable American resource. Peterson and Fisher saw North America and its inhabitants at a turning point, Weidensaul writes, and their book became part of the important force initiating change in public awareness of wild America.

It is this conservation movement which is responsible for so many of the environmental victories in the United States since the publication of *Wild America* at both local and national levels. The Wilderness Act was passed by Congress in 1964, the National Environmental Policy Act and the creation of the Environmental Protection Agency in 1969, the Clean Air Act a year later (in time to celebrate the first Earth Day), followed by the Clean Water Act in 1972 and the Endangered Species Act in 1974. The National Wildlife Refuge System has almost quintupled in size since Peterson and Fisher crisscrossed the country in 1953, and the federal wilderness system, which came into existence in 1964, now encompasses more than 106 million acres.

~

*Scott Weidensaul is the author of
more than two dozen books,
including* The Ghost with Trembling
Wings *(2002) and* Living on the
Wind, *which was a 1999 Pulitzer
Prize finalist. He lives in the
Pennsylvania Appalachians.*

~

Scott Weidensaul first read *Wild America* as a child, and as a seasoned naturalist and writer himself, the author of more than two dozen books, decided to try to discover whether Peterson and Fisher's diagnosis of America's wilderness health is still accurate. He follows their route, but at a more leisurely pace, and not in their single, one hundred-day journey but in a series of trips to the major sites they visited, from Cape St. Mary's, Newfoundland ("the easternmost prow of North America"), down the eastern seaboard to the Florida Keys, across the Rio Grande Valley into Mexico's Sierra Madre, and back up along the West Coast, with stops in California, Oregon, Washington, and finally Alaska. In fifteen detailed chapters, he visits dozens of national parks and wilderness sites, from the Great Smoky Mountains through the Dry Tortugas and the Grand Canyon to the Olympic Peninsula and the Pribilof Islands, three hundred miles west of the Alaskan mainland out in the Bering Sea.

In Weidensaul's journey he raises fundamental and pressing questions about the contemporary state of America's waterways, forests, and wildlife populations. He reminds readers of how far North Americans have come, and of how far they have yet to go, in order to preserve the most valuable legacy they pass on to future generations. His story is beautifully written, balanced in its account, and as important as any other volume on current affairs. Part memoir, part jeremiad, *Return to Wild America* does for the environmental movement at the beginning of the twenty-first century what *Wild America* did for conservation in the second half of the twentieth.

The losses are easy enough to record. In Florida, Weidensaul explores the Everglades, "one of the most manipulated landscapes in America," which, by the time Peterson and Fisher visited it, had already undergone half a century of dredging and draining. In his travels through the state, Weidensaul notes Florida's explosive growth (from nine million to sixteen million people in a twenty-year period—thanks in large part to the development of air conditioning—and headed to a projected population of twenty-three million by 2025) and laments its loss of eight million acres of forest, wetland, and farmland since Peterson and Fisher visited the state. Weidensaul also notes the recovery of certain species—the alligator and the cattle egret, for example—and spends time in Corkscrew Swamp, the largest stand of virgin bald cypress forest on the planet (and just minutes from the fast-growing Naples metropolitan area) and marvels at the biological diversity of Fakahatchee, in the heart of nearby Big Cypress National Preserve, the largest state park in Florida. Likewise, he camps out on the Dry Tortugas at the furthest edge of the Florida Keys, witnesses the rich bird life (sooty terns, brown noddies), and records the damage which visitors have done to the fragile coral reefs surrounding the islands, another example of the unintentional but nonetheless damaging effects humans often have on the biosphere. The decline in the California sea otter population in the 1990's, Weidensaul later notes, may be traced to the introduction of flushable kitty litter.

Weidensaul witnesses destruction of America's natural resources wherever he hikes and camps. Half of all Americans live within a day's drive of Shenandoah National Park, he writes, so the air pollution and acid deposits are understandable. It is the downside of the resurgence of interest in natural resources, as Californians have witnessed in Yosemite and other parks: Fascination with dwindling wilderness areas means more visitors, which means more congestion and thus more pollution. (National parks, Weidensaul notices, are "often surprisingly close to the schlock and profligacy of the modern age," walled up by "so many ugly, impossibly congested gateway communities.") Much of the damage to national parks comes from improperly managed natural forces, however, such as white-tailed deer destroying plant diversity and nonnative species and diseases moving in from other regions (witness sudden oak death syndrome, like the earlier American chestnut blight).

He finds a corrected balance in a number of places, such as the lower Rio Grande Valley in Texas. This valley was once the most biologically diverse ecosystem in North America. In their visit in 1953, James Fisher recorded 132 species of birds, more than he had ever seen in a single day in a lifetime of birding. In their three-month trip, Peterson and Fisher set a new record for the most species of birds spotted in a single year. Growth and development have changed the Rio Grande Valley, and now conservationists are trying to build an ecological corridor along the river, "a linked and functional chain of natural land preserving most of the region's biological wealth." Ecotourists, such as the avid bird watchers who flock to the region during migratory periods, help this effort at the same time they aid the region's economy. The developments in the Rio Grande Valley, Weidensaul finds, are also going on in wilderness areas across the United States. Such success stories pepper his account—black bears returning to the Northeast, peregrine falcons nesting in Manhattan's Central Park, the ivory-billed woodpecker miraculously coming back into the swamps of eastern Arkansas, jaguars reappearing in the Southwest, the marbled murrelet and northern spotted owl surviving in the Pacific Northwest. He describes the often decades-long struggles which have resulted in many of these victories, such as the efforts to save the California condor, as well as the expansion of the elephant seal colony at San Simeon.

The battles are never easy. In the Pacific Northwest, Weidensaul chronicles the history of habitat loss, the deep cuts into the wilderness made by the timber industry in the past century, and the way politics can often trump the scientific certainty that the loss of biodiversity is a loss for the whole planet. In the Kalmiopsis Wilderness of Oregon, Weidensaul hikes into the wild and ponders "the complexities of history, ecology, economics, and politics that now drive the debates over both fire and water in the West." He concludes that, while society has come a long way since Peterson and Fisher visited the area, "we're still scratching the edges of what we need to know in order to rectify the mistakes of the past and prevent making even bigger and costlier blunders in the future." Similar thoughts plague him as he ponders the effects of global warming along the coast of Alaska. There are no simple answers, Weidensaul knows, and a lot of hard questions must be asked. The news media hardly help; a recent report on the effects of climate change in California by a team of scientists, he notes, was reduced to the story of the threat to the wine industry. Again and again Weidensaul analyzes the interplay of economics, politics, and culture in this complex story of the American wilderness.

If there is a villain in his journey, it is the George W. Bush administration in Washington, "the most environmentally hostile administration and Congress in generations." Inadequate funding for environmental protection is only the most obvious problem; more serious is the relaxation of land, air, and water standards in recent years. Weidensaul is concerned that the administration now proposes outsourcing more than half the National Park Service jobs—"not only entrance staff and maintenance jobs but professional positions like biologists, archaeologists, and museum curators." If there are heroes in *Return to Wild America*, they are precisely such men and women who make up the administrative and scientific core of national parks. These managers and biologists who spend their lives studying the fragile ecosystems of wild places not only maintain them but also work with others to improve them. Their stories lie at the heart of Weidensaul's account.

What is unique about *Return to Wild America* is its reach. There have been numerous studies in recent years of regional problems, individual efforts focusing on particular species or environmental issues. (Weidensaul has read the relevant literature—and written some of it himself.) He has taken the half-century anniversary of Peterson and Fisher's *Wild America* as the opportunity to back away from the local and specific issues to see the whole American wilderness canvas—wildlife, parklands, water, land use. He does this, furthermore, in all of North America, and some of his best stories concern conservation efforts in Mexico's Sierra Madre and on the Alaskan coast. The result is an overview which is invaluable. *Return to Wild America* is not only a detailed history of environmental use and misuse but also a plan and a plea for what Americans can do in the twenty-first century to help protect the remaining wildlife and wildlands of North America.

David Peck

Review Sources

Booklist 102, no. 4 (October 15, 2005): 14.
Kirkus Reviews 73, no. 19 (October 1, 2005): 1072.
Library Journal 130, no. 14 (September 1, 2005): 175.
Natural History 114, no. 7 (September, 2005): 64.
Publishers Weekly 252, no. 33 (August 22, 2005): 51.
Science 310 (December 2, 2005): 1432-1433.
Science News 168, no. 22 (November 26, 2005): 351.
The Seattle Times, November 27, 2005, p. J8.

THE ROAD TO REALITY
A Complete Guide to the Laws of the Universe

Author: Roger Penrose (1931-   )
Publisher: Alfred A. Knopf (New York). Illustrated.
  1,099 pp. $40.00
Type of work: History of science and science
Time: From the big bang (about fourteen billion years
  ago) to 2005
Locale: The universe (with speculations about other uni-
verses)

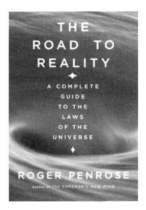

*This comprehensive narrative elucidates how scientists
have used mathematical principles in such revolutionary
theories as relativity and quantum mechanics to understand the matter and movements of the universe's contents,
from subatomic particles to galaxies*

Principal personages:
> ALBERT EINSTEIN (1879-1955), the physicist whose theory of general
> relativity Penrose considers the twentieth century's greatest achieve-
> ment
> STEPHEN HAWKING (b. 1942), the mathematical physicist who combined
> relativity theory and quantum physics to create a new understanding
> of black holes
> PAUL DIRAC (1902-1984), the physicist who made important contribu-
> tions to relativistic quantum physics, quantum electrodynamics, and
> quantum field theory

Throughout the history of science, a productive tension has existed between mathematicians and scientists. Such early natural philosophers as Pythagoras believed that
mathematics was the key to unlocking the secrets of the natural world, and author
Roger Penrose sees this Pythagorean approach as the first great breakthrough in science. However, another ancient Greek philosopher, Plato, even more enamored of
mathematics than Pythagoras, denigrated the world of the senses as illusory, while ex-
alting the world of mathematical forms and propositions as perfect, exemplary, and
"unassailably true." The contrast between the truths and beauties of this mathematical
(or Platonic) world and the complexities and paradoxes of the physical world, which
surprisingly often can be explained in terms of mathematical laws, is a major theme of
The Road to Reality. The twenty-five-hundred-year search for these laws has resulted
in significant successes, while also revealing what remains to be discovered about
how physical principles may be interrelated and perhaps united.

    Other scientists have written general accounts of modern physics and cosmology,
but what distinguishes Penrose's approach is his use of sophisticated mathematics
that, he believes, is essential for a serious lay reader to understand the basic laws of

Roger Penrose became interested in general relativity in the 1950's. From 1973 to 1998, he was Rouse Ball Professor of Mathematics at the University of Oxford. His previous books include The Emperor's New Mind *(1989), which won the COPUS Prize for science writing. He and physicist Stephen Hawking shared the 1975 World Prize for their joint contributions to fostering an understanding of the universe.*

the universe. Despite his publisher's warnings that his highly mathematical treatment would drastically restrict sales of his book, Penrose maintained, perhaps quixotically, that he could gradually introduce novices to the complexities of the modern mathematics needed for a genuine understanding of advanced physics by a step-by-step process from simple number theory, geometry, and algebra through complex numbers and the calculus and finally to such difficult topics as topology, manifolds, groups, bundles, and infinities.

Judging by such successful earlier popularizations as *The Emperor's New Mind* (1989), Penrose has the talent to make esoteric scientific ideas, such as his controversial explanation of human consciousness through quantum theory, accessible to a general readership. He is also well respected for his work in general relativity and for his contributions, in collaboration with Stephen Hawking, to black holes and big bang theory. Penrose has been knighted for his achievements in science, and he spent eight years writing *The Road to Reality* so that as many readers as possible would share his enthusiasm for mathematical physics. This *vade mecum* of all that he thinks is important in modern physics and cosmology will certainly enlighten scientists, mathematicians, and students who are pursuing technical professions, but amateurs should be cautioned that much of the material and many of the mathematical exercises may be beyond their grasp.

The title of Penrose's book has provoked criticism and discussion. If humans are traveling on the "road to reality," what is their goal? Is it some Platonic world of perfect forms or a "theory of everything" (TOE), the so-called Holy Grail of modern physics? Penrose himself sees mathematicians as explorers of a world of equations that has objectivity transcending "mere opinion." Furthermore, the physical world has mysterious connections to this mathematical world, and the main thrust of his book is to explore these remarkable connections. In his book's subtitle, Penrose presumptuously proposes that he will provide the reader with a "Complete Guide to the Laws of the Universe." As a mathematical physicist and a reductionist, he believes that ultimately the theories of all the sciences will be explicable in terms of basic physical principles. Perhaps this is why he makes no mention of such important biological laws as Gregor Mendel's mathematical principles of inheritance or Charles Darwin's laws of natural and sexual selection.

In short, Penrose does not treat that many laws of scientific disciplines other than physics, thus provoking the concerns of chemists, biologists, and psychologists. On the other hand, he concedes that many important scientific laws have yet to be discovered and that some laws of this universe may, in principle, be inaccessible to human reason.

Although the thirty-four chapters of *The Road to Reality* are not formally divided into parts, an analysis of its contents and themes reveals a tripartite structure. Chapters 1 through 16 are devoted to an explication of the mathematical ideas that will be needed in the second part, chapters 17 through 27 show how such scientists as Isaac Newton, James Clerk Maxwell, Albert Einstein, Paul Dirac, and Richard Feynman have used these mathematical ideas to deepen the modern understanding of the universe. The final part, chapters 28 through 34, deals with speculative ideas about space, time, and matter that have a tenuous relationship with observational data and that may (or may not) be verified (or discounted) in the future.

Throughout his book, and especially in the mathematics section, Penrose uses diagrams and drawings to illustrate the equations of complex and hypercomplex numbers, the calculus, surfaces, manifolds, groups, and tensors. In this way readers who are not comfortable with equations can still gain some insight into the mathematical truths Penrose is exploring. On the other hand, historians of mathematics will find that Penrose's analysis of the past is distorted, as his interest in these old discoveries is not about how they were created and understood at the time but about their relevance to modern beliefs and practices. In other words, the first third of his book does not constitute a balanced history of mathematics but a treatment slanted toward his mathematical and physical interests. For example, he is particularly fond of what he calls "magical complex numbers," that is, numbers involving the square root of negative one (symbolized by "i"), because these numbers have proved useful in analyzing periodic motions in the macroscopic world and the motions of subatomic particles in the quantum world. He also devotes many pages to analyzing topological surfaces and spaces (called manifolds), because some of these, such as Riemann's surfaces, enable mathematicians (and later, physicists) to study spaces that curve in various ways.

After his highly abstract tour through ancient and modern mathematics, Penrose uses the ideas, equations, and diagrams he has analyzed in concrete applications to the physical world. His narrative approach will irritate historians of science, because he discusses the achievements of such scientists as Galileo Galilei and Newton not in the context of their times but as they relate to twenty-first century concerns. For example, Penrose interprets Galileo's discoveries in dynamics through a "fiber bundle" interpretation of space-time, an approach alien to the seventeenth century but relevant to modern gauge theories of particle interactions.

Although Einstein is Penrose's scientific hero par excellence, he thinks that the modern idea of space-time came not from Einstein but from his teacher Hermann Minkowski, who showed that space and time are not independent ideas but are inextricably intertwined in Einstein's four-dimensional picture of phenomena. So impressed is Penrose by the profound truths revealed by Einstein's special and general theories of relativity that he believes that the other pivotal physical theory of the twentieth century—quantum mechanics—must be reconciled with relativity theory, and not vice versa.

Penrose admires the effectiveness of quantum ideas in explaining the interactions of light and matter as well as the behavior of electrons in atoms and molecules, but he is troubled by the paradoxical connections between quantum ideas and reality. Are the mysterious quantum jumps of electrons in atoms real? Is the probabilistic interpretation of the wave function, which is used to describe the behavior of electrons in atoms and cats in boxes, valid? His mathematical analysis of "Schrödinger's cat" (in which a cat, confined with a deadly quantum device, may be both dead and alive before the box is opened) and "nonlocal entanglement" (in which the measurement of the spin of one of an entangled pair of electrons can be instantaneously communicated to its distant partner) may seem more like science fiction than genuine science, but he insists that his "quanglement" explanation conveys what information can and cannot be transmitted by quantum effects.

Penrose greatly admires Dirac, whose equation for the electron correctly predicted the positron's existence, but he is critical of the "standard model" that tries to account for the other fundamental particles that have been discovered (and some that have not). He finds this model arbitrary and overly complicated, failing as it has to unite the quantum theory of particle physics with the requirements of relativity. The standard model is also an example of a quantum theory of interacting fields, and this quantum field theory, which began with Dirac and was developed by such physicists as Werner Heisenberg and Feynman, has been successful in accounting for many experimental results of particle interactions. Nevertheless, Penrose is bothered by this theory's mathematical inconsistencies, and he thinks that it might have to be modified in order to bring it in line with the gravitational principles of general relativity.

Throughout the first twenty-seven chapters of his book, Penrose tries to give an evenhanded account of ancient and recent accomplishments in mathematics and physics, but in the final seven chapters he gives free rein to his own controversial theories of the universe, while criticizing the speculative theories of others. For example, he finds fault with those cosmologists who try to explain the remarkably uniform distribution of matter in the universe by a period, very soon after the big bang, in which the expansion rate dramatically accelerated (the so-called inflation theory). He accuses these "inflationists" of ignoring the profound puzzles raised by the second law of thermodynamics in analyzing the universe's early history.

Judging by some initial reactions to his book, the most controversial target of Penrose's criticism is the highly popular string theory. To its ardent supporters, this theory constitutes a revolution in physics comparable with general relativity and quantum mechanics. To its detractors, including Penrose, it has had little or no observational support. Furthermore, its basic idea—minuscule loops of energy in ten or eleven dimensions—would require experimentally unattainable energies to verify. Penrose also believes that string theorists will be unable to solve the problem of an unacceptable multiplication of excessive degrees of freedom, though he concedes that such theorists as Edward Witten have discovered some impressive mathematical relationships that may indicate that something fascinating may be "going on behind the scenes."

Even though it has garnered little support from most physicists, Penrose favors his own twistor theory, on which he has worked for more than forty years, to explain Nature's scheme for uniting the quantum physics of the very small with the curved-space geometry of the very large. The mathematics behind twistor theory has a complex number structure, and its guiding principle is nonlocality. Penrose states that the twistor itself can be thought of as a light ray in ordinary space-time, this ray provides a causal link between events. Some theorists build their theories from what they consider most essential, and Penrose has a strong feeling that physical laws must be expressed through combinatorial principles as basic as the counting of causal links.

Despite his enthusiasm, Penrose's twistor theory, like string theory, is based more on mathematical and aesthetic arguments than observational data, and the reader who has followed him through a thousand pages of complex mathematical and physical analyses might find it frustrating to discover, at the end of this journey, that Penrose admits that the string, twistor, and other theories he has discussed are far from a final theory of the universe.

Even though he does not arrive at a theory of everything, he still feels that this tour of past, present, and future theories has been meaningful because he has shown the fruitful interplay between mathematical ideas and material realities, which was his principal goal. For the future, he believes that a radically new perspective created by a new Einstein is what is needed to solve the paradoxes of quantum mechanics in the context of general relativity.

An interesting phenomenon followed the publication of *The Road to Reality*. It has generated much discussion on the Internet, in which Penrose himself has participated. Some enthusiasts have called it, after the Bible, the best book ever published, and, even though the twenty-first century is young, others have called it this new century's most important scientific book. On the other hand, detractors view the book as deeply flawed and have pointed out its serious errors, particularly in the chapters on high-energy physics and quantum field theory. Penrose and his publisher set up a Web site (www.roadsolutions.ox.ac.uk) to handle both corrections of the book's text and the solutions to the book's exercises. The often emotional exchanges of opposed opinions over the book show that Penrose has touched on something that is of deep concern to many people. Whether mathematical physicists will eventually discover *the* road to reality, as Penrose believes, or whether the ultimate mysteries of the universe will forever be beyond human grasp are questions that this book does not resolve. In the long histories of mathematics and physics, searchers exploring the deepest secrets of the universe have often encountered the pain of the impossible as well as the magnificent failures of their most cherished ideas.

Robert J. Paradowski

Review Sources

American Scientist 93, no. 5 (September/October, 2005): 459-460.
Discover 26, no. 6 (June, 2005): 27.
Laser Focus World 41, no. 6 (June, 2005): 196.
Library Journal 130, no. 3 (February 15, 2005): 154-155.
Nature 431 (October 14, 2004): 741-742.
The New York Times Book Review 154 (February 27, 2005): 14.
Publishers Weekly 252, no. 5 (January 31, 2005): 62.
Science 307 (February 11, 2005): 852-853.
Skeptic 11 (January 1, 2005): 78.

RULES FOR OLD MEN WAITING

Author: Peter Pouncey (1937-   )
Publisher: Random House (New York). 210 pp. $22.00
Type of work: Novel
Time: 1987
Locale: Rural Massachusetts

Pouncey's novel about the ways that aging Scottish professor of history Robert MacIver devises to spend his last days

Principal characters:
> ROBERT MACIVER, the protagonist, an elderly historian and widower who must develop some structure to his life while waiting to die
> MARGARET, his dead wife, once a well-known painter
> DAVID, their son, a medic who is killed in Vietnam
> LIEUTENANT SIMON DODDS, the leader of a British platoon during World War I, as created and written by MacIver
> SERGEANT BRADDIS, a murderer and opportunist in MacIver's war story
> PRIVATE TIM CALLUM, an artist and Braddis's enemy in MacIver's war story

Rules for Old Men Waiting distinguishes itself as a rare first novel in a number of ways. Some of its more interesting distinctions include the age and pedigree of the book's author, Peter Pouncey. The author was born in China to English parents and trained in the classics at English preparatory schools and Oxford; he became a professor of classics and a dean at Columbia University and then president of Amherst College. Sixty-seven years old by the time of the publication of *Rules for Old Men Waiting*, Pouncey worked on his slim novel for more than twenty years.

The narrative of *Rules for Old Men Waiting* follows a peculiar structure. The reader realizes almost immediately what the "waiting" in the title refers to: The protagonist, eighty-year old Scot Robert MacIver, terminally ill, recently a widower, is at the end of his long life and is waiting quietly for his death. Most of the narrative, however, does not concern MacIver in his twilight life but instead focuses largely on his reminiscences of times past. A significant portion of the novel is also given to a story of World War I constructed by MacIver as a means of passing the time during his last, lonely days.

MacIver is passing those last days at the house in the country that has always been his family's rural escape. A "traditional cape house" that is "older than the Republic," MacIver's wife dubbed it "Night Heron House" in honor of a bird they once encountered. The MacIvers permanently move into Night Heron during the last months of Margaret's battle with cancer, so that her last days will pass in the place she loves.

Peter Pouncey was born in China to expatriate English parents. Because of World War II, the family was relocated and separated several times but eventually arrived in England, where Pouncey later attended Oxford University. He came to the United States in the 1960's and became a professor of classics, first at Fordham and later Columbia College. He later served as president of Amherst College.

With her death in early spring, MacIver is lost. In many ways the decaying house reflects the decline, fall, and decay of MacIver himself. The opening lines of the novel note that the "house and the old man were well matched, both large framed and failing fast." In the days after Margaret's death, MacIver considers the features of the house that need addressing: the roof, the siding on the windward side, the boiler, the gutters, and the porch. Just as MacIver "let the house go," he also lets himself go. For months after Margaret's death, he eats irregularly, does not keep up with housework, avoids the doctor, and spends most of his time sleeping. It is only when the porch collapses beneath him that he finally admits to himself, "I must retrench." To make some sense of his last days, and to make them worthy of Margaret, MacIver realizes he must have some rules.

He must, he decides, "Keep personally clean," make the bed daily and clean the house twice a week, and dress warmly; he must also "Eat regularly," and "Play music and read." Most important, he must "Work every morning." MacIver is a historian and academic by training and vocation; his most important work was in interviewing and describing how the government mistreated veterans of World War I who were victims of mustard gas attacks.

Indeed, the notion of history—on both the personal and the global scale—is woven throughout the text. MacIver's quest to do justice by the veterans of World War I comes into focus when one learns that his father died in the war. In a sense, then, his attempts to trace the histories of damaged veterans and tell their stories is also in some way an attempt to become closer to the father he lost as a small boy. Similarly, the structure of the novel—the frame set with the dying MacIver as he either remembers the past or fabricates a story in the tempestuous conflict of World War I—befits a historian trying to create order in the wake of the chaos of everyday life.

Pouncey's prose is at its best when MacIver is reveling in past glories and suffering under past sorrows; in his descriptions of his triumph as a Scottish rugby player who won the national game against England, in the details of his romancing of his wife, Margaret, and the pain each felt with the death of their son, David, who served as a medic during the Vietnam War, MacIver comes alive as a fiery Scot, too large for his garb as an American academic, quick to temper and to passion. In this way the reader truly understands the bitter and the sweet of looking back on a long life that has been fully lived. In MacIver's present at Night Heron House, however, Pouncey does, upon occasion, tend to veer into the elegiac and wax perhaps a bit too poetically; similarly, his crafted World War I story lacks the immediacy and the vitality that MacIver's own past contains.

The creation of a story depicting a conflict between a murderer and an artist on the front lines of World War I is the work that MacIver sets himself. The hallucinations he felt in his lowest hours of starvation and exhaustion, he believes, have revealed his rage against all that has gone wrong in his life—a dead father, a dead son, and a wife who preceded him to death—as well as his obsession with World War I. MacIver decides, then, to confront his demons head-on and begins constructing a story as his daily work. His villain is Sergeant Braddis, who is not content with bullying his own men in the trenches. At night he steals out into enemy territory and assaults other soldiers, looting the dead as he goes. Braddis's enemies are the talented and youthful artist Tim Callum; the platoon commander Lieutenant Simon Dodds; and the older, quieter private, gamekeeper Charlie Alston.

Interspersed with the narrative of MacIver's final days in Night Heron House and with his memories of past events, the war story seems at first to have little to do with MacIver's passions. The characters are not aviators like his father or veterans permanently disabled by gas attacks and then pawned off by the government. Rather, the war plot revolves around an initial friction between Braddis and Callum. Braddis tries to bully Callum over the private's drawings, and Callum reacts by bringing in the lieutenant, who is astute enough to understand the darkness that lies at the center of Braddis's being and courageous enough to try to put an end to his looting and bullying. Before long, Braddis has plotted and carried out a battlefield murder of the lieutenant. Only Callum and his fellow private and friend Alston suspect Braddis. Callum carries the fight to Braddis out in the barbed wire- and foxhole-strewn No Man's Land between the trenches. In the end both men are killed in their struggle against each other.

Although the story ostensibly has little to do with either MacIver's life with his wife or his work as a historian, in essence it has everything to do with them. As is slowly revealed throughout the novel, MacIver's life has been shaped by two dominant forces: war, on one side, countered by his wife, Margaret, on the other. As a young boy, MacIver's father, despite his promise to come back to his son from the war alive, is slain. Reaching his maturity, MacIver serves as a lieutenant commander in the Navy during World War II and actually commands a small vessel during an engagement that won the day, at the cost of several of his men. MacIver's son, David, is taken by war, as well; and MacIver's professional focus as an academic historian was in telling the story of the gassed veterans. Even his favorite game, rugby, is played as a kind of war, man against man, team against team.

Over the years, MacIver is forced to realize that a darkness lies in him, as it perhaps does in many men. An Army major who accompanied MacIver's boat during its assault on the German position during the war asks MacIver, "You love what you do, don't you," and it is only later that MacIver understands that Lockeford was posing the question, "How can you radiate such exultation at the outcome, when you have just lost seven men whom you obviously cared about?" At some level, MacIver has a Braddis in him, a rage-torn man who exults in the destruction of unchecked violence.

However, Margaret has served in his life as a polestar to steer him away from the rage that could destroy him. When his anger at their son's death threatens to destroy him, it is Margaret's intervention—and the realization that he might lose her—that brings him forth from grief. Through her art, gentleness, and appreciation for all that life has to offer, MacIver realizes the inadequacy of his own temper-fueled responses to life's vagaries. In his last days, MacIver realizes that it is "the real women who gentle our condition," and that without them "we are all rampaging in Braddis Land." This is made particularly clear in MacIver's memories of first meeting Margaret at a gallery.

Throughout MacIver's life, injustice—or rather, events that he perceives to be unjust—has gone unpunished. The veterans suffering from gas never receive the credit and care they are due; the governments that war and rob him of his father and his son never seem to learn their lessons. In his fabrication, however, evil is confronted, and injustice is faced by a greater courage. It is significant that MacIver makes his faithful Private Callum an artist, just as his wife was an artist. Both are creators of beauty rather than destroyers such as Braddis and perhaps MacIver himself.

Just as Callum's avocation is important, so, too, is the heirloom watch that Lieutenant Dodds carries. Its significance is made manifest in the plot in that it more or less becomes a smoking gun. It is through discovering Dodds's watch on Braddis that Callum comes to understand what Braddis has done. After Callum has confronted Braddis and the two of them are dead, Alston takes the watch to the commanding officer and asks on Callum's behalf that it be delivered back to the lieutenant's grandfather. The watch seems to symbolize several things at once. It seems to be saying, on one hand, that one is never free of history, that one forges one's way into the future dragging the vast chains of yesterdays behind. At the same time, it is perhaps an imperative that people make the most of their time, for it is fleeting and swift.

Written in a descriptive, elegiac prose, *Rules for Old Men Waiting* is about far more than how one should live one's last few weeks on Earth. Rather, in the examples set forth by MacIver's departed wife, Margaret, and son, David, and in consideration of the difference they made in others' lives through their work and compassion, one learns to live life every day. In this way, when one finally reaches those final days of waiting, one's memories are not stories of personal failures and what might have been but sweet reminiscences of all the bounties of life.

Scott Yarbrough

Review Sources

Booklist 101, no. 14 (March 15, 2005): 1266.
Kirkus Reviews 73, no. 4 (February 15, 2005): 194.
The New Republic 233, no. 13 (September 26, 2005): 36-37.
The New York Review of Books 52, no. 10 (June 9, 2005): 46-48.
The New York Times 154 (May 17, 2005): B1-B6.
People 63, no. 19 (May 16, 2005): 59.
Publishers Weekly 252, no. 12 (March 21, 2005): 37.
The Times Literary Supplement, June 17, 2005, p. 21.

SALONICA, CITY OF GHOSTS
Christians, Muslims, and Jews, 1430-1950

Author: Mark Mazower (1958-   )
Publisher: Alfred A. Knopf (New York). 490 pp. $35.00
Type of work: History
Time: 1430-1950
Locale: Salonica, Greece

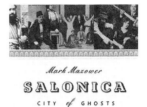

This historical portrait examines the northern Greek port city of Salonica from the end of the Byzantine era through the city's reconstruction following World War II

Principal personages:
> SAINT DIMITRIOS, a Christian martyr and the patron saint of Salonica, son of the city's chief military commander during the early fourth century
> MURAD II, the Ottoman sultan who conquered Salonica in 1430
> MAHMUD II, the sultan who ruthlessly disbanded the janissary corps
> ABDUL HAMID II, the last sultan of the Ottoman Empire
> RAPHAEL ASCHER COVO, the chief rabbi in Salonica for twenty-six years during the nineteenth century
> MUSTAFA KEMAL ATATÜRK, the founder of the Turkish Republic
> MAX MERTEN, the leading Nazi functionary in northern Greece
> JOHN MURRAY, the author of the *Handbook for Travellers in Greece* (1840), a work that epitomized the Romantic and Victorian view of Greek society

Despite being modern Greece's second largest city after Athens, the northern port city of Salonica, or Thessalonike, has been the subject of surprisingly few book-length studies. Aside from tourist guides and travelogues, most recent works discussing Salonica have been personal memoirs, such as Leon Sciaky's *Farewell to Salonica: City at the Crossroads* (2003) or Erika Kounio-Amariglio's *From Thessaloniki to Auschwitz and Back, 1926-1996* (2000), highly focused studies of specific moments in the city's history, or works restricted to a single aspect of the city's past, such as Steven Bowman and Isaac Benmayor's collection of eyewitness accounts, *The Holocaust in Salonika* (2002). As a result, Mark Mazower's *Salonica, City of Ghosts* fills an important gap by tracing the development of the city in the broadest possible way, from the Renaissance through the twentieth century. This book is likely to stand for some time as the definitive history of Salonica, particularly for its sensitive examination of the area's diverse religious traditions. The result is a vivid portrait of Salonica's fascinating and, at times, tragic history.

Mazower approaches his subject with an historian's eye but also with a poet's spirit. Interspersed among all the data drawn from Salonica's written records are a number of memorable personal notes. These include a letter to the editor of a newspa-

∼

Mark Mazower is a professor of history at Columbia University and is Anniversary Professor of History at Birkbeck College of the University of London. His research interests include the modern history of the Balkans; the social, cultural, and psychological effects of the Nazi period on Europe; the rise of nation-states; and the history of minority cultures. He is the author of such books as Inside Hitler's Greece: The Experience of Occupation, 1941–44 *(1993),* Dark Continent: Europe's Twentieth Century *(1999), and* The Balkans: A Short History *(2000).*

∼

per written by an English serviceman in World War II that touched off a debate about the correct pronunciation of the city's name, lyrics from the music of the Greek underworld and hashish dens known as *rembetika*, and lines by forgotten poets responding to the way in which their city was changing because of war or destruction. While historians thus find all the names, dates, and major events that they could possibly wish in *Salonica, City of Ghosts*, its greatest contribution may derive from author's ability to evoke this city's unique spirit of place. Glimpses into daily life provide insight into what it must have been like to live, work, worship, struggle, and argue in such a cosmopolitan community. Mazower introduces his work with only the briefest survey of Salonica during the nearly two millennia that it served as a crossroads of the Hellenistic, Roman, and Byzantine worlds. His primary goal is to bring the reader quickly to the beginning of the Renaissance, providing the backdrop for what will be five of the city's most complex centuries.

A constant theme of *Salonica, City of Ghosts* is to provide an antidote to attempts begun in the early twentieth century by residents and the Greek government to present this city as essentially—and almost purely—Greek, Christian, and Byzantine in spirit. Throughout most of the city's history, it was far more multicultural in nature than its Greek inhabitants readily admit. Even today, there are abundant traces of the city's Turkish and Jewish heritage lurking around corners or behind facades.

Salonica's fall to the Ottomans in 1430 began a period of occupation that, unlike subsequent conquests, proved to be relatively tolerant of different cultures, even by modern standards. Although the city's Christian inhabitants were horrified to see a number of their most cherished churches rededicated as mosques, the Ottomans also opened the community to the cultural richness that would characterize its later development. For instance, they welcomed the Sephardic Jews who had been expelled from Spain by the edict of Ferdinand and Isabella in 1492. Within a very short time, Jewish residents actually made up the largest ethnic community living in Salonica, beginning a chapter in the city's history that would have tragic consequences during World War II.

As Mazower points out, however, it would be a mistake to romanticize the harmony in which Jews, Muslims, and Christians lived together in Salonica throughout the sixteenth and seventeenth centuries. Although there was a great deal of mutual (and, at times, unconscious) cultural influence, there were also inevitable tensions, hostilities, and persecutions. Many Christians were sold into slavery. Other Christians as well as Jews led a meager existence, barely scraping by. Nevertheless, the city's important geographic location, just south of the Balkan range on a pathway that connected western Europe with Istanbul, meant that local citizens were continually exposed to a mélange of cultures that extended even beyond Salonica's diversity. Merchants from Egypt, Vlachs from Romania or Moldova, exiles from Albania, fisherman from Italy, and political emissaries from a host of other cities and nations would pass through the city's winding streets, each with something to contribute to and borrow from Salonica's expanding cultural heritage.

The Ottomans also enriched Salonica in far more tangible ways. Introducing the Muslim charitable institution known as the *vakf*, the Ottomans helped expand the city's commercial strength and physical beauty. A *vakf* was a benevolent endowment that occurred when a benefactor initiated some type of enterprise, then relinquished rights to capital and profits of the enterprise in exchange for anticipated benefits in the afterlife. Because the *vakf* was also exempt from most taxes, such endeavors tended to thrive with great prosperity, enriching Salonica through the production of goods and also, at times, splendid physical structures. Human nature being what it is, however, many "donors" discovered ways of diverting this charitable tradition to their own benefit. Surrendering ownership of a business in name only, they took steps to ensure that members of their family would remain associated with the *vakf* indefinitely as managers and highly paid employees. Thus, in addition to its many other cultural contributions, Salonica also introduced the European world to the modern concept of the tax loophole.

A singularly influential period of Salonica's history occurred during the expansion of the military unit known as the janissary corps. An elite military force established by Sultan Murad I, the janissaries originally consisted of prisoners of war and young Christian males pressed into service. Rigorously trained, converted to Islam, and then employed as a garrison throughout the city, the janissary corps soon became a potent military and social power.

> In their own minds, the janissaries were the protectors of the masses, the voice of hard-working Muslim artisans and traders, stepping in when the rich—be they land-owners, Ottoman officials or Frankish merchants—tried to exploit the poor. Baron de Tott, a knowledgeable observer of the empire, saw them as the natural opponents of "despotism." And it is true that whenever a sudden downturn in the market or a failure of the harvest threatened the city with starvation, the janissaries found themselves speaking for its consuming classes. . . . Yet the janissaries made unconvincing Robin Hoods. With their violent tempers, esprit de corps, rivalrousness and swaggering aggression they were as liable to fall on each other, beat up innocent Christians or ransack taverns as to worry about the food supply.

In time, however, entrance to the janissaries came to be treated as little more than a hereditary right. The high discipline of the garrison declined, natural-born Muslims were allowed to enter its ranks, and with lax discipline, the less savory aspects of this elite body came to outweigh its military advantage. Although the corps remained in existence until 1826, when the sultan Mahmud II finally disbanded the unit and allowed the remaining janissaries to be slaughtered in the city's White Tower (then known as the "Tower of Blood"), their most influential period in Ottoman history was already long past. In many ways, however, the janissaries were emblematic of Salonica's ability to mingle a number of different cultures in a way that was simultaneously ethically diverse, highly efficient, and ruthlessly violent.

As the Ottoman Empire weakened and eventually collapsed, the religious mix that had characterized Salonica since 1430 began shifting again. When Greece attained independence during the 1820's—resulting in the establishment of a Greek state that did not yet include Salonica—the tenuous relationship between Christian and Muslim residents of the area declined precipitously. A series of Balkan wars eventually brought Salonica into the new Greek nation and compelled many Muslims to leave an area that had been home to their families for generations. Islamic influences in the area's culture began to decline almost immediately, while Jewish and Christian cultural influences continued to spread even more widely. With the end of World War I, the final dissolution of the Ottoman Empire, and the rise of the Turkish Republic, it was anticipated that the exhausted states of the Balkan region would develop some sort of détente. The result, however, was a further isolation of Muslim and Christian cultures through the entire region. More than a million Christians living in Turkey were relocated to Greece; approximately half as many Muslims were removed to Turkey. Christian Greece and Muslim Turkey, despite all of their similarities in food, music, and basic worldview (similarities that are usually denied by each culture or else attributed to "theft" of native traditions by the other culture), simply turned their backs on one another.

Certainly the darkest parts of Mazower's book are the relatively brief final chapters dealing with Salonica's Jewish population during the Nazi period from 1941 through 1944. This is an episode in the city's history that Mazower knows particularly well, having treated it in a book-length study called *Inside Hitler's Greece: The Experience of Occupation, 1941-44* (1993). The Nazi presence in Greece occurred at roughly the same time as the rise of the death camps, and the Jewish inhabitants of Salonica were systematically transported to their deaths. Even in this time of catastrophe, however, the city's unique nature became apparent.

> Salonica was very different from Athens. . . . Something less than 5 per cent of Salonica's Jewish population escaped deportation compared with perhaps 50 per cent in the Greek capital a year later. This was partly because the Jews of the Macedonian capital were far more numerous, more obtrusive and less assimilated than Athens; helping a few thousand mostly Greek-speaking Jews in a city of nearly half a million was considerably easier than helping 50,000 Sefardim in a city half the size. . . . According to the German records, approximately 45,000 people reached Auschwitz from Salonica. Within a few hours of arriving, most of them had been killed in gas chambers.

Mazower thus indicates that Salonica's rich cultural diversity is part story of inspiration, part cautionary tale. As the City of Ghosts has demonstrated for more than five hundred years, even sharply divergent cultures can attain a surprising level of harmony, learning from one another and becoming stronger by frequent interaction. Tensions are, however, an inevitable part of all human associations, and so diverse societies have a great need to maintain open dialogue, commercial contact, and a healthy amount of diligence if they hope to prevent these tensions from erupting into mutually destructive conflict.

Salonica, City of Ghosts contains numerous photographs and other illustrations, a useful glossary, and valuable annotations that will assist readers in continuing their studies of this unique city.

Jeffrey L. Buller

Review Sources

Booklist 101, no. 14 (March 15, 2005): 1262.
History Today 55, no. 1 (January, 2005): 58.
Kirkus Reviews 73, no. 3 (February 1, 2005): 168.
Library Journal 130, no. 7 (April 15, 2005): 103.
The Nation 280, no. 23 (June 13, 2005): 35-37.
The New York Review of Books 52, no. 11 (June 23, 2005): 40-43.
The New York Times Book Review 154 (May 8, 2005): 19.
Publishers Weekly 252, no. 8 (February 21, 2005): 164-165.
Weekly Standard 10, no. 19 (January 31, 2005): 39.

SATURDAY

Author: Ian McEwan (1948-   )
Publisher: Nan A. Talese/Doubleday (New York). 289
    pp. $26.00
Type of work: Novel
Time: February 15, 2003
Locale: London

This novel follows a day in the life of a London neuro-surgeon and his family as they encounter the anxieties and realities presented by the terrorist attacks of September 11, 2001

Principal characters:
> HENRY PEROWNE, a successful, forty-eight-
>   year-old neurosurgeon
> ROSALIND PEROWNE, his wife, a lawyer for a London newspaper
> DAISY PEROWNE, their twenty-three-year-old daughter, an award-
>   winning poet
> THEO PEROWNE, their eighteen-year-old son, a talented blues guitarist
> JOHN GRAMMATICUS, Rosalind's widowed father, a distinguished poet in
>   his seventies
> LILIAN PEROWNE, Henry's mother, who is suffering from dementia and
>   living in a suburban nursing home
> JAY STRAUSS, Henry's American colleague and squash partner
> BAXTER, a small-time thug who invades the Perownes' lives

The journey Ian McEwan has taken from the sensation of his early work to the nearly universal acclaim that has greeted the achievements of *Atonement* (2001) and *Saturday* has been fascinating. He first gained attention in the late1970's and early 1980's for the story collections *First Love, Last Rites* (1976) and *In Between the Sheets* (1978) and the novels *The Cement Garden* (1978) and *The Comfort of Strangers* (1981). Written in a style that might be described as existential gothic— populated by deranged narrators, distinguished by acts of violence and sexual obsession that included incest, sadomasochism, fetishism, infanticide, dismemberment, entombment, and pornography—these books earned him both a well-deserved reputation as "a master of menace" and "a connoisseur of catastrophe" as well as the nickname "Ian Macabre." The writers who seemed to inspire him were Edgar Allan Poe, André Gide, Albert Camus and Jean-Paul Sartre. The world McEwan created felt hermetically sealed; the impulse seemed to be to shock; the focus was the tortured psyches of his characters.

These books earned awards as well as attention, but by the mid-1980's McEwan's ambition and vision began to outgrow his early style and voice. Briony Tallis, the thirteen-year-old aspiring novelist in the first section of *Atonement*, seems to offer a self-portrait of the young McEwan when she decides that her goal will be to imitate "Mrs. Woolf," to abandon the techniques of the nineteenth century novel to devote herself to capturing the stream of consciousness. "To enter a mind and show it at work, or being worked on," she thinks, "and to do this within a symmetrical design—this would be an artistic triumph."

Writing *A Child in Time* (1987), a novel about a kidnapping and its consequences, McEwan decided that the stream of consciousness and symmetrical design were not enough. In an interview, he de-scribed the novel as a turning point, where "politi-cal, moral, social, comic, and other possibilities moved in" to combine with his efforts to capture the "flow of thought." His inspira-tions became the American writers he calls "the Senators"—Saul Bellow, John Updike, and Philip Roth—as well as Virginia Woolf. The change could not have been more startling, or more salutary.

Ian McEwan has published story collections, novels, a play, and screenplays. Among his honors are the Somerset Maugham Award for First Love, Last Rites *(1976), the Whitbread Novel Award for* A Child in Time *(1987), the Booker Prize for* Amsterdam *(1998), and the National Book Critics Circle Award for* Atonement *(2001).*

Violence and the threat of violence have remained an essential aspect of Mc-Ewan's fiction. *The Innocent* (1989) contains a gruesome killing, *Amsterdam* (1998) involves a suicide pact that becomes a double murder, and the moral violence in *Atonement* is accompanied by detailed descriptions of wounds and deaths in World War II. In his work after *The Innocent*, however, the violence no longer feels either willful or grotesque. Instead, McEwan's fictional world has expanded, gained breadth and depth through its engagement with the physical and social realities that surround and shape his characters' fates and consciousness. The portrait of occupied postwar Germany in *The Innocent*, the description of Berlin and Eastern Europe following the fall of the Berlin Wall in *Black Dogs* (1992), the treatment of Margaret Thatcher's En-gland in *Amsterdam*, the examination of the life of an English manor house between the wars and of London during and after World War II in *Atonement*—all offer the same combination of careful attention to the particulars of the external world and to the flow of thought that characterizes the best work of Woolf and the American "Sen-ators."

The impulse is to explore, represent, comprehend the complexity of living in a meticulously described modern world. The focus is on the fragility of peace and happiness, on how easily a life, a love affair, a marriage, a family, a friendship, a com-munity can be shattered by an unexpected twist or turn of circumstance and experi-ence.

Like Woolf's *Mrs. Dalloway* (1925), whose themes, images, characters, and con-cerns it so artfully echoes, *Saturday* describes a day in the life of a well-to-do Lon-doner. Like Bellow's *Herzog* (1964), which provides McEwan's novel with its epi-graph, *Saturday* presents that day through the eyes and mind of its main character. Henry Perowne has everything: a wife he loves and desires after twenty-five years of marriage, a close relationship with two talented children of whom he is understandably proud, a satisfying and successful professional career, a beautiful home in the fashionable Fitzrovia section of London, a Mercedes S500. The pattern of McEwan's previous work—the pattern of most fiction since the mid-nineteenth century, in fact—will lead readers to expect that his contentment will be shaken, if not shattered, before the novel ends. They will not be disappointed.

Although Perowne is happy, with an enviable life, he is also a middle-aged modern man living in a Western capital in the spring of 2003. Through his thoughts, memories, and experiences in the course of the day the novel traces, McEwan masterfully captures the mixed emotions, the private and public anxieties, that are an inevitable part of the way even the most privileged live now. In the wake of World War I and in the midst of her own intimations of mortality, Mrs. Dalloway thought that "this is what she loved; life; London; this morning in June," but also that "she always had the feeling that it was very, very dangerous to live even one day," that "this later age of the world's experience had bred in them all, all men and women, a well of tears." In the wake of September 11 and the midst of his own intimations of mortality, Perowne awakes before dawn, goes to the window of his bedroom, looks out on Fitzroy Square, and feels the same ambivalence. He thinks that "the city is a success, a brilliant invention, a biological masterpiece" but also asks himself "what days are these? Baffled and fearful . . ." Recalling the biography of Charles Darwin that he was reading before he went to sleep the night before, Perowne is haunted by the thought of "how easily an existence, its ambitions, networks of family and friends, all its cherished stuff, solidly possessed, could so entirely vanish."

These thoughts are suddenly interrupted when he sees a fire in the sky. At first he thinks it is a meteor or a comet. When he hears a rumbling sound, he realizes that it is a plane in flames, hurtling toward Heathrow Airport, and he imagines that the terrorist attack on London that has been expected since September 11, 2001, has begun. The day is February 15, 2003, when a million people are scheduled to march in London, and millions more will take to the streets around the world to protest the invasion of Iraq that seems inevitable.

As Perowne moves through his Saturday, the story of the plane that unfolds in the background and the march that is going on around him become both symbols and immediate sources of the dangers that threaten to engulf him, his family, and his world. In the course of the day, he talks to his son, has sex with his wife, watches and listens to reports about the plane, observes the crowds massing for and dispersing after the demonstration, gets into an automobile accident, plays squash with a friend, visits his mother in a nursing home, attends a rehearsal of his son's band, shops for a family reunion, returns to his house to cook dinner, welcomes his daughter back from Paris, and greets his father-in-law. The novel's themes converge when he and his family are then confronted by the consequences of an accident that it would spoil the riveting last seventy-five pages of the novel to reveal.

Throughout the large and small events of his day, Perowne observes and thinks. He is a surgeon and a scientist, so he never stops analyzing the material world around him. (However, McEwan's desire to convince one that he can imagine the point of view of such a man leads to a half dozen pages, mainly at the beginning of the novel, in which he is carried away by his research. In these pages he uses dozens of medical terms without explanation—trigeminal ganglion, multi-level lumbar laminectomy, vestibular schwannoma, posterior frontal glioma, pilocytic astrocytoma, pruritus and mu receptor—that will leave most readers lost.) Perowne's travels provide the occasion for vivid descriptions of contemporary London, its places and its people, as well as a series of brilliantly rendered incidents and conversations.

Perowne also thinks about the past and the future, about his childhood, the early years of his marriage, and each of the members of his family; about his ideas concerning the war, the media, the demonstration and terrorism; about youth and age, security and fear, self and others, individuality and community, and the eroding boundaries between public and private life; about music and literature. In the process, McEwan creates a convincing portrait of a flawed but good modern-day Everyman.

Unlike *Atonement*'s Robbie Turner, who imagines himself at fifty as a physician whose sensibility will be shaped both by his commitment to science and his continued reading of great literature—"Birth, death, and the frailty in between. Rise and fall— this was a doctor's business, and it was literature's too"—Perowne is one of those scientists who are as immune to the power and appeal of literature as a way of understanding the world as they are to religion. He loves music and appreciates art, but his medical studies left him little time for such reading when he was younger, and nothing he has read since has led him to think he is missing much.

Since she was a girl, on the other hand, his daugher, Daisy, has memorized poems that she can quote at will. As a way to stay connected to her, over the years Perowne has tried to follow Daisy's recommendations, reading classics as well as recent novels and poetry. He finds, however, that he does not want to "have the world reinvented; he wants it explained." He does not want to be "a spectator of other lives, of imaginary lives. . . . The times are strange enough. Why make things up?"

In the end, this novel so grounded in contemporary reality turns into an allegory in which McEwan both acknowledges the power of the objection and provides a stunningly convincing answer to the question of what fiction has to offer in modern times. In the end, the plane that caused everyone so much anxiety turns out to have nothing to do with terrorism in London. In real life, that would come later—on July 7, 2005, when bombs exploded in the Underground and on a bus within blocks of the scene of most of the action of *Saturday*. The next day, an op-ed piece by McEwan appeared in both *The Guardian* and *The New York Times*. *The New York Times* titled the article "The Surprise We Expected."

Bernard F. Rodgers, Jr.

Review Sources

The Atlantic Monthly 295, no. 3 (April, 2005): 107-110.
Booklist 101, no. 12 (February 15, 2005): 1036.
Harper's Magazine 310 (May, 2005): 87-92.

The Nation 280, no. 14 (April 11, 2005): 33-38.
The New York Review of Books 52, no. 9 (May 26, 2005): 12-14.
The New York Times 154 (March 18, 2005): E37-E44.
The New York Times Book Review 154 (March 20, 2005): 1-11.
Newsweek 145, no. 12 (March 21, 2005): 60-61.
Review of Contemporary Fiction 25, no. 2 (Summer, 2005): 132-445.
The Spectator 297 (January 29, 2005): 38.
Time 166, no. 26 (December 26, 2005): 172.

SCHOOL OF THE ARTS

Author: Mark Doty (1953-   )
Publisher: HarperCollins (New York). 109 pp. $23.00
Type of work: Poetry

This finely textured, meditative collection of poetry examines how it is possible for individuals to come to terms with both desire and loss

Mark Doty began honing his craft as a poet during the 1970's but did not publish what he considers his first collection of poetry, *Turtle, Swan*, until 1987. His third collection, *My Alexandria*, was published in 1993 and won the National Book Critics Circle Award for poetry. The volume also won the *Los Angeles Times* Book Award for poetry and the T. S. Eliot Prize for the best book of poetry published in the United Kingdom. With these honors, Doty has established himself as one of the leading American poets of his generation. He has been praised by fellow poets and critics alike for his ability to convey compassion for those who are in need of healing, those who have fallen through the cracks of society. Throughout his poetry, Doty always has strived for clarity of purpose, for a precise vision that is welcoming for the reader.

He also does not shy away from uncomfortable subject matter. Doty was devastated in 1994 by the death of his lover, Wally Roberts, from complications related to acquired immunodeficiency syndrome (AIDS). His 1996 memoir, *Heaven's Coast*, details the tortured experience of losing Roberts to AIDS. As in his poetry, Doty found a way to move on, to come to terms with loss in the act of writing. Doty understands that without the creative outlet he would not have survived such a loss. Doty published his fourth collection of poetry, *Atlantis*, in 1995. The volume concerns itself with the havoc that comes from major tempests loosed upon the world. For all that is left in ruins, it points out, there is a new beauty that has been created. The poet recognizes the rage that comes from loss and devastation, but he is mature enough to realize that grief can lead to an unexpected cleansing of the soul.

Over the years, Doty has forged an extraordinary body of work that speaks to the core of what makes the human spirit tick. For his seventh volume of poetry, *School of the Arts*, he wrestles with the eternal themes of release and renewal. Always graceful, even in the darkest and most bitter of moments, he searches for the reservoir of resiliency that keeps humankind moving forward. There are twenty-seven poems included in this collection. A number of poems have "Heaven" in the title. In each of these poems, the idea of heaven means something different. In the poem "Heaven for Stanley," heaven is involvement in the creative process, in moving forward. The Stanley of the poem is the great American poet Stanley Kunitz. It is revealed in the poem that Kunitz is an avid gardener. Doty recognizes that there can be no better way to illuminate the creative process than by describing what a gardener does. As Doty

~

Mark Doty is the author of several highly regarded volumes of poetry, including Turtle, Swan *(1987),* My Alexandria *(1993),* Atlantis *(1995),* Sweet Machine *(1998), and* Source *(2001). He also is the author of the powerful and revealing memoirs* Heaven's Coast *(1996) and* Firebird *(1999). His honors include the 1994 National Book Critics Circle Award for* My Alexandria.

~

sees it, Kunitz "could be forever pleased/ to participate in motion." The garden is "all furious change," and the gardener would have it no other way. One poet comes to the realization that another poet—a master poet—finds heaven in the "budding and rot and then the coming up again." The abstract heaven, the religious heaven, does not come into play. Doty is more interested in the heaven that can be found down here on Earth, in the act of creation. As he sees it, art and literature can serve as a form of salvation.

For this collection, Doty has stripped down his poetry. All unnecessary contrivances have been removed and the poems whittled down to bare essence. The poet has arrived at middle age without the distractions of youthful exuberance. There is a subtlety in Doty's poetic voice. How the passing of time can overwhelm a person if he or she does not make peace with the past is one of the central themes of the collection. It also is obvious in *School of the Arts* that Doty has allowed a more relaxed approach to his poetry. The poet has concluded that perfection in anything is nearly impossible and that as he wrestles with middle age there must be a way to temper the anxieties that could undermine any form of peace of mind. There is always the process though, always the need to struggle with personal insecurities. No one can get through life unscathed.

School of the Arts reveals a new maturity of the poet and the person. He juggles such themes as change and loss with the dexterity of someone who has grown wiser with the passing of years. The five "Heaven" poems give the collection an invisible structure, a foundation from which to turn in all directions. The poet does not impose a heaven on these poems but allows loved ones to conjure up their own vision of what heaven would be for them. The poems "Heaven to Beau" and "Heaven to Arden" are concerned with two marvelous dogs. It is obvious in each of these poems that Doty has a great respect and love for his pets. Dogs appear in other poems in the collection as well. In "Ultrasound," the poet speaks with great poignancy about an important visit to the veterinarian. There also is a wonderful understated power to the poem "Stairs," in which his elderly dog Arden must now sleep outside in the garden because he can no longer climb the stairs and sleep at the foot of the bed. Over time, Arden had to make do with the garden, learn to make the most of the situation. A new routine was established, and a new phase was just around the corner. Although it broke the poet's heart to watch his dog attempt to climb the stairs, he observes how Arden adjusted to his failing by forgetting that "he ever wanted to" climb "something so awkward." Arden would "wedge his muzzle/ into a hole he'd made in the sliding screen door,// push it to the left, and sleep all night in the garden,/ on the gravel beneath the spread of a Montauk daisy." The dog had found a solution to the changes that come with the passing of time.

For his memoir *Firebird* (1999), Doty found the courage to delve into the tortured past that was his childhood. His father was a monstrous figure, and his mother became an alcoholic. At an early age, Doty learned how grief can play a major part in daily life. Over time, he learned that it was possible to have a new beginning out of the grief of the past. For him to survive, it was mandatory for him to rise above circumstances. During his high-school years, he wrestled with his sexual orientation. For all the turmoil of these years, Doty found salvation in art and literature. He became fascinated with poetry. He has stated that poetry can be best described as a "door into the inner life." For Doty, creativity would become his "life-raft." Because it is almost a given that life will be hard at times, the poet found it necessary to look to poetry to serve as a "way to keep our spirits going in the face of difficulty." There is comfort in the very act of creation. As Doty sees it, art and literature can make life bearable. Out of the struggle of his family life, out of the struggle of coming to terms with being gay, the poet rose out of the ashes like a firebird. He found stability in literature, in books, and in being creative.

The creative spirit beats strong in the *School of the Arts*. Most of the twenty-seven poems included in the volume have been published previously in respected literary publications such as *Lyric*, *The New Yorker*, *Rattle*, *Shenandoah*, *The Threepenny Review*, and *The Virginia Quarterly Review*. Three of the poems from *School of the Arts* had been commissioned by a foundation or institute. Throughout the collection, the reader is introduced to the world of Doty as the poet observes birds in flight, the wonderful faces of those who make New York City such a fascinating place, a small-town art auction, gay bars, the pleasure of gardening, aging dogs, and a plane that comes very close to crashing. Out of each of these observations or experiences, Doty illuminates the agony and the ecstacy of the human condition. There is no cheap sentiment, no easy solution to what ails individuals. There are poems that speak about mortality, but Doty does not allow them to slip into platitudes. He honors those loved ones who he has loved and lost. He recognizes the need for a "school of the arts" that will teach him how to carry on in the face of tragedy. The arts have given Doty much to savor. At an early age, he learned the value of art and literature. Ever since, Doty has attempted to be a credit to the creative process, to pass on what he has learned about how to live a dignified life. Doty has dedicated *School of the Arts* "To God." Faith is never far away from the surface in the collection. For Doty though, faith is not a blind exercise. He always is the skeptic, and seems to live in a tangle of both the spiritual and the erotic. Doty always seems to be contemplating whether faith can fit squeezed between the bookends of joy and despair. He lives in the world with true passion and continues to find reasons to be creative. Out of his willingness to remain vulnerable to what the world around him has to offer, Doty has crafted the intelligent and powerful collection of *School of the Arts*.

Jeffry Jensen

Review Sources

Booklist 101, no. 14 (March 15, 2005): 1259.
The Daily Telegraph, April 16, 2005, p. 10.
Gay & Lesbian Review 12 (November/December, 2005): 45.
Library Journal 130, no. 2 (February 1, 2005): 82-83.
Los Angeles Times Book Review, March 27, 2005, p. 10.
Publishers Weekly 252, no. 10 (March 7, 2005): 65.
The Times Literary Supplement, September 2, 2005, p. 21.
The Virginia Quarterly Review 81, no. 4 (Fall, 2005): 295-296.

SEIZE THE FIRE
Heroism, Duty, and the Battle of Trafalgar

Author: Adam Nicolson (1957-   )
Publisher: HarperCollins (New York). Illustrated. 341
  pp. $26.95
Type of work: History
Time: The early nineteenth century
Locale: Great Britain, Spain, and France

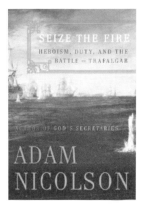

Nicolson explores the nature and appeal of heroism and its ties to violence through an examination of Lord Horatio Nelson's great victory at Trafalgar on October 21, 1805

Adam Nicolson has taken the occasion of the two hundredth anniversary of the Battle of Trafalgar to write a brilliant meditation on war, heroism, and violence. Nicolson brings real skill to his appointed task. He is a gifted narrative historian whose previous book was a best-selling account of the creation of the King James Bible. He is also a sailor and has published a splendid account of a voyage in a forty-two-foot ketch along the coasts of Scotland and Ireland. In *Seize the Fire*, Nicolson writes with both imagination and authority about the most celebrated naval battle of the age of sail.

Trafalgar invites an epic treatment. It was the decisive naval confrontation of the Napoleonic Wars. In one savage afternoon of combat, on October 21, 1805, Lord Horatio Nelson and the remarkable group of captains he termed his "band of brothers" destroyed the Franco-Spanish fleet Napoleon had collected to safeguard his long-planned invasion of Britain. His fleet gone, Napoleon consoled himself by marching his Grande Armée off to victory over the Austrians and Russians at Austerlitz. England had been spared, however, and the British would continue to harass the French emperor until his final defeat at Waterloo in 1815. Fittingly, a veteran of Trafalgar, HMS *Bellerophon* carried Napoleon off to exile at St. Helena.

The bare fact of victory does not by itself account for Trafalgar's place in history. It was a smashingly one-sided triumph. The British fleet captured or sank eighteen French and Spanish ships while losing none of their own. Nelson's men killed ten times as many of their enemies as they lost themselves; more than six thousand Frenchmen and Spaniards perished, as opposed to about six hundred British sailors. Shaping both the battle and its mythology was the outsized figure of Horatio Nelson. His legendary determination to come to grips with the enemy and his romantic fearlessness inspired his men to feats of self-sacrificial bravery. Fiction could not do justice to the image of the one-eyed and one-armed British admiral driving two columns of ships into the heart of the enemy fleet, defiantly pacing his quarterdeck, wearing a uniform all too conspicuously covered with the decorations of a distinguished career. Nelson's wounding, and his lingering death in the hold of his flagship, HMS *Victory*, was described in exacting detail by survivors and invariably portrayed in patriotic ico-

Adam Nicolson is the author of
Seamanship (2005), about his
voyage around Scotland and Ireland
in a forty-two-foot ketch, and God's
Secretaries (2003), an acclaimed
study about the composition of the
King James Bible. Nicolson is the
winner of the Somerset Maugham
and William Heinemann Prizes. He
lives in England with his family.

nography as Christ-like. Nelson was, indeed, the savior of his country. His signal to his fleet before the battle, "England expects every man to do his duty," and his words as he lay dying, "Thank God, I have done my duty," expressed his warrior's code. Nelson's call to duty became both his epitaph and a charge to his countrymen as he took his place as the greatest British hero of the nineteenth century. A grateful nation looked away from the admiral's scandalous private life; the Nelson of Trafalgar became the idealized exemplar for the stoic English gentlemen who upheld Queen Victoria's empire.

Nicolson has not written a traditional military narrative of the Battle of Trafalgar. As he describes the maneuverings of the fleets on the fateful 21st of October, he offers his readers fascinating digressions on the construction and operation of eighteenth century warships, the living conditions of ordinary seamen, the tactics and hazards of ship-to-ship combat, and the military culture of the Spanish, French, and British navies. This last is the most important aspect of the book. For all Nicolson's self-evident delight in describing Nelson's sailing ships, the most advanced technological marvels of their day, he is most concerned with the military ethos that guided the combatants at Trafalgar. Nicolson is interested in the moral dimension of battle; he wants to explore why people fight and how they understand and justify their actions. Nicolson argues convincingly that moral qualities inherent in the Royal Navy, epitomized by Nelson, gave the British victory.

The navies that fought at Trafalgar were strikingly different. They reflected the nations that sent them into battle. Nicolson notes that, because of this, the Battle of Trafalgar was probably won before it was fought.

Spain as a great power was decaying. Its political culture was conservative and torpid, ruined by generations of reliance on the treasure fleets that regularly arrived from its colonies. The aristocrats who ruled Spain were unimaginative and resistant to reforms that might have energized the country. A middle class scarcely existed in the country. Most of the population lived in hopeless poverty, prey to famine and disease. The Spanish navy was as hollow as the Spanish state. The Spanish possessed a number of large, well-constructed ships, but the government could neither staff nor maintain this fleet. The crews of the Spanish ships were drawn largely from peasants and beggars conscripted into service. They were poorly fed and rarely paid. Only a small percentage of any Spanish crew were actual sailors who knew their business. The Spanish officers were aristocrats who had little to do with their underlings. They considered the actual running of their ships to be beneath them. Lower level functionaries such as pilots handled all matters involving seamanship. The officers were warriors who commanded the soldiers on board. Their duty began and ended with battle. This was a recipe for naval disaster. The French commanders whose duty it was to work with the Spanish considered them hopeless as useful allies.

The French navy had its own problems. Traditionally the French navy had been of-ficered by the aristocracy. The French aristocracy was not as hidebound as the Span-ish, but breeding often counted for more than competence. Influenced by the Enlight-enment, French officers studied the science of navigation, but their learning remained more abstract than practical. This aristocratic elitism was challenged by the French Revolution. Discipline dissolved as the old regime collapsed. Support and mainte-nance for the navy, imperfect under the monarchy, fell apart. Some measure of order was reestablished by Jacobin commissars who used terror to hold officers and men to their tasks. The overthrow of the Jacobins improved morale somewhat, but the navy did not get the peace it needed to rest and refit. Twelve years of attrition in largely un-successful warfare eroded the navy's effectiveness. The French fleet at Trafalgar was worn out, materially and morally. The French admiral who commanded at Trafalgar, Pierre-Charles-Jean-Baptiste-Silvestre Villeneuve, was an aristocrat who prudently dropped the "de" before his last name in 1793. A practicing Catholic and refined intel-lectual who could quote freely from the great French tragedians, Villeneuve was a man out of place in a revolutionary world. He clearly had no use for his upstart master Napoleon; the emperor, in turn, did not trust him and had dispatched a replacement. Villeneuve, brave but conflicted, embodied the weaknesses of the French navy. On the day of Trafalgar he would accept what he knew was an unequal battle out of a fa-talistic sense of honor.

The British navy was very different from its opponents. It reflected the dynamism of British society. Spain and France were demographically stagnant in the eighteenth century; their populations grew very slowly, the Spanish increasing by 50 percent and the French only 30 percent. By contrast the British population doubled, growing at twice the rate of continental Europe. Britain had boomed economically, enabling it to employ gainfully all its citizens. An agricultural revolution spared Britain the famines and plagues still common elsewhere. Mercantile enterprise prospered in Britain's cit-ies. An industrial revolution unleashed new and powerful commercial forces. Adam Smith and his *Wealth of Nations* (1776) spoke for a robust capitalism that had put Britain on the cutting edge of world economic development. Britain's maritime em-pire both supported and was supported by its thriving commerce. As Nicolson points out, Britain's economic success made it possible to support the expenses of a navy second to none. The British navy was made possible by trade and then extended that trade.

This navy reflected Britain's comparative modernity. Although eighteenth century Britain was far from egalitarian, there was far more room for social mobility in British society than elsewhere in Europe. Many British naval officers came from the growing middle class. Nelson himself was the son of a vicar. For these men, the navy offered an opportunity to raise their station. Like their peers on shore, however, they had to work for success. British officers were expected to pass exacting examinations with every elevation in rank. Unlike their counterparts in Spain and France, they were im-mersed in the rigors of practical seamanship. By the time a man rose to be captain of his own ship, he was familiar with every aspect of its operation. He was also now pre-pared to pursue his fortune. The alluring prospect of prize money encouraged initiative and aggressiveness in British officers. A rich ship taken from the enemy brought an officer a substantial sum of cash. Readers of Jane Austen's novels are familiar with this spirit of naval entrepreneurship. One of Austen's brothers served under Nelson. The aristocratic officers of the Spanish and French navies fought for honor; their sense of self or position in society was not diminished by a respectable defeat. The middle-class officers of the British navy fought to win; only by capturing prizes could they finance a secure position ashore.

The capitalist determination with which the British navy pursued victory led to tactics that confounded and appalled their enemy. The French preferred to fight at a distance, aiming their guns for the masts and rigging in order to cripple a ship. This style of naval warfare minimized casualties but also precluded decisive results. The British chose instead to bear down on their enemy and fight murderous ship-to-ship duels. The carnage wrought by these close-quarters cannonades could be shocking, with scores of men ripped to pieces by solid shot and splinters. Such ferocity brought results. The loser in this kind of combat rarely got away. The British could accept the risks of such tactics because of the superior discipline and training that they imposed on themselves. A typical Spanish gun crew could get off a shot once every five minutes; an ordinary British gun crew could do the same every ninety seconds and the best among them in a third of that time. At Trafalgar, both sides knew that if the British got in amid the Franco-Spanish fleet, they would blast it apart. It is a measure of the courage of the French and Spanish that day that they stood and fought.

Nelson was the avatar of this aggressive and bloody way of war. He was not blind to the horrors that he unleashed. On some primal level, he and his captains relished the release that such unrestrained violence gave after long months of disciplined monotony aboard ship. Their enemies regarded the British, with their high crime rate and taste for bloody sports such as boxing, as a peculiarly violent people. Nelson's passion for battle and reckless courting of danger seemed to express a national pugnacity. Nelson, however, understood himself differently. He was an exponent of controlled violence. His brutal tactics were intended to serve an ideal. He fought with a fervor that reflected another widely noted characteristic of his countrymen— an intense religious enthusiasm stoked by the Great Awakening. Nelson was an ideological warrior who genuinely abhorred the French Revolution and Napoleon's imperial designs. He saw himself and his "band of brothers" as engaged in a chivalric defense of England and its traditional values. Till the day he died heroically at Trafalgar, Nelson drew inspiration from William Shakespeare's *Henry V* (pr. c. 1598-1599). He ensured his lasting fame by sacrificing himself as freely as any knight of yore. This idealism redeemed the ruthlessness of Nelson's methods. After the battle, the British captains, who had killed so many of their enemies, risked their lives in a storm to save the survivors. It is a measure of Nicolson's literary achievement that he captures so well the paradox that the most exquisite humanity can flower amid the cruelty of war.

Daniel P. Murphy

Review Sources

The Atlantic Monthly 296, no. 3 (October, 2005): 121-126.

Booklist 101, no. 22 (August 1, 2005): 1985.

Kirkus Reviews 73, no. 11 (June 1, 2005): 627.

The New York Review of Books 52, no. 17 (November 3, 2005): 55-58.

The New York Times Book Review 154 (September 4, 2005): 26.

The Wall Street Journal 246, no. 35 (August 19, 2005): W6.

1776

Author: David McCullough (1933-   )
Publisher: Simon & Schuster (New York). 386 pp.
    $32.00
Type of work: History
Time: 1776
Locale: North America and London

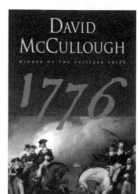

   Pulitzer Prize-winner McCullough reconstructs the year
when thirteen British colonies became the United States of
America, tracing the course of the Revolutionary War and
those who shaped it, especially George Washington, Wil-
liam Howe, Henry Knox, and Nathanael Greene

   Principal personages:
   GENERAL GEORGE WASHINGTON, the Virginia planter who became the
      commander in chief of the Continental Army
   GENERAL WILLIAM HOWE, the commander of the British army in the
      American colonies
   NATHANAEL GREENE, a Quaker and the youngest general officer in the
      Continental Army
   HENRY KNOX, a Boston bookseller and colonel in the Continental Army
      charged with retrieving guns from Fort Ticonderoga
   JOSEPH REED, a colonel and adjutant general of the Continental Army, a
      confidant of George Washington
   CHARLES LEE, Washington's second-in-command, a former British offi-
      cer and the only professional soldier on Washington's staff
   CHARLES CORNWALLIS, a British general
   HENRY CLINTON, a British general
   JAMES GRANT, a British general
   BENJAMIN RUSH, a signer of the Declaration of Independence and medi-
      cal doctor to the Continental Army
   JABEZ FITCH, a Connecticut lieutenant and diarist
   JOHN GREENWOOD, a sixteen-year-old fifer in the Continental Army and
      diarist

   In a companion volume to his best-selling biography *John Adams* (2001), David
McCullough closely examines a year of near-mythic status in the American collective
memory: 1776. It was the year that the Continental Congress, meeting in steamy Philadelphia, decided, "these united colonies are, and of right ought to be free and independent states." It was also the year that the American Revolution began in earnest
and was nearly lost. With his strong sense of narrative and his gift for capturing the
humanity of his subjects, McCullough leads readers through a well-known story with
both style and grace.
   McCullough structures the book into three large subdivisions. The story opens
in England, October 26, 1775, with King George III of England addressing the Brit-

ish Parliament on the war in the North American colonies. McCullough takes issue with the commonly held notions of the king, often more known for the madness of his later years (thought to have been brought about by porphyria triggered by arsenic ingestion) than for his intelligence and hardworking leadership of his country. Mc-Cullough offers the British perspective on the events in faraway North America first, re-creating the debate in Parliament over the king's decision to quash the rebellion.

From his description of the situation in Britain at the end of 1775, McCullough turns to the situation in Boston. After the opening Battles of Lexington and Concord in April, 1775, the colonials had engaged the British in what was commonly known as the Battle of Bunker Hill. Although technically a British victory, there were one thousand British casualties in the skirmish. In July, 1775, when George Washington arrived to take charge of the colonial troops, the British soldiers were under siege in the city, with supplies and food running dangerously low.

McCullough uses his opening chapters to summarize the state of the opposing armies and to introduce some of his major characters: Washington, Nathanael Greene, Henry Knox, and William Howe. Washington, a Tidewater planter, was also an experienced soldier and surveyor,

David McCullough is a well-known and much honored writer of American history. He received Pulitzer Prizes for his books Truman *(1992) and* John Adams *(2001) and National Book Awards for* The Path Between the Seas: The Creation of the Panama Canal, 1870-1914 *(1977) and* Mornings on Horseback *(1981). He has also received the National Book Foundation Distinguished Contribution to American Letters Award and the National Humanities Medal.*

serving with distinction under Edward Braddock in the French and Indian War. Mc-Cullough reminds readers of Washington's background: "Like other planters of the Tidewater, Washington embraced a life very like that of the English gentry. English by ancestry, he was, in dress, manner, and his favorite pastimes, as close to being an English country gentleman as was possible for an American of his day, and intentionally." That Washington would risk so much to take command of what appeared to be no more than a "rabble in arms" speaks to his deep commitment to the American cause.

Greene, according to McCullough, was an unlikely candidate as a general: he was a Quaker, had a limp, and had never been in a battle. He was just thirty-three years old. Although he had little formal schooling, he educated himself through reading. His correspondence is rich with description of Washington, the war, and the meaning of life. Some of McCullough's most memorable passages in *1776* are from Greene's pen. Likewise, Greene's friend Knox, a well-known Boston bookseller, had a damaged hand, a Loyalist wife, and no experience as a soldier. Yet Knox proved to be one of the most ingenious and intrepid among Washington's force, bringing cannons from the captured Fort Ticonderoga in upstate New York across many miles and in terrible weather to the battle at Boston.

McCullough is not content to focus solely on the Americans, however. He writes evenhandedly about the British generals Howe, Henry Clinton, John Burgoyne, and Charles Cornwallis. Howe had served under General James Wolfe, who called him "the best officer in the King's service." As commander of the British troops in Boston, he showed great courage. As McCullough writes, "At Bunker Hill, assuring his troops he would not ask them 'to go a step further than where I go myself,' he had marched in the front line. . . . After one blinding volley during the third assault, he had been the only man in the front line still standing."

The first section of the book closes with the March "miracle of Dorchester," when, in a surprise move, the Continental Army occupied the high ground surrounding Boston and began a bombardment that ended with the evacuation of British troops from the city. McCullough summarizes Washington's accomplishments in the siege of Boston:

> He had . . . bested Howe and his regulars, and despite insufficient arms and ammunition, insufficient shelter, sickness, inexperienced officers, lack of discipline, clothing and money. . . . He had kept his head, kept his health and his strength, bearing up under a weight of work and worry that only a few could have carried.

The second section of the book, "The Fateful Summer," describes the movement of the war southward from Boston to New York, where the British and the Americans fought for control of the city through the late summer of 1776. In this struggle, the Americans fared less well than in Boston. "The Battle of Long Island," McCullough writes, "had been a fiasco. Washington had proven indecisive and inept. In his first command on a large-scale battle, he and his general officers had not only failed, they had been made to look like fools." Even Washington's brilliant night evacuation of his men, although impressive, could not remove the stain of defeat from the encounter. If there is a weakness in the narrative of *1776*, however, it is in this middle section. Although McCullough describes the strategies of both the Americans and the British straightforwardly, the pacing is slower than in the first or third sections. Nonetheless, these pages clearly show the extraordinarily narrow margin that separated the American cause from utter defeat.

In "The Long Retreat," the final section, the pace quickens. McCullough details the final months of the year, as Washington and his army retreated into New Jersey. These were the "times that try men souls," according to Thomas Paine in *The American Crisis* (1776-1783). The British, along with Hessian troops, moved steadily into New Jersey as well, threatening Philadelphia and the Continental Congress. Finally, the American troops and the British troops found themselves, with winter setting in, on opposite sides of the Delaware River. Washington and others understood that time was crucial to their cause. Joseph Reed, Washington's adjutant general, wrote to the commander on December 22, urging him to take action: "Our affairs are hastening fast to ruin if we not retrieve them by some happy event. Delay with us is now equal to total defeat." It was out of this desperate need to act that Washington decided on a surprise attack on the Hessian troops at Trenton on Christmas. In a blinding blizzard,

Washington managed to move his troops across the Delaware River at night on December 25. In forty-five minutes after the attack began, Washington's troops had surrounded the Hessians, who surrendered.

Washington again moved his troops, before the British could retaliate. On January 2, 1777, troops led by Greene and another group led by Hugh Mercer surprised the British near Princeton, and a heated battle ensued. Alexander Hamilton and his men surrounded Nassau Hall on the Princeton College campus, where some two hundred British were garrisoned, capturing them all.

According to McCullough, for the British, the defeats at Trenton and Princeton were no more than skirmishes; for the Americans, the victories were vital. They revitalized the patriot cause with revolutionary zeal. Although there were many long years ahead for Washington and his army, the events of the closing days of 1776 kept the cause alive.

McCullough maintains that the year 1776 served as a training ground for Washington, Greene, and Knox, the only general officers still in the Continental Army by the time of the last battle, fought in Yorktown, Virginia, in 1781, when American and French troops surrounded British troops led by Cornwallis. For Washington, McCullough writes, "experience had been his greatest teacher from boyhood, and in this his greatest test, he learned steadily from experience. Above all, Washington never forgot what was at stake and he never gave up."

By the end of the book, however, it is also clear how much chance played its role in the quest for American independence. In the pivotal year of 1776, McCullough concludes that "often circumstance, storms, contrary winds, [and] the oddities or strengths of individual character had made the difference" in the nearly miraculous success of the American colonies to establish themselves as an independent nation.

At its heart, *1776* is a story of men and action. Through diaries, letters, contemporary newspaper articles, and standard historical accounts, McCullough has woven together compelling portraits and a seamless narrative. He is often able to capture the essential humanity of one of his characters through just a few words or a particularly apt quote from primary material. Moreover, he moves the action without sacrificing his characterizations. Nonetheless, some critics have found *1776* light on analysis and narrow in scope, and others have criticized McCullough for giving the Declaration of Independence and its framers short shrift. Readers interested in a wider view of the year 1776 ought to consider reading *John Adams* along with *1776*. In this considerably longer book, McCullough spends ample time on the Continental Congress and the larger philosophical issues of the day.

The events of this book are well known to anyone who has finished high school-level American history. When an audience already knows the outcome of a book, it is a rare writer who can infuse the narrative with page-turning suspense. McCullough is just such a writer. With skill and grace, he allows the participants in the events of 1776 to speak through their long-silent diaries and letters, offering modern-day readers a glimpse into the earliest days of the United States of America.

Diane Andrews Henningfeld

Review Sources

Booklist 101, no. 13 (March 1, 2005): 1100.
The Daily Telegraph, July 5, 2005, p. 26.
Entertainment Weekly, May 27, 2005, p. 143.
Kirkus Reviews 73, no. 7 (April 1, 2005): 404.
Library Journal 130, no. 7 (April 15, 2005): 102.
The New York Times 154 (May 24, 2005): E1-E9.
The New Yorker 81, no. 14 (May 23, 2005): 87-90.
Newsweek 145, no. 21 (May 23, 2005): 42-46.
The Washington Times, June 7, 2005, p. A02.

THE SEVENTH BEGGAR

Author: Pearl Abraham (1960-   )
Publisher: Riverhead Books (New York). 335 pp. $26.00
Type of work: Novel
Time: The twentieth century
Locale: The eastern United States

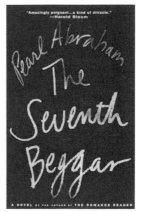

This novel sheds light on the ultra-Orthodox, almost mystical Hasidic world and establishes it firmly as part of mainstream America

> *Principal characters:*
> NAḤMAN OF BRATSLAV, the charismatic
>   founder of a nineteenth century Hasid
> JOEL, a modern-day Hasidic Jew and
>   would-be mystic
> ADA, Joel's sister
> JAKOBJOEL, Joel's nephew, also a would-be mystic
> LILITH, a vision JakobJoel encounters at the grave of Naḥman
> YANKEL YANKEVITCH, a wedding jester

Pearl Abraham follows closely in the footsteps of the 1978 winner of the Nobel Prize in Literature, Isaac Bashevis Singer, whose short stories brought Jewish culture before the eyes of so many Americans. Unlike Singer, Abraham writes full-length novels. Her newest, *The Seventh Beggar*, is made up of multifaceted, multigenerational stories that link myth with faith.

Thematically, the novel's plot line concerns the power of stories and the limits of creation and originality. Stories, old and new, happy and sad, long and short, intersect the plot and deeply influence the characters' lives. *Sippurei maʿasiyot* (1815; *The Tales of Rabbi Nachman*, 1956) by Naḥman of Bratslav, the still controversial nineteenth century founder of the Bratslav-kabbalist Hasid, which retains followers today, is central to the action of *The Seventh Beggar*, a title inspired by one of the spiritualist's homilies.

The plot's fundamental stories concern two modern-day Hasids on the East Coast of the United States: JakobJoel, called Joel, a brilliant yeshiva student of the Berditchev Hasidim who dies in a flash flood, and his namesake nephew, JakobJoel, who has moved out of his upstate New York Hasidic community to live a secular life, attending Massachusetts Institute of Technology (MIT) in Boston. Although JakobJoel has never even met his uncle, the two men live parallel lives.

As a troubled seventeen-year-old in Monsey, New York, Joel finds himself fed up with rote learning and goes against the wishes of his father, Rabbi Moshel, and the teachings of his popular rabbi grandfather, the "Berditchever," by stealthily reading Naḥman's book. To an outsider, the distinction between Joel's yeshiva and its rival Bratslav-kabbalist Hasid might seem inconsequential, but the youngster's study of the

~

Pearl Abraham is the author of
The Romance Reader (1995) and
Giving Up America (1998). She
has taught at Sarah Lawrence
College, the University of
Houston and at New York
University. She lives in New
York City.

~

Bratslav writings is considered dangerous within his community. Indeed, traditional rabbinical advice would reserve such readings for men over age forty.

Joel's father, deeply devout and supportive, and his warm, caring mother worry as Joel, hitherto a well-behaved and deeply religious child, begins to experience seizures. He then takes an abrupt Yom Kippur pilgrimage to visit Master Naḥman's grave in the Ukraine. While there, Joel experiences a nighttime vision in the form of a young woman named Lilith who appears to him by Naḥman's grave and attempts to seduce him. It remains unclear whether Lilith (the name given a biblical temptress), with whom the young scholar becomes sexually obsessed, is real or a vision. Joel learns later that she has tempted many men through the ages.

Upon his return to New York, the seventeen-year-old begins indulging his secret fixation in dangerous ways by isolating himself from society, starving through fasting, and by meditating for hours as he turns evermore inward. One evening, he is attacked by hoodlums at a rival yeshiva after combining meditation and masturbation. His consequent expulsion from his own yeshiva forces him to withdraw even more. Before his reputation is irreparably sullied, his parents attempt to arrange his marriage. Beginning at this point, Abraham ingeniously uses the life of Joel's nephew JakobJoel to illustrate the devastated family in the aftermath of Joel's death not quite halfway through the novel.

Joel's counterpart and nephew, JakobJoel, at a temporal remove of twenty years, finds himself in a mind-set similar to that of his uncle. It is scientific curiosity, however, and not religious inquisitiveness that lures this young man away from his community during the mid-1990's. Like Joel, JakobJoel fights his sexual urges, refusing at one point to date a woman who might cause him to become sexually aroused and thus interfere with his research at MIT. His work involves interfacing with Cog, a female robot in the artificial intelligence (AI) laboratory.

In their quest for spiritual and intellectual fulfillment, both Joel and JakobJoel are haunted by ghosts they intuit rather than visualize. Joel's ghostly mentor, so to speak, is Naḥman, a great-grandson of the Ba'al Shem Tov, the founder of Hasidism, who through interior dialogue guides Joel in his everyday life and especially in matters pertaining to his quest for spiritual fulfillment. Conversely, JakobJoel experiences inner conversations with the ghost of his late Uncle Joel, who resides perched on JakobJoel's shoulder.

Both men attempt to fashion a creature, a being in the manner of Mary Shelly's Frankenstein, or a golem, the otherworldly servant of Jewish legend. Unknown to Joel's father and to his sister Ada, Joel obsessively uses the legendary Kabbalist form of memorizing various permutations of the Hebrew alphabet—Kabbalists believe that the alphabet was used by God to create the world—to create, by transposing the letters, the female form of Lilith, whom he envisioned in the Ukraine. Joel meditates for hours on end.

At this point, one questions whether Joel is insane, especially when one considers his seizures. Indeed, Joel lies, mesmerized, in his alphabet-lined bedroom, summoning up the scribes of old who spent their days with ink and feather quills, writing passionately. He experiences intense feelings of jealousy that their knowledge must have brought them far closer to God then he could ever hope to be. Ultimately, Joel's insistence on absolute privacy forces him underground, literally, into an oversized, otherworldly drainpipe in which he sits, meditating, hidden as cars drive on the roadway overhead. This drainpipe represents the Hasidic belief in the necessity of spiritual descent before spiritual ascent. Trapped for days in heavy rains that symbolize the roiling primordial waters of creation, Joel eventually drowns.

Interestingly, Abraham chooses not to answer the reader's query about Joel's sanity, prompting one to wonder whether Joel is indeed sane or whether he suffers from a form of epilepsy which brings about religious ecstasy such as that experienced by Joan of Arc, or as presented in Gian Lorenzo Bernini's famous Baroque sculpture *Ecstasy of St. Teresa*. Or, one wonders, could Joel possibly be a true religious mystic with a mind powerful enough to create a golem, an artificial intelligence, of sorts?

After his death, Joel's family is devastated. Their only hope for psychic relief rests in Ada's newborn son, JakobJoel. The youngster, like his uncle before him, will also attempt to create a form of artificial life. At MIT, JakobJoel centers his scientific research on Cog. During his interactions with Cog, JakobJoel finds the inspiration to write (create) the Book of Cog as a means of enhancing her as a being by bestowing her with sentience. His opening line recalls the biblical Book of Genesis as it describes the basic computational binary system: "In the beginning there were zeros and ones, unordered and without meaning. And Cog hovered above, where memory stood empty and void. . . ."

Although Abraham often places her characters in dreamlike landscapes, they remain wide awake and full of life. Ada, Joel's sister and JakobJoel's mother, acts as a level-headed intermediary within the "real" world for both preternatural men. It is rare in literature to see such a close brother/sister relationship and, for that matter, such a close mother/son bond. Ada, a dress designer who adapts designer fashions for Hasidic women, turns out to be the most successful character in this novel. Unlike her brother Joel and her son JakobJoel, the intensely intelligent Ada believes in living a tuned-in, happy life and cares little at all about what others think of her. A no-nonsense counterbalance to Joel's passion and JakobJoel's sophomoric naïvety, Ada manages to use the art of design to intermingle the splendor of her religion with the wonder of the world as she adapts current fashion to traditional Jewish standards of modesty.

Although Ada also exhibits otherworldly tendencies, she refuses to indulge them. Her efforts at precognition, however, do allow her to locate her brother in the drain pipe after he disappears. She suffers a severe bout of postpartum depression after JakobJoel is born from her initial union with Joel's best friend, Arron—again within the primordial drainpipe waters. It is as if she has to come to terms with the death of her much beloved brother to care for the baby whose name, transposed, he shares.

Another of Abraham's fully developed characters, Yankel Yankevitch, is the wedding jester who enhances the novel's theme of storytelling. His duty is to make the bride and groom laugh and the wedding guests cry, by writing personalized rhymes and by telling entertaining tales. To everyone's horror and outrage, Yankel concocts a very unfunny story of the Holocaust at the wedding of Ada and Arron and effectively casts the shadow of doom over this emotionally overwrought family.

Throughout the novel, Abraham brilliantly manages to hold to her overarching theme of storytelling. Near the beginning, Joel attempts to "get a handle," so to speak, on the Bratslaver by diagraming a box-within-a-box sequence to keep track of the master's works. Abraham very effectively utilizes this construct, much akin to the Russian nesting doll, in this highly complex literary effort. She emphasizes that, no matter how far humankind has advanced technologically, stories, whether oral, written, or visual, remain highly significant when it comes to how world events, people's lives, and exceptional work are passed along.

Stories in *The Seventh Beggar* remain, indeed, central to each young scholar. Rabbi Naḥman of Bratslav, the author of the legendary fabulist folktale of the seven beggars, dies before he can finish his analysis of his final story. However, after he is reincarnated as his nephew JakobJoel's ghostly mentor, Joel completes the story as JakobJoel has a vision of his Uncle Joel at a bluegrass festival in the Berkshires Mountains of Massachusetts. The full text of Naḥman's "The Seven Beggars," which details seven physically deformed beggars that two children meet in their journey through a forest, appears in the conclusion of the book.

Abraham, who broke literary ground by introducing readers to the Hasidic world in the innovative novel *The Romance Reader* (1995), about a young girl who rebels against her family by surreptitiously reading romance novels, returns once again to this fascinating world, similar to the one in which she was raised, in her ambitious and innovative *The Seventh Beggar*. She succeeds in the Herculean task she set for herself: examining the human construct of storytelling and the limits to which people will go in their effort to create, and also the dangers inherent in this attempt to, essentially, usurp God's powers by shifting the boundary between the written word and the word made flesh, so to speak, in their quest for innovation. While the author cleverly stitches the many subplots and themes together that bring the Hasidic world to life, she also binds this ultra-Orthodox, almost mystical existence to everyday American life. For instance, father and son visit the Home Depot to purchase the materials necessary to build a hut, the once-a-year religious practice that helps Jews remember their nomadic ancestors who wandered in the desert. Abraham, incidentally, also provides a recipe for a most delectable chicken soup.

M. Casey Diana

Review Sources

Kirkus Reviews 72, no. 14 (July 15, 2004): 643.
Publishers Weekly 252, no. 1 (January 3, 2005): 34-35.

SHAKESPEARE
The Biography

Author: Peter Ackroyd (1949-   )
Publisher: Nan A. Talese/Doubleday/Random House
   (New York). Illustrated. 572 pp. $32.00
Type of work: Literary biography
Time: 1564-1616
Locale: Stratford-upon-Avon, Lancashire, and London,
   England

Drawing on contemporary documents and later leg-
ends, Ackroyd situates William Shakespeare within the his-
tory, geography, and stagecraft of Elizabethan and Jaco-
bean England

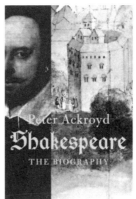

Principal personages:
   WILLIAM SHAKESPEARE, a poet and play-
      wright
   JOHN SHAKESPEARE, his father
   MARY ARDEN SHAKESPEARE, his mother
   ANNE HATHAWAY, his wife
   RICHARD BURBAGE, an actor
   WILL KEMPE, a comic actor
   ROBERT ARMIN, a comic actor
   ROBERT GREENE, a dramatist
   CHRISTOPHER MARLOWE, a playwright
   FERDINANDO, LORD STRANGE, the fifth earl of Derby, patron of the
      theater

Peter Ackroyd's *Shakespeare: The Biography* does not warrant the definite article
of the subtitle implying what the dust jacket states, that this is the definitive biography
of the playwright. That designation belongs to Park Honan's more modestly titled
work, *Shakespeare: A Life* (1998). The strength of Ackroyd's book lies in placing
William Shakespeare within the context of his world; it is flawed, however, by questionable statements of fact and interpretation that can mislead the general reader for
whom the work is intended.

Ackroyd is best when he shows how the world Shakespeare made in his plays reflects the world that he found. In *King John* (pr. c. 1596-1597) a smith listens to the
gossip of a tailor. Ackroyd points out that when Shakespeare was growing up in
Henley Street, Stratford-upon-Avon, his next-door neighbor was a tailor, and next to
the tailor lived Richard Hornby, a smith. *Henry IV, Part II* (pr. 1598) includes the
character William Visor of Woncote, who probably takes his name from the real
wool-dealer George Vizer of Woodmacote (pronounced Woncote), with whom
Shakespeare's father very likely dealt, as John Shakespeare supplemented his income

Peter Ackroyd has won many awards for his fiction and biographies. Subjects of the latter include Charles Dickens, William Blake, Geoffrey Chaucer, and T. S. Eliot. Among Ackroyd's other books are volumes of poetry, a history of London, and a study of transvestism.

by trading in wool illegally. Shakespeare calls Visor an "arrant knave," perhaps suggesting that relations between John Shakespeare and George Vizer were not always amicable. Ackroyd notes that a William Fluellen lived in Stratford; the name resurfaces in *Henry V* (pr. c. 1598-1599). One of Falstaff's confederates is Bardolph, whose name probably derives from another Stratford resident, George Bardolph.

Shakespeare's country origins are reflected in his language as well. Michael Wood's *In Search of Shakespeare* (2003) makes this point, too. Although only a few pages of Shakespearean manuscript survive, word forms in the printed early quartos and even the First Folio may reflect the author's spellings, which in turn suggest a Warwickshire accent. Shakespeare's vocabulary similarly derives from the English Midlands, as when in *Antony and Cleopatra* (pr. c. 1606-1607) he calls gadflies "the breeze." In *Othello, the Moor of Venice* (pr. 1604) Cassio tells Montano, "Let me go, sir, or I'll knock you o'er the mazzard," using the Warwickshire word for head.

Shakespeare's world continued to intrude upon his imagination when he came to London. In *Twelfth Night* (pr. c. 1600-1602) Antonio recommends that Sebastian lodge at the Elephant, an inn located in "the south suburbs" of the capital of Illyria, where that play is set. The Elephant was an actual inn that stood near the Globe Theatre in Southwark, London. Shakespeare was writing *Henry IV, Part II* in 1597 at the same time that he was renovating his newly acquired house in Stratford, New Place. This play contains references to construction. *Coriolanus* (pr. c. 1607-1608) opens with a food riot, an event that Shakespeare did not find in his source, Plutarch. However, he could have seen such rioting outside his front door in Stratford at the time he was composing this tragedy.

Shakespeare's London contemporaries found their way into his plays just as did the residents of his Stratford youth. It is probably no accident that the French herald in *Henry V* is named Mountjoy. By 1601 Shakespeare was living in the house owned by the Huguenot wig-maker Christopher Mountjoy, who may have helped him with the French scenes in that play. Incidentally, Ackroyd's biography highlights what a small world London was in 1600, despite its population of some two hundred thousand. At the request of Mountjoy's wife, Shakespeare encouraged one of Mountjoy's apprentices, Stephen Belott, to marry her daughter, Mary Mountjoy. After the wedding, Stephen and Mary became tenants of George Wilkins, who may have collaborated with Shakespeare in the writing of *Pericles, Prince of Tyre* (pr. c. 1607-1608). Wilkins certainly wrote a novel that may be the source of the play, unless it was based on Shakespeare's romance. The publisher of the first quarto of *Pericles* was Henry Gosson, who stood surety for Wilkins when he was accused of beating a pregnant prostitute.

Other of Shakespeare's contemporaries also served as models for characters in his work. *Love's Labour's Lost* (pr. c. 1594-1595) seems replete with topical allusions.

Armado in that play may be based on the poet Gabriel Harvey, Moth on the writer Thomas Nashe, and Holofernes on the lexicographer and translator John Florio. Ackroyd notes that the steward in *Twelfth Night*, Malvolio, may satirize the comptroller of the royal household, Sir William Knollys. Polonius in *Hamlet* (pr. c. 1600-1601) may mock William Cecil, Queen Elizabeth's Lord Treasurer. Cecil opposed the earls of Essex and Southampton; the latter is the most popular candidate for the fair youth of Shakespeare's sonnets, and in the chorus preceding act 5 of *Henry V*, Shakespeare praises Essex. Stephen Greenblatt in *Will in the World* (2004) suggests that the dramatist Robert Greene may have served as a model for Falstaff.

Ackroyd also reminds readers how much Shakespeare was a man of the theater. Shakespeare's company, the Lord Chamberlain's Men, competed with the Lord Admiral's Men, whose theater, the Rose, stood near the Globe in Southwark. When the Lord Chamberlain's Men staged Hamlet, the Lord Admiral's Men revived Thomas Kyd's play about revenge, *The Spanish Tragedy* (pr. c. 1588). After the Lord Admiral's Men had produced popular pastorals, Shakespeare replied with *As You Like It* (pr. c. 1599-1600). In 1599, Philip Henslowe, manager of the Lord Admiral's Men, paid Thomas Dekker and Henry Chettle for a play titled "Troyeles & creasse daye"; a few years later Shakespeare's company staged *Troilus and Cressida* (pr. c. 1601-1602). *Macbeth* (pr. 1606) capitalized on the recent Gunpowder Plot of 1605; *The Merchant of Venice* (pr. c. 1596-1597) followed hard upon the execution of Elizabeth's Jewish physician Roderigo Lopez in 1594.

Further, as Ackroyd notes, Shakespeare was writing for a particular company, so he tailored roles to his actors. In *Henry VI, Part II* the rebel Jack Cade performs a morris dance because Will Kempe, who played that role, was famous for his dancing skills. At the end of *Henry IV, Part II*, Shakespeare promises that the popular Falstaff will reappear in *Henry V*. Will Kempe, who was the first Falstaff, left the Lord Chamberlain's Men before *Henry V* was staged, so Falstaff is not a character in that work after all.

Kempe's successor in comic roles was Robert Armin, whose approach to acting was more subtle and reflective than Kempe's. Hence, one sees a change in the nature of the clown in Shakespeare's later plays, as reflected in Touchstone (*As You Like It*) and King Lear's Fool when compared to the earlier Bottom (*A Midsummer Night's Dream*, pr. c. 1595-1596) and Dogberry *(Much Ado About Nothing*, pr. c. 1598-1599). Armin had a good voice, which Shakespeare uses to advantage in *Twelfth Night*, for example, where Feste is given four songs.

In a larger sense, too, Shakespeare's world influenced his work. Ackroyd observes that culture in the sixteenth century was still oral in nature, in which the greatest writers turned to the theater. There was no popular market yet for print. Even so great a poet as Edmund Spenser had to rely on patronage to survive. Hence, the best writers turned to that oral medium, the stage. When the culture of print emerged in the eighteenth century, the outstanding writers turned to prose fiction. Shakespeare's world was also cruel. The theater of cruelty that is *Titus Andronicus* (pr. 1594) reflects reality. Titus has his hand cut off on stage. John Stubbs, in fact, had his right hand cut off for writing against Queen Elizabeth's proposed marriage to Francis, Duke of Alençon, brother of King Henry III of France, in 1579. *Henry VIII* (pr. 1613) shows the origins of England's break with Rome, and the play was staged in the very room where Katherine of Aragon had been tried.

Though good at presenting the historical and theatrical milieu in which Shakespeare wrote, Ackroyd says little about the works themselves. While he is writing a biography rather than a critical analysis, such taciturnity, especially from one who is himself a writer, disappoints. What he does say about the plays sometimes is misleading. Thus, he comments that the last speech is given to the highest ranking character on stage. This is not the case in *The Two Gentlemen of Verona* (pr. c. 1594-1595), *Love's Labour's Lost*, *The Merchant of Venice*, and *Othello*. The quarto and Folio versions of *King Lear* (pr. c. 1605-1606) assign the last speech to different speakers (Albany in the quarto, Edgar in the Folio), so who outranks whom? Ackroyd writes that in his plays Shakespeare takes a lenient attitude toward the breaking of oaths, an attitude that Ackroyd links to Shakespeare's family's Catholicism. Not only is this Catholicism not proved, but rarely do the plays condone the breaking of promises or violations of loyalty. Indeed, quite the reverse is true. Ackroyd observes that all scenes between the two sexes in Shakespeare show hostility; again, the facts do not support this contention. Ackroyd claims that Othello is Spanish; the play makes clear that the character comes from Mauritania.

Ackroyd wants Shakespeare to be an early bloomer. The first definite references to Shakespeare in the London theater date from 1592, when the playwright was twenty-eight. That is rather old for a genius to begin his career; Christopher Marlowe died at the age of twenty-nine. Ackroyd therefore dates some plays to the late 1580's; he even ascribes an early and now lost *Hamlet* (c. 1587) to Shakespeare, though the most popular candidate for authorship is Thomas Kyd. To bolster his case, Ackroyd repeatedly assumes that ambiguous allusions in this period refer to Shakespeare. In *The Teares of the Muses* (1591) Edmund Spenser refers to "our pleasant Willy." Ackroyd wants this Willy to be Shakespeare, even though the line continues, "ah is dead of late." This desire to make Shakespeare a playwright by the age of twenty-three also compels Ackroyd to regard what are called bad quartos not as memorial reconstructions but rather as early drafts and to assign some questionable works to the young writer. Despite its strengths and its lovely illustrations, this book can mislead general readers, while scholars will find in it nothing new that is good, and nothing good that is new.

Joseph Rosenblum

Review Sources

Booklist 101, no. 21 (July 1, 2005): 1890.
Kirkus Reviews 73, no. 13 (July 1, 2005): 715.
Library Journal 130, no. 13 (August 15, 2005): 83-84.
New Statesman 134 (September 5, 2005): 36-37.
The New York Times Book Review 155 (October 23, 2005): 8-9.
Publishers Weekly 252, no. 27 (July 11, 2005): 75.
The Times Literary Supplement, October 28, 2005, pp. 24-25.

SHALIMAR THE CLOWN

Author: Salman Rushdie (1947-   )
Publisher: Random House (New York). 398 pp. $26.00
Type of work: Novel
Time: About 1939-2000
Locale: Los Angeles, Kashmir, France, New Delhi, London, and San Quentin State Prison

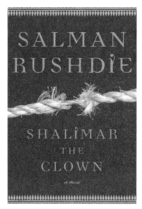

This novel tells the story of a love triangle and bloody personal revenge in the global village, specifically within the context of Kashmir conflicts and worldwide Islamic terrorism

Principal characters:
> NOMAN SHER NOMAN, also known as
>   SHALIMAR THE CLOWN, a Kashmiri actor
>   and later terrorist killer
> BOONYI KAUL NOMAN, his wife, a beautiful dancer
> MAX OPHULS, United States ambassador to India, Boonyi's lover
> INDIA OPHULS, Max and Boonyi's daughter
> PEGGY OPHULS, a World War II English undercover agent, later Max's wife
> OLGA "OLGA VOLGA" SIMEONOVNA, India's Los Angeles apartment manager
> ZAINAB AZAM, an Indian film star, Max's last lover
> KHADAFFY ANDANG, India's gentlemanly Filipino neighbor, a terrorist "sleeper"
> PYARELAL KAUL, Boonyi's father, a Kashmiri Hindu pandit
> ABDULLAH SHER NOMAN, Shalimar's father, a Kashmiri Muslim *sarpanch* (headman)
> FIRDAUS BEGUM NOMAN, Shalimar's mother, a snake sorceress
> ANEES NOMAN, Shalimar's older brother who joins the Kashmiri liberation front
> NAZARÉBADDOOR, an old Gujar prophetess in Pachigam, Shalimar and Boonyi's village
> BOMBUR YAMBARZAL, a headman in Shirmal, the neighboring village
> HASINA "HARUD" KARIM YAMBARZAL, a widow who marries Bombur
> ZOON MISRI, Boonyi's friend, raped by the Gegroo brothers
> HAMMIRDEV SURYAVANS KACHHWAHA, a colonel, later general, of Indian armed forces in Kashmir
> MAULANA BULBUL FAKH, a repressive "iron mullah," later leader of Muslim terrorists in Kashmir
> ABDURAJAK ABUBAKAR JANJALANI, a Filipino Muslim terrorist leader, Shalimar's friend
> WILLIAM TILLERMAN, Shalimar's attorney, concocts the "sorcerer's defense"

Salman Rushdie's previous works include the Booker Prize-winning Midnight's Children *(1995) and* The Satanic Verses *(1998), winner of the* Whitbread Prize; a short-story collection, East, West *(1994); and three works of nonfiction, including* Imaginary Homelands *(1991). He has often been mentioned for the Nobel Prize in Literature.*

Probably no one is better than Salman Rushdie at depicting the interconnected human variety of the world at the end of the second millennium. As he says in *Shalimar the Clown*, his ninth novel, "Everywhere was now a part of everywhere else," and "Everyone's story was a part of everyone else's." The rich fabric of human interconnection is Rushdie's grand theme, a kind of literary U.N. he shares with numerous other writers, especially other Anglo-Indian authors. East meets West. North meets South. Transients, migrants, and immigrants converge and merge in a simmering stew of in-between, of dislocation and suspension, an intercultural limbo whose mecca in *Shalimar the Clown* is Los Angeles.

Such human interconnection takes a particularly violent turn in *Shalimar the Clown*, which shows not only American power to do damage abroad and arouse animosity but also the ability of avengers to strike across decades and thousands of miles. Possibly Rushdie had in mind the fatwa against his life, provoked by his 1988 novel *The Satanic Verses*, when he contemplated *Shalimar the Clown*. The fatwa, however, was only one early shot in the war against Western ways launched by Islamic fundamentalists which included the terrorist attacks of September 11, 2001, and others. *Shalimar the Clown* thus has immediacy and relevance, as the rise of extremist terrorism is one of the topics Rushdie covers in his many-faceted novel. This work also concerns other matters, particularly the ongoing destruction of disputed Kashmir, to which Rushdie has family ties; the novel is dedicated to his late Kashmiri grandparents. The centerpiece of *Shalimar the Clown* is a case of personal revenge, not programmatic terrorism, though Rushdie's point might be that terrorism has a personal face.

The pieces of *Shalimar the Clown* do not always fit together clearly, and its main characters are also creaky. Even Rushdie's vaunted style, with its Shakespearian playfulness and extravagance, fails at times, such as when he makes some embarrassing efforts at rendering broken English and dialect. Mostly, however, his imaginative, engaging style carries the novel along and makes the pieces sound good, whether they make perfect sense or not.

The main action of *Shalimar the Clown* involves a love triangle and an extended pursuit of personal revenge by one of its aggrieved parties. Max Ophuls, married U.S. ambassador to India, falls in love with Boonyi Kaul Noman, a beautiful Kashmiri dancer who also is married. With the help of a sleazy embassy aide, Max entices Boonyi to New Delhi. There she hopes to advance her career, but Max makes her his mistress, enjoys her for a while, and then leaves her pregnant. Max's wife, Peggy, outraged by his habitual womanizing, leaves him but adopts Boonyi's baby, Kashmira, whom Peggy renames India. Boonyi returns in disgrace to her Kashmiri village, Pachigam, where she is declared *mritak* (one of the living dead), shunned, and spends the rest of her life alone in an abandoned mountain hut. Meanwhile, Boonyi's husband, Noman Sher Noman, also known as Shalimar the Clown, vows deadly revenge against Max, Boonyi, and the baby. Taking a circuitous route through several terrorist organizations, he spends years training, killing professionally, and whetting his knife for the upcoming big events.

Stripped down, the plot sounds like a melodrama, possibly a Kashmiri version of the "Madame Butterfly" story, first penned in 1898 by John Luther Long. Rushdie enriches his novel with an epic cast of characters and numerous side events, embedding the operatic plot in the context of history and culture. He also complicates the plot by narrating the novel out of chronological order, beginning in modern-day Los Angeles, harking back to Kashmir before the troubles, harking further back to World War II France, returning to Kashmir to trace its dissolution into strife, and then returning to California for the novel's ending. This method of narration enables Rushdie to begin and end the novel at key dramatic moments (though the ending is left hanging), to trace the historical context of current events (including terrorism), and to juxtapose parallels between late-twentieth century "ethnic cleansing" and the Nazis' "final solution."

Rushdie's method of narration also helps explain the main characters and their motivations. For example, the World War II exploits of Max and Peggy in the French Resistance explain their heroic status and how they were thrown together, attracted to each other, and married. Unfortunately Peggy, "the Grey Rat" (as she is dubbed by the Nazis), proves to have little interest in sex after marriage, which might in part explain why Max is such a womanizer. The cultural practices of the Kashmiris, especially the declarations of *mritak* and shunning of women who have been sexually besmirched, also help explain the extreme reactions of Boonyi and Shalimar.

Shalimar is a case study of what goes into making a terrorist. His sense of being personally wronged, solidified by vows of revenge, leaves him a walking sore spot. Concurrently he experiences the breakdown of supportive traditional culture. Originally Shalimar the Clown is part of his village's traditional *bhand pather* troupe, whose livelihood for generations has been performing old legends and clown stories to much acclaim. During Shalimar's generation the *bhand pather* performances fall out of favor, with serious economic, cultural, and psychological consequences. Finally, traditional culture is largely replaced by a culture of violence that sucks young men into its factions and that consumes both Shalimar's village and family. Eventually Shalimar the Clown has nothing to live for except the pleasure of killing.

Despite these explanations, the main characters, for the most part, fail to generate enough identification with their feelings. Little is revealed about the complex emotions Shalimar must go through to get from clown to killer. A character of Raskolnikovian potential, Shalimar goes to some extent unrealized and underdeveloped. The development of the other main characters shows similar weaknesses. Maybe they command little identification or empathy because they are shallow, do not show much forethought or conscience, and bring their problems on themselves. The motivations for some of their actions, which seem to merely drive the plot, also challenge the imagination. For example, both Max and Boonyi get what they want, then reverse themselves and do not want it. In contrast to their complete turnarounds, Shalimar the Clown's single-minded, fanatical pursuit of revenge never lets up.

Similarly, it is hard to infer why the mismatched Max and Peggy stay together for so long, why Max is appointed U.S. ambassador to India (supposedly his Alsace origin qualifies him, though he is also said to be a smart, charming fellow), why Max immediately falls for an obscure Kashmiri dancing girl (there must have been tastier prey nearby in New Delhi), why Max the former ambassador knows so little about Indian film stars, and why Max the former antiterrorism chief knowingly hires his former lover's husband to be his personal body servant.

In *Shalimar the Clown* Rushdie's forte seems to be not so much depth as dazzling breadth, exemplified by his extensive knowledge of cultures. The novel is full of colorful supporting characters who, while mostly one-dimensional, evoke the range of ethnic groups from which they come: "Olga Volga," India's Los Angeles landlady, potato sorceress from old Russia; pandit Pyarelal Kaul, peaceful dispenser of Hindu wisdom and mythology; Nazarébaddoor, old Gujar prophetess who traces her ancestry back to a migration from ancient Georgia; Firdaus Noman, snake sorceress who traces her ancestry back to Alexander the Great; Anya and Max Ophuls, Sr., Max's cultured Jewish parents, serenely playing their grand piano even as the Nazis come for them; Talib the Afghan, one-eyed terrorist leader who keeps a boy lover, Zahir, and believes in executing homosexuals; William Tillerman, Shalimar's sharp lawyer who designs the "sorcerer's defense" and loads the jury with women; and the Blood King, three-hundred-pound inmate who first attacks Shalimar, then helps him escape prison. Two of the most interesting characters are military opponents in Kashmir, both of whom commit atrocities and are absolutely convinced of their rightness: Maulana Bulbul Fakh, "iron mullah" and terrorist leader who, when killed, seems to disintegrate into "disassembled machine parts," and Hammirdev Suryavans Kachhwaha, pompous England-returned Indian army leader who dies from a king cobra snakebite after Firdaus Noman puts a snake curse on him.

Rushdie is also good at capturing the feel of a culture. His writing brims with etymologies, mythologies, allusions, historical background, and cultural details. In *Shalimar the Clown* Kashmir in particular gets his loving attention. Before it became disputed territory, Kashmir is described as an earthly paradise, a pristine land of mountains, lakes, gardens, and agricultural abundance. It is also a storied land of myth and history, the stories recounted in a rich oral tradition and in the *bhand pather* performances. Finally, it is a peaceful land where Hindus, Muslims, and even a few Jews live together in harmony. These descriptions turn the fate of Kashmir after it becomes disputed territory into the true tragedy of the novel.

At the opposite end of the cultural spectrum is the popular culture created by the media, its mecca in Los Angeles. Rushdie interlaces *Shalimar the Clown* with references to the films, television, popular music, and news coverage. The media facilitate the spectacular rise and fall of Max's reputation and influence Shalimar's lawyer to devise the "sorcerer's" or "Manchurian" defense (the latter named after the 1959 Richard Condon novel *The Manchurian Candidate*). References to the media naturally predominate *Shalimar the Clown*'s episodes set in New Delhi and California, but Rushdie also shows how films and television contribute to the demise of traditional culture in Kashmir. Boonyi is beckoned by the bright lights of the big city, Hasina Yambarzal operates her popular television tent, and the Indian and Pakistani governments use the media for propaganda purposes.

While the title *Shalimar the Clown* might be ironic, it suggests a central trope for the novel: acting. The shallow concept of character promulgated by the media, and perhaps illustrated in the novel's main characters, seems to be based on acting. Both Max and Boonyi enjoy relative success in their ventures because they are superb actors, Max a diplomat of consummate charm and beautiful Boonyi able to attract even his sophisticated eye. Shalimar, with his acting and acrobatic abilities, makes an easy transition into undercover living, assumed identities, professional killing, and terrorism. The main characters' name changes and metamorphoses suggest a superficial but fluid sense of identity that Rushdie seems to link to the media and, rightly or wrongly, the city of Los Angeles, where all of the novel's main characters except Boonyi end up. Some residents of Los Angeles might not be pleased with Rushdie's description of their city, but the depiction does help provide a symbolic focus to the ongoing clash between fundamentalist Islam and the Great Satan.

Harold Branam

Review Sources

Booklist 101, nos. 19/20 (June 1, 2005): 1713.
Kirkus Reviews 73, no. 11 (June 1, 2005): 608.
The Nation 281, no. 10 (October 3, 2005): 28-32.
The New York Review of Books 52, no. 15 (October 6, 2005): 8-11.
The New York Times 154 (September 6, 2005): E1-E7.
The New York Times Book Review 155 (October 23, 2005): 16.
The New Yorker 81, no. 26 (September 5, 2005): 152-155.
Publishers Weekly 252, no. 29 (July 25, 2005): 39.
The Wall Street Journal, September 9, 2005, p. W6.

A SHORT HISTORY OF TRACTORS IN UKRAINIAN

Author: Marina Lewycka (1946-   )
Publisher: Penguin Press (New York). 294 pp. $25.00
Type of work: Novel
Time: From the 1910's to the 1990's
Locale: England, Germany, and Ukraine

In 1990's England, two estranged sisters of a Ukrainian family join forces to rescue their elderly father from a sexy new Ukrainian refugee

Principal characters:
NADIA, the narrator, aged forty-seven
VERA, her older sister
NIKOLAI MAYEVSKYJ, their engineer father, aged eighty-four
LUDMILLA MAYEVSKYJ, their deceased mother
VALENTINA, sexy Ukrainian divorcé, aged thirty-six
STANISLAV, Valentina's son, aged fourteen
BOB TURNER, ERIC PIKE, and BALD ED, Valentina's boyfriends
MARGARITKA ZADCHUK, Valentina's girlfriend
LAURA CARTER, a lawyer representing Nikolai
VOLODYA DUBOV, Valentina's Ukrainian husband
MIKE LEWIS, Nadia's husband
MARGARITKA, Valentina's new baby

People who enjoy watching those daft British comedies on television will likely enjoy reading *A Short History of Tractors in Ukrainian*, a funny, slightly offbeat novel written along the lines of the situation comedy formula, right down to one or two characters who speak broken English and use endearments such as "Ah, holubchik. My little pigeon." The situation in the novel is classic: A dirty, doting old man falls for a sexy, gold-digging bombshell less than half his age. His two daughters, themselves considerably older than the bombshell, engage her and their father in a long, drawn-out struggle to save him. The plot is full of twists and surprises, with each of the thirty-one chapters corresponding to an episode in a comedy series and the author showing great ingenuity in developing them. Though close to being caricatures, the characters nevertheless give a highly entertaining satirical view of modern-day England.

Author Marina Lewycka has said that she set out deliberately to entertain in *A Short History of Tractors in Ukrainian*, after writing several novels with big ideas and serious themes that failed to get published. She certainly succeeded in her intentions, producing a novel that won the 2005 Bollinger Everyman Wodehouse Prize for Comic Fiction and was short-listed for the 2005 Orange Prize for Fiction (an international award for women writing in English). Lewycka's experience as a university lecturer on public relations probably helped her carry out her intentions, as her characters and their dialogue remind one of television advertisements built around slogans and sound bites and repeated every hour. Although Lewycka drew on popular culture in writing *A Short History of Tractors in Ukrainian*, her six books on elder care suggest more serious intentions in the novel than first appear.

In fact, some readers expecting only entertainment might be put off by Lewycka's inclusion of material echoing her Ukrainian refugee family history. A late product of World War II's destruction, Lewycka was born in 1946 in a German refugee camp and moved with her family to England a few years later. The Ukrainian refugee family in her novel has a similar history. Lewycka's father actually did write a book on the history of tractors, as the old widower in the novel is doing, and Lewycka dedicated the novel to the memory of her mother. Although the novel is not strictly autobiographical and draws on only the outlines of Lewycka's family history, it includes references to Stalinization, the 1930's Ukrainian famine, the ravages of World War II, the work camps in Germany, the massacre at Babi Yar, and other atrocities that might not seem to fit into a comic novel. Yet this horrific background does fit, with minimum clashing and disruption, as do the tractor history and episodes of elder abuse.

Lewycka uses her comic-writing talents to catch and hold her readers' attention, as in the opening lines: "Two years after my mother died, my father fell in love with a glamorous blond Ukrainian divorcée. He was eighty-four and she was thirty-six. She exploded into our lives like a fluffy pink grenade." Readers are hooked by page 2, where the old man compares his new love, Valentina, to "Botticelli's Venus rising from waves. Golden hair. Charming eyes. Superior breasts. When you see her you will understand." The old man, Nikolai, is speaking by phone with his younger daughter, Nadia, the novel's narrator, and what she understands ("The randy old beast!") is obviously different from what he thinks she understands. The novel includes lots of phone calls and, while remaining anchored in Nadia's point of view, lots of play with different perspectives. These features are symptomatic of the media-dominated world whose fantasies Lewycka satirizes.

For example, the eighty-four-year-old Nikolai, a former engineer with seventeen patents and intellectual interests, has apparently been watching too much television and has bought into the flesh market of the sexual revolution. As he says, "Snag is, hydraulic lift no longer fully functioning. But maybe with Valentina . . . " He is transfixed by Valentina's breasts, which she lets him fondle (though later she will not let her new baby breast-feed). If his hydraulic lift malfunctions, Valentina says, "Squishy squashy husband want make oralsex." Oral sex is recommended by Mrs. Zadchuk, Valentina's friend, as a legally binding way of consummating the marriage. According to Mrs. Zadchuk, oral sex is all the rage in England and in all the newspapers.

Nikolai is not the only male who succumbs to Valentina's charms. Over the course of the novel, she has liaisons with several other men—Bob Turner, Eric Pike, and Bald Ed are named—and the paternity of her new baby remains a mystery. Her former

Of Ukrainian descent, Marina Lewycka was born in 1946 in a German refugee camp and raised in England. She lectures on public relations at Sheffield Hallam University and is the author of six books on elder care.

Ukrainian husband, Volodya Dubov, shows up to reclaim her. Even in her casual encounters with men, even the police, Valentina knows her power to melt them down quickly. With the help of dyed hair, breast enhancement surgery, and piles of cosmetics, Valentina comes well armed for the battles of the flesh market: "She yanks up her T-shirt top to display those ferocious breasts bursting like twin warheads out of an underwired, ribbon-strapped Lyrca-panelled lace-trimmed green satin rocket launcher of a bra." Flaunting her superiority, Valentina scornfully refers to Nadia as "this bad-news peeping no-tits crow." Part of the charm of the novel is the broken English some characters speak, which tends to get right to the point.

Despite her awesome arsenal, Valentina is herself a victim of global village fantasies. An economic refugee and opportunist, Valentina apparently flees the struggling Ukraine for Britain because she fantasizes about sharing in the rich material benefits of the consumer society. To accomplish her goal, she needs a permanent visa, hence a British husband, and is willing to marry a decrepit old pensioner. Unfortunately, Valentina has overestimated Nikolai's monetary resources, which she quickly exhausts by buying old luxury cars (a Rover and a Rolls-Royce), a new stove, a new vacuum cleaner, and other accoutrements of the good life, including boil-in-the-bag dinners. Valentina has to get jobs working in a nursing home by day and in hotels at night, and soon the housework piles up. She abuses Nikolai verbally and physically, and he messes his pants and hides in his room out of fear.

Valentina seems to be an example of the gangster capitalist type said in the novel to emerge after the fall of the Soviet Union and to dominate the new Ukraine. The novel refers to such gangster capitalist types as recycled communist *apparatchiks*, greedy people who will take on any guise to exploit the society in which they live. Valentina seems to have made herself into a gross parody of Western values, probably imbibed from the media. It is hard to feel any sympathy for Valentina, yet told from her point of view the novel would be entirely different. Underneath, Valentina is a desperate woman who will do anything to stay in the West, and she does care for and look after her kids. In a self-made sense, she is one of those beautiful prostitutes who Dubov, her Ukrainian husband, says is poor Ukraine's main export to the West.

As the novel moves along, the sad modern history of the Ukraine comes more to the fore. The stark contrast between Nikolai's two daughters, Vera and Nadia, is explained by that history. Vera (Faith) is a child of the 1930's and 1940's who endured the horrors of Stalinization, famine, World War II, and work camps in Germany as these were visited on her family. Flung from place to place, she hardly ever saw her father and waited long hours at the fence for her mother to return from longer hours of labor. Now Vera is a shrewd, flint-hard divorcé and sophisticated woman who lives well in her London flat and can take care of herself (and any would-be opponents). Vera recognizes the new family situation right away and is ready to deliver the death blow to Valentina and her father.

On the other hand, Nadia (the name *Nadezhda* means "hope") is a peacetime baby, born after World War II, who flourished on the orange juice, milk, and cod-liver oil dispensed by the British government. A child of the 1950's and 1960's, with memories of the Beatles and antiwar protests, and now a happily married woman who lives in Cambridge and lectures on sociology at Anglia Polytechnic University, Nadia is a mushy liberal who supports good causes and buys her clothes from Oxfam. She finds it ironic that, as a feminist, she is defending her randy old father against an exploitative woman. Soon, though, Nadia is acting like the most chauvinistic refugee basher, reading up on immigration and deportation laws, hiring lawyers, and writing letters to the Home Office. Such distressing behavior raises questions about how deep her values are and how she would act if she found herself in the same situations as Vera and even Valentina: Is Nadia only another creation of the modern media who can afford the luxury of political correctness?

If the novel's characters represent the new postcommunist Ukraine and a previous Ukraine decimated by communism and World War II, the novel also recalls a still earlier Ukraine—a rural land of small farms and simple country folk. Memories of this supposedly idyllic motherland, Ukraina, color the thinking of the older characters. Nikolai even associates Valentina with Ukraina, "breathing in the remembered scent of mown hay and cherry blossoms" (but Nadia catches "the distinct synthetic whiff of New Russia"). The imagery of their speech also reflects a rural background: "The Ukrainian community in Peterborough has disowned her [Valentina]. . . . They say she sold her mother's goat and cow to buy grease to put on her face to attract Western men. They speak rubbish. Her mother had chicken and pigs—she never had a goat or a cow."

Nostalgic memories of old Ukraina only serve to intensify the sadness of the modern Ukraine. The rich, flat farmland of old Ukraina, which once made it the breadbasket of Europe, also left it susceptible to Joseph Stalin's farm collectivization and overexport of products—policies which (along with purges) led to the 1930's Ukrainian famine. As Nikolai points out in his history, the tractor helped make these disasters possible. Even worse, the design of tractors lent itself to redesign as tanks, which also found it easy to negotiate the flat Ukrainian landscape. The modern nightmare actually started when Americans used tractors to overfarm the Midwest and create the Dust Bowl, which led to the fall of the stock market, which spread depression and chaos around the world, which led to the embrace of fascism and communism.

Nikolai's history of tractors thus stands at the center of Lewycka's novel and offers an interpretation of modern history. His history of tractors also suggests a parallel to the history of modern media, another creation of technology, and issues a warning. If the humble tractor had such power to affect recent history and spawn disasters, what are the modern media—with their power to enshrine fantasies around the world—doing right now?

Harold Branam

Review Sources

Booklist 101, nos. 9/10 (January 1-15, 2005): 820.
Entertainment Weekly, March 4, 2005, p. 78.
Kirkus Reviews 72, no. 23 (December 1, 2004): 1108-1109.

THE SINGULARITY IS NEAR
When Humans Transcend Biology

Author: Ray Kurzweil (1948-   )
Publisher: Viking (New York). 652 pp. $30.00
Type of work: Medicine, psychology, science, and technology
Time: From the period after the big bang (about fourteen billion years ago) to the initial spread of nonbiological human intelligence throughout the universe (probably in the twenty-second century)
Locale: Earth, with speculations about the rest of the universe

The exponential growth of technologies, especially artificial intelligence, Kurzweil says, will lead to a pivotal event, the Singularity, when human intelligence will merge with vastly superior machine intelligence, a union that will allow solutions to problems ranging from pollution and poverty to human mortality

> *Principal personages:*
> RAY KURZWEIL (b. 1948), an inventor, artificial intelligence (AI) enthusiast, and futurist
> GORDON E. MOORE (b. 1929), a leading inventor of integrated circuits and longtime chairman of Intel, whose predictions of the exponential growth of computer power deeply influenced Kurzweil
> ALAN M. TURING (1912-1954), an English mathematician and computer scientist who developed a pragmatic test for differentiating human from machine intelligence
> MARVIN MINSKY (b. 1927), an American mathematician, computer scientist, and Kurzweil's mentor
> JOHN R. SEARLE (b. 1932), an American philosopher and a chief critic of Kurzweil's reductionist views on human consciousness and machine intelligence

Ray Kurzweil is a self-proclaimed superoptimist about technological progress. According to some of his critics, he is unrealistically confident about the future of artificial intelligence (AI), but according to such supporters as Marvin Minsky and Microsoft founder Bill Gates, Kurzweil is insightfully extending scientifically observed trends of the twentieth century into the future. In such earlier books as *The Age of Intelligent Machines* (1990) and *The Age of Spiritual Machines: When Computers Exceed Human Intelligence* (1999), Kurzweil develops themes and makes predictions that he develops even more extensively in *The Singularity Is Near: When Humans Transcend Biology*.

Moore's Law, a central theme of Kurzweil's earlier books, is also at the center of this new one. Computer engineer Gordon Moore noticed early in his career that the number of transistors on a single integrated circuit (IC) was doubling every year, a trend that has continued and has become known as Moore's Law. A consequence of this law has been the phenomenal growth of computer power, with a concomitant reduction in costs. Kurzweil believes that not only computers but all information-related technologies will experience similar exponential growth. He has codified his belief in a theory he has called "the law of accelerating returns," which explains how salient events in the evolution of technology occur at increasingly shorter time intervals.

∽

Ray Kurzweil was educated at the Massachusetts Institute of Technology. His many successful inventions led to his induction into the Inventors Hall of Fame. He received the half-million-dollar MIT-Lemelson Prize, the world's most prestigious award for innovations. His previous books have won several awards, and twelve universities have bestowed honorary degrees on him.

∽

What is novel in Kurzweil's twenty-first century publications is his emphasis on a future period during which the ceaselessly accelerating augmentation of machine intelligence will irreversibly transform not only human life but also human nature. This period—when *Homo sapiens* breaks the bonds of its genetic past and ascends to unimaginable heights of health, intelligence, even immortality—Kurzweil calls the Singularity. Shortly before the appearance of *The Singularity Is Near*, Kurzweil published, with Terry Grossman, a doctor interested in life extension, *Fantastic Voyage: Live Long Enough to Live Forever* (2004), in which the two argue that new discoveries in genomics, biotechnology, and nanotechnology will allow humans to overcome bodily diseases and organ decline and to live in good health indefinitely. Kurzweil, who takes 250 supplement pills every day, hopes to preserve his good health until biotechnologists have learned how to conquer aging.

Throughout *The Singularity Is Near*, Kurzweil sprinkles autobiographical clues that help to explain his optimism. For example, as a child growing up in Queens, New York, he read Tom Swift stories, which imbued him with the unshakable conviction that humans have the power to solve whatever problems they encounter. When he was fifteen, he invented a teaching machine based on pattern recognition, and his correspondence with Minsky at the Massachusetts Institute of Technology led to his attending that school, where he studied computer science. His education reinforced his veneration for human creativity and his certitude that ideas can change the world. In 1974 he founded Kurzweil Computer Products, whose chief goal was to construct a machine that could read printed texts. He then invented a "Reading Machine for the Blind," of which blind musician Stevie Wonder purchased the first model. The friendship that arose between Kurzweil and Wonder led to the founding of Kurzweil Music Systems, which made music synthesizers that accurately mimicked the sounds of many traditional instruments.

The Singularity Is Near, which draws on the author's experiences as an inventor and maker of pattern-recognizing machines, is structured in nine chapters, prefaced by a prologue and concluding with an epilogue. Periodically interspersed in these chapters are Socratic dialogues in which historical, modern-day, and futuristic characters lightheartedly discuss the weighty analyses preceding them. Kurzweil even imagines a debate between bacteria during the early stages of life on Earth about the wisdom of their joining together, as this might lead to the evolution of such problematic life-forms as *Homo sapiens*.

Early in this book, Kurzweil introduces the reader to his visionary theory of technological evolution as a process of creating patterns of increasing complexity and order. He strongly disagrees with previous forecasters of future technological development who relied on an "intuitive linear view of history," whereas he favors an exponential view. He divides the trajectory of evolution into six epochs, the first four of which refer to the past and present. His Epochs Five and Six are concerned with speculative future developments. In Epoch One atoms and molecules made their appearance. Epoch Two was a period during which life and the precise digital mechanisms for reproducing it appeared. In Epoch Three, early animals' capacity to recognize patterns became highly sophisticated because of their complex brains, which eventually allowed humans to understand the world through abstract models. In Epoch Four, Kurzweil analyzes the evolution of human-created technologies, from simple machines to advanced computers capable of sensing, storing, and evaluating elaborate patterns of information.

Central to the book's thesis is Epoch Five, during which, Kurzweil conjectures, the biological intelligence of human brains will be initially augmented and then transcended by nonbiological intelligence (this is the Singularity). During the sixth and final epoch, this nonbiological intelligence will spread beyond Earth into the rest of the universe. As the title of his book makes clear, Kurzweil believes that the Singularity of Epoch Five is near. By using a Moore's Law-like extrapolation, he calculates that the hardware and software to model human intelligence will be in place by the end of the 2020's. In other words, he believes that this is when AI machines will pass the Turing test, in which a human interrogator, in electronic contact with an unseen computer and human, is unable to tell the difference between the two. So sure is Kurzweil of the correctness of this prediction that he has a twenty-thousand-dollar wager with a skeptic.

Because his law of accelerating returns is so important to his analyses and predictions, Kurzweil devotes pages to proving that revolutionary technological achievements have been occurring in shorter and shorter times. Unlike Charles Darwin, who tried to eliminate any notion of hierarchical order in his theory of evolution, Kurzweil strongly insists that technological evolution inevitably leads to better machines, and these "higher" machines are appearing at an accelerated rate. For example, it took about fifty years for the telephone to become widely integrated into society, but such integration for the cell phone took only a decade. In 1990 it cost about ten dollars to sequence a base pair in the deoxyribonucleic acid (DNA) molecule, whereas in 2004 it cost only a few cents.

The reason, according to Kurzweil, that technological evolution differs so dramatically from random biological evolution is that intelligent humans can orchestrate the evolution of machines. It took millions of years of biological evolution to produce a human brain, but Kurzweil thinks that it will take only decades for humans to reverse-engineer the human brain to create "strong AI" (artificial intelligence that exceeds human intelligence).

To achieve the computational capacity of the human brain, several new technologies will be necessary. Kurzweil believes that nanotubes, very tiny, elongated structures made from carbon atoms, are the most likely technology to prolong the exponential growth of computer power when ICs are no longer viable. The ability to scan the brain is increasing exponentially and, by using brain-scan information, scientists will be able to simulate neuronal networks that will be functionally equivalent to certain brain regions.

As helpful as these new tools are for modeling the brain, Kurzweil recognizes the importance of understanding the brain from within, and this is where nanobots become essential. Nanobots are very tiny robots, about the size of a human blood cell. By populating the brain with billions of nanobots, scientists will finally be able to grasp the awe-inspiring details of the tiniest brain components and how they work.

According to Kurzweil, three overlapping revolutions will usher in the Singularity, which he predicts will occur in 2045: genetics, nanotechnology, and robotics (GNR). The genetic revolution will allow science to cure degenerative diseases, conquer cancer, and reverse aging. Nanotechnology will allow the inexpensive, molecule by molecule creation of innovative biological and physical artifacts. Some of these tiny machines have already been made, and Kurzweil sees no difficulties in eventually manufacturing molecular devices that will remove toxins from the environment and travel within the human bloodstream to perform various diagnostic and therapeutic tasks. Robots will also play a significant role in the Singularity revolution. According to Minsky, such intelligent robots will become people's new children.

Once nonbiological intelligence appears, it will evolve much more rapidly than biological intelligence. The Singularity will constitute a change more far-reaching than any previous revolution in human history. Kurzweil envisions a utopian symbiotic society of the human and artificial in which nanobots in human bodies will maintain organs in optimum states of health, and nanobots in brains will allow humans to expand their intelligence trillionfold and to change personalities at will. If wars do occur in this Kurzweilian world, they will be more benign than previous wars, waged with robotic systems that are smaller, faster, lighter, and smarter than present military technologies.

Ultimately, nonbiological intelligence will grow to such an extent that the Earth will be too small to contain it, says Kurzweil, and he thus predicts that nonbiological astronauts, and not biological humans, will be the colonizers not only of this galaxy but also, eventually, of the entire universe. His analysis of such a cosmic future leads him to the interesting conclusion that humans are most likely unique in the universe. If the law of accelerating returns is valid, then it applies throughout the universe to many other extraterrestrial civilizations. At least some of these advanced civilizations should have gone far beyond the Singularity, and they therefore should have made contact with Earth. Because they never have, Kurzweil concludes that they do not exist, and it is humankind's duty to spread human intelligence throughout the cosmos. If the speed of light is an unconquerable limit, then this will take billions of years, but Kurzweil hopes that ways around this limitation may be found.

Kurzweil calls himself a Singularitarian, and many have seen him as the father of a movement. Some have interpreted his vision as a new religion, with its promise of immortality through technology. He responds that his ideas and values are not substitutes for those of traditional religions, as his vision is not a matter of faith but of understanding technological trends. Nevertheless, his ideas, if they become realized, will transform religions, as they will all institutions. Throughout these revolutionary changes Kurzweil emphasizes that two ethical principles will be preeminent for all: respect for consciousness (his version of the biblical Golden Rule) and the significance of knowledge.

Though he is an unrepentant optimist, Kurzweil recognizes that technologies have not always resulted in unmixed blessings to humanity, and so he analyzes the "deeply intertwined promise and peril of GNR." In one example he gives, nanobots, particularly if they can self-replicate, could escape into the environment and cause serious damage. Similarly, nonbiological intelligence could escape human control and become totalitarian, leading to the annihilation of biological intelligence. These and other dangers Kurzweil minimizes, believing in the technological fix because, by the time such technologies reach a potentially perilous stage, humans will have created the technologies that will eliminate their detrimental potential. He is more concerned about the negative influence of Luddites and antitechnologists than about the actualized dreams of technophiles.

From responses to his earlier writings, Kurzweil is well aware that he has a plethora of critics. Toward the end of this book he presents his responses to "a panoply" of criticisms. His responses to these criticisms have to be read while keeping in mind that he controls how such critiques are formulated. For example, he spends considerable space responding to John Searle's arguments attacking his belief that the brain's mind is simply a computer program, which means, of course, that there is no barrier to the creation of conscious thinking machines. For Searle, a computer program merely manipulates symbols, whereas a human brain attaches meaning to them. Kurzweil finds Searle's arguments "tautological," and he insists that Searle does not have a correct understanding of future computer programs that will be based on the reverse-engineering of the brain.

Kurzweil is a futurist, but he insists that he is not writing science fiction. The scientist and science-fiction writer Isaac Asimov once said that he wrote his stories as finger exercises for the future. Similarly, Kurzweil wrote this book so that society can begin to analyze today the implications that the Singularity will have for future. Philosophers have pointed out that Kurzweil makes a logical error in his many extrapolations. Sir Karl Popper has called this the inductivist error. An example of a classic inductivist error is the way in which physicists once extrapolated their many observations of electrons to conclude that all electrons are negatively charged; this conclusion was proved false with the discovery of the positron, the positively charged electron.

Writers who are aware of the history of technology have challenged Kurzweil's optimism. Edward Tenner, in his *Why Things Bite Back: Technology and the Revenge of Unintended Consequences* (1996), analyzes numerous examples of the adverse effects of introduced technologies. Cautionary tales such as Mary Shelley's *Frankenstein* (1817) and Aldous Huxley's *Brave New World* (1932) have warned readers about the arrogance of scientists who overestimate the benefits of technologies while minimizing their hazards. Some of the readers of *The Singularity Is Near* think that the Singularity could bring about human extinction rather than a utopia. Kurzweil disagrees with these pessimistic views, and he has a simple response to his many critics: Wait and see if the Singularity actually occurs.

Robert J. Paradowski

Review Sources

Booklist 102, no. 2 (September 15, 2005): 8.
Computer 38 (November, 2005): 96.
Information Week (October 17, 2005): 72.
Kirkus Reviews 73, no. 14 (July 15, 2005): 778.
The New York Times 155 (October 3, 2005): E6.
Publishers Weekly 252, no. 29 (July 25, 2005): 66.
Science News 168, no. 13 (September 25, 2005): 207.
The Wall Street Journal 246, no. 67 (October 1, 2005): P8.

SLOW MAN

Author: J. M. Coetzee (1940-   )
Publisher: Viking Press (New York). 265 pp. $24.95
Type of work: Novel
Time: 2005
Locale: Adelaide, South Australia

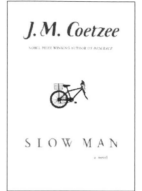

Following a bicycling accident that costs him a leg, a retired photographer falls in love with his nurse and is visited by an intrusive novelist

Principal characters:
PAUL RAYMENT, a sixty-year-old former
   photographer
MARIJANA JOKIÉ, a Croatian-born nurse
DRAGO JOKIÉ, her sixteen-year-old son
MIROSLAV JOKIÉ, her husband, a car assembly plant worker
LJUBICA JOKIÉ, the youngest Jokié child
BLANKA JOKIÉ, the oldest of the three Jokié children
MARIANNA, a blind, unmarried woman
ELIZABETH COSTELLO, a famous Australian writer
MARGARET MCCORD, Rayment's former lover

For the first twelve of its thirty chapters, *Slow Man* reads like a retake of J. M. Coetzee's *Disgrace* (1999). A proudly solitary older man is dramatically humbled, forced to acknowledge his vulnerability and dependency on others, particularly women. In *Disgrace*, after accusations of sexual harassment cause him to lose his academic position in Cape Town, fifty-two-year-old David Lurie ends up moving to his daughter's small, secluded farm and finding redemptive work in a shelter for abandoned animals.

The eponymous slow man of Coetzee's new novel is Paul Rayment, a retired, sixty-year-old photographer. In the first sentence of *Slow Man*, he is knocked off his bicycle and sent flying through the air by a careless young driver. He has barely recovered consciousness, in a hospital bed, when a surgeon extracts his consent to amputate his right leg. Rayment, who is divorced and childless and has no close living relatives, stubbornly refuses to be fitted for a prosthesis and balks at regimens of physical therapy. Returning to his empty apartment in South Australia, he is tended to by a succession of unsatisfactory caregivers before settling on a Croatian nurse named Marijana Jokié. Rayment falls in love with her and imagines that she might be willing to abandon her jealous husband, Miroslav, for him.

Rayment's new physical disability forces him to reflect on the relationship between mind and body and on how his options have been suddenly and radically reduced. Convinced that his life is frivolous, that he has been merely sliding through the world, Rayment longs for a child of his own, someone who would endow his existence with

transcendent value. He befriends Marijana's troubled sixteen-year-old son, Drago, and offers to
pay for his tuition at a prestigious boarding
school. The patronizing gesture causes turmoil
within Drago's family. When the boy has a falling
out with his parents, Rayment invites him to move
in with him. Fantasizing a new household in
which he has displaced Miroslav as paterfamilias,
Rayment attempts to win the trust of Ljubica and
Blanka Jokié, Drago's younger and older sisters.

On page 79, *Slow Man* takes a metafictional
turn when Elizabeth Costello, a character in two
of Coetzee's earlier books, *The Lives of Animals*
(1999) and *Elizabeth Costello* (2003), rings the
doorbell of Rayment's flat in Adelaide. An accomplished and respected novelist, she insinu-
ates herself into his aimless life, while claiming,
ambiguously, that he in some sense came to
her. "*Who is this madwoman I have let in my
home?*" asks Rayment, who feels overpowered
by the presumptuous, seventy-two-year-old intruder. "*How am I going to rid myself of her?*"

*J. M. Coetzee introduced the
character of Elizabeth Costello in*
The Lives of Animals *(1999) and
brought her back in* Elizabeth
Costello *(2003), which was
published just before he received
the Nobel Prize in Literature. He
was awarded the Booker Prize
twice, for* Disgrace *(1999) and* Life
and Times of Michael K *(1983). His
other books include the novels*
Waiting for the Barbarians *(1980),*
Foe *(1986), and* The Master of
Petersburg *(1994) and the memoirs*
Boyhood: Scenes from Provincial
Life *(1997) and* Youth *(2002). A
native of South Africa, Coetzee
moved to Australia in 2002.*

Costello reveals an uncanny knowledge about
details of Rayment's existence, and she analyzes
his current situation as if he were a character in a
developing plot for her next novel, or perhaps as
if he were a muse she is studying for inspiration.
Rayment, who rebuffs the advances of a married
former lover, Margaret McCord, reluctantly allows Costello to move into his apartment. When
she offers to arrange a tryst with a sexually hungry blind woman she calls Marianna,
Rayment accedes, but the awkward encounter is marred by his sense that he and his
partner are performing for Costello.

The visiting author chides Rayment about his behavior toward his nurse, Marijana,
and her family. Disappointed by his deficiency of passion and his failure to act deci-
sively, as if demanding for her book a more assertive hero, Costello accuses Rayment
of being slow and cold. Exhorting him to make himself worthy of being the protagonist of a novel, she admonishes him to "please stop dithering." Rayment joins aloof
personalities found throughout Coetzee's oeuvre who, no longer able to take for
granted their own autonomy, are forced to acknowledge the integrity of the Other—
man, woman, or beast. "You treat me like a puppet," complains Rayment, who feels
like a character rebelling against his tyrannical creator. "You treat everyone like a
puppet. You make up stories and bully us into playing them out for you." Rejecting
the traditional role of omniscient author, Costello insists that her relationship to

Rayment is more complicated, that he has the power to take control of his own life. She, in fact, urges him to do so. "The moment you decide to take charge, I will fade away," says the writer to Rayment, who might be nothing but a figment of her imagination. Or has Rayment merely conjured up Costello out of his own loneliness and despair?

The setting of *Slow Man*, in Adelaide, reflects the fact that, three years after the publication of *Disgrace*, Coetzee, one of South Africa's most celebrated authors, moved to Australia. Though Costello was born in Australia and is one of its most eminent literary figures, most of the other characters in the novel are, like their author, immigrants. For reasons Rayment assumes had something to do with political conflict in the Balkans, Marijana and Miroslav Jokié left Croatia twelve years previously. Though both studied at the Art Institute in Dubrovnik, relocation to a foreign country diminished their economic and social status. Skilled and respected artisans in their homeland, the Jokiés in Australia are hobbled by an incomplete command of their thickly accented English. Marijana earns a living by cleaning up after Rayment and other maimed and ailing employers, and Miroslav works at an automobile assembly plant.

Rayment, however, is also an outsider. Born in France, he was brought to Australia at the age of six by his mother and the stern Dutch husband she married after the death of her son's father. Rayment does not feel at home in either France or Australia. He notes that, though the country is his residence rather than his home, he can at least pass for Australian. "That, as far as I am concerned," says Rayment, who might in this be speaking for the peripatetic Coetzee, "is all there is to it, to the national-identity business: where one passes and where one does not, where on the contrary one stands out." Viewing Australia as a nation of immigrants, Rayment does not stand out, in fact takes modest comfort in not being outstanding. His most emphatic assertion of national identity comes in his devotion to collecting photographs of Australia made during the nineteenth century, as if to prove that the frontier country in which he resides has a history and that he is part of it.

In South Africa, Coetzee grew up speaking both Afrikaans, the language of his father's people, and English, the language of his mother's. He also studied French and wrote his doctoral dissertation, at the University of Texas, on Samuel Beckett, a translingual author who moved between English and French. In his essays and his fiction, Coetzee has always been sensitive to the ways in which particular languages both enable and limit thought. He fashions Paul Rayment as a linguistic alien, a man incapable of expressing his most fundamental intuitions in either his native French or his adopted English. While assuring Costello, in faultless English, that he is fluent in her language, Rayment notes that he will never fully possess it: "But English came to me too late. It did not come with my mother's milk. In fact it did not come at all. Privately I have always felt myself to be a kind of ventriloquist's dummy. It is not I who speak the language, it is the language that is spoken through me."

Thus, built into *Slow Man* is a self-consciousness about its own medium, words, as well as about the illusions on which its fiction is constructed. When Rayment's collection of historical photographs of Australia is stolen and their images altered, Coetzee challenges the reader to consider the distinctions between reality and replica and how one's representations of the past, which is all one has of the past, are mutable.

So, too, does the entire novel provide a reflexive interrogation of its own processes and powers.

Impatient with metafiction, fiction that lays bare its own devices, some reviewers reacted negatively, even angrily, to Coetzee's novel. Authors and characters exist in distinct ontological dimensions, and there are those who cannot countenance a mingling of the two—who wince when, for example, the "toon" characters mix with live-action humans in the 1988 film *Who Framed Roger Rabbit*. By shattering the reader's belief in the reality of Paul Rayment, the insertion of Elizabeth Costello into the story reduces *Slow Man* for some to a tedious intellectual exercise. In her earlier appearances in Coetzee's fiction, Costello had at least been used to advance such themes as animal rights, evil, faith, and eros. With *Slow Man*, where her principal function appears to be to antagonize the fictional Rayment, some readers also respond with antipathy. "I am not an amenable subject," declares Rayment, refusing to submit to Costello's script. Some reviewers have similarly resisted the authority of Coetzee's text.

However, Coetzee's narrative strategy of blurring the boundaries between the fictional universe and the "real" world can trace its lineage at least as far back as the moment in part 2 of Miguel de Cervantes' *Don Quixote de la Mancha* (1615) when Don Quixote reads part 1 of the novel (1605), in which he is himself the main character. Like Luigi Pirandello's *Sei personaggi in cerca d'autore* (1921; *Six Characters in Search of an Author*, 1922) and John Fowles's *The French Lieutenant's Woman* (1969), *Slow Man* is a metafiction that demands an active role in the literary experience. Just as Rayment is goaded out of passivity into taking charge of his life, so is the reader forced to assume a kind of authority for the text in hand. Coetzee refrains from resolving the dilemmas he provides for his characters, and his readers. On the final page of *Slow Man*, when Rayment literally kisses off on Costello, the author who would take responsibility for his existence, it is up to each reader, humbled by a lesson in individual insufficiency, to face the future without illusions.

Steven G. Kellman

Review Sources

Booklist 101, no. 21 (July 1, 2005): 1875.
The Boston Globe, October 2, 2005, p. D6.
The Christian Science Monitor, September 27, 2005, p. 14.
Library Journal 130, no. 14 (September 1, 2005): 128.
Los Angeles Times, September 24, 2005, p. E1.
The Nation 281, no. 16 (November 14, 2005): 40-43.
The New Republic 233, no. 15 (October 10, 2005): 31-33.
The New York Times Book Review 155 (October 2, 2005): 20-21.
Publishers Weekly 252, no. 34 (August 29, 2005): 34-35.
Time, September 12, 2005, p. 62.
The Times Literary Supplement, September 2, 2005, pp. 9-10.
The Washington Post, September 25, 2005, p. T06.

SMALL ISLAND

Author: Andrea Levy (1956-   )
First published: 2004, in Great Britain
Publisher: Picador (New York). 438 pp. Paperback
    $14.00
Type of work: Novel
Time: From the 1930's to 1948
Locale: Jamaica, London, the English countryside, India,
    and Burma

*The lives of a middle-class English couple and a pair of
Jamaican immigrants become enmeshed in London after
World War II*

Principal characters:
    HORTENSE ROBERTS, an educated Jamaican
        woman who follows her husband to
        England
    VICTORIA "QUEENIE" BUXTON BLIGH, an English woman abandoned by
        her husband after World War II
    GILBERT JOSEPH, Hortense's husband a Jamaican immigrant to England
    BERNARD BLIGH, Queenie's husband, a bank clerk
    ARTHUR BLIGH, Bernard's elderly father who refuses to speak
    MICHAEL ROBERTS, a distant cousin of Hortense, with whom she is in
        love

Small Island presents the stories of four people who come together in London in the 1940's. The narrative unfolds through sections titled "Before" and "1948," which contain first-person narratives from the four main characters. The story opens with Bernard and Queenie Bligh, a middle-class couple living a dull life in a staid, sere marriage.

Queenie is the only daughter of a rural butcher and his wife. Although as a child she was smart and did well in school, her education was limited by her parents' need for her help on the farm. Dismayed by the blood and gore of her father's trade, she has fled to London to live with her widowed aunt. Her aunt sends the teenage Queenie to elocution lessons, buys her lovely clothes, and puts her to work in the shop she owns. While working there, Queenie meets Bernard Bligh, an older bank clerk. Bernard's father, Arthur, had returned from World War I psychologically damaged, and Bernard and his mother had to care for him as if for a child. When Bernard's mother died in her forties, Bernard assumed the care of his father.

Bernard courts Queenie in a taciturn fashion. The two have little in common, and Queenie had dreamed of a more romantic and exciting suitor. When her aunt suddenly dies from a stroke and her family assumes she will return to the farm, Queenie agrees to marry Bernard. Bernard does not want his wife to work, which initially seems like a wonderful luxury to Queenie. Her days, however, are spent caring for Arthur, and Bernard does not allow her to make changes in their musty old home. Bernard is a perfunctory sexual partner, and their sexual relationship is a boring chore to Queenie. Although they both hope to have children, Queenie does not become pregnant.

The other main characters, Hortense and Gilbert Joseph, are Jamaican immigrants to England. Born of a peasant mother and a well-to-do, respected married man, Hortense was sent as a small child to live with her father's cousin and his wife. Their son, Michael, a year older than Hortense, is a handsome, spoiled, and charismatic young man. Although Hortense is in love with him, he looks upon her as a little sister. After a scandal involving a married white woman, Michael leaves for England to join the Royal Air Force (RAF). Hortense later learns that Michael's plane has been lost, but she refuses to believe that he is dead.

Gilbert Joseph is one of nine children of an alcoholic Jewish father and a Jamaican mother. Brought up to revere England as Jamaica's mother country, Gilbert is one of many islanders who join the RAF. He is eager to fight the Nazis, believing that if they are conquered, discrimination in the world will end and life in Jamaica will be better. He hopes to study law after his service ends but is encouraged to become a baker instead. After he is shipped back to Jamaica, a series of financially disastrous ventures with his childhood friend make him want to return to England.

Andrea Levy was born in London in 1956. She studied textiles and weaving in college and did not begin writing until 1988. Small Island, *winner of three prestigious British awards—the Whitbread Book of the Year, the Orange Prize for Fiction, and the Commonwealth Writers' Prize—is her fourth novel and the first published in the United States.*

Hortense is sent to a teacher training school in Kingston. There she befriends Celia, who wants to marry Gilbert and go to England with him. After Hortense cruelly reveals to Gilbert that Celia's mother is mentally unbalanced, Gilbert abandons Celia. Hortense promises to give Gilbert money to return to England if he marries her and promises to send for her after he is settled. Within a few weeks they wed. Hortense is completely innocent in sexual matters, and their marriage is unconsummated when Gilbert leaves.

In London, the Blighs' staid lives are turned upside down by World War II. Queenie is determined to help the poor families who have lost their homes in the air raids, despite Bernard's irritation. When he refuses to let her bring a homeless family to live with them, she defiantly takes a job in the refugee center, begins working long hours, and becomes emotionally involved in her clients' lives.

Bernard eventually joins the RAF. Assigned to the Repair and Salvage Unit, he serves in India and then Burma. While Bernard is away, three RAF pilots—one of whom is Michael Roberts, Hortense's cousin—are temporarily lodged at the Blighs' home. Queenie is charmed and aroused by the flirtatious Jamaican, and they spend a passionate night together, Queenie's first fulfilling sexual encounter.

Queenie takes Arthur to stay at her family's farm in order to shield him from the worst of the bombings. One afternoon, he wanders away and is found by Gilbert, who is stationed nearby. When Gilbert brings Arthur back to the farmhouse, Queenie at first mistakes him for Michael. Gilbert, Queenie, and Arthur meet again in town and encounter a great deal of hostility when they enter a tea shop. Their determination to sit together in a motion-picture theater, where blacks are expected to sit separately in the upper balcony, sparks a riot outside in which Arthur is killed.

Away in the service, Bernard suffers considerable taunting from one of his comrades for his naïve and puritanical attitudes about sex. After the war, Bernard goes to a whorehouse and has a sexual experience unlike any he could imagine having with his wife. Afterward, he feels ashamed and guilty. On the ship back to England, he discovers a sore on his genitals and is convinced he has syphilis. Unwilling to admit this to Queenie, he finds lodging and a job in Brighton and does not contact his wife.

After Arthur's death, Queenie returns to London. One night, Michael appears at her door, asking if he can stay with her until his ship sails for Canada. They spend three impassioned days and nights together before Michael leaves.

Alone, unemployed, and unsure whether Bernard is dead or missing, Queenie ignores the reproaches of her neighbors and begins renting rooms in her crumbling London home to "colored" lodgers, including Gilbert. After being rejected for many jobs because he is black, Gilbert finally is hired as a postal driver. After several months, he sends for Hortense. Their life together does not begin well when Gilbert oversleeps and fails to meet her ship. Hortense, who expects to live in a stately home, is horrified to find a tiny, dirty room up several flights of stairs in the Blighs' dilapidated house. When Gilbert tries to join her in bed, Hortense recoils, and he is forced to sleep in the chair.

Their lives continue in this fashion, Hortense remaining angry and arrogant while Gilbert resigns himself to a lonely and sexless marriage. Queenie is welcoming and friendly to Hortense, taking her new boarder to local shops and helping Hortense when she is not too proud to ask for help. Hortense, who prides herself on her manners, elocution, and appearance, is confused and offended when people cannot understand her accent.

After being gone five years, Bernard unexpectedly returns. During a bout with the flu, he was visited by a doctor, who assured him that he had not contracted syphyllis. Bernard is horrified that Queenie is renting out rooms in his family home and insists that the lodgers leave.

Gilbert fears that he and Hortense will not be able to afford a better place to live, but Hortense is confident that she will easily get a job as a teacher and their financial problems will be over. Gilbert insists on going with her on a long bus ride to an interview despite her scornful assurances she can find the appointed place on her own. Knowing well how Hortense will fare, he waits outside for her. When she comes out, distraught and ashamed that she was rudely rebuffed, his joshing but concerned comforting causes her finally to open up to him. Gilbert then takes her to see the famous sights of London about which she has read in books, and they visit a tea shop. He suggests she look for a job sewing and admits to her that he had once hoped to study law.

When Gilbert and Hortense return to the house, they find Bernard in their room. Furious, Gilbert confronts Bernard, verbally and then physically. Hearing the fight, Queenie comes upstairs and shocks Bernard by taking the lodgers' side against him. Suddenly, Queenie is gripped by pain and asks Hortense to help her downstairs. In her bedroom, Queenie unwraps the huge bandage she has bound tightly around her stomach, and Hortense realizes that Queenie is pregnant. Assisted only by the inexperienced Hortense, Queenie gives birth to a black son. Both Bernard and Hortense assume it is Gilbert's child, but he finally convinces them that he has not been there long enough to be the father. Queenie and Bernard achieve a reconciliation of sorts, each admitting to their indiscretions.

A friend of Gilbert offers him and Hortense a chance to live in his large old house in exchange for fixing it up. Gilbert worries that Hortense will think the rundown house is not good enough, but she is delighted and eager to make it their home. That night, for the first time, she lets Gilbert share her bed.

Small Island, an engaging story of two very different couples, is also about two diverse cultures. The Jamaicans consider themselves more sophisticated than the inhabitants of the islands surrounding them and assume the English will recognize them as such. They also expect England to be both beautiful and welcoming, its people cultured and educated. They are shocked to find discrimination and shortages, a cold, drab environment, and poorly educated, unsophisticated people. They are frequently taunted by Britons, who often think Jamaica is part of Africa and that Jamaicans are jungle-born primitives. When Queenie says she is not ashamed to be seen on the street with Hortense, the Jamaican woman cannot understand why—it is she who is dressed in gloves and a hat, while Queenie wears a dowdy gray coat and no ornamentation. The Jamaica left behind is not an island paradise, however: The division between rich and poor, upper class and lower class, is as prevalent there as the discrimination they meet in England.

Much of the Jamaicans' story reflects the life of the author's parents—also named Gilbert and Hortense—as immigrants. Her father served in the RAF and returned to England in June, 1948, on the SS *Empire Windrush*, part of the first wave of Caribbean immigrants to Great Britain.

Among the most vivid and gripping sections of the book are Levy's descriptions of wartime Londoners hiding in the shelters, the dispossesed poor roaming the streets looking for help, Queenie's injury in a rocket attack—all are intensely descriptive passages. Levy also sensitively illuminates the different forms of prejudice experienced by Jamaican servicemen and black servicemen from the United States. The coincidences that bind the couples together, and the story's resolution, may be too contrived for some readers, but overall the book is beautifully written and engrossing.

Irene Struthers Rush

Review Sources

Entertainment Weekly, March 11, 2005, p. 107.
Kirkus Reviews 73, no. 4 (February 15, 2005): 192.
The New York Times Book Review 154 (April 3, 2005): 17.
Newsweek 145, no. 14 (April 4, 2005): 54.
Publishers Weekly 252, no. 10 (March 7, 2005): 50.
School Library Journal 51, no. 8 (August, 2005): 151-152.

SNAKES AND EARRINGS

Author: Hitomi Kanehara (1983-   )
First published: Hebi ni piasu, 1983, in Japan
Translated from the Japanese by David James Karashima
Publisher: Penguin Books (New York). 120 pp. $18.00
Type of work: Novel
Time: 2002
Locale: Tokyo

Snakes and Earrings | Hitomi Kanehara

*A self-destructive young woman drifts into a nihilistic
youth culture and dangerous love triangle*

Principal characters:

LUI NAKAZAWA, a nineteen-year-old Japanese woman from a respectable family
AMA, short for AMADA KAZUNORI, Lui's tough, hot-tempered young lover, whose snakelike split tongue exerts an irresistible influence over her
SHIBA-SAN, the owner of a Tokyo tattoo parlor, who provides Lui with a pierced tongue and an elaborate tattoo in exchange for sadomasochistic sex

Hitomi Kanehara's *Snakes and Earrings* begins as the young and beautiful "Barbie Girl" Lui finds herself mesmerized by the split, snakelike tongue of a young man named Ama. Although Lui is never quite certain whether it is Ama or his enviable tongue that attracts her, she immediately enters into a sexual relationship with him. The next day Ama takes Lui to a tattoo parlor called Desire, owned and operated by Ama's friend Shiba-san, who will begin the piercing process that will culminate in a tongue just like her lover Ama's. The reasons for Lui's immediate partnering with Ama, as well as the reasons for her fascination with acquiring a snakelike tongue, remain ambiguous. Although Lui's motivations with regard to a number of situations will, to some extent, remain mysterious, such questions of meaning and motivation are at the core of this novel.

One can interpret Lui's wish for a forked tongue as part of a desire to feel acute pain, arising from her conviction that there is nothing for her in which to believe and nothing for her to feel. Often detached from her emotions, Lui experiences a desire to have her tongue pierced which can be viewed as an effort to secure at least the reality of her own body, and the pain it feels, in a world empty of any reliable meaning. The pointlessness of her life throughout the story seems to be related to her status as a rootless young woman and part-time "freeter" in the Japanese economy. Her adoption of a counterculture lifestyle, however, leaves her adrift. Despite her efforts to awaken her flesh through the use of pain, she feels strangely disembodied.

Her drinking binges, self-starvation, and peculiar love affairs, along with her obsessional interest in body piercing, seem to amount to nothing of any particular signif-

Hitomi Kanehara left school at the age of eleven and left home by the age of fifteen. She wrote her first novel, Snakes and Earrings, *when she was twenty years old. In 2002, she became one of the youngest authors to win the Akutagawa Prize, Japan's highest literary honor for new writers. She lives in Tokyo.*

icance. She finds it difficult to attach any actual meaning or recognizable human motive to anything she does. The transgressive aspects of her behavior do suggest, however, that she is determined to identify herself as a nonconformist, in flight from mainstream Japanese society, which would regard her alteration of her body as a violation of the tradition of filial piety. Even as the underworld of tattoos and piercing have a deviance Lui might read as liberating, this world at the same time seems little more than an aspect of the modern consumer industry. Her pursuit of such countercultural symbols acquires some of the banality associated with modern recreational shopping.

After Ama introduces Lui to Shiba-san, she begins a clandestine sadomasochistic sexual relationship with him, evidently motivated by little more than a desire to trade sex for Shiba's tattoo and piercing services. Like the tongue-piercing, however, sex with Shiba involves levels of pain that shock her out of her apathy. Although Shiba is far more abusive as a sexual partner than Ama, both men have violent tendencies. When a local gangster makes a pass at Lui on one of the dense, neon-lit streets of the Shinjuku district, Ama loses control and beats the gangster to a bloody pulp, pulling out two of the man's teeth to give to Lui. Lui begins to feel that Ama could one day kill her as well. Even though she is unsure of her feelings for him, she decides to protect him from the possibility of arrest for this crime by making sure he changes his appearance.

Although Ama is increasingly devoted to her and emotionally dependent on her, it is clear their relationship does not awaken any similar feelings in Lui, who instead begins a depressive descent into alcoholism and anorexia, all the while increasing the size of the hole in her tongue by inserting larger studs. Her inability to connect emotionally with Ama is demonstrated in her continued encounters with Shiba, in secret, for brutal sex. Attracted to his violence, Lui also desires the cosmetic alterations of her body Shiba can provide. In addition to Lui's pierced tongue, Shiba creates an elaborate tattoo on her back that joins the mythical figure of a dragon with that of a kirin, or unicorn. Significantly, Lui asks that the dragon and the kirin both be made eyeless because of a superstitious belief that sightlessness will keep these treasured tattoos from escaping her skin. This reminds the reader that, rather than her increasingly alcohol-fueled life with Ama, or Shiba's rough sex, it is the imprints on her flesh that have an overriding importance for Lui.

It is possible that Lui's double life with her two lovers would eventually have been disrupted by her escalating anorexia and alcoholism, but it is the sudden disappearance of Ama that precipitates a crisis. The routine of Lui's life with her lover comes to a halt when she learns he has been brutally tortured, raped, and beaten to death. Ama's death produces a number of different reactions from Lui. Whatever grief she may have felt for a man she is not sure she knew or loved is almost immediately translated into the pain she causes herself to endure when she introduces a lower-gauge stud in her tongue in order to further advance the splitting process. She also asks Shiba to tattoo eyes into the mythical animals on her back, a gesture that seems to suggest she has not only given them their spiritual freedom but that she has also set Ama and herself free.

During this period of unconventional mourning for Ama, Lui finally becomes fully conscious of the defects in their relationship—such as the fact that she never knew, or particularly cared to know, his real name or anything about his family or his job. The recognition of her own incuriosity and lack of affect feeds into a self-loathing that has surfaced throughout the narrative, suggesting that Lui has always, to some extent, been aware of her personality disorders. Although Lui realizes she failed to develop a real bond with Ama, to commemorate his love for her she smashes his courtship gift of the gangster's two teeth into a powder, which she downs with her ever-present bottle of beer. This incident, like so many in Lui's narrative, remains enigmatic in terms of motive and meaning.

Such rituals as the smashing of the gangster's teeth seem to exert a strange healing effect on Lui. Another healing aspect of Lui's response to Ama's death is her effort to develop a greater emotional intimacy with Shiba. Complicating her relationship with him, however, is her discovery of evidence that suggests it was Shiba who committed the sexually sadistic murder of Ama. Although Lui realizes she is very likely living with her former boyfriend's twisted killer, she destroys the evidence that may lead to his arrest, putting the disturbing crime behind her with surprising equanimity. Once again, an initial interpretation of Lui's behavior may suggest that she is operating on an extremely shallow and superficial plane. Underneath the surface, however, there is the suggestion that Ama's death held deep and important psychological ramifications for her. It was Ama who was her guide and mentor on her journey into this nihilistic countercultural underworld, and his death has somehow allowed Lui to begin to rise out of it.

Throughout the story, Kanehara has employed imagery of lightlessness as a way to describe Lui's situation, indeed, as a way to describe the rest of her character's life. Lui anticipates her future as pitch-black, filled with shadows and ashes, or as an exitless tunnel. She is seeking to create an underworld of dark materiality, without sunshine, love, or laughter, in which there is nothing spiritual and in which she herself is little more than a shadow. Ama's grisly death at the hands of Shiba, however, and the tattoos, piercings, and the sexual abuse she receives at his hands returns to her a nascent will to live.

After Ama's death, when Shiba introduces eyes into the faces of the mystical creatures he has tattooed on her back, Lui intuitively and instantly understands that he will no longer abuse her and that he will instead look after her and love her. The final lines of the novel incorporate a welcoming sunlight for the first time, in direct opposition to the metaphors of lightlessness that had previously characterized the narrative. On the day the novel concludes, in an ambiance of powerful morning sunlight, Lui chooses water instead of beer to drink, the flow of the cool water down her throat leading her to feel as if suddenly a life-giving river had grown inside of her.

Euphoric amid the experience of water and light, Lui nevertheless is still, to some extent, seeking a split tongue of the kind inspired by Ama. Her pursuit returns the narrative to the issue of the painful body piercings that began her journey. It may be that she will continue to transform her tongue into a snakelike shape. Whether or not she will decide her tongue piercing is little more than an empty consumer preference, Lui knows her journey into the world of tattoos and piercing has not been simply meaningless or defiantly deviant. By the end of the narrative, the reader is allowed to consider all of her risky, masochistic behaviors as, on a deep level, healing-related. Perhaps they are even part of a larger spiritual process, so that her pursuit of her forked tongue at the end of the novel is, surprisingly, placed within a context of an ultimate quest for health and wholeness. Additionally, the imagery of the snake, the dragon, and the kirin point to totem animals that traditionally carry mythical powers and virtues. These may suggest that Lui herself has been in search of such positive attributes.

Deploying a direct, pull-no-punches prose style that does not shy away from graphic sexual passages, *Snakes and Earrings* shocked readers in Japan with its unblinking depiction of the dark side of a Japanese youth culture utterly estranged from traditional beliefs or values. Kanehara's youth and gender particularly contributed to the public's surprise at her ability to present a stark but powerful picture of the depression and dissociation of a generation coming of age in a demoralized, post-"bubble" economy. Beyond its relevance for modern-day Japan, her astute psychological study of a disaffected personality can also be appreciated within a global context; Kanehara's young people are denizens of a pervasive contemporary counterculture that transcends national boundaries.

Margaret Boe Birns

Review Sources

Artforum, June-September, 2005, p. 52.
Booklist 101, no. 16 (April 15, 2005): 1432.
Entertainment Weekly, May 27, 2005, p. 146.
The Guardian, May 30, 2005, p. 8.
Kirkus Reviews 73, no. 6 (March 15, 2005): 307.
Library Journal 130, no. 5 (March 15, 2005): 72.
The New York Times, March 27, 2004, p. A4.

SØREN KIERKEGAARD
A Biography

Author: Joakim Garff (1960-   )
First published: SAK, Søren Aabye Kierkegaard: En
   Biografi, 2000, in Denmark
Translated from the Danish by Bruce H. Kirmmse
Publisher: Princeton University Press (Princeton, N.J.).
   Illustrated. 867 pp. $35.00
Type of work: Biography
Time: 1813-1855
Locale: Copenhagen and environs; briefly Berlin

This account of the life and work of Denmark's most
distinguished philosopher-theologian includes the contro-
versies that swirled around him all of his life

   Principal personages:
   Søren Aabye Kierkegaard, an existentialist Christian who challenged
      the State Church
   Michael Pedersen Kierkegaard, his prosperous merchant father
   Peter Christian Kierkegaard, his older brother, who became bishop
      of Aalborg
   Regine Olsen, his fiancé
   Emil Boesen, his trusted friend
   Meïraron Goldschmidt, the editor of *The Corsair*, in which he sati-
      rized Kierkegaard
   Jakob Peter Mynster, a powerful dignitary of the State Church, called
      "a poisonous plant" by Kierkegaard
   Hans Lassen Martensen, a tutor of the young Søren who was angered
      by his later silence on theological issues
   Nikolai Frederik Severin Grundtvig, a theologian denigrated by
      Kierkegaard as a "world-historical rowdy" and a "bellowing black-
      smith"
   Jens Finsen Giødwad, Kierkegaard's friend who handled his pseudon-
      ymous works at the printer's
   Rasmus Nielsen, a philosophy professor and disciple of Kierkegaard
   Johan Ludvig Heiberg, a man of letters whom Kierkegaard tried to
      cultivate as a friend but later turned against
   Hans Christian Andersen, a famous writer sneered at by
      Kierkegaard
   Israel Levin, a literary scholar who acted as Kierkegaard's secretary
   Poul Martin Møller, a philosophy professor and important influence
      on Kierkegaard
   Peder Ludvig Møller, Kierkegaard's brilliant but most detested antag-
      onist

∾

Joakim Garff is an associate professor at the Søren Kierkegaard Research Center at the University of Copenhagen and the coeditor of a project to publish definitive new Danish-language editions of all of Kierkegaard's writings.

∾

Søren Aabye Kierkegaard (the name means, roughly, "churchyard") was born in Copenhagen on May 5, 1813, the seventh child and fourth son of Michael and Ane Kierkegaard. Michael was a merchant who had been born into a poor family in Jutland but had made his way to Copenhagen and commercial success. His first wife had lived for only two years after their marriage. A year after her death, Michael married his serving maid, whom he had impregnated in a moral lapse that haunted him till his death. The oldest child, Maren Kirsten, died at the age of twenty-four and the second son, Søren Michael, died when he was twelve.

Søren Aabye's childhood under his father's severe Christianity formed what he called the "dark background" of his life, and he identified his father as the source of his lifelong melancholy despite his having been the "best of fathers." Author Joakim Garff finds in their relationship the "fund of artistic capital" that Kierkegaard later exploited in his pseudonymous writings. When Søren entered school in 1821, he became a tease and a "smart aleck" and was well known for his cheating, but the demanding curriculum (the matriculation examination in Latin, for instance, covered eleven thousand lines of poetry and 1,250 pages of prose) guaranteed considerable mastery of the subject matter. When he entered the university in 1830 he had excellent marks. His private tutor, Hans Lassen Martensen, observed of Kierkegaard that he was exceptionally bright but suffered from "an irresistible urge to sophistry." As early as 1835, Kierkegaard was excoriating the ordinary Christians he observed, "victims" of the Church's "suffocating atmosphere."

Two men who played important roles in Kierkegaard's early life were Johan Ludvig Heiberg and Poul Martin Møller. Heiberg reigned in Copenhagen's literary and social circles, and Kierkegaard began a study of Johann Woldfgang von Goethe—especially of *Faust* (1808-1832)—in hope of ingratiating himself with the Heiberg cult, but it was Martensen's essay on *Faust* that won Heiberg's favor and Kierkegaard's permanent bitterness. Møller, however, rejected the common rationalist approach to Christianity, expounding a personal vision that Kierkegaard found more congenial. Møller's interest in psychology, especially in the way that affectation reveals a person's self-deception, is reflected in Kierkegaard's later treatments of irony.

In 1838 Kierkegaard's father died, and by 1840 Kierkegaard was engaged to the lovely Regine Olsen, nine years his junior. Regine loved Kierkegaard passionately, but in 1841 Kierkegaard hurt her deeply by ending the engagement, probably fearing that marriage would work against his writing career. For him the difficulties of this time were mitigated by the successful defense in September, 1841, of his dissertation "On the Concept of Irony" and a four-month interlude in Berlin.

The publication in 1843 of *Enten-Eller* (*Either/Or*, 1944) under the pseudonym Victor Eremita occasioned a lot of speculation about its authorship as well as the contempt of Heiberg, who clearly knew who the author was. It was the essay on "The Seducer's Diary," with its clear ties to the Regine affair, that most angered Heiberg. From this point on in his career, Kierkegaard did an about-face and wrote against Goethe and Georg Wilhelm Friedrich Hegel, the reigning gods of the Heiberg circle. Garff devotes a lengthy exposition to *Gjentagelsen* (1843; *Repetition*, 1933), a murky text prompted by Kierkegaard's obsession with the aborted affair with Regine and which Garff describes as "steeped in ironic and silly posturing." Out of *Repetition*, however, developed what is probably Kierkegaard's most important work, *Frygt og Bæven* (1843; *Fear and Trembling*, 1939), attributed to one Johannes de Silentio. In his consideration of the story of Abraham and Isaac from Genesis, Kierkegaard sketches four scenarios, all intended to veer away from the clichéd interpretation that the journey to Mount Moriah was "only a trial" and to give it existential urgency. Abraham becomes for Kierkegaard the "knight of faith," an example of the paradox of the "teleological suspension of the ethical."

Begrebet Angest (1844; *The Concept of Dread*, 1944) is well described by Garff as "extremely complex" and "at some points close to unreadable." It is psychology mixed with dogmatics, teasing out the ties sexuality has to hysteria and aggression, and Garff superbly explicates "The Seducer's Diary" as an introduction to the new work. The tantalizing question that remains is: Did Regine seduce Kierkegaard? Garff achieves an eloquent conclusion to the myth of Adam and Eve and the serpent: "The serpent is the emblem of the actual play of seduction; it represents seduction as an independent and alien power that chooses its agents and possesses them."

When Meïr Aron Goldschmidt published a friendly reference to Victor Eremita in his journal *The Corsair* in November, 1845, he initiated some good-natured badinage exchanged with Kierkegaard, but the latter went too far in his liberties. Goldschmidt had bought a fancy coat, complete with fur collar and black braid, and when Kierkegaard met him on the street he told him the coat was too flashy. Already a little self-conscious about the coat, Goldschmidt was so hurt that he sent it back to have the braid removed. Kierkegaard continued to patronize Goldschmidt, who came under the influence of Peder Ludvig Møller (not to be confused with Poul Martin Møller, who died in 1838) and under a pseudonym wrote a well-received novel titled *En Jøde* (1845; *The Jew of Denmark*, 1852). In the painful aftermath of this event, Kierkegaard told Goldschmidt that people wanted to identify him as the author of the novel but attributed *The Corsair* to Peder Ludvig Møller. Both Goldschmidt and Møller panicked at this for fear that editorship of *The Corsair* would damage Møller's career.

Møller's brutal—and perceptive—attack on Kierkegaard in his yearbook *Gæa* was answered by Kierkegaard in a salvo published in *Fædrelandet* five days later, on December 27, 1845. The ensuing complications in *The Corsair* before Goldschmidt closed it down defy quick summary, but Garff states the frictions clearly: "Kierkegaard was the eccentric and the genius who admired and envied Møller for his erotic audacity; Møller was the eroticist and child of the proletariat who admired and envied Kierkegaard for his genius and his financial independence; Goldschmidt was the ambitious Jew who also admired and envied Kierkegaard, but who hated his arrogance and patronizing manner."

Garff notes that "everything Kierkegaard touched turned to writing," and that observation leads to his fascinating discussion of the possibility that Kierkegaard's apparent graphomania was related to epilepsy. Garff describes Kierkegaard's melancholy and what he called his "painful prison" of "self-enclosedness" as "aesthetically productive factors" that he welcomed. Much of Garff's thesis depends on Kierkegaard's deep interest in the writings of Adolph Peter Adler, whose books were often marked by an astonishing number of repetitions in a manner similar to Kierkegaard's own practice of repeating lines. No proof exists that either Adler or Kierkegaard suffered from epilepsy, but Adler had an olfactory episode of the kind that patients with temporal lobe epilepsy have been known to experience. Garff cites accounts from eyewitnesses that suggest attacks such as that may have occurred to Kierkegaard. One final bit of evidence lies in the common prescription of valerian root for epilepsy and the fact that when Kierkegaard was evaluated at Royal Frederik's Hospital in October, 1855, the same root was found in his blood.

Kierkegaard's views on social issues hardened into, in Garff's words, "the harsh testiness of an old man." He feared that increasing knowledge of psychology and of social factors would diminish the general sense of individual responsibility, transforming sin into a malfunction of "physiology" and ethics into an "illusion." On questions of government, he was dead set against what he called "leveling," or anything approaching communism: "Of all tyrannies, a people's government is the most excruciating, the most spiritless, the absolute ruin of everything great and holy," and "the true image of Hell." He worried about the collapse of individuals in a social hierarchy into an undifferentiated mass he called "the public," to his mind "the most dangerous of all powers and the most insignificant." Accompanying such a collapse is the growing phenomenon of alienation, the individual's separation from the crowd, a development that Kierkegaard paradoxically approves of insofar as it leads individuals to look after their own religious growth, free from authorities.

Kierkegaard had powerful antagonists in the two prominent churchmen, Jakob Peter Mynster and Hans Lassen Martensen. The latter's *Den Christelige Dogmatik* (1849; *Christian Dogmatics*, 1866) represented precisely the approach to Christian faith against which Kierkegaard railed. Besides, it was a big success, whereas Kierkegaard's *Sygdommen til Døden* (1849; *The Sickness unto Death*, 1941) was a flop both commercially and professionally. Mynster and Martensen's preaching leads to "respected positions in society" and is all "tarted up as Christianity," but it is "lowliness and despisedness," not social status, for Kierkegaard, that define Christians. Although Kierkegaard and Mynster were both conservatives, Kierkegaard was far to the left of Mynster, who "regarded Christianity as a great source of reassurance and relief, while Kierkegaard saw it as a scandalous reversal of all human and cultural values, a permanent conflict with the world." Mynster had urged Kierkegaard in 1846 to become a country pastor, but Kierkegaard came to interpret Mynster's interest as a ruse to relocate him away from the center of intellectual life.

Garff gets to the center of Kierkegaard's differences with the churchmen in his explication of Kierkegaard's concept of cultivation. Once an attribute to be admired in, for instance, the grand figure of Goethe, "the refined epitome of cultivated society," cultivation becomes invested in Kierkegaard with snobbishness and what Garff calls, in his relaxed and ingratiating style, "the dubious odor of the hoity-toity and the artsy-fartsy." Given his extreme doctrinal differences from these titans of the Church, it is no wonder that Kierkegaard nourished his undoubted leaning toward self-pity and saw himself as a martyr to Christianity.

Worn out by a lifetime of polemic, Kierkegaard made his last journal entry on September 25, 1855, confessing his "most extreme degree of weariness with life." His physical ailments became so taxing he had to be hospitalized on October 2. He was dizzy, suffered from urinary incontinence, coughed up blood, and completely lost the use of his legs. What, exactly, his medical problem was cannot be determined, but Garff speculates that it was some progressive neurological disease, perhaps Guillain-Barré syndrome. Kierkegaard never left the hospital, and his death came on November 11.

Garff explains in his preface, "It is my intention not only to tell the great stories in Kierkegaard's life but also to scrutinize the minor details and incidental circumstances, the cracks in the granite of genius, the madness just below the surface, the intensity, the economic and psychological costs of the frenzies of writing, as well as the profound and mercurial mysteriousness of a figure with whom one is never really finished." There can be no doubt of Garff's success, and for once the adjective "magisterial" seems fully appropriate.

Frank Day

Review Sources

Booklist 101, no. 5 (November 1, 2004): 447.
The Christian Century 122, no. 18 (September 6, 2005): 37-41.
New Scientist 186 (April 16, 2005): 55.
Publishers Weekly 251, no. 51 (December 20, 2004): 55.
The Times Literary Supplement, January 28, 2005, pp. 3-4.
The Wall Street Journal 245, no. 24 (February 3, 2005): D8.

SPECIMEN DAYS

Author: Michael Cunningham (1952-   )
Publisher: Farrar, Straus and Giroux (New York).
   305 pp. $25.00
Type of work: Novel
Time: Approximately 1880, 2005, and 2155
Locale: New York City

   Cunningham's three loosely interlocked stories of the hard side of life in New York City in the past, the near present, and the future create a fable for the present time

   Principal characters:
   LUCAS, a twelve-year-old deformed boy in "In the Machine" who falls in love with his dead brother's girlfriend and thinks his brother has become a ghost
   CATHERINE, a young woman who had been engaged to Simon, Lucas's older brother who was killed in a factory accident
   CAT MARTIN, a forensic psychologist in "The Children's Crusade" who is drawn to a strange boy who calls her at a crisis center
   "LUKE," the name the ten-year-old boy says he likes when Cat finally meets her caller, who is involved with a terrorist group
   SIMON, Cat's boyfriend, whom she abandons as she becomes obsessed with helping the deranged boy
   CATAREEN, in "Like Beauty," an alien who knows her life on Earth is limited
   SIMON, a "simulo," or artificial man
   LUKE, a strange adolescent prophet whom Catareen and Simon meet after they escape New York
   WALT WHITMAN, the nineteenth century American poet whose works are quoted throughout the three stories by the young boys and whom Lucas thinks he glimpses walking in New York

   Specimen Days, Michael Cunningham's first novel since his Pulitzer Prize-winning *The Hours* (1998), presents a bleak portrait of life in the past, present, and future. The novel is divided into three novella-length stories set in three different time periods. The main setting for each is New York City. The stories are loosely bound together by recurring devices.
   The major uniting device is that each story, or section of the novel, has a strange young boy who repeatedly quotes stray lines from the poems of Walt Whitman. In the first story the boy's name is Lucas; in the second the unnamed boy says he likes the name Luke; in the third it is Luke. Whether any of these boys are cognizant of why they have memorized and repeat these lines of poetry is unclear, especially as the lines do not have obvious relevance to the situations in which they are invoked. Whitman

"haunts" the novel, reminiscent of the way Virginia Woolf unites the text in *The Hours*, though not so clearly. Whitman himself is not a true character here, but phrases from his poetry are used as a repeated motif, presumably intended to contrast Whitman's openness and his love of life and humankind with the narrow and sordid existence evinced in most of the characters in *Specimen Days.*

Along with a Whitman-quoting boy, each story features as the major characters a man and a woman (although in the futuristic story, "Like Beauty," neither of them is actually human), with the man called Simon and the woman's name some version of Catherine. They are not the same persons, or even reincarnations of the same person, but in each story the man and woman fit the general roles of "boyfriend" and "girlfriend," and the three pairs confront some of the same types of problems. In none of stories do the couples end up together.

A third connecting device is the appearance at some point in each story of an unusual little bowl, presumably the same shining bowl in each story. Someone comes across the bowl by chance and is instantly struck by its beauty. The finder then passes it on to someone he or she cares about.

Michael Cunningham is the author of the best-selling novel The Hours *(1998), which won the Pulitzer Prize and the PEN/ Faulkner Award and was adapted into an Academy Award-winning film in 2002. His other works include* A Home at the End of the World *(1990) and* Flesh and Blood *(1995).*

Lucas, for example, in "In the Machine," buys the luminescent bowl from a boy on the street, despite its high cost in relation to his poverty, and takes it as an offering to Catherine, who had been his brother Simon's girlfriend. She recognizes that it is meant as a love token from Lucas himself, and she does not want to accept it, but he leaves it to her anyway. The bowl incident in each piece is brief but significant in that at least one person has seen it as an object of beauty in the midst of an otherwise bleak set of personal circumstances and has shared this beauty with someone else.

"In the Machine" is set sometime from 1870 to the early years of the twentieth century. The story highlights the problems associated with the Industrial Revolution and its costs to society, especially to the underpaid factory workers at their tedious, repetitive jobs, always at the mercy of their bosses. Simon, Lucas's older brother, was a fatality of such a job, a week before he was to marry Catherine. He caught his shirt on the machine he operated and was summarily sucked into the machine and mangled to death. Lucas, at age twelve, replaced him at the machine. Lucas's mother is ill and mentally deranged; so is his elderly father. The level of their poverty is shockingly portrayed by their lack of food; they literally do not have enough to keep them alive. The money Lucas receives for ten or more hours a day at the machine is abysmal. Lucas is isolated at the machine, unable to talk to other workers because of the noise and the constant pressure to do the job more quickly. He has no one to ask when he might receive his pittance of money, or if his pay is similar to theirs.

Given such life circumstances, it is not surprising that Lucas begins to lose touch with reality and to imagine that Simon's ghost inhabits the machine and is just waiting for Lucas to come join him inside it. Lucas has few outlets for respite from the job or from the perpetual parental crisis at home. Each night he tries to memorize a line from the book of Whitman's poetry that his teacher had loaned him and that he had not returned when he had to quit school to work in the factory.

Lucas begins to focus on Catherine. He sees her once on the street and stops, uninvited, a few times at her apartment. Catherine is kind and once offers him something to eat. Lucas does not know what to say to her and finds himself compulsively reciting random lines of Whitman's poetry. She listens to him with some confusion but not without sympathy. As she begins to suspect the boy's fantastic need for her, especially when he brings her an expensive-looking little bowl, she recognizes that he should not come to see her again and tells him so.

As the story ends, Lucas has some premonition that Catherine is in danger, and he deserts his job to search for her. He finds her miraculously escaping from the sewing factory where she has been working. The building is on fire, and amid the wild flames young women workers are leaping from upper floor windows. The scene is obviously meant to resemble the Triangle Shirtwaist fire in New York in 1911, in which 163 of the factory's immigrant women workers were killed because the employer had locked all the doors. In the story, however, it is identified only as the Mannahatta Company. Lucas believes that the sewing machines wanted to absorb the women but were too puny to do so, and thus the fire was the only way the machines could get them. Lucas believes he has saved Catherine and that his life had been meant for exactly that purpose. He then feels his own heart stop, and dies, or thinks he does, looking up at a glittering horse made of stars in the sky above the fiery building.

"The Children's Crusade," the second story, takes place in an early year of the twenty-first century. Cat Martin is an African American forensic psychologist for the New York Police Department (NYPD). She spends much of her time taking crisis phone calls. She begins to get repeated anonymous calls from what sounds like a young boy. On one occasion the boy, who quotes Walt Whitman, seems to warn her of an impending suicide bombing. A terrorist attack is then reported. According to witnesses on the street, a boy with a pipe explosive strapped to his body hugged a passerby, killing both of them.

Another boy calls, recites more Whitman, and there is another bombing. Then yet another caller recites Whitman. Cat phones the English department at New York University and is put in touch with Professor Rita Dunn, a Whitman scholar, but no matter how much they discuss it, neither of them can see what the poetry has to do with the bombers or the bombings. Cat and her coworkers, particularly her friend Pete, desperately try to track the calls and to locate the third boy. Cat's tension is made more poignant and disturbing because she has suffered the loss of her own young son. Because of her relentless work, she spends less and less time with her boyfriend, Simon, and then scarcely thinks about him.

When the police finally locate where the third boy lives, Cat goes there and finds all the walls of the dreary apartment completely covered with pages of Whitman's poetry. The boy will not tell her his name. She suggests that she call him Smokey, because he said he once had a dog he liked named Smokey. He says instead that he likes the name Luke. He keeps talking about "the family," repeating that the family says he is to use the bombs. Cat realizes that he has been brainwashed by an unidentified someone who tells the boys that Whitman says we do not die, we only go into the grass, and that out of love they should wear the pipe bombs and hug people.

Cat takes the boy home with her, contrary to all the rules of the crisis center or police procedures. From an automatic banking machine she withdraws the maximum amount of money allowed, $500 from her checking account and $500 from her savings. She buys two bags of groceries with her Visa card, her last purchase in New York except for that of two train tickets at Penn Station. Cat and the boy get on the train, on the way to someplace, somewhere. They will probably be tracked down. She thinks that she understands that the message of the person or persons behind using the boys for random bombings is that nobody is safe, no one is ever safe.

The third story, "Like Beauty," recapitulates the themes of loss and horror suggested in the other two stories but with the twist that it is set 150 years in the future. Michael Cunningham's first foray into science fiction is totally dystopian, with the only ray of hope offered by the brief joining together of an unlikely trio. Catareen is a four-and-a-half-foot-tall green lizard from a far-off planet; Simon is a simulo, a robotic simulated man; Luke is a Whitman-quoting child prophet whom the other two pick up on their way somewhere west as they try to escape the omnipresent oppressive rulers of New York who seek to kill them. Catareen and Luke find an old spaceship and leave the planet; Simon is left behind.

The moral of Cunningham's fables seem to be that one needs to be better than one has been, or is being, or the future will be even much worse. One needs more Whitmanesque love and compassion for all one's fellow creatures.

Lois A. Marchino

Review Sources

Booklist 101, no. 17 (May 1, 2005): 1501.
Kirkus Reviews 73, no. 11 (June 1, 2005): 600.
Library Journal 130, no. 9 (May 15, 2005): 104-105.
The Nation 280, no. 23 (June 13, 2005): 44-46, 48.
The New Republic 233, no. 6 (August 8, 2005): 35-37.
The New York Times 154 (June 14, 2005): E1-E9.
The New York Times Book Review 154 (June 26, 2005): 12.
People 63, no. 24 (June 20, 2005): 49.
Time 165, no. 24 (June 13, 2005): 58.

SPRING FORWARD
The Annual Madness of Daylight Saving Time

Author: Michael Downing (1958-   )
Publisher: Shoemaker & Hoard (Washington, D.C.).
    202 pp. $23.00
Type of work: History
Time: 1907-2005
Locale: The United States

SPRING FORWARD

The Annual Madness of Daylight Saving Time

MICHAEL DOWNING

The history of Daylight Saving Time legislation in the United States is related together with the political, practical, and nonsensical reasons behind it

Principal personages:
> BENJAMIN FRANKLIN, an American statesman, writer, and scientist
> ROBERT GARLAND, the president of the Pittsburgh (Pennsylvania) Chamber of Commerce and regarded in the 1940's as "the father of daylight saving time in the United States"
> WARREN G. HARDING, the president of the United States, 1921-1923
> EDWARD KING, a U.S. congressman from Illinois during the 1910's
> MARKUS MARKS, the first president of the National Daylight Saving Association and leader of the Merchants' Association of New York
> RICHARD M. NIXON, the president of the United States, 1969-1974
> FRANKLIN D. ROOSEVELT, the president of the United States, 1933-1945
> JAMES STRONG, a U.S. congressman from Kansas beginning in 1919
> WILLIAM WILLETT, an English architect whose 1907 pamphlet launched the modern daylight saving movement
> WOODROW WILSON, the president of the United States, 1913-1921

The detailed analysis of a seemingly small thing has been a trend at the turn of the twenty-first century. Mark Kurlansky devoted more than four hundred pages to *Salt: A World History* (2002), following his *Cod: A Biography of the Fish That Changed the World* (1997). Dava Sobel's *Longitude* (1995), John McPhee's *The Founding Fish* (2002), and Philip Ball's *Life's Matrix: A Biography of Water* (2000), written by true polymaths, show the heights to which this form can soar, pulling together history, literature, philosophy, and science in wonderfully engaging prose. In 2005, two more authors have attempted to join this noble roster with similar books: David Prerau, with *Seize the Daylight: The Curious and Contentious Story of Daylight Saving Time*, and Michael Downing, with *Spring Forward: The Annual Madness of Daylight Saving Time*. In Downing's case, a tremendous amount of research has been devoted to uncovering the history of Daylight Saving Time, and he is eager to share everything he knows.

Most people in the United States turn back their clocks one hour in the fall (that is, they "fall back") and ahead one hour in the spring (they "spring forward"), without having any clear sense of the history of what they are doing. Few know exactly when the clocks are supposed to be adjusted, although federal law mandates when the change will occur. Practically no one understands what the term "daylight saving" means, as Downing found in an informal survey of his friends and acquaintances: "Were we saving daylight when the sunrise was earlier or when it was later? Unclear. When had Americans started to fuss with their clocks? Also unclear. Who saved what when?"

Michael Downing is the author of four novels: Breakfast with Scot *(1999),* Perfect Agreement *(1997),* Mother of God *(1990), and* A Narrow Time *(1987). His nonfiction includes* Shoes Outside the Door: Desire, Devotion, and Excess at San Francisco Zen Center *(2001). He teaches creative writing at Tufts University in Massachusetts.*

As Downing points out, much of what people think they know about Daylight Saving Time is wrong. For example, most people think farmers had something to do with it, because farmers wanted more sunlight in which to get their work done. Although this argument was put forth by a series of city-dwelling congressmen in support of Daylight Saving, farmers were among the first opponents of the plan. After all, they explained to anyone who would listen, a farmer might set his watch ahead one hour, but that would not change the time at which a cow was ready to be milked. Cows that were milked at 5:30 in the morning during the winter would need to be milked at 4:30 during Daylight Saving Time—no advantage to the milker. Under Daylight Saving, a train might leave the station at noon, the moment that had been called "eleven o'clock" during the winter. Moving the clocks did not speed the sun's movement, and grain that needed a certain amount of sunlight for the morning dew to dry before it could be harvested might not be ready to meet that train. Downing traces a century of farmers' consistent objections to Daylight Saving, showing how in this regard, as in many others, rural citizens were outvoted by their city neighbors.

Another popular idea is that Daylight Saving Time was created to protect schoolchildren, or to give them an extra hour of family time before bed. In fact, like farmers, schoolchildren have been used as evidence on both sides of the debate, presenting what Downing calls an "emotionally charged issue [which] defied rational analysis." The first mention of schoolchildren in the Daylight Saving Time debate did not come until 1942, when President Franklin Delano Roosevelt had declared War Time, a year-round Daylight Saving plan meant to save energy and increase war-related production. Coincidentally, it was a group of Idaho farmers, wanting to revert to Standard Time so they could get the fall harvest done at reasonable times, who pointed out that western Idaho schools had begun opening as late as ten o'clock in the morning so that children would not have to travel in the dark. "For the next fifty years," Downing writes, "communities across the country would attribute many early-morning pedestrian and school bus accidents to the untimely darkness created by Daylight Saving." In the 1970's, data seemed to show an almost imperceptible increase in early-morning fatalities involving school children, and data in the 1990's seemed to show a more dramatic decrease in afternoon and evening fatalities with Daylight Saving. Again, the data are almost beside the point. As Downing demonstrates, the debate over the past century has been driven more by emotion and misinformation than by facts.

No one really knows, for example, whether Daylight Saving saves energy—a reason given for its adoption during World Wars I and II and during the energy crisis of the 1970's. Benjamin Franklin had noticed in the eighteenth century that most Londoners slept through the first hour or two of daylight and then complained about the cost of candles they burned to light their homes in the evenings. In 1784 he published a humorous letter to the editor in a Paris newspaper, calling for a tax on windows shuttered after sunrise to discourage Parisians from wasting daylight. It did not take long for skeptics to notice that people who got up before the sun had to light candles in the morning, even though they did not need as many in the evening. Were candles conserved? During World War I, Daylight Saving had been adopted primarily as a way to conserve coal, and Sidney Colgate of Colgate & Company testified confidently before Congress in 1919 that "There are hundreds of thousands and even millions of tons of coal saved annually by this daylight-saving bill." When pressed, he could support this claim only with the idea that it was "a self evident fact." President Richard Nixon called in 1973 for a two-year run of year-round Daylight Saving Time in response to the fuel shortage, but during the plan's first month the Edison Electric Institute was unable to demonstrate any energy savings, and the strategy was scrapped. In May, 2001, Congress held hearings to settle once and for all whether Daylight Saving Time produces energy savings. The conclusion stated by California Congresswoman Lynn Woolsey, and standing deftly as the last sentence of *Spring Forward*, was "I am more confused than I was when we started."

If the obvious reasons for Daylight Saving are false or incomplete, why does it exist at all? Any system for measuring time, whether it is called Daylight Saving Time (Downing is comically insistent that it not be called "Daylight Savings"), God's time, War Time, Standard Time, Universal Time, or Single-Double Summer Time, is merely a rough way to describe where the sun is overhead at a given moment. It is more convenient than accurate, as one can see by realizing that it is noon in Boston, in Pittsburgh, and in Detroit at the same moment, although the sun is not in the same place in the sky above each of these cities. Through much of the nineteenth century most people did not travel far from home, and most areas of the United States kept their own time based on the sun, so that "when it was (apparently) noon in Chicago, it was 11:39 A.M. in St. Paul and 12:31 P.M. in Pittsburgh; when it was noon in Washington, D.C., it was 11:43 A.M. in Savannah and 12:24 P.M. in Boston." It was the railroads, Downing reveals, who created Standard Time in 1883 and set their timetables accordingly. Cities were free to follow along or not. Only after Standard Time was widely adopted could the idea of Daylight Saving Time, an hour's variation off the standard, be considered.

While it is unclear whether Daylight Saving saves or costs lives, and whether it saves or costs energy, discussion of adjustments to time and time zones has remained passionate and steady at local, state, and federal levels of government for more than a century. Readers will hardly be surprised to learn from *Spring Forward* that much of the debate has centered on business. From the beginning, store owners liked the plan because it gave customers more daylight hours after work for shopping. The film and theater industries hated it because most people prefer to see shows after dark. Baseball teams profited from the extra hour of sunlight, especially before stadiums had lights, and thousands of golf courses were built. Restaurants felt that their dinner business was harmed by the shift. Whatever stirring testimony has been given about patriotism and child safety, it has been Chambers of Commerce who have led the fight all the way.

Downing does his best to make this analysis of legislation and time zones engaging. He has a good ear for lively prose and a hearty appetite for amusing and ridiculous anecdotes and characters, such as the man who complained that the extra hour of sunlight was making his lawn turn brown. Although Downing has uncovered many, many facts, statistics, and quotations, the book bogs down about halfway through and begins to seem repetitious. As is often the case with complex congressional debate, the disagreements over the 1918 legislation sound very much like the disagreements over the 1966 legislation, which sound very much like the disagreements over the 1973 legislation.

Organization is a problem in a story this complicated, and while some chapters are focused on a particular slice of time ("Millennial Fever") or a particular theme ("Capitol Sports"), others read like a compilation of leftover bits. Chapter 8, "Men of the Hour," for example, begins with Roosevelt's call to adopt Daylight Saving Time after the 1941 attack on Pearl Harbor, backs up in time to discuss British and French attitudes toward Daylight Saving going back to 1909, backs up again to discuss the controversy over who should get credit as "father" of Daylight Saving in the United States, considers England and Winston Churchill again, and gives the history of Daylight Saving in Russia from 1917 to 1991—all in eighteen pages. In this chapter, as is much of the second half of the book, the details piling atop one another begin to feel formless, and it is difficult to follow the arc of the story.

Still, the book is entertaining and occasionally hilarious. The century-long argument over Daylight Saving provides a window into how Congress works, the influence of business on daily life, and the strangely American confidence that enables individuals to make sweeping statements about complex issues without worrying about facts. The topic of Daylight Saving remains fascinating, and it remains controversial. Since *Spring Forward* went to press, Indiana has continued in its role as the most time-muddled state, passing legislation in early 2005 that called for all the counties in the state to observe Daylight Saving together (previously, each county could decide for itself) and then requesting federal hearings to ask whether the entire state might be moved into the Central time zone. Then the Energy Policy Act of 2005 extended Daylight Saving from the second Sunday of March to the first Sunday of November starting in 2007, setting the stage for another round of letters to the editor sure to provide amusing material for Downing's second edition.

Cynthia A. Bily

Review Sources

Booklist 101, no. 14 (March 15, 2005): 1249.
The Boston Globe, April 2, 2005, p. C1.
Publishers Weekly 252, no. 11 (March 14, 2005): 57-58.
The Wall Street Journal 245, no. 63 (March 31, 2005): D8.

STALIN
A Biography

Author: Robert Service (1947-   )
Publisher: Harvard University Press (Cambridge, Mass.).
    718 pp. $30.00
Type of work: Biography
Time: 1878-1953
Locale: Russia and the Soviet Union

This scholarly synthesis acknowledges positive aspects of Joseph Stalin's personality and accomplishments while emphasizing his lust for power, his cruel indifference toward human suffering, and his stubborn commitment to Marxist-Leninist ideology

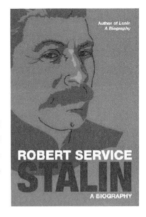

Principal personages:

JOSEPH STALIN (born IOSEF DZHUGHASHVILI), the dictator of the Soviet Union from 1924 to 1953

VLADIMIR LENIN (born VLADIMIR ULYANOV), a communist theorist and leader of the Soviet Union from 1917 until his stroke in 1922

LEON TROTSKY (born LEV BRONSTEIN), Stalin's rival who advocated a theory of continuous revolution

GRIGORI ZINOVIEV, the leader of the Communist International who was executed in the Great Terror

LEV KAMENEV, a communist leader who was executed in the Great Terror

NIKOLAI I. BUKHARIN, a communist theorist and proponent of moderation who was executed in the Great Terror

VYACHESLAV MOLOTOV, a foreign minister of the Soviet Union from 1939 to 1956

NIKOLAI YEZHOV, the head of the NKVD (secret police) during the Great Terror of 1937-1938

LAVRENTI BERIA, the head of the NKVD from 1938 until after Stalin's death

GEORGI K. ZHUKOV, a famous World War II Soviet marshal

GEORGI MALENKOV, Stalin's associate and later Prime Minister

NIKITA KHRUSHCHEV, Stalin's associate and later secretary of the Communist Party from 1953 to 1964

NADEZHDA (NADYA) ALLILUEVA, Stalin's second wife who committed suicide

Author Robert Service acknowledges that several excellent biographies of the Soviet dictator have previously been published, but he believes that they have all failed to describe adequately the dictator's complexities and contradictory qualities. *Stalin: A Biography*, therefore, "is aimed at showing that [Joseph Stalin] was a more dynamic and diverse figure than has conventionally been supposed." A complex human

Currently a history professor at Oxford University, Robert Service is an expert in modern Russian history and an outspoken critic of Marxist-Leninist ideology. His previous books include The Bolshevik Party in Revolution *(1979),* The Russian Revolution, 1900-1927 *(1986),* Lenin: A Biography *(2000), and* A History of Modern Russia, from Nicholas II to Vladimir Putin *(2003).*

being not reducible to a single dimension, Stalin "was a bureaucrat and a killer, he was also a leader, a writer and editor, a theorist (of sorts), a bit of poet (when young), a follower of the arts, a family man and a charmer." Despite some humane qualities, however, he was "as wicked a man as has ever lived," displaying paranoid tendencies, abnormal compulsions to dominate and seek vengeance, and an absence of moral qualms about causing the deaths of countless persons, including former friends and associates.

Having previously published and edited at least eight books about modern Russian history, Service is very familiar with the mountain of primary and secondary sources relating to Stalin's life and career. At least two-thirds of the book's footnotes refer to Russian-language materials not translated into English. This is the first major biography of Stalin to appear since the large-scale opening of Soviet archives after the breakup of the Soviet Union, although the vast majority of significant discoveries have already been revealed in works such as *Inside the Kremlin's Cold War* (1996), by Vladislav Zubok and Constantine Pleshakov, one of the hundreds of sources to which Service referred. Even if the biography has few surprises, it is filled with fascinating details and is at least as interesting and readable as the earlier works of Richard Conquest, Robert Tucker, and others.

Service argues that an examination of Stalin's early life is essential to understanding his mature personality and behavior. Born Iosef Dzhughashvili, the boy grew up in a household filled with an extreme degree of capricious violence, and it is reasonable to infer that "little Joseph must have grown up assuming that this was the natural order of things." The evidence clearly indicates that his father was a brute who was frequently drunk. According to his daughter, Svetlana, Stalin once threw a knife at his father in an attempt to stop a beating of his mother. Even his pious mother was not averse to giving a young boy a brutal thrashing. Without relying on psychoanalytic theory, Service observes that persons bullied in childhood frequently grow up looking for others to bully. He further observes: "Not everyone beaten by parents acquires a murderous personality. Yet some do, and it would seem that more do than is true for general society."

Service holds that Stalin's development was also influenced by the broader culture in which he lived during his formative years. In his native land of Georgia, people sometimes engaged in practiced long-standing group feuds and approved of revenge-taking as a virtue. Even more significantly, Stalin's boyhood experiences as a relatively poor son of an unhappy cobbler left him with a strong sense of bitterness toward persons of wealth and prestige. His seminary training for the Orthodox priesthood probably reinforced his tendency toward dogmatic, dualistic, and authoritarian tendencies. In addition, he acquired many of his ideas and values from specific books that he read, particularly Niccolò Machiavelli's *Il principe* (1513; *The Prince*, 1640) and biographies of Ivan the Terrible, who became one of Stalin's heroes.

Reflecting an anticommunist point of view, Service argues that Stalin's inclinations and unconscious needs predisposed him to be attracted to the Marxist-Leninist ideology. For an angry young man who assumed that conflict was normal and wanted to dominate others, the ideology was a perfect fit. It provided a moral justification for taking revenge and establishing a dictatorship under a revolutionary vanguard in the name of the proletariat. In short, the ideology "allowed him to give vent to his chronic viciousness."

Service refutes the commonly held thesis that Stalin played only a minor role in the Bolshevik Revolution of 1917 and the Civil War. On the issue of nationality, he praises Stalin's moderate encouragement of federal autonomy for large non-Russian nationalities. On the question of violence, Stalin was a part of a subculture that endorsed terror as a means to a utopian end. Service observes that perceptions about Stalin's early career often have their origins in the writings of Leon Trotsky, who did not have much to say about Stalin's violent proclivities during these years. As Trotsky was also an "enthusiastic perpetrator of terror," he had no reason to emphasize the matter. Service writes: "It was only because all the other communist leaders applied the politics of violence after the October Revolution that his maladjusted personality did not fully stand out." Still, he recognizes that Stalin's cruelty toward opponents was "excessive even by Bolshevik norms."

With the beginning of the First Five-Year Plan in 1928, Stalin's use of terror became increasingly prominent. Numerous intellectuals and scientists were tried and condemned for "anti-Soviet" activities in 1929-1930. When the Kulaks (moderately prosperous farmers) resisted the collectivization of agriculture, the result was the so-called Peasant Holocaust, in which entire families were evicted from their homes and either transported to Siberia or allowed to die of cold and starvation. This process of collectivization, according to Stalin's own admission, required the deaths of about ten million persons. Service accepts the conventional view that the resulting state-controlled farms were extremely inefficient in producing food, in contrast to the "revolution from above" in manufacturing and transportation, which successfully transformed the Soviet Union into a modern industrial country.

In December, 1934, the murder of the party leader of Leningrad, Sergi Kirov, gave Stalin an excuse to issue a decree authorizing extraordinary *troiki* (three-men panels), which delivered summary "justice" against political enemies without recourse to the courts. Based on circumstantial evidence, Service suspects that Stalin might have ordered the murder. Just six months earlier, Stalin had praised the way that Adolf Hitler had exploited an alleged antigovernment plot in the infamous Night of the Long Knives.

Using the dreaded *troiki*, the NKVD, or secret police, quickly responded to Kirov's murder by exiling more than six hundred persons suspected of association with anti-Stalinist elements. In May, 1935, members of the Communist Party were required to turn in their membership cards, and those unable to prove their loyalty were purged from the party. All former supporters of Trotsky were sent to labor in the Gulag for a minimum of three years. In 1936, the secretariat announced discovery of "terrorist activities of the Trosyskist-Zinoviev block." Former Communist leaders such as Gregori Zinoviev, Lev Kamenev, and Nikolai I. Bukharin were either tricked or coerced into making confessions, after which they were quickly executed. Service estimates that during the Great Terror of 1936-1938, the NKVD seized approximately one-and-a-half million individuals, of whom only about two hundred thousand were eventually released.

Like the majority of historians, Service disagrees with J. Arch Getty's thesis that the Great Terror did not arise from Stalin's initiative. In fact, Stalin and Yezhov established quotas for the number of persons to be arrested before investigations were made. Although many of those arrested were used as forced laborers, the NKVD was instructed to execute about half of the prisoners—three quarters of a million people. Service writes that Stalin personally ratified the arrests of some forty-four thousand individuals listed in 383 albums. In November, 1938, the Great Terror ended when Stalin replaced Yeshov with Lavrenti Beria, who was also known for his ruthlessness. Terrorism continued until Stalin's death, but it was practiced at a diminished rate.

In contrast to Nikita Khrushchev, who blamed the violence and fear almost exclusively on Stalin's personality cult, Service writes: "The Great Terror, while being instigated by the single-minded leadership of Joseph Stalin, was also a reflection—however distorted a reflection—of the mind-set of Bolshevism." This provides one of the reasons that Stalin never had much trouble getting others to cooperate with his coercive measures. Even if Khrushchev, as Moscow City Party Committee, had a "decent side," Service observes that he nevertheless participated in the murderous activities of the Great Terror.

Service thinks that the Bolsheviks actually had no choice but to disallow free expression and brutally suppress opposition. Because of mass discontent, the political and economic order created by the Bolsheviks was inherently unstable, and it could not have survived free elections in which competing political parties had to appeal to voters. In a word: "Without dictatorship the USSR as a communist order would have fallen apart." Although it is never possible to prove what might have happened, later history gives considerable support for this controversial hypothesis, which provides some insight into why Stalin was able to command the support and loyalty of so many subordinates who were eventually disgraced and either killed or exiled.

While recognizing that Stalin was never a man of philosophical reflection, Service finds that he was highly intelligent as well as "a fluent and thoughtful writer." As an editor of *Pravda* in the early years, he demonstrated competence as a journalist. In his *Foundations of Leninism*, nine lectures delivered in 1924, he generally "succeeded in codifying the ragbag of writings, speeches, and policies of Lenin's lifelong *oeuvre*." Service particularly praises Stalin's book *Marxism and the Problem of Linguistics* as a "healthy anecdote" to the theory, then dominant in the Soviet Union, that languages are class-specific phenomena.

Service also maintains that Stalin's foreign policies were usually rational from the perspective of Soviet objectives and the available information. The Soviet-Nazi agreement of 1939 made sense as a means of buying time. Before the German invasion of June 22, 1941, Stalin unwisely ignored the warnings of Marshal Georgi Zhukov and others because he believed that Hitler would not be foolish enough to become involved in a two-front war, and also because he assumed that a successful operation would have to begin early in the summer. Concerning Stalin's mysterious withdrawal on June 29, Service writes that it will never be known exactly what happened. Perhaps Stalin was suffering from depression and expected to be deposed, or perhaps he withdrew to show how much his leadership was needed. Stalin had good reasons for not assisting the Warsaw uprising of August, 1944, although he probably was also motivated by the desire to gain political dominance over Poland. For the beginning of the Cold War, Service puts most of the blame on Stalin's expansionist policies, but he convincingly argues that the leader of North Korea, Kim Il-Sung, was primarily responsible for the outbreak of the Korean War.

While covering Stalin's life and career, Service presents a great deal of information about the politics and organization of the Soviet Union. Although he classifies the Soviet Union as a totalitarian state, he insists that neither Vladimir Lenin nor Stalin exercised unlimited power. Both men had to gain the support of other influential members of the party, and both "were constrained by the nature of the regime which they had created." Certainly they possessed great prerogatives in formulating public policy, but their decisions had to be compatible with the needs of a one-ideology, one-party state. The entire enterprise, according to Service, was doomed to ultimate failure: "Lenin had invented a cul-de-sac for communism; Stalin drove the party through it." Without Stalin's brutal leadership, the experiment might have produced less suffering. It also might have ended earlier than it did.

Thomas Tandy Lewis

Review Sources

Booklist 101, no. 14 (March 15, 2005): 1262.
Contemporary Review 286 (May, 2005): 318.
The Economist 34 (January 8, 2005): 74.
Library Journal 130, no. 10 (June 1, 2005): 142.
The New Leader 88, no. 2 (March/April, 2005): 17-19.
New Statesman 133 (October 18, 2004): 50-51.
The New York Times 154 (April 13, 2005): E10.
The New York Times Book Review 154 (June 12, 2005): 22-23.
Publishers Weekly 252, no. 8 (February 21, 2005): 164.
The Times Literary Supplement, December 24, 2004, p. 14.
The Washington Post Book World, April 17, 2005, p. 3.

STAR DUST

Author: Frank Bidart (1939-   )
Publisher: Farrar, Straus and Giroux (New York). 96 pp.
    $20.00
Type of work: Poetry

This collection combines a chapbook published in 2002,
Music Like Dirt, *with a long poem to explore the necessary*
relationship between creation and destruction

Frank Bidart is known for his unusual, startlingly original representations of the problem of guilt, which is related
to the issue of creativity and the human desire to make. His
first poems looked at the family myth as the locus for this
problem, but his more recent work provides a variety of
dramatic monologues and narrative poems about obsessed characters. The stories he
tells are not represented in conventional narrative form but at the edges of language—
broken, elliptical, interrupted by other narratives.

Bidart at first wanted to be a film director. While at University of California, Riverside, though, he became interested in poetry, and his attention was compelled by the
modernists, especially by Ezra Pound's *Cantos* (1917-1970). After trying to write
without much direction, he asked Richard Howard for advice on his poetry, and
Howard decided to publish Bidart's early poems as *Golden State*, which appeared in
1973. This first collection dealt with the family myth and Bidart's own familial struggles; it also introduced the first of Bidart's developed personae, "Herbert White,"
child murderer. This kind of extended poem about a tortured, conflicted individual—
sometimes dramatic monologue, sometimes third-person narrative—is the poet's
specialty. Bidart's narrative character descriptions are not like other dramatic monologues; rather they throw pieces of a life together in a chaotic fashion, details and dialogues and letters and events, to create a coherent chaos from which glimpses of a personality emerge. *Star Dust* is Bidart's seventh book of poetry.

Bidart's style almost defies description. A conglomeration of parts that might
make the reader think of William Carlos Williams's Paterson, a Bidart poem nevertheless has a unified voice that comes through its fragments—Matthew Gilbert com-
mented, "[The poems] constitute a hauntingly raw voice that finds itself through an
exhilarating array of prosodic techniques." It is this combination of fragmentation
and unity that is Bidart's unique contribution. He is almost universally acclaimed by
postmodernist poets and critics and praised by many more traditional writers as well.

Star Dust is an experimental exploration of creativity. The collection *Music Like
Dirt*, which forms its first part, was the first chapbook ever to be a finalist for the Pulitzer Prize. *Star Dust* pairs the chapbook with a long, free verse poem about the life of
Benvenuto Cellini. The more accessible, though still challenging, poems in the first
part play off against the long and difficult exploration of Cellini's life and art, which is

part dramatic monologue, part other unidentified voices.

Even the poems in the first part of the book are sometimes elusive, dragging veils of suggestion with every word. The first poem, "For the Twentieth Century," plays with repeatability and finishedness; more traditionally coherent than some of the other poems, it describes the speaker's desire to "pluck again from the thousand/ technologies of ecstasy// boundlessness" which prompts him to "push the PLAY button," bringing forth the voices of the dead. The twentieth century brought technology, changing artists' work into "form whose infinite/ repeatability within matter/ defies matter—." The reader sees the preservation as both victory and defeat at once, a contradiction which is a common effect in Bidart's work. The poem leaves the reader with a sense of disjunction: One desires to replay the past, and to do it all one has to do is push Play, but the machine replays the past without the life of the past. Technology, then, offers no salvation.

Frank Bidart was born into a farming family in California and graduated from the University of California at Riverside. His many awards include a Guggenheim Fellowship, a Lannan Literary Fellowship, a Wallace Stevens Award, and the Shelley Award from the Poetry Society of America.

The poems in this section have a number of subjects but seem always to come back to the same issue—that human beings desire infinity, recognize their finitude, try desperately to create for themselves some kind of eternity but are balked by the matter, or materiality, of the world. In all the poems there is this balance between desire and limitation, and many resonant ironies are evoked by the conflict. It is the desire to make that makes people human.

In "Advice to the Players," the speaker issues a series of statements divided by bullets—looking like aphorisms or quotations. Each statement is a pronunciamento on making as a necessity and a curse. "Advice" begins:

> There is something missing in our definition, a vision, of a human being: the need to make.
> •
> We are creatures who need to make.
> •
> Because existence is willy-nilly thrust into our hands, our fate is to make something—if nothing else, the shape cut by the arc of our lives.

This odd arrangement of statements segues into the relationship between parents and children in their approach to making their lives and the difficulty of finding clarity in the making. The plain, direct language of this section seems to make of it a thesis statement for the book, which in general is reaching and indirect, especially in the long poem.

"The Third Hour of the Night," according to its author, is part of a long project based on the Egyptian "Book of Gates" from the sarcophagus of Seti I; the series follows the twelve territories of the underworld the sun must pass through each night before it rises again. Each hour has its gate, as it is the border of a territory. The first two poems were published years earlier; Bidart does not see the group as a sequence that will be published together. This poem first appeared in the October, 2004, issue of *Poetry*, sparking controversy—many readers found it inappropriate to include only one poem in the journal, and some did not like the poem. It is rich and obscure and has the poet's trademark piecework and layered representation of narrative. It also includes graphic descriptions of violence, including rape and murder. This focus on blood and pain is, of course, nothing new for Bidart; some of his earlier narratives focused on extremes of violence, and some of his earlier subjects were even less law-abiding than Cellini.

The basic narrative in "Third Hour" is the life of Cellini, while other narratives, mythic, historical, literary, flow over and through it. Cellini was a sixteenth century Italian Renaissance Man: a celebrated sculptor, goldsmith, warrior, and writer but also a revenge-killer, in and out of trouble with authorities. The need to create in him was balanced by the need to destroy, making him, for Bidart, a good example of the sheer energy that characterizes the artist. This energy, this desire to create, is amoral and flows into all containers. The most violent part of the poem appears to describe a rape and murder and is based, according to Bidart in an interview, "on the words of an Australian sorcerer, found in a book by Mircea Eliade on the history of religions." In the passage, close to the end of the poem, the rapist appears to kill the woman, but then brings her back to life and tells her she will die in two days, which she does. According to Bidart, "The passage is clearly about the will to power." He goes on to explain that this is a parody of what Cellini does when he saves a statue of Perseus and brings the art back to life.

The passage and the explanation illustrate the difficulties of this poem: It would be easy to assume that the "I" describing the rape, in graphic and repellent detail, is Cellini, whose first-person account of major life events accounts for much of the poem. It takes a while for the reader to realize that this is a life of Cellini at all, because he does not appear until one is well into the poem. Events in the artist's life are narrated in the first-person voice through quirky, intense descriptions, and the poem concludes with an italicized section about the overwhelming, amoral flow of creativity that characterizes Cellini and by extension the artist in general.

> *Eater, become food*
>
> *All life exists at the expense of other life*
> *Because you have eaten and eat as eat you must*
>
> *Eater, become food*
>
> *unlike the burning stars*
> *burning merely to be*

Creativity seems irrevocably linked to destruction, consumption, even self-consumption. Yet this insatiable urge to create is at the heart of humanness.

It is clear that Bidart's work is not for all readers of poetry. Those used to the more accessible work of modern-day writers will not appreciate the links of history, myth, personal experience, literature, and art that are difficult to follow and require the reader to return again and again to the poem. Those who like Ezra Pound will like Bidart; those who prefer T. S. Eliot are less likely to. The sheer energy and verve of Bidart's scope will appear to many readers and compel them to revisit the work. The question is whether Bidart's complex and layered work will last. In fifty years, will students study him, eagerly returning for more enigma, more ambiguity? There is no way of answering that question, or of determining which among the thousands of poetry books that emerge to applause every year will have staying power.

To approach "Third Hour," a short biography of Cellini is useful—it opens the poem to those to whom he is only a name and a vague impression. Nothing, though, will supply all the background needed to enter the world of these poems. The sheer force of their voice is needed to call the reader into them, and for many this is effective.

In general, *Star Dust* is a conjunction of opposites. It erases borders between genres, and it takes in all sorts of ordinarily nonpoetic materials. It introduces a kind of postmodern dramatic monologue—a "monologue" that is actually polyvocal, polyvalent. *Star Dust*, however, does not have the more artificial of the common characteristics of postmodernism—there is not a sense of randomness or arbitrary selection of materials. The book is not one thing; one poem will be relatively accessible to the typical poetry reader, while the next may withhold its secrets after many readings. For many, the difficulties of the work are challenging and exciting enough to compel the study that is required to enter the world of the writer. Bidart's work is hailed by critics for its grandeur, its inclusiveness, and its inventive, original forms. His special gift seems to be to have a single voice come through all the rags and patches. He first fell in love with Ezra Pound's *Cantos*, and he seems to be practicing a kind of vorticism himself—the power that makes the rose form on the page out of the iron filings is the magnet of his vision.

Janet McCann

Review Sources

The New York Times 154 (July 24, 2005): 11.
The New York Times Book Review 154 (July 31, 2005): 18.

STILL LOOKING
Essays on American Art

Author: John Updike (1932-   )
Publisher: Alfred A. Knopf (New York). Illustrated. 222
    pp. $40.00
Type of work: Fine arts
Time: The nineteenth and twentieth centuries
Locale: The United States

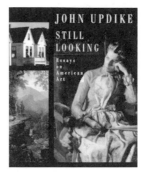

*One of America's most distinguished writers provides
commentary on the works of major American artists whose
careers have been highlighted in major exhibitions during
the period from 1990 to 2004*

Principal personages:
> JOHN SINGLETON COPLEY, an American painter
> MARTIN JOHNSON HEADE, an American painter
> WINSLOW HOMER, an American painter
> THOMAS EAKINS, an American painter
> JAMES MCNEIL WHISTLER, an American painter
> ALBERT PINKHAM RYDER, an American painter
> FREDERICK CHILDE HASSAM, an American painter
> ALFRED STIEGLITZ, an American photographer
> MARSDEN HARTLEY, an American painter
> ARTHUR DOVE, an American abstract artist
> ELIE NADELMAN, an American sculptor
> EDWARD HOPPER, an American painter
> JACKSON POLLOCK, an American painter
> ANDY WARHOL, an American multimedia artist

For nearly half a century, John Updike has been producing books of fiction, poetry, and criticism at a rate that would make a dime-novel writer envious. In Updike's
case, however, the products of his labors continue to be elegantly styled, insightful,
and, with rare exceptions, of the highest quality. Whether he is constructing a novel,
commenting on foreign literature, or writing about his family, he engages his readers
with his witticisms and his ability to make his prose or his poetry, when he chooses to
write some, serve his bidding. His productivity has matched his breadth of knowledge, as he has published, on average, one book each year since 1957. Therefore, it is
hard to think of another living writer who deserves the sobriquet "America's most
distinguished man of letters."

Still Looking, Updike's 2005 contribution to his canon of distinguished nonfiction, demonstrates that he is as perceptive about American visual arts as he is about
American life. This volume collects eighteen of the more than fifty essays Updike
has published since the appearance of his first book of art criticism, *Just Looking:*

Essays on Art, in 1989. Most were written for *The New York Review of Books* and other prestigious publications, though a few were produced for inclusion in exhibition catalogs or for collections of art criticism. Two essays cover "theme" exhibits: one on representations of landscape painting, another on realism and impressionism in America. The remaining sixteen focus on the careers of individual artists. All were written after Updike visited major exhibitions in cities across the United States.

To give the book a sense of coherence, Updike has arranged his pieces in a loose chronological order, beginning with the eighteenth century painter John Singleton Copley and ending with the iconoclastic mid-twentieth century pop-art guru Andy Warhol. Most essays extend to three thousand words, allowing Updike to produce commonsense critiques of individual works and comment on the significance of an individual or movement in the context of the historical development of the visual arts in America. Updike's running commentary demonstrates how individual paintings, photographs, or sculptures display something about an individual artist's development. Reading the essays gives one a sense of what motivated artists as disparate as Winslow Homer, Albert Pinkham Ryder, Marsden Hartley, or Arthur Dove. One comes to understand, too, what drove James McNeil Whistler to leave his native America—for reasons much different from Copley's a half-century earlier—or why sculptor Elie Nadelman or photographer Alfred Stieglitz are important in the history of American art even if their work has been neglected or, in the case of Stieglitz, overshadowed by his relationship with his wife, the more famous Georgia O'Keeffe.

One of America's leading writers of fiction, John Updike has also published several volumes of poems and a number of critical essays on literature and art. His work has won the Pulitzer Prize, the National Book Award, the National Book Critics Circle Award, and the Howells Medal.

One learns how, as with Whistler, Jackson Pollock's being thrust into the public role of the artist affected his work and why mid-nineteenth century artists such as Thomas Eakins and Childe Hassam worked within what might at first seem a rather limited range of subjects. Under Updike's penetrating gaze, not only do the pictures and statuary speak to readers; the artists who painted or sculpted them are also made human. Nowhere is Updike's love of art and artists more evident than in the two essays on Edward Hopper, a painter with whom Updike seems to share some affinities. Both are chroniclers of everyday American life, finding the subjects for their art in places outside the big cities. While every essay manages to reveal something about its subject, these two seem especially poignant, as if Updike has found a kindred spirit in this artist who paints ordinary people in ordinary situations and manages to suggest something extraordinary about their lives. Anyone familiar with Updike's fiction will immediately recognize the parallels.

Those readers more familiar with the world of the visual arts than literature may be skeptical about Updike's qualifications for producing such books. In an age when celebrities in one field are often asked to offer criticism in areas for which they have no special competence, it is refreshing to know that Updike is, in fact, qualified for his role as art critic. After graduating from Harvard University in 1954, he spent a year in Oxford at the Ruskin School of Fine Art, and he has managed to read widely in the field while maintaining his schedule as a writer of fiction and literary essays. For this reason, the essays in *Still Looking* are not only insightful but also erudite. Further, Updike is willing to take on other art critics, especially those who have bought into the recent movement in critical theory that considers all art political and insists that a painter's worth be judged not only by formal mastery of technique but also by his or her opposition to dominant (read "conservative") political trends.

The best example of Updike's quarrel with postmodern critics is his essay on American impressionists and realists. It is as much about what he considers wrongheaded in modern-day criticism as it is about late nineteenth century painting. Cleverly titled "Walls That Talk Too Much," this piece is a stinging critique of academics and professional curators who have bought into new Leftist criticism, who (in Updike's view, at least) clutter and obscure visual art by burying it under a mountain of textual commentary intended to instruct viewers on what they should be seeing, and letting them know when artists are deficient in their social and political vision. His prose drips with sarcasm in describing those who prepare the exhibition catalogs and the written commentary affixed to the museum walls beside the paintings. These critics who claim superiority over the artists in knowing how society should have been depicted by these creative geniuses end up drafting "mural commentary" that faults the realists for their "'genteel euphemism' in soft-pedalling the grim faces of an American in the throes of urbanization, industrialization, and mass immigration." "The Realists," Updike says in tongue-in-cheek fashion, "with their pretensions to honest democratic and urban perspectives, disappoint the wall-inscribers repeatedly." He is clearly on the side of the painters whose creations speak more honestly than their postmodernist critics: "To reproach the American Realists with optimism and euphemism is to denigrate the affirmative message that art brings to us all." Updike encourages those who wish to appreciate what these artists have accomplished to look to the paintings, not the commentary. "Viewed without reference to the hectoring comments on the walls" one might discern that the paintings in this exhibit "less describe social conditions between 1885 and 1915 than provide a luminous and benignly noncommittal view of the human condition in general, as it perennially manifests itself beneath blue skies, on crowded streets, and in furnished rooms." This view of the purpose of art could be extended to most of the works included in *Still Looking*.

By contrast, what may be most refreshing about the art criticism in *Still Looking* is that it seems unpretentious. In the personal essay that serves for an introduction to the volume, Updike explains how his mother's purchase of a simple seascape led him to an interest in and love for art. The wonder that he felt as a child when gazing on a painting by a competent but far from famous midwestern artist is sustained in his reviews of works by American masters. Just as he does in his fiction, Updike peppers his critical work with lively comparisons and vivid imagery that captures readers' attention. For example, he says that the figure of the shark in Copley's famous painting *Watson and the Shark* is "oddly dignified, with the bulging brow and watchful eye of a senior statesman." He describes the feeling of silence evoked by Hopper's *Sun in an Empty Room* as being like "that of an old-time public library." He notes how unusual it is for the Nadelman exhibit catalog to have been written by a single critic "in this day of catalogues composed like Dagwood sandwiches of disparate essays." The language draws readers into his narrative, and the narrative constantly suggests the joy that one should experience in viewing great art.

Because the subjects of these essays were determined by those who commissioned Updike to write them and by art exhibits that Updike visited, there is a certain eclecticism in the choice of artists which may bother some who would wish to see other artists included. Certainly women artists are notable by their absence. Only in the essay on Stieglitz does Updike discuss the work of a woman painter for more than a paragraph, commenting on Georgia O'Keeffe's personal and professional relationship with the photographer and art promoter who became her husband. Moreover, these eighteen essays were composed to stand alone, and Updike makes no effort to revise them to create a thematic strand throughout his book. In fact, some of the commentary on exhibition dates and availability of peripheral materials that museum-goers might purchase remains in these selections. One might have wished that Updike had eliminated the topical information to give the volume a greater sense of "timelessness." That would have been unfortunate, however, because as they stand, these eighteen pieces demonstrate what can be done when a great writer turns his attention to an often overlooked and underrated form of art: the occasional essay. Given his subject, assigned a definite word length, and placed under pressure to deliver his work by a certain time, Updike manages to turn a form of journalism into something that meets the criterion for great literature suggested by the eighteenth century man of letters Dr. Samuel Johnson: that which teaches by delighting.

Furthermore, on a larger level, there is a strong link running through all the essays: the growth of American visual arts as a distinct national art form, related to Western European art but not simply derivative. Updike, ever a champion of all things American, misses no opportunity to demonstrate how America shapes the work of these men, and how they made America—its beauty and its ugliness—visible to the world. Containing more than two hundred reproductions, most in color except when the originals are black-and-white photographs, *Still Looking* is a visual feast for readers as well, allowing them to see for themselves many of the paintings Updike describes. The volume can serve as a short course in American art history, perhaps not complete but certainly informative and at times provocative.

Laurence W. Mazzeno

Review Sources

Booklist 102, no. 2 (September 15, 2005): 18.
Choice 43, no. 1 (September, 2005): 1-3.
Kirkus Reviews 73, no. 17 (September 1, 2005): 964.
Library Journal 130, no. 18 (November 1, 2005): 76.
The New York Times 155 (December 6, 2005): E1-E8.
The New York Times Book Review 155 (December 25, 2005): 14-15.
Poets and Writers 33, no. 6 (November/December, 2005): 32-38.

THE SUCCESSOR

Author: Ismail Kadare (1936-   )
First published: Pasardh'si, 2003, in Albania
Translated from the French of Tedi Papavrami by David
    Bellos
Publisher: Arcade (New York). 207 pp. $24.00
Type of work: Novel
Time: 1981
Locale: Tirana, Albania

An investigation into the mysterious death of the successor to Albania's communist dictator builds to an exposure
of the dark realities of modern totalitarianism

Principal characters:
>   SUZANA, a woman whose two romances have been undermined by her
>   politically ambitious father, known as the Successor
>   THE SUCCESSOR'S SON, who also feels he has been sacrificed to his
>   father's power and status
>   ADRIEN HASOBEU, the minister of the interior, the likely replacement to
>   the Successor, suspected of eliminating him as a rival
>   THE GUIDE, another murder suspect; terrifying and powerful head of
>   state, now blind and increasingly paranoid
>   THE ARCHITECT, yet another suspect, responsible for renovating the
>   Successor's home in a way that challenged the power of The Guide
>   THE WIFE OF THE SUCCESSOR, his partner in life and politics, who is
>   directly responsible for his murder
>   THE SUCCESSOR, at one time designated to become the next Guide, who
>   appears as a tormented spirit from the afterlife

Ismail Kadare's *The Successor* is based on an actual historical incident—the mysterious death, in 1981, of Mehmet Shehu, the designated successor to Albania's longtime communist dictator Enver Hoxha. Informed by the author's conversations with
Shehu's only surviving son, this incident is the basis for Kadare's enigmatic blend of
surrealism, fabulation, and historical investigation. Structured as a classic "locked
room" murder mystery, a number of characters in the novel are suspected of murdering the man known as the Successor and expected to follow in the footsteps of the nation's leader.

Before turning to the various possible characters who have reason to murder the
Successor, however, Kadare re-creates the sense of maddening and indissoluble mystery that pervaded Albania in the 1980's, by means of the plaints of foreign intelligence agents who cannot understand the first thing about a country that had deliberately made itself inaccessible under the rule of its intransigent totalitarian leader. This
theme of uncertainty is continued in subsequent chapters, as one considers various
characters suspected of the crime. Under consideration first are the Successor's son

Ismail Kadare is Albania's most prominent poet and novelist and is acclaimed worldwide as one of the most important writers of the modern day. In 2005, he won the first Man Booker International Prize, which recognizes the body of work of a living author and his outstanding contribution to world literature.

and daughter, whose lives have been affected not only by the Successor's death but also by the choices their father had made while still alive. The Successor's daughter, Suzana, was forced to break off two romantic relationships because her father felt her liaisons undermined the security of his political position. She and her brother agree that blood ties were not nearly as strong her father's political ambitions and ideology. The interpretation of the Successor's motives, however, are so fluid and so subject to the winds of opinion that by the end of the novel the daughter is stunned to find that there is a wholly false consensus that, rather than forcing her to break off her latest relationship, her father actually encouraged the match in order to serve his own political agenda. In either scenario, however, it is the Successor's political agenda that is paramount.

After the Successor's death, Suzana hallucinates a vision of her father as a returning spirit, a mystical turn given greater play in the response of the Successor's son to his father's death. As with Suzana, the son's resentment of his father's greater loyalty to the Communist Party than to his own family supplies him with a motive for murder. After his father's death, the son becomes less a suspect than a kind of mystic, drawing close to a mysterious aunt, who may be a ghostly spirit visiting the bereaved family amid talk of a family curse. It is clear that the son's ideas run counter to the modernity of communist Albania, which has militantly placed itself in the vanguard of the Enlightenment project's rejection of the lore of magic, ghosts, and curses associated with Albania's past. The mystical motif introduced by the son is carried forward as well by his prognostications of various psychics, particularly an Icelandic visionary, and, eventually, an uncanny visitation by the murdered Successor himself.

The first section of the novel establishes two motifs: the way in which communist political interests dominate even the family's personal life and relationships, and the possibility of supernatural influences that exist in direct opposition to communist ideology. While avoiding, significantly, the interior life of the Successor's wife, Kadare proceeds to explore the inner lives of characters who, in one way or another, have appeared actually to confess to the murder of the Successor. The first suspect is Adrien Hasobeu, the minister of the interior and the Successor's most likely replacement. While armed with a revolver, and having admitted to snooping around the Successor's sealed residence at the request of the Guide, it is possible that Hasobeu's inability to actually assassinate the Successor leads to his being placed in handcuffs and accused of masterminding a conspiracy against the Guide, an accusation that, in the end, even he half-believes.

Of greater certainty, however, is that Hasobeu has been the subject of a typical purge directed against those who are perceived as becoming too powerful or too independent, or who have simply become casualties of an irrational change in the political winds. To add to the arbitrariness of the situation, Hasobeu's sudden reversal of fortune is accompanied by a possible posthumous rehabilitation of the Successor, who in an Alice-in-Wonderland way, is on the brink of being declared a martyr of the revolution, murdered by reactionary insurgents.

How, or if, the Successor fell from favor, whether he died through murder or suicide and the nature of those who killed him, varies from day to day, depending on whether the Guide has, arbitrarily, deemed the Successor a despicable traitor or a loyal servant of the Communist Party.

Even if the increasingly demented and now-blind Guide has not been directly responsible for the murder of the Successor, he has nevertheless for some time been planning the Successor's death. He depicts himself in a grandiose way as a psychic with the power to foretell a death that will in due time be given some rationale not yet apparent. The Guide also confuses the situation by providing a tape of a speech supposedly made before the death of the Successor, in which the Successor is given absolution for his various crimes and deviations, a ploy which allows the Guide to wriggle free of any suspicion of murder. In confusing the time line of actual events, the tape is less an explanation than a disturbing new addition to the general atmosphere of fear and uncertainty. It becomes evident that it is not only one murder that Kadare's narrative puts under investigation but also the fate of truth itself when it is routinely sacrificed to power or expedience.

A third suspect is an architect who has renovated the Successor's residence. The Architect has been made aware of an addition to his plans, that of a secret passage which leads from the Guide's residence to that of the Successor. Although this passageway could implicate the Successor in a possible political assassination plot orchestrated by the Guide, it has been conveniently covered with plaster, relieving the Architect of any obvious association with the crime. Despite the fact that he is now in the clear as far as anyone knows, the Architect confesses privately to his wife that he is, in fact, the Successor's murderer. Insulted and threatened by the Successor with relegation to a cooperative farm, the Architect suggests that he has exacted his revenge by turning the Successor's residence into a luxurious showplace superior to the Guide's home and calculated to inspire the Guide's murderous envy. He knows his superior achievement will make the Successor an unacceptable rival to the Guide, compounded by the way in which, in a society where property is collective, the renovated residence challenges the establishment by being remade to bear some resemblance to the private mansions of Western Europe. The Architect feels it is he who has supplied the Guide with psychological and political motives powerful enough for him to arrange for the elimination of his Successor.

The narrative, which began with a volley of theories on the part of watchful but baffled foreign intelligence agents, ends with the testimony of the deceased himself.

Earlier in the novel, the Icelandic medium has suggested that the Successor's death involved rival women in his personal life, a theory that was generally derided given the widespread belief that it was politics and not personal life that shaped the destinies of those members of the inner party who ruled communist Albania. From the region of a hellish afterlife, however, the Successor recalls that on the night in question it appeared to him that his first love, his comrade-in-arms during World War II, had mystically invaded the person of his wife. Although all the suspects have in one way or another wished death on the Successor, it is his obliging wife, the Successor suggests, who fulfills a request to die he first articulated decades earlier. Remembering how, when in a fever, he begged his first love to care for him enough to murder him, so that he would not die at the hands of the monstrous Nazis, he suggests that this profound death wish was at last granted almost forty years later.

Although it is, of course, possible that his politically dedicated wife was acting loyally under orders from the Guide, it is the Successor's own conviction that his wife's foremost motive for murdering him in 1981 was the product of a loving wish to save him from the ordeal of public execution by the party, in a way uncannily similar to his situation during World War II, when the goal was to be saved from the Nazis. This explanation of his wife's actions suggests that for the Successor, the Communists were ultimately not a victorious advance over the Nazis but were also in reality a virtual continuation of the Nazi totalitarian regime.

Fulfilling a flippant remark made by a member of the politburo earlier in the novel, in which the Successor was imagined as a lost soul wandering in one of the circles of a medieval version of hell, the narrative reveals in the end that the Successor is truly a damned soul wandering in a hellish void. This underworld, populated by successors and their guides and locked into a peculiar intimacy involving a perpetual struggle for mastery, is, the Successor warns us, also an underworld in which its lost souls are ever-ready to return from the dead to blight humanity with their dark and unending struggles for power.

The novel's conclusion confirms one of its major themes, involving the way in which archetypal or eternal patterns surface within the particulars of a historical time and place. Throughout the narrative, Kadare has introduced references to past historical situations and authoritarian leaders which, whether Egyptian, ancient Greek, Roman, Chinese or Medieval European, all parallel the regime of the present Guide, undermining the theoretical modernity of the new communist dictatorship. The ancient tales of the distant past surface in a way that undermines the conviction that modern Albania has begun at a zero hour that eliminated all relationship with past patterns. Additionally, the mention of spells and curses—even the mention of the wild rain and gusts of wind on the night of the Successor's death—suggest the possibility of demonic presences that have not been overcome by the modern regime.

Kadare's style blends the rational with irrational, the historical with mythological, the recognizably real with the surreality of the dream. Kadare has indicated that the greatest influence on his work was William Shakespeare's *Macbeth* (pr. 1606), which he encountered at a young and formative age. This work, set in medieval times and replete with witches, ghosts, prophecies, remorseless crime, and blind political ambition, not to mention ambiguity with regard to not only morality but to truth itself, became the template through which Kadare interpreted his own historical period. Additionally, in his exploration of a historical moment symbolic of Albania's political situation in the twentieth century, Kadare indicates alternatives to modern socialist realism, such as ancient Greek tragedy, the Bible, or premodern folkways, all of which insinuate a sense of timeless evil into a society that had prided itself on its progressive, revolutionary ideology.

Margaret Boe Birns

Review Sources

Booklist 102, no. 5 (November 1, 2005): 24.
Kirkus Reviews 73, no. 19 (October 1, 2005): 1048.
Library Journal 130, no. 16 (October 1, 2005): 66.
Los Angeles Times, October 23, 2005, p. R7.
The New York Times Book Review 155 (November 13, 2005): 62.
Publishers Weekly 252, no. 37 (September 19, 2005): 43.

THE SUMMER HE DIDN'T DIE

Author: Jim Harrison (1937-   )
Publisher: Atlantic Monthly Press (New York). 277 pp.
  $24.00
Type of work: Novellas
Time: 2005
Locale: Upper Peninsula Michigan, Montana

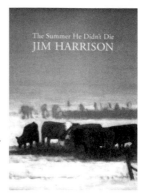

The three novellas in this collection are all about people in search of happiness and meaning: whimsical Upper Peninsula backwoods logger Brown Dog, three wives of well-respected men who have affairs with the same man, and the author himself

Principal characters:

> BROWN DOG, a part-Anishnabe-Chippewa Indian woodsman in *The Summer He Didn't Die* who decides to fight authority in his quest to help his stepdaughter
> DELMORE, his uncle
> BERRY, his stepdaughter, a mentally disabled victim of fetal alcohol syndrome
> GRETCHEN, the lesbian social worker who is the recipient of Brown Dog's affections
> BELINDA, Gretchen's dentist friend, with whom he has a brief affair
> MARTHA, a woman in *Republican Wives*, trapped in an unfulfilling marriage, who tries to kill her lover, the poet Daryl
> FRANCES, Martha's friend since before college and during it, who also has slept with Daryl
> SHIRLEY, a lifelong friend of Martha and Frances who has also slept with Daryl
> DARYL, an intellectual poser, poet, and seducer
> JIMMY, the narrator of *Tracking* who grows up in Michigan and becomes a writer

During the heyday of magazine fiction in the late nineteenth and early twentieth centuries, the novella was one of the more favored forms. Longer and providing more depth than the short story, a novella nevertheless did not require the commitment of time demanded by the reading of a long novel. Many of the fiction classics associated with the era are novellas: Henry James's *The Turn of the Screw* (1898), Joseph Conrad's *Heart of Darkness* (1899), and Thomas Mann's *Der Tod in Venedig* (1912; *Death in Venice*, 1925) are all examples. Other than occasional forays by writers such as William Faulkner and Philip Roth, however, the novella, perhaps too long for the modern magazine market, largely languished in the later twentieth century and into the twenty-first.

It is appropriate that Jim Harrison, who has so often written of fish-out-of-water characters and walking anachronisms, turns frequently to the novella when writing his prose. *The Summer He Didn't Die* is his fifth collection of novellas. The first and titular work in the volume brings back Harrison's backwoods logger and pulp-wooder Brown Dog, a part-Anishnabe-Chippewa Indian from the wild Upper Peninsula of Michigan. Brown Dog muddles his way through life in constant rebellion against the forces of unflinching and unnatural authority that work to derail his existence and ongoing search for love and sex. This character first appeared in Harrison's 1990 collection of novellas, *The Woman Lit by Fireflies*. Affable, optimistic, and endearing, Brown Dog has not changed much since his introduction, although his circumstances have: To avoid a jail sentence, he has been forced to marry the imprisoned Rose, his friend's sister, so that he can be able to care for her teenage son and her mentally disabled adolescent daughter, a victim of fetal alcohol syndrome.

Jim Harrison taught briefly at the State University of New York, Stony Brook, but has largely supported himself and his family through his writing. He has published five collections of novellas, seven novels, and ten collections of poems. He has also written screenplays, food columns, and a memoir. He is a past winner of a Guggenheim Fellowship and a grant from the National Endowment for the Arts.

Brown Dog's simple, existentialist lifestyle becomes complicated in a variety of ways in "The Summer He Didn't Die." He falls in love with Gretchen, his social worker, a lesbian who is not romantically interested in Brown Dog. He has an affair with Gretchen's friend Belinda, a dentist who eventually decides that she and Brown Dog are not compatible. He is then hired, briefly, to escort Belinda's former flame Bob, a journalist, around the Upper Peninsula as he researches an article on down-and-out American Indians. Next, Brown Dog finds that his stepdaughter, Berry, is to be removed from his custody and sent to a special school. Although unable to perform intellectual exercises or achieve in school or even hold a conversation, Berry is conversant with nature and at ease in the wilderness. Brown Dog often witnesses her speaking to wild dogs, birds, and snakes.

Again and again in the various tales that Harrison has told about Brown Dog, the action boils down to Brown Dog's casual rebelliousness in the face of a blind and unfeeling bureaucracy. In "The Summer He Didn't Die," Brown Dog decides to spirit Berry away into Canada with the help of his full-blooded Anishnabe-Chippewa Uncle Delmore, Gretchen, and a group of Canadian Chippewas. If Berry, in a way, represents a return to a pre-civilization form of humanity who is integrated into nature rather than separated from it, then Brown Dog's flight with her to a Native American community is, in a sense, a flight from all that is cruel and indifferent in modern civilization. It represents a return to a time and place where matters are settled by the human heart in accord with the laws of nature, not societal codes and regulations.

The second novella, "Republican Wives," focuses on three women who have a lot in common. All in their late thirties, they have known one another since childhood, attended the same college, and belonged to the same sorority. They have all married very successful men who turned out to be unsatisfactory husbands. More recently, each has had an affair with Daryl, a disaffected, self-important, counterculture aesthete and writer. The three friends—Martha, Frances, and Shirley—have known Daryl since college, when he first managed to seduce each of them even though they had sworn an oath that "none . . . would ever sleep with this monster." After Daryl, in what seems to be a moment of mean-spirited reprisal, reveals to the friends' three husbands that he has slept with their wives, Martha poisons him with crushed-up antidepressant drugs in his coffee. Before long Martha has fled to Mexico, where her friends soon join her to help her understand how to get her life back in order.

"Republican Wives" manages to do several things at once. On one hand, it pokes fun at upper-class American life, with its materialism and crass capitalism. The story poses the age-old question: Can money buy happiness? If so, why are these women so eager to enter into an affair, one at a time, with a man they loathe? The novella also pokes fun at the archetype of the smug and condescending literary artiste. At the same time, the central focus of these women's lives—although perhaps unrealized by any of the three of them—is shown to be the friendships they have with one another.

The third piece in Harrison's collection, "Tracking," is only a novella in terms of its length; it does not exactly create a fictional story. The account it provides, in a clipped, precise, third-person narrative, mirrors closely Harrison's biography as most recently related by the author in his memoir *Off to the Side* (2003). "Tracking" begins with a young man, Jimmy or Jim, growing up in rural Michigan whose intellectual curiosity is slowly stoked until he has determined to become a writer. He attends the University of Michigan, marries young, earns a master's degree, teaches briefly at State University of New York, Stony Brook, wins poetry awards, eventually turns to fiction, and finally makes money once Hollywood takes an interest.

The title of the novella-memoir implies that, again and again, Jim tries to make sense of who he is and what he is to become, based on where he is. The narrator notes that, more than any other occupation, travel has taught him the most: "If your own personality was almost carelessly absolved and you were open and interested, the stories floated into the mind in amazing quantity. There seemed to be a place in every culture for the writer as listener and most people wanted to be heard."

Like "The Summer He Didn't Die" and "Republican Wives," "Tracking" is divided into three parts; the segments of "Tracking" divide the writer-narrator's life: "What the Boy Saw," "What the Man Saw," and "What the Older Man Saw." Part of what the narrator learns over his long career and various misadventures is the importance of family. Spending a night with two elderly fishermen who helped him fix his broken truck during one spell of wanderlust, "it occurred to him that there were no obligations to art or anything else except to support his wife and daughters. Above all else he was still his father's son." In other words, "place" is not somewhere to be visited but rather something one constructs from the love of other people, to take along with one.

The reader of *The Summer He Didn't Die* is tempted to connect its three works thematically, as Faulkner famously did with the collection of short stories and novellas *Go Down Moses* (1942). Often, placing such artificial frameworks on collections of shorter works is to do the author a disservice. Nonetheless, there are certain thematic elements that carry through each of these texts. At some level, each of the protagonists—Brown Dog, Martha, Frances, Shirley, and Jim—is looking for some fleeting phantom of happiness, a will-o-the-wisp that will bring enlightenment and fulfillment. The unsophisticated and stumbling Brown Dog may be the one most adept at enjoying the wonders that each day brings, but even he is in a constant search for love. The three Republican wives hope to find happiness and meaning in life through sex with a man who represents everything their stolid and secure husbands are not. Jim seeks to find artistic transcendence somewhere just down the road.

What each of these characters does, in response to the simple human elusiveness of their dreams, is to gather family about them. Over the course of "The Summer He Didn't Die," Brown Dog goes from being a single, forty-nine-year-old man with no responsibilities to someone willing to flee his native land and become a fugitive from the law to save his adopted daughter. In "Republican Wives," the one man that Martha can count on is her father, a representative of how men behaved in prior generations, when loyalty and honesty counted. Further, although none of the women have sisters, they each fly to Martha's side immediately when she is in trouble. In a sense, the care the women show one another reveals that their deepest relationships are not between themselves and their husbands but rather among the three of them. Even their dalliances with Daryl are shared. Although "Tracking" is more of a portrait of the artist as a young man than it is a work focused on family, Jim nevertheless learns in it that his family is what is most important to him—above fame, above riches, and above artistry.

Scott Yarbrough

Review Sources

Booklist 101, no. 21 (July 1, 2005): 1876.
Kirkus Reviews 73, no. 10 (May 15, 2005): 558-559.
Library Journal 130, no. 12 (July 1, 2005): 74.
The New York Times Book Review 154 (August 7, 2005): 11.
Publishers Weekly 252, no. 21 (May 23, 2005): 53.

SWEETNESS AND LIGHT
The Mysterious History of the Honeybee

Author: Hattie Ellis
First published: 2004, in Great Britain
Publisher: Harmony Books (New York). 243 pp. $23.00
Type of work: History and science

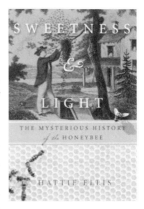

Ellis explores the history of the working relationship honeybees and humans have shared over thousands of years

The title of Hattie Ellis's delectable treatise on the honeybee, *Sweetness and Light*, is derived from a quote from Jonathan Swift's satirical *The Battle of the Books* (1704): "We have chosen to fill our hives with honey and wax; thus furnishing mankind with the two noblest things, which are sweetness and light." Taking readers on a wide-ranging journey through time and around the globe, Ellis examines how people have hunted, robbed, and, finally, tamed bees to obtain the "sweetness and light" they produce. Her engaging discussion of the social history, popular science, ancient myth, and quaint folklore buzzing around this industrious insect provides an close-up look at not only the inner workings of the hive but also the symbiotic relationship humans and bees have shared since the Stone Age. Ellis does a remarkable job of distilling thousands of years of science, history, and anthropology into less than 250 pages, portraying the "common" honeybee as anything but common.

Ellis claims that *Apis mellifera* is "the most studied creature on the planet next to man"—and the most successful of all the subspecies of bee. Centuries of observations by farmers, aristocrats, clergymen, writers, and scientists have contributed to the knowledge of bee biology, lore, and husbandry. Ellis's fluid prose and playful wit make this sometimes arcane information accessible to the modern reader as she sprinkles her narrative with fascinating and often quirky tidbits about the secret life of bees. For example, when calm, bees hum at the pitch of middle C. They can live in colonies of up to a hundred thousand individuals. Bees cannot see red but can see yellow, green, and blue, colors that are associated with rosemary, thyme, and lavender, which are favorite sources of nectar.

A bee's sense of smell is tied to its memory. For twelve days after a bee has visited a certain flower, the insect "remembers" the scent and returns repeatedly to the bloom to collect pollen and nectar. A female worker bee processes only one-quarter ounce of honey during her brief, six-week life span. A gallon of honey could provide enough fuel for a bee to fly seven million miles. Employing a complicated dance, a bee can communicate to the rest of its hive the distance, direction, quantity, and quality of sources of nectar. Ellis also notes the odd likelihood that bees may have evolved before flowers. Such a possibility is surprising, considering that the modern honeybee's survival is intimately intertwined with that of blossoming plants. Each depends on the other for "the twin necessities of existence, of reproduction and food."

In addition to being the "necessities of existence," reproduction and food also dictate the social structure of the colony. Taking readers within the walls of the hive, Ellis reveals the remarkably efficient division of labor that is essential to the smooth operation of the community, which consists of a queen, male drones, and thousands of female worker bees. The queen is the center of the life of the hive. After mating with drones in flight, she stores sperm in her body that will last her lifetime. She is the only egg-producing female in the community, laying up to an astonishing two thousand eggs per day.

~

Hattie Ellis writes about the relationships among people, places, and food. Her previous books include Trading Places *(1999), portraits of specialty shops and their owners, and* Eating England: Why We Eat What We Eat *(2001). To tell the story of bees, she traversed the globe from Nepal to New Zealand, Paris to Tahiti, and New York to Utah. She lives in England.*

~

The drones' sole purpose is to mate with the queen. Once a drone accomplishes this important mission, he dies. The remaining drones who did not mate with the queen loiter around the hive and are fed and supported by the workers. It may seem that the drones lead a charmed, if idle life. However, just as in human society, there is no such thing as a free lunch within the bee community. When the workers are readying the hive for the winter, they stop feeding the drones and even bar them from entering the nest. The drones die of exposure and starvation. If the queen is the heart of the hive, the workers are its soul and by far the busiest bees in the colony. Not only do they go on wide-ranging reconnaissance flights to locate and bring back nectar, ultimately transforming it into honey, they also clean the cells, feed developing larvae, repair the nest, pack the cells with pollen, keep the hive at a consistent temperature by flapping their wings, and patrol the entrance to the hive.

Understanding the social structure of the hive has no doubt aided humans in domesticating bees over the centuries, but why were people attracted to the insects in the first place? Ellis speculates that early humans associated sweetness with good nutrition and quick energy, advantages that served active hunter-gatherers well. Although honey may have fulfilled a practical need to boost physical activity, it also offered a sensual benefit—the taste was pure pleasure. Neolithic cave paintings depict Stone Age people risking life and limb—not to mention considerable exposure to numerous stings—just for a mouthful of the nectarous comb. Ellis also conjectures that both ancient and modern humans associate sweetness with nurturing. If her supposition is true, then honey is a supreme example of the psychological and spiritual power of comfort food.

Over the centuries, people have also looked on honey metaphorically, as food for the soul as well as for the body. When humans first learned to domesticate bees, they began to attach mythological significance to the insects, giving birth to a large body of legend, folklore, and religious and cultural rituals. One of the most compelling chapters in Ellis's book is titled "Organization and Magic," which traces the influence of the honeybee on ancient Egyptian civilization. Ellis notes that archaeological evidence reveals that the Egyptians were among the first apiarists and that the beekeeping practices they originated five thousand years ago are still in use today. Honey was so prized in Egyptian culture that only the rich could afford it. It was also extolled in Egyptian literature. Ellis quotes a poem written by the daughter of Prime Minister Rekhmire: "The little sycamore, which she hath planted with her hand, it moveth its mouth to speak. The whispering of its leaves is sweet as refined honey." Honey was used medicinally to dress wounds and as a remedy for poor dentition. The Egyptians may not have known why it worked to fight infection, but modern science has since shown that honey possesses antibiotic properties. The Egyptians also used honey as a preservative in the embalming process, and the generative power of the bee was celebrated in their religious beliefs relating to the afterlife. Ellis quotes from a funerary ritual: "Going about as a bee, thou seest all the goings about of thy father." Finally, honey was used as an offering to the gods, including Pharoah, whose royal hieroglyph includes a symbol for the bee.

Folklore and superstition surrounding bees survived well into the eighteenth century, lasting until the rise of rationalism during the Enlightenment took the bee out of the spirit world and put it under a microscope. Instead of envisioning the bee as an all-seeing soul, as the ancient Egyptians did, Dr. Edward Bevan, a British inventor and beekeeper, emphasized the bee's effect on the intellect, noting that the bee "tends to enlarge and harmonize the mind, and to elevate it into worthy conceptions of Nature and its Author." Ellis reports on a number of innovations in beekeeping during the 1800's, particularly the invention by Lorenzo Langstroth of the moveable frame hive in 1852. Langstroth's innovation enabled the beekeepers to harvest honey by removing the comb easily, which in turn allowed apiarists to produce much larger quantities of honey than they could when they housed bees in skeps. Ellis calls Langstroth's discovery a "eureka moment" and a "revolution in beekeeping." Other apiarists built on Langstroth's work and, to keep up with the news on the latest inventions and innovations, formed associations and published their own scientific journals.

Modern interest in bees has not been limited to the scientific realm or even to beekeeping circles. Twentieth century artists, most notably architects, were inspired by the structure of the honeycomb. Ellis cites Antonio Guadi's invention of the parabolic arch as an example of an architectural feature that was patterned on wild comb. The buildings designed by Frank Lloyd Wright reflect the hexagonal form of the comb, specifically the Honeycomb House in Stanford, California. In addition to architecture, bees also captured the interest of filmmakers such as Victor Erice, a Spanish director who produced *Spirit of the Beehive* in 1973. Bees have also appeared prominently in works of modern literature. Ellis notes that Sylvia Plath's father, Otto, an expert on bees, influenced her work. A apiarist herself, Plath wrote several works in which the bee appeared as a central image, including "The Beekeeper's Daughter."

Of the many beekeepers Ellis profiles in her book, perhaps the most memorable is Brother Adam, an intrepid twentieth century Benedictine monk and member of the Buckfast religious community in England. In an attempt to rid hives of the devastating Isle of Wight disease, an illness that suffocates bees and maims their wings,

Brother Adam instituted a cross-breeding program that included using Italian queens. Influenced by the work of another monk, Gregor Mendel, Brother Adam sought better ways of breeding bees in order to make them more gentle, increase honey production, and build up their immunity to disease. His quest took him all over the world, including an ascent up Mount Kilimanjaro, Africa's highest peak, when he was eighty-nine. When he died at ninety-eight, he was held in high esteem among apiarists for his groundbreaking work in bee genetics and breeding.

Through much of her book Ellis portrays bees as the quintessence of "sweetness and light," but she also looks at not-so-benevolent bees. In the 1950's, the search for the perfect bee was in full swing. While Brother Adam was working with docile strains in England, other geneticists were experimenting with more aggressive species, primarily *Apis mellifera scutellata* from southern Africa. Queens from this strain were crossbred in South America with the hope that they would increase honey production. Thriving in warm climates, large swarms rapidly traveled into the southern part of the United States. Their nasty natures and propensity for stinging earned them the title "killer bees" in press releases. Ellis notes that their spread has changed beekeeping practices. Because of the threat of killer bees' deadly stings, beekeepers now have to wear thicker suits and work in pairs. Amateur beekeeping is no longer safe, and backyard hives are disappearing from the landscape. If there is a bright side to this scenario, it is that the Africanized bees cannot survive in cold weather, which may halt their spread into the northern United States.

Ellis makes it clear that although bees are an important part of Earth's ecosystem, pesticides, diseases, and other environmental hazards are causing the insects to leave backyard apiaries in droves. What will happen to the close relationship bees and humans have shared over the millennia when the bees leave the neighborhoods? In her gem of a book, Ellis emphasizes the interconnectedness of all living things and demonstrates that if people allow the honeybee to fly out of their lives, they will lose touch not only with the natural world but also with themselves.

Pegge Bochynski

Review Sources

Booklist 101, no. 12 (February 15, 2005): 1044.
Forbes 175, no. 5 (March 14, 2005): 117-119.
Kirkus Reviews 72, no. 24 (December 15, 2004): 1179.
Publishers Weekly 252, no. 3 (January 17, 2005): 44.

THE TENDER BAR
A Memoir

Author: J. R. Moehringer (1964-   )
Publisher: Hyperion (New York). 368 pp. $24.00
Type of work: Memoir
Time: 1972-2001
Locale: Manhasset, Long Island, New York; Arizona;
    New York City; New Haven, Connecticut

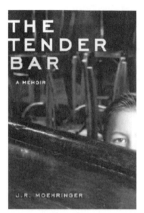

*In this coming-of-age memoir, a fatherless boy is guided
to manhood by a rough collection of neighborhood bar
patrons*

> *Principal personages:*
> JOHN JOSEPH MOEHRINGER, JR., known as
>   J. R., a journalist recalling his childhood
>   and young adulthood
> DOROTHY MOEHRINGER, J. R.'s mother
> JOHN JOSEPH MOEHRINGER (JOHNNY MICHAELS), a popular disk jockey
>   and J. R.'s absent father
> CHARLES MAGUIRE (CHARLIE), Dorothy's brother, a bartender at
>   Dickens/Publicans
> STEVE, the owner of Dickens/Publicans
> SIDNEY, a rich college classmate who becomes J. R.'s girlfriend

Pulitzer Prize-winning journalist J. R. Moehringer is the son of a fiercely devoted Irish mother and a mercurial, disinterested Italian father. His parents separate when he is a baby, and his father abandons his son physically, financially, and emotionally. His mother, Dorothy, moves back into her parents' ramshackle house in Manhasset, Long Island, in which her brother, Charlie, her married sister, Ruth, and Ruth's six children also live. J. R. listens to the radio to hear the voice of his father, a popular disc jockey known as Johnny Michaels. Living in a household dominated by women, J. R. craves validation from men and talks back to his father's radio voice, pretending they are having a conversation.

Dorothy works long hours, always striving for enough money for her and J. R. to move into their own apartment. Occasionally she succeeds, and for a time they have a place of their own, but financial crises always send them back to the chaotic family home. J. R.'s cousins also move in and out, as their parents, Ruth and Harry, separate and reunite.

Although their house is one of the most dilapidated in town, J. R.'s grandfather is quite well-off. He had retired after acquiring an impressive stock portfolio, but he is so cheap that he digs in trash cans for discarded newspapers to check on his stocks. Worse, he is as stingy with affection as with money, rarely speaking a kind word to anyone and never calling his wife anything but "Stupid Woman."

J. R. is intelligent and an avid reader; books provide the only respite from his crowded, chaotic, noisy home. His mother realizes how much he longs for a father. Hoping to provide him with at least male companionship, Dorothy asks Charlie to take J. R. to the beach with him and his buddies.

J. R. Moehringer, winner of the Pulitzer Prize for feature writing in 2000, is a national correspondent for the Los Angeles Times *and a former Niemann Fellow at Harvard University. He lives in Denver, Colorado.*

Charlie, a heavy gambler, is a flamboyant bartender at one of Manhasset's most popular bars, Dickens (later called Publicans), and all of his friends are employees or regular patrons of the bar. Charlie and his buddies soon accept their young charge and become almost as much of a constant in the boy's life as his mother. Thus begins J. R.'s journey to manhood, the path littered with salty language, strewn with chauvinistic attitudes, and watered by alcohol but also providing him with admiration, encouragement, and a refuge from his problems.

Bars and churches were the most prominent establishments in Manhasset, Moehringer recalls. A church stood at one end of the main street and Dickens/Publicans Bar at the other end. These he find to be equally impressive and important temples. The predominantly Irish neighborhood happily patronizes Dickens/Publicans, where most of the staff is Irish, each drink is a long pour, and every third drink is free. Dickens/Publicans attracts an eclectic crowd from the neighborhood and beyond, from Wall Street tycoons to the unemployed, pontificating intellectuals to the barely coherent.

> Everyone has a holy place, a refuge. . . . For better or worse, my holy place was Steve's bar. . . . I grew up 142 steps from a glorious old American tavern, and that has meant all the difference. . . . For the first twenty-five years of my life, everyone I knew either sent me to the bar, drove me to the bar, accompanied me to the bar, rescued me from the bar, or was in the bar when I arrived. . . . At some point the bar itself became my father, its dozens of men melding into one enormous male eye looking over my shoulder, providing the needed alternative to my mother, that Y chromosome to her X.

Mother and son are extremely close and loving. As much as he depends on his mother, J. R. also feels a huge responsibility to take care of her, despite Dorothy's efforts to allay his concerns. As a young child, he decides to become a lawyer so that he can put his mother through college; his grandfather had refused to allow his daughters to pursue higher education. J. R. worries obsessively about his mother, their finances, and their future, fearing that if he is not perfect, he will fail his mother as his father had done. In Dickens, he finds a different dynamic: The men there applaud him as much for losing as for succeeding.

When J. R. is a young teenager, Aunt Ruth and her children move to Arizona. Looking for a new start, Dorothy and J. R. follow. However, Aunt Ruth soon returns to New York, leaving Dorothy and J. R. somewhat adrift. With their relatives gone, Dorothy decides that J. R. would be better off with family during vacations, and he returns to his grandparents' home every summer. There, he has few social outlets beyond Uncle Charlie and his drinking buddies, and he lives for the days that Charlie gets up early enough and in a good enough mood to take him to the beach.

In Arizona, J. R. meets two additional men who have a significant impact on his life. Bill and Bud run a local bookstore in an unorthodox fashion: They spend most of their time in the back room reading, seldom appearing at the cash register to wait on customers. They are quite unlike Charlie and his friends—antisocial and interested in nothing but reading. However, J. R. charms them, and they become his mentors, steering him toward great writers, significant books, and the music of Wolfgang Amadeus Mozart. They help J. R. improve his grammar and soften his accent, encourage him to dress better despite their own careless wardrobes, and give him a part-time job at a time when his mother desperately needs more money. Most important, they encourage him to prepare for college—not just any college, but Yale.

Back in New York as a teenager, J. R. has another mentor: His older cousin Sheryl gets him a summer job in the law firm where she works. He feels that he has truly become a man—taking the train to Manhattan every day to a prestigious office, sending money to his mother in Arizona. To Sheryl, however, being a man is mainly about appearances: what he wears, how he smokes a cigarette, what newspaper he reads on the train, and, especially, how well he can drink. Sheryl happily adopts her underage cousin as her drinking buddy, and he begins drinking regularly and heavily at sixteen years of age.

During his childhood, J. R.'s father had visited only him once, then dropped from sight. In his senior year of high school, J. R. determines to find him. Calling radio stations and combing though phone books from throughout the United States yield no results. He tries to keep his search a secret, sure his mother will be angry, but once she finds out she offers to help him. The next day, he receives a call from his father, who is surprised to learn that J. R. is not dying—the lie his mother told Johnny's sister in hopes of making Johnny call. Once Johnny is convinced that J. R. is not looking for financial support, he agrees to fly to Arizona to see his son.

Their meeting is strained, and Johnny makes conversation by telling—perhaps inventing—stories of his glamorous life and rich, famous friends. Only one story impresses J. R.: the story of his name. Although Johnny is Italian, Moehringer is not an Italian name. Johnny's father, a Sicilian immigrant, believed that the Germans who owned the factories on New York's Lower East Side would not hire Italians, so he took the name of a German neighbor who had died, Franz Moehringer.

J. R. is admitted to Yale University on a full scholarship and thinks his life from then on will be perfect. He quickly realizes, however, that he is an outsider. A poor boy in the midst of wealth and breeding, he launders and irons other students' clothes to earn extra money. His penchant for using the longest, most pretentious words he can find earns him a series of near-failing grades on his essays. He falls in love with Sidney, a rich girl who alternately adores him and abandons him. The one aspect of college life in which J. R. discovers he can keep up is drinking. Soon his grades plummet, and he is on the verge of being expelled.

Somehow, he regains his focus on school, brings his grades up, reunites for a time with Sidney, and gets a job in a bookstore-café. Briefly, his life is as perfect as he had always dreamed. After graduation, he plans to live at his grandfather's house and write a novel. His mother, however, insists that he get a real job to pay his bills. Almost against his will, he is hired in the Home Fashions department of the Lord and Taylor department store, where his fabrications about the merchandise soon make him the department's top salesperson. One morning, waking up after a drinking binge, he sends a job application to *The New York Times*. Fully expecting a rejection letter, he is startled to be offered a job as a copyboy.

At the *Times*, he feels he is in his element, surrounded by people who love both words and alcohol as much as he does. His duties as a copyboy include only menial tasks, but he always holds the hope of impressing an editor and receiving an assignment that would lead to a reporter's job.

For years J. R. had taken notes of conversations overheard in Dickens/Publicans, hoping to capture its essence in a novel one day. He moves to a tiny, odoriferous apartment above a Greek restaurant and tries every night to work on his novel before retreating to Dickens/Publicans. Soon the bar's denizens become his editors and best critics. The smallest error in his writing at the *Times* brings scorn and shame, but when patrons at the bar find an error, they turn it into a joke or a better story.

J. R. finally receives a thirty-day tryout as a reporter and is devastated at the end when he is told that he will not be offered a reporter's job. Although he is encouraged to find a job at a smaller paper to hone his obvious talent, he continues as a copyboy and falls more deeply under the influence of alcohol. He realizes that his drinking is no longer a social pastime but a desperate search for oblivion, yet he continues. Not until one of Dickens/Publicans' regulars nearly kills him in a bar fight does he end his addiction to the bar that fostered his dependence on alcohol. He leaves New York to pursue a career in journalism in Colorado and later stops drinking.

With *The Tender Bar*, Moehringer tells his story with wit, warmth, and wisdom. Rather than novelize Dickens/Publicans, he captures what it meant to him by letting its characters tell their own stories, reconstructed from scribbled notes, interviews, and help from his mother's diaries, letters, and recollections. Although another person might have seen the crowd at Dickens/Publicans as a harmful influence, Moehringer accepts these men for what they gave him and takes responsibility for his own behavior. He also discovers that as much as the men in the bar taught him about being a man, he learned all the basics—"toughness, persistence, determination, reliability, honesty, integrity, guts"—from his mother's example.

His memoir is not only a tender salute to the men whose company he so craved but also a tender homage to the mother who let him find his way.

Irene Struthers Rush

Review Sources

Booklist 101, no. 22 (August 1, 2005): 1969.
Kirkus Reviews 73, no. 14 (July 15, 2005): 779-780.
Library Journal 130, no. 14 (September 1, 2005): 142.
The New York Times 154 (September 1, 2005): E1-E7.
The New York Times Book Review 154 (September 11, 2005): 12.
Newsweek 146, nos. 9/10 (September 5, 2005): 74-75.
People 64, no. 12 (September 19, 2005): 59.
Publishers Weekly 252, no. 26 (June 27, 2005): 50.

TESTOSTERONE DREAMS
Rejuvenation, Aphrodisia, Doping

Author: John Hoberman (1944-   )
Publisher: University of California Press (Berkeley).
  381 pp. $25.00
Type of work: Medicine, science, and sociology
Time: The twentieth and twenty-first centuries
Locale: The United States

Hoberman examines the history of human testosterone enhancement and its impact on modern American society

In *Testosterone Dreams: Rejuvenation, Aphrodisia, Doping*, author and sociologist John Hoberman investigates modern attitudes toward improving the mental, physical, and sexual abilities of humans. Testosterone, a fountain of youth of sorts, has inspired dreams of running faster, thinking quicker, enhancing sexual pleasure, and bulking up diminishing muscle mass. Termed as a "charismatic hormone," synthetic testosterone has become increasingly available and accepted in mainstream America; it is sold as a rejuvenating drug, a sexually stimulating drug, and as a doping steroid drug that builds muscle mass and vastly increases athletic performance.

Hoberman provides a comprehensive overview of the hormone's synthesis, begun in 1935, by raising and then answering such highly charged questions as: When have testosterone drugs been viewed as harmful? Why now, and not when it gained first attention in the 1940's, has testosterone become fashionable? How does the pharmaceutical industry market such drugs? How are changing medical technologies affecting how men and women think about their respective sexual identities?

The mass market failed in its original efforts to market testosterone after World War II (a time that, amazingly, saw women taking the drug to increase factory work performance) for religious and moral reasons. Testosterone formulas, which today are readily available via mail order or the Internet, have been on the market since the 1930's. The synthetic male hormone was touted as far back as 1937 by those seeking to profit, as sports fans watched records being smashed by athletes on testosterone-based anabolic steroids. Methyltestosterone, available in pill form and marketed as testosterone replacement therapy, was sold to promote sexual stimulation and enhance productivity at work for aging males.

However, the hormone was viewed early on as dangerous and failed to become a mass-market phenomenon, Hoberman hypothesizes, because of the era's sexual conservatism. Doctors of the day saw little advantage in providing a method for their aging male patients to increase sexual activity and enjoyment. Today, thanks to major changes in social perception of sexual enjoyment into old age not as an embarrassment but as a right, and marketing strategies that define the natural decrease in tes-

John Hoberman is the author of Darwin's Athletes: How Sport Has Damaged Black America and Preserved the Myth of Race *(1997) and* Mortal Engines: The Science of Performance and the Dehumanization of Sport *(1992). He is a professor of Germanic Studies at the University of Texas at Austin.*

tosterone and estrogen as "deficiencies," hormone therapy has become legitimized as a socially acceptable form of enhancement. Its money-making potential has also been discovered.

In Olympic competition, doping has increased tremendously over the last forty years. Hoberman insists that while the media might portray steroid abuse in terms of isolated incidents, the truth is that abuse runs rampant throughout the whole Olympic structure and includes not only athlete dopers but also medical practitioners, sports officials and federations, and even, in the second half of the twentieth century, the International Olympic Committee (IOC). According to the author, it is not just at the institutional level that testosterone-based drugs are abused. Indeed, pharmacological performance enhancement has become normal for increasing numbers of athletes, while the doctor/patient relationship inherent in athletic doping serves as a model for physicians who now offer to enhance their everyday patients' mental, physical, and sexual lives.

The use of testosterone enhancement will precipitate a crisis of human identity in the twenty-first century, says Hoberman. Among its social and ethical implications, of primary concern is the idea that as pharmaceutical companies find more and more uses for enhancement drugs, the boundaries between illicit doping and socially acceptable forms of drug-assisted productivity—such as drugs to help tired workers stay awake and more productive at work—will shift, together with the perception of such drug use, from acceptable to compulsory.

Numbered among the reasons people could come to feel obligated to dope themselves are military, professional, and sexual. The author compares pilots on long flights under the World War II policy of dispersing Benzadrine to professional Tour de France cyclists. In no way does he paste the heroic Lance Armstrong with the steroid label of shame, but he severely criticizes Armstrong's use of an altitude chamber to boost his red-blood cell count as a "doping procedure." To be competitive in today's world, athletes could feel compelled, if not downright obligated to teammates, managers, and owners, to consume anabolic steroids, especially in certain sports communities such as professional cycling, where athletes have legitimized their use. Indeed, late into the twentieth century, the East German Olympic teams practiced compulsory doping in their efforts to gain recognition and medals, all in the effort of what Hoberman terms "sportive nationalism," the attempt to increase a country's international prestige through the presentation of their elite athletes' physical fitness.

Hoberman calls the major league baseball practice of taking drugs to increase athletic performance the worst doping scandal of the twentieth century. In 1998, Americans were amazed to see ballplayers Mark McGwire, who had recently gained twenty-five pounds of muscle mass, and Sammy Sosa surpassing the record for most home runs in a season.

Beyond professional athletics, steroid abuse today is invading the neighborhood YMCA and brings in its wake a whole set of health issues. The use of steroids among adult males may include breast development, atrophied testicles, reduced sperm count, enlarged prostate, liver and kidney problems, high blood pressure, increased risk of stroke and heart attack, and increased aggressiveness. In growing adolescent bodies, steroid use may cause stunted growth and severe depression that could end in suicide.

Doping in the workplace has also become rampant, as the business world reacts to increasing competition. As in many athletic programs, consuming enhancement drugs could become compulsory or even obligatory in a show of company loyalty and fear over losing one's job to younger, perhaps more chemically enhanced coworkers. For instance, if one worker takes Zoloft to stay alert and get more work done, what is to stop another employee from using the same device? Does a tired employee owe it to his or her employer to work to the highest capacity possible? Under such perceptions, a functional argument thus emerges proposing drug use—and steroid use particularly—in cases of physically demanding work, to increase American productivity. Other occupational users such as bouncers and prison guards, or others in jobs who encounter physical threats, use steroids to increase their size and aggression, in an effort both to threaten and protect.

Hoberman brings to light the hidden use of hormone doping by police officers who claim that steroid abuse by their colleagues throughout United States, and in other parts of the world, also goes unreported. In professional roles that involve physical strength and assertiveness, significant numbers of policemen abuse anabolic steroids in an effort to "beef up." Consequently, they often wind up playing criminal roles themselves when enormously high testosterone levels—sometimes as high as fifty times greater than normal—lead to hyperaggressiveness.

In the sexual arena, hormone replacement therapy (HRT) has helped place women under a social obligation to stay younger, first in an effort to provide satisfaction for their sexual partners, then to avoid the health problems associated with aging, and after that to seek sexual satisfaction for themselves. Today, testosterone can be prescribed to boost older women's sexual appetite in order to match demands in the bedroom now made on them by their Viagra-taking partners. In this vein, testosterone has, in recent years, been prescribed to remedy the natural decline in testosterone levels of aging men undergoing the so-called andropause, the controversial marketing of the male menopause suffered by many men over age sixty-five.

Testosterone Dreams also examines the medical community's complicit role in the increased use and abuse of testosterone, in which doctors and drug companies foster a climate of permissiveness and self-medication. For instance, *Testosterone* magazine coaches those interested in taking performance-enhancing drugs, especially anabolic steroids, on how to fake symptoms to fool doctors into writing prescriptions. Doctors, free to prescribe medications for any use they see fit, often legally prescribe

such medications for uses other than intended—a practice called "off-labeling."
Antiaging therapy is a particularly apt term doctors use to prescribe testosterone in an
effort to circumvent the Anabolic Steroids Control Act of 1990. In addition, the use of
human growth hormone (HGH) is prescribed in this off-label manner for conditions
that have nothing to do with therapies for which it received Food and Drug Administration approval. Where, Hoberman asks, does therapy end and performance enhancement begin?

Synthetic testosterone is currently a frequently prescribed off-label drug, placing
members of the public in the role of human guinea pig. Hoberman likens testosterone
therapies to today's medical dosing of inattentive kids, gastric-bypass surgery, and in-
fertility treatments. Frankly fearful of physicians who listen more to their patients'
demands rather than to their own sense of what is right, he insists such physicians
have become beauticians rather than healers. The author also blames competition
among pharmaceutical companies that drives testosterone sales in the attempt to produce a rival market to the phenomenally profitable female hormone market.

In *Testosterone Dreams*, readers get a long, hard look at pharmaceutical promo-
tional campaigns aimed at creating new markets for testosterone products. Hoberman
strongly takes the stand that drugs should be used to treat illness and not to enhance
healthy bodies. In this effort, he effectively combines the history of medicine, sports,
and sex in the United States, covering not only steroids but also providing an overview of historical events that precipitated today's social climate. His book presents a
frightening portrayal of patients' fantasies and the pharmaceutical marketplace that
fuels such desires. His work reveals the dark side of medicine that remains complicit
in increasing athletic performance, and how that increased performance, in turn, sets
the bar higher and higher in other areas of society. Americans have internalized the
belief in individual self-improvement. After all, it is only natural to strive to do more
and to want to do it better. Sports fans want faster times and longer home runs from
great athletes, who show that it is possible to transcend normality, mediocrity, and
perhaps even the bounds of nature itself becoming godlike in the effort. What,
Hoberman asks, about the so-called purity of sports?

Insisting that steroid use is the natural outcome of the hypercompetitiveness of the
entire American culture, Hoberman's book proposes that the future will bring the battle between a liberal medical ethos that embraces medical interventions to enhance
life functions and the traditional sense that death should follow birth in a natural progression, without the intervention of measures to artificially enhance and prolong life.
Anyone considering any form of enhancement should read it.

M. Casey Diana

Review Sources

The New Yorker, April 18, 2005.
The Times Literary Supplement, July 1, 2005, p. 31.

THEM
A Memoir of Parents

Author: Francine du Plessix Gray (1930-   )
Publisher: Penguin Press (New York). 544 pp. $30.00
Type of work: Biography and memoir
Time: The twentieth century
Locale: Russia, France, New York

*This brutally candid yet loving account describes two
eccentric, strong-willed, narcissistic Russian-born immigrants who became giants in America's postwar fashion
industry and New York City's social scene but whose
parenting skills left much to be desired*

Principal personages:
> FRANCINE DU PLESSIX GRAY, an author
> TATIANA LIBERMAN, her mother
> ALEXANDRE LIBERMAN, her stepfather
> BERTRAND DU PLESSIX, her father
> VLADIMIR MAYAKOVSKY, a Russian poet and Tatiana's lover
> MARLENE DIETRICH, a German actress and Liberman family friend

Clearly this saga of two larger-than-life characters and a daughter's unfulfilled
need for their attention makes for an engrossing, thought-provoking read. Rather than
merely chronicle long-forgotten ancestors, the narrative of *Them* dramatizes lives
transformed by revolution, war, and rapid social change. As demonstrated in works as
disparate as *At Home with the Marquis De Sade: A Life* (1998) and *Divine Disobedience: Profiles in Catholic Radicalism* (1970), author Francine du Plessix Gray is a
thorough researcher and master storyteller who excels in capturing the uniqueness of
her subjects as well as environmental factors shaping their personalities.

Focusing on European émigrés who made lasting marks on the clothing and publishing industries during the mid-twentieth century, she brings to life an almost forgotten cultural landscape. Tatiana Iacovleva du Plessix Liberman never lost her essential Russian-ness. Growing up in a family of artists and intellectuals left destitute
by the Bolshevik Revolution, she recited poetry on street corners in her early teens in
return for edible handouts from Red Army soldiers. She contracted tuberculosis during the famine year of 1922 and three years later at age nineteen moved to Paris to live
with Uncle Sasho (a charismatic artist and explorer), Aunt Sandra (a gifted opera
singer), and a loving but strict grandmother, Sofia Petrovna Iacovleva, called Ba-
bushka. After a steamy romance with famed Russian poet Vladimir Mayakovsky,
who considered her his muse and eventually committed suicide, she married a less exotic suitor, Bertrand du Plessix, and gave birth to her only child nine months and two
days later. After catching her husband with another woman, she took up with a Russian émigré six years her junior, Alexandre Liberman.

∽

*Francine du Plessix Gray, a
frequent contributor to* The New
Yorker, *excels at writing both
fiction and nonfiction. Especially
recommended are her books* World
Without End *(1981)* Hawaii: The
Sugar-Coated Fortress *(1972), and*
Simone Weil *(2001).*

∽

Alex, just five in 1917, retained vivid memories of street demonstrations, red flags, and likenesses of the czar burning in effigy. His father, Simon, though not a Bolshevik, was a trusted functionary in Vladimir Lenin's regime. In charge of harvesting the state's timber, he traveled abroad on trade missions and received permission to enroll Alex in an English boarding school (where he picked up a slight accent that he retained all of his life). After Simon fell out of favor following Lenin's death, the family moved to France. Alex became the first Jew to attend Les Roches, a private school where he excelled at rugby.

His mother, Henrietta, was emotionally immature and embarrassingly licentious well into her middle age. Stressed over impending exams and Henrietta's nagging, Alex almost died of bleeding ulcers; for the rest of life he could only eat bland food. During the harrowing months following the fall of France in 1940, Alex, Tatiana, and Francine were in frequent danger before fleeing to the United States. The two-week voyage took place in January, 1941, in the dead of winter. Meeting the *Carvalho Araujo* was Tatiana's biological father, Alexis Evgenevich Iacovleff, who had divorced her mother when Tatiana was nine. Once an inveterate gambler and vagabond, he had remarried, taken the name Al Jackson, and settled into a routine production job at Kodak in Rochester, New York. Unbeknown to Francine, her mother had decided to send her off with this complete stranger until she and Alex got settled in New York City.

Meanwhile, Tatiana found employment at Saks Fifth Avenue. Before long she was presiding over a millinery salon in the fashionable department store. Dubbed "Countess Tatiana" (she always had a weakness for titles), she deliberately refrained from learning proper English because, as her boss Adam Gimbel claimed, her exotic speech would sell more hats. Her keen sales sense stemmed in part from the certitude of her opinions. She would tell most customers, "Thee sees hat for you" rather than let them select. Underneath a veneer of bravado and garrulousness lurked shyness and insecurity. She never once, for instance, asked Gimbel for a raise.

Alex had no such reticence. Having worked at the French periodical *Vu*, he found a job in *Vogue*'s art department and soon was designing its covers, sometimes displaying Tatiana's hats. In rapid order he took charge of *Vogue* and eventually mogul Condé Nast's entire publishing empire. Nicknamed the Silver Fox, he was particularly adept at ingratiation but could be deliberately cruel to underlings. One victim was Diana Vreeland, once his rival at *Harper's Bazaar*. Parenthetically, Alex's professional career does not figure into the narrative as much as one might expect, given its historic importance, but others have covered that ground in books Gray cites in her endnotes.

A 70th Street brownstone became home to the Libermans beginning in December of 1942, finally offering a semblance of permanence. Alex, though unfailingly deferential to Tatiana, ran the household. Servants performed the mundane tasks. Francine's favorite was cook Mabel Moses, who taught her a love of black music by whisking her off to the Savoy Ballroom in Harlem. Unable to converse meaningfully with Tatiana, Francine made Alex her confidant. He clearly enjoyed that role, just as he relished, Gray recalled, "being both my mother's Superman and the absolute slave of her whims." Every few months Tatiana would exclaim, "Didn't we have the luck of the devil finding him?"

Francine often sat silently as her mother stared into a dressing table mirror, scrutinizing herself and applying makeup with great deliberation. In fact, that is how she designed her millinery creations (thirty for the spring season, thirty for the fall). Alex went through a similar grooming ritual with his mustache, which the author regarded as "a dual token of his asexuality and his often Byzantine slyness." Alex bragged about being monogamous despite temptations readily available to one so powerful. One suspects he may not have been as asexual as his stepdaughter imagined, just as it stretches credulity to imagine Tatiana a virgin on her wedding night, as she claimed.

Francine's first serious trauma resulted from her not being told of her father's death; Tatiana eventually delegated that task to someone else. Being exiled to Rochester upon arrival in the United States was another jolt. When Tatiana and Alex got married in 1942, they neglected to invite the twelve-year-old Francine to the ceremony. On weekends and holidays they preferred the company of friends to time alone with her. More days than not, they left her in the care of baby-sitters while pursuing their social climbing. Saturdays were usually given over to marathon high-stake bridge, canasta, and backgammon games. Christmastime meant a party for a hundred guests and hand-wrapping presents for each.

On rare occasions the threesome patronized the Horn and Hardart automat, where Francine loved selecting food items displayed behind glass in chrome coin-operated machines. When she broke her leg in Colorado, her mother and stepfather called twice a week but did not visit her in the hospital. When Francine was sixteen, Tatiana encouraged her to date a twenty-eight-year-old drunken Russian aristocrat (again displaying her weakness for titles) and insisted on selecting Francine's first formal dress. "I pliantly acquiesce[d]," the author explained about the hated gown, "for her love has been so hard-won that the smallest confrontation could destroy it." Oblivious to her daughter's embarrassment, Tatiana compared a friend's raincoat to a contraceptive. In 1976 Gray got a measure of revenge by publishing a fictionalized memoir called *Lovers and Tyrants*. "How could you?" her mother exclaimed, then added, "Tell the truth this way?" Becoming a successful writer liberated Francine from her parents' emotional grip, although researching *Them* brought back vivid memories, including one when she was fifteen near their summer cottage in Stony Brook, Long Island.

So the three of us trooped toward the bulrushes, and Alex loaded his film as I took off my bathing suit, feeling, at that particular moment vaguely offended. Was this *right*? Was it *honorable* of any mom and dad to photograph their daughter stark naked on the beach? What would Aunt Nada and Uncle Pat think of this? What if someone outside the family were to see these shots? . . . Once my clothes were off and Alex started shooting, my parents grew particularly solicitous and tender. "Are you all right, are you comfortable?" Alex asked. "You look ravishing," Mother exclaimed.

The author never reflected on the incident until she stumbled upon the nude photos a half-century later. Even then, she could only speculate about her parents' motivation. While they were connoisseurs of pornography, their behavior was more chaste than smarmy, as if they were aesthetically admiring a prized possession. They offered to disrobe themselves if that would make Francine more comfortable. She demurred; after all, it was one of those rare moments when she had their undivided attention. In fact, the emotion she felt upon baring all was more pride than embarrassment. Francine felt a similar elation dancing for Alex's father, Simon, a disciple of Nikolai Berdyaev, who believed in a benevolent Divine Will and the ideal of an egalitarian society. On Thursday afternoons they would converse and then play Russian folk music on the Victrola. Francine would transform herself into a "fiery gypsy," twirling a scarf and whirling around the study while Simon stomped his feet and shouted, "Faster! Faster!"

As they grew older, Tatiana and Alex displayed accentuated character flaws. Callously dumped by Saks after custom-made hats became less profitable, Tatiana became dependent on drugs, especially Demerol, and drank so heavily that she created scenes. Alex would bring home dirty movies, and Tatiana would announce that they were retiring to watch the "ah-ah girls," a reference to the panting porn stars.

Once his position at Condé Nast Publications was secure, Alex put most of his creative energies into being an artist and sculptor and had no scruples about using his clout to publicize and market his work. Both Tatiana and Alex commonly cut off friends for whom the couple no longer had use; still it was a shock when after his wife's death, Alex "excised my family out of his life," Gray writes, with "surgical meanness." For years she believed her stepfather to be the nicest man she had ever met. She had experienced guilt feelings that loving her stepfather was a mark of disloyalty to her real father. Alex, however, turned from a doting to an indifferent grandfather, no longer wanted Francine's friends around, and sold the brownstone and valuables without consulting her. He married Filipino nurse Melinda Pechangco, who stroked his vanity until his self-absorption reached new heights. An Annie Leibovitz photo of them kissing appeared in a 1993 issue of *Vanity Fair*, one of many illustrations interspersed throughout the book that illuminate the Libermans' glamorous lifstyle as well as the ravages of old age.

While Gray's parents were described by some reviewers to be dreadful monsters, her book conveys some excitement at being the daughter of people whose acquaintances included artist Salvador Dalí, designer Christian Dior, and actress Claudette Colbert, plus a plentiful supply of friends, relatives, surrogate parents, and servants who fawned over her. She lived with Justin and Patricia Greene while attending a private school near Greenwich Village. In contrast to her parents, the Greenes were a model, she notes dryly, for "life-as-it-should-be" (at least in the eyes of a neglected kid).

It is a tribute to Gray's talents that minor characters vividly spring to life. The Marlene Dietrich vignettes are gems. Once the actress leaned over while cooking, and Francine noticed that she had nothing on under a cotton shirt but a tampon string dangling between her famous legs. Sometimes Dietrich attended parties looking like a dominatrix in a nursemaid's uniform she normally wore while with her grandchildren in Central Park. Gray's announced intention in writing of her parents was to strike a balance between ruthless severity and compassionate tenderness, traits, she concluded, that "were at the heart of my mother's own character." She hoped to excise painful personal memories and record for posterity not just Tatiana's appalling side but her admirable hospitality toward both scions of fashion and needy Russian-born hangers-on. Addressing her deceased mother, she intoned: "Despite your cowardice, your deceitfulness, your arrogance, what force and shrewdness and power of survival you passed on to me!"

Chief among the memoir's many merits is its unhesitating self-criticism. A *Publishers Weekly* reviewer praised it as "an instructive model on how to write a difficult book honestly." If the author resented not being the center of her parents' universe, she provides ample proof that in their own peculiar way they adored her. Once a woman slapped young Francine, and Tatiana hit her back, saying, "No one slaps my daughter's face!" "What a good time we had together," Gray quips, "whenever they gave me time!"

James B. Lane

Review Sources

Booklist 101, no. 16 (April 15, 2005): 1426.
Kirkus Reviews 73, no. 4 (February 15, 2005): 209-210.
The New York Times 154 (May 10, 2005): E6.
The New York Times Book Review 154 (May 29, 2005): 8.
People 63 (May 30, 2005): 45.
Publishers Weekly 252, no. 10 (March 7, 2005): 58.
Time 165 (May 23, 2005): 75.

THIS I BELIEVE
An A to Z of a Life

Author: Carlos Fuentes (1928-   )
First published: En esto creo, 2002, in Mexico
Translated from the Spanish by Kristina Cordero
Publisher: Random House (New York). 331 pp.
   $27.00
Type of work: Essays
Time: 1600-2005

A finely wrought collection of short personal and political essays, presented alphabetically, on Fuentes's musings about everything from Amor to Zurich

Principal personages:
   ANNA AKHMATOVA (1889-1966), a Russian poet persecuted by Joseph Stalin
   LUIS BUÑUEL (1900-1983), a French filmmaker, innovator of Surrealist cinema
   FRANZ KAFKA (1883-1924), a Czech novelist
   HONORÉ DE BALZAC (1799-1850), a French novelist
   WILLIAM FAULKNER (1897-1962), an American novelist
   MILAN KUNDERA, Czech novelist, Fuentes's friend
   SILVIA LEMUS, Fuentes's second wife
   CARLOS FUENTES LEMUS, Fuentes's son, who died of hemophilia-related complications
   OCTAVIO PAZ, a Mexican writer, social critic, and Fuentes's contemporary

Carlos Fuentes has been called Mexico's greatest living novelist. As a distinguished essayist, novelist, diplomat, and scholar, Fuentes is well-versed in myriad subjects. Although *This I Believe* defies easy categorization, it is a work of tremendous maturity and wisdom. Equal parts memoir, political manifesto, and literary criticism, *This I Believe* is also a work of daring, with a bravura in its insights that only one of Fuentes's stature can pull off successfully. Fuentes, a child of diplomats, was raised in Mexico and the United States. Since the 1930's he has witnessed fascism, totalitarianism, democratization, and terrorism, all with the discerning and compassionate eye of a genuinely universal being.

In these forty-two essays, Fuentes takes on, without hesitation, subjects that range as far and wide in their scope as might a global circumnavigation. The essays cover reminiscences about his amorous exploits in "Sex," where Fuentes calls his earlier self "a passenger of sex, a privileged but fleeting actor amongst a circle of beautiful women," and explorations into the larger world of love. In "Amor," he displays his ability to see love metaphorically, as in this opening:

In Yucatan, you never see the water. It flows underground, beneath a fragile sheath of earth and limestone. Occasionally, that delicate Yucatec skin blossoms in eyes of water, in liquid ponds—the *cenotes*—that attest to the existence of a mysterious subterranean current. For me, love is like those hidden rivers . . .

Love is not only the romantic, gentle kind; it can also be the "love of evil." Fuentes writes: "I do not doubt . . . that [Adolf] Hitler loved Germany. But in *Mein Kampf*, he made it clear that the notion of loving his country was inseparable from the hatred of all those things he perceived to be at odds with Germany." Here, Fuentes recognizes that all things human, even that most powerful emotion of love, have multiple meanings and dark underbellies to them.

In "Children," he moves from the political and public to the deeply personal, in this case, the tragic loss of his son, Carlos Fuentes Lemus (to whom he dedicates this book). While he writes of his other children, daughters Cecilia and Natasha, it is upon his son, Carlos, he focuses most of his attention. Carlos was born a hemophiliac, and "from a very early age, he had to receive injections of the coagulating agent he lacked." His childhood was punctuated with pain, though he pursued painting, then later photography and po-

The son of diplomats, Carlos Fuentes was raised in Mexico and the United States, has served as Mexican ambassador to France, and is acting professor-at-large at Brown University. He was awarded France's Legion of Honor and was the first recipient of the Latin Civilization Award, presented by the presidents of Brazil, Mexico, and France. His novels include La muerte de Artemio Cruz *(1962;* The Death of Artemio Cruz, *1964),* Terra nostra *(1975; English translation, 1976), and* Gringo viejo *(1985;* The Old Gringo, *1985).*

etry. In this essay, Fuentes includes one of his son's poems and describes how he and his wife were left "with the reality of all that is indestructible."

It is in the very intertwining of the personal with the political that Fuentes impresses with his fearlessness. In "Friendship," he looks back on his "gang," his *chorcha* in grammar school. He remembers one boy whom he defended against bullying because of the boy's physical deformities. This boy later, as a man, was tortured to death under Chilean dictator Augusto Pinochet's regime. "It is a time for a return to friendship but with the knowledge that friendship demands cultivation on a daily basis if it is to bear its marvelous fruits." Fuentes sees true friendship as "dignified modesty," as a comfortable embracing of shared silence. He recalls learning through famed filmmaker Luis Buñuel the value of silence between friends. "Eventually," he states, "I realized that knowing how to be together without saying a word was, ultimately, a superior form of friendship."

The essay "God" takes the form of a dialogue between two unidentified voices, arguing either for or against the existence of God. The dialogue is cleverly antagonistic and rhetorical, with exchanges about the big bang theory ("Do you mean to say that

God inhabited the Universe before the Big Bang, and then, one day, for a little fun, ordered a . . . universal explosion, knowing that everything would end, not in some kind of final explosion but in one final sob?") In "God," Fuentes breathlessly references poet T. S. Eliot; philosopher Friedrich Nietzche; artist Gianlorenzo Bernini; the Aztec God of Wind, Ehecatl; and British poet John Milton. Interestingly, the author considers himself an agnostic, and so the writing of both "God" and "Christ" came as a surprise to him.

One of the challenges in reading *This I Believe* is keeping up with Fuentes's expansive references to other writers, as well as philosophers, politicians, revolutionaries, scientists, and luminaries from other fields. The effect is one of authority, but the book also fosters an appreciation of the work of a Renaissance man with far-reaching tastes and interests. Through his facility with such a broad range of subjects, he models what it means to be a citizen of the world, not an isolated, ignorant victim of others more powerful or better informed. Fuentes, however, is not one to look down upon the uneducated or upon those uninvited to the great banquet of globalization. "Mexico" is a love letter to his native country. "And so I return to the kingdom of small things in Mexico because they are the greatest . . . the modesty of an artisan, the pride of a cook. The melancholy of a singer and the cry of a rebel. The discretion of lovers. The inborn courtesy of good Mexicans." He exalts the "beautiful and the steadfast," while denouncing "the toxic progression of the ugly—the garbage, chaos of the city." In the end, he sees Mexico as a phoenix rising from its own ashes.

Fuentes insists on political responsibility and activism. As a Latin American, he feels profound outrage at the atrocities of the United States government in the name of democracy and freedom. In "Globalization," one of the most important essays in the collection, he insists that

> Charity begins at home, and the first thing that we must ask ourselves, as Latin Americans, is this: what resources do we have to establish the foundations for a progress that, beginning with the local village, will allow us to eventually become active agents and not passive victims of rapid-fire global movement?

He views globalization as a highly volatile phenomenon. It tears asunder developing nations, furthering impoverishing the poor while empowering the already too powerful. "Tribalism. Reductive, chauvinistic nationalism. Xenophobia. Racial and cultural prejudices. Religious fundamentalism. Fratricidal wars." Here lie the dangers of globalization without respect to differences, to the potential of local action.

Fuentes's literary influences are evidenced in such essays as "Faulkner," "Balzac," "Shakespeare," and "Kafka," in which he not only sings these writers' praises but places their work within the greater context of literary, social, and political theory. Take, for example, in "Kafka," the following statement: "The Kafkaesque 'hero' only wishes to be embraced by power. But by subjecting himself to it, he unwittingly scratches at its mask. He reveals the arbitrary basis upon which power rests thanks to his clumsiness, not his intelligence."

Recognition of the individual's relative powerlessness underscores other, more overtly political essays on Fuentes's profound commitment to the rights of all people, regardless of position. In "Novel," the author explores the interrelationship between literature and history. History gives birth to the novel, while the novel allows the individual to see history "in a clearer light, so that we may be authentically historical." He sees, through the rich lens of the novel, humanity as inherently incomplete. The novel, and thus literature, offers common ground for those "greatest" values which humans share with one another.

"Urbanities" is Fuentes's unabashed declaration of love for cities. He proclaims, "I love cities. Nature makes me too anxious." Paris, Venice, Prague, and Cambridge are among his favorites, cities to which he returns over the decades to dine with old friends or stroll along beloved boulevards. Paris is "where beauty and life coalesce so perfectly," where he feels he lived most fully. It is where his son, Carlos, was born, a city where little changes, immortalized by novelist Marcel Proust, chanteuse Edith Piaf, and poet Guillaume Apollinaire. Fuentes pledges his allegiance to those cities that bore witness to his intellectual growth, his education, and coming-of-age as a young man. He then turns to the post-September 11, 2001, New York City, believing that "no one can destroy the energy of New York." Though he declares a preference for cities over nature, Fuentes ends this essay with a plea for more cognition of maintaining the balance between nature and urban life so that future generations are not condemned to a life without nature.

As a lifelong advocate of education, Fuentes includes "Reading" as the "R" entry. For him, reading goes beyond a private act of intellectual pleasure or edification. The ability to read is nothing less than the elevation of a culture. He makes a distinction between libraries within the "purely oral culture, inside the head of an Indian, and the memory of a postmodern, post-Communist, postcapitalist, posteverything suprayuppie." He goes on to point out that both groups still possess the ability to choose "between silence and voice, memory, and oblivion, movement and paralysis, life and death," for the absence of stories and suppression of the creative imagination is a deadly form of paralysis. "The global village of mass communication" Fuentes writes of can be a tool for enlightenment or cause for fear and tyranny. He emphasizes the necessity for compassion, for casting a discerning eye on the media, and for remaining vigilant against oppression.

This fine compendium of essays concludes with "Zebra" and "Zurich." The former begins with a tribute to the zebra, then veers off into the sightings of fantastic creatures such as mermaids, the guitar-fish, "capable of sinking an entire ship with its mighty horn," and the denizens of fantastic literature such as Dracula ("who fornicates without love"), Frankenstein, and finally, Kafka's character Gregor Samsa, who awakens one morning to find himself transformed into a cockroach. The conclusion of the last essay cements Fuentes's place in literary history as one who can write with genuine depth on just about anything. In the twilight of his life, Fuentes looks courageously back at past loves, past victories, past mistakes with an endearing and empowering tenderness.

Nika Hoffman

Review Sources

Booklist 101, no. 8 (December 15, 2004): 690.
Kirkus Reviews 72, no. 24 (December 15, 2004): 1180-1181.
Library Journal 130, no. 4 (March 1, 2005): 84.
The New York Times Book Review 154 (June 12, 2005): 28.
Publishers Weekly 252, no. 2 (January 10, 2005): 46.
The Times Literary Supplement, November 19, 2004, p. 37.
The Washington Post Book World, January 30, 2005, p. 15.

THIS IS A VOICE FROM YOUR PAST
New and Selected Stories

Author: Merrill Joan Gerber (1938-   )
Publisher: Ontario Review Press (Princeton, N.J.).
  219 pp. $24.00
Type of work: Short fiction
Time: From the 1950's to 2005
Locale: Boston, Las Vegas, and California

Thirteen stories tell of middle-class life, focusing primarily on family and relationships, all narrated from a female point of view

Merrill Joan Gerber has published seven novels for adults, nine for young adults, three nonfiction works, and now *This Is a Voice from Your Past*, her sixth collection of short stories. In spite of this output and numerous awards, her work is little-known. One might speculate that she has been unfairly cast as a "women's writer" because many of her stories first appeared in *Redbook*, or because such works frequently touch on domestic issues. Whatever the cause, it would be nice to think that this will be Gerber's breakthrough book.

At least four of the stories collected here focus on the dynamics of family life and thus represent a large portion of Gerber's work. "Latitude" and "Approval" concern the same couple, Martha and Will. In "Latitude," the young couple endures Sunday dinner with Will's parents, Edna and Harry, who fiercely opposed their son's marrying Martha, claiming that she was unfit for him. At last they have grudgingly accepted the union, but old tensions and oppositions linger, despite the granddaughter who has helped mollify them. Will remains resentful and expresses his anger in sullen passive aggressiveness. The rift has narrowed slowly by a series of gestures: Martha's cutting Edna's hair, ritual Sunday dinners, Harry's desperate search for a screwdriver to lend Will, and finally a parting hug and kiss shared by the two women.

In "Approval" Martha's parents visit her and Will, and Will is again aloof and preoccupied. Tension and disapproval lurk just beneath the surface when a homeless man comes to the door asking for work. Will's polite treatment of the "bum" unleashes abuse from Martha's father, who, it turns out, briefly deserted his family during the Depression. When Will mysteriously disappears, her father's warnings about the dangers of "bums" make Martha's hands tremble with fear. Will returns shortly, having left only long enough to give the homeless man their leftovers, but this gesture provokes further attack. Finally, Martha can stand no more: She accuses her father of leaving because he did not want his family, whereas Will wants his. Then, however, she reaches out with a consoling word, reminding her father that he did return—and letting her insights into her parents' bitter marriage pass unsaid.

*Merrill Joan Gerber has
received numerous awards for
her short fiction, including the
Andrew Lytle Fiction Prize, an
O. Henry Award for "I Don't
Believe This," a Pushcart Prize
for* King of the World *(1990),
and the Harold U. Ribalow Prize
for fiction in English on a Jewish
subject. She teaches creative
writing at the California
Institute of Technology.*

"We Know That Your Hearts Are Heavy" and "A Daughter of My Own" feature Janet and Danny, a couple very similar to Martha and Will. "A Daughter of My Own" centers on an archetypal mother-daughter conflict—the birth of the first grandchild and the mother's offer of help. Unfortunately, mother takes over, so much so that her presence in the tiny apartment becomes oppressive. Janet finally explodes, forcing her mother to leave early. The parting scene at the airport is touching and complicated, with Danny holding the baby for the first time and Janet trying desperately to reassure her mother that she loves her.

Far more complicated is "We Know That Your Hearts Are Heavy," which describes an extended family during the only occasion to rival a wedding for turmoil—a funeral. Janet's rich Uncle Benny has died, and predictably, old arguments and wounds surface. Gerber skillfully depicts family members getting on one another's nerves as seven people sleep in a one-bedroom apartment. No one sleeps well; breakfast is a disaster. Afterward, talk turns to Benny's estate and the promises he made to two poor relations—but there is no will, and none of Benny's good intentions will be realized.

These stories honestly depict the complicated, maddening, angry, and occasionally consoling institution known as the family. Gerber unflinchingly probes family dynamics, how resentments linger, anger boils over, expectations sour. Like the pigeons vying for shelter on the window ledge outside Janet's office, members crowd one another, jockey for position, make room, fly off, return. Gerber offers no solutions, allows no cheap sentiment, gives no assurances that today's truce will result in peace, but the family is affirmed. If that is "women's writing," then readers need more of it.

Failed or doomed relationships are dramatized in "Cleopatra Birds" and "Honeymoon" and suggested in "See Bonnie & Clyde Death Car." In all three, the women characters betrayed by men absent even when physically present. In "Cleopatra Birds," the husband, Davy, cares more about fishing and raising birds than for his wife. She, a student of African dance, eventually leaves with her African lover, buying Davy a pair of rare Cleopatra pheasants—a symbol of their mutual betrayal. "Honeymoon" is an emotionally complex study of a doomed marriage—a young woman drawn to an older man by his maturity and confidence. From the beginning the reader perceives that Rand's interest in Cheryl is sexual and monetary; she is his shill at the blackjack tables. His wedding gift to her is a pair of cheap "love light" earrings that, poignantly, do not show up in her "wedding photo," a Polaroid taken of her alone by a young couple she meets on her solitary trip to Hoover Dam.

Gerber successfully portrays the emotional complexity of her narrators, using the tension in their voices, the fibs they tell themselves, and telling metaphors, objective correlatives of their inner condition. Lynn in "See Bonnie & Clyde Death Car" is typical. Having vowed never to visit Las Vegas again, she finds herself there with Phil, hoping the nickel slots will affirm her desperate pursuit of luck, that Phil will find happiness, that the two of them will always be together. Gerber skillfully builds tension as Lynn loses steadily at the slots, empathizes with the pathetic desperation of a woman who leaves her wedding ring on a machine and does not return to claim it, and hysterically panics over the loss of her own purse. At the story's end, she and Phil admire Bonnie and Clyde's car—he because they lived dangerously, she because they died together in love. Their fate is left trembling at the end of the story.

"Tell Me Your Secret" and "My Suicides" are not entirely successful, perhaps because they depart from the emotional territory Gerber understands most deeply. "Tell Me Your Secret" is set amid the in loco parentis days of 1950's college life, when female students had strict curfews, and getting off campus overnight had to be arranged by lies. Against her better judgment, Fanny agrees to attend a party thrown by a faculty member, knowing that she is setting herself up for seduction. It is a defiant gesture, carried out despite the news of her grandmother's death. Perhaps too predictably, the dangers the college warned her about become real. "My Suicides" details the four suicides in the narrator's life, contrasting them a bit too obviously with the unsuccessful attempt by her aunt, which led only to a lingering death. Also obvious is the symbolism of a peahen and her chicks, apparently looking for the lost peacock. Intended as a symbol of the people abandoned by those who commit suicide, it is used too blatantly at the end.

The remaining four selections could be called horror stories but not in the Hollywood sense. These spring from the genuine terrors of life in the suburbs. "This Is a Voice from Your Past," begins with a phone call from a former classmate, the talented Ricky, who, their creative writing teacher asserted, was a genius. The narrator (Janet again), has carved out a modest career as a writer, enough so that thirty years later Ricky imposes himself on offers of assistance, ruthlessly deceiving, lying, betraying, accusing, and finally threatening until his very absence is an ominous presence. Gerber skillfully guides readers through the steps of this evolving nightmare, leaving them, like Janet, in a state of paranoid suspense.

"I Don't Believe This" opens with a macabre detail straight out of the news: Carol's husband's cremated remains had ended up a dumpster. The ashes she scattered could have belonged to anyone or anything, a fitting end for the ironically named Bard, whose life was a series of blunders, a bad joke that made him an abusive husband. Carol's sister, the narrator, had been caught in the middle when Carol and the children fled to a shelter, and Bard called daily to try to cajole, intimidate, or charm information from the narrator regarding their whereabouts. When Bard finally makes good his suicide threats, he leaves his wife in guilt-ridden relief. The story ends as strangely as it began: Carol's children use their father's clothes to make a dummy they hang from a tree for their Halloween display.

"Night Stalker" plays on the fears a serial killer arouses in Sylvie, an assistant in a hospital's leukemia research lab, who responds with cautionary maneuvers in response to news bulletins about the killer. She especially misses the dogs her husband took when they separated. At story's end, she buys a basset pup, not just for herself but also to cheer a leukemia victim who visits her lab. Death stalks the story, but the ending is anticlimactic.

Nothing is anticlimactic in "Dogs Bark," the most intense and horrific story in the collection. The narrator and her husband live next door to a family with three huge dogs that bark at the slightest provocation, or none at all, disturbing their academic lives, ruining sleep, destroying their love life, driving them to the edge of insanity. Gradually a war between the neighbors rises in pitch and intensity; attempts at understanding and compromise lead nowhere. The police are called, to no avail, for the law offers more protection to the dogs' owners than to the aggrieved neighbors, and reconciliation becomes impossible as a legal case waits in limbo and the narrator becomes increasingly frantic. Finally, resolution seems possible when the case comes to court, but the dog owners are fined a paltry one hundred dollars, and nothing in the settlement quiets the dogs or ends the other tortures—blaring radios, a demoniac sprinkler, the disappearance of the narrator's cats—that the dog owners inflict. In desperation, the couple takes matters into their own hands and poison the dogs, but after a two months of blissful peace, the barking returns. The neighbors have bought a huge, slavering mastiff.

This story is bone-chilling in its ever-rising tension. The reader feels the anger, frustration, injustice, and looming insanity that the characters experience. The smooth-talking neighbor becomes a demoniac figure, shmoozing the police, pretending to be reasonable, feigning reconciliation. Is he? Does the story have another side? Are the narrator and her husband the crazy ones, unreasonable in their expectations of quiet, unable to ignore a din that seems to bother no one else? The ambiguity of the situation, the incrementally rising tensions, the near hysteria that the narrator feels as the situation spins increasingly out of control create heart-pounding anxiety in the reader. Throughout, the "law is an ass," fueling the couple's rage and playing on the reader's suspicion that to become involved with the police and judiciary is to enter a Kafka-esque world of nightmare and hallucination. If anything, Gerber's irrational world is more real that Franz Kafka's bizarre allegories, for it springs not from a fevered imagination but from the suburban world known too well.

Here, then are thirteen stories to command a reader's attention and respect. Not all are of the highest quality, and four are reprints from previous collections, even though this is not a "best of" collection. This book is enjoyable not for its literary experiments or flashy technique but for its good, solid writing, flashes of metaphorical brilliance, and insights into the ordinary lives most of people live. Frank O'Connor's dictum that the short story deals with those on the margins of society is here proven inadequate. Normal lives, too, have their dramas, and Merrill Joan Gerber is their poet.

Dean Baldwin

Review Sources

Antioch Review 63, no. 3 (Summer, 2005): 598-599.
Booklist 101, no. 13 (March 1, 2005): 1136.
Kirkus Reviews 73, no. 2 (January 15, 2005): 71.

TOOTH AND CLAW
And Other Stories

Author: T. Coraghessan Boyle (1948-   )
Publisher: Viking Press (New York). 284 pp. $26.00
Type of work: Short fiction
Time: 2005, the 1920's, and 1702
Locale: New York's Hudson River Valley; Southern California; Isle of Unst, Scotland; suburban Connecticut; Godamuri and Midnapore, India; central Florida; Maine; Patagonia; New England

Most of the fourteen stories in this collection continue Boyle's darkly humorous exploration of contemporary American life, especially the reckless loves and addictions of klutzy young men, but a few stories venture wildly off into time, space, and other species

Principal characters:
"JIMMY," a generic-type troubled man in a bar
ROBBIE BAIKIE, a Scot who falls in love with a bird lady
JULIAN FOX, a married man who falls in love with a dog lady
THE REVEREND J. A. L. SINGH, the capturer of two wolf children in India
BOOMER, a disc jockey who challenges the record for going without sleep
ZACK, a risk-taker who takes a back road during a blizzard
JACKSON PETERS REILLY, a home buyer in a fancy Florida development
RAYMOND LEITNER, a young alcoholic sinking into homelessness
LESTER, a young man of many wrecks
BOB FERNANDO CASTILLO, a Patagonian sheep rancher
JAMES "JUNIOR" TURNER, the winner of a wild cat in a bar
SARAH KNIGHT, a traveler on horseback from Boston to New York
JOHN CADDIS, an eighth-grade teacher who gets involved with drugs

In ten novels and six previous collections of short fiction, T. Coraghessan Boyle has established himself as one of America's most imaginative and entertaining writers. He is especially noted for his breezy colloquial style, his satire of American fads and movements, and his dark sense of humor. His most enduring character type is the young, white, American male, a kind of loose cannon who speaks in his own voice, reveals his various shortcomings (which usually involve alcohol, drugs, or sex), and as often as not becomes his own worst enemy. Boyle's women characters, in contrast, tend to be intrepid and resourceful, showing few signs of ever having been repressed. These trademark attractions continue in *Tooth and Claw, and Other Stories*, Boyle's seventh collection of short stories, all of which have been previously published in leading magazines. Some of these fourteen stories push the imaginative horizon far

T. Coraghessan Boyle is the author of novels and collections of short stories. His novel World's End *(1987) won the PEN/Faulkner Award, and he received the 1999 PEN/Malamud Award for Excellence in Short Fiction.*

afield, ranging to other continents or centuries, examining relationships with other creatures, or taking dark humor to the verge of tragedy.

The collection gets off to an appropriate start with "When I Woke Up This Morning, Everything I Had Was Gone," which has a generic quality about it. The story, like two or three of the others, is set in a bar, specifically the bar at Jimmy's Steak House. The unnamed male narrator meets another man at the bar who seems to have been drinking nonstop for weeks or months. They introduce themselves, the other man consulting a sign for the bar and saying, "Just call me Jimmy." "Jimmy" then tells the narrator a horrific story that explains why he is drinking like a fish: His college-age son died in a fraternity hazing incident, forced to consume too much alcohol and then choking on his own vomit. The next week, the narrator meets another man in the same bar who he thinks is Jimmy's brother. The other man has another sad story to relate, this one about an alcoholic old woman, a family friend, who froze to death outside his front door. The narrator is a good listener to these twin tales of woe, but meanwhile he is nursing his own wounds. Despite its different strands, the story holds together remarkably well, the parallels, the generic name Jimmy, and the unifying elements of drink and the bar suggesting a common suffering humanity, even if, ironically, somewhat self-pitying and maudlin.

Other stories provide variations on these motifs. A number of stories feature sad sacks, men who have been around for a while but seem not to have gained much wisdom from their years. For example, another man who ends up crying in his scotch is Robbie Baikie, a big, hulking Unst Islander in "Swept Away": "The light of the westering sun . . . laid the glowing cross of our Saviour in the precise spot where Robbie's shoulder blades conjoined. He heaved a sigh then—a roaring, single-malt, tobacco-inflected groan it was, actually—and finally those massive shoulders began to quake and heave." Robbie's crucifixion comes from falling in love with a visiting American woman, an eager ornithologist who has near-perfect legs, face, and figure. He is saved from being swept away with her in a storm but not from the storm of remembrance that racks him daily as he "sits even now over his pint and his drop of whisky in the back nook at Magnuson's."

Robbie, the Shetland sheepman, is not as simple as some of the sad sacks in the other stories. In "The Kind Assassin," Boomer, a struggling disc jockey at KFUN, lets himself be talked into an on-air publicity stunt even sillier than his radio persona—trying to break the world's sleep-deprivation record. When he sets a new record, he cannot understand that the quest was only hype and, like Franz Kafka's hunger artist, wants to keep going. The biggest believer in hype, however, is Jackson Peters Reilly, a divorced snowbird who, in "Jubilation," buys property in an expensive central Florida housing development allied with a theme park. To market itself, the housing development draws on typical theme-park fantasies, using cartoon characters such as Gulpy Gator and Chowchy and giving its home models names such as Casual Contempos, Little Adobes, and Courteous Coastals. Jackson not only adopts the development's terminology but soon is trying to enforce its code restrictions on his neighbors. Reality, nonetheless, has a way of asserting itself, here in the form of mosquitoes, hurricanes, and other hazards of nature.

Still another group of stories centers on young men who are even dumber and hence dangerous to themselves and others. In the final story, "Up Against the Wall," recent college graduate John Gaddis moves back in with his parents (always a comedown). He finally finds a job in a miserable ghetto school teaching eighth-grade English but, to forget his daily battle, also gets involved with drugs and a bad crowd. When his mother saves him by confronting him with incriminating tape recordings, he feels trapped like his father, his life over. He could have ended up like Raymond, the homeless young man in "Here Comes" who is a slave to alcohol, who sees his homeless friends brutally murdered, and who crawls back to beg his disgusted girlfriend, who threw him out, to take him in again.

Another problem with these young men is that they are out to prove themselves and impress people, especially young women. In "All the Wrecks I've Crawled Out Of," which begins with the line "All I wanted, really, was to attain mythic status," young Lester brags throughout about his "wrecks both literal and figurative, replete with flames, blood, crushed metal and broken hearts, a whole swath of destruction and self-immolation, my own personal skid marks etched into the road of my life and maybe yours too."

In "The Swift Passage of the Animals," young Zach sets off for a weekend getaway at a mountain lodge with Ontario, a young divorcé he met three weeks before. Zach, who fancies himself a risk-taker, decides to impress her by taking a winding back road during a blizzard. Unfortunately, he proves to be like one of those animals on which Ontario is an expert, who became extinct through their stupidity. For the survival of the species, she gets a separate room at the lodge.

Animal behavior is also the focus of the collection's title story, "Tooth and Claw." Again, the story begins in a bar, where James "Junior" Turner, to impress the onlookers and especially Daria the waitress, is drawn into a game of Horse for a wild cat, an African serval. He wins, to the delight of Daria, who accompanies him home. "So," he thinks proudly, "I had a cat. And a girl." The phrasing has an ominous symbolic equivalence that reverberates through the rest of the story. What the wild cat does to his bedroom, where they turn it loose, is pretty much what Daria does to him. He begins to think of her as "a prime mover" in his life, but she spends only a couple of nights with him, announces that she has a regular boyfriend away at college, and says goodbye. He is left with a ripped-up bedroom and a raging wild creature with which—at the story's end—he comes to identify and tries to set free.

Animals play an important role in still other stories from the collection. Besides the ornithologist who is for the birds, a woman in "Dogology" is going to the dogs and entices a married neighbor, fittingly named Julian Fox, to accompany her. She is a graduate student whose thesis has been rejected by her committee, and she is determined to show them up with a groundbreaking study of dogs from the dogs' perspective, running with the pack on all fours, howling at the moon, and helping protect the den. In separate sections of the story, her behavior is paralleled with that of wolf children from 1920's India. Like Boyle's epigraph from Charles Darwin and his title *Tooth and Claw*, the connections between humans and animals in these stories point to an underlying Darwinian nature of existence.

The ultimate Darwinian scenario is played out in "Chicxulub," which describes the extinction of dinosaurs caused by an asteroid or comet striking the earth. This earth-shaking event is used in the story as a metaphor for parental loss of a child, but the literal fact that such cosmic events could happen at any time and wipe out civilization is a bit rattling. However, in "Blinded by the Light" Boyle takes a similar premise and uses it to comic effect. Here "the sky is falling" in the form of cancer-causing rays coming through a hole in the ozone layer at the South Pole, or so says American expert John Longworth, Ph.D. He is preaching to Patagonia, Chile, whose proximity to the South Pole puts it in imminent danger. When he messes with the daughter of a Patagonian sheep rancher who comes after him with a gun, the expert temporarily puts his campaign to save the world on hold. Boyle's ability in these two stories to take a similar premise and argue it both ways is a measure of how he can stretch his imagination.

These two stories and others in the collection, such as "The Doubtfulness of Water: Madam Knight's Journey to New York, 1702," also show that Boyle does his research. The factual information in the stories, such as the big words Boyle sometimes slips in, rings true. His ability to insert himself and his readers into his settings, however remote, and to participate in the lives of his characters, however bizarre, shows that he can take almost any factual information and run with it the way a writer of fiction should.

Harold Branam

Review Sources

Booklist 101, nos. 19/20 (June 1, 2005): 1711.
Entertainment Weekly, September 16, 2005, pp. 94-95.
Kirkus Reviews 73, no. 12 (June 15, 2005): 650-651.
Library Journal 130, no. 12 (July 1, 2005): 74.
The New York Times Book Review 154 (September 11, 2005): 8.
The New Yorker 79, no. 34 (November 10, 2003): 106-115.
Publishers Weekly 252, no. 26 (June 27, 2005): 37.

TRAWLER
A Journey Through the North Atlantic

Author: Redmond O'Hanlon (1947-   )
Publisher: Alfred A. Knopf (New York). 339 pp. $25.00
Type of work: Natural history and travel
Time: 1998
Locale: Scrabster and Stromness, Scotland, and the Arctic region of the North Atlantic Ocean

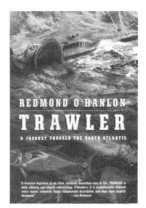

A middle-aged writer risks his life in order to fulfill a lifelong dream—shipping aboard a trawler in the North Atlantic in the hurricane season

Principal personages:
    REDMOND O'HANLON, an editor and travel writer with a zeal for some of the world's most inhospitable regions
    LUKE BULLOUGH, a biologist and doctoral student, Redmond's guide to the wonders of the ocean's depths
    JASON SCHOFIELD, the obsessive captain of the *Norlantean*

Although not nearly as old as the sea itself, literature about the ocean and its inhabitants has been part of written language from the very beginning. In the ancient world it ranged from Homer's *Odyssey* (c. 750 B.C.E.)—where its implacable hero meets grueling terrors on his voyage home—to the biblical story of Jonah, whose spate of ill fortune would become an epithet for any sailor associated with bad luck. In more recent times, the literature of the sea has expressed itself in forms both real and imagined. There are innumerable published accounts of ocean voyages and the transformative effect of the sea upon writers; the best known and the one that virtually created its own genre is *Two Years Before the Mast* (1840) Richard Henry Dana, Jr.'s coming-of-age tale of life on the brig *Pilgrim*. Undeniably, there is something about the nature of water that ceaselessly inspires authors to write about it, beyond the fact that it is both a means of livelihood and a source of recreation.

It is common knowledge that water covers three-quarters of Earth's surface. Ironically, even as evolution reveals it to be the source of all life on the planet, it remains a region little understood and the last great unexplored frontier on earth. On or near the ocean's surface, plant organisms in this biological matrix manufacture much of the atmospheric oxygen that is so vital to life on earth. At or near the bottom of the ocean, however, roam creatures as strange as any to be found in science fiction. In this area of perpetual gloom, life thrives in the vicinity of volcanic vents, a region once deemed to be a biological void. Of more immediate importance, though, is the fact that, in an age of diminished arable land and a rising world population, the oceans represent an enormous and mostly unknown protein resource. It is this fact that forms the backdrop to Redmond O'Hanlon's book *Trawler: A Journey Through the North Atlantic*.

~

A much admired writer, Redmond O'Hanlon has proven his abilities in both literature and science. He is a fellow of the Royal Society of Literature and the Royal Geographical Society. O'Hanlon is best known for such travel books as Into the Heart of Borneo *(1984),* In Trouble Again *(1988), and* Congo Journey *(1996).*

~

O'Hanlon, who has fashioned a career by writing about his experiences in such inhospitable places as the Congo and the Amazon, would seem to be the ideal person to challenge the North Atlantic Ocean. Although he was once a member of an elite British military group known as the Special Boat Service, he also has a considerable reputation as a credentialed scholar. His doctoral thesis concerned the relationship between nature and Joseph Conrad's writings, and for fifteen years O'Hanlon served as the natural history editor of *The Times Literary Supplement*, one of the most distinguished literary publications in the English language. *Trawler*, unlike Dana's classic work, is not about a young man matching his physical prowess against the power of the sea. Indeed, O'Hanlon readily admits that he looks and feels every bit of his fifty-one years, and his frequent bouts of physical incapacity constitute the book's most humorous episodes. In a very real sense, *Trawler* is an ironic response to the usual firsthand account of a sea voyage.

Most such real-life narratives are solidly rooted in time and, as in Dana's book, are often presented as extended journal entries. Not so with O'Hanlon. Given the importance of this voyage, one would think that, at its inception, he would inform the reader as to the precise date that he boarded the *Norlantean*, the ship that figures so prominently in his tale. Instead, it is casually revealed in an aside that the trip takes place during a cold January somewhere north of Scotland. Rarely does the author clearly distinguish one day from the next. While Luke Bullough, the biologist-crewman and doctoral student who serves as O'Hanlon's guide, states that a trawler is expected to return to port after ten days with a full hold, fouled gear forces O'Hanlon's vessel to return with less than a full load. O'Hanlon has stated in an interview that the entire voyage lasted two weeks, something one would be hard-pressed to find by reading his text.

Why is the author so coy regarding time frames in a genre that is usually constituted by them? Given his literary credentials, one can only conclude that this was a conscious choice on O'Hanlon's part, and one that addresses two time-related issues that come into play in the book. When Dana came to write his narrative, he was attempting to describe the Herculean tasks performed by himself and his fellow crew members during an epic twenty-four-month excursion. In the modern, mechanized merchant fleet, a voyage of such length would be both impractical and unprofitable. A trip lasting several weeks aboard a fishing trawler can never compare to a lengthy voyage around Cape Horn, with its repeated scenes of exhausted men struggling with sodden canvas in raging seas.

Life is not shown to be much safer on O'Hanlon's trawler than it was on the old square riggers, especially when captains such as the one who commands the *Norlantean* are so far in debt that they are willing to put both vessel and crew in the path of hurricanes. It is for this reason that trawler fishing has the highest mortality rate of any industry in Britain. O'Hanlon emphasizes the fact that the goal of a trawler captain is to fill the hold of his or her vessel with as much marketable fish in as little time as possible, a practice that results in relatively brief but intense voyages measured in weeks. O'Hanlon accentuates the effectiveness of his narrative by diminishing any discussion of the length of the voyage and by introducing a wealth of material in reference to that narrow time frame. Another significant reason for this approach is the fact that O'Hanlon is reprising in text the very process enacted on every trawler voyage: Crew members do not sleep until a haul of fish is gutted and packed. The more successful a voyage is, the more captain and crew must work.

Jason Schofield, the obsessive captain of the *Norlantean*, is motivated to keep his crew busy in order to pay off his two-million-pound debt. In an industry where one may only manage to sleep three hours in every thirty-six, the distinction between one day and the next—or even between night and day—has little significance. O'Hanlon recognizes this and cleverly enhances his narrative by carefully deploying text as a means of reflecting this aspect of trawler life. Rather than simply describe the enervating effects of sleep deprivation upon himself and his fellow crewmen, he demonstrates this by liberally quoting his shipboard conversations.

At the beginning of the voyage, O'Hanlon presents a fairly straightforward description of the crewmen and his interactions with them. From them, he learns how they cope with the ever-present dangers of the sea, the uncertainty of being able to survive by it, and the separation from loved ones that the occupation demands. Toward the end of the trip, however, O'Hanlon and his young mentor lose all restraint in their conversations as sleep deprivation loosens their tongues, a fact observed by O'Hanlon himself: "Because right now I'd say anything! Anything! I can't stop! I've *never* felt like this before: the boss, the organizer, you know, the internal *tough guy* that we sometimes resent but always obey, the Mister Big who directs our thoughts, Luke—he's gone! He's ceased to exist!"

One should exercise some caution when reading these extensive conversations, which make up much of the book's text. It strains one's credulity to accept what O'Hanlon offers as the verbatim talks he had with the crewmen. Unless he somehow recorded every conversation or is gifted with a perfect memory—which seems unlikely—then one must conclude that these are reconstructions based upon imagination and memory. These dialogues are artfully crafted, and this is reinforced by the fact that in the one just quoted the ebb and flow of the conversation mirrors the storm raging outside: long swelling rhapsodies are occasionally broken by short sentences or spasmodic interjections.

This literary quality is also suggested by the fact that O'Hanlon adopts a peculiar persona for the book, one that plays down his physical and rhetorical skills. Thus, when he is entered into the ship's books as a neophyte crewman, he spends more time describing his bout with nausea than he does the ship itself. This is no doubt a reflection of his actual experience. Seasickness is an almost universal phenomenon in such tumultuous seas and one that seriously threatens the success of the voyage. If he became too ill, the captain would be forced to return to port. The fact that O'Hanlon is reduced to the helplessness of a newborn also suggests a literary association, an ironic allusion to the notion of rebirth. Indeed, he describes himself as "dribbling like a baby." O'Hanlon's physical weakness and his tendency to daydream fuse into a kind of shipboard persona, one the crew christens "Worzel." It is an allusion to a rather dimwitted character from British television. He is far removed from the ex-warrior and published scholar, the twin qualities that helped secure his position on the vessel. O'Hanlon presents himself a kind of befuddled Walter Mitty, one who has suddenly found himself in the most frightening of all nightmares: realizing the hazards of actually living his most treasured fantasies. It is an effective device, for O'Hanlon has passed the threshold into a strange new world full of deep-sea monsters that have only recently come to the attention of science.

While Luke's nominal position on the vessel is to gather data on the life cycle and distribution of different species of fish for commercial purposes, he as a scientist is in the enviable position of being at the leading edge of his profession. A crewman's belief that a fish called the black butt is breeding in an area known as Hatton bank may seem trivial to most readers, but Luke immediately seizes upon it. By determining how and where such creatures breed, the fishing industry can better realize a sustainable yield: harvesting enough of a particular species of fish to make it commercially viable while at the same time ensuring that enough remain for the future. In an age of diminished food sources, such research is vital.

What makes *Trawler* such an enthralling experience is how well O'Hanlon communicates the thrill of discovery in the ocean's depths. There is the Greenland shark, whose flesh is so poisonous that Icelandic fishermen must bury it before it can be eaten, or the distended features of such oddities as rabbit fish or the roughhead grenadier. O'Hanlon's well-chosen photographs illustrate far better than any description how different life must be in order to survive kilometers below the surface. Although O'Hanlon only proved to be a middling crewman, his evocation of contemporary life at sea succeeds admirably. *Trawler: A Journey Through the North Atlantic* is nearly as engrossing as the ocean itself.

Cliff Prewencki

Review Sources

Booklist 101, nos. 9/10 (January 1-15, 2005): 805.
The Economist 369 (November 22, 2003): 83.
Kirkus Reviews 72, no. 22 (November 15, 2004): 1082.
The New York Times Book Review 154 (January 23, 2005): 20.
Publishers Weekly 251, no. 47 (November 22, 2004): 49.
Science 305 (August 27, 2004): 1242.
The Spectator 293, no. 9144 (November 8, 2003): 66-67.
The Times Literary Supplement, November 7, 2003, p. 12.

THE TROUBLE WITH POETRY
And Other Poems

Author: Billy Collins (1941-   )
Publisher: Random House (New York). 88 pp. $23.00
Type of work: Poetry

Collins's poems celebrate the world and all of its beauties, including poetry, jazz, and daily life, while they recognize mortality

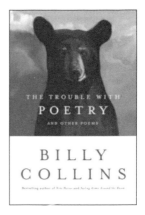

The Trouble with Poetry is Billy Collins's seventh collection of poems, his first since he completed his tenure as United States Poet Laureate in 2003. One of the special projects he instituted during his laureate was "Poetry 180," an effort to engage high schools in daily readings of American poems. In his Internet notes to the project, he urges schools to recruit a variety of readers ranging from faculty and staff to students, and not just students with literary bents. He also encourages schools not to turn the poems into assignments in analysis; instead he suggests that the project should simply offer young people something they rarely experience—the pleasure of hearing an accessible poem, one read simply for the sake of pleasing its hearers. Although "Poetry 180" is aimed at high schools, its goals might well represent Collins's overall poetic goals as they are translated into the poems he writes, poems which celebrate the beauties of the quotidian—the things he loves, ranging from jazz to poetry, to the look of the lawn from the kitchen window. Implicit in his work is the idea that readers may enjoy these things as well, particularly if the poem nudges readers into noticing their beauty. This is why, in the introduction to his collection *The Apple That Astonished Paris* (1988), he teasingly protested those who would to "tie the poem to a chair with rope/ and torture a confession out of it."

Thus the poems in *The Trouble with Poetry* will seem like pleasantly familiar ground to Collins's fans; they offer his direct language, his sly humor, and his joy in the world which surrounds him. One of Collins's habits is to address the reader directly and familiarly, more typical of the usage of nineteenth century novelists than of twenty-first century poets. For Collins, the direct address becomes an invitation into the poem. "You, Reader" serves as this collection's dedication and suggests that the reader may be sorry to discover that Collins wrote the poem rather than the reader himself. Collins's point is that the things he included in the poem were already in the reader's mind—the details of the room and the dining table, the music on the radio. As he speculates playfully about the relationship between the salt and pepper shakers on the table, the poet concludes that their relationship is like the poet's relationship with the reader; they are simultaneously friends and strangers.

The fabric of Collins's world is woven of familiar threads as well. In an earlier volume he suggested that he felt like the amanuensis of the day, a sort of poetic court re-

Billy Collins has written seven volumes of poetry and edited two others. He is Distinguished Professor of English at Lehman College of the City University of New York. He served as poet laureate of the United States from 2001 to 2003. He was selected New York State Poet in 2004.

porter, recording the day's details. In this volume, too, one sees the weather and wallpaper and hears the radio playing Cole Porter. No wonder Collins elects to dedicate a poem ("Eastern Standard Time") to his fellow residents in the Eastern time zone who share breakfast hours and work schedules with him, while residents of other time zones may already have gone to bed.

In the midst of all these familiar themes, a few poems here introduce territory which seems foreign to Collins's usual stances. In "The Drive," for example, the speaker finds himself in a car directly behind another car, the driver of which begins to speak badly of "you"—some friend of the speaker. The speaker becomes progressively more and more angry as he listens to the driver's abuse until he finds himself mentally marking the driver's skull with the sort of dotted lines that indicate cuts of meat on a chart as he imagines locating some particular region which could harbor all this ill will. The poem ends with the ambiguous picture of the speaker, who metaphorically wears a butcher's cap and apron while riding along, a garb one is unaccustomed to seeing on such a genial poet. An equally uncomfortable poem is "The Revenant," in which the speaker is "the dog you put to sleep." From his canine afterlife, the dog reveals his longstanding hatred of the master and everything associated with him—his friends, the toys he provided, even the maddening jingling of his dog tags. The dog's venom is relieved at the end by a reappearance of Collins's whimsy—in the afterlife dogs write poetry (and cats write prose).

As this volume's title indicates, Collins continues to examine poetry and poets with gentle humor. In "Monday," for example, he begins, in his guise of the day's secretary, by indicating that everything is in its proper place this morning. Birds inhabit trees, toast pops from the toaster, "and the poets are at their windows." As the poem goes on to catalog the places of clerks, proofreaders, chefs, and fishermen, it notes, too, that the place for a poet, whether American or Chinese, is at a window, looking out at a world in which "there is always something to see" from which the poet can make a poem. In "The Student," Collins has fun with the arbitrary rules imposed by his imaginary poetry instruction book (the rules no less arbitrary than some found in real instruction books).

In "The Introduction" he pokes fun at a cliché of the poetry reading: "I don't think this next poem/ needs any introduction—/ it's best to let the work speak for itself" the poet says and then goes on to explain a dozen words from the poem, each more arcane than the last. Perhaps he is right to suspect that many hearers will be unfamiliar with the term for the study of worms—"helminthology." As for the trouble with poetry, in the title poem Collins suggests playfully that poetry leads to more and more poetry; indeed, reading a poem encourages the reader to write a poem himself, and in doing that the poet may well also be moved to steal a bit from other poets, as Collins himself does at the end of this poem, borrowing an image from the American Beat poet Lawrence Ferlinghetti, whose book *A Coney Island of the Mind* (1958) evidently sustained Collins through high school.

In an interview on National Public Radio on November 6, 2005, Collins said that the great theme of all poetry is death, that poets urge readers to seize the day, because humans have so few days to seize during their short life spans. Collins's poems certainly urge the reader to celebrate the world, but this volume seems to address mortality more directly than Collins's past work, perhaps because the poet has himself claimed (in "Care and Feeding") that he is "420 in dog years," and advancing age makes him consider the inevitable. In the deceptively playful poem "Flock," for example, an epigraph informs the reader that three hundred sheepskins were required for each copy of the Gutenberg Bible. Collins goes on to picture the sheep, penned and waiting. He notes that one of them "will carry the news/ that the Lord is a shepherd" and adds, ironically, "one of the few things they already know."

"Building with Its Face Blown Off" presents a familiar picture from television news, a picture as stark as the poem's title. Collins describes the scene, shameful somehow in the way it reveals the inner life of the building, its bedrooms and bathrooms, and then he pulls back to suggest the details of warfare—crows, a military statue, smoke rising. At last, in a far country, a couple shares a peaceful picnic under a tree. The speaker's quiet shock at both the blown-up building and the heedless couple may seem surprising in the voice of the herald of daily-ness, but the things he has treasured in ordinary life are the very things which war destroys.

Some of Collins's dealings with death are more personal. In "Reaper" he passes a scythe-carrying man on the roadside, and even though the man is not wearing Death's traditional black robes (he is dressed, in fact, like an ordinary workman), his glance is so piercing that the speaker says there is nothing for him to do but to keep driving, to "turn off the radio,/ and notice how white the houses were,/ how red the barns, and green the sloping fields." In short, he is moved to seize the day. In "The Order of the Day," the speaker describes a day in which everything seems especially brilliant— the sunlight, the cat, and "you," the person making coffee in the kitchen. The day is especially vivid "because I knew we were all going to die,/ first the cat, then you, then me . . . " and finally even the sun. At that point the speaker considers whether he has the right order. The cat looks very healthy, and "your" smile seems to suggest immortality. Traditionally the idea of sleep carries with it suggestions of death, as Collins notes in "Breathless." There he pictures the various sleeping postures favored by different people—face up, on the stomach or, like the speaker himself, on one side. He proposes that this is the way he would like to be buried, dressed in fresh pajamas and ready to rest.

"Lanyard" may be the most affecting of these poems. It is a lament for the poet's mother and a recognition of the inevitable inequity of the exchange between child and parent. "She gave me life and milk from her breasts,/ and I gave her a lanyard" he says, recalling how, out of boredom, he wove the plastic strips for a crafts project at camp to make a gift for his mother, who had no use for a lanyard (if indeed anyone needs such an item). He goes on to enumerate his mother's sacrifices for him, the ones most parents make for their children and repeats the sad refrain of "lanyard" in ironic counterpoint. This poem, he says, is not intended to say the obvious, "that you can never repay your mother." Instead he notes the even sadder truth that in the egotism of childhood he imagined that his gift was sufficient to repay hers.

The music Collins loves, jazz and the great popular music of the 1930's and 1940's, carries in it the same melancholy that informs much of Collins's poetry. In "Theme," the poet pictures the sort of idyllic spring day which often inspires his poems. This one is so lovely that he longs to add something to the great themes of the world's poems, themes which all seem to touch on mortality. One by one he considers them and then rejects each, finding himself unable to add anything to such lofty ideas as "the pursuit/ of the moth of eternal beauty." At last he is left with "the fall from exuberant maturity/ into sudden, headlong decline," a theme so unnerving that he is left at the piano, picking out a one-finger version of Cole Porter's "Easy to Love." That song, he says, combines the lover's facade of nonchalance with the recognition that his love is hopeless. That nonchalance is much like Collins's own, and love's melancholy is one of the many sadnesses that touch people who love the world. The trouble with poetry, Collins seems to say, is the much the same as the delight of poetry—it teaches one to seize the day before it inevitably slips into night.

Ann D. Garbett

Review Sources

Booklist 102, no. 2 (September 15, 2005): 20.
Entertainment Weekly, November 25, 2005, p. 105.
Library Journal 130, no. 17 (October 15, 2005): 60-61.
The New York Times Book Review 155 (January 8, 2006): 19.
Publishers Weekly 252, no. 32 (August 15, 2005): 34-35.

TRUTH AND CONSEQUENCES

Author: Alison Lurie (1926-   )
Publisher: Viking Press (New York). 232 pp. $25.00
Type of work: Novel
Time: The early twenty-first century
Locale: Corinth University, located in a college town in
the American Northeast

*The novel chronicles the disintegration of a marriage,
illustrating the destructiveness of chronic pain on both the
sufferer and the caregiver*

> *Principal characters:*
> ALAN MACKENZIE, a professor of architec-
> tural history
> JANE MACKENZIE, his wife, director of the
> Matthew Unger Center for the Humanities
> DELIA DELANEY, a fellow at the center and a writer of fairy tales, poetry,
> and spiritual essays
> HENRY HULL, Delaney's husband, a former poet

Using the same setting as her *War Between the Tates* (1974), Alison Lurie has placed *Truth and Consequences* in the college town of Corinth, loosely modeled after Ithaca, New York, the location of Cornell University, where Lurie has taught in the English department for more than thirty years. As with many of her other novels, including her Pulitzer Prize-winning *Foreign Affairs* (1984), Lurie focuses in *Truth and Consequences* on middle-class professional couples from academia as they struggle through the vicissitudes of everyday life and endure midlife crises.

Alan MacKenzie, a professor of architectural history, is an acknowledged expert on eighteenth century architecture, a creator of follies, models of architectural ruins, and a recently named fellow at the Matthew Unger Center for the Humanities, which his wife, Jane, directs. For sixteen years the two have enjoyed a satisfying marriage, being friends, lovers, and helpmates to each other. Their marriage had been stress-free and untested until Alan, priding himself on his vitality and welcoming the opportunity to display it at a departmental picnic, plays volleyball, injuring his back. Fifteen months later, he cannot sit for an entire meal, moans when he gets up, and no longer drives a car. He has tried physical therapy, pain pills, acupuncture, injections of cortisone, a back brace, and surgery, but nothing has helped. The drugs, both prescription and over-the-counter, have added the side effects of constipation, headaches, sleeplessness, and fatigue to his original complaint. The chronic pain has altered his entire life. He questions his love for Jane, gains twenty pounds, and has become self-centered, irritable, and depressed. He has drifted away from his usual friends, who cannot understand his preoccupation with pain, and seeks support and solace from fellow pain sufferers.

Alison Lurie is the author of children's books, nonfiction, and novels. She received critical and popular acclaim for The War Between the Tates *(1974) and the Pulitzer Prize for her novel* Foreign Affairs *(1984), which was also nominated for a National Book Critics Circle Award and an American Book Award.*

Alternating chapters provide the different viewpoints of Jane and Alan as their marriage deteriorates. Therefore, the reader witnesses the change both in Alan's life and in Jane's. Jane married a vigorous and confident man, once imagining him as her prince, and now has an invalid for a husband for whom lovemaking is too painful. The transformation in Alan has been so complete that she, one day, fails to recognize him: "Someone was getting out of a taxi, paying the driver, and then starting slowly down the long driveway: an aging man with slumped shoulders, a sunken chest, and a protruding belly, leaning on a cane . . . there was something about him that made her uneasy and a little frightened. He reminded her of other unwelcome figures: a property tax inspector . . . an FBI official."

Instead of being his wife, she has become his personal assistant, putting on and removing his shoes, retrieving newspapers, getting ice packs and pillows, and going to the store for requested items while neglecting her own gardening interests. Her personality is also altering; previously responsible and composed, she is often irritable and indignant about her added burden. She feels guilty when she sees him as a "pale, fat, weak, greedy, demanding person" and selfish when she resents Alan's requests because, after all, he is in constant pain. Pain has become the central feature of their marriage and has taken its toll: "For months Jane has been wonderful to Alan, and Alan has been grateful. But now she was tired of being wonderful, and Alan, she suspected, was tired of being grateful."

Probably incapable of meeting the physical demands of teaching, Alan fortunately is named one of the five fellows at the center. Another fellow is Delia Delaney, a southern writer who specializes in fairy tales. On one hand, Delia is beautiful, suggesting with her red-gold hair, rosy skin, and her silver-gray eyes a Botticelli painting. On the other, she is narcissistic, manipulative, and needy. She arrives at the center making demands, insisting on exchanging offices, commandeering a couch from a reception room, and appropriating the office's lime green poster paper for her drafts. People fall under her spell and rush to accommodate her: Susie, Jane's assistant, types her handwritten manuscripts, and Alan allows her to hide in his office when she wants to avoid requests for autographs or interviews. Jane seems alone in her dislike of Delia. Like Alan, Delia has her weakness; she suffers from migraine headaches, although Jane sometimes wonders if they are real or imagined. Delia uses her fragility to procure favors and sympathy from others but especially from Henry Hull, her own husband, who eases Delia's life at the center and elsewhere. He fulfills the role of personal assistant to Delia, in much the same way that Jane does for Alan. Perhaps it is inevitable that the care-getters, Alan and Delia, are drawn to each other and that the caregivers, Jane and Henry, are drawn to each other as well.

First encountering Delia at a reception at his house, Alan is immediately attracted to her and, at her request, shows her both follies, including the unfinished one that no one is invited to see. For the fifteen minutes that they are together, he forgets about his pain. With offices across the hall, Delia and Alan soon become close, sharing not only a knowledge of pain but also an interest in creative projects. Alan feels Delia understands his physical suffering and his artistic nature better than Jane does. He is interested in follies, reduced reconstructions of famous sites but portrayed in ruins, a project that Jane finds tasteless given the recent destruction of the Twin Towers in New York. Under Delia's influence, he starts the preliminary drawings for a new sculpture series, "fragments of domestic architecture," later titled "Doors and Windows constructions," which Jane cannot appreciate. She reflects that they are "All empty, like their marriage . . . nobody there, nothing left." Delia, however, applauds his projects. She introduces him to a gallery in New York, which leads to a show of his drawings and a commission in Connecticut to build a folly.

Their friendship soon turns to love, at least for Alan; for Delia he is just another one of her conquests. He is inspired by her kiss, which feels "as if a burning butterfly had brushed his cheek," and afterward he resumes preparation of his public lecture with unexpected enthusiasm. Even though she does not share his interpretation of their relationship, as he will learn later, she rekindles his interest in his work: "It was because of her that he had crawled out from under the heap of dirt and stones that his life had become, and dared to commit himself to art and to love." Meeting in New York, she seduces him—almost, first asking him to massage her feet, then instructing him to move up higher to her knees and then higher. However, she establishes limits: "I can't bear to be invaded. Never in any way. . . . But anything else—everything else."

Delia argues for the benefits of enduring pain. For her, artists create out of their suffering: "In the end you have to accept your affliction as a gift. . . . Inspiration comes from a dark, distant place, and it can't come without pain." Delia has turned her painful childhood into art. L. D. Zimmern, a lecturer at the center and a literary critic (familiar to readers of *The War Between the Tates*), argues that once Delia left West Virginia, where her life "was so intense, so violent, so primitive," her writing weakened. Alan, during a night filled with pain and drug-induced confusion, establishes a new artistic direction for himself, affirming that "Delia was right . . . this gift he had received was a by-product of pain and illness."

Just as Alan needs Jane to assist with physical tasks, Jane needs support emotionally. This she receives from Henry, who can empathize because of his own caregiving role. The two meet by chance in a grocery store, altogether innocently, but "there was something about the glance he had given her." Sharing an interest in fresh, wholesome produce, they then meet a few times at the local farmers' market. Although she suspects that she loves Henry because of her "bright dizzy feeling of flying and floating whenever she thought of him," she dutifully accepts her obligation to

Alan until the afternoon she walks into Delia's office and finds a disheveled Alan hiding behind the curtains. Soon after, she and Henry begin a romantic relationship which is consummated in a hay-filled barn.

After a brief stay with her parents, Jane decides not to see Henry and returns, unasked, to Alan, thinking that her place is with her husband. A nonmarriage ensues. Although Alan has promised to avoid Delia, he does not. Delia soon abandons the center for North Carolina, arguing that she is unable to work because the cold northern winters increase her migraines, and her fans are too demanding of her: "They all crowd around like hunting dogs, shoving and barking, wanting to eat me alive." However, before she leaves, she carefully ensures that her paychecks will continue. Henry remains in Corinth, partly because of Jane but also because he discovers that his seven-year marriage to Delia was not technically a marriage, as Delia had forgotten to divorce her previous husband.

Even though Alan has received only three short notes from Delia in the months of her absence, he is unwilling to believe that he was exploited until there is an announcement in the paper about Delia's marriage to Wally Hersh, a wealthy but also old and bald trustee of the Unger Center. As Delia later explains to Alan, she had to secure her future because fans are so fickle. Although Alan has some professional and artistic success as a "newly fashionable installation artist," he has neither Delia nor his wife, who has married Henry. One cannot help but think that Jane and Henry, ordinary though they might be, are more fortunate than the creative types.

The novel provides an in-depth look at the demanding nature of chronic pain and the draining effects of caregiving. Lurie also addresses other complex issues in *Truth and Consequences*: the relationship between pain or suffering and the creative process, the possibly narcissistic nature of artists, and the obligation of the artist to his or her fans, who, in reality, are a source of the artist's income.

Barbara Wiedemann

Review Sources

Booklist 102, no. 1 (September 1, 2005): 65.
Kirkus Reviews 73, no. 14 (July 15, 2005): 758.
Library Journal 130, no. 13 (August 15, 2005): 69-70.
Los Angeles Times, October 30, 2005, p. R9.
The New Leader 88, no. 5 (September/October, 2005): 28-30.
New Statesman 18 (October 31, 2005): 52-53.
The New York Times 155 (October 14, 2005): E41.
The New York Times Book Review 155 (October 30, 2005): 14.
Publishers Weekly 252, no. 31 (August 8, 2005): 209.
The Washington Post, October 16, 2005, p. T2.

UNDERSTANDING IRAQ
The Whole Sweep of Iraqi History, from Genghis Khan's Mongols to the Ottoman Turks to the British Mandate to the American Occupation

Author: William R. Polk (1929-   )
Publisher: HarperCollins (New York). 221 pp. $23.00
Type of work: Current affairs and history
Time: From prehistory to 2005
Locale: Iraq

A brief history of Iraq, concentrating on the twentieth and early twenty-first centuries, particularly America's involvement with that nation

> *Principal personages:*
> NURI SAID, the Iraqi prime minister, 1941-1958
> ABDUL QASIM KARIM, the "Sole Leader" of Iraq, 1958-1963
> SADDAM HUSSEIN, the president of Iraq, 1979-2003
> GEORGE H. W. BUSH, the president of the United States, 1989-1993
> GEORGE W. BUSH, the president of the United States, 2001-

William R. Polk, in *Understanding Iraq*, subtitles his work as *The Whole Sweep of Iraqi History, from Genghis Khan's Mongols to the Ottoman Turks to the British Mandate to the American Occupation*, but the volume focuses upon Iraqi from the early twentieth century. Polk's aim, as he states it in the preface, is to place present-day events in their historical context in order to illuminate the present. Well qualified for his task, the author first visited Iraq in 1947 and has written several volumes on the Middle East.

Iraq was one of the earliest places where humans made the transition from nomadic hunter-gatherers to settled agriculturalists. Millennia later, c. 3000 B.C.E., in ancient Mesopotamia, bound by the Tigris and Euphrates Rivers, the world's first civilization was created by the Sumerians, who built cities and irrigation projects and invented writing. Because of the lack of geographical barriers, Mesopotamian societies were often the victims of foreign invasions, beginning in the twenty-fourth century B.C.E. About 1100, the Assyrians seized power, ruthlessly relocating the population, a policy Saddam Hussein would later use. The Assyrians were succeeded by the Neo-Babylonians, and then the Persians, who coined the name "Iraq" from the Persian *eragh*, meaning "the lowlands." Alexander the Great humbled the Persians, followed by the Macedonian Seleucids, the Parthians and the Romans, and the Persian Sasanian Empire.

Much changed with the coming of Islam. By the time of his death in 632, Muhammad, the Prophet of Allah, had fashioned a religious community or *ummah* that en-

~

*William R. Polk earned a Ph.D. at
Harvard University and was a
member of the Policy Planning
Council of the Department of State
during the Kennedy administration.
The author of numerous books,
including* The Elusive Peace: The
Middle East in the Twentieth
Century *(1979) and* Neighbors and
Strangers *(1997), Polk has received
Rockefeller, Ford, and Guggenheim
Foundation Fellowships.*

~

compassed most of Arabia. However, the community divided over Muhammad's successor.
Sunnis trace their tradition to Abu Bakr, the first
caliph, while Shias look back to Ali, Muhammad's son-in-law, who was murdered in 661.
His supporters became known as or "Partisans of
Ali" (*Shias* in Arabic).

Under the Abbasid dynasty, Baghdad became
one of the world's great cities. However, Turks
from Central Asia captured it in 1055. The city
survived and prospered until the arrival of Hu-
lagu, the Mongol grandson of Genghis Khan,
who sacked Baghdad in 1258, reportedly killing
eight hundred thousand of its inhabitants. Two
new Islamic dynasties emerged in the fifteenth
and early sixteenth centuries. The Shia Safavids ruled in Persia, and the Sunni Ottoman Turks conquered Constantinople in 1453, destroying the Byzantine Empire. Iraq
was the violent borderland between the two empires, inhibiting economic growth and
deepening the divisions between Sunnis and Shias. Iraq was too poor to attract much
attention from its Ottoman rulers. For the British, Iraq was of significance only when
France or Russia threatened its imperial interests.

World War I and the discovery of oil in Iran changed the geopolitical realities of
the region. The war led to the dismantling of the Ottoman Empire, allied to defeated
Germany, and the creation of many of the modern Middle East nations, including
Iraq. During the war, Britain occupied Iraq to protect Iran's oil, crucial for the British
military, but at the cost twenty thousand British casualties. The postwar British occupation of Iraq, sanctioned as a League of Nations' "mandate," met with rebellion, and
British occupation forces rose to 133,000 troops. Britain opted to work mainly with
the Sunni minority. The British selected the Arab Revolt's Faisal as Iraq's king, although he was a foreigner, little known in Iraq.

Iraq was an artificial creation, divided under the Ottomans into three provinces.
Britain used airplanes and bombs, machine guns, and poison gas to enforce its rule,
terminating its mandate in 1932. Iraq joined the League of Nations, but the British
continued to rule Iraq indirectly by controlling the monarchy. At the outbreak of
World War II, the Iraqi army, becoming the arbiter of Iraqi politics, forced the British-
backed regent to flee, but British forces defeated the Iraqi military because of the new
government's pro-German sentiments. Under Nuri Said, who became prime minister
in 1941, oil funds were used for economic development, but the Said regime was
tainted by what many Iraqis believed to be undue British influence.

Nuri Said was an Iraqi nationalist but not an Arab nationalist. From neighboring
Syria came the pan-Arab Baath movement, which took root in the Iraqi army. In July,
1958, Iraqi military elements seized Baghdad, killing the king and Nuri Said. Abdul
Karim Qasim became the "Sole Leader," but in February, 1963, the military executed
Qasim. The new Baathist government divided over the issue of pan-Arabism, and

Colonel Abdus-Salam Arif seized power in November, 1963, but died in a helicopter crash in 1966. His brother, Abdur-Rahman Arif, took control, but in 1968, while he was out of the country, the army established a dictatorship with General Hassan al-Bakr as president. Saddam Hussein, a cousin of al-Bakr, was appointed vice president, becoming the de facto ruler by the mid-1970's and president in 1979. Polk argues that Saddam had no particular ideology: All that mattered to him was power. Fearing enemies, and Polk claims that paranoia was endemic in Iraq, a small state with large oil reserves, Saddam, a Sunni, forcibly relocated Shias and Kurds. He also cultivated middle-class support through social programs. By 1980, health and educational opportunities had increased significantly, and Polk gives Saddam credit, but oil made it possible.

The British had established the Iraq Petroleum Company (IPC). When Qasim attempted to reduce IPC's profits, he met opposition and in retaliation joined the Organization of Petroleum Exporting Countries (OPEC). In 1972, Saddam nationalized the IPC, possibly his most popular action, given resentment of foreign domination of Iraq's oil. Revenues rose rapidly, from one billion dollars in 1973 to twenty-six billion by 1980, but the Iraq-Iran War, begun by Saddam in retaliation for Iran's Ayatollah Khomeini's urging of Iraq's Shias to rebel, brought an end to prosperity. Opposition to the war nearly toppled Saddam from power, but he was saved by American money arms. Polk notes that United States aided Saddam although it was known that his regime was engaged in developing nuclear weapons and had used banned chemical weapons. American support was in response to Iran's Islamic revolution and the fear of upheaval in the Middle East with its oil reserves. A cease-fire was agreed to in 1988, but the war devastated Iraq's economy.

Peace increased the supply of oil but resulted in a fall in the price from $26 per barrel to $11. In desperate need of money, Saddam turned on Kuwait, arguing that Kuwait was a disloyal province of Iraq, a commonly held Iraqi view, and Kuwait, by exceeding OPEC production quotas, had driven down the price of Iraq's oil. Saddam believed that foreign governments would accept an Iraqi conquest of Kuwait once it was over, but he was detested in the West, not least because of his recent gassing of four thousand Kurds. Also, Polk argues, the neo-conservatives in the George H. W. Bush administration, who were supporters of Israel, advocated a hard line against Iraq because of Saddam's support of the Palestinians. Saddam did not fear his Arab neighbors, and America's ambassador to Iraq intimated that the United States did not involve itself in border disputes. Iraq invaded Kuwait in August, 1990. The consequence was what Polk calls "American Iraq," because since 1990 the United States has been the major influence upon Iraq.

Saddam expected that condemnations of his invasion of Kuwait would fade, but they did not, and the reason, Polk argues, was oil more than morality. The Gulf War began on January 17, 1991, but the outgunned Iraqi army was no match for the American-led coalition, and the ground war lasted only three days, from February 24 to 27. Bush ended the conflict without Saddam's removal from power, justifying his decision because he feared a long American occupation of a hostile Iraq, a statement, Polk points out, that proved to be not only a justification but also a prediction.

However, Saddam's Republican Guard had not been destroyed, probably to prevent a disintegration of Iraq leading to Iranian hegemony in the region, and with American acquiescence, Shia and Kurdish uprisings were brutally repressed. Iraq was placed under United Nations sanctions, forced to dismantle all weapons of mass destruction, and imports and exports were restricted. In 1995 a "Food for Oil" program was adopted, but the regime diverted most of the aid into the military and Saddam's personal survival in the face of American demands for "regime change." Saddam apparently abandoned the quest for weapons of mass destruction in the early 1990's, although most observers believed the contrary, and the George W. Bush administration later would use the alleged existence of mass destruction weapons to justify a second Iraq war.

Saddam survived the 1990's. Oil exports were up, and regime change had failed, but the latter became an early goal of the George W. Bush administration. Iraq offered, perhaps sincerely, to allow American troops and Federal Bureau of Investigation agents into Iraq to verify that there were no weapons of mass destruction, but it was too late. The world changed after September 11, 2001, and the administration was committed to regime change. War began on March 20, 2003, and on April 16, Bush declared Iraq liberated. However, there was no peace. Polk faults the administration for the war and also for the subsequent occupation. The senior American officials demobilized Iraq's army of a half million men, who returned home with little possibility of employment but with their weapons. Food, water, and electricity were in short supply, and looting was prevalent. War was one thing, nation building—justified by Bush as bringing democracy—was something else. Insurgents attacked coalition troops, blew up United Nations headquarters in Baghdad, and murdered Iraqis who cooperated with the occupation.

The Bush administration blamed the insurgency upon foreign Islamic militants, but Polk doubts that foreigners played a major role, believing the insurgency to be mainly a native Iraqi resistance to the new occupiers, similar to the resistance to the British in the 1920's. In 2004 it was decided to reconstitute the Iraqi army and police to eventually replace the coalition forces, something Polk doubts will be easily achieved, noting that the French in Algeria, the Russians in Chechnya, and Americans in Vietnam found it impossible to defeat native insurgencies.

In the concluding chapter, "Whose Iraq?" Polk posits several possible futures: a Shia-fundamentalist Iraq, an American-controlled Iraq, a secular-Sunni Iraq, a Saddam-type Iraq under a dictator, a U.N.-mandate Iraq, or possibly two or three Iraqs. After two years of war, Polk claims that most Iraqis view the United States less as a democratic liberator and more as a traditional imperialist, concerned with Iraq's oil rather than Iraq's people. Polk argues that the longer the American involvement, the more inevitable will be the emergence of another dictator. If a democratic Iraq does materialize, it will be from internal evolution and not be imposed by outsiders, and it can only grow from the bottom up and not be implemented from the top down.

The author doubts Bush's claim that Saddam's Iraq was allied with Osama bin Ladin and al-Qaeda to further international terrorism, given that Saddam's regime was secular rather than religious, and his primary aim was self-preservation rather than spreading Islamic fundamentalism. If anything, America's war in Iraq has increased the threat of terrorism because Iraq has become a lightning rod for disaffected Muslims. Bush's commitment to remain in Iraq, to "staying the course," can only be counterproductive, not only costing billions of dollars and thousands of lives but also subverting America's democratic ideals. Polk suggests an exit strategy, including a public American commitment to abandon any future domination of the Iraqi economy including oil and an admission that the war cannot be "won" in any accepted sense. American troops should eventually be replaced by multinational United Nations peacekeeping troops, which might give Iraqis the opportunity to develop a true civil society.

Understanding Iraq is less an objective history than an impassioned critique of current American policy, but by adding a historical dimension to the debate over American goals in Iraq and the Middle East, Polk has performed a valuable service, whether one fully agrees with his analysis or not.

Eugene Larson

Review Sources

Booklist 101, no. 16 (April 15, 2005): 1427.
Foreign Affairs 84, no. 3 (May/June, 2005): 148.
Kirkus Reviews 73, no. 5 (March 1, 2005): 280.
Publishers Weekly 252, no. 12 (March 21, 2005): 47.

V. S. PRITCHETT
A Working Life

Author: Jeremy Treglown (1946-   )
Publisher: Random House (New York). 334 pp. $26.00
Type of work: Literary biography
Time: 1900-1997
Locale: England, the United States, and various locales in
    Western Europe and Russia

This study chronicles the life and work of Pritchett, explores his many travels and how he transformed them into articles and books, follows the development of his fiction, and surveys his extensive output of literary reviewing and essays

> *Principal personages:*
> V. S. PRITCHETT, a short-story writer and essayist
> WALTER PRITCHETT, his father
> CYRIL, KATHLEEN, and GORDON, his siblings
> EVELYN PRITCHETT, his first wife
> DOROTHY PRITCHETT, his second wife
> JOSEPHINE and OLIVER, their children

V. S. Pritchett, routinely referred to by his initials, VSP, was probably considered the foremost literary essayist of his generation, was certainly one of its most celebrated writers of short fiction, and was unquestionably one of the busiest authors of the twentieth century. His range was extensive. At one time or another he wrote novels, short stories, travel books and articles, book reviews, translations, both brief and lengthy literary essays on a wide range of subjects, several volumes of biography and autobiography, journalism, and even turned his hand at film, both wartime propaganda and features. He married twice, fathered two children, had many affairs, traveled extensively, won many awards, and generally received the praise of his colleagues.

Victor Sawton Pritchett was born in 1900 into a lower-middle-class English family. His parents' families were both socially mixed. His paternal grandfather was a congregational minister, his maternal grandfather a stable boy and his wife a barmaid. The family moved frequently, often just ahead of the bailiffs, as VSP's Micawber-like father, Walter, who was chronically broke and in and out of bankruptcy all of his life, searched for suitable employment. Author Jeremy Treglown remarks that Walter proved to be a model for several of his son's best fictional characters. In spite of their rocky beginnings, all of VSP's siblings turned out well. Cyril became a woman's clothing buyer, Kathleen was a ceramicist and married a printer for the Bank of England, and Gordon also made a success in the clothing trade. Both of his brothers served in the military during World War II.

VSP's schooling was often disrupted by the family's frequent moves, but he eventually ended up in Alleyn's School in Dulwich, where he developed his proficiency in foreign languages. He was forced to leave school at sixteen by his father and went to work sorting skins on the London docks. He later would remark that he was lucky to have avoided the middle-class treadmill. Born at the turn of the twentieth century, VSP's childhood was thoroughly Edwardian, a sensibility that influenced his subsequent literary career in many ways. It was the world of H. G. Wells, Rudyard Kipling, Arnold Bennett, and John Galsworthy, the inheritors of the great Victorian literary institutions. Although VSP later wrote about the modernists who came after, his own fiction was firmly grounded in the older tradition.

~

Jeremy Treglown is the author of Roald Dahl: A Biography *(1994)* and Romancing: The Life and Work of Henry Green *(2000), which won the Dictionary of Literary Biography Award. He is now a professor of English at the University of Warwick. Editor of* The Times Literary Supplement *from 1982 to 1990, he is a fellow of the Royal Society of Literature.*

~

   Even though VSP had rejected the Christian Science of his father, it was in *The Christian Science Monitor* that his earliest writing appeared. After having had to maintain a day job, even working in a photographer's studio while living for two years in Paris, it was a relief finally to be able to pay the bills, even if only just, through the sole efforts of his pen. Early in 1923 the newspaper sent VSP to Ireland as a correspondent, where he met and later married his first wife, Evelyn, a marriage that would cause him a great deal of personal pain and would end in a bitter divorce. Despite the unpleasantness, Ireland proved to be a lasting source of material, especially for his short fiction and even later a travel book, *Dublin: A Portrait* (1967).

   Immediately after their marriage in early January, 1924, the Pritchetts set off for Spain, sent by the *Monitor*, where VSP covered the political events following the recent coup. Then they traveled to the United States and Canada, and to Spain again, Sicily, and southern Italy, and finally back to Ireland. All the while VSP collected impressions, honed his prose style, and savored the atmosphere of these foreign places that would show up in his later works of fiction and travel pieces. His first book, *Marching Spain* (1928), came out of these early travels. Their peripatetic life did much to feed his wanderlust, a feature of his life until his old age. Although his marriage was falling apart, being constantly on the move agreed with him, and it proved useful to his growing output of fiction, novels as well as short stories. *Clare Drummer* appeared in 1929, *The Spanish Virgin, and Other Stories* in 1930, and a second novel, *Shirley Sanz*, in 1932. He also kept up a consistent stream of articles and journalism.

   Through the late 1920's the *Monitor* remained his chief source of consistent income, but VSP reviewed extensively for the *New Statesman*, the *Spectator*, and the *Fortnightly Review* and was doing some translating for pennies a word. He also published some ten stories between 1930 and 1932. This substantial output established his career, but much of this early work VSP later disavowed.

   Treglown points out that VSP never really became a "Spanish Civil War Writer" like so many of his contemporaries, but his knowledge of the people and typography of Spain made him sought-after to cover the events there during the conflict. In 1935 he was sent by the *Fortnightly Review* as a correspondent and reported on not only the war but also on the effect it was having on the people in, for its time, a fairly balanced way. Treglown's remark about his not becoming a "Spanish Civil War Writer" is based primarily on his not becoming especially partisan in his reports.

VSP met Dorothy Roberts in 1934, when he was thirty-three and she nineteen. They began an affair at once. His marriage to Evelyn was over, and he was ready for another. Dorothy and Victor were married in October, 1936, and their first child, a daughter, Josephine, was born a year later. A son, Oliver was born two years after that. Although his second marriage was also challenging at times, especially because of his affairs and her drinking, husband and wife managed to stay together for the rest of his life.

Treglown remarks that VSP emerged from World War II not only as Britain's leading man of letters but also as the greatest writer-critic since Virginia Woolf. He did his bit for the war effort, of course, as nearly everyone did in Great Britain at the time, by assuming official tasks at the Ministry of Information and at other governmental offices while reviewing and broadcasting on the radio on topical issues. At the BBC the canteen became for him a kind of international club, as the broadcast service attracted numerous writers and artists of every stripe. He traveled all over the island reporting on ordinary working people. He also collaborated with filmmakers on wartime documentaries and wrote propaganda, such as the pamphlet "Transport in War Time." His keen eye for detail and his reporter's skill at recounting the telling story made him an especially effective author for such otherwise mundane work. Treglown cites his anonymous illustrated booklet *Build the Ships: The Official Story of the Shipyards in Wartime* as a fine example of this sort of writing and one that still reads well today.

In addition to his official and semiofficial work for the government, VSP was also a very busy essayist, and his ongoing series for the wartime *New Statesman* provided for many people a literary education. His persona and accessible literary style made a perfect fit for the newly egalitarian demands of the times. Finally his working-class background paid off handsomely. His voice, once a detriment on the BBC, now became an asset: It was sincere, not too cultivated, and sensible. He became just the voice to report on the social changes in language and national identity and for the need for a new common culture that did not separate the classes. He spoke for the common person and kept his topics close to the world of most listeners. The radio brought him a larger audience than he had enjoyed before the war, and his writings made him the most eagerly read British literary critic and essayist of his time.

His wartime activities made the rest of his career and opened up new markets for his work, especially in the United States, where by the early 1950's he was regularly published by *The New Yorker*, *The New York Times*, and later *The New York Review of Books*. His American publications also proved to be financially lucrative as well.

The end of the war allowed VSP to return to his fiction, and there was pressure for him to deliver his much-awaited new novel. The Pritchetts returned to London after living in the country, and once again he was close to his sources of income. Although his reputation was secure, his income still was not, and he threw himself back into his nonstop work schedule. He did not abandon his civic duties, either, and was early on involved with the United Nations Educational, Scientific, and Cultural Organization (UNESCO). He also chaired an exhibition of modern British books for the National Book League, and he campaigned for royalties from Britain's free public libraries. *Mr. Beluncle* finally appeared in 1951 and became his most celebrated novel.

VSP was also busy as a father and husband, coping with the demands of his growing children and the increasingly erratic behavior of his wife. In 1953 he made a triumphant visit to the United States, where he discovered that he was both well known and well respected. Treglown calls him a transatlantic hit. While in the States he met and began an affair with another younger woman, the last of his serious lovers. It eventually precipitated a crisis in his marriage, but like the others, VSP and Evelyn managed to weather it, as they would her drinking problem.

After *Mr. Beluncle* VSP abandoned the novel, which must have cost him some pain because as a young writer it had been his goal to become a writer of long fiction. Now he concentrated on the short story, which he wrote and published regularly, eventually collecting them into highly regarded volumes (three between 1974 and 1980), and he became recognized as a master in the field. His essays now appeared on both sides of the Atlantic, earning him praise and, increasingly, much-needed money. By the 1960's VSP was a celebrity of sorts, and when he went to California to teach at the University of California at Berkeley, he appeared on the set of his fellow countryman's film *The Birds* (1963), which Alfred Hitchcock was filming north of San Francisco. VSP was even asked to make some suggestions on screenwriter Evan Hunter's script.

Back home, VSP resumed his steady output of travel pieces, mostly for *Holiday* magazine, literary essays, and short stories. In 1968 he published the first of his autobiographical works, *A Cab at the Door*. In the same year he was made a Commander of the British Empire, one step down from knighthood, appointed Zisskind Professor at Brandeis University in New York, and invited to give the Clark Lectures at Kings College, Cambridge University. The beginning of the 1970's found VSP embarking on a new career, that of biographer. *George Meredith and English Comedy* (1969) became, in Treglown's assessment, the trial run for the three that would follow: *Balzac* (1973), *Turgenev* (1977), and *Chekhov* (1988). Biographies offered VSP an opportunity to write at length about writers he admired and had written about before, to explore the psychology of authorship, and to speculate about his subjects' lives and works. They were novels without dialogue.

As VSP entered his ninth decade, he finally began to slow down. He was feted, awarded honors, and much photographed and painted. He had become a national treasure. The final years of his life were not without their travails, however. In the last story in the last of his books, called "The Image Trade," the story of an aging writer and a photographer, he worried over the gap between self and reputation, though his reputation was now out of his hands. VSP had a stroke in April, 1995, and although he enjoyed outings with his children and grandchildren, he became increasingly addled. He was moved into a nursing home in December, 1996, where he suffered a second major stoke a month later. VSP died in Whittington Hospital on March 20, 1997. His wife died of cancer four years later.

In *V. S. Pritchett: A Working Life*, Treglown has written an engaging and thorough biography which not only covers the subject's life but, as the subtitle suggests, his work as well. Because Pritchett converted many of his life experiences into his writing, Treglown's emphasis is both enlightening and necessary and provides a comprehensive overview of both. As he did in his previous study of Henry Green, Treglown also surveys the literary and social events of his subject's time, which provides the reader a background for understanding VSP's work and also a general understanding of British literary culture of the period. This biography is thoroughly researched and written in an accessible and graceful style. It is a first-class piece of work.

Charles L. P. Silet

Review Sources

Booklist 101, no. 11 (February 1, 2005): 930.
The New York Review of Books 52, no. 7 (April 28, 2005): 8-12.
The New York Times Book Review 154 (January 23, 2005): 22.
The New Yorker 81, no. 3 (March 7, 2005): 81.

VINDICATION
A Life of Mary Wollstonecraft

Author: Lyndall Gordon (1941-   )
Publisher: HarperCollins (New York). 562 pp. $30.00
Type of work: Biography
Time: 1759-1797
Locale: London, Dublin, France

This extensively detailed biography of Wollstonecraft's life as a woman living in eighteenth century England and Europe covers her struggle to overcome adversity and rise to notoriety

Principal personages:
MARY WOLLSTONECRAFT, a writer
GILBERT IMLAY, her lover, the father of her
    first child
WILLIAM GODWIN, her husband, the father of her second child
MARY GODWIN, her second child
ELIZABETH (BESS) WOLLSTONECRAFT BISHOP, Wollstonecraft's sister
MARGARET KING, Wollstonecraft's charge when she worked as a
    governess
FANNY BLOOD, a friend of Wollstonecraft
EVERINA WOLLSTONECRAFT, Wollstonecraft's sister

Mary Wollstonecraft is not a well-known author, historical figure, or literary character despite the numerous publications about her writings and her life. She is best known for her work *A Vindication of the Rights of Woman* (1792) which was not her first publication but her third. Wollstonecraft was born in London as the second daughter of seven siblings in an average middle-class family of the eighteenth century. Her father was an abusive, irresponsible man who did little to provide for his family. His lack of financial support for his family and his abusive nature toward his wife and children had a great impact upon Wollstonecraft's life. The lack of resources for formal education or training forced Wollstonecraft to learn as much as she could on her own.

Given her family's lack of financial resources for a suitable dowry, her meager self-education, and a desire to escape a dysfunctional family setting, Wollstonecraft pursued courses of employment available to women of her social status. She began work as a lady's companion for roughly one year before she was forced to return home to care for her dying mother and her siblings. While caring for her siblings, she also managed to rescue her married sister, Bess, shortly after the birth of her child from what biographer Lyndall Gordon alludes to as a sexually abusive marriage. In need of some means of support, Mary and Bess set out to found a progressive school and boardinghouse. Their venture was successful enough to provide a means of sup-

*Lyndall Gordon has authored
highly acclaimed biographies of
famous authors such as T. S. Elliot,
Charlotte Brontë, and Henry James.
She has won the James Tait Black
Memorial Prize for Biography and
the Cheltenham Prize for Literature.
Gordon is a fellow of the Royal
Society of Literature and a senior
research fellow at St. Hilda's
College in Oxford, England.*

port, and Mary was able to have her other sister, Everina, join them at the school. At this point Wollstonecraft's life as a teacher was beginning to look more promising until the death of her dear friend Fanny Blood, to whose aid Wollstonecraft rushed in Portugal. When she was finally able to return to England, Wollstonecraft discovered that her sisters had let the school and boardinghouse fall into a financial shambles. She was forced to close the school and then took a position as governess in the home of Viscount and Lady Kingsborough in Ireland.

Of all the positions Wollstonecraft held, that of governess appears to be the one she detested most, yet her ideas on the education of women had a profound impact on her charges, especially on Margaret King, who went on to study and practice medicine in Spain. After working several years as a governess, Wollstonecraft was able to resign thanks to a generous gift from an acquaintance. She repaid her debts and moved to London to begin a new life as a writer. She was somewhat secretive in this endeavor, perhaps out of fear that she would fail but more likely because success might bring her eldest brother and father to lay claim to her earnings. The lack of substantial income either from her family or through her own pursuits, as well as her apparent loathing for positions of servitude, appear to be driving forces behind her desire to pursue an independent course as a writer. While marriage was a common means for women to obtain financial support, Wollstonecraft's lack of a substantial dowry left her few choices. Although it can be argued that marriage as relief from financial burdens is not necessarily a choice either, and given the circumstances of the eighteenth century when women were considered property with few rights, it can easily be seen that this was no option for a free-thinker such as Wollstonecraft.

Wollstonecraft was able to support herself through her writings and appears to have been comfortable in the life she created for herself in London. Eventually, she chose to go to Paris to report on the events of the French Revolution. Gordon notes that there are discrepancies among accounts of the circumstances surrounding this decision. Without additional primary source documentation, Wollstonecraft's exact reasons for leaving for Paris will remain mysterious. Once in France, Wollstonecraft found old acquaintances from England and was eventually introduced to Gilbert Imlay, best described as an American profiteer and Wollstonecraft's first love. Wollstonecraft shed societal conventions of the time to become romantically involved with Imlay. As a result of their affair, she became pregnant. While she and Imlay never legally wed, they were able to purport a marriage to protect Wollstonecraft from persecution in France as an English spy or traitor during one of the bloodiest periods in French history.

Through the pregnancy, forged marriage, and birth of their daughter, Imlay seemed to distance himself further and further from Wollstonecraft, despite his stream of letters that continually proclaimed his love and devotion to her and the child. His excuse for the physical distance was his need to work hard in order to make a life back in the United States possible for them all, a dream Wollstonecraft held dearly. Upon her eventual realization that Imlay did not return the intensity of her love for him and he had also had relationships with several other women, Wollstonecraft, who had a history of depression, attempted suicide twice.

In what seems a last-ditch effort to restore the relationship, Wollstonecraft embarked on a business trip for Imlay, to reclaim money from a failed business transaction. Her travels took her to Norway and then to Germany and, while her relationship with Imlay was never restored, her experience led her to writing another well-received work, *Letters Written During a Short Residence in Sweden, Norway, and Denmark* (1796). Back in London once again and forced to find a way to support herself and her small daughter, Wollstonecraft again pursued a course in writing. Through her London acquaintances she was reintroduced to William Godwin, also a writer, and a new relationship was formed. When she once again found herself pregnant, she and Godwin married, and Wollstonecraft delivered another daughter. Tragically, a week later Wollstonecraft died from puerperal fever, known at the time as childbirth fever. Her second daughter, Mary Godwin, would, as Mary Wollstonecraft Shelley, write *Frankenstein: Or, The Modern Prometheus* (1818).

The story of Mary Wollstonecraft reads like a Charles Dickens novel showcasing the miserable life of a main character who overcomes numerous obstacles to live a somewhat happy existence. In Wollstonecraft's life, she never found the security she desired. While she did experience perceived happiness in her final months, her life tragically ended in an early demise. Her beginnings in the household of an abusive father and complacent mother struggling at poverty's door were not uncommon among contemporary society. However, Wollstonecraft's concern for her family, as well as her altruistic actions on behalf of her dear friend Fanny Blood's family despite her own disadvantaged childhood, indicate a resourcefulness that is not common. Wollstonecraft's ability to make a way for herself through controversial writings shows brilliance that she herself described as genius.

This is not the story of a radical woman attempting to foment a revolution in women's rights. It is the story of a someone who overcame numerous obstacles to make her way through life and in the process left a mark on history. In part, she was able to pursue the literary course she took because of her shaky social status. If her father had provided a better life for her and her brothers and sisters, it is possible to suspect that she would not have been pushed to greatness. It is through her struggles to overcome one disastrous event after another that she developed such a keen sense of study and observation that give her the impetus to write.

It is unfortunate that, given the amount written about Wollstonecraft's life, inaccuracies seem common. For example, one source will note she only had one child, while another source correctly notes she had two. Gordon alludes to some of the discrepancies in the other works and attempts to correct inaccurate assumptions about Wollstonecraft's life and work through extensive research of primary documents such as letters, diaries, and recently discovered documents. Because of Gordon's authoritative refutation of facts about Wollstonecraft's life in other works, at times the reader who is new to Wollstonecraft may find some passages difficult to read through. In some cases, background presentations of people or historical events seem lengthy and distracting from the life of such a significant woman. People and events surrounding Wollstonecraft, however, greatly influenced the course of her actions and her writing.

Gordon has written an extraordinary literary biography, focused on the details of Wollstonecraft's life and her struggles to overcome numerous obstacles. The book also provides an extensively researched history of how she was motivated to write each of her works. *Vindication: A Life of Mary Wollstonecraft* is more than just a story of one women's life; it is also a historical summation of her writings. Gordon's biography of Wollstonecraft is not the first work about her to use the word "vindication" in the title. A previous fictional account of Wollstonecraft's life by Frances Sherwood was simply titled *Vindication* (1993). *Vindication: A Life of Mary Wollstonecraft* was relatively well received, despite one comment that a biography by Claire Tomalin, *The Life and Death of Mary Wollstonecraft* (1978), is a better story on the life of Wollstonecraft.

Susan E. Thomas

Review Sources

Booklist 101, no. 18 (May 15, 2005): 1629.
Kirkus Reviews 73, no. 6 (March 15, 2005): 333.
Library Journal 130, no. 7 (April 15, 2005): 99.
The Nation 280, no. 23 (June 13, 2005): 52-57.
The New York Review of Books 52, no. 19 (December 1, 2005): 55-58.
The New York Times Book Review 154 (May 29, 2005): 5-6.
Publishers Weekly 252, no. 15 (April 11, 2005): 43.
The Washington Post, July 3, 2005, p. T04.
Weekly Standard 10, no. 33 (May 16, 2005): 31-34.

A WAR LIKE NO OTHER
How the Athenians and Spartans Fought the Peloponnesian War

Author: Victor Davis Hanson (1953-   )
Publisher: Random House (New York). 397 pp. $30.00
Type of work: History
Time: 431-404 B.C.E.
Locale: Greece and the Mediterranean Sea

*This history describes how various aspects of the cata-
strophic Peloponnesian War of the fifth century B.C.E.
brought to an end the golden age of Greece*

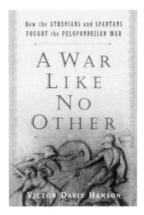

Principal personages:
    PERICLES (c. 495-429 B.C.E.), an Athenian
        political leader for thirty years who was
        responsible for the decision to go to war
        with Sparta
    THUCYDIDES (460-395? B.C.E.), an Athenian general, later exiled, and
        historian of the Peloponnesian War
    ALCIBIADES (450-404 B.C.E.), a controversial but talented Athenian gen-
        eral who fought for and against both Athens and Sparta
    LYSANDER (d. 395 B.C.E.), a Spartan admiral who defeated the Athenians
        in naval battles
    CLEON (d. 422 B.C.E.), a demagogic Athenian politician who came to
        influence after the death of Pericles
    NICIAS (470-413 B.C.E.), an aristocratic and conservative Athenian gen-
        eral who was responsible for the Athenian defeat on Sicily
    XENOPHON (428-354 B.C.E.), a Greek historian who continued
        Thucydides' narrative of the Peloponnesian War
    PLUTARCH (c. 50-120 C.E.), a Greek writer of the Roman era who wrote
        short biographies of Alcibiades, Lysander, Nicias, and Pericles

Victor Davis Hanson has written widely on ancient Greece and also upon war, ancient and modern, both as an academic and as a journalist. In *A War Like No Other*,
Hanson discusses the Peloponnesian War, one of the most famous, and widely written
about, of all wars prior to the nineteenth century. The Greek city-state of Athens,
along with members of its empire and its many allies, and Sparta, the other iconic
polis of ancient Greece, and its Peloponnesian League allies and other supporters, engaged in a bitter contest that lasted for almost four decades, from 431 until 404 B.C.E.,
and arguably brought to a tragic end the Golden Age of Greece. The war has had many
chroniclers, beginning with the Athenian general Thucydides, who took part in the
war but was cashiered by Athens's democratic government. More recently Donald
Kagan authored a four-volume work, *The Peloponnesian War* (2003). A reader might
fairly ask, what can Hanson say that has not been said many times before?

Victor Davis Hanson is the author of such works as The Western Way of War *(1989) and* The Wars of the Ancient Greeks *(2004). He is Director Emeritus of the classics program at California State University, Fresno, and a classics scholar at Stanford University's Hoover Institution. The recipient of the Eric Brendel Memorial Award for journalism, Hanson has also been a National Endowment for the Humanities Fellow, an Onassis Fellow in Greece, and Shifrin Professor at the U.S. Naval Academy.*

A War Like No Other is a history of the Peloponnesian War "like no other" history of that war. Instead of writing a narrative history of the conflict, Hanson focuses upon certain themes, explicating them at considerable length. Thucydides, whose narrative ended in 410 B.C.E., several years before the war's conclusion, composed a year-by-year account and wrote about the war's justice and morality, as in his famous dialogue between the Athenians and the inhabitants of the little island of Melos, in which the former argue that might always makes right. Kagan's work focuses upon the diplomacy and politics of the war from the top down. While not ignoring the major political figures, such as the Athenian statesman Pericles and the controversial turncoat Alcibiades, *A War Like No Other* looks at the conflict from the bottom up and the impact it had upon the civilian farmers of Attica and the lower-class rowers on the triremes, the Greek ships. These varied topics are discussed in separate chapters, and it can be claimed that the parts are greater than the whole. However, taken altogether, if the reader brings some knowledge of the background and the course of the war, a semi-narrative emerges, as Hanson has arranged his topics within a general chronological framework.

Hanson, the historian-journalist, is pointedly writing to a post-September 11, 2001, audience. In his opening chapter, "Fear," the author explicitly connects the events of Greece in the fifth century B.C.E. to the early twenty-first century when the United States, the modern Athens in its superpower status and democratic ideology, found itself in an intractable war against terrorists in the Middle East. Parallels in history are problematic, and no reputable historian would claim that the present precisely replicates the past. Still, Hanson argues in a subsection titled "Athens and America," today's reader, particularly in the United States, might well gain some insight into the present and its many challenges by considering the ancient world's most famous war, when another democratic empire went to war—and lost. When wars begin, Hanson points out, there are many unforeseen and unintended consequences.

Was the Peloponnesian War inevitable? Pericles, the leader of Athens, claimed it was. Athens was democratic and expansionist, depending upon trade to fuel its economic and political systems. Sparta, conversely, was a rural oligarchy, long dominated by militaristic values. Initially, the advantages lay with Athens, with its wealth, its formidable human resources—Athens was by far the largest city in Greece with a population of 250,000 to 300,000—and military experience, particularly in naval warfare. Sparta depended upon its heavy infantry, the hoplites, and the phalanx formation, which was formidable in formal battles fought on relatively level ground.

However, Athens had recently constructed its Long Walls, connecting Athens to its seaport of Piraeus. Secure behind its walls, Athens would merely wait until Sparta gave up the fight.

When Sparta and its allies invaded Attica, the area around Athens, in 431, the intent was that by destroying the crops and the farms, the Athenians would be either starved out or forced to come out and fight. However, as Hanson, who still lives on his family's farm in California, observes, it is not easy to cut down and destroy olive trees and grape vines or burn grain fields. The Spartans tried but with no success. However, Pericles also miscalculated in assuming that Athens could readily accommodate thousands of farmers and their families fleeing the countryside to find refuge behind the walls. Again, unintended consequences arose when a plague descended in 430-429— the specific disease is unknown, although Thucydides' description is explicit—that caused the death of a hundred thousand Athenians, including Pericles. Hanson's discussion of the plague, including the chaos that followed, raises the question of what might happen to today's society in the event of an outbreak of deadly disease, whether intentionally caused or otherwise. Its impact on Athenian military capacity was profound, resulting in more deaths in the plague than it suffered in battle, a parallel to the 1918-1919 flu epidemic that killed more people than did World War I, which just preceded it.

In his chapter titled "Terror" the author discusses the transition from hoplite warriors with their heavy armor to the employment of irregular troops, which to regular soldiers violated the traditions of Greek warfare. The response of the hoplites was to kill troops in retreat and murder civilians and other noncombatants, something that Hanson claims rarely, if ever, happened in earlier Greek history. When the anticipated formal battles did not occur, both sides reverted to raiding the towns and farms of their opponents, a policy of terror against civilians that pre-figured the bombing of cities of World War II and, Hanson notes, the killing of 150,000 civilians in Lebanon between 1975 and 1985, or "the Lebanonization of Greece," when innocent Greeks were seized, held for a time, and then executed when thought propitious.

The world was turned upside down in other ways. More people died on the sea and in urban sieges, when those who surrendered after the city fell were invariably executed, than in formal hoplite battles. Also, in the course of the long war, which took place all over the Mediterranean Sea and beyond, or wherever there were Greeks, hundreds of thousands of slaves gained their freedom when their masters were defeated by their opponents, and conversely, thousands of free Greeks were enslaved when captured in the conflict. In addition, over the course of the war, any ideological purity was cast aside in spite of the rhetoric of Pericles and others about the democratic Athens being the school of Hellas. One of the major events of the war was the Athenian invasion of the island of Sicily, where its opponent was equally democratic Syracuse. In that Sicilian campaign, Athens and its allies lost forty-five thousand warriors in just over two years.

Horses played a major role in the Sicilian campaign, although not to Athens's advantage. Riders and their horses are portrayed on the Parthenon friezes that Britain's

Lord Elgin removed from Greece in the early nineteenth century and have since been dramatically exhibited in London's British Museum. In reality, as Hanson states, the riders would have been no more than five-and-a-half feet, and weighed about 120 pounds, and their small horses only about thirteen-and-a-half hands at the withers. It was a smaller world two millennia ago, if not a less violent world.

Ultimately the war was decided upon the sea. The Athenian fleet had destroyed the Persian navy in 480 B.C.E. at the battle of Salamis, and Pericles' initial strategy assumed that Athens would retain control of the sea against land-locked Sparta. So long as Athens ruled the waves, it could import food and other supplies and thus withstand any Spartan siege. There were numerous naval battles in the course of the Peloponnesian War, and Athens won many of them, with its citizen oarsmen drawn from the lower classes in Athenian society, unlike the hoplite soldiers, most of whom were land-owning farmers. The trireme ships, with their three banks of oars, could not stay long at sea and were beached at night to rest the crew, and they were too small and unsteady to transport infantry troops. Naval battles meant either ramming or grappling, and the rowers usually could see nothing of what was taking place on deck or the surface of the waves. In just the last decade of the war, fifty thousand sailors died, many by drowning, others captured and executed.

Pericles' strategy proved inadequate, particularly as the war entered its third decade. Greece's archenemy, Persia, provided monetary support to the Spartan alliance. Ironically, the war's greatest naval tactician emerged on the Spartan side, and Lysander led the Spartans to victory at the naval battle of Aegospotami in 405, destroying or capturing 170 Athenian ships, most of them on shore. Predictably, the Athenian survivors were executed. Lacking a navy, the following year, in 404, Athens was forced to surrender. Democracies do not always emerge victorious. The Athenian defeat, Hanson contends, was a failure of enlightened leadership after the death of Pericles and the disastrous decision to invade Sicily.

In reality, there were no victors. In the fourth century, Sparta declined, and it was the Macedonians under Philip II and his son, Alexander the Great, who became the masters of Greece. One of the virtues of *A War Like No Other* is its accessibility to a nonspecialist reader. Hanson uses many colloquial terms and phrases in his discussion of the Peloponnesian War, such as "unintended consequences," "old habits die hard," and "ethnic cleansing," phrases not likely to have been common in ancient Greece. It could be argued that by using such current expressions, Hanson is making an ancient war more relevant to the present, making the Peloponnesian War in all of its idealism and deceit, glory and violence, seem as close as the day's newspaper or television news. Ultimately the war was a tragedy, and hubris, or excessive pride, was partially its cause, as the dramatists of the era—Aeschylus, Sophocles, and Euripides—so poignantly illustrated in their tragedies.

Eugene Larson

Review Sources

Booklist 102, no. 2 (September 15, 2005): 21.
Commentary 120, no. 4 (November, 2005): 104-108.
Kirkus Reviews 73, no. 16 (August 15, 2005): 897.
The New York Times 155 (October 11, 2005): E9.
The New York Times Book Review 155 (October 23, 2005): 15.
Publishers Weekly 252, no. 28 (July 18, 2005): 196.

THE WATCHER IN THE PINE

Author: Rebecca Pawel (1977-　　)
Publisher: Soho Press (New York). 308 pp. $24.00
Type of work: Novel
Time: 1940
Locale: Rural Potes, Spain

Carlos Tejada and Elena Fernandez, newlyweds, leave their metropolitan lifestyle to live in rural Potes, where they find themselves facing not only the challenges of assimilation but also a murder mystery

Principal characters:
>CARLOS TEJADA ALONSO Y LEÓN, a lieutenant of Potes's Guardia Civil
>ELENA FERNANDEZ, Carlos's wife and a Red sympathizer
>SERGEANT MÁRQUEZ, a resentful member of the Guardia
>CORPORAL BATTISTA, one of the Guardia
>LIEUTENANT CALERO, Tejada's murdered predecessor
>ANSELMO MONTALBÁN, a missing innkeeper
>BÁRBARA MONTALBÁN, the wife of Anselmo
>SEÑOR ALCALDE, the mayor of Potes
>SEÑOR ROSAS, the regional director of Devastated Regions
>COLONEL SUÁREZ, the head of the Guardia Civil in Santander
>FEDERICO ÁLVAREZ, a carpenter in Tama
>MARTA ÁLVAREZ, Federico's wife
>SIMÓN, TERESA, and ROMÁNITA ÁLVAREZ, the Álvarez children
>JESULÍN MONTALBÁN, the Montalbáns' youngest son, killed by the Guardia
>LAURA MÁRQUEZ, a girlfriend of Jesulín and the love of Calero
>BENIGNO ROMÁN MÁRQUEZ, a teacher and Laura's brother
>FATHER BERNARDO, the town priest
>DOMINGO ROLDÁN, an informant
>DOLORES SEVERINO and PEDRO VARGAS, captured Maquis
>ANTONIO MILAGROS, a shepherd who helps Elena

In *The Watcher in the Pine*, Rebecca Pawel introduces the reader to unlikely newlyweds, Carlos Tejada and Elena Fernandez, their new home, and a murder mystery. Pawel courageously and seamlessly switches between Carlos's and Elena's points of view, giving the novel richness and creating an intimate relationship between the characters and the reader.

The story begins in 1940, as Carlos and Elena move to Potes, a rural village in the mountains of northern Spain. Carlos has just been promoted to lieutenant of the Guardia Civil. Potes was devastated by the Spanish Civil War, leaving it with few functional buildings and little love for the Guardia. Many of the villagers lost love

ones at the hands of the Guardia after being accused
of being Reds or Red sympathizers. Carlos quickly
learns that the village's mountains are filled with
militant Maquis (Red Guerillas), who ambush the
Guardia performing their nightly patrols, and that
much of the town sympathizes with the Maquis's
ideals. On his first day as lieutenant, Carlos discovers that his predecessor, lieutenant Calero, was killed
during his patrol, presumably by the Maquis. Carlos
realizes he must immediately stop the Maquis and
solve the murder of Calero with a staff of five
grossly incompetent officers, as well as help Elena
settle into rural life.

*Rebecca Pawel is a high school
Spanish teacher in Brooklyn,
New York. She received
nominations for the* Los Angeles
Times *Book Prize and the
Anthony Award. Pawel won the
Edgar Allan Poe Award for Best
First Novel from the Mystery
Writers of America for* Death of
a Nationalist *(2003).*

Finding unsuitable the converted jail cells that
they had been given as living quarters, Carlos moves
Elena and himself to the Fonda, the local inn and
tavern run by the Montalbáns. Bárbara Montalbán
is not happy to accommodate any Guardia and only
reluctantly allows them to stay. Elena overhears a
conversation between patrons of the tavern and
learns that Bárbara's husband, Anselmo Montalbán, has been missing for some time.

As Carlos struggles to establish himself in his
new position, Elena also struggles to create a new
life for herself in Potes. Pregnant, she desperately tries to make friends in the village
but is met with suspicion and resentment, to which she becomes accustomed as a
Guardia's wife. To complicate the matter, she herself is a Red sympathizer whose
brother fled the country to escape a Guardia firing squad. Elena remembers her
mother telling her before her wedding, "You can't stay on both sides, Elenita. And if
you marry him, you'll become one of Them." Pawel tenderly illustrates and personal-
izes Elena's constant internal battle between loving her husband and hating the career
that defines him.

Already frustrated, when Carlos tries to hold people for questioning about recent
events he discovers that there are not enough holding cells. He visits the town mayor,
Señor Alcalde, and the director of devastated regions, Señor Rosas, in the hopes of
building new cells, and learns not only that is the town unable to devote the labor
needed for building a new jail but also that building supplies and a dynamite shipment
have been stolen by the Maquis. Realizing the implications of dynamite at the Maquis's disposal, Carlos contacts the commander of the Guardia Civil in Santander,
Colonel Suárez, for additional officers to secure the town and recover the supplies.

Meanwhile, Elena, unsuccessful in befriending villagers, ventures out to the neighboring town of Tama to order furniture from the carpenter, Federico Álvarez. Elena's
anonymity in Tama allows her to socialize freely with the Álvarezes. She ingratiates
herself into the family, helping their son Simón with algebra and their daughters,

Teresa and Romonita, to mend a broken doll. Elena talks at length with Marta Álvarez and learns that Bárbara Montalbán's youngest son, Jesulín, was killed by lieutenant Calero because the woman the lieutenant loved, Laura, loved Jesulín. Elena also learns that Bárbara's older son, Baldo, was imprisoned by the Guardia and relocated to a work camp in a different region. Elena inquires about the education system in Potes, and Marta explains that the town's teacher, Laura's brother Román, was accused of being a Red and killed.

A former teacher, Elena offers to tutor the Álvarez children and decides to talk with the village priest, Father Bernardo, about starting a school. Father Bernardo agrees that Potes desperately needs a school, but there is no money or workforce to build one and no one left to teach. When Elena offers to help create a school however she can, the priest agrees to form a committee to petition the mayor for a school and appoints Elena its chairwoman. She and the priest agree to meet the following morning to tour the forest and the town cathedral. While walking through the forest, Elena and the priest make the gruesome discovery of a torso suspended in the bushes. After they wrestle the body out of the roots, the priest identifies it as that of Anselmo Montalbán. Elena and the priest return to the inn to inform Bárbara. Although Bárbara does not say so, Elena knows that she holds the Guardia responsible for her husband's murder.

Since the discovery of the body, Elena feels a connection to Anselmo and attends his funeral, even though she is neither invited nor welcome. After the service, Elena, remaining alone in the cemetery, finds the grave of Román, the schoolteacher, and realizes he may be related to Sergeant Márquez, based on the surname on his tombstone.

Meanwhile, Carlos receives the additional officers he has requested and, with the increased staff, the Guardia are able to conduct searches and recover the missing dynamite in an abandoned farmhouse deep in the mountains. To add to this good fortune, a peasant, Domingo Roldán, appears in the station and informs Carlos of a secret meeting of the Maquis to occur that week. The Guardia launch a surprise raid, and a shootout ensues. Only two of the Maquis survive; a fifteen-year-old girl, Dolores Severino, whose father died in the crossfire, and Pedro Vargas, a devoted Maquis. Realizing the girl's trauma, Carlos asks Elena to speak with her. Elena immediately takes pity on the child, bringing her changes of clothing and agreeing to deliver messages to her siblings and her fellow prisoner Pedro. Elena also befriends Pedro and discovers that they are able to discuss literature, opera, and music, which Elena has not been able to do with anyone in the village. When Carlos finds out about this relationship, he becomes jealous and condemns Elena for associating with a Red terrorist. In the heat of the battle, Elena tells Carlos she sympathizes with their cause and hates the fact that he, her husband, is a Guardia. Carlos retaliates by saying that when their baby is born it will be given to his parents to raise so that Elena will not be able to brainwash the child. He then storms out of the inn.

Elena knows that under the new Spain within which they live, a woman has no rights in regard to her children and Carlos could legally take her child from her. Terrified and alone, she is startled by men looking for her husband in the tavern below their apartment. She opens the door and is met with a rag doused in chloroform, then kidnapped. Carlos, not knowing of his wife's peril, visits Father Bernardo and receives advice on rectifying the argument. With new hope, Carlos returns home to discover his wife is gone. He finds a ransom note demanding weapons, ammunition, and the return of the dynamite. The note explicitly states there is to be no house-to-house search, or Elena will be killed.

In a state of confusion, disbelief, and terror, Carlos rushes to the Guardia post and calls an emergency meeting. To his dismay, Sergeant Márquez orders a house-to-house search and begins dividing officers into teams. When Carlos protests, Márquez locks him in a jail cell, with Battista standing guard. Claiming that Carlos is currently unfit to lead, Márquez appoints himself the temporary lieutenant. Carlos sees this as mutiny and, after the officers leave to conduct the search, disarms Battista and escapes to stop the search and find Elena before she and the unborn baby are harmed.

Elena awakens alone in darkness and manages to cut the rope that binds her hands by rubbing it against a rock in the wall. Freed and unguarded, she escapes the makeshift holding cell and begins to descend the mountaintop where she was held. During her escape she suffers extreme pains and realizes she is in labor. Luckily, she finds a shepherd, Antonio Milagros, who takes her in and fetches his wife to assist in the delivery. As Elena is giving birth, a desperate Carlos hears a woman in agony. He follows the screams and recognizes them as Elena's. Thinking she is being tortured, Carlos is about to kill Milagros when he is told that Elena has just given birth to their baby son.

Reunited, Carlos tells Elena of the mutiny and reflects on how lucky Elena was in her escape. Thinking aloud, he begins to review Márquez's constant resentment toward him and starts to theorize about Márquez's involvement in Elena's kidnapping. Elena tells Carlos that she discovered a possible connection between Márquez and the murdered schoolteacher, Benigno Román Márquez, who was Laura's brother. Together, they hypothesize that Márquez may have murdered Calero to avenge Román's death.

Through simple language, Pawel slowly builds layers of connections and intrigue as Elena and Carlos suggest that possibly the Maquis knew of Márquez's actions and blackmailed him into helping them with the smuggling ring, or perhaps he orchestrated the ring and received a share of the profits. Finally, they conclude that Márquez may have organized the kidnapping and violated the ransom demands, claiming to be following orders, to show the Maquis that he did not have much pull at the Guardia in an attempt to sever his ties with them.

Ensuring Elena's safety, Carlos arrests Márquez and brings him to Colonel Suárez in Santander, seeking a court marshal. After Carlos explains his theory to the colonel, who reviews Márquez's record, Suárez agrees to hold him while he awaits trial. After Márquez's arrest, Bárbara Montalbán confirms that Márquez was Laura and Román's uncle, that he had killed Calero, and that he organized the Maquis smuggling ring, forced her husband to be a part of it, and then turned on him, resulting in Anselmo's death. She agrees to testify to the Guardia if it means prison for Márquez.

After nearly losing his family, Carlos realizes that his position places all of them in jeopardy and offers to leave the Guardia. Elena, thrilled by the prospect, refuses to allow Carlos to quit because she knows that he loves his job. She realizes his career makes him who he is—the man she loves. Pawel reveals what constitutes a person and marriage through Elena putting aside her ideology and seeing Carlos for the person he is instead of the uniform he wears.

Sara Vidar

Review Sources

Booklist 101, no. 8 (December 15, 2004): 712.
Kirkus Reviews 72, no. 2 (January 15, 2005): 87.
Publishers Weekly 251, no. 48 (November 29, 2004): 26.

WHITE GOLD
The Extraordinary Story of Thomas Pellow and Islam's One Million White Slaves

Author: Giles Milton (1966-   )
Publisher: Farrar, Straus and Giroux (New York). Illustrated. 316 pp. $25.00
Type of work: History
Time: 1715-1738
Locale: North Africa

Milton uses the memoir of Thomas Pellow, an English boy kidnapped by Muslim corsairs in 1716, to explore the little-known story of the million Europeans held as slaves in North Africa in the seventeenth and eighteenth centuries

Principal personage:
   THOMAS PELLOW, an Englishman who wrote of his experiences as a slave in Morocco Moulay Ismail, the sultan of Morocco

Giles Milton in *White Gold: The Extraordinary Story of Thomas Pellow and Islam's One Million White Slaves* explores a fascinating and little-known history. Much has been written about the slave trade organized by Europeans to purchase slaves in Africa for transportation to their plantations in the New World. Largely forgotten is the fact that slavery existed in many other parts of the world, involving millions of victims. Among these victims would be Europeans captured and enslaved by Muslim corsairs.

For centuries, the wars between Christians and Muslims in the Mediterranean region had produced captives who were forcibly enslaved. The sleek war galleys that alternately protected or preyed upon shipping were driven by slaves chained to their oars. This continued a grim maritime tradition in the Mediterranean Sea that could be traced back to the days of the Romans. The Islamic world, however, nourished a demand for slaves that went beyond such military needs. The Ottoman Turkish sultans required a constant supply of Christian boys to be disciplined into their elite regiments of janissaries. Arab slavers maintained a trading network that spanned continents. In the seventeenth and eighteenth centuries, Muslim raiders from the North African ports of Algiers, Tunis, Tripoli, and Sale preyed on European shipping lanes and seacoasts. They were known collectively as the Barbary pirates. Throughout the Muslim world, these corsairs were celebrated as heroes, waging jihad against the infidel. The raiders themselves were happy to combine piety with the pursuit of plunder.

At the peak of their pride and power, the Barbary pirates ranged outside the Mediterranean into the North Atlantic and as far as the English Channel. No European at

~

In addition to White Gold,
*Londoner Giles Milton has also
written* Samurai William *(2004),*
The Riddle and the Knight
(2001), Big Chief Elizabeth
(2000), and the best-selling
Nathaniel's Nutmeg *(1999).*

~

sea, or who lived near the sea, was safe. Even Americans, trading with the mother country, were attacked and carried off to North Africa. Despite the burgeoning military strength of Europe in the age of Louis XIV and the duke of Marlborough, the Europeans proved unable to mount an effective defense against these piratical depredations. Incompetence, disunity, and distraction on the part of their governments all combined to leave the people of Europe vulnerable to the Barbary raiders. To the extent that the European governments considered the plight of their captive subjects, they pursued appeasement of the pirates, offering bribes for safety and purchasing slaves from their captors. Thus the Barbary pirates became the terror of their age. They took on the grim role played by the Vikings in an earlier period. Across Europe, people living near the water prayed to God for deliverance from the Moors.

One of the many victims of the Barbary pirates was a young Cornish boy named Thomas Pellow. After enduring twenty-three years as a slave in Morocco, he would live to escape and dictate the story of his experiences. Milton makes brilliant use of Pellow's narrative as a window into the cruel treatment of European slaves in North Africa. He places Pellow's account into a rich historical context, with digressions on such topics as Moroccan palace politics, European efforts to ransom Christian slaves, and European attitudes toward slaves who mitigated their conditions by converting to Islam. The result is a truly engrossing read. Milton brilliantly alternates between microcosm and macrocosm in his book, and he delivers a moving meditation on the surprising capacity of some people to endure in the face of fearsome tribulation.

Thomas Pellow, at the age of eleven, signed on as a cabin boy aboard a merchant ship captained by his uncle. Aside from Pellow and his uncle, the crew consisted of just six men. They were carrying a load of salted fish from England to Catholic Italy. Their ship was unarmed. At the time that they departed England in 1715, shippers were under the impression that the Royal Government had concluded an agreement with the sultan of Morocco. Unfortunately for Pellow and his shipmates, this diplomatic rapprochement had fallen through. On the voyage home, in the summer of 1716, off the coast of northwest Spain, two shiploads of Moroccan corsairs from Sale attacked and captured their vessel. Two other British ships were taken with them. In all, fifty-two English mariners were made prisoners. They were confined in the holds of the pirate ships and carried off to Sale. While the two corsair vessels were becalmed off the sandbar that guarded the harbor of Sale, the prisoners were almost unexpectedly rescued. A British warship suddenly hove into sight, firing at the pirates. The two corsair ships broke up on the sandbar, throwing pirates and captives together into the water. Then the British ship sailed away as mysteriously as it had appeared, leaving Pellow and his fellow Englishmen in the hands of the Sale raiders.

The prisoners were marched from Sale to Meknes, capitol of the Moroccan Sultan Moulay Ismail, a tyrant as remarkable for his cruelty as for his ambition. The sultan was a crafty survivor of the brutal dynastic politics of seventeenth century Morocco. Through a Darwinian process of elimination, he defeated various brothers and nephews to claim the Moroccan throne. His only security in power lay in terrorizing his subjects. He formed an army of black slaves. African boys from south of the Sahara Desert were kidnapped by slaving expeditions and brought north, where they were subjected to a merciless training program. By the time it was complete, these black soldiers were utterly ruthless and fiercely loyal to Moulay Ismail. Pellow on a number of occasions witnessed arbitrary executions carried out by members of the black army at the sultan's behest.

Moulay Ismail himself often did his own killing. European diplomats were shocked to be received by the sultan while he was still soaked in the blood of his victims. He was proud of his strength with a sword and sometimes practiced his skill by lopping off the heads of the slaves who helped him mount his horse. Moulay Ismail wanted to be regarded as the equal of the great European monarchs. A tangible expression of this desire was the construction of an enormous palace at Meknes, intended to be the largest royal residence in the world. The palace was a complex of buildings that stretched for miles. Moulay Ismail dreamed of a continuous line of construction three hundred miles from Meknes to Marrakesh. The long-lived sultan never finished his mighty pile, but what he did complete was awe-inspiring. Within the walls were apartments for two thousand concubines and barracks for ten thousand soldiers. The stables alone were the size of a city. The palace was famous for the intricate luxury of its decoration. All of this magnificence was built by Christian slaves working fifteen hours a day. Poorly fed, continually mistreated, thousands of these slaves were buried in the foundations of Moulay Ismail's dream palace.

It was to this palace that Pellow and his fellow captives were led. Moulay Ismail himself came out to inspect and purchase his new slaves. To the horror of the Englishmen, he suddenly drew his scimitar and struck off the head of one of the two corsair captains who had taken them. The sultan did not believe that this man had put up a good enough show in the fight off Sale. As Moulay Ismail looked over his new slaves, his attention for some reason was drawn to young Pellow, who was led aside, along with a few others. The rest of the slaves were marched off to labor on the sultan's construction projects. Pellow's uncle died there some months later, worn down by malnourishment and disease.

After a brief stint working in the sultan's armory, Pellow was given to one of Moulay Ismail's sons. The prince, recognizing Pellow's intelligence, tried to persuade him to convert to Islam. When the boy refused, the prince had him repeatedly beaten and denied all food but bread and water. Pellow endured this torture and privation for months before he finally gave in and converted. Accepting Islam improved Pellow's situation somewhat, though he remained a slave. It unfortunately also alienated him from his compatriots back at home. Europeans regarded slaves who turned Muslim as apostates, making no allowances for circumstances or duress in these conversions. These slaves were never ransomed. Hearing of Pellow's conversion, Moulay Ismail ordered that he be taught to speak and write Arabic. The prince failed to do this. Brooking no disobedience, even in a son, Moulay Ismail had one of his black guards break the prince's neck.

Pellow now was put to work in the sultan's palace. The most dangerous job that he held was doorkeeper to the sultan's harem. No outsider could look on the sultan's women and live. Not even the sultan himself was given access to the harem between dusk and dawn without prior notice. One night the sultan tried to visit his harem. The terrified gatekeepers let him in, but Pellow would not let him in through an inner door, despite curses and threats. The next day the complaisant doorkeepers were executed, and Pellow was rewarded. He became a personal attendant to the sultan. Moulay Ismail even gave him a wife, with whom he had a daughter.

In 1720, Moulay Ismail made Pellow a soldier. He appointed him one of the captains of a troop of six hundred converted slaves sent to garrison a fort two hundred miles from the capitol. Pellow was glad of the opportunity to get so far away from the dangerously mercurial sultan. For the rest of his captivity in Morocco, Pellow would serve in the imperial army. He took part in punitive campaigns against rebels and a slaving expedition across the Sahara.

Moulay Ismail died in 1727. There then followed the usual dynastic wars. Pellow saw hard and dangerous service in these conflicts. He was wounded. The unsettled conditions in Morocco heightened the urgency of his desire to get away. He had always wanted to go home. Word that his wife and daughter had died while he was away campaigning cut the only possible tie holding him in North Africa. He began actively to plan his escape. This was a very dangerous enterprise. Only his luck saved his life after two failed attempts. Finally, Pellow made a break for the coast on foot, disguised as a traveling physician. After nearly being murdered by bandits, he found a small port with two European ships at anchor. The sailors treated him kindly, and one of the vessels took him to Gibraltar, where he was welcomed and given passage back to England. Twenty-three years after he had been enslaved, Pellow was reunited with his parents in Cornwall.

Pellow's story ultimately had a happy ending. Such was not the case for most of the Europeans enslaved by Muslim corsairs. The Barbary pirates continued their raids until the American and British navies finally broke their power in the early nineteenth century. Ironically, the British vice admiral who commanded the fleet that in 1816 forced the Barbary pirates to renounce slaving was named Sir Edward Pellow, a distant relation of Thomas Pellow. Milton finishes his book by describing a walk through the crumbling ruins of Moulay Ismail's palace. Time has not been to kind to Moulay Ismail's dream. An earthquake wrecked the palace in 1755, and the elements have over the centuries eroded away much of what was left. What passed for Moulay Ismail's glory is long gone. Milton's *White Gold* will keep readers from forgetting the Europeans enslaved to labor on the Moroccan sultan's cruel folly.

Daniel P. Murphy

Review Sources

Booklist 101, no. 18 (May 15, 2005): 1620.
Library Journal 130, no. 12 (July 1, 2005): 97-98.
New Statesman 133 (June 14, 2004): 51-52.
The New York Times Book Review 154 (August 21, 2005): 7-8.
Publishers Weekly 252, no. 18 (May 2, 2005): 187-188.
The Spectator 295, no. 9175 (June 12, 2004): 42-43.
The Times Literary Supplement, November 26, 2004, p. 33.

WHO SHE WAS
My Search for My Mother's Life

Author: Samuel G. Freedman (1956-   )
Publisher: Simon & Schuster (New York). 337 pp.
  $ 25.00
Type of work: Biography
Time: 1938-1974
Locale: New York City

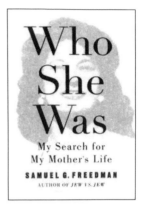

*This intimate biography of Freedman's mother cap-
tures a young Jewish woman's experience of family, her
East Bronx neighborhood, and World War II from the
1930's to the 1950's*

Principal personages:
ELEANOR HATKIN, the author's mother
FANNIE HATKIN, her younger sister
SOL HATKIN, her father, a working-class Jewish immigrant
ROSE HATKIN, her mother
CHARLIE GRECO, her Italian boyfriend whom her mother refused to let
  her marry
LEONARD (LENNY) SCHULMAN, the Jewish suitor whom Eleanor married
  to please her mother

Samuel G. Freedman has written other books about the American Jewish experience, but *Who She Was: My Search for My Mother's Life* is a more deeply intimate
story, written after Freedman revisited his mother's grave for the first time in twenty-
six years after her death. His mother, Eleanor (Hatkin) Freedman, was diagnosed with
breast cancer when Samuel was fourteen years old and died while he was in college.
When he realized, at age forty-five, that his mother was a stranger to him, Freedman
regretted his rejection of her during her illness. (He had gone so far as to pretend that
he did not know her when she visited his campus.) At her grave, he felt compelled to
seek to understand his mother—not just as his mother, or his father's wife, or someone who died young and painfully—but as a person in her own right. He asks, "What
did it mean to have come of age during the Depression, World War II, the Holocaust?" and "Who was my mother before she became my mother? Whom did she
love? Who broke her heart? What lifted her dreams? What crushed her spirit? What
did she want to be? And did she ever get to be it in her brief time on earth?" To answer
these questions became a need that led Freedman to write this book as an act of penance for his years of neglect.

As his mother shared little of her past or family lore with him, Freedman used his
skills as a professional journalist to reconstruct his mother's life. He contacted potential sources through Internet services and letters to one thousand alumni of the college
she attended. He consulted genealogists; school, medical, and immigration records;

legal documents; newspapers and magazines of the period; archives; and other historical sources. He used his mother's own short stories about her childhood, his personal memories, and those of Eleanor's brother and sister. The yield was a wonderful mix of anecdotes from relatives, Eleanor's high school and college classmates, former boyfriends, letters, postcards, diaries, yearbooks and autograph books, home movies, and photographs. Yiddish sayings and photographs (especially the photographs—pictures of Eleanor with her family, Fannie and Eleanor clowning on their roof, Eleanor with her girlfriends at Coney Island, with her boyfriend, Charlie, and with her first husband, Lenny) add life and poignancy to the text. Writing the biography as a novel, in the context of the American Jewish experience during the Depression and World War II, actually increases its realism.

Samuel G. Freedman is the author of four earlier books, including the National Jewish Book Award-winning Jew vs. Jew: The Struggle for the Soul of American Jewry *(2000). He teaches journalism at Columbia University and contributes regularly to* The New York Times.

Eleanor's story is essentially the tale of a woman growing up, finding love, experiencing regret and disillusionment, and finally, trying to make the best of it. It begins in February, 1938, with Eleanor's first day of high school, just before her fourteenth birthday. She is portrayed as a "star," adored by her family yet bored, defiant, and ashamed of her parents. Longing for a better life than her parents have been able to eke out during the Depression—a refrigerator, nice clothes, and "steak on Sunday and turkey on Thanksgiving"—she dreams of becoming a scientist, like her heroine Madame Curie. She has outgrown the childhood joys of her Jewish working-class neighborhood of East Bronx (now South Bronx), and her world seems as "cramped and confining" as the narrow daybed she shares with Fannie, her younger sister.

Freedman re-creates both the dreary, cramped, and cold tenement-house apartment where Eleanor lives with her family and the neighborhood—its tenements, storefront synagogues, trolley cars, peddlers and street musicians, men looking for work, and children jumping rope on the sidewalks. Rose, Eleanor's unhappy, careworn, Polish immigrant mother, has been in America for twenty years and still longs for her homeland. She pinches pennies to send money to her relatives overseas and helps her sister's husband and children immigrate to Uruguay. Her sister remains in Poland. Sol, Eleanor's father, works in a shoe factory in Lower Manhattan, loves America, and finds purpose in life and escape from his domineering wife by working for the Jackson Democratic Club. Rose keeps a kosher house, and Sol goes regularly to synagogue, but Eleanor associates Judaism with "superstition in the Old World and hypocrisy in the New" and resists going to synagogue. She is close to her sister Fannie, who, in contrast to Eleanor, is dutiful, undemanding, and content with her world.

In high school Eleanor excels in a predominantly Jewish group of 150 honors students in a school of 3,000 students. She has a crush on Hy Keltz, a graduating senior who is handsome and athletic, but poorer than Eleanor and not as bright as she. She pursues him, and when he takes a full-time job as a deliveryman after graduation, she enjoys an idyllic summer, dating Hy, going to the New York World Fair, and picnicking and renting bikes in Central Park with her friends. Meanwhile, the Nazis are taking over Eastern Europe, and Rose's preoccupation with her relatives trying to survive in Europe increases the friction between her and Eleanor. The description of Rose's desperate efforts to get information about her family in Nazi Europe and stay in touch with her sister's family in Uruguay is touching. Political turmoil preceding the United States' entry into the war is reflected in pro-Nazi and anti-Semitic rallies and isolationist and radical left-wing orators. Throughout the book, the war and the plight of European Jews are persistent themes, updated through newspaper headlines and conversations. They offer a grim backdrop to Eleanor's teenage world. In her senior year, she edits the school paper, belongs to the Honor Society, drama club, literary society, yearbook staff, and infirmary squad. She is the only girl in calculus class. Also, she is beautiful. Eleanor graduates first in her class, but when she wins numerous medals at graduation for outstanding academic achievement, the conflict between her and her mother resurfaces. She publicly humiliates Rose and denies her the parental pride she would relish by shoving the medals at her in a dismissive gesture. Her romance with Hy ended, she lets another boy take her to the prom. In his words, she "wants a little more out of life than an average fella can give her."

When she is forced to work part-time to help support the family in 1941, Eleanor abandons the liberal arts education she had pursued at Brooklyn College for the more practical business curriculum at City College. Uninspired and overwhelmed, she becomes an average student. War is declared on December 7, and young men begin enlisting. Rationing begins, Sol becomes an air-raid warden, and Eleanor loses her scholarship when she decides to work full-time and attend night school. One weekend in 1942, she meets Charlie Greco, who, "for an Italian guy . . . seemed mighty Jewish." A deliveryman who dreams of owning his own company, Charlie grew up on the Jewish streets in East Harlem, and his closest friends are Jewish. Even though Eleanor may lose her family for dating a non-Jew, she begins hanging out with Charlie and even brings him home, insisting they are "just friends." As defense industry jobs are opening up, Eleanor gets a full-time job in a factory, where she becomes friends with Jewish radicals, tolerant of interfaith marriages. Charlie enlists in the Navy in September, 1943, and Eleanor and her girlfriends lament the shortage of men; but Eleanor has never done better financially, and the family is able to rent a bigger apartment in a better neighborhood.

In January, 1944, Jack, whom Eleanor dated briefly and has been writing to, comes home on furlough. Freedman portrays his mother "famished for a man's caress, aching to confirm her allure," and "straining against the very rules Jack honored," when he takes her out. Freedman wonders if she has gone "to that rare gynecologist willing to prescribe an unmarried patient a diaphragm." Jack is a gentleman and believes Eleanor is a daring, but nice, girl. He continues to write. When Hy comes home on leave, he also dates Eleanor but leaves her when she tries to seduce him. Eleanor sends him love letters and a Dear John letter to Charlie. When Hy returns from the war, he buys a grocery store and proposes to Eleanor, who cannot see herself working in the store and turns him down. When Eleanor breaks up with someone, she purges "her photo album of every snapshot of him."

She calls Charlie when he returns home to renew their love affair. They decide to get married, and she is welcomed by his family, but Rose has not "raised her daughter to fall in love with the enemy," and when she threatens to kill herself if they marry, Charlie backs down. Eleanor and Charlie part, and Eleanor continues to live "under the roof of the woman who had ruined her life, too paralyzed by hate and hurt to move away." Charlie begins seeing Selma, another Jewish girl. To the relief of her mother, Eleanor marries Lenny Schulman on the rebound—"a Jewish young man with prospects, finishing a degree at NYU and already enrolled in podiatry school." He is her ticket out of her mother's house. Having heard of Eleanor's wedding, Charlie elopes with Selma, but for years he continues to carry Eleanor's picture in his wallet.

Eleanor and Lenny settle down to a busy regime of school and work. Eleanor finally graduates from night school with a degree in business administration, throws herself into her work, and with the aid of the G.I. Bill, supports Lenny in podiatry school. Lenny's deceit, infidelities, and strange sense of humor spell doom for the marriage—"It was not just that Lenny had broken his vows but that he had broken her spell, the hold that her beauty had exerted over every other man in her life." After four years of marriage, Eleanor and Lenny are able to get an annulment by sticking to a certain legal script. During this time, Eleanor calls Charlie at work to tell him she wants to marry him if he'll get a divorce, but he says it's too late. She has begun seeing a machinist, David Freedman, who, with some misgivings, marries her in a religious ceremony as a concession to her parents. Freedman, who knows little about his parents' courtship, says, "As I recognize now, my mother hurtled into marriage to my father and thus into our life as a family as a damaged and desperate person." Their courtship was an "unsentimental mixture of pressure, falsehood, attraction, and mutual convenience."

The reconstruction of his mother's life is grounded in history, but Freedman tells the story as a novel. Although he acknowledges that he cannot be certain of what was happening inside his mother's head and heart "at every second of her young womanhood," he freely attributes motives, ideas, and attitudes to Eleanor. She emerges a courageous but cold, calculating, and unfulfilled woman—"someone whose life peaked at seventeen. And if there's anything sadder than dying at fifty, then it's having peaked at seventeen and living to fifty with that knowledge." Eleanor left a note with her will that ends, "I have fantastic children & they helped give me a good & happy life." Perhaps her son's portrait is colored by his own complex emotions. In sharing his personal memories, emotions, questions, and doubts, Freedman reveals himself as much as his mother. Even though the focus of the story is Eleanor's life before he was born, the reader is aware of his presence, "brooding" over every scene, and his commentary raises questions at times about whether issues between his mother and himself have truly been resolved. This is a strength, rather than a weakness, of the book. One continues to be involved with this mother and son long after the book is finished.

Edna B. Quinn

Review Sources

Booklist 101, no. 15 (April 1, 2005): 1338.
Kirkus Reviews 73, no. 2 (January 15, 2005): 99.
The New York Times Book Review 154 (April 24, 2005): 30.
Publishers Weekly 252, no. 10 (March 7, 2005): 60.

WHY BIRDS SING
A Journey into the Mystery of Bird Song

Author: David Rothenberg (1962-   )
Publisher: Basic Books (New York). 258 pp. $26.00
Type of work: Natural history
Time: 2000-2003
Locale: Various countries

Rothenberg examines various hypotheses explaining birdsong, from the mechanistic view that song is communication between birds seeking mates to the possibility that birds enjoy singing and find their own songs beautiful

Principal personage:
DAVID ROTHENBERG, a composer, writer,
ecologist, musician, and philosopher

David Rothenberg has gained international fame in an unusual way: He is a composer and jazz clarinetist who improvises to the accompaniment of natural sounds. In 2000, he began to play live with singing birds, and his experiences prompted him to seek answers to many questions: What meanings can birdsong have? Why do some birds speak in simple peeps, while others give voice to complicated song motifs? Do birds sing merely mechanically, for finding mates and defending territory, or can they feel joy when they sing?

In *Why Birds Sing*, Rothenberg asks these questions repeatedly, tackling them in each chapter in different ways. If the book is read in a single sitting, the repetition of the questions can become wearying, as though Rothenberg thought the chapters might be read in isolation. The table of contents makes this unlikely, as the chapter titles are floridly metaphorical ("To Drink the Sound," "The Opposite of Time"), diminishing their usefulness for keyword searching in library catalogs.

However, the repetitions amid the various approaches in all ten chapters may have been intentional, as Rothenberg more probably intended his writing to imitate music: He excels at analyzing the reiterations and improvisations within the simplest of bird songs and the most complex of human symphonies. His prose is jazzy and rhapsodical—"I laugh, and the bird laughs some more. His laugh is a melody, a saxophone laugh, a Charlie Parker laugh"—and his arrangement of themes may be equally intentional, only apparently unpremeditated.

One chapter, for instance, summarizes centuries of research and speculations into these questions, though further summaries appear throughout the rest of the volume, as though enhancements on later motifs felt more appropriate to Rothenberg than rigorous orderliness. Indeed, as a compendium of the literature on birdsong, the book is valuable and thorough. Rothenberg asserts that there is more nature writing on birds than on any other animals, and his evidence ranges from the Roman writer Titus

∿

David B. Rothenberg, associate professor of philosophy at the New Jersey Institute of Technology, is a composer and clarinetist known for his integration of improvisation with the sounds of nature. Besides releasing several albums, he has written and edited books on natural history and philosophy. Rothenberg is the editor of the Terra Nova book series published by MIT Press.

∿

Lucretius Carus (c. 94-55 B.C.E.) to philosophers Immanuel Kant and Henry David Thoreau to poets John Keats, Walt Whitman, and T. S. Eliot to polymath George Meredith. In the ensuing chapter, Rothenberg looks at various theories, from the scientific studies of ornithologists to the populist, lyrical musings of nineteenth century naturalists, as to why birds sing.

Elsewhere, Rothenberg codifies birdsong from a professional musician's point of view, and the black-and-white illustrations include reprints of the musical notations of many naturalists who tried to capture avian tunes via transcription. Rothenberg covers the history of sound recording equipment and of birdwatchers' use of it to capture birdsong. Rothenberg rhapsodizes over the dadaist printouts of sonograms (graphs of sound spectrograms); he likes his science mixed with aesthetics. He describes the "playback experiments" of scientists such as Cambridge University zoologist W. H. Thorpe, who studied chaffinch songs for decades, and his student, University of California, Davis ornithologist Peter Marler, who would play all kinds of recorded bird songs to chaffinches in captivity and note their responses.

Rothenberg encapsulates neurobiological studies in which songbird brains and syrinxes are removed for examination. Studies of canary brains, for instance, disproved the long-held hypothesis that adult brains continue to develop new neurons, a discovery that has benefited medical science. In another chapter, he describes remarkable human compositions influenced by the music of birds: Wolfgang Amadeus Mozart's "Musikalischer Spass," Antonio Vivaldi's "Il Gardellino" ("The Goldfinch"), Ludwig van Beethoven's Sixth Symphony, the "Pastoral," Olivier Messiaen's "Quartet for the End of Time" and "Catalogue d'Oiseaux," and those of more recent musicians who use state-of-the-art musical equipment to sample and mimic bird songs, such as Magnus Robb and Pamela Z.

Rothenberg is convinced that birds sing for joy and know their music is beautiful. So why is he obsessed with explaining why birds sing? The problem seems to be that most scientists do not want to anthropomorphize birds—to assume that because humans can enjoy making music, birds can too. Rothenberg argues the opposite: that those scientists are too anthropocentric in their presumption that humans have aesthetic faculties not to be found in the rest of the animal kingdom. "No scientist worth his data set really wants to tell you why birds sing. There's enough to examine in the quest to figure out *how* birds sing, and especially how complex behavior is learned in a very short time. . . . But the patterns don't explain why the song is there."

The lay reader who is not a musician or an ethologist will most enjoy the anecdotes with which Rothenberg shores up his arguments. Stories of interactions between people and birds are charming:

In southeastern Australia they tell a story about the superb lyrebird, widespread in the hills of the states of Victoria and New South Wales. This species possesses a shared and learned sense of song that is passed down from generation to generation. In the 1930's in Dorrigo, New South Wales, a flute-playing farmer kept a young lyrebird as a pet for several years. In all that time, the bird learned to imitate just one small fragment of the farmer's flute playing. . . . After a time, the farmer released the bird into the forest. Thirty years later, lyrebirds in the adjacent New England National Park were found to have flutelike elements in their song, a sound not heard in other populations of superb lyrebirds. . . . It is now seventy years since a lyrebird learned these fragments, and today the flute song has been heard a hundred kilometers from the original source. A human tune is spreading through the lyrebird world.

Such tales, particularly of birds who mimic, such as the starling and the mockingbird, are plentiful. Rothenberg writes much about the remarkable starling, an irritant to birdwatchers but a delight to laboratory scientists, as researchers at the University of Indiana found:

Only the five birds that had extensive daily contact with people learned to mimic human sounds. They would recognize simple phrases and recombine them in odd ways. "Basic research," one said. "Basic research, it's true, I guess that's right." One bird, which needed to have its claws treated for an infection, squirmed while held, screaming, "I have a question!"

Another bird would imitate the sound of the fluorescent light above his cage, especially one time when the power was out, as if yearning for the light to come back. A third copied a teapot's whistle, and when [researcher Marianne] Engle got a new, non-whistling kettle, the bird would still whistle whenever the pot was placed on the stove. These birds knew more than the realm of sounds surrounding them—they could place the sounds in a context. These stories suggest that birds' ability to imitate a wide range of sounds may have something to do with a sense of themselves in an environment. . . . Social species like starlings seem to use songs in subtle interactive ways that are far more nuanced than attraction or defense.

Another species, the marsh warbler, relies entirely on mimicking, and imitates birds it hears when it migrates back and forth between northern Europe and east Africa. An amazed birdwatcher discovered it is "the one bird in the world who can recount its migratory path as a kind of songline, where the journey is mapped into the music itself."

Many of the facts readers will encounter may surprise and intrigue. For instance, birds that need to defend their territory tend to have more complex and splendid songs. On the other hand, these birds that sing as part of a "sonic arms race" do not need beautiful songs, only songs identifiable from a great distance; the beauty is gratuitous. Some species have simple songs and do not sing often; those that produce complex and variable songs, such as the mockingbird, tend to sing for hours a day. Also, very few kinds of animals employ vocal learning. Humans, whales and dolphins, and birds do, which implies that natural selection works against vocal learning, perhaps because it attracts predators, perhaps for some undiscovered reason. (Naturalist Charles Darwin believed that animals have an innate aesthetic sense and feel emotions.) The satin bowerbird of Australia, famous for the mating bowers he builds and decorates with blue flowers, bottle tops, ball-point pens, or other items to attract a mate, will actually kill other blue birds if it cannot find anything else blue; the color is essential for attracting a mate to the nest.

Rothenberg's emphasis on beauty and poetry is notable even in the index, which includes such terms as "exaltation," "fun," and "sublime." His book is meant to persuade, and readers who readily accept that birds enjoy singing, just as horses enjoy running and dogs enjoy playing, will be convinced with ease. Whether he will persuade ornithologists matters more to Rothenberg than it will to the casual reader. Rothenberg wants to poeticize science for the lay reader, but he also entreats scientists to accept poetry in their speculations as well as crunched numbers. He is likelier to influence mavericks and interdisciplinarians than hidebound ethologists.

His tone ranges from the exuberant to the plaintive to the contentious: "There are no answers at the end of bird song papers, just further dreams and guesses as to the elusive reasons why." He concludes on a personal note:

> Why must they [human and bird] both sing? By this point it's more Zen koan than question. . . . I play along with birds to enter a new kind of improvisation, with a musician from another species. I want to engage, to interact, to create together, not to sign my territory or find a mate. What does he want? Who does he think I am?

Most readers will likely be caught up in Rothenberg's yearning and frustration and be satisfied by the rapturous musings on his years of study. This is certainly a book ethologists will enjoy and ponder, and musicians will find the accompanying CD of the same title (published separately by Terra Nova Music), which contains twelve tracks of his music set to birdsong, stimulating and provocative. Both academic and public libraries will find the volume a good investment.

Fiona Kelleghan

Review Sources

Booklist 101, no. 14 (March 15, 2005): 1253.
The Boston Globe, May 15, 2005, p. D6.
The Chicago Tribune, May 29, 2005, p. 1.
Discover 26, no. 7 (July, 2005): 76.
E Magazine: The Environmental Magazine 16, no. 3 (May/June, 2005): 62.
Kirkus Reviews 73, no. 3 (February 1, 2005): 170-171.
Library Journal 130, no. 4 (March 1, 2005): 109.
Los Angeles Times, March 1, 2005, p. F6.
Publishers Weekly 252, no. 8 (February 21, 2005): 167.

WICKETT'S REMEDY

Author: Myla Goldberg (1972-   )
Publisher: Doubleday (New York). 326 pp. $25.00
Type of work: Novel
Time: 1918
Locale: Boston

This multidimensional tale re-creates the Boston of the early twentieth century—one locus of the flu epidemic that killed more than half a million Americans

Principal characters:

LYDIA KILKENNY WICKETT, an Irish American shopgirl who marries a medical student from a prosperous family
HENRY WICKETT, her first husband, who succumbs early to the 1918 flu epidemic
FRANK BENTLEY, her second husband, a Navy prisoner and volunteer for the flu-research project on Gallup's Island
MICHAEL KILKENNY, her beloved brother, who also dies of flu
QUENTIN DRISCOLL, Henry's business partner, who steals the remedy and turns it into soda pop
DR. JOSEPH GOLD, the head of the Gallups Island flu-research project

In 2000, Myla Goldberg created a nationwide sensation with her first novel, *Bee Season*, later made into a film starring Richard Gere. Not one to rest on her laurels, Goldberg recently told an interviewer that she wanted her second novel "to be as humanly different from 'Bee Season' as possible." She explained, "I think it's really important to push yourself into as many different directions as possible." The result was *Wickett's Remedy*, a highly original work whose approach is indeed different from that of *Bee Season*.

In *Wickett's Remedy*, Goldberg re-creates the world of the 1918 epidemic of Spanish influenza, which by various estimates killed between twenty-two million and fifty million people worldwide and from five hundred thousand to eight hundred thousand people in the United States. According to Goldberg, who thoroughly researched the subject for her novel, the epidemic killed more Americans than were killed in all twentieth century wars combined. Until the recent publication of several nonfiction works, the 1918 epidemic had virtually faded from public memory. That, Goldberg speculates, is because it coincided with, and was overshadowed by, World War I, which was "manmade," whereas the disease was beyond human control. "I think when you can't control something," she says, "the instinct is to forget about it as soon as possible."

The inability of medical science and government policy to control the disease, or even fathom its origin, is a prominent, and skillfully conveyed, theme of *Wickett's*

Myla Goldberg's first published novel, Bee Season *(2000), was a critical and commercial success and was a runner-up for the Hemingway Foundation/PEN Award. A film version premiered in 2005. Goldberg's short stories have appeared in such literary journals as* Eclectic Literary Forum *and* American Writing. *She also wrote the audiobook* The Commemorative *(2001) and the travel book* Time's Magpie: A Walk in Prague *(2004).*

Remedy. Goldberg's literary methods are a large factor in the novel's originality. With them, not only does she communicate how swiftly the epidemic caught the nation unaware, but she also creates impressive portraits from the era: the men's clothing store where her protagonist works; a hospital full of dying flu victims; a research facility where medical workers grope for the cause and a solution; and, simultaneously, the public's feverish enthusiasm for the war "over there."

Goldberg creates this tapestry by weaving together several techniques: the core story; articles culled from newspaper archives of the period; marginal "comments" on the story from the collective voice of the dead; cheerleading memos from the business firm whose founder pirated the "remedy" of the title and turned it into soda pop. All of this combines to give the novel a large scope in a comparatively small space—326 pages.

As with any novel, at the heart of *Wickett's Remedy* is the story involving its human characters. Lydia Kilkenny, a young Irish American woman of South Boston, has resolved to leave "Southie" for a better life. After graduation from school, "when her girlfriends found jobs behind sewing machines," the ambitious Lydia goes to work in the stockroom of a department store, where she learns everything she can about the operation. When a sales position opens up in the men's clothing department, she is prepared. Unexpectedly, when working in that new capacity, she meets Henry Wickett, a shy young medical student who charms her with eloquent love letters. Lydia marries him, convinced that her future is now secure.

Soon after the wedding, however, Henry abruptly quits medical school, determined to pursue journalism instead. To Lydia's distress; he volunteers for the Army, expecting to be assigned as a war correspondent. When he fails the physical examination, the insouciant Henry changes his plan: He will now sell a home remedy—Wickett's Remedy—by mail order and send a healing letter with each bottle. To him, of course, the letters are the real point of the enterprise. On a handshake, to supplement the mail-order operation, he grants one Quentin Driscoll exclusive permission to market the remedy to drugstores. This plan, too, is stymied when Henry suddenly dies, an early victim of the still-unrecognized flu epidemic.

Devastated, Lydia returns to her close-knit family in South Boston, only to find the unstoppable flu cutting down many of her neighbors and family members, including her beloved brother. One day, carrying a sick neighbor boy to the hospital, she discovers that she can make a difference in the world through simple acts of kindness, such as bringing water to a dying patient. In volunteer work at the hospital, she finds a new vocation, and though not quite a real nurse, she lands a nursing assignment on Gallup's Island in Boston Harbor, where medical researchers plan to experiment with human subjects to learn how influenza is transmitted.

The human subjects are Navy convicts who have volunteered in order to escape life in the Deer Island Naval Prison. Lydia quickly realizes what is happening to the men who will be deliberately infected and, unlike her professional colleagues, she comes to feel excruciating sadness for the prisoners. Yet, amid her turmoil, she finds new love with one of them, Frank Bentley.

Meanwhile, as Henry's widow, Lydia has become the business partner of Quentin, who fails to honor the handshake agreement and instead turns the remedy into the commercially successful "QD Soda." This part of Lydia's story—her vain struggle to bring Quentin to account and his engulfment in moral guilt many decades later—is told mainly through letters (Quentin ignores those from Lydia) and QD Soda company memos, interspersed with the authentic news articles Goldberg collected during her research. All the while, the marginal comments from the chorus of the dead provide correctives and wryly humorous critiques of the characters' perceptions.

Critical response to Goldberg's blend of literary elements has been uneven. Most reviewers have given high marks to the core story of Lydia, Henry, and Frank but have balked at the other elements—the letters, articles, and, most particularly, the marginal chorus comments, even while acknowledging Goldberg's courage in departing from the model of her wildly successful first novel. (Anne Jolis of the Pittsburgh *Post-Gazette* praised Goldberg's "heartening example of the risk-taking rarely seen by today's young female authors.") Generally, the complaint has been that these added elements distract readers from the core story. A reviewer for the *Raleigh News and Observer* speculated that the tale "might have been more gripping if so much energy hadn't been leached from it by the chorus, the newspaper clippings from the time, the imagined scenes of men going off to World War I, the "Wickett's Remedy" pieces, and all the other efforts to create a virtuoso, Dos Passos-esque performance." (Goldberg says her use of news articles was inspired by a similar technique in the 1937 *U.S.A.* trilogy by John Dos Passos.)

While no reviewer denies that Goldberg did meticulous research, or that she expertly portrays the period and locale of her story, the result still does not seem to fit what reviewers expect a novel to be. "We turn to fiction, though, for something different: not just the facts but the feelings; not just the documents but the texture of the experience," explained a critic for *The New York Times*. Another writer was disappointed because "There is no well-defined problem-resolution cycle but, instead, just the tragedies and travesties of one character's life." One reviewer actually seemed to rejoice at the elimination of human characters she considered inconvenient and unappealing, and to wish even more had been eliminated.

Moreover, no matter how Goldberg insisted on her determination to take new risks—"Why write if you're not taking risks, especially when you're young?"—the critical and popular success of her first novel made it inevitable that reviewers would hold her second novel to the same standard. Whereas they found the characters of *Bee Season* intensely portrayed, those of *Wickett's Remedy* were perceived as flat and poorly delineated. Whereas the plot of *Bee Season* was perceived as tightly focused, that of *Wickett's Remedy* was criticized as diffuse and cluttered. Whereas the successful techniques of past authors inspired her to use the same techniques—news articles from Dos Passos, marginal "chorus" comments from Vladimir Nabokov's *Pale Fire* (1962)—they are not perceived as successful in *Wickett's Remedy*.

Again, her multidimensional approach has been adversely compared with more straightforward works by Katherine Anne Porter and William Maxwell, both of whom lost loved ones in the 1918 flu epidemic. Porter's *Pale Horse, Pale Rider* (1939) and Maxwell's *They Came Like Swallows* (1937) were compact, classically formal accounts of personal experience. In contrast, a critic argued that "Despite all that Goldberg has going on in this novel, it fails to hang together in any compelling way." Another reviewer (unlike the one who noted that Henry "happily" dies early on) complained that "Goldberg's opening chapters—like her title—prove misleading. Both Henry and the remedy swiftly disappear."

Here is a possible key to an alternative evaluation of this novel, which apparently fails to meet so many critics' expectations: Is the title misleading—or is it ironic? One of the novel's larger themes is the illusory sense of control initially held by science, government, and the general public. In the core story, there is no "Wickett's Remedy" because Wickett dies young and the remedy is quickly stolen and converted into a sugary confection. Just so, on the public level, there is no remedy for the ravaging flu epidemic. Just so, on the global level, World War I did not prove to be Woodrow Wilson's "war to end all wars."

Far from distracting the reader, the newspaper articles give a strong indication of just how helpless the public was in the face of a killing disease—and how the public eventually came to understand its helplessness. These headlines progress from hopeful to hopeless: "New Serum Bars Pneumonia," announces an early headline. Patriotically, one story is headed, "Influenza No Match for the Army." Later headlines read discouragingly, "Bride in Gas Mask at Upton Wedding" and "Under City Ordinance All Public Meetings Banned." Another story lists "Games for Stay-at-Home Children." Another announces, "Whole Country in Grip's Grasp," and toward the end, another reads, "Fails to Find Influenza Cure: Joint Board Endorses None of the Vaccines at Present in Use." Finally, the rah-rah company memos are playfully subversive parodies of opportunistic business practices masquerading as Horatio Alger legends.

The news articles, chorus comments, and company memos all serve to illustrate an environment, just as filmmakers sometimes provide so-called establishing shots or pull the camera back from a house to a cityscape, from a planet to a galaxy. Instead of distracting the reader, the headlines provide the context in which certain individual characters—Lydia and Frank in particular—attempt to live a life of integrity and to retain their humanity despite uncertainty about what is happening around them or why, and without much ability to control events. It can be argued that such a context reveals these characters as even more admirable than their actions already show them to be.

Goldberg's array of elements in *Wickett's Remedy*—and the story they conspire to tell—are indeed complex, but readers may not necessarily agree with critics that these elements rob the story of clarity. The reader needs a great deal of information about a forgotten phenomenon of a bygone era, but the details provided by Goldberg do not amount to clutter. The emotions—and the individual fates—portrayed in the story are plainly spelled out by the main narrative and strongly hinted at by the other story elements. There might have been other ways to present both the characters and their milieu, but it can be argued that Goldberg's method is both effective and—despite the borrowings of technique—highly original.

Meanwhile, if Goldberg has noticed the bad reviews at all, they have done nothing to dampen her enthusiasm for going in new directions and taking risks: *USA Today* reported that "Her next novel will be set in the present for a simple reason: 'I haven't done that yet.'"

Thomas Rankin

Review Sources

Booklist 101, no. 22 (August 1, 2005): 1991.
Kirkus Reviews 73, no. 14 (July 15, 2005): 755.
Library Journal 130, no. 12 (July 1, 2005): 68.
New York 38, no. 31 (September 12, 2005): 74-75.
The New York Times Book Review 155 (September 18, 2005): 19.
Newsweek 146, no. 12 (September 19, 2005): 62.
Publishers Weekly 252, no. 29 (July 25, 2005): 40.
San Francisco Chronicle, October 2, 2005, p. F1.
Time 166, no. 13 (September 26, 2005): 76.

A WILD PERFECTION
The Selected Letters of James Wright

Author: James Wright (1927-1980)
Edited by Anne Wright and Saundra Rose Maley, with
Jonathan Blunk
Publisher: Farrar, Straus and Giroux (New York). 633
pp. $40.00
Type of work: Letters
Time: 1946-1979

*This selection of Wright's letters includes conversations
on the craft of poetry with major poets of the second half of
the twentieth century*

It is indicative of the scope of this collection of James
Wright's letters that the title, *A Wild Perfection*, comes not
from Wright himself but from a letter to him from fellow
poet Stanley Kunitz, quoted by Wright in a letter to yet another poet, James Dickey. The
community of postmodern American poets suggested by that triangle is at the heart of
A Wild Perfection: It is, in a phrase coeditor Saundra Rose Maley borrows from
Mortimer Adler and uses as the title of her introduction, "The Great Conversation." The
conversation goes beyond the twentieth century and beyond America. In his letters to
friends, Wright works out quarrels and queries with the writers he is reading: Plato,
Catullus, Horace, Leo Tolstoy, Rainer Maria Rilke, Georg Trakl, and others. Yet many
of the recipients of his letters also constitute virtually any critic's short list of major
American poets of the late twentieth century: alphabetically, A. R. Ammons, Robert
Bly, Louise Bogan, Dickey, Richard Eberhart, Donald Hall, Galway Kinnell, Kunitz,
Denise Levertov, Philip Levine, Robert Lowell, J. D. McClatchy, John Crowe Ran-
som, Kenneth Rexroth, Theodore Roethke, M. L. Rosenthal, Anne Sexton, Leslie
Marmon Silko, W. D. Snodgrass, Allen Tate, Diane Wakoski, and Austin Warren.

Few, however, will turn to the letters of a poet to read about other poets. Readers
pursuing biographical information about Wright will find it in *A Wild Perfection*, but
they may find more than they bargained for. To be sure, they will find dates and details about the poet's life from just before his enlistment in the Army in the summer of
1946 to his cancer surgery just three months before his death in March of 1980. Tan-
gled among the details of the life of James Wright are also philosophical reflections
on the nature of human existence, literary criticism, the craft of writing, love, the academic life. Sometimes these reflections are offhand comments squeezed from the
moment. Other times they are polished essays, as carefully wrought as his poems, his
reviews, or his college lectures.

Even the essays appear as digressions in a coherent story of Wright's adult life,
much as the cetology chapters of Herman Melville's *Moby Dick* (1851) punctuate
the forward movement of the sailor's yarn. (Wright admitted, in a February 1, 1958,

letter to his dissertation director, Wayne Burns, that he loved a good "yarn.") The presence of a "plot" in *A Wild Perfection* is no accident: Maley indicates in her introduction that "readability as part of a narrative" was a selection criterion suggested by her editor at Farrar, Straus and Giroux, Jonathan Galassi. While Wright scholars may seize piecemeal on this or that nugget of correspondence, fitting it into a context already constructed, the general reader may, with pleasure and profit, read the whole book seriatim and follow the development of one of America's best twentieth century poets.

∽

James Wright was born in Ohio. After serving with the U.S. Army in postwar Japan, Wright attended Kenyon College and later the University of Washington, where he studied with poet Theodore Roethke while earning his Ph.D. In 1971, his Collected Poems *received the Pulitzer Prize.*

∽

While a book of letters that can be read like a novel has its merits, the editors could have offered more helpful contextualization, even to the reader who knows a great deal about Wright. For instance, Wright's March 13, 1964, letter to Macalester College President Dr. Harvey Rice bubbles with effusive superlatives: "I have never been so moved for so many truly personal reasons as I am moved by your letter." What in Rice's letter to Wright could have prompted such language? Nothing in Wright's letter offers a clue, and the editors are silent. Fourteen pages later, in a May 28 letter to his estranged wife Liberty, Wright tells the whole story: President Rice had attended a lecture Wright gave to an honor society, wrote him a commendatory note, and had copies sent to the dean of students and to Wright's department chair. What had touched the poet was not just the administrative act itself, though it was kind enough, but the context of the previous six years of what Wright perceived as neglect at the University of Minnesota, where he had been denied tenure. So necessary is the May 28 explanation to the March 13 thank you that, at the very least, a cross-reference should have been made for the reader who has no intention of reading this volume as a linear narrative.

Wright's letters were not written with an eye toward publication, which gives them a stark, sometimes startling intimacy and brutal honesty. "Brutally honest" is a cliché, but it is the right cliché, which Wright may have approved. He came to know the brute part of himself, what philosopher Friedrich Nietzsche called the Dionysian (though Wright identified Nietzsche as a "German poet"). Wright knew the beast, and did not flinch in its presence. Yet sometimes the honesty of these letters is almost painful, not just because they reveal uncomfortable truths, which they sometimes do (such as his nervous breakdown at age fifteen, recalled at age thirty; the disintegration of his first marriage; several outbreaks of his catathymic depression; his angry and obscene blowup with James Dickey after a bad review), but also because they exemplify one of the most pandemic diseases of twentieth century writers: self-consciousness. Even in business and personal correspondence, Wright is a conscious craftsman, struggling to master a form, even when that form is the personal letter. The downside of that struggle is that some letters become solipsistic, infinite-regress letters about writing letters. The advantage, however, is that in the process Wright reveals some of the s crets wrested from that struggle, secrets about the nature of the personal letter in particular, and English prose in general, in what may be the last generation of American letter writers.

The notion that letters such as Wright's are no longer possible in the age of e-mail is entertained in Maley's introduction and elaborated by David Orr in his *New York Times* review of *A Wild Perfection*. The death of the personal letter, however, was similarly predicted with the advent of the telegraph, the technology of which did, indeed, influence English prose style (the staccato rhythms and short sentences dictated by the sheer cost per word led to a style still sometimes called "telegraphic"). If letters such as those of James Wright are never seen again, it is because there will never be another James Wright. It has nothing to do with the technology of the typewriter, or pen and ink.

Or perhaps, in one respect, it does. The aforementioned self-consciousness of Wright's letters extends to an awareness of the physical medium in which he wrote, and Wright felt a difference between the pen in which he first drafted his poems and the typewriter with which he hammered them into shape. To poet and editor Donald Hall, Wright said the following in March of 1956, a paragraph which makes no sense unless one understands his distinction between writing and typing:

> I know I haven't sent you anything new for a while. To tell the truth, I haven't even typed much, though I've been writing like hell, mostly stuff that isn't coming off. I can't say that I feel barren—far from it. But I'm going through some odd stage in which changes, which I don't understand, are taking place. I don't want to sound like *Letters to a Young Poet*, but it's the truth.

Many writers have left records of those agonizing failures of inspiration, but that is not what is going on here. The muse on March 22, 1956, was sending Wright all he could handle, but the angel of revision, the goddess of editing, seemed unavailable. The form, which Wright always expressed as something external to the poet, would not come.

Wright's struggles with poetic form, which *A Wild Perfection* details admirably, were the struggles of his generation of poets, the post-1945 poets who made that bizarre compound "postmodernist" necessary in American letters. In a lifelong dialogue with Robert Bly, whose war against the iamb in English-language poetry he joined with reservations, Wright played the role of a French neoclassic *raisonneur*. Genuinely grateful for what he considered Bly's tutelage, Wright nevertheless feared that Bly's extremism on the issue of poetic meter would blunt or waste his powers. Furthermore, as he wrote to Louis Simpson (while congratulating him for winning the 1964 Pulitzer Prize for poetry), "there isn't enough strict iambic verse in the English language to bother resisting; anyway, Wyatt already resisted it." That is, the moment iambic pentameter was established as the "natural" English verse form, in Sir Thomas Wyatt's translation of book 4 of Vergil's *Aeneid* (c. 29-19 B.C.E.; English translation, 1553), it was already doomed.

Wright's quarter-century conversation with James Dickey is similarly precarious, specially as it began with a July 6, 1958, blast against Dickey, ostensibly because a review of Dickey's had slighted Philip Booth but manifestly also because it had slighted Wright's poetry. Wright's immediate retraction, his temporary "resignation" as a poet, a few weekends of rest at Bly's farm, all unfold alongside a growing respectful interchange with Dickey. The editors present the original offending letter in its entirety and do not edit out Wright's stumbling over his apologies in the next few letters to Dickey. Avoiding both sensationalism and Bowdlerization, *A Wild Perfection* reveals both the ugliest and the most beautiful elements of Wright.

The index of the book is a marvel of detail, yet it is not exhaustive. It seems to have been prosecuted in the unwarranted assumption that the only readers of Wright's letters would be devotees of American poetry. A great number of proper nouns appear in Wright's letters that do not show up in the index. It is clear from Wright's letters that he had at least a passing interest in college football—but a reader could not tell that from the index. Surely the only reason that baseball great Dizzy Dean is indexed is that Wright wrote an elegy for Dean's death in 1974, which appears in an appendix of unpublished poems at the end of the volume.

That appendix itself is worth the price of the book. Jonathan Blunk has carefully selected all the poems to which Wright specifically refers in his letters. They appear in the form in which they then existed. Many are unpublished, and those that were published later appear here in earlier incarnations.

Wright, despite his anguished lashings of self-hatred and occasional erosions of will (mostly thanks to alcoholism, which he was able to stave off in the last decade of his life), was a deeply humane presence in American poetry in the second half of the twentieth century, and *A Wild Perfection* admirably captures the personal and intellectual charism that made his loyal friends—themselves major figures in American letters—love him as fiercely as he loved life, America, and poetry.

John R. Holmes

Review Sources

American Poetry Review 34, no. 4 (July/August, 2005): 23.
The New York Times Book Review 154 (August 28, 2005): 14.
Publishers Weekly 252, no. 19 (May 9, 2005): 57.

WILLIAM EMPSON
Volume I: Among the Mandarins

Author: John Haffenden (1945-   )
Publisher: Oxford University Press (New York). 695 pp.
$45.00
Type of work: Literary biography
Time: 1906-1940
Locale: The United Kingdom, Japan, China, and the
  United States

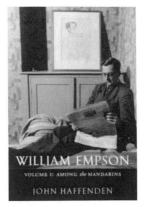

The first in what will be a two-volume biography of one
of the twentieth century's foremost literary critics covers
the years from his birth in 1906 through the beginning
stages of World War II in 1939-1940

Principal personages:

WILLIAM EMPSON, a British literary critic
I. A. RICHARDS, a British literary critic, Empson's most important influence and mentor
DOROTHEA RICHARDS, the wife of I. A. Richards, a keen observer of Empson's personal foibles
T. S. ELIOT, a seminal Anglo-American poet and critic who admired Empson's work
W. H. AUDEN, a major British poet, a friend and supporter of Empson
F. R. LEAVIS, an influential British literary critic who first supported and then attacked Empson's scholarly publications
HUMPHREY JENNINGS, a British literary intellectual, Empson's lifelong friend

Even though his name might not be recognized outside the ranks of those concerned with the history of literary criticism in English, William Empson's accomplishments as a superb textual analyst as well as gifted poet make him a figure of modern as well as historical significance. Building on his mentor I. A. Richards's insights into how readers actually respond to words, Empson in *Seven Types of Ambiguity* (1930) began to apply his own remarkable critical abilities to the interpretation of the literary text as the site of a complicated and quite possibly indeterminate series of meanings, a process that he would continue to develop and refine throughout the course of his career. This New Criticism, as it would come to be called, became the dominant method of textual study in the 1940's and remained so well into the 1970's. Although subsequently eclipsed by first structuralist and then poststructuralist developments in literary theory, the New Criticism remains a source of useful critical techniques well worth the attention of anyone interested in the formal properties of literary works.

As John Haffenden emphasizes, Empson's freewheeling critical procedures were in many respects significantly different from those of more rigidly empirical practitioners of the New Criticism such as F. R. Leavis and John Crowe Ransom. Empson respected the creative complexity of the writer's linguistic process and, in opposition to what became the orthodox version of the New Criticism, did not attempt to reduce the text to a finite set of meanings recoverable by those equipped with the proper critical apparatus. This aspect of *Among the Mandarins* is an important contribution to a more nuanced understanding of how New Criticism originated and should prompt some rewriting of the standard accounts of its inception.

John Haffenden is a professor of English literature at the University of Sheffield, England. A fellow of the Royal Society of Literature, he is the author of The Life of John Berryman *(1982) and has edited several volumes of William Empson's collected poetry and prose.*

Thus Empson remains a generative force in literary studies and so a likely subject for biography. John Haffenden, a friend of Empson whose *The Life of John Berryman* (1982) demonstrates his own abilities as both biographer and critic, has in the first part of what will be a two-volume work covered Empson's career from his birth in 1906 to his return to England from a teaching post in China in 1940. Haffenden has been engaged in researching this project for more than two decades, and if there are any serious omissions in his account of Empson's life, times, and companions, they were not noticed by this reviewer. From his account of several centuries of family history to his groundbreaking inquiries into Empson's hitherto somewhat obscured sojourns in Japan and China during the 1930's, Haffenden provides an exhaustively detailed and often surprisingly dramatic narrative of a story of achievement in both life and literature.

Empson's childhood years are not well documented, and in its early chapters *Among the Mandarins* relies too heavily on formulations of the "Empson must have felt" and "Empson may well have thought" variety in attempting to imagine his responses to familial and school events. In the absence of more direct biographical evidence, Haffenden supplies an extensive—and at times excessive—amount of information about the history of the Empson clan and those people and institutions with whom young William came into contact. Occasionally, as when the question of Richards's salary is afforded detailed attention, such digressions seem utterly pointless. More frequently, as in a twenty-five-page description of Empson's involvement with a fledgling literary magazine, the subject is obviously relevant but is considered at such exhausting length that one begins to wish Haffenden would step up the narrative's pace.

Fortunately, subsequent developments in Empson's literary and academic careers are both more intrinsically interesting and far better documented. His undergraduate years at Magdalene College, Cambridge, were marked by recognition of his abilities as both student and writer, which made him a figure of note to his contemporaries and thus the subject of some revealing recollections. The portrait that results is one of a young man determined to go his own way in sampling what life has to offer, whether that be new forms of prose and poetry or a wide variety of sexual experiences, and when he graduated with honors in 1929 a bright future seemed to lie ahead.

In that same year, however, not long after Empson had been appointed to a fellow-ship at Magdalene, one of the servants at the College discovered contraceptives in his living quarters. The incident could have been handled with discretion in a way that would have left no permanent blot on his record. Unfortunately, Magdalene's ad-ministration chose to take a hard line by canceling his fellowship and removing his name from the college's rolls, a decision that in effect turned Empson into a kind of academic stateless person. Although *Seven Types of Ambiguity* was critically (if not commercially) well received upon its publication in 1930, and Empson as a con-sequence enjoyed some success as a freelance writer in London, it was clear that at the moment there were no prospects of an academic post for him in the United Kingdom.

With the help of Richards, Empson obtained a position as professor of English language and literature at the University of Literature and Science in Tokyo, just at the time when extreme right-wing nationalistic sentiment was emerging as the dominant force in Japan's political life. Haffenden titles the chapter dealing with this experience "The Trials of Tokyo" and is at pains to refute previous accounts which have presented Empson's time in Japan as a kind of mutual love feast be-tween himself and his hosts. As his biographer makes clear, Empson was often be-wildered and repelled by developments in contemporary Japanese society, although he was also deeply appreciative of its artistic heritage and in the classroom proved an effective and conscientious teacher. He left the country in 1934 with decidedly mixed emotions, well aware of its growing militarism and yet hoping that it would eventually reject what he saw as a perversion of the best aspects of its cultural tradi-tions.

Back in London, Empson resumed his career as a freelance writer and began to prepare a collection of his poems for publication. Here and elsewhere *Among the Mandarins* does an excellent job of conveying its subject's progress as an increas-ingly serious writer of verse, making good use of the alternate drafts and journal com-ments in Empson's papers. It will be interesting to see if Haffenden's advocacy re-sults in a rise in Empson's stock as a poet. Certainly the work quoted here stands up well in comparison with that of T. S. Eliot and W. H. Auden, contemporaries of Empson who took his poetry seriously and with whom he shares a number of themes and techniques.

Haffenden's treatment of Empson's literary criticism is not quite as satisfactory, primarily because of the mass of not always pertinent detail that too often clogs the in-tellectual arteries of *Among the Mandarins*. Its account of the critical reception of *Seven Types of Ambiguity* and the equally influential *Some Versions of Pastoral* (1935) is excellent, but the content and character of the books themselves are not pre-sented as fully as they might be, to the point that readers unfamiliar with these works will have some difficulty in understanding why they are important. Their engagement with the interpretive possibilities of sensitive reading is as challenging and exhilarat-ing now as it was when they were first published, but this openness to multifaceted critical judgment is somewhat lost in the thickets of contextual detail with which Haffenden surrounds them.

In 1937, after three years of struggling to support himself as a freelance writer, Empson accepted a teaching position at the National Peking University in China. His timing could not have been worse; after years of provocation and bullying, Japan had just embarked on a full-scale offensive into China's northern provinces that forced the relocation of his university to a series of safer venues in the country's interior. Although the majority of the faculty and students were safely evacuated, the institution's physical resources, and in particular its library, had to be left behind, and as a consequence Empson found himself forced to rely upon his memory for most of the works that he taught in his courses on English literature.

Fortunately, Empson had been educated at a time when the memorization of texts was still considered a normative part of their study, and so he was able to cope with a situation which subsequent generations of academics, reliant upon the instant retrieval facilities of the information age, would find impossible. Living in temporary and often unsanitary housing, inadequately fed, and frequently bombed by Japanese planes, Empson nonetheless survived these conditions and in a sense transcended them. He experienced reducing education to its essentials as a kind of Spartan regime that pared away the distractions of normal university life and forced one to concentrate on what was truly important. Although the two chapters on his 1937-1939 period in China are marred by some of the excessive detail that is the only serious negative feature of *Among the Mandarins*—a long digression into Chinese provincial politics is particularly tedious—they on the whole present a fascinating portrait of a somewhat unlikely hero coping with conditions that would have defeated a lesser person.

The conclusion of *Among the Mandarins* finds Empson in the United States, where in the fall of 1939 he took a temporary job writing radio scripts in Boston and unsuccessfully sought a college-teaching position. Empson was frustrated by what he saw as American ignorance of world events, particularly the suffering of China, and returned to London at the beginning of 1940 psychologically well prepared for the city's ordeal during the imminent Battle of Britain.

Haffenden will continue this story in a forthcoming sequel, and it is safe to say that the project when finished will constitute the definitive biography of William Empson. *Among the Mandarins* is a work to be welcomed and admired, particularly for its effective advocacy of his importance as a poet, although one may hope that its concluding volume will be somewhat less encumbered with factual digressions and will more clearly address the issues raised by Empson's literary criticism. To conclude with some corny but relevant—especially for a critic who delighted in linguistic possibilities—wordplay, the at times ponderous prolixity of *Among the Mandarins* needs to be succeeded by a more down-to-earth approach to what Empson himself did and why it deserves, as it surely does, attention.

Paul Stuewe

Review Sources

The Economist 375 (June 4, 2005): 79.
London Review of Books 27, no. 10 (May 19, 2005): 3-5.
New Criterion 23, no. 9 (May, 2005): 73-74.
Publishers Weekly 252, no. 20 (May 16, 2005): 53-54.
The Spectator 297 (April 30, 2005): 37.
Sunday Times, May 1, 2005, p. 50.
The Times Higher Education Supplement, April 15, 2005, p. 26.
The Times Literary Supplement, July 1, 2005, pp. 4-6.
The Washington Post Book World, June 19, 2005, p. 15.

THE WORLD REPUBLIC OF LETTERS

Author: Pascale Casanova
First published: La République mondiale des letters,
  1999, in France
Translated from the French by M. B. DeBevoise
Publisher: Harvard University Press (Cambridge, Mass.).
  420 pp. $35.00
Type of work: Literary criticism and literary history

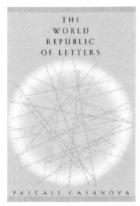

Casanova examines inequalities in a global literary
realm that exists independently of political and economic
realms

Certain men and women of letters have created imaginary republics—sometimes vast societies—in their writings. Isaac Asimov, in his Foundation series, listed more than seventy separate worlds in a loose hierarchy, including capitals of space sectors, trading and agricultural planets, a "world of strange fashions," and of course Terminus, the Encyclopedia Planet. William Faulkner invented Yoknapatawpha County, home of the Snopes, Sartoris, and Compson clans. Now, in *The World Republic of Letters*, Pascale Casanova has mapped a global realm of authors themselves.

Like political republics—and those invented by Faulkner, Asimov, and others—this world republic of letters has its history, its major and minor characters, its capital (Paris), and its provinces. This is a place—and a state of mind—whose centuries-long development Casanova relates in *The World Republic of Letters* and carries further than it has been carried before.

Like political republics, the literary republic envisioned by Casanova runs largely on economics. Her predecessors in this line of thought have described the world of letters largely in economic terms. As early as 1827, Johann Wolfgang von Goethe anticipated that a global literary culture would be generated by "a commerce of ideas among peoples." In the 1920's, Paul Valéry likened it to the French stock market, the Bourse. The late French sociologist Pierre Bourdieu, one of Casanova's most immediate intellectual models, conceived of "social capital" (class membership) and "cultural capital" (education and knowledge) as having force equal to that of economic capital. Casanova, however, stands apart from her predecessors in reworking a nationally based concept of "symbolic and literary capital" to present it on an international scale.

Like many worlds portrayed in economic metaphors, Casanova's world republic of letters assumes a conflict model of human endeavor. In her view, the literary world has its winners and losers, as does the economic arena; but literary success is determined in large part by how close one lives to acknowledged literary centers such as New York, London, or, especially, Paris. Those born in the backwaters of this

∽

Literary critic Pascale Casanova is a researcher at the Center for Research in Arts and Language in Paris. Her previous work Beckett the Abstractor *(1977) won the Grand Prix de l'Essai de la Société des Gens de Lettres.*

∽

literary republic are doomed to obscurity unless they resort to tricks and stratagems to win public recognition—stratagems that may include relocating to one of the literary centers, as did the American expatriates living in Paris during the 1920's, such as Gertrude Stein, Ernest Hemingway, Malcolm Cowley, and E. E. Cummings.

In allying themselves with the avant-garde, writers from the literary provinces partake of its "literary capital," which Casanova says "is both what everyone seeks to acquire and what is universally recognized as the necessary and sufficient condition of taking part in literary competition."

What are the components of literary capital? Casanova cites a study in which Priscilla Clark Ferguson identifies these components, including literacy rates, annual numbers of books published and sold, numbers of publishers and bookstores. The nations that score high on these components—usually those with literary histories spanning several centuries—have accumulated the most "literary capital." Literary capital also rests on judgments and reputation; as Valéry pointed out, this too gives literary capital something in common with the financial stock market. Casanova adds, "Language is another major component of literary capital. . . . Certain languages, by virtue of the prestige of the texts written in them, are reputed to be more literary than others, to embody literature." The elitist tendencies of the republic are unmistakable, although as Casanova shows, it has also been the salvation of many writers from "deprived" areas.

How did the world republic of letters come into being? This is Casanova's main subject in the first half of her book. As she sees it, four separate phases mark the republic's development. First, the Renaissance and Reformation movements launched an offensive against a culture dominated by the Latin language and the Catholic Church. In 1549, Joachim du Bellay published an essay, "The Defense and Illustration of the French Language," which Casanova describes as a "declaration of war against the domination of Latin." Casanova, a Frenchwoman, credits du Bellay with starting the vernacular revolution, though actually Dante Alighieri's *De vulgari eloquentia* (c. 1306; English translation, 1890), a defense of vernacular language, preceded du Bellay's work by 243 years. From the 1550's to 1700 and beyond, France accumulated "literary assets" largely by beating the dominant Latin culture at its own game—translating and imitating classical models, standardizing the French language, and perfecting poetic form. By the reign of Louis XIV, French had supplanted Latin as the literary language.

Italy, too, though not a unified nation until the nineteenth century, became a "recognized literary power," along with France and followed by Spain and England. Eventually Germany, which, unlike France and Italy, had no classical literary heritage from antiquity, found a new source of "literary capital"—its own folk culture, initially championed by Johann Gottfried von Herder (1744-1803). The notion that a people's traditional oral culture would reveal its unique soul—its "genius"—has sparked literary enterprise both in emerging nineteenth century European nations and in "postcolonial" nations of the twentieth and twenty-first centuries.

In this phase also, the modern European states began to emerge. This led to a second phase—literary nationalism—in which authors tied their fortunes to the rising nation-states. Literature, and language itself, became powerful political tools. Casanova argues, however, that when this phase is accomplished, nation-states delude themselves into thinking that literature is not a political instrument but a wholly autonomous enterprise. This leads to the third, modernist phase, in which literature declares its independence and ceases to support the political apparatus. In this spirit, the French Symbolist poets described their work as entirely useless in the political sense—with which assessment much of bourgeois society agreed. Meanwhile, according to Casanova, "dominated" nations in Africa, Asia, and Latin America are forced to continue the struggle for literary recognition and authority.

In the fourth phase, the dominant culture receives a new infusion of ideas and spirit, as authors who had been excluded from that culture—and exempt from its standards and constraints—find themselves newly recognized and rewarded. Casanova cites the twentieth century examples of James Joyce and Faulkner, notable revolutionaries in literature, who struggled to prominence from the "dominated" regions, and indeed became the avant-garde.

Paradoxically, it was the rivalry among national literatures that led to the emergence of what Casanova calls an "international literary space" by asserting literary values independently of national political agendas. In an autonomous transnational realm where literary endeavor could (at least theoretically) be judged on its own terms, writers might win readership and admiration outside their own generally conservative national constituencies. The new constituency was a literary avant-garde, with Paris at the helm because of its enduring autonomy and its exceptional hospitality to the avant-garde.

In the second half of her book, Casanova relates the stratagems that writers on the literary periphery have used to seize a position in the literary center. She contends, however, that these writers' struggles have been obscured by "the fable of an enchanted world . . . where universality reigns through liberty and equality." In an impressive display of learning, she supports her argument with examples from all over the "literarily deprived" world—North Africa, Latin America, Eastern Europe, East Asia—and from all ages since the mid-sixteenth century. She addresses the modernism of Henrik Ibsen and W. B. Yeats as well as the most recent postcolonial literary strategists; from "assimilationists" such as V. S. Naipaul and E. M. Cioran to "rebels" such as Pablo Neruda and Chinua Achebe.

It may help readers to know that in this book Casanova, a scholar associated with the Center for Research in Arts and Language in Paris, is presenting a work of comparative literature, a discipline that strives to establish a taxonomy of literature as it searches for affinities of literary strategies across time and space. She successfully demonstrates the remarkable consistency of those strategies among writers living decades, even centuries, and continents apart. Thus, a strong drive for international acceptance characterizes initially "marginalized" writers as diverse as Joyce, Ibsen, Samuel Beckett, Jorge Luis Borges, Gabriel García Márquez, and Salman Rushdie. It is this drive that has fueled literary innovation for more than a hundred years, as younger writers educate the public taste to accept unfamiliar literary subjects and techniques. They become a new avant-garde, beating Paris—or other centers such as London and New York—at their own game just as, centuries ago, the French beat the dominant classical Latin culture at its own game. In being more "modern" than Paris, these writers transform the standard for literary modernity. Thus, the international literary avant-garde provides aspiring writers an alternative to their peripheral origins, even while demanding that these writers accept its own supremacy as the price of literary recognition.

Perhaps because of its glaring inequalities, however, Casanova seems reluctant to acknowledge this positive aspect of the world literary republic. Moreover, her classification systems make her appear unwilling to concede the literary excellence of authors who would not make the political choices she approves. In chapters titled "The Assimilated" and "The Rebels," she catalogs "two great families of strategies" for escaping the literary backwaters and achieving international recognition. The first of these, assimilation into a dominant culture—especially one that has colonized one's native land—she scorns as "the lowest level of literary revolt," a gambit for an author who "can thus refuse the fate of becoming a national writer." An example is Naipaul, born in the West Indies of a family that had immigrated there from India. Casanova describes him as having adopted an assimilationist position "at once conservative, disillusioned, and impossible" owing to his "betrayal of his own kind, whom England had once colonized." Ungraciously, she dismisses his accomplishments by saying, "The traditional character of his stories and novels is the direct consequence of this pathetic search for identity."

Casanova's real heroes are the "rebels," including Franz Kafka, Joyce, and Faulkner. For whatever reason, she offers rather contrived explanations of how these authors fought their way into the mainstream. Here, for example, is her highly overblown description of Faulkner's revolutionary impact:

> Though he enjoys a great reputation in the highest circles of the literary world and ranks among the great literary revolutionaries, Faulkner is still a figure with whom all writers in countries on the periphery can identify. . . . In putting an end to the curse of backwardness that lay over these regions, by offering the novelists of the poorest countries the possibility of giving acceptable literary form to the most repugnant realities of the margins of the world, Faulkner has been a formidable force for accelerating literary time . . . . in his hands, a violent, tribal civilization, impressed with the mark of biblical mythologies, opposed in every respect to urban modernity (which was typically associated with the stylistic avant-garde), became the privileged object in one of the most daring exercises in style of the century. Faulkner singlehandedly resolved the contradictions in which writers from disadvantaged countries found themselves mired, lifting the curse of imposed literary hierarchies and bringing about a prodigious reversal of values. With a single stroke he wiped out the accumulated backwardness of literatures that hitherto had been excluded from the literary present, which is to say from stylistic modernity.

Faulkner did not "put an end to the curse of backwardness that lay over these regions" any more than the hero of Howard Fast's novel *Spartacus* (1951) put an end to slavery. Faulkner did, as Casanova reports, inspire younger writers in lands as diverse as León, Algeria, and Latin America. However he himself, with complete sincerity, specifically disavowed any such programmatic intent as Casanova suggests.

Casanova wants her book to be "an instrument for struggling against the presumptions, the arrogance, and the fiats of critics in the center." In describing "these regions" in the terms she chooses, does not Casanova however betray some ambivalence toward the "poorest countries" she wishes to champion? She also overlooks the fact that writers at the center are as capable of innovation as those from the backwaters. After all, French authors such as Marcel Proust and Alain Robbe-Grillet exerted a strong innovative influence throughout the twentieth century, and it was Jean-Paul Sartre who took Faulkner under his wing. The center can be liberated from within as well as from the outside.

Thomas Rankin

Review Sources

London Review of Books 26, no. 18 (September 23, 2004).
The Nation 280, no. 1 (January 3, 2005): 21-23.
New Left Review 31 (January/February, 2005): 71.
New Statesman 134 (April 11, 2005): 50-51.

WOUNDED

Author: Percival Everett (1956-   )
Publisher: Graywolf Press (St. Paul, Minn.). 207 pp.
   $23.00
Type of work: Novel
Time: 2005
Locale: Southwestern Wyoming

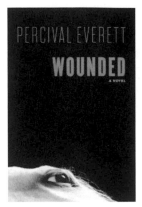

Tentatively reconnecting with other people after a period of self-imposed isolation, one man learns a bitter lesson about the abiding intolerance toward minorities in modern America

Principal characters:
> JOHN HUNT, the first-person narrator, an African American rancher and horse trainer
> GUS, John's uncle and housemate since the death of John's wife Susie
> MORGAN REECE, a college instructor and neighbor
> BUCKY EDMONDS, the local sheriff
> DAVID THAYER, a gay college student
> HOWARD THAYER, David's father, a Chicago tax attorney and John's old college friend
> ELVIS MONDAY, a local American Indian rancher

One of a number of novels that reflect Percival Everett's interest in the culture of the American West, *Wounded* focuses on one man's rediscovery of himself as a result of his reengagement in the lives of others. Cut off from the larger world in part because of geographical distance (his ranch is thirty miles from the nearest town), in part because of race (he is one of very few African Americans in the rural West), and in part because of the psychological and emotional walls that he has built around himself since the death of his wife Susie six years earlier, John Hunt must redirect the course of his life when he is forced to respond to events in the local community.

First, he answers a call from the local sheriff to visit in jail Wallace Castlebury, an apparently aimless, friendless young man "dumber than a bucket of hair." A hired hand on John's ranch, Castlebury is accused of the brutal murder of a gay college student, an apparently senseless crime reminiscent of the real-life murder of University of Wyoming undergraduate Matthew Shepard in 1998. Shepard's death—he was savagely beaten and left to die in freezing temperatures along a rural road—focused international attention on the issue of hate crimes in the United States and provided the subject for the play *The Laramie Project* (2000) by American dramatist Moises Kaufman, director of the groundbreaking Tectonic Theatre Project.

For a time, John reluctantly serves as Castlebury's only contact with the outside world; and John's involvement in the case does not end with Castlebury's cellblock suicide. The shocking nature of the crime of which he is accused pushes the little town of Highland, Wyoming, into the national spotlight, just as Shepard's murder exposed Laramie to the broad glare of publicity. Soon people from other parts of the United States begin arriving to attend a rally to condemn the violence sometimes bred from bigotry.

Among them are twenty-year-old David Thayer, the son of an old college chum of John when he was an art history student at the University of California at Berkeley, and his partner, Robert. Although the rally is canceled because of snow, David returns to town a couple of months later, after Robert cheats on him, and he decides to put aside his studies at the University of Illinois for a semester. He is drawn back to Wyoming partly because he responds to the dramatic landscape and partly because he is attracted to John.

Percival Everett is a prolific writer noted for his experimentation with various fictional genres, including realism, fantasy, parody, and children's literature. A professor of English at the University of Southern California, Everett earned critical approbation with his first novel, Suder *(1983), and since then has solidified his reputation as a writer who resists categorization.*

The laconic rancher is also an object of interest to his neighbor, Morgan Reece, a part-time community college instructor who has moved back home to take care of her ailing mother. Although he finds her attractive, John is reluctant to get involved with another woman because he blames himself for his wife's death. Susie was killed by one of the horses that John was training, perhaps in an attempt to prove to her husband that she was not afraid. If any romance is to blossom, Morgan must take the initiative.

It is clear that John is more comfortable with animals than with people. The first half of the novel is peppered with bits of wisdom that he has acquired from his years of training horses, such as the dictum that "the horse isn't supposed to make decisions." It comes down to control; John believes that he understands and can therefore control horses, but people are another matter.

The landscape is also an object of fascination and a source of comfort for John, who responds deeply to the "dramatic land, dry, remote, wild." His ranch is just east of the Red Desert, which encompasses six million acres in the southwest corner of Wyoming. "Every time I come up here and look at that," John tells David at one point in the novel, "I know my place in the world." John himself admits that he has "no affection necessarily for the history of the people" of the West. "It [is] the land for me," John affirms. It may, however, be the sheer inhospitality of the landscape that necessitates some sort of communal bonding; to survive in this space, people need to band together in common cause.

This is one lesson that John finally learns. As the novel progresses, his ranch becomes a kind of sanctuary. After Susie's death, John took in his seventy-nine-year-old Uncle Gus, who had spent eleven years in prison for the killing of his wife's white rapist. In short succession, John brings home a crippled coyote pup, the only surviving member of her family, whose lair had been torched in a senseless act of destruction. David Thayer arrives to heal the wounds of his broken relationship. Morgan Reece takes up residence after the death of her mother.

Just as horses find him to be a calming force, people are drawn to John's quiet authority. A man of few words but strong of character, independent of mind, and compassionate to those victimized by others, John Hunt fits the mold of the archetypal Western hero. As a man whose deeds are more eloquent than his words, as a rugged individualist in whose care the welfare of others rests, John joins the ranks of such heroic figures as the title character of Owen Wister's classic novel *The Virginian* (1902), which is also set in Wyoming, and the tough protagonists in the popular cowboy novels of American fiction writers Zane Grey and Max Brand.

John's critical reengagement in human affairs reaches a head when it eventually becomes clear that a group of neo-Nazis has taken up residence in the area and that they are the ones responsible for a series of violent acts against minorities, including cattle mutilations and racial slurs written in blood in the snow on a nearby Indian reservation—and, as will be discovered at the novel's end, the death of the gay college student of which Wallace had been accused. They extend their string of malevolent acts by kidnapping David, who has driven to town to get some medicine for Gus. The local authorities, including the slow-witted sheriff, fail to pursue his disappearance aggressively. Then John and his uncle take matters into their own hands.

John's evolving, increasingly complicated relationship with David is central to the plot. Time and time again, John intercedes on the young man's behalf. When David's homophobic father, Howard, arrives at the ranch with his twenty-something girlfriend in tow, David, still reeling from Robert's infidelity, throws his father's philandering in his face. In the middle of the night, after a drunken argument with his father, David wanders, partially dressed, outside into the snow. Singlehandedly John tracks him down in the subzero temperatures.

When he finds him, John takes David to the temporary shelter of a nearby cave to help forestall hypothermia. This cave, the subject of John's recurring dreams, is of major symbolic significance in the text. In fact, the novel begins with the narrator's attempt to define the essential nature of caves, including what might be regarded as their most frightening aspect—"that one can enter." Emblematic of the deep recesses of selfhood, the cave represents something in John or something in his relationship with his wife that prevents complete intimacy between the two; he wants to explore the cave, but Susie is scared by the very thought of penetrating its interior. Yet, eventually this very same cave provides the setting for John's first sexual experience with Morgan; it is also in this cave that John strips down to warm the nearly frozen David with his body heat, and David, delirious from the cold, responds to their naked embrace with a kiss on the mouth.

John's confused reaction to this act is representative of the difficulty many people have with the issue of sexual orientation, especially when it challenges their preconceptions regarding the nature of manhood. In trying to find David on his own, John acknowledges his own complicated affection for the young man. There is between the two an attraction that John does not fully understand, but it makes Morgan uncomfortable despite the fact that John has proposed marriage to her.

In setting out to find David, John also asserts the code of the Old West that it is perfectly justifiable to be one's own agent of justice. Alone, he rushes out in the snow to rescue David from the cold; later, with only his uncle beside him, he sets out to rescue David from his kidnappers.

Thus, John Hunt joins other self-contained characters in Everett's Western novels, individuals who find their ultimate purpose in compassionate defense of the welfare of others. David Larson, a transplanted southerner in *Walk Me to the Distance* (1985), a novel set in Wyoming during the Vietnam War era, participates, however reluctantly, in the lynching of a mentally handicapped man who rapes a Eurasian child abandoned to his initially involuntary care. Bubba, an African American tracker in *God's Country* (1994), a novel set in the Old West, repeatedly defends the orphan girl Jake from predators and also determines to avenge the massacre of an innocent American Indian tribe. Robert Hawks, an African American hydrologist in *Watershed* (1996), a novel set in the modern-day West, slowly takes up the cause of a Native American group whose water supply is being poisoned by a federal project. All four fit the mold of the code hero who is willing to make sacrifices for the greater good. In each case, action is taken on behalf of an oppressed individual or minority group.

Suffering massive internal injuries from the beating that he endured at the hands of the three "rednecks" that have been terrorizing the community, David does not survive his attack. Neither do his killers. While John rushes the unconscious David to the hospital, Uncle Gus and some of their American Indian neighbors take matters into their own hands to prevent any repetition of the group's destructive behavior.

Elvis Monday, one of the Indian ranchers bedeviled by the neo-Nazis, delivers the novel's final message when he tells John, in justification of their disposal of this cadre of right-wing extremists: "Everyplace is the frontier." John nods in agreement, and the reader is left to consider the proposition that in a day and age when hate crimes against minorities are more and more common and established governmental safeguards appear less and less effectual, it may be the final recourse of victimized groups—blacks, Indians, and gays—to defend themselves by all necessary means.

As signaled by the novel's title, a single man, "wounded" by the course his personal life has taken—particularly the loss of his wife, finds the strength to shelter and defend others "wounded" by prejudice and bigotry. In taking a stand, John rediscovers himself. Like the three-legged coyote pup that he adopts, John admits near the end of the novel, "I can't recognize my own tracks until I stop moving."

S. Thomas Mack

Review Sources

Booklist 101, no. 22 (August 1, 2005): 1991.
Entertainment Weekly, September 2, 2005, p. 85.
Kirkus Reviews 73, no. 12 (June 15, 2005): 654.
Library Journal 130, no. 12 (July 1, 2005): 66-67.
Los Angeles Times, August 28, 2005, p. R2.
The New York Times Book Review 155 (September 18, 2005): 22.
Publishers Weekly 252, no. 28 (July 18, 2005): 183.
The Washington Post, September 4, 2005, p. T4.

THE YEAR OF MAGICAL THINKING

Author: Joan Didion (1934-   )
Publisher: Alfred A. Knopf (New York). 240 pp. $24.00
Type of work: Memoir
Time: From the 1960's to 2004
Locale: New York, Los Angeles, Hawaii, and Paris

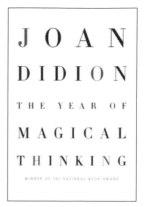

Didion is unsparingly candid in this account of her coming to terms with the sudden death of her husband, the grave illness of her daughter, and the grief attached to both

Principal personages:
> JOAN DIDION, a novelist and essayist
> JOHN GREGORY DUNNE, a novelist, journalist, and Didion's husband of forty years
> QUINTANA, their daughter

> Life changes fast.
> Life changes in the instant.
> You sit down to dinner and life as you know it ends.
> The question of self-pity.

These are the first words in Joan Didion's new book, *The Year of Magical Thinking*. They are also the first words she set down a day or two after her husband, John Gregory Dunne, died of a "sudden massive coronary event" at dinner in their New York apartment on December 30, 2003. They are words that recur throughout the book, as if prompting the stream of reflections that emerge during Didion's yearlong struggle with Dunne's death and the splintering of her life. It was not until October 4, 2004, that she began to write the book in earnest, but these initial sentences, spilled onto her computer in the wake of Dunne's collapse, and while their only daughter lay comatose in a hospital across town, contain the germ of the memoir's narrative and the main line of its inquiry. How does one live through such wrenching changes? How does one avoid self-pity at such losses? How does one endure the temporary insanity of grief? How does one mourn in a culture that has no time for death, makes no allowance for grief, and fears talking about either? Whatever else she does here, Didion talks about death, about grief, and in shattering, immediate ways. Hers is an eloquent testimony to what many have doubtless experienced but few have been able to describe with so much power and penetration.

Didion has famously said that she does not know what she thinks until she writes it down. All of her instincts as a journalist tell her that when she is uncertain about what something means, the best plan is to "read, learn, work it up, go to the literature." This is what she does following Dunne's death. She spends months finding her way to information, cobbling together whatever seems helpful: from poets and psychologists, doctors and etiquette writers. She researches her husband's case, grills

*Joan Didion, a longtime anxious
observer of American politics and
culture, has written five novels and
eight books of nonfiction. She is a
regular contributor to* The New
York Review of Books *and* The
New Yorker. The Year of Magical
Thinking *received the National
Book Award for nonfiction.*

physicians about her daughter's condition, sifts through the assembled medical facts, retraces the chronology of events, even rereads her husband's novels. She works it all up and writes it all down, producing a narrative that she hopes will give meaning to death's meaninglessness, a narrative that will tell her how to think about losing her partner of forty years and how to handle the threat of losing her only child.

Didion's first collection of nonfiction, *Slouching Towards Bethlehem* (1968), began with her confession that the title essay was a way, in a time of cultural crisis, "to come to terms with disorder." *The White Album* (1979), written a decade of cultural atomization later, began with her claim that "we tell ourselves stories in order to live." In this memoir, the motive behind Didion's writing remains the same: She is clearly trying to tell herself a story that will allow her to go on in the face of a life now wildly disordered.

While she pursues this rational business of compiling facts and shaping information, while she appears to be handling things intelligently and with admirable poise and efficiency (the social worker on that first evening at the hospital calls her "a pretty cool customer"), she is actually going crazy. She is, she says, thinking magically, and "magical thinking," which characterizes Didion's behavior for the year of 2004, is thinking that is simply irrational. It is thinking like a child, where what is wished for can happen, what is imagined must be true, what cannot be accepted is therefore not true. She knows this is crazy but cannot proceed otherwise. Only when she receives the autopsy results, almost a full year later than she should have, can she finally admit the fact of Dunne's death, the fact of his being gone for good. For months she has nursed the belief that if she did not read the obituary notice, he would not be dead. She could not throw out Dunne's shoes because he would be returning and would need them; she could not throw out the broken alarm clock or the Buffalo pens long gone dry because he would be back and would want them. She lives by signs, probing everything for symbolic meaning. His dictionary opened to a particular page must signify something, and inadvertently turning over the page means she has lost the crucial message. She lives ritualistically, doing things that will ensure his return, ignoring evidence that says he will not. This, she discovers, is the madness of grief at work, and even though it subsides by the end of this first year, it is a genuine state of madness while it lasts and one which she explores with harrowing precision.

What Didion is most at pains to convey is that grief is not what one expects it to be. It is not the same as mourning, and it does not hit at once. As the initial shock of a sudden death recedes, grief roars in and completely alters the landscape of ordinary existence: It "comes in waves, paroxysms, sudden apprehensions that weaken the knees and blind the eyes and obliterate the dailiness of life." It is unpredictable and without any forward movement. One is passive before its onslaughts, caught up vertiginously in great surges of pain and panic. It is, she is glad to read in Sigmund Freud's "Mourning and Melancholia" (1917), a real mental derangement but one not treated as a pathology because it is known to pass; it is eventually overcome. But how? When? It may not be a pathological state, but so great is her disorientation that she nevertheless imagines she might be pathologically bereaved.

Oddly enough, more helpful than the clinical observations of psychologists is what Didion finds in a 1922 volume of etiquette by Emily Post. Post's pronouncements on death and dying are direct, practical, instinctively right in their awareness of the unique kind of mental and physiological suffering someone in Didion's position experiences. Yet reassuring as it is for her to find someone speaking from a time when death was not swathed in euphemisms or wholly eclipsed, all of Post's knowing advice about heated milk and sunny rooms cannot change the dark reality of grief: "Nor can we know ahead of the fact (and here lies the heart of the difference between grief as we imagine it and grief as it is) the unending absence that follows, the void, the very opposite of meaning, the relentless succession of moments, during which we will confront the experience of meaninglessness." That kind of existential pain, a pain that cannot be accurately imagined or successfully prepared for, is what Didion's memoir tries to communicate.

Compounding this emotional turmoil is the fact that her daughter, having defied the odds to pull through the December crisis (a case of a healthy and newly married young woman suddenly facing death, as ordinary flu turns to extraordinary septic shock) has now, several months later, again fallen seriously ill in Los Angeles. Didion flies out to the West Coast, where she is swept up in what she calls the vortex effect, the track to the past, caught unawares and pulled into the rich shared life she and Dunne knew in the twenty-four years they lived in Los Angeles. Now the city is full only of ghosts, reminders of past happiness, a quarter-century's history that threatens at every intersection of Wilshire Boulevard to overtake and undo her. Her heart stops when she passes the theater where they saw *The Graduate* in 1967, or when she buys bottled water at a Rite-Aid pharmacy on the spot of the old Bistro restaurant where they celebrated Quintana's third birthday. Hard as these memories are for Didion to revisit, and much as she tries to shield herself from being sideswiped by them, for the reader these are some of the most moving passages in the memoir, these clear-eyed vignettes of Didion and Dunne, writing together in the big old house on Franklin Avenue, entertaining together in Malibu, polishing film scripts together in Hawaii.

What is clear is that theirs was truly a joint literary career. As she says, they were rarely apart in forty years, living and working together, their personal and professional lives wholly (and apparently harmoniously) integrated. Dunne was her first reader, her principal editor; she was his. They trusted each other as they did no one else. Beyond the writing, Dunne was what tethered his wife to the world. Her notorious emotional fragility, the fearfulness she admits she was born with, the anxiety only partly hidden behind her exceedingly crafted prose—this is what Dunne neutralized and made functional. He handled all telephone calls, kept in touch with friends, made all arrangements. Without him, the isolation and sense of detachment becomes overwhelming. What she has lost is her sense of control, always something on which she had at best a slim purchase. Now, with her husband dead and her daughter close to death (Quintana died in August, 2005, after the memoir had been written, and this fact is not mentioned here), Didion realizes the widespread belief that people can control much of anything in their lives is scandalously false. In spite of what her daughter's doctors insisted, one cannot "manage" things; in spite of the wish to protect those one loves, one cannot make people safe. There are limits to what one can control.

There are limits to what writing can control, too—even Didion's writing, which has always seemed such an artifact of control, so calculated and ironically distanced, so spare yet gravid with implication. Spare, lean, detached—these are terms critics seem unable to resist attaching to her prose, and they characterize her writing here, too, though the style is even more stripped down than usual: It feels raw, less writerly. This is appropriate. She is writing out of a place of exposed nerves and chaotic emotions. She has said that she was not so much writing a book as trying to sort things out for herself; it was only later, as she began to think about structure, that she realized it could even be a book. The structure she came up with reflects the original impulse behind the writing: a nonlinear narrative of twenty-two short sections which keep coming back to that fatal night of December 30 and trying again, from a different angle, to identify just what happened and why, trying to determine if it might have unfolded differently and how. There are pages of fugitive lyricism, but far more show Didion at her most pared back, reporting, itemizing ("let me try a chronology here"), the uninflected and reiterated declarative sentences shedding even her typical less-is-more chic.

What she is trying to create in all of this, she says, is something that will "collapse the sequence of time, show you simultaneously all the frames of memory that come to me now, let you pick the takes, the marginally different expressions, the variant readings of the same lines. This is a case in which I need more than words to find the meaning." Like T. S. Eliot before her, she has gathered these fragments, the many strands of the memoir, to shore up against her ruin. Beyond that act of assembling and remembering, she can only do what Dunne once told her to when they were swimming into the cave at Portuguese Bend. The tide had to be just right to catch it as it moved through the rocks: "You had to feel the swell change. You had to go with the change." Go with the change. That is what Didion hopes she can do, what she hopes writing this memoir has allowed her to do.

Thomas J. Campbell

Review Sources

Booklist 101, no. 22 (August 1, 2005): 1950.
Commentary 120, no. 5 (December, 2005): 86-88.
Harper's Magazine 311 (November, 2005): 97-102.
Kirkus Reviews 73, no. 14 (July 15, 2005): 774.
Library Journal 130, no. 14 (September 1, 2005): 140-141.
Ms. 15, no. 3 (Fall, 2005): 74-75.
New Statesman 134, no. 4763 (October 24, 2005): 49-50.
The New York Review of Books 52, no. 16 (October 20, 2005): 8-12.
The New York Times 155 (October 4, 2005): E1-E6.
The New York Times Book Review 155 (October 9, 2005): 1-11.
Newsweek 146, no. 15 (October 10, 2005): 63.
Publishers Weekly 252, no. 26 (June 27, 2005): 48.
Time 166, no. 15 (October 10, 2005): 56-57.

BIOGRAPHICAL WORKS BY SUBJECT

2006

BEATLES, THE
    Beatles, The (Spitz), 41
BLACKMUN, HARRY
    Becoming Justice Blackmun
        (Greenhouse), 45

CANSECO, JOSÉ
    Juiced (Canseco), 412
CLEMENS, SAMUEL LANGHORNE. See
    TWAIN, MARK

DIDION, JOAN
    Year of Magical Thinking, The
        (Didion), 897
DREISER, THEODORE
    Last Titan, The (Loving), 443

EMPSON, WILLIAM
    William Empson (Haffenden), 882
EQUIANO, OLAUDAH
    Equiano, the African (Carretta), 209

FLEMING, THOMAS
    Mysteries of My Father (Fleming), 572
FORD, HENRY
    People's Tycoon, The (Watts), 640
FOWLES, JOHN
    Journals: Vol. 1, The (Fowles), 408
FRANKLIN, BENJAMIN
    Great Improvisation, A (Schiff), 313
FUCHS, DANIEL
    Golden West, The (Fuchs), 305

GALBRAITH, JOHN KENNETH
    John Kenneth Galbraith (Parker), 397
GIULIANI, RUDOLPH
    Prince of the City, The (Siegel), 669
GOULD, JAY
    Dark Genius of Wall Street, The
        (Renehan), 173

GRAY, FRANCINE DU PLESSIX
    Them (Gray), 805

HALL, DONALD
    Best Day the Worst Day, The (Hall), 54
HARRISON, GEORGE
    Beatles, The (Spitz), 41
HATKIN, ELEANOR
    Who She Was (Freedman), 864
HAWTHORNE, SOPHIA PEABODY
    Peabody Sisters, The (Marshall), 631

IVAN THE TERRIBLE
    Ivan the Terrible (De Madariaga), 392

JACKSON, LAURA RIDING. See
    RIDING, LAURA
JOHNSON, B. S.
    Like a Fiery Elephant (Coe), 473
JOHNSON, SAMUEL
    Defining the World (Hitchings), 177

KENYON, JANE
    Best Day the Worst Day, The (Hall), 54
KIERKEGAARD, SØREN
    Søren Kierkegaard (Garff), 755

LENNON, JOHN
    Beatles, The (Spitz), 41
LEWIS, C. S.
    Narnian, The (Jacobs), 580
LIBERMAN, ALEXANDRE, and
    TATIANA
    Them (Gray), 805
LOISEAU, BERNARD
    Perfectionist, The (Chelminski), 649
LOWELL, ROBERT
    Letters of Robert Lowell, The (Lowell),
        456

CATEGORY INDEX

2006

ANTHROPOLOGY. *See* SOCIOLOGY, ARCHAEOLOGY, and ANTHROPOLOGY

ARCHAEOLOGY. *See* SOCIOLOGY, ARCHAEOLOGY, and ANTHROPOLOGY

AUTOBIOGRAPHY, MEMOIRS, DIARIES, and LETTERS
American Ghosts (Plante), 13
Best Day the Worst Day, The (Hall), 54
Dictionary Days (Stavans), 181
Glass Castle, The (Walls), 296
Golden West, The (Fuchs), 305
If This Be Treason (Rabassa), 362
Istanbul (Pamuk), 387
Journals: Vol. 1, The (Fowles), 408
Juiced (Canseco), 412
Letters of Robert Lowell, The (Lowell), 456
Matter of Opinion, A (Navasky), 530
Mysteries of My Father (Fleming), 572
Tender Bar, The (Moehringer), 796
Them (Gray), 805
Wild Perfection, A (Wright), 878

Year of Magical Thinking, The (Didion), 897

BIOGRAPHY. *See also* LITERARY BIOGRAPHY
American Prometheus (Bird and Sherwin), 17
Beatles, The (Spitz), 41
Becoming Justice Blackmun (Greenhouse), 45
Boss Tweed (Ackerman), 84
Dark Genius of Wall Street, The (Renehan), 173
Defining the World (Hitchings), 177
Equiano, the African (Carretta), 209
Finding George Orwell in Burma (Larkin), 251
Great Improvisation, A (Schiff), 313
Ivan the Terrible (De Madariaga), 392
John Kenneth Galbraith (Parker), 397
Joseph Smith (Bushman), 402
Lee Miller (Burke), 447
Mao (Chang and Halliday), 507
Matisse the Master (Spurling), 526
Old Ball Game, The (Deford), 617
Peabody Sisters, The (Marshall), 631

TITLE INDEX

2006

AUTHOR INDEX

2006